THE

MINOR PROPHETS;

WITH

NOTES,

CRITICAL, EXPLANATORY, AND PRACTICAL,

DESIGNED FOR BOTH PASTORS AND PEOPLE.

BY

REV. HENRY COWLES.

"Understandest thou what thou readest? And he said, How can I, except some man should guide me?"—ACTS 8: 30, 31.

NEW YORK:
D. APPLETON AND COMPANY,
443 & 445 BROADWAY.
1867.

PREFACE.

THE Christian commentator, assuming that the Scriptures are from God, infers their inestimable value to mankind. Assuming also that God speaks to man in love and for his good, he infers that originally, to common hearers and readers, his words must have been readily intelligible. Hence he finds his work to be, comprehensively, to get possession of the same means for understanding the words of God which were enjoyed by those first hearers and readers, including specially the language in which God spake, the historic facts to which he alludes, and the scenes in nature and common life from which he drew his illustrations. So much he must have in order to a clear and full understanding for himself of the ancient words of God to men.——Then it remains only to put his readers in possession of his views of the Sacred Word. To do this he may lead them over all the ground which he himself has travelled, *i. e.*, through the original Hebrew, unfolding its laws of etymology, syntax, and usage of words, and also through all the details of historic investigation: or he may place before his readers for the most part only the results at which he has arrived. In the former case, he writes for scholars only; in the latter, for readers of all classes.——I have adopted mainly the latter method, aiming to meet the wants, not of Hebrew scholars only or chiefly, but of all English readers. I have had in view somewhat specially those who have been and are yet to be trained to thoughtful study of God's word in Sabbath schools and Bible classes, and indeed all those laymen and women who love the Sacred Scriptures, and who naturally wish to know their full and precise meaning.——While in the main it has been my plan to give results only, and not the processes by which I reach them, yet points of great practical interest and value, *e. g.*, those prophecies respecting the Messiah and his kingdom which yet remain in part to be fulfilled, I have deemed it important to discuss fundamentally and thoroughly, so that the reader may see what principles of interpretation I adopt, and why,—and also to what results they have led me. A superficial treatment of these points ought to be eminently unsatisfactory.

The commentator has his option whether to restrict his work mainly to the unfolding of the exact sense, or to speak more or less fully of the practical and moral applications of the truth which he brings out. These moral applications are, of course, of the utmost importance to every reader; yet usually God has left each reader to make them for himself, and adapt them to his own case. Hence I have thought it cannot be unwise for me to follow for the most part the same method—assuming that God's word as it came from his lips will have power on men's hearts when the full sense of it is clearly apprehended. I have therefore spoken of the moral bearings and applications of the truth only in fewest words, suggestively and by no means exhaustively, and rather as a specimen and illustration of the practical use to be made of the divine word. By this method, the work is much reduced in size and expense; is brought within the means and the time for reading of a much greater number; and still, it is hoped, without lessening its moral and spiritual value.

The study of the Bible has been to me, above all other studies, my life-work and my life-joy. Through divine mercy and a fore-ordering providence, my attention has been turned and held very considerably during forty years past to the study of the Hebrew Scriptures, and especially to the writings of the prophets. At the urgent suggestion of friends, and under a strong conviction of the need of a commentary on these books adapted to all readers, I entered, three years ago, upon the preparation of these volumes, fully purposed to spare no pains, first to reach the exact and full thought in these sacred words, and then to present it with whatever clearness, brevity, and force I could command.——These years of study and writing have been to me a continual feast. Such a profusion of literary and poetic beauties as lie here, is one of God's great benefactions, yet is not to be named in comparison with the value of these truths fresh from the infinite mind of our divine Father, and from his parental heart. It is a luxury to see the lines of evidence converging to a focus to certify the exact meaning of God's word, and to bring out that meaning in sunlight before the mind. It ought to be and is a luxury even more rich to feel the presence and the power of such truth upon the heart. The writer has gone through these prophetic books with a growing sense of the richness and fulness of their provisions for both the mind and the heart, earnestly wishing that his readers may partake of this feast, and drink deeply at these fountains.

This volume is sent forth in the hope that it may aid the studies and refresh the souls of those who prize the Sacred Word, and rejoice in the growing sway of light and love under the great Redeemer's reign.

It has been thought best to begin with the minor prophets. The notes on the remaining prophets, upon the same general plan, have been prepared for the press, and may appear at some future day, if it should seem desirable.

The reader will be careful to observe that in the notes, italic words are *emphatic;* but in the sacred text, as in all English Bibles, they indicate that there are no corresponding words in the original Hebrew. Hence they are often the opposite of emphatic,—a more just translation dispensing with them altogether.

The author has aimed to give either a translation, more or less free, or a paraphrase, in all cases where he has been compelled to differ from the received version. These passages are usually indicated by marks of quotation.

OBERLIN, *Ohio*, *Sept.*, 1866.

GENERAL INTRODUCTION TO THE PROPHETS.

The Mosaic system comprised institutions and agencies for sustaining the religious life of the Hebrew people. The priests and the Levites were religious orders, held responsible for this service. In the degenerate ages of the nation, the forms of their religion lost their spiritual power, and those religious orders seem to have gone down morally in the general declension. Hence there arose a demand for a new order of men, and prophets appeared, holding their individual commissions direct from the living God. Singled out by his special call, they went forth with his definite messages, calling upon the people to hear his voice, and turn from their sins to righteousness. Hence it resulted, from the very circumstances which called into existence the order of prophets, that their main work should be to preach reform; to rebuke the prevalent sins of the nation; to denounce their idolatry, their self-righteousness, their heartless formality, and their oppression of the poor; to threaten impending judgments, and to call the people back to their forsaken God.

A portion of them (not all) have left in writing more or less of the messages sent by them from God to the people. Some, whose position is quite prominent in the history (*e. g.*, Elijah and Elisha), have left no books of their own. Others, whose names are not in the historic annals, have left valuable writings. Manifestly each followed, in this respect, his own word from the Lord—the Lord in his wisdom using these servants of his for the work which he most needed done and which they were best qualified to do.

It is manifest, both from the history and from the tenor of these recorded prophecies, that with few if any exceptions they first bore their messages from God to the people, with the living voice, in the form of direct address. It may be safely assumed that those portions were committed to writing which embraced prophecy yet to be fulfilled, or which would be specially useful, either to the Jewish or the Gentile Church, along the course of future ages.

These writings of the Hebrew prophets are now before us—rich treasures of truth and experience from the ancient past, God's own words, given to "holy men of old, who spake as they were moved by the Holy Ghost." Noble men were they, of martyr spirit, of Christian heroism, of faith and courage inspired by the sense of a special mission from the Most High; men whose record the world cannot afford to lose, nor the Christian Church to drop from her living thought. With what power of logic have they set forth the claims of God upon his rational creatures! How have they depicted the ingratitude, the meanness, the folly, and the madness of sin! With what solemn and thrilling words have they spoken of the judgments which God would send, and did, upon guilty nations, Jew and Gentile, in retribution on sinners, whom no warning from his voice availed to reclaim, and whose sins even the great forbearance of God could not longer endure! How pertinent and forcible are the moral lessons which come down to us from such living examples! Do proud rulers question whether there be an infinite Moral Governor of the universe? Do they doubt whether he takes note of the sins of mighty nations, and holds both them and their rulers to a strict moral accountability? Do they vainly think to set justice at naught, and trample down the helpless—no God from on high regarding and avenging? Or do they presume that he is too tender-hearted or too weak to punish, so that strong men and proud nations shall feel it?

On all these and on all kindred points, the logic of facts

affords demonstration, not only convincing, but appalling. It must be morally wholesome to study such testimonies from the actual ways of God in the teaching past. It were madness to ignore them.

Here also, coupled with these terrible retributions from God upon persistent sinners, are the most touching invitations to return in penitence, and the richest promises of pardon to the humble and the contrite. You are impressed as you read with a sense that these words of promise are freighted with a wealth of love unknown in human hearts, and truly worthy of a God. Whoever with honest mind shall take in their full significance, and not abuse it, will surely find in it a blessing.——It was one of the special functions of those ancient prophets to minister to the faith and hope of the few yet found faithful among the many faithless. To them, and primarily for their sake, God spake, through his servants, of the great things then in the future of his Zion. The Messiah yet to come; the work he should achieve while yet among men in the flesh; the mission of the Holy Spirit; the conversion of the Gentiles; the fortunes of the Jews—at first mostly cast off for their unbelief, but ultimately brought in through great mercy; the abrogation of the sacrificial system; the outgoing of the gospel to the distant nations of the earth; the mission of truth and its triumphs in every land, and the final victory of Christ over all opposing powers: these things are grouped together into these glorious visions of the then distant future—a grand and sublime panorama of the Christian age in whole, making revelations even to us who live midway in their fulfilment, such as no lover of his race and lover of Christ can contemplate without being quickened anew in faith and love for the prayer and the work to which Christ calls him. How earnestly do these prophecies invite the most careful study! We do not wonder that Peter should endorse and commend them to his Christian brethren, saying: "We have also the word of prophecy made more sure (*i. e.*, by its incipient fulfilment), whereunto ye do well that ye take heed as to a light that shineth in a dark place until the day dawn, and the day-star arise in your hearts" (2 Peter: 1,

19). Truly this "prophetic word" does shed forth a glorious light upon the future history of our world, a place otherwise utterly dark to mortal vision; and equally true is it that in giving due heed to this light, and in bringing our souls fully under its illuminating power and its inspiring influence, a glorious "day" dawns upon us; the day-star of faith and hope arises, and we wake to the work of the millennial age, to joyful anticipations of its approach, and to a sense of the ocean fulness of its blessings for a world redeemed.

Yet, rich in gospel truth and inspiring to faith as this prophetic word truly is, no portion of the Scriptures is so little read, so little studied, and so little understood. Nowhere else in human language does there lie such a mass of half-buried and almost unknown treasures. True, they come to us in a language now long unspoken, but diligent labor can unlock its meaning; in figures somewhat unfamiliar, yet not unintelligible; with allusions to history then past, and to life-scenes then present, which need from us some careful research to bring them within command for ready use. These circumstances make labor for the commentator; yet when his work is well done, the resulting profit to the diligent reader will be richly remunerative.

HOSEA.

INTRODUCTION.

Hosea prophesied "in the days of Uzziah, Jotham, Ahaz, and Hezekiah, kings of Judah, and in the days of Jeroboam, the son of Joash, king of Israel." This covers a long period at the very least, for, from the death of Jeroboam to the accession of Hezekiah, was fifty-six years; to which must be added whatever years he prophesied before Jeroboam's death and after Hezekiah's reign began. Jeroboam reigned forty-one years (2 Kings 14:23), and Hezekiah twenty-nine. How much of either of these reigns fell within the prophetic life of Hosea there are no positive data to show; probably several from each. Various allusions to events past, then passing, or very near, locate the greater part of this book within the sixty-two years lying between the death of Jeroboam and the fall of the kingdom. Jeroboam's was the last long and vigorous reign, and hence the only one in Israel worthy of being named in this introduction. The ensuing period had two seasons of anarchy, one of eleven years and the other of nine; besides the reign of Zachariah, six months; of Shallum, two months; of Menahem, ten years; of Pekahiah, two; of Pekah, nineteen, and of Hoshea, the last, nine. If, now, the reader recalls the facts stated in the history, that these six kings belonged to five different dynasties; that four of them fell by conspiracy, and a fifth with the final fall of his kingdom; and that not one of them bears any other record than that of "doing evil in the sight of the Lord, departing not from the sins of Jeroboam, son of Nebat, who made Israel to sin," he will have valuable data for estimating the deplorable state of morals, piety, and civil government at this time. During this same period Isaiah and Micah were prophesying, chiefly in Judah, and Amos, like Hosea, mostly in Israel. The latter were shut up by the force of circumstances to one main effort to convict the people of their great sins, and to call them to repentance toward God as the only means of saving either the government or the people from utter ruin.—— Hence the prophecies of Hosea are full of rebuke and expostulation against sin, and of demonstrations of God's loving-kindness and pity toward his people. It is preëminently *the* book in the whole Bible for times of spiritual declension and sore apostasy—God's voice of warning and entreaty to any people who once walked in fear and love before him, but who have become deeply corrupt in heart and life. Must it not also have many points of forcible application to the great American people—a nation eminently favored of God, but grievously apostate from his fear and honor?

In style, Hosea is preëminently concise and abrupt, abounding in historical allusions and also in sudden transitions, which involve more or less obscurity. Yet the book will yield a rich reward for close and earnest study. Let the reader come to it as to God's own words, through one of his faithful but long and sorely-tried servants, remembering his own closing testimony: "Who is wise, and he shall understand these things; prudent, and he shall know them; for the ways of the Lord are right, and the just shall walk in them; but the transgressors shall fall therein."

CHAPTER I.

THE book opens with events peculiar to Hosea's prophetic ministry—the taking of a wife whose lewdness symbolized the infidelity of the nation to God, their Maker and Husband; and the birth and naming of children whose names were significant before the people of their relations to Jehovah.

1. The word of the LORD that came unto Hosea, the son of Beeri, in the days of Uzziah, Jotham, Ahaz, *and* Hezekiah, kings of Judah, and in the days of Jeroboam the son of Joash king of Israel.

The reader may wisely peruse the history of the period covered by these reigns as recorded 2 Kings 14:23 to 18:12, and also in 2 Chron. chapters 26–31. The record is a dismal one—revolutions, anarchy, conspiracies, universal idolatry, and outbreaking wickedness.

2. The beginning of the word of the LORD by Hosea. And the LORD said to Hosea, Go, take unto thee a wife of whoredoms and children of whoredoms; for the land hath committed great whoredom, *departing* from the LORD.

It has been questioned whether this taking of a lewd wife were a real transaction. Some suppose it existed only *in vision*. The laws of prophetic interpretation forbid this view. The command is, "Go, take;" and nothing less than the strongest reasons can justify us in rejecting the obvious sense of such language. Besides, what could be the use of such a thing, if done only in vision; and especially, what could be the use of it *to the people?* Yet further, and more to our purpose as interpreters of God's word—if the Lord meant only that Hosea saw or should see this thing *in vision*, why did he not *say* so? Cases in which things were to be done in the actual life of the prophets for the greater effect as *symbols* before the people, occur frequently in Ezekiel, and occasionally in other Old Testament prophets. But see this subject discussed more fully in the Appendix—Dissertation I.

A second question, of less importance, is, whether Gomer was a lewd woman *before* marriage. On the one hand, the language does not absolutely demand the affirmative, while yet it is the more obvious sense of the words. On the other hand, the negative is supported by the circumstance that, so interpreted, the case better symbolizes the idolatry of Israel, inasmuch as the Lord entered into covenant with them while yet they were mostly pure from this great sin. It is not necessary, however, that the symbol should fit at all possible points. The one main point is the grievous guilt of such adultery. I pass this question, simply expressing my opinion that she had been lewd before marriage, and was taken as a wife upon a promise of conjugal fidelity. It is well to note carefully that the Lord gave the reasons for this remarkable command—viz.: because the land had become wholly adulterous and apostate from God. Of course, adultery here means specially *idolatry*. By the worship of idols the people had put other gods before Jehovah. They had faithlessly broken their solemn covenant to fear and serve the Lord alone. This covenant can find no better symbol among human relations than that by which one man and one woman "become no longer twain, but one flesh." The marriage relation, closer and more endearing than any other, comes nearest to a perfect symbol of the covenant relation between God and his chosen people. It is therefore used with great pertinence, beauty, and force. ——The fact is humiliating to the people of God that this symbol should find its most abundant occasion for use, not on the bright side of this marriage relation, but on the dark—the shameful infidelities and apostasies of the people in the times of Hosea, Jeremiah, and Ezekiel. The same idea, and mostly on its bright side, underlies the forty-fifth Psalm, and (as the Jews must have understood it) the Book of Canticles; but its fuller development waited till flagrant sin called it forth.

Let us not pass this point without taking note of the keenness of the domestic trial to which Hosea was subjected at his very entrance upon the prophetic work. We sometimes think of this work as bringing the prophet into near and honored relations to Jehovah—as, indeed, sublimely grand and glorious. We are liable to forget that for even such prophets to live godly was to suffer. Isaiah shrank from the work; Jonah fled, to escape its responsibilities; Jeremiah felt heavily on his heart the message burdens he bore from God to the people; and to Hosea was allotted this bitter affliction—a wife unfaithful to her marriage vows—that he might be a living representative of the great sin of the people against their divine Husband; and perhaps, also, that his own experience of domestic wrong and wretchedness might give him a keener sense of the cruel guilt of the nation's idolatry, and might help him to sympathize with the feelings of Jehovah under such abuse.——These trials in the prophet's mission have a vital bearing on the question of his essential honesty. No selfish motive could have moved him to such a life-work. To rebuke sin in an age of such outbreaking and universal wickedness, and to be subjected to such domestic affliction for the sake of more vividly illustrating the apostasy of Israel from their God involve and imply an honest, self-sacrificing devotion to the will of God, and quite preclude the supposition of his being an impostor.

3. So he went and took Gomer the daughter of Diblaim; which conceived, and bare him a son.

4. And the LORD said unto him, Call his name Jezreel; for yet a little *while*, and I will avenge the blood of Jezreel upon the house of Jehu, and will cause to cease the kingdom of the house of Israel.

5. And it shall come to pass at that day, that I will break the bow of Israel in the valley of Jezreel.

The word Jezreel has a two-fold significance; the one drawn from its etymology, the other from its history. By its etymology it means *the Lord will sow*, or *the Lord's sowing*. We have this sense in v. 11. Great shall be the day when the Lord shall sow or plant his people in their own land. By historical allusion, the word carries us back to the city bearing that name, the royal residence of Ahab; to the blood shed there by Jehu, and to the avenging of that blood upon his posterity. See 2 Kings 10 : 11, 14.——Naming the prophet's first child Jezreel denoted that this avenging was near at hand. Jehu by promise was to hold the throne to the fourth generation. Jeroboam II. was the third in that line; his son, Zachariah, was the fourth and last. A wicked reign of six months ended his life and the dynasty of Jehu. See 2 Kings 15: 8–12.

The kingdom of the house of Israel was to cease soon. It ceased fifty-one years after the death of this king, Zachariah. It may be asked, Did not the Lord (2 Kings 10: 30) approve of Jehu's deeds in destroying the house of Ahab? And if so, why should he now avenge that blood on the house of Jehu? The true answer seems to be that he *in part* approved it, and therefore in part rewarded Jehu—that is, by giving him the kingdom to the fourth generation. But he could not approve his spirit, which was far from being right before God; nor could he approve of his "taking no heed to walk in the law of the Lord God of Israel with all his heart, departing not from the sins of Jeroboam," 2 Kings 10: 31. Hence these judgments on his house.——"Breaking the bow of Jezreel," is breaking their military power—the bow being then the chief weapon of war. That this was done especially in the valley of Jezreel is every way probable, though there is no definite record of the event. This valley, since called *Esdraelon*, has been one of the most noted battle-grounds in history. Here Deborah and Barak fought and conquered; here Gideon scourged and drove the Midianites; here Ahab gained a great victory over Ben-hadad. Here have fought Romans, Crusaders, Egyptians, and Frenchmen. It is more than supposable that in this famous valley the enfeebled hosts of Israel made their last stand against the Assyrian power.

6. And she conceived again and bare a daughter. And *God* said unto him, Call her name Lo-ruhamah: for I will no more have mercy upon the house of Israel; but I will utterly take them away.

"*Lo-ruhamah*" is literally "not compassionated"—not a subject of mercy. This use of the negative *Lo* implies not merely the absence of mercy, but the presence of wrath. The sense is not suspended at the point of mere negation, but goes over to the opposite side. Here it means that the people had incurred Jehovah's *frown*. He would not any more show mercy to the people of the ten tribes in such form as to arrest and turn aside his impending, long-deserved judgments. On the contrary, he "would utterly take them away" into captivity.——As to the last clause, the marginal reading suggests another possible sense of the original. viz.: "that I should altogether pardon them." The original Hebrew verb means to take away, and is sometimes used for the taking away of sin. But the connecting particle gives this as the course of thought: "I will not again show mercy to the house of Israel, *for* I will utterly take them away," *i. e.*, from their land. This is my purpose.

7. But I will have mercy upon the house of Judah, and will save them by the LORD their God, and will not save them by bow, nor by sword, nor by battle, by horses, nor by horsemen.

There was still in Judah some true fidelity to God; he would therefore yet have mercy on them. The expression—"Save them *by* the Lord their God, and not by sword or battle," is beautifully concise and forcible—as if Jehovah were himself the engines of war, the sword and the bow, that should save them. The might of his arm is finely contrasted with the might of human prowess in war.

8. Now when she had weaned Lo-ruhamah, she conceived, and bare a son.

9. Then said *God*, Call his name Lo-ammi: for ye *are* not my people, and I will not be your *God*.

"Lo-ammi" signifies *not my people*, and as said above of Lo-ruhamah, it implies that they are in a state of positive rejection. God was about to disown them—so utterly had they rejected him by their abounding persistent idolatry, by forsaking the worship of God, and by most flagrant immoralities.——How impressive to Hosea must have been all the scenes and sounds of his household! Often as he spake or heard spoken the names of these two children, the thought came—*No mercy! Not my people!* A like testimony it must have borne to the people among whom he was sent as the prophet of the living God.

10. Yet the number of the children of Israel shall be as the sand of the sea, which cannot be measured nor numbered; and it shall come to pass, *that* in the place where it was said unto them, Ye *are* not my people, *there* it shall be said unto them, *Ye are* the sons of the living God.

11. Then shall the children of Judah and the children of Israel be gathered together and appoint themselves one head, and they shall come up out of the land: for great *shall be* the day of Jezreel.

Here is a sudden transition from extreme judgment to the fulness of mercy. "The Lord keepeth not his anger forever." Remarkably is it his method, whether by prophet or apostle, to blend threatening with promise, and to follow the sternest denunciations with outbursts of pity and love.——The general sense of the passage is—God hath not forsaken his church utterly and forever. Notwithstanding this ruin now coming on Israel, the Lord shall yet have a people, countless as the sands, united also and prosperous, the true Israel and Judah.——A number "as the sands of the sea" is, of course, indefinitely great, denoting the highest prosperity and a vast increase of population, compared with the Israel then present.——What is spoken of here as currently "said to them" must be construed as said, because *true.* The truth of it, rather than the saying of it, is the thing specially affirmed. Whereas ye formerly were not my people, ye shall, in the future time referred to, be really the sons of the living God.——No special stress can be given to the words "in the place where," as defining any particular locality. It is used adverbially to mean that *instead of—in place of*—their not being God's people, they shall really *be* his sons.

That Israel and Judah "gather together and appoint themselves one head," looks by historical allusion to the sad history of the recent past, since the revolt under Jeroboam, and means to say that in this good time coming, that sore breach shall be healed, the rival kingdoms become one, and "Ephraim no more envy Judah, nor Judah vex Ephraim." The Church of God, in those times, shall be one in love, and strong in its union.——To "come up out of the land" is the classic phrase for the exodus from Egypt, and implies that God will work a like deliverance of his people from their bondage, whatever the form of that bondage may be. When we find a manifest historical allusion, we must accept it as illustrative, and not look for a precisely literal fulfilment. In the present case, we are not to look for the geographical land, out of which they come up. It is rather a moral *state*, and no land or country whatever.——The "day of Jezreel" is here the day of the Lord's sowing, or, in our English idiom, *planting* His people—with reference to the etymology of the word Jezreel. Looking historically to the planting in Canaan, under Joshua, it means that God will do a similar thing again. Great shall be the day when the Lord thus lays anew the foundations of his Zion, and rebuilds Jerusalem —plants his people in their new estate, and puts a new face upon his earthly kingdom. It does not necessarily follow that this planting is the locating of his ancient people in the land of Canaan.

Having now noted the sense of the several expressions, it remains to consider the meaning of the whole passage.——Here we must not fail to take account of the fearful things God had just spoken against Israel: "I will cause to cease the kingdom of the house of Israel;" "I will break the bow of Israel;" "I will no more have mercy on the house of Israel, but will utterly take them away," *i. e.*, into captivity; "Ye are not my people, and I will not be your God."——All this has the aspect of rejecting Israel, utterly and forever.—Yes, and the Israel of the ten tribes *was* substantially rejected. But a new Israel comes up, a new or at least a modified sense is given to the word Israel, so that it now means not merely those born of Jacob, or those who were of the kingdom of the ten tribes, but the *real people of God;* or, as the etymology of the word implies, those who have a princely power with God through prayer. See Gen. 32:28, and Hos. 12:3, 4. This play on the different senses of a word, the one, perhaps, historical, and the other drawn from its etymology, is by no means foreign to the style of Hosea. We have seen it already in the word Jezreel.

The general interpretation here indicated involves great questions and results, and should, therefore, be carefully stated and well supported.——Let it, then, be considered,

(1.) The literal and old sense of *Israel*, in this passage, is *simply impossible*. To hold, as some good men have done, that the ten tribes did return in vast numbers with the Jews under Zerubbabel, their "one head," and that the richness of this glorious promise had its fulfilment then, is to struggle in vain against the whole array of authentic history. Ezra and Nehemiah have told us (Ez. 2:1 ff., and Neh. 7:6 ff.) how many did return; about 50,000, all told. They have shown us that these were mostly of the tribes of Judah and Levi, the lineal descendants of those who belonged to that kingdom, and not to the kingdom of the ten tribes (see Ez. 2:1, and Neh. 7:6). Hence they leave no place there for the ten tribes, and, much more, no place for a multitude of them, like the sands of the sea. And yet more, the ten tribes are now plainly lost from the view of authentic history, leaving no ground to suppose they can ever be discovered among the living tribes of the earth. Therefore it is not too much to say that this prophecy, *if applied to the kingdom of the ten tribes*, has never been fulfilled, and never can be. We are amply justified, therefore, in looking for some other sense of the word "*Israel.*"

(2.) The construction above given, which supposes the word to be used here for the true people of God, is in harmony with the peculiar style of Hosea, as has been already stated.

(3.) It is abundantly endorsed by the New Testament. (*a.*) By its use of the terms Israel, Zion, the temple, &c., &c. Thus Rom. 9:6, "They are not all Israel which are of Israel," *i. e.*, they are not all God's true people who are lineally born of Israel—a case, therefore, in which we have precisely the same new second sense of the word Israel, which is claimed for Hosea in this passage. Again, this same apostle closes one epistle—full of the doctrine that "all who are Christ's are Abraham's seed," by invoking "peace upon the Israel of God." So Mount Zion (Heb. 12:22) is the whole Christian church: Christians (2 Cor. 6:16) are God's temple.——(*b.*) This construction is sustained by the whole doctrine of the New Testament in reference to the relation of Gentiles to the church and kingdom of God. The great battle of the apostolic age was fought over this very question, whether *Gentiles could come in with Jews* as heirs of God's promises, and really entitled to the blessings foretold in prophecy for Israel.——(*c.*) But more particularly, Paul (Rom. 9:25, 26) quotes this very passage from Hosea to prove that the "vessels of mercy" to whom God "makes known the riches of his glory," are "not of the Jews only but also of the Gentiles." That is, he assumes that in this very passage

Hosea embraces Gentile Christians under the name *Israel;* and, of course, that it is fulfilled in the New Testament age, and not exclusively before—in the Gentiles, and not otherwise. This ought to be decisive.

(4.) While some of the prophets, *e. g.*, Isaiah, speak of the Gentiles by name as coming into the church and sharing in the great blessings of the latter days; others, like Hosea, predict the same great blessings, but never name the Gentiles, and give them no share except as they come in under the name *Israel.* We must, therefore, either say that they rule out the Gentiles from the pale of these blessings and give them to the lineal Israel, and to Israel only; or we must admit that they modify the sense of the word Israel, and use it to include all the real children of God in the latter days.

Finally, we have the great fact that just at the point where the Israel of the ten tribes was being cast off for their hopeless idolatry and incurable corruption, a larger, richer promise is made to the "children of Israel" than the literal Israel ever had before or since, or ever can have. Moveover, what time the old Israel became lost to history, a new Israel appears; Gentiles come into the church of God; the world opens to the mission of the Gospel, and lies at the feet of the Prince of Peace: and so his Israel becomes as the sand of the sea; his people are the "sons of the living God;" old antipathies give place to the oneness of love; under their one head, they come up from their last house of bondage, and great beyond all former thought is "the day of Jezreel."——For all this let us sing in words furnished to the church for this occasion by Isaiah (chap. 12). "O Lord, I will praise thee; though thou wast angry with me, thine anger is turned away, and thou comfortedst me. Behold God is my salvation; I will trust and not be afraid; for the Lord Jehovah is my strength and my song; he also is become my salvation."

CHAPTER II.

In this chapter, the Lord exposes and rebukes the sins of his people, and threatens retribution, vs. 1–13; then turns to promises of effective discipline and of restoring mercy, vs. 14–23.

It is noticeable that throughout this chapter, the adulterous mother, Israel, is spoken of in the third person, and the Lord declares what he will do to her in judgment and for her in mercy. Remarkably, and as if to give a more impressive sense of her horrible guilt, her children are introduced—are apprised of the unnatural crime of their mother, and are exhorted to plead with her to put away her sins. What a family scene must be the reality presented in this symbol—the children appealing to their mother to desist from her adulterous life, and to put an end at once to all its indications! It is manifestly the purpose of God, in this message by Hosea, to paint a life-scene of the crimes of his covenant people in their relations to himself.

1. Say unto your brethren, Ammi; and to your sisters, Ruhamah.

Say to your brethren, Ammi; to your sisters, Ruhamah. Drop the negative particle from the names, Lo-Ammi, Lo-Ruhamah; sound the sweet words, "*my* people;" "the pitied and beloved"—as if to suggest that the heart of the Lord still yearns to make them again his own, and to give the freest flow to his great and deep compassions.——The persons exhorted to do this may be supposed to be the few yet found faithful among the many faithless. The Lord calls on them for one more effort to reclaim the nation.

2. Plead with your mother, plead; for she *is* not my wife, neither *am* I her husband: let her therefore put away her whoredoms out of her sight, and her adulteries from between her breasts;

3. Lest I strip her naked, and set her as in the day that she was born, and make her as a wilderness, and set her like a dry land, and slay her with thirst.

"Plead with your mother," ye children of shame; go and tell her you cannot bear the disgrace and pain of her unnatural crime; tell her that her God disowns her as a wife, and puts her away for her lewd idolatry. Such is this strain of fiery rebuke.——The last clause refers to the incitements to lewdness common with bad women. "Out of her sight," should read, "from her face," corresponding to "from her breasts" in the parallel member of the sentence. The original has the same form of expression in each case. The face and the bosom are alike used for incitement to lewd passion;—paint, ornament, and lascivious expression in the one; exposure of person in the other. In the spiritual application, God frowns upon and would put away every form of inducement to idolatry in Israel; every thing that in any age naturally tempts his people to sin.

4. And I will not have mercy upon her children; for they *be* the children of whoredoms.

Closely following out the symbol, the Lord appeals to the heart of the mother, as if he would say: Though you have lost all sensibility to your own welfare, yet think of your children. I will not have mercy on them; your unnatural crime comes down on them with perpetual curses. Can a mother's heart resist such an appeal?

5. For their mother hath played the harlot: she that conceived them hath done shamefully: for she said, I

will go after my lovers, that give *me* my bread and my water, my wool and my flax, mine oil and my drink.

The adulterous mother is here seen, going after her infamous paramours—as one who *lives* on the wages of her shameless crime. This is turning over and over the leading symbol, to put in still new light the shameful sins of the chosen people against their God, and to show why he ought to and must visit them with terrible retribution.——The fifth and sixth verses stand related as cause and result: "*Because* their mother hath committed lewdness," "*therefore* will I hedge up her way," &c.

6. Therefore, behold, I will hedge up thy way with thorns, and make a wall, that she shall not find her paths.

7. And she shall follow after her lovers, but she shall not overtake them; and she shall seek them, but shall not find *them*: then shall she say, I will go and return to my first husband; for then *was it* better with me than now.

God will trouble her in every way; she shall follow *hard* (so the original) after her lovers for help, but in vain, till affliction and want bring her back to reason and to her forsaken God.

8. For she did not know that I gave her corn, and wine, and oil, and multiplied her silver and gold, *which* they prepared for Baal.

9. Therefore will I return, and take away my corn in the time thereof, and my wine in the season thereof, and will recover my wool and my flax *given* to cover her nakedness.

Vs. 8 and 9 are correlated thus: "*Because* she did not know," &c., "*therefore* will I take away," &c.——"Did not know that *I* gave her" all, where the original makes the pronoun *I* emphatic.——God multiplied to Israel silver and gold, which they wrought into images of Baal. This is one point of aggravation in all sin. Men take the gifts of God and pervert them into means of sinning the more against him; work them into idols to worship instead of Jehovah. ——Baal was one of the most ancient of the gods worshipped in the East. He is supposed by many to represent the sun; by others, the planet Jupiter, as the almoner of good fortune. He was worshipped by the people of Phœnicia and Tyre, and from them, at a very early age, and in the reign of Ahab especially, his worship passed over to the Jews.

10. And now will I discover her lewdness in the

sight of her lovers, and none shall deliver her out of mine hand.

"Discover," in the sense of *expose* her nakedness before her lovers—terribly significant of the fearful judgments God knows how to send on his apostate people!

11. I will also cause all her mirth to cease, her feast days, her new moons, and her sabbaths, and all her solemn feasts.

These were seasons of special joy to the Hebrew people, and stand here to represent *all* joy.

12. And I will destroy her vines and her fig-trees, whereof she hath said, These *are* my rewards that my lovers have given me: and I will make them a forest, and the beasts of the field shall eat them.

The heathen regarded their idol gods as the givers of their vines and fig-trees. Israel says the same thing. Those idol gods are her lovers, to whom, in her spiritual adultery, she gives her heart and her confidence.

13. And I will visit upon her the days of Baalim, wherein she burned incense to them, and she decked herself with her ear-rings and her jewels, and she went after her lovers, and forgat me, saith the LORD.

This strain of rebuke and threatening culminates with the general declaration—"I will visit upon her for the guilt of her days of Baal worship." "Baalim," in the plural, refers to the numerous images of Baal, or as others hold plausibly, to the diverse modes of his manifestation. "Decking herself with ear-rings and jewels, and going after her lovers," carries out the symbol—a harlot, plying all the shameless arts of a common prostitute.

14. Therefore, behold, I will allure her, and bring her into the wilderness, and speak comfortably unto her.

This verse is, for the chapter, the transition point between rebuke and threatened retribution for the sins of idol worship on the one hand, and promises of effective discipline and of restoring mercy on the other.——"*Behold*," calls special attention to the great things God now proposes to do.——"*Therefore*," reminds us to ask *why?* What is the reason for the promises of good that follow?——Some have found a difficulty here, inasmuch as the grievous sins of Israel seem to be no natural reason for giving the blessings hereafter promised.——But the reasons, viewed fundamentally, lie deeper than the sins of Israel, even in God's covenant love and faithfulness. He cannot bear that his own Israel should sink hopelessly under her sins into ruin. Therefore his pity moves him to discipline and to mercy.——"Will allure her"—in a good sense; persuade her, draw her by the sweet attractions of love.

This "bringing her into the wilderness," Dr. Henderson, following his principles of literal interpretation, finds fulfilled in God's taking the whole Hebrew people into captivity to Babylon and Assyria. Apparently he fails to notice that they were *driven* not *drawn* thither, and also that neither Babylon nor Assyria are known in Scripture as "the wilderness."——Dismissing, therefore, this literal view of the language, I prefer to assume an historical allusion to the exodus from Egypt. God means—"I will do to Israel *again* what I did when I took them by the hand and led them out of the house of bondage, and out of the land of idol gods, into the wilderness, and there spake to them face to face"—spake most effectively "*to their heart*," as the last clause reads in the original. We may fitly recall the fact that this wilderness-life was to the Hebrew people a great and most effective theatre of moral discipline. No generation in all their history was so true to God or so much beloved of him as that which had its training in the wilderness, and went in under Joshua to the land of Canaan. God here promises to do a like thing to his covenant people again.——With allusion probably to this passage, yet amplifying it, Ezekiel (20: 35, 36) says: "And I will bring you into the wilderness of the people, and there will I plead with you face to face. Like as I pleaded with your fathers in the wilderness of the land of Egypt, so will I plead with you, saith the Lord." This confirms the idea of an historical allusion to the scenes of the exodus.

15. And I will give her her vineyards from thence, and the valley of Achor for a door of hope: and she shall sing there, as in the days of her youth, and as in the day when she came up out of the land of Egypt.

"From thence"—from such a scene of moral discipline, God will give her her vineyards—with historical reference to the grapes of Eshcol, which ancient Israel found on entering Canaan. Blessings come after, and out of, efficient moral discipline.——"The valley of Achor" is still another historical allusion. The word *Achor* means by its etymology, *trouble:* in history it was the place of trouble to Achan. See Josh. 7: 24–26. So the troubles of Israel shall be her "door of hope."——"And she shall sing there"—with declared reference to the joy of the Hebrews when, led by Moses and Miriam, they sang songs of deliverance on the hither side of the Red Sea.——So joy comes from sanctified sorrow. Moral discipline that really turns the heart from sin to God, is evermore a well-spring of blessings.

16. And it shall be at that day, saith the LORD, *that*

thou shalt call me Ishi; and shalt call me no more Baali.

17. For I will take away the names of Baalim out of her mouth, and they shall no more be remembered by their name.

The true and full sense of these verses is seen in the fact that "*Ishi*," my man, and "*Baali*," my lord, were both sometimes used to mean *my husband*. But the word Baal had become so dangerously associated with idol worship that Jehovah forbade the use of it, even to express an innocent relation. So there is sound wisdom in forestalling all those temptations which steal upon us under the laws of mental association. God would take away from us every thing that may work, through the power of those laws of thought, to beguile us into sin.

18. And in that day will I make a covenant for them with the beasts of the field, and with the fowls of heaven, and *with* the creeping things of the ground: and I will break the bow and the sword and the battle out of the earth, and will make them to lie down safely.

This covenant which God makes with the lower animals, debars them from harming his people. I find here an allusion to vs. 12, where God gives the beasts of the field license to devour the vines and fig-trees of his sinning people. This covenant recalls that license, and even lays them under bond to spare to God's penitent people the fruits of the earth. Sense: God's providence becomes their shield and refuge.

19. And I will betroth thee unto me for ever; yea, I will betroth thee unto me in righteousness, and in judgment, and in loving-kindness, and in mercies.

20. I will even betroth thee unto me in faithfulness: and thou shalt know the Lord.

This betrothal assumes that her long-persistent adulteries had ended in *divorce*. Now the marriage covenant is renewed—renewed "*forever;*" renewed "in righteousness, in judgment, in loving-kindness, and in great mercy;" where the reiteration is intended to heighten the sense of God's great love in this transaction. Remarkably, it culminates *in faithfulness;* as if to say, This covenant must stand, and be broken no more.——"Thou shalt know the Lord," is one of the most expressive phrases possible to human language, implying to know God in all the great elements of his character, and in all the experiences of his spiritual power; to know with a knowledge other and better far than theory; to know with the heart brought fully under the power of Jehovah's presence and love.

21. And it shall come to pass in that day, I will hear, saith the LORD, I will hear the heavens, and they shall hear the earth;

22. And the earth shall hear the corn, and the wine, and the oil; and they shall hear Jezreel.

This extraordinary passage means, comprehensively, that God will hear the prayer of his people for the earthly good they may need and shall ask of him. The *manner* of saying this gives us what we may call a circle of prayer. "Hearing," means hearing *and answering* the requests made. "Jezreel" stands here for the people whom God plants in the land. Hence, the form of the thought is: This people call for corn and wine and oil, and in a sense cry unto these things, and are heard and answered: the corn and wine cry to the earth; the earth to the heavens; and the heavens to God. God hears the heavens; the heavens hear the earth; the earth hears the corn, and the corn hears the people whom God plants in the land. The agencies of providence that lie between God and his praying people, which must be all put in operation in order to give them corn and wine, are beautifully put into the links of this chain of prayer.

23. And I will sow her unto me in the earth; and I will have mercy upon her that had not obtained mercy; and I will say to *them which were* not my people, Thou *art* my people; and they shall say, *Thou art* my God.

"I will sow her unto me," still keeps up the sense of the word "Jezreel." "*Unto me*," shows that this planting of God's people shall be for himself and not for another; no more for Baal. "In the earth," might have been as well expressed by "in the land," the allusion being to the fact that of old God had given to his people a land, specially their own by covenant promise.——I will now and onward have mercy on her who was rejected from my mercy, bearing the name *Lo*-Ruhamah: I will say to Lo-Ammi, Thou art Ammi—beautifully expunging the negative; and he [my people] shall say, My God!——This is the concise, yet strongly expressive form of the original.

Thus closes this richly instructive passage. Its whole strain is one glorious testimony that our God, in the midst of wrath, remembers mercy.

CHAPTER III.

This short chapter embraces one theme only—the prophet's relation to a wife—adduced as the occasion of a remarkable prophecy of the future of the Jewish people.

1. Then said the Lord unto me, Go yet, love a woman beloved of *her* friend, yet an adulteress, according to the love of the Lord toward the children of Israel, who look to other gods, and love flagons of wine.

A question arises here, rather curious than vital to the general sense of the chapter—whether this woman was or was not Gomer, the wife brought to our knowledge in the first chapter.——On the supposition that she was the same, it seems somewhat remarkable that the statements are so indefinite, with no clear allusions to the Gomer before introduced; yet, despite of this difficulty, the evidence preponderates in favor of their identity. The Lord here says, "Go, *love*," not *take* a woman; the latter being the usual formula for entering the first time into the marriage relation. He says simply "a woman," not "thy wife;" indicating a state of separation and semi-divorce, such as would naturally result from the lewdness of Gomer. She is further described as "beloved of *a friend*," as the original has it (not "*her*" friend), a sort of free-love relationship, and yet an adulteress; and, of course, not living with this friend in lawful wedlock. A further point in the description is, that this case corresponds to the love of the Lord toward the children of Israel, who look (in the Heb. *turn*) to other gods. Inasmuch as this is part of the description of this woman, it should be allowed the more weight in identifying her. Its whole force goes to show that she was Gomer, since it was the same Israel with whom the Lord had been in covenant, to whom he now returns in his great loving-kindness. And this is the very point made in this chapter. This main feature, therefore, forbids us to think here of any other woman than Gomer.——Our translation renders the last word of this verse, "flagons of wine." Modern scholars agree in rendering the Hebrew word *grape-cakes; i. e.*, grapes dried and pressed into the form of cakes. They were customarily offered in the worship of idols, and then eaten by the worshippers. Another instance of the general policy of making idol-worship every way attractive to the senses and animal appetites.

2. So I bought her to me for fifteen *pieces* of silver, and *for* an homer of barley, and an half homer of barley.

It was common among the Jews, indeed it is in all the East, to this day, to buy a wife. Whether the price named here was the standard one is of no special importance; if it were, our means of fixing the value of a "piece of silver" are very imperfect. The amount of barley was about fourteen bushels.——This buying does not necessarily forbid the supposition that she had been his wife before. It does imply that she had forfeited that relation, and could properly return only as one justly divorced. To show this seems to be the chief or sole intent in this second verse.

3. And I said unto her, Thou shalt abide for me many days; thou shalt not play the harlot, and thou shalt not be for *another* man: so *will* I also *be* for thee.

The prophet implores her to desist from her former crimes. Probably the true sense of the verse is better given by omitting the word "*another*," which has nothing to correspond to it in the Hebrew. "Thou shalt not be *for man*"—any man;—the special point being to represent a state of Israel described in the next verse as without any worship of either the true God or idols.

4. For the children of Israel shall abide many days without a king, and without a prince, and without a sacrifice, and without an image, and without an ephod, and *without* teraphim:

5. Afterward shall the children of Israel return, and seek the LORD their God, and David their king; and shall fear the LORD and his goodness in the latter days.

Here is an exceedingly interesting prophecy, to the effect that the children of Israel shall remain a long time without king or prince, without sacrifice, images, or any insignia of worship, whether true or false, required or forbidden. Images and teraphim (household gods) must be put in the latter class. The ephod was the outer robe of the high priest.——Cured of idolatry, yet not converted to the worship of the true God, they were to remain long in this peculiar, extraordinary state. Considering how strong their national passion has been to have a king and some established ceremonials of worship, either divine or idolatrous, this prophecy is surely such as no human sagacity could or would have made. Yet, ever since their own Messiah came in the flesh, or, more definitely, since the fall of their city under the Roman arms (A. D. 70), this has been precisely their condition.——"Afterwards"—somewhere in the times yet future—"they shall return and seek the Lord their God and David their king." Hosea is not alone in giving to David's greater Son the name David. Jeremiah (30 : 9) says—"They shall serve the Lord their God and David their king, whom I will raise up to them." Ezekiel likewise (34 : 23, 24, and 37 : 24, 25). David, considered as king, was a special type of the Messiah, so that the transfer of his name to the latter is natural.——To "fear the Lord" is the current phrase of the Old Testament for real piety —naturally so under a dispensation of "law as a schoolmaster." In this passage, the Hebrew verb which means, primarily, *to fear*, is followed by a preposition, meaning *toward* or *unto*, showing that this fear does not repel away from God, but rather draws toward him. The precise sense seems to be—to draw near to God in reverential fear and trust.——This view is confirmed by the addition of the word *goodness*, which cannot be a thing for Christians to *fear*, in the usual sense of this word. On the contrary, it draws them very near to his feet in the spirit of filial confidence and hope.—— In this spirit the children of Israel shall seek and approach the Lord "in the latter days." The time here designated can be no other in this case than the Gospel age. The phrase, "latter days," almost invariably has this sense.——The phrase, "the children of Israel," can have no special reference here to the ten tribes, but rather comprises all the Hebrew people, without distinction between Israel and Judah.—The ultimate conversion of the Jews is, therefore, distinctly foretold in this passage. It must come to pass in the latter days. It has not been yet, and therefore waits its fulfilment in the future.

It may be asked—Why interpret chapter iii. throughout, of the lineal Hebrew race, and not chapter i. likewise?

Ans. (1.) Chapter iii. bears this interpretation—has received, and is yet receiving a most striking fulfilment on this principle. Not this, but its opposite, is true of chapter i. It cannot be interpreted throughout of the lineal children of Israel. The facts of history forbid it.

(2.) Chapter iii. demands this construction. The entire scope of the chapter, so far as it is prediction, gives us precisely the anomalous condition of the Hebrew race, from the fall of Jerusalem down to their ultimate conversion; nothing more, nothing else.——On the contrary, in chapter i. there is no close connection of thought, holding the interpreter to the people of the ten tribes, or even to the lineal Hebrews. The last two verses may be applied without violence to a new and other Israel.

(3.) In general, the construction given to chapter i.: 10, 11 is justified, on its own proper grounds, to be determined in view of what it is, and of its relations to history and to the doctrine of the New Testament. So of the construction given above to chapter iii. It must be interpreted in view of what it is.——Such I hold to be the true theory of interpreting all prophecy.

CHAPTER IV.

THE Lord sets forth the great sin of the people; charges it largely to the account of the priests, whose flagrant neglects of duty he exposes and denounces, vs. 1–11; shows that idolatry is folly, v. 12, and begets licentiousness, vs. 13, 14. He solemnly warns Judah to avoid the sin and doom of Ephraim, vs. 15–19.

1. Hear the word of the LORD, ye children of Israel: for the LORD hath a controversy with the inhabitants of the land, because *there is* no truth, nor mercy, nor knowledge of God in the land.

The word rendered "controversy" often means an occasion for civil process in law—a case of crime so aggravated that it should come before the judges.——The word which, applied to God, is so well rendered mercy, might better, when applied to man, be rendered kindness, inasmuch as real mercy—the richest favors shown to the utterly vile and guilty—though found abundantly in God, can scarcely be predicated at all of men. Hence, kindness is, in this passage, the better rendering.——The Lord can have no peace with any people who misuse and abuse one another—truthless, unkind, and discarding the knowledge and claims of their God.

2. By swearing, and lying, and killing, and stealing, and committing adultery, they break out, and blood toucheth blood.

The Hebrew of this verse is a model of brevity and force—its infinitives absolute, standing naked, and as compact as possible.——"Swearing, lying, murdering, stealing, committing adultery"—they are outbreaking in all. Scorning restraint, they break over all bounds.——"Blood toucheth blood" in the strong sense that the streams from the first murdered man meet and mingle with the streams from the second, and scarcely can there be found a spot clean of the gore of murder.

3. Therefore shall the land mourn, and every one that dwelleth therein shall languish, with the beasts of the field, and with the fowls of heaven; yea, the fishes of the sea also shall be taken away.

Under such wickedness the whole land suffers; society is paralyzed; even beasts, fowls, and fishes sympathize and suffer under the general affliction.

4. Yet let no man strive, nor reprove another; for thy people *are* as they that strive with the priest.

Worst of all is the hopeless moral infatuation of the people. It is all in vain for one man to reprove another for sin. The people are like him who resists the judicial decisions given by the priest acting as judge, under God. Of him the law of Moses said (Deut. 17:12), "The man that will do presumptuously, and will not hearken unto the priest that standeth to minister there before the Lord thy God, or unto the judge, even that man shall die, and thou shalt put away the evil from Israel."——This sin is referred to as the height of defiant hardihood against God. Such were the people of Israel at this time.

5. Therefore, shalt thou fall in the day, and the prophet also shall fall with thee in the night, and I will destroy thy mother.

This abrupt change of person to direct address is for the sake of greater force. "Thou"—the people—"shalt fall," by awful judgments from God.——"The prophet" here is the false prophet who had misguided and deluded the people, and must perish with them.——No special stress should be given to his falling by night, and the people by day. Judgments fall thick; life is no longer sacred; men are dying day and night.——"Thy mother" is either the capital, the mother city, or the state, involving the nationality; probably, in this case, the latter. The nation was, in fact, utterly destroyed very soon.——The Hebrew word "destroy" carries here the strong idea—brought to perpetual silence.

6. My people are destroyed for lack of knowledge: because thou hast rejected knowledge, I will also reject thee, that thou shalt be no priest to me: seeing thou hast forgotten the law of thy God, I will also forget thy children.

From this doom the knowledge of God, exerting its legitimate influence, would have saved them—a glorious but just testimony to the value of this knowledge in sustaining the vital life of society.——Again the prophet accosts the priests directly, as if they stood in his eye, and fearlessly says, "Thou art the man!" "Because thou hast rejected knowledge, I have rejected thee from being a priest for me; thou hast forgotten the law of thy God; I, even I, will forget thy children."——God's *forgetting* their children means more than it expresses. For God to *forget* to protect and bless is to give up to unmingled curses. The turn given in this language is fearfully significant of retribution.——The Hebrew makes God's agency emphatic: "I, yea, *I*, will forget thy children."

7. As they were increased, so they sinned against me: *therefore* will I change their glory into shame.

"They" refers to the priests. The "increase" might be either in numbers or in wealth and honor; probably not either alone, but all. The more they prospered, by so much the more they sinned against God. Hence he would convert their glory into disgrace. The desolations of war and captivity soon fulfilled this threatening.

8. They eat up the sin of my people, and they set their heart on their iniquity.

By "sin," in this passage, some suppose the sin-offerings of the Mosaic law to be meant, and eating them to be the sin committed by the sons of Eli. See 1 Sam. 2 : 12–17.——The usual sense of the word is, however, preferable, and is fully sustained by the parallel clause, which is, literally, "They lift up their soul to their iniquity;" *i. e.*, they are interested and pleasurably excited by the sins of the people. They *eat* them, in the sense of enjoying them as hungry men enjoy a feast.——How horribly corrupt these priests must have been! So far gone in sin that they loved to have all the people sin!——The Hebrew verbs rendered "*eat up*" and "*set*" are future, implying not only that they have done, but will yet do this; are committed, past reclaim, to these sins.

9. And there shall be, like people, like priest: and I will punish them for their ways, and reward them their doings.

No wonder God has judgments in store for them, from which their superior dignity and rank shall by no means shield them.——Such is the import of this verse. As the people were doomed to desolating judgments, so also are the priests. Their office shall not conduct the lightnings of Jehovah's wrath *away* from their heads, but rather *down upon* them.

10. For they shall eat, and not have enough: they shall commit whoredom, and shall not increase: because they have left off to take heed to the LORD.

Resuming from v. 8 their eating the sins of the people, God now declares—They shall eat, but shall get no good of it; this being the sense of the words rendered "not have enough;" literally, "shall not be satisfied."

Adulterous life gives no increase of family—the natural consequences being the opposite of this. Barrenness was accounted one of the greatest calamities.——These sins are due to the fact that they have ceased to honor and fear Jehovah.

11. Whoredom and wine and new wine take away the heart.

This verse is a grand moral adage—an axiom in the philosophy of human life.——The "*heart*," in Hebrew usage, is sometimes wise and understanding, in reference to the intellectual faculties, and sometimes includes the moral purposes of the soul, as when God is said to be served with the whole heart.——"Taking away the heart," therefore, is robbing a man of his good sense, his moral stamina—of all that makes his manhood of any account. After whoredom and wine have done their work upon him, he is practically more brutish than rational and human. Hosea has a similar use of the word "heart" (7:11): "Ephraim is like a silly dove *without heart*"—lacking even natural sagacity to avoid the snare.

12. My people ask counsel at their stocks, and their staff declareth unto them: for the spirit of whoredoms hath caused *them* to err, and they have gone a whoring from under their God.

As if to prove how utterly whoredom and wine have robbed the people of their good sense, the Lord adduces their confidence in idol gods. "*My* people"—who ought to ask counsel of me—"ask counsel of their sticks of wood"—a justly contemptuous name for a wooden god; "and their staff"—a divining rod, makes revelations to them as an oracle.——This divining rod has been common among the miserable superstitions of heathenism, and is not unknown in nominally Christian lands.——"Whoredom" in this connection seems to be literal, sensual; not the spiritual whoredom of idolatry. The essential spirit of licentiousness has plunged them into error and folly, so that, from "being *under* their God," in a state of humble dependence and moral purity, they have gone utterly into this most imbruting sin. Idol worship in all ages and countries has been intensely licentious, mixed up with abominations too foul to be named.

13. They sacrifice upon the tops of the mountains, and burn incense upon the hills, under oaks and poplars and elms, because the shadow thereof *is* good: therefore your daughters shall commit whoredom, and your spouses shall commit adultery.

High places and groves of great natural beauty and sublimity have always been favorite localities for idol worship—as said here —"because the shadow thereof is good"—pleasant and attractive, it being the policy of Satan always to cluster around his worship all possible sensuous attractions.——Therefore the daughters and wives of the Hebrew idolaters became licentious and corrupt. This is only the natural consequence of such idolatry, practised amid such temptations to lewdness.

14. I will not punish your daughters when they commit whoredom, nor your spouses when they commit adultery: for themselves are separated with whores, and they sacrifice with harlots: therefore the people *that* doth not understand shall fall.

Some prefer to read interrogatively—"Shall I not punish," &c.? But the usual sense of the Hebrew words is simply declarative—"I will not." The sense seems to be—I will not punish your daughters and wives for sins for which you are mainly responsible. So long as you lead them into such scenes of temptation, and allure them on by your own example, upon yourselves and not upon them shall fall my heaviest judgments.——"Themselves are separated," &c., refers not to the daughters and wives, but to the fathers and husbands. The change of person is peculiar, but not uncommon in Hosea. The prophet is showing why the fathers and not their daughters, the husbands and not their wives, should be specially punished. They seek retired places with vile women; they offer idolatrous sacrifices with harlots—a class of women, as the Hebrew shows, *consecrated* to pollution in the idol temples.——Therefore this people, so utterly void of understanding, moral sense, and reason, shall fall, *i. e.*, into ruin.

15. Though thou, Israel, play the harlot, *yet* let not Judah offend; and come not ye unto Gilgal, neither go ye up to Beth-aven, nor swear, The LORD liveth.

Thus far in this chapter the sins of Israel, the ten tribes, have been portrayed. Here the prophet turns to admonish Judah to shun such crime and its consequent ruin.——Gilgal was one of the centres of idol worship, as was also Beth-aven, house of vanity, which was probably the place long known as Bethel—house of God. The change of name represents the change from the worship of Jehovah to the worship of mere nothings, vanities.——Both Gilgal and Bethel had been associated with the true worship of God; Gilgal ever since the rolling up of the heap of stones there on entering Canaan, and the circumcision of all the people there (Josh. 4 : 20 and 5 : 9), and Samuel's holding his circuit court there (1 Sam. 7 : 16); and Bethel, from that eventful night when the Lord met the youthful Jacob there (Gen. 28 : 16–19). This appropriation of God's house (Bethel) to the devil's worship is one of his own Satanic arts, kept up through all time.——"Nor swear," in the profane way of idol worshippers, "The Lord liveth." It seems to have been common to blend with idolatry some of the forms of recognizing the true God. This he abhorred.

16. For Israel slideth back as a backsliding heifer: now the LORD will feed them as a lamb in a large place.

"Sliding back" is not strong enough to represent the original word. The figure supposes a young heifer under the yoke (for the female was put to real work in the East), but resisting, refractory, yerking her head away, and running back—a very different sort of action from that gradual down-hill sliding which is commonly associated with the English word, backslide. It is unfortunate that the word backslide, taken from the Bible to describe a state of Christian experience, should by usage fall so far short of the Bible sense. It means here that Israel is persistent, stubborn, half frantic in her rebellion against God—a state of heart and life utterly far from true piety.——Now, *i. e.*, very soon, the Lord will give Israel a vast range of wilderness for her wanderings—will cast her forth from her land as a lamb might be cast forth from his secure and peaceful fold, to roam at large, homeless and unprotected. The passage predicts the captivity of the ten tribes to Assyria, but keeps up the figure of the refractory heifer, only changing from the heifer to the lamb as being more defenceless, and more wretched when lost and wandering alone. The heifer tears herself away; God lets her go, a wandering lamb, into a hopeless captivity.

17. Ephraim *is* joined to idols: let him alone.

The Hebrew word for idols implies things made with the toilsome but fruitless labor of human hands.——Ephraim is *joined* to them in the strong sense of being closely united and *adhering*, so to speak, to those senseless things.——"Let him alone," cannot, in this connection, be the declaration of God's purpose to abandon Ephraim and withdraw his Spirit, as has been supposed by some; but is God's command to Judah to desist from all society with Ephraim and leave him to sin and suffer alone. The general course of thought in the context, as well as the phrase itself, require the latter construction.——Here, for the first time in Hosea, we have the word "Ephraim" used for the kingdom and people of the ten tribes—a usage due to the great preponderance of this tribe in population and also in dignity as having the capital, Samaria, and as having furnished the first king, Jeroboam.

18. Their drink is sour: they have committed whoredom continually: her rulers *with* shame do love, Give ye.

"Drink," here, is not common drink, is certainly not cold water. The original is always *strong, intoxicating drink*, or the drinking itself—the carousals. The verb* which our translators have rendered "*is sour*," is used very frequently in the general sense of passing away, departing; and also in the special sense of departing from God, apostatizing, becoming degenerate. These two senses indicate the two constructions between which our choice is to be made. The general sense is here the more probable, as when Agag, using the same word (1 Sam. 15 : 32), said, "The bitterness of death *is past*." Hence I translate closely thus: "Their carousals are over; they plunge into lewdness; their shields (rulers) love shame." The better to bring out the sense, I paraphrase the verse thus: "When their carousals are past, their passions are sharpened for baser whoredom: their rulers, who ought to be their shields and safeguards against such baseness, are themselves so corrupt as to love what is only their shame."

The second construction is worthy of being suggested. By it, the first verb, rendered "*is sour*," has the sense of becoming apostate, thus: "He (Ephraim) becomes the more apostate from God through strong drink; so they plunge the deeper into whoredom,"

* סוּר.

&c. In this construction this verb looks toward its cognate * in v. 16: *There* Israel is refractory, like an unbroken heifer; *here* he becomes the more refractory as to God through strong drink. This verb unquestionably bears the sense of departing from God, becoming apostate and refractory, as may be seen in Deut. 11 : 16: "Ye *turn aside* and serve other gods." Ps. 14 : 3: "They are all *gone aside;* they are altogether become filthy," &c. But especially Jer. 5 : 23, where those two cognate verbs are brought together as parallel: "This people hath a *revolting* † and a rebellious heart; they are revolted ‡ and gone." This passage entirely confirms the close cognate relationship between these two verbs—that in v. 16, and this in 18.——The rendering of the verb with its noun in the first clause is more easy on the first construction above given, else the second of the two would be preferable. The ultimate sense is essentially the same, testifying to the fearfully demoralizing influence of strong drink toward lewdness in the orgies of idolatry.

The second verb in this verse, expressing the practice of lewdness, is made intensive by the usual repetition of the finite verb by means of the infinitive.——The reader will notice that my translation of the last clause differs from that of our English Bible in two respects, making "shame" the object of the verb, and entirely omitting the words "*Give ye.*" This last change follows the best critical authorities as to the original text. These omit this word rendered "Give ye" as spurious, or, as some conjecture, attach it to the previous verb, and thus reduplicate its two last radicals. The very apposite sense thus obtained in the place of one very obscure and inept, justifies this choice between the authorities for the original text.

19. The wind hath bound her up in her wings, and they shall be ashamed because of their sacrifices.

The whirlwind affords a common figure for those providential agencies with which God overwhelms and sweeps away the wicked. See Ps. 58 : 9; Prov. 1 : 27; Isa. 40 : 24, and 66 : 15, &c.——Here a bold poetic imagination gives to the whirlwind real life, and wings in which the guilty nation is enfolded, to be borne away to its final doom—captivity. Zechariah (5 : 5-11) has the same figure in a slightly different dress.——"They shall be confounded because of their sacrifices" to idol gods which cannot save. Their objects of confidence shall utterly fail them; the idols in which they trusted shall prove their curse.——So evermore must all the hopes of the wicked perish! That on which they rely for help shall become the millstone to sink them—the fire to scorch and blast them, for ever and ever!

* סָרַר. † סוּר. ‡ סָרַר.

CHAPTER V.

In general, the course of thought is the same in this chapter as in the fourth; rebukes for sin, threatening of near judgments, in which God's own hand should be specially manifest. Judah is spoken of more frequently than in chapter iv., and hence, Judah being less hardened than Ephraim, the strain of remark gives more intimations of hopeful repentance.

1. Hear ye this, O priests; and hearken, ye house of Israel; and give ye ear, O house of the king; for judgment *is* toward you, because ye have been a snare on Mizpah, and a net spread upon Tabor.

The priests and the king are specially called to attend to this message, because the threatened judgments were to fall first and most heavily on them. The word "judgment" in the original has the article, and should have in English—"for *the* judgment"—the one predicted and near impending—"is specially destined for *you*." The reason given is, they have ensnared the people into sin—"have been a snare," such as is laid to catch birds, "on Mizpah," &c. Mizpah and Tabor were "high places," locations for idol worship; the former east of Jordan, the latter west.

2. And the revolters are profound to make slaughter, though I *have been* a rebuker of them all.

The verb rendered "to make slaughter" is most commonly used for the slaughter of animals—rarely for the slaying of men; and in reference to animals, more often for purposes of sacrifice, less often for food. Here we may best take the most common sense. ——The word rendered "revolters," is used both in the concrete, meaning revolters, and in the abstract, revolting, departure from right, sin. The latter sense seems preferable here. I paraphrase thus: "They," the priests and the king, "make their sins deep, even in their slaying of animals for sacrifice;" they deviate widely from righteousness and from God, even in their religious ceremonies.——"But I will chastise them all." The sense given in the English version *may* be the true one: the one given here seems the more probable as being more in harmony with the course of thought, and equally in harmony with the usual sense of the words. The Lord assures them that their sacrifice of animals after the law of Moses, whether mixed up with idol worship and all manner of wickedness, or standing by itself, yet used as a cloak for their sin, would avail them nothing. They might go deep into it; it could be accounted only as so much the greater sin, and could by no means screen them from the judgments of God.

3. I know Ephraim, and Israel is not hid from me: for now, O Ephraim, thou committest whoredom, *and* Israel is defiled.

The special pertinence of the declaration "I know Ephraim," &c., comes from the thought in the verse preceding—the attempt to cover up idol worship and all wickedness, with the established religious rites of the Mosaic system. What if they do put on the fairest semblance of true worship, slaughtering animals by the thousand—"I know them;" I see through their hearts; Ephraim is full of whoredom (idolatry).——True it is that men only insult God the more when they assume that they can cover up sin by the forms of religion. To assume that God cannot see through this covering, is an insult to his omniscience; to assume that he can ever accept such hypocrisy, is an insult to his holiness.

4. They will not frame their doings to turn unto their God: for the spirit of whoredoms *is* in the midst of them, and they have not known the LORD.

A great moral truth lies here—that when men have given themselves up heartily to sin and the spirit of sinning rules, and they do not care to know God, then they will not make any honest efforts to turn to God; they will not shape their external doings so as to facilitate the turning of their hearts from sin to holiness. The reason why they will not is given here—the spirit of sinning is in them as the ruling power of their heart and life. They have not known the Lord, and do not intend to think or to learn of him.

5. And the pride of Israel doth testify to his face: therefore shall Israel and Ephraim fall in their iniquity; Judah also shall fall with them.

The pride of Israel is a true witness against him to the point here charged; for pride seals the evidence that the heart is hardened and perverse. When a sinner is proud in his sin and of his sin, he gives the strongest evidence of being fully committed and awfully hardened.——Therefore shall Israel and Ephraim fall under the judgments of God.——Judah comes in here, and henceforward through the chapter, as having shared in the guilt of Ephraim, and consequently as bound to share her doom.

6. They shall go with their flocks and with their herds to seek the LORD; but they shall not find *him;* he hath withdrawn himself from them.

In the day of their calamity they may summon to their help the most costly forms and services of religious worship, but all in vain. There comes a time when it is too late to cry even for mercy. The Scriptures repeatedly affirm this awful truth, as *e. g.* Prov. 1:24–31. When mercy has been abused too long, and patience in God ceases to be a virtue, then retribution must take its course—else law were a farce, and the throne of justice would sink into contempt.

7. They have dealt treacherously against the LORD: for they have begotten strange children: now shall a month devour them with their portions.

The charge of treachery looks to their violation of their covenant vows to be the Lord's. One proof of this perfidy was that they had begotten children of foreign mothers, by intermarriage or by adulterous connection with the heathen round about them. This, God had most explicitly forbidden, Ex. 34:16.——The time of their destruction hastens on; within one month they shall perish "with their portions"—their idol gods whom they had chosen as their helpers and refuge.

8. Blow ye the cornet in Gibeah, *and* the trumpet in Ramah: cry aloud *at* Beth-aven; after thee, O Benjamin.

The enemy are near; let the war-cry ring out the alarm on the very hill-tops where the idol temples stand. "Cry aloud at Beth-aven"—that place once sacred as *Bethel*, the house of God; now desecrated by idol-worship into *Beth-aven*—house of vanity—nothings.——"After thee, O Benjamin," it seems most natural to take as the very words of the outcry. "The foe is *after* thee," or behind thee, close upon thee.

9. Ephraim shall be desolate in the day of rebuke: among the tribes of Israel have I made known that which shall surely be.

The judgment on Ephraim should be sweeping and exterminating, putting an end to her nationality, and leaving her desecrated land a desolation.——"Rebuke" here refers to deeds, not words; to the judgments of war, subjugation, captivity.——The last clause refers to the warnings God had given to the people of the ten tribes by the mouth of Hosea and other prophets. What they had said from the Lord was wholly true, and should surely come to pass.

10. The princes of Judah were like them that remove the bound: *therefore* I will pour out my wrath upon them like water.

The "bound" referred to is the *landmark* by which contiguous estates were defined. In the absence of fences these "bounds" were relied on in practice. The sin of removing them is the greater because so easily done and so difficult of detection. The Mosaic law severely denounced this sin. (See Deut. 19:14 and 27:17.) It became a proverb to signify a man of no conscience and no honor.

11. Ephraim *is* oppressed *and* broken in judgment because he willingly walked after the commandment.

Ephraim is crushed utterly under the divine judgments because he heartily consented to walk after *the* commandment of Jeroboam, son of Nebat, who bade the people worship the golden calves at Bethel and at Dan. (1 Kings 12 : 28–33.) This is the commandment referred to as the first fatal step—the occasion of the sad relapse which was so soon to end in the utter ruin of the people and the kingdom.

12. Therefore *will* I *be* unto Ephraim as a moth, and to the house of Judah as rottenness.

This strong language implies sapping the nation's vitality and leaving it utterly powerless.

13. When Ephraim saw his sickness, and Judah *saw* his wound, then went Ephraim to the Assyrian, and sent to king Jareb: yet could he not heal you, nor cure you of your wound.

This "sickness" and "wound" are of the body politic. The sense is that each kingdom, conscious of its weakness and danger, sent to the Assyrian power for help, but to no good purpose.——Before the word "sent," *Judah* should be supplied. Ephraim went to the Assyrian king, and Judah sent, &c. The history takes note of both these facts. Ephraim (2 Kings 15 : 19, 20), threatened by Pul, king of Assyria, "gave him a thousand talents of silver, that his hand might be with him to confirm the kingdom in his hand." Judah (2 Kings 16 : 7), threatened by Rezin of Syria, sent to Tiglath-Pileser of Assyria for help. In neither case was this call for help of any avail.——"Jareb" is not the proper name of any king, but is a verb, meaning one who should interpose, or, in modern phrase, *intervene.* This was precisely what Ahaz king of Judah sought of the Assyrian king, that he should *intervene* and help himself against Rezin of Syria.

14. For I *will be* unto Ephraim as a lion, and as a young lion to the house of Judah: I, *even* I, will tear and go away; I will take away, and none shall rescue *him.*

The connection of thought is—No good can come of Assyrian help, "*for* I will be unto Ephraim as a lion," &c.,—the lion being a symbol of power that turns not from its purpose for any. Compare Ps. 50 : 22: "Consider this, ye that forget God, lest I tear you in pieces, and there be none to deliver." The symbol should not be forced so as to carry over to the Almighty *all* the qualities of the lion—not his ferocity, not his heartless cruelty, but only his great power which none can evade, none escape, none withstand.

——The *manner* of the lion is carried out here to a remarkable extent. He tears his prey in pieces; goes away; comes again; then takes some of it with him to his place, and none can rescue from his grasp.——There were points analogous to this in the ways of God toward Ephraim and Judah, as the prophet proceeds to show.

15. I will go *and* return to my place, till they acknowledge their offence, and seek my face: in their affliction they will seek me early.

Especially in this respect would the Lord be as a lion to those kingdoms. He would send one fearful scourge; then retire as it were to his place to watch and wait for the moral result. For God's purpose in sending these afflictions was never vindictive, was never merely to destroy, but only to constrain them to seek his face in repentance.——The verb rendered "acknowledge their offence" means primarily to be guilty; then to bear one's guilt in the sense of suffering punishment or chastisement for it. The latter seems clearly to be the sense here. There is no decisive usage to sustain the interpretation—"acknowledge one's offence."——The Lord, having sorely chastised them, would wait till they had borne the infliction, and had been brought by it to seek his face. He is sure that in their affliction they will seek him *early*, or earnestly, as one who is up betimes in the morning to a work lying near his heart. So the original implies.——Here the chapter closes, but the course of thought passes over to the next unbroken.

CHAPTER VI.

In this chapter we have calls to repentance, assurances of God's great mercy, but this mercy is grieved by the fickleness of God's degenerate people. It closes with continued details of aggravated wickedness.

1. Come, and let us return unto the Lord: for he hath torn, and he will heal us; he hath smitten, and he will bind us up.

With unsurpassed beauty and force, the Lord himself gives his people the very words with which they may exhort each other to return to him. The marvel is that in the figure the Lord is no more the lion, but an angel of mercy, coming down to bind up the wounds himself has made! And it is he himself that declares this—testimony, therefore, that could not be better. Indeed, we could not reasonably accept any other. For who else could know, or who else could make us believe, that the same God who hath torn will also heal—the same who hath smitten will also bind up? Such are the wondrous things of God's mercy.

2. After two days will he revive us: in the third day he will raise us up, and we shall live in his sight.

The general sense is clear. God will *soon* revive us if chastisement has wrought its proper fruits. Various conjectures have been made to answer the question, Why does he say so definitely, "After two days," "on the third day?"——Some have found here, as they suppose, an allusion to the resurrection of Christ. But this passage has the air of historic allusion and not of prophecy; and historic allusions look to the past, and not to the future. The manner of this passage is not that of *prophecy*, foretelling some future event to occur after two days or on the third, but it is rather that of a statement shaped by the thought, then present to the mind, of some analogous event in past, well-known history. Such an event I find substantially in the case of the pestilence sent on Israel for David's sin of numbering the people. (See 2 Sam. 24.) When for this sin three forms of judgment were proposed to David for his choice, he chose the pestilence, as coming more directly from the hand of God, saying, "Let us fall now into the hand of the Lord, for his mercies are great, and let me not fall into the hand of man." This pestilence continued three days, no more. The Lord became a lion to tear, so long;—then turned to revive and restore. This case, supposed to have been before the mind of Hosea, would fitly account for his naming two and three days. Hosea abounds, beyond most of the sacred writers, in historic allusions. ——A case much less closely parallel may be seen in the plague of darkness on Egypt of three days. And there may be a tacit allusion to the fact that three days is about the extent of human endurance under extreme privations and hardships, as *e. g.* the case of the Egyptian found by David's men. (1 Sam. 30:11, 12.) The sentiment would then be that God is wont to arrest his judgments before human endurance is quite exhausted.

3. Then shall we know, *if* we follow on to know the LORD: his going forth is prepared as the morning; and he shall come unto us as the rain, as the latter *and* former rain unto the earth.

Our translators apprise us that they found no word in the original for "*if*." It is more true to the original and equally pertinent sense to read it, "Then let us know, let us follow on to know the Lord," &c., *i. e.* encouraged by these demonstrations of his mercy, let us seek to know, yea let us follow on earnestly to know the Lord.——"His going forth," in this connection, is not his going in general, but his going forth in the revelations of his great mercy —his outgoing, as the sun comes to light after the darkness of storm or of night—the original word being currently used for the rising of the sun. David uses it in his exquisite nineteenth psalm, saying of the sun, "His *going forth* is from one end of the heavens and his circuit to the other end thereof." So God's coming forth in the displays of his mercy "is prepared as the morning," equally sure in its place, and nothing in nature more fitly represents the revelations of his mercy as they rise on benighted souls. ——The next figure also is rich in beauty and in blessings.——"He shall come unto us," corresponding in sense to his "going forth," "as the great rain" (often called the "former rain"), "and as the latter rain that water the earth." This is a precise translation of the original.——The former rain, succeeding a long dry season, falling from the middle of October to the middle of December, prepared the ground for seed-sowing, and if abundant, gave assurance of harvests. The latter rain fell in March and April, maturing the crops, and continuing in some seasons quite to their early harvest, from which fact it takes its Hebrew name.

Those who have "tasted that the Lord is gracious" will appreciate the fitness and force of these illustrations, and will not wonder that the most beautiful and beneficent things in nature are clustered together to set forth the munificent loving-kindness of the Lord.

4. O Ephraim, what shall I do unto thee? O Judah, what shall I do unto thee? for your goodness *is* as a morning cloud, and as the early dew it goeth away.

Alas! that there should ever be occasion to turn so abruptly from the glory of God's mercy to the meanness of man's sin!—from the enduring love and the well-ordered going forth of his light and salvation, to the fickleness of man's best resolutions, and to the inconstancy of his most hopeful professions!——The antithesis between this verse and the preceding one should be noted. The morning light, gloriously outbreaking from the east, is God's love-shining out on the darkness of the sin-stricken soul. The morning cloud and the early dew, hopeful and sweet for a moment, but soon gone up as if they had never been, are the goodness of God's inconstant people. We cannot wonder that the Lord should exclaim: "O Ephraim, what shall I do unto thee?" By what new and untried appliances shall I bring stability out of fickleness, and make your wavering steps steadfast?

5. Therefore have I hewed *them* by the prophets; I have slain them by the words of my mouth: and thy judgments *are as* the light *that* goeth forth.

As to the figures in this verse—"hewing them by the prophets," "slaying them by the words of my mouth"—we may fitly remember that Solomon says: "The words of the wise are as goads and as nails" (Eccl. 12:11), and Paul (Heb. 4:12) speaks of "the word of God as sharper than any two-edged sword, piercing even to the dividing asunder of soul and spirit," and also (Eph. 6:17) of "the sword of the Spirit, which is the word of God." The Lord signifies here that he has used sharp and cutting words in his messages to the people—has, in fact, exhausted the power of earnest language to pierce the hard shell of their heart and reach live flesh.——"Thy judgments are as the light"—clear, impressive, awe-inspiring as the lightnings of heaven—for so the word *may* signify. The instances of this usage are comparatively rare, however, and the common sense, light, is pertinent and forcible. God had made his displeasure toward their sins clear as the light.

6. For I desired mercy, and not sacrifice; and the knowledge of God more than burnt-offerings.

"Mercy" here represents the whole circle of moral duties toward man, as in the next clause, "the knowledge of God" stands for that which is practical, not theoretical only, and comprises all right affections toward God.——The people had shown themselves far more ready to offer sacrifices than to *do right* toward either God or man. The Lord, on the contrary, held sacrifices in low esteem, but held in the highest esteem mercy toward man and the intelligent worship and homage of the heart toward God.

See a similar doctrine taught in the Old Testament, Ps. 40:7–9 and 50:8–23; Isa. 1:11–17, and Micah 6:6–8.

Our divine Teacher on two several occasions endorsed the sentiment of this verse most emphatically, Matt. 9:13, and 12:7; "Go ye and learn what that meaneth; I will have mercy, and not sacrifice"—said, in this case, to show why he ate with publicans and sinners—viz., to save their souls.——"But if ye had known what this meaneth—'I will have mercy, and not sacrifice,' ye would not have condemned the guiltless;" said in rebuke of the Pharisees for their judgments in regard to keeping the Sabbath.——This form of statement should not be pressed to mean that God had never required sacrifice and burnt-offerings; this would not be true.

This doctrine needs often to be revived and reiterated, so prone are men to put the forms and ceremonies of religion in the place of real kindness and justice toward man, and honest heart-worship of God. American slaveholding Christianity is a striking case in point—an effort to conform Christianity to the demands of the time by framing a system of religion and morals with mercy and even justice left out, and the real knowledge of God woefully perverted.

7. But they like men have transgressed the covenant; there have they dealt treacherously against me.

The word rendered "men" is, in Hebrew, *adam*, and may be either a proper noun, meaning Adam, or a common noun, meaning *man*. Hence this clause has been construed three ways: (1.) "They, like common men, have transgressed the covenant"—the point being that *they*, being priests, princes, and a people long trained of God, have yet broken their covenant, as common men might do; or, (2.) "They are like men who break covenant"—the point here being that they break their covenant with God as men are wont to break their covenants with each other, accounting obligation to God no more sacred than a man's obligation to his fellow; or, (3.) "They, like Adam, have broken covenant;" their obligation, like his, being all the more sacred by reason of their intimate and honored relations to the glorious God.

Of these various interpretations, none bad, the last has in its favor the obvious antithesis between "they" and "Adam," which stands out strongly in the original, inasmuch as the use of the personal pronoun in Hebrew is not common, and is, therefore, usually somewhat emphatic where introduced as here.——A parallel case of the use of Adam as a proper and not a common noun, is found Job 31:33: "If I covered my transgressions as Adam" did, etc. ——"*There*," in the phrase, "there have they dealt treacherously," refers to the kingdom of the ten tribes, where the great mass had proved utterly treacherous toward God.

8. Gilead *is* a city of them that work iniquity, *and is* polluted with blood.

From general charges of sin, the prophet here becomes specific. ——Gilead (often called Ramoth-Gilead) was a prominent city of refuge (see Deut. 4:43) on the east of Jordan. The cities of refuge made special provision for the residence of the priests, who, indeed, were needed there to hold civil courts and determine questions of manslaughter, which naturally came to trial there. But this city was full of bloody violence—as the last clause of the verse has it— "tracked or footstepped with blood." Murderers left their bloody footprints along its streets.——It appears from 2 Kings, 15:25, that Pekah, in conspiring against and murdering Pekahiah, had with him fifty men of the Gileadites. To this fact the prophet may allude. From such a city he might get fit materials for conspiracy and murder.

9. And as troops of robbers wait for a man, *so* the company of priests murder in the way by consent: for they commit lewdness.

This might be closely translated thus: "As robber-gangs waylay men, so bands of priests commit murder on the way to Shechem, for they work out deep-laid schemes of crime."——Shechem (by mistake of our translators taken as a common noun) was another city of refuge, inhabited largely by priests therefore, who waylaid travellers coming to the city—perhaps the implication is, such as were fleeing thither for refuge—so horribly did they pervert the functions of justice committed to their hands!——The last word does not mean lewdness, but intentional, studied crime—all the more guilty in the view both of God and man for the amount of thought and deep-laid plot that entered into it.

10. I have seen an horrible thing in the house of

Israel: there *is* the whoredom of Ephraim, Israel is defiled.

It is in view of such particulars as these that the Lord now exclaims, "I have seen horrible things in the house of Israel!"——"Whoredom" seems here to be idolatry, the mother sin of all sins in the land.

11. Also, O Judah, he hath set an harvest for thee, when I returned the captivity of my people.

This verse has caused commentators much perplexity. The questions have been, whether the "harvest" appointed of God for Judah betokened blessings or calamities; and, if the latter, how it can correspond with bringing back their captives—a fact which naturally and usually indicates blessings.——The first word, well rendered "also," implies that the Lord had something for Judah *of the same sort* which he was about to bring on Ephraim; and there can be no doubt that the strain of the previous context assumes the near coming of fearful judgments on Ephraim.——Then further, prophetic usage very uniformly makes the harvest a symbol of judgments. (See Jer. 51:33; Joel 3:13; Rev. 14:15–20.) These considerations go far to show that the passage must predict judgments on Judah—naturally, a great slaughter. It only remains to see how this can comport with the Lord's bringing back the captives of his people. The history recorded 2 Chron. 28:1–15 solves this remarkable problem, meeting all its difficulties, and readily accounting for its apparent incompatibilities.

Ahaz, king of Judah, reigned wickedly; for which God delivered him into the hand of the king of Syria, who smote him and took many captives to Damascus. God also delivered him into the hand of the king of Israel, who smote him with great slaughter. "For Pekah slew in Judah one hundred and twenty thousand in one day, because they had forsaken the Lord God of their fathers." He also took away two hundred thousand captives, women, sons, and daughters, and brought them to Samaria.——Here was a fearful harvest in the sense of a great slaughter. Yet, contrary to all human expectation, it was closely connected with God's interposition to bring back the captives of his people, for the history proceeds to say that when the captives were brought into Samaria, a prophet of the Lord was there by the name of Oded, and that he went before the host of Israel and expostulated with them earnestly, and finally persuaded them to send all the captives home. Hence, although God brought back their captives, yet a harvest was set for Judah in the usual sense of an immense slaughter of their people.

CHAPTER VII.

Speaking of Ephraim, this chapter continues to portray his treachery, blindness, intense passion in sinning, and extreme folly. It should be specially noted that throughout this and the succeeding chapters to the twelfth, Ephraim, the kingdom of the ten tribes, is the theme of remark, Judah being scarcely mentioned. The historic events alluded to fell within the last years of the kingdom—some of them in the reign of Hoshea, its last king.

1. When I would have healed Israel, then the iniquity of Ephraim was discovered, and the wickedness of Samaria: for they commit falsehood: and the thief cometh in, *and* the troop of robbers spoileth without.

The time specially referred to, when the Lord sought to heal Israel, and the indications were hopeful, may probably have been when they sent home their Jewish captives, as in 2 Chron. 28: 9–15—historically coincident with the events referred to in the close of the previous chapter. At that time "certain of the heads of the children of Ephraim" acknowledged the guilt of their nation, and spake sensibly of "God's fierce wrath against Israel." But these hopeful appearances soon passed away; the nation proved false to Jehovah and false to even common morality; thieves break into houses and robbers plunder abroad.——So it often happens that the deepest wickedness comes to light only under the special efforts which the Lord makes to heal and restore. When wicked men will not be healed, and only become the more infatuated and determined, and the more outbreaking in their sin for all the labor of love which God bestows upon them to reclaim them, they are fast verging to the brink of ruin. How painfully discouraging even to infinite patience and pity!

Some suppose that the period specially referred to as one in which the Lord would have healed Israel, was during the reign of Jeroboam second. This reign was one of general prosperity. (See 2 Kings 14: 23–28.) He restored the coast of Israel on the north, as had been foretold by Jonah: "For the Lord saw the affliction of Israel that it was most bitter, for there was not any shut up, nor any left, nor any helper for Israel; and the Lord said not that he would blot out the name of Israel from under heaven; but he saved them by the hand of Jeroboam, the son of Joash."

Manifestly here was one special effort to heal Israel. Hosea may have thought of more than one. The Lord is wont to repeat such efforts of reclaiming mercy.

2. And they consider not in their hearts, *that* I remember all their wickedness: now their own doings have beset them about; they are before my face.

Literally—"They do not *say* to their heart, I remember all their wickedness. Now their own doings invest them—lie on the outside surface as a garment—palpably before my face, with no concealment."

3. They make the king glad with their wickedness, and the princes with their lies.

Their king and princes, instead of frowning upon the wickedness of the people, were in full sympathy with it, and could be drawn in to rejoice in it all.

4. They *are* all adulterers, as an oven heated by the baker, *who* ceaseth from raising after he hath kneaded the dough, until it be leavened.

"Adulterers," probably in the literal, not the symbolic sense. Idolatry fostered lewdness.——The figure of an "*oven*," as used in vs. 4, 6, 7, demands special notice. Of course, we must go far back of the modern stove-oven in which the heat is generated and used at the same time. In the kind of ancient oven here referred to, as also in those used commonly before the age of stoves, the heating is done *before* the baking, and the excellence of the oven consists in its power to *hold heat*, and give it up gradually for baking purposes. Precisely at this point the figure applies. The baker gets up an intense heat, and then takes out his fuel and lets it rest till the first intense heat is somewhat abated. He trusts his oven to hold heat while his dough is rising; indeed, by closing his oven with his fuel in, he may keep the heat confined there so that he can sleep all night, and yet find every thing ready for flaming out in the morning.——So these wicked men are perpetually heated up with the hot passions of sin. They do not need new incitements continually. The old fires, smothered for a time, flame out again on the first occasion. The heart of wicked men *holds heat*—the heat of sinful passion—like an oriental oven.——The last clause of v. 4, should read, "ceaseth from firing up," *i. e.*, his oven, "after the kneading of the dough, until it is risen." Once intensely heated, it can be trusted to rest, and indeed to bake only the better therefor.

5. In the day of our king the princes have made *him* sick with bottles of wine; he stretched out his hand with scorners.

"The day of our king" would naturally be his birth-day, or perhaps his coronation-day—devoted, therefore, to special festivities. On that day, "the princes made him sick (intoxicated) with the *heat* of wine," not "bottles." "He stretched out his hand with scorners," Belshazzar-like; for when men are inflamed with wine, they are wont to scoff at things sacred.

6. For they have made ready their heart like an

oven, while they lie in wait: their baker sleepeth all the night; in the morning it burneth as a flaming fire.

7. They are all hot as an oven, and have devoured their judges; all their kings are fallen: *there is* none among them that calleth unto me.

The special form of wickedness spoken of here is that of plotting the destruction of their princes, judges, and kings. That such conspiracies were shockingly common, the brief history of this period shows.

The verse may be rendered thus: "For they bring their hearts close together as in the oven, in their plots; all night their baker sleeps" (so perfectly is the plot laid); "in the morning he burns as with the fiery flame." [The baker represents the managing spirit of the plot.] "All of them are hot as the oven: they devour their judges," as fire devours; "all their kings fall" (before such conspiracies), "and none among them call unto me"—to the fear of God and to repentance for such wickedness.

8. Ephraim, he hath mixed himself among the people; Ephraim is a cake not turned.

The "people" here are the heathen nations. Ephraim had mixed himself with them by means of entangling alliances, but more especially by importing their idol-worship. The figure of "a cake not turned," is suggested by the oven. The kind of oven thought of here seems to be different from that in mind in the previous verses. The most ancient mode of baking was to heat the naked sand with a fire; then remove the fire, and lay on the dough. This, of course, must soon be "turned." To this our verse alludes. Another form of oven was a hole excavated in the earth and walled up; and still a third, bearing the name given here, vs. 4, 6, 7, was made of brick, besmeared within and without with clay.

"A cake not turned" in the first-named sort of oven, would naturally be burned on one side, and raw on the other—all worthless—spoiled by bad baking. The *fact* of its being spoiled, rather than any particular analogy in the *mode* of doing it, seems to be the thought of the passage.

9. Strangers have devoured his strength, and he knoweth *it* not: yea, gray hairs are here and there upon him, yet he knoweth not.

As usual in the Scriptures, "strangers" are foreigners—born in other lands. Indications of decrepitude and of death near at hand are on him, and he is not aware of it.

10. And the pride of Israel testifieth to his face: and they do not return to the LORD their God, nor seek him for all this.

The same expression as to pride occurred above (5 : 5). Pride is working his ruin. The judgments of God fail of leading him to return in penitence.

11. Ephraim also is like a silly dove without heart: they call to Egypt, they go to Assyria.

A "silly dove," means one open to seductive influences—easily drawn into the fatal snare. So, "without heart," means without wisdom or sense to suspect and avoid danger. Ephraim plunges into danger, as appears by his sending to Egypt for help and going to Assyria. This was putting his head within the jaws of the lion. God had warned him against this course; he would not hear.

12. When they shall go, I will spread my net upon them; I will bring them down as the fowls of the heaven; I will chastise them, as their congregation hath heard.

With the figure of the dove still before the mind, the Lord says —"When they fly off to Assyria or Egypt for help I will spread my net over them; I will bring them down as by the shafts of the fowler; I will chastise them, as hath been heard from the lips of the prophets in their congregation," where those prophetic messages were publicly read.

13. Woe unto them! for they have fled from me: destruction unto them! because they have transgressed against me: though I have redeemed them, yet they have spoken lies against me.

"Fled" still keeps up the figure of the dove. The people utterly turned away from God, and this became their ruin. God had redeemed them often from their enemies—from Pharaoh, and from the strong nations on their borders; yet they would prove false to all their professions of penitence and fidelity.——In the original the verb translated "have redeemed," is in the tense commonly called the future, but perhaps better, the imperfect or incomplete—indicating in this case not only that God *had* redeemed them, but would now and hereafter—this being the permanent state of his mind toward them. The clause might be fitly paraphrased, "Though I would gladly redeem them at any time, as I have often done already, yet they only speak lies against me."

The passage puts in forcible contrast the loving faithfulness of God, still warm and sure, on the one hand; and, on the other, the treachery and utter infidelity of his people. The original makes this contrast the more palpable by writing out in full the pronouns "I" and "they." These pronouns are not usually written in Hebrew except for the sake of emphasis.——"Redeemed" is the usual word for the deliverance God wrought for his people from Egypt. (See Deut. 7: 8, and 13 : 5, and Micah 6 : 4.)

14. And they have not cried unto me with their heart, when they howled upon their beds: they assemble themselves for corn and wine, *and* they rebel against me.

Under their affliction, when they howled upon their beds, in their anguish, they would not sincerely cry unto God. They assembled in their idol temples to implore corn and wine of their false gods; and so they rebelled yet the more grievously against Jehovah.——The last three verbs, "howl," "assemble," "rebel," are in the imperfect—incomplete tense, implying not only that they *had*, but *would yet*. They were doomed to "howl;" it was fully in their heart to "assemble," and to "rebel."

15. Though I have bound *and* strengthened their arms, yet do they imagine mischief against me.

The word rendered "bound" means to chasten and correct. God had in this way taught them, and he had also made their arm strong in war; yet they only do and will plot revolt and wrong against him. Here also the last verb is in the imperfect, denoting a state of mind yet active and fixed.

16. They return, *but* not to the Most High: they are like a deceitful bow: their princes shall fall by the sword for the rage of their tongue: this *shall be* their derision in the land of Egypt.

If they turned, in any sense, it was not to the Most High. The original most naturally reads, "They will turn to a *no-god*"—to one *not* the Most High, but the opposite—one infinitely low and mean. So in the words, Lo-Ammi, Lo-Ruhamah, the negative particle gives the opposite sense—a people *rejected* from being mine—to whom mercy is denied.——"A deceitful bow" makes the arrow miss the mark, and therefore cannot be trusted. So with Israel.——"The rage of their tongue" is their insolence of language, probably in boasting of help from Egypt, despite of God's warning to the contrary. When they shall have come into Egypt, captive and weak, this proud boasting will be their special derision. Hoshea, the last king of the ten tribes, sought help from Egypt against the king of Assyria, but only to his shame and ruin. (2 Kings 17:4.)——So shall it ever be with all who depart from God!

CHAPTER VIII.

ISRAEL is still the subject of rebuke, and of threatened judgment—the prophet bringing forth to view her sins, her resort to idol gods and to foreign alliances, to the rejection of her own ever-living God, and showing that this policy must be utterly ruinous.

1. *Set* the trumpet to thy mouth. *He shall come* as an eagle against the house of the LORD, because they have transgressed my covenant, and trespassed against my law.

This verse is remarkably in the peculiar style of Hosea—abrupt and bold. "To thy mouth the trumpet;" [the foe comes down] "as an eagle upon the house of the Lord, because they [my people] have broken my covenant and sinned against my law."

The blast of the trumpet, long and loud, was the alarm for war. The coming of the foe is compared with the swoop of the eagle, when, from his lofty height, he comes down upon the temple. This coming down on the temple may suggest that even this sacred symbol of Jehovah's presence in the land cannot shield it from the fierce invader.

The eagle in his flight is frequently, in Scripture, a symbol of swiftness and of terrible conquest. Thus, Deut. 28:49: "The Lord shall bring a nation against thee from far, from the ends of the earth, as swift as the eagle flieth." Also, Lam. 4:19: "Our persecutors are swifter than the eagles of heaven."——This fearful foe comes because the nation has so utterly apostatized from their God.

2. Israel shall cry unto me, My God, we know thee.

Grievously as they had departed from God, they still made high religious professions, vainly claiming to know the true God. So in later times they said, "We have Abraham to our father." "Have we not prophesied in thy name?"

The English translation renders it "*shall cry*," as if the thought were future only. The Hebrew imperfect rather means the past running on into the future. They have done, and still do.

3. Israel hath cast off *the thing that is* good: the enemy shall pursue him.

The repetition of the name "Israel" is expressive. The same people, Israel, who claim to know the true God, have, in truth, scornfully repelled all that is good; *i. e.* both God and his blessings. Hence, enemies shall pursue him; or, as the original word means, chase him down.

The verb rendered "cast off" has, for its primary sense, to be foul, nauseous, loathsome; then, to reject and cast off *as* loathsome. The latter is the sense here. With loathing has this Israel, who claims to know me, spurned away all good, even God himself.

4. They have set up kings, but not by me: they have made princes, and I knew *it* not: of their silver and their gold have they made them idols, that they may be cut off.

From Jeroboam of Nebat onward they have set up kings after their own heart, with no regard to God's will. So of their princes; *they* have made them, and without my approval—the word "know" being used here in this not infrequent sense.

They had made idol images out of their silver and gold, to the end that they might be cut off; *i. e.* not of *their intention*, but of God's purpose, and of both natural and actual *result*. The ruin of the nation was both a righteous and a natural retribution for this sin—natural because idolatry and its associate vices were essential rottenness in the bódy politic.

5. Thy calf, O Samaria, hath cast *thee* off; mine anger is kindled against them: how long *will it be* ere they attain to innocency?

"Thy calf, Samaria," is the golden one set up by Jeroboam (see 1 Kings 12 : 26–33), out of which grew the idol worship of the kingdom of the ten tribes. Samaria, the capital, here represents the whole kingdom; the calf was properly theirs.

The verb rendered "cast off" is the same that is used and so rendered in v. 3, but manifestly here with a slight modification of meaning;—there, in the sense of repelling with loathing; here, in the sense of being loathsome, abominable. There is no word for "thee," as found in the English translation, which unfortunately fails to give the true sense.——There is great force and beauty in this play upon the two kindred meanings of the same word. Thus, v. 3: "With loathing has Israel rejected God and all real good;" v. 5: "Truly and intensely loathsome is thy calf, Samaria." Thou hast thrust from thee thy God and all his blessings, as things loathsome; the really loathsome thing is *thy calf.*

To this construction the next clause fits perfectly: "Mine anger is kindled against the worshippers of that abominable calf."——The last clause is literally rendered, "How long will they be impotent as to moral innocence?" *i. e.* with no recuperative moral power to return to sense, and to the reasonable worship of the true God?——In how many cases, throughout all ages, must a holy and compassionate God deplore the same moral impotence in wicked men! Inasmuch as God was constantly acting upon them toward "innocency," we must understand this verse to imply that there was no conscience, and no moral sensibility in them, to respond healthfully under the divine efforts made for their recovery.

6. For from Israel *was* it also: the workman made it; therefore it *is* not God: but the calf of Samaria shall be broken in pieces.

The aggravation of this case was that the calf "came out *from Israel*"—from God's chosen people. "A workman made it" with his human fingers, so that it is no god at all. On the contrary, according to the expressive Hebrew, "it shall become fragments."——The prophets were wont to expose the ineffable folly of idol-worship and of all trust in idols, by referring to their origin as nothing higher or other than human workmanship. A mere man made it, made all there is of it; and can that senseless, helpless thing be *God?*

7. For they have sown the wind, and they shall reap the whirlwind: it hath no stalk: the bud shall yield no meal: if so be it yield, the strangers shall swallow it up.

They—the idol-worshippers—in forsaking the true God for idols, have sown the wind; and how vain a thing this is, any one will see who will suppose himself actually attempting to do it.——The passage becomes terribly forcible when this sowing of wind, vain and empty as it would seem to be, brings forth for its harvest the *whirlwind*—one of the most fearfully destructive agencies in nature.

The idea of a harvest is still kept up, and the prophet proceeds to say, "There is no stalk to it; its shoot will not produce meal; or, if it should, foreigners shall devour it."——"Strangers," in the Bible, are always foreigners; not merely those with whom we have no personal acquaintance.

8 Israel is swallowed up: now shall they be among the Gentiles as a vessel wherein is no pleasure.

The last verb of the verse preceding gives the leading thought of this verse. All Israel is "swallowed up;" not only will a foreign foe swallow up all the harvests of the land; the very *nation* is swallowed up, and its nationality is to become extinct.——"Now," *i. e.* shortly, they shall be among the nations as a vessel of no value, for which nobody cares; a potsherd, a piece of broken crockery, simply useless.

9. For they are gone up to Assyria, a wild ass alone by himself: Ephraim hath hired lovers.

As showing how low they have sunk in general esteem among the nations of their time, the prophet goes on to say, "They have gone to Assyria for help"—wild, wayward, solitary and friendless as the wild ass that has no affinities for other animals, and little, at best, for his own species.

In the words "Ephraim hath hired lovers," the idea of his marriage relations to Jehovah reappears. This going to other nations and not to God for help, is the baseness of an adulteress, forsaking the home and the love of her husband, and sunk so low that, instead of being hired for prostitution, she herself hires her paramours. Ephraim in his distress goes for help, not to his God, who would have joyfully relieved him with no thought of pay, but to heathen nations, and pays them enormously. See a case of such exaction, 2 Kings 15:19, 20, where Menahem, king of Israel, gave to Pul of Assyria one thousand talents of silver, and "exacted the money of Israel, even of all the mighty men of wealth, of each man fifty shekels of silver, to give to the king of Assyria." Hoshea also, the last king, paid tribute, 2 Kings 17:3.

10. Yea, though they have hired among the nations, now will I gather them, and they shall sorrow a little for the burden of the king of princes.

This verse has perplexed commentators, especially because of the difficulty of determining the root and the exact sense of the verb rendered, in our version, "sorrow." Without entering upon minute Hebrew criticism, let it suffice that I find here threatening, not promise, the former only being in harmony with the strain of the context; and therefore I derive the verb from the root * which means to writhe, to be in pain, etc. The sense of the passage then is, "Although Ephraim hires foreign help [in the line of ungodly national alliances], yet now will I gather them" (*i. e.* group them all under this scourge), "and they shall soon be in anguish under the burden of exactions imposed by the king of princes."

This "king of princes" is the Assyrian who said (Isa. 10: 8), "Are not my princes altogether kings?" Several kingdoms were then his tributaries.

The received version unfortunately gives the sense of "sorrowing *a little*," instead of sorrowing severely, VERY SOON, as the original obviously means. The marginal reading—"in a little while"—should have gone into the text. The verb is very intensive.

11. Because Ephraim hath made many altars to sin, altars shall be unto him to sin.

The verb rendered "to sin," in the phrases "made altars *to sin;*" "altars shall be to him *to sin;*"—is the same in both clauses. If taken in precisely the same sense in both cases, it would give this as the meaning of the verse—"Because Ephraim has multipled idol altars for purposes of sin, they shall be to him the occasion of more and greater sin."

I suggest a slight modification in the sense of this verb on its second occurrence—a usage quite common in Hosea. This verb, *to sin*, means primarily, to miss the mark, to misdirect, and consequently to fail of one's object, and so to reap disaster rather than

* חול

profit. Modifying this verb, therefore, on its second occurrence, we have this sense—"Because Ephraim multiplied altars *for sin*, altars shall be to him *for ruin.*" He meant to deviate from right: he shall thereby, in fact, miss happiness. He meant to wander from God: he shall really wander from all good.

Such a play upon two well-known senses of the same word is one of the beauties of the style of Hosea. The verb rendered "cast off," in vs. 3 and 5 above, is another case in this chapter. To make the mutual relation of "cast off," v. 3, to "cast off," v. 5, the more obvious, the verb in each case stands at the head of its verse; as in the verse before us correspondingly, "to sin" is the closing word in each clause.

12. I have written to him the great things of my law, *but* they were counted as a strange thing.

This had been the chief aggravation of the sin of Ephraim. God had sent to him in writing the great things of his law—its great truths, principles, and rules of life; yet he had practically accounted them as foreign and unworthy of his thought or care. This is the monster sin of all those in Christian lands who repel the light of God's word, and sin on as if no Bible had ever been given them. Jesus said (John. 15: 22), "If I had not come and spoken unto them, they had not had sin; but now they have no cloak [excuse] for their sin."

The original verb, "have written," is in the tense which implies incomplete action. God had written, and had yet more to write.

13. They sacrifice flesh *for* the sacrifice of mine offerings, and eat *it; but* the LORD accepteth them not; now will he remember their iniquity, and visit their sins: they shall return to Egypt.

"As to the sacrifices of things dedicated to me, they sacrifice flesh, and then eat;—Jehovah does not accept them"—*i. e.* abhors them. The sacrifices referred to were professedly made to God, but made before the golden calves, or in the worship of Baal or other idols. It should be remembered that Jeroboam's original plan was professedly to change the *place* and, slightly, the *form* of worship, rather than *the* God to be worshipped. Bringing forth his two calves of gold, he said: "It is too much for you to go up to Jerusalem; behold thy gods, O Israel, which brought thee up out of the land of Egypt."——By a form of retribution, strikingly in line with the sin which was borrowed from Egypt, they were doomed to return to Egypt. Some of them soon fled thither to escape the Assyrian arms, and, contrary to their intentions, never returned again to their native land. The whole nation returned again to a state of captivity and oppression analogous to their former one in Egypt.

14. For Israel hath forgotten his Maker, and buildeth temples; and Judah hath multiplied fenced cities: but I will send a fire upon his cities, and it shall devour the palaces thereof.

These temples were for their idols.—The sin of Judah, in multiplying fenced (fortified) cities, lay in making strong cities rather than the Almighty God their hope and refuge. God would soon send a fire upon their strong cities and consume all their lofty palaces.

CHAPTER IX.

EPHRAIM is still the subject; the strain of rebuke for sin is more and more mingled with announcements of near impending judgment.

1. Rejoice not, O Israel, for joy, as *other* people: for thou hast gone a whoring from thy God, thou hast loved a reward upon every corn-floor.

The first clause means precisely—"Rejoice not, O Israel, unto the point of exultation, as other nations may." Comparatively speaking, it was legitimate for the latter to exult in their prosperity, and in the abundance of their fruits; but not so for Israel. She had sinned against so much light and against obligations so sacred, it was madness for her to exult in her blessings. God would surely tear them away, and leave her to desolation.——So terrible a thing it is to sin against great mercies! He who does it should take this admonition. Rejoice not as others may fitly do, for there will soon be an utter end to blessings so ungratefully and so fatally abused.

The idolatry of Israel is here, as heretofore, spoken of as adultery. The original word for "reward" is currently used for the hire of harlots. It is spoken of here as being "on every corn-floor," because, like the heathen about them, idolatrous Israel had sunk so low as to attribute her corn and wine to Baal's favor and not to Jehovah's. Hence she paid her offerings to Baal—here thought of as the harlot-hire of her spiritual adultery.

2. The floor and the winepress shall not feed them, and the new wine shall fail in her.

Passing from the sin to the curse for sin, God declares that these blessings—the fruits of the earth—shall fail them. Neither the corn-floor nor the wine-press shall supply them food; the new wine shall prove false—shall *lie* to them, as the original has it. The last words ("in her") mean either in the wine-press, or in the land; —sense, shall *lie* to the people.

3. They shall not dwell in the LORD's land; but

Ephraim shall return to Egypt, and they shall eat unclean *things* in Assyria.

The land, sacred so long as the land of promise, and subsequently so long the land of Jehovah's presence and power, would spew them out as unfit to live in it. Egypt and Assyria were their only fit abode. It would seem that many individuals from the ten tribes fled to Egypt for refuge from the impending storm of Assyrian invasion, hoping to return soon. Others, the greater portion, were borne away into Assyria, and there doomed to eat things unclean and abominable to a Jew—fit retribution on them for eating so long and against so much light, in idol temples.

4. They shall not offer wine-*offerings* to the LORD, neither shall they be pleasing unto him: their sacrifices *shall be* unto them as the bread of mourners; all that eat thereof shall be polluted: for their bread for their soul shall not come into the house of the LORD.

According to the Mosaic ritual (Num. 15: 5, 7, 10) wine was poured out in certain sacrifices. The prophet here says, they shall offer it no more to the Lord; if they do, he will not accept it.

"The bread of mourners" was deemed unclean, as was also whatever had been near a dead body.——"Bread for their soul" probably means bread for sustenance, for the physical life. It had been customary to feast upon large portions of what was offered in sacrifice to God. The prophet here declares that this shall be no longer. The food for their subsistence should no more come into the sacred temple of Jehovah. He could no longer have such fellowship with his apostate people as this communion in bread would imply.——Another construction of this last clause (not preferred, however) may be noticed.—Their bread shall be *for themselves alone;* it shall not come into the house of the Lord. So Gesenius and Henderson.

5. What will ye do in the solemn day, and in the day of the feast of the LORD?

A rendering more true to the original, and giving better the exact sense, would be—"What will ye do *for* the day of solemn assembly, and *for* the day of the feast of the Lord?" They could no more have them in the remote land of their captivity. They would sadly miss those seasons of great public rejoicing. (See Hos. 2: 11.)

6. For, lo, they are gone because of destruction: Egypt shall gather them up, Memphis shall bury them: the pleasant *places* for their silver, nettles shall possess them: thorns *shall be* in their tabernacles.

The reason why they could not have those national festivals is given—*For* they have fled their country because of impending destruction. They shall die and be buried in Egypt—whither some had fled, never thinking to lay their bones there.—Memphis is specially named because it was a noted burying-place of Egyptians, as its tombs and mummies are proving at this day.——The clause rendered "pleasant places for their silver," seems to mean, their costly and most valued property—the original words making prominent the two ideas—*desire* and *money*,—that which men love, and which costs silver. Those things nettles shall inherit, and of course, occupy. Desolation comes over whatever was fairest and most valued.

7. The days of visitation are come, the days of recompense are come; Israel shall know *it:* the prophet *is* a fool, the spiritual man *is* mad, for the multitude of thine iniquity, and the great hatred.

This "visitation" is for judgment. "Recompense," parallel to it, is retribution for their great sin.——"Israel shall know it" experimentally; know it in such a way as precludes not only all mistake, but all indifference and insensibility.——The "prophet" here must be the false one who had misled the people. He is shown to be a fool by the failure of all his predictions and promises.——"The spiritual man"—literally, "the man of the spirit"—represents the class who professed to be filled with some superhuman spirit, but were utterly far from God and his Spirit. These men have been known by various names—magicians, sorcerers, soothsayers, &c., down to "spiritists." It is here said of him that he is "frantic," beside himself, because of the greatness of their iniquity (and of its resulting punishment), and of the great hatred—*i. e.* felt by God against such sin. Its sense is—In the days of God's visitation, the false prophets, who had so long deceived the people, were appalled, their folly exposed, and themselves driven mad with vexation, chagrin, and shame, before the dreadful wrath of Jehovah upon his people.

8. The watchman of Ephraim *was* with my God: *but* the prophet *is* a snare of a fowler in all his ways, *and* hatred in the house of his God.

Our translators seem to have understood the first clause to speak of God's true prophets, and as standing on the side of God. But both the context and the grammatical construction oppose their view. The course of thought here respects the false, not the true prophet, and the form of the word requires us to render, not "the watchman of Ephraim," but "Ephraim was watching," *i. e.* looking for and awaiting good from with my God. Despite of his great sin, Ephraim was full of hope and expectation of good from Jehovah—probably with reference to help against their foreign enemies —which help might have come had not the false prophet been as the snare of a fowler over all his ways, and the occasion of God's hating them the more even for their coming into his temple.——In this manner repeatedly is this grievous apostasy of the people ascribed largely to the terribly pernicious influence of corrupt priests and false prophets. Truly there can be no power for evil so active and so fatal as a corrupt ministry—as flagrant sin in those who speak for God and of him to men.

9. They have deeply corrupted *themselves*, as in the days of Gibeah: *therefore* he will remember their iniquity, he will visit their sins.

The sin of Gibeah at the time referred to may be seen, Judg. 19:22–25. An appalling history! Alas for the dreadful corruption of the land of Ephraim, if it was fitly compared to those scenes in Gibeah of Benjamin! Good reason why God should remember their iniquity and visit retribution upon the whole land!

10. I found Israel like grapes in the wilderness; I saw your fathers as the first ripe in the fig-tree at her first time: *but* they went to Baal-peor, and separated themselves unto *that* shame; and *their* abominations were according as they loved.

The true light for seeing their sins can be had only through contrast with the bright days of their early national history. Hence this historical sketch.——As one finds grapes in the wilderness, himself weary and hungry, and not expecting luscious fruit amid such barrenness, and therefore is filled with joy at the discovery, so the Lord found Israel. The first ripe figs in their first bearing year furnish the next beautiful figure. But the fatal mischief was, they went after idol gods, and plunged into the vices associated with idol worship. First at Baal-peor, in the wilderness; see Num. 25.——"Separated themselves unto that shame," means that they set themselves apart by consecration as the Nazarites under their vows—the original word being precisely this—they became Nazarites, not to a noble principle or a worthy purpose, but to that *shame!* The last clause thus—"They became abominable, like their paramours, lovers;" referring to the idol gods to whom they gave their homage.——So evermore men become like the God they worship; abominable and vile like their idols, or pure-minded and loving, like Him whose nature is purity and whose name is love.

11. *As for* Ephraim, their glory shall fly away like a bird, from the birth, and from the womb, and from the conception.

With the significance of the word Ephraim in mind, viz., fruitful in offspring (see Gen. 41:52), the reader will readily trace the drift of thought in this and the subsequent verses.——"Ephraim," the populous—"their glory" (a dense population), "shall take wings as a bird, so that there shall be no birth, no womb, no conception." ——This construction of the preposition before the last three nouns is admissible by usage and pertinent to the course of thought. The received translation gives it precisely this construction in the next verse.

12. Though they bring up their children, yet will I bereave them, *that there shall* not *be* a man *left:* yea, woe also to them when I depart from them!

Literally "bereave them *from man*," *i. e.* so that they shall not live to manhood; none shall come to man's estate. The curse of God's departing from them shall fall on that which has been their chief glory, as it is wont to do. Barrenness shall take the place of numerous families and a dense population.

13. Ephraim, as I saw Tyrus, *is* planted in a pleasant place: but Ephraim shall bring forth his children to the murderer.

Ephraim as well as Tyre had a delightful country, surroundings of beauty and prosperity; but what can these avail to stay the wrath of God against their sin?——The language in this verse and the next is plain.

14. Give them, O Lord: what wilt thou give? give them a miscarrying womb and dry breasts.

The holy indignation of the prophet is kindled, and for once he gives it expression.

15. All their wickedness *is* in Gilgal: for there I hated them: for the wickedness of their doings I will drive them out of mine house, I will love them no more: all their princes *are* revolters.

The speaker in this verse, as also in verse 13, is the Lord.—— Gilgal, as was remarked on Hosea 4:15, was noted for its idol worship. There the sins of the nation might be supposed to be concentrated. God abhorred this great sin, and in this sense hated the sinners—would drive them from his temple and show them favor no more.——Reference is again made to the wicked life and pernicious influence of the chief men, all of whom were refractory—rebels against God—this being the sense of the last word in the verse.

16. Ephraim is smitten, their root is dried up, they shall bear no fruit: yea, though they bring forth, yet will I slay *even* the beloved *fruit* of their womb.

Ephraim now appears under the figure of a fruit-bearing tree, smitten with death, dried up, to bear fruit no more. Then dropping, or rather changing the figure, God declares that if they have children born to them, he will slay even their dearest and most loved offspring.——So terrible are the curses that must come down on those who sin so persistently, and against so great light and so rich mercies.

17. My God will cast them away, because they did not hearken unto him: and they shall be wanderers among the nations.

"My God will reject them from being his people." "They shall be wanderers among the nations," with no settled habitation, no loved home—a prophecy eminently improbable when spoken, but eminently true for ages on ages. The ten tribes have long since lost all distinct nationality. Their posterity, if yet living, are wandering among the nations, unknown and of no account in history. Even the Jews are often known simply as "wanderers." "The wandering Jew" is his style, both in common parlance and in more stately history.——So signally are the words of prophecy fulfilled, and so terribly do the judgments of God scourge and desolate those whom his great mercies fail to reclaim!

CHAPTER X.

THE same general subject continues; the sin of Ephraim and its just punishment, vs. 1–11; a call to repentance and a new life, v. 12; judgments still more near and dire, vs. 13–15.

1. Israel *is* an empty vine, he bringeth forth fruit unto himself: according to the multitude of his fruit he hath increased the altars; according to the goodness of his land they have made goodly images.

I paraphrase thus: "A vine pouring itself abroad, in luxurious growth, is Israel; he makes fruit for himself; according to the abundance of his fruit he has multiplied altars; according to the goodness of his land have they, the people, made good images."

The word rendered "empty" does not appear anywhere in use in the intransitive sense of being empty, but does sometimes in the transitive sense of *making* empty. Its usual and primary sense is that of pouring out abroad.——The course of thought forbids the sense of barren, fruitless, since the very point made is the abundant wealth of Israel, perverted the more to idolatry and sin. The more God gives them, the more they give to idols; the richer their land and its products, the richer shrines and altars go up for Baal.——So sinful men everywhere are wont to pervert the earthly gifts of God, till more gifts only make them more wicked and more ungrateful to the Giver; and so more mercy in this line becomes only the greater curse, and sinners themselves compel their God to turn from blessings to retribution.

2. Their heart is divided; now shall they be found faulty: he shall break down their altars, he shall spoil their images.

"Their heart is smooth," *i. e.*, treacherous, deceitful, the verb here having this its primary sense. Among the various meanings of this word the idea of *dividing* is secondary and remote, growing out of the use of *smooth* stones in casting the lot for the purpose of *dividing* between rival claimants. There seems to be no good reason here for departing from the primary sense of the word. ——"Now shall they be punished," not merely "found faulty." The verb means first to sin, and then naturally to suffer for sin, to bear punishment, as here.——"*He*," who "shall break down their altars," &c., is God, named last in the closing verse of the previous chapter, but naturally present in thought in this connection.——It is altogether legitimate that his judgments should fall on the idol altars and images, as here said.

3. For now they shall say, We have no king, because we feared not the LORD; what then should a king do to us?

The last clause should read—"As to the king, what shall he do *for* us? *i. e.*, to help us.——The time to which this applies would naturally be in some of the seasons of anarchy when they had no king, and the tone is that of discouragement, tending to despair. Now they shall say, "We have no king, for we have not feared the Lord," and therefore this judgment of anarchy has come upon us; what help now can we have from the king?

4. They have spoken words, swearing falsely in making a covenant: thus judgment springeth up as hemlock in the furrows of the field.

"They speak mere words" (unreliable), "swearing falsely, making covenants," in both of which their words go for nothing, and hence "the judgments of God spring up as the poisonous poppy in the furrows of the field." This plant was peculiar for spreading rapidly, especially in a ploughed field, and for being injurious as a poison. In this view the point of the figure would be the rapidity with which the judgments of God on the people spring to light on every hand, and the fearful devastations and mischiefs they bring upon the land.——Or possibly the sense may be—Justice as determined among men, either publicly or privately, is perverted to become as the deadly poisonous poppy in the furrows of the field.—— This figure appears twice in Amos, viz., 5:7 and 6:12. "Ye who turn judgment to wormwood, and leave off righteousness in the earth." "For ye have turned judgment into gall" (the same

Hebrew words as in Hosea), "and the fruit of righteousness into hemlock."——Now since Amos prophesied somewhat earlier than Hosea, the latter may have taken up this figure from his brother prophet, changing it only as a mind of higher poetic culture and a more vivid imagination would naturally do.

5. The inhabitants of Samaria shall fear because of the calves of Beth-aven: for the people thereof shall mourn over it, and the priests thereof *that* rejoiced on it, for the glory thereof, because it is departed from it.

Beth-aven, house of idols (literally, of nothings, nonentities), is instead of Bethel, house of God,—the name being changed to indicate the fearful fact that the people had ceased to be a house of God, and had become a house of idols, after Jeroboam of Nebat set up his golden calf there. The sentiment of this verse is, that the people of Samaria should be put in fear because of these calves. So far from finding peace and help from their new gods, they should find only peril and alarm.——"The people thereof" who "shall mourn over it" are the worshippers of these calves. The next clause should read—"And his priests" (those of the calf) "shall be thrilled with terror," or perhaps "shall leap as men frantic with terror, on account of them, because of his glory" (that of the calf), "for it is departed as into captivity."——Sentiment—shame, confusion, and horror shall come on all the worshippers and priests of these calves, under the force of God's awful judgments on the land for this sin.

6. It shall be also carried unto Assyria, *for* a present to king Jareb: Ephraim shall receive shame, and Israel shall be ashamed of his own counsel.

"It" (the calf) "shall be carried into Assyria for a present to the king that intervenes," *i. e.*, who is called in to defend the kingdom against the Syrian power, but who, instead, becomes the conqueror and devastator of the ten tribes. See 5:13. Then Ephraim and Israel shall be confounded by the result of their own counsels. Their expected helper becomes their actual destroyer.

7. *As for* Samaria, her king is cut off as the foam upon the water.

"As for Samaria, her king is cut off as chips on the face of the waters"—as if he were as insignificant as a floating chip, and as easily taken away and destroyed. The original word demands the sense chip, and not foam.

8. The high places also of Aven, the sin of Israel, shall be destroyed: the thorn and the thistle shall come up on their altars; and they shall say to the mountains, Cover us; and to the hills, Fall on us.

"Aven" is here the Beth-aven of v. 5—the locality of one of the golden calves—long time known as Bethel. See notes on 4: 15. Its high places, on which idol altars and temples stood, should be destroyed.——"The sin of Israel," is said of the calf at Bethel, as being the occasion and manifestation of her sin of idolatry. The growth of thorns and thistles in places once so much frequented and so magnificent in works of art, gives a vivid sense of utter desolation. The doom of the people would be so terrible that they would choose death rather than life, and hence would cry to the mountains, "Cover us," and to the hills, "Fall on us!"—strong poetic conceptions, but terribly significant of their awful doom.

9. O Israel, thou hast sinned from the days of Gibeah: there they stood: the battle in Gibeah against the children of iniquity did not overtake them.

"More than in the days of Gibeah, hast thou sinned, Israel;"—thy sins are greater than theirs; for which, see Judges, chap. 19–21. Of course, her doom is more terrible. "There (in Gibeah) they stood;" a remnant, even six hundred men, survived, from whom the tribe was again filled up. The battle in Gibeah against the children of iniquity (those wicked men) did not overtake and exterminate them. Ephraim need not expect to come off so well, for of her no remnant shall survive to replace the fallen and rebuild the kingdom.

10. *It is* in my desire that I should chastise them; and the people shall be gathered against them, when they shall bind themselves in their two furrows.

The received translation of the last clause scarcely gives an intelligible sense. The passage has vexed commentators the more because the reading of the original, both in its vowels and consonants, is in dispute.——Omitting the details of this matter, suffice it to say that I prefer to read after the margin—sins not furrows, and hence to render the entire verse thus:—

"It is in my purpose to chastise them, and the nations shall be gathered against them when they shall be bound for their two sins,"—these sins having reference to the two golden calves at Bethel and at Dan. In the same sense, the "high places of Aven" are called "the sin of Israel" (v. 8). The idea is that, to chastise them, God will bind them fast because of these sins of calf-worship, and will then gather the nations (Syrians and Assyrians) together to fall upon them.——So construed, the sense is vigorous, and entirely in accordance with both the significance of the several words and the grammatical construction.

11. And Ephraim *is as* an heifer *that is* taught, *and* loveth to tread out *the corn*, but I passed over upon her fair neck: I will make Ephraim to ride; Judah shall plough, *and* Jacob shall break his clods.

To understand this verse readily, we need to bear in mind that in the East, cows (heifers also) as well as oxen were put under the yoke and to the plough. They were also used for threshing, and under the Mosaic law—"Thou shalt not muzzle the ox that treadeth out the corn" (Deut. 25: 4), the latter may be supposed the more pleasant service. Threshing, moreover, was a common symbol for the exercise of oppressive power, or for the infliction of severe suffering.——Hence I render—"Ephraim is a well-trained heifer, loving to thresh" (*i. e.*, without a figure, *to oppress*), "but I passed along over the beauty of her neck" (never yet galled with a yoke); "I will yoke Ephraim; Judah shall plough; Jacob shall harrow."——Some render—I will put a rider on Ephraim, *i. e.*, for a driver. Our English version quite misses the sense in saying—"I will make Ephraim to ride," the idea being that he shall *draw* and *work*, not ride.——These figures, taken from the occupations of agriculture, are significant and forcible.

12. Sow to yourselves in righteousness, reap in mercy; break up your fallow ground: for *it is* time to seek the LORD, till he come and rain righteousness upon you.

With this new figure before the mind, the prophet turns here to exhort both Israel and Judah to repentance and to works of righteousness.——Here, as is very common in Hebrew, the second of two successive imperatives should be rendered in the future as a promise. "Sow for yourselves, for righteousness; thus shall ye reap according to your piety." The "reaping in mercy" must be *promise*, not *command*.——"For righteousness" is the literal rendering, meaning, sow what will naturally produce the fruits of righteousness. The word rendered "mercy" must refer to man, not to God, and is therefore piety. The Hebrew phrase means—according to the measure of your piety.——"Break up your fallow ground;" make all due preparation for the harvest of blessings you need and should seek.——"For it is time to seek Jehovah until he come and teach you righteousness." The verb rendered in our version to "rain" means to rain in a very few cases, to teach in a much larger number. In the conjugation used here it always means to *teach*, never to *rain*. And since in this latter half of the verse the figure is dropped, and the prophet says without a figure—"it is time to seek the Lord," it is more consonant with the strain of the clause to translate this word without a figure, "teach," rather than with a figure, "rain."

13. Ye have ploughed wickedness, ye have reaped iniquity; ye have eaten the fruit of lies: because thou didst trust in thy way, in the multitude of thy mighty men.

Resuming the figures of husbandry, the prophet says—"Ye

have ploughed wickedness," &c., in the same sense as Paul (Gal. 6 : 7), "Whatsoever a man soweth, that shall he also reap;" or Solomon (Prov. 1 : 31), "They shall eat of the fruit of their own way," &c. ——Ephraim had trusted, not in the Lord, but in the way of her own choice, and in the multitude of her mighty men. The Lord is now about to show her the folly of such trust.

14. Therefore shall a tumult arise among thy people, and all thy fortresses shall be spoiled, as Shalman spoiled Beth-arbel in the day of battle: the mother was dashed in pieces upon *her* children.

"Tumult" is the panic-cry of men smitten with fear. "Shalman" is abbreviated for Shalmaneser, king of Assyria (see 2 Kings 17 : 3), the same who conquered the kingdom of the ten tribes, besieged and took Samaria, and bore the people away into captivity. ——"Beth-Arbel" is probably Arbela of Galilee.——The fearful judgments which have been spoken of repeatedly throughout chapters 4–10 culminate here. The time is just at hand, and the manner and form of the visitation are no longer couched in symbols, but are announced in the plainest speech.

15. So shall Beth-el do unto you because of your great wickedness: in a morning shall the king of Israel utterly be cut off.

Bethel, the centre and hence the symbol of calf-worship, is here used for the scourge sent of God to desolate the land. The sentiment is that their sin at Bethel becomes their ruin.

The king of Israel referred to here, I assume to be Hoshea, the last in the kingdom of the ten tribes,—especially because the whole tenor of chapters 7–14 implies that the destruction of the kingdom was very near, and because chap. 13 : 10, 11, implies that the king is already cut off.——"In a morning," is in the Hebrew—"in *the* morning;" and therefore cannot well mean that his being cut off should occur in the morning hour of some indefinite day; but either in *the next* morning; or taken adverbially, *very soon*—as the Hebrews were wont to signify the doing of a thing early by a verb formed from this same word, which means the morning dawn.——There seems to be no objection, either grammatical or historical, to the sense—in the next morning—to-morrow morning;—for it is plain that this prophet continued to bear messages to the people *after* the last king, Hoshea, was cut off. The history (2 Kings 17 : 3–6) shows that this king was shut up and bound in prison, and that *after this*, the king of Assyria seized the whole country, besieged Samaria, and took it after a siege of three years. But this last king appears no more on the face of the history;—"he is utterly cut off."

CHAPTER XI.

The strain of rebuke and of forewarning of judgment having continued with only brief interruptions from the beginning of chapter 4, till we are brought almost to the very day in which the king of Israel should be cut off, the course of thought now turns to reminiscences of love, and to the most touching expressions of pity and grief over the impending ruin of Israel.

1. When Israel *was* a child, then I loved him, and called my son out of Egypt.

Thinking of the nation as having a lifetime, analogous to that of the individual, running through infancy and youth to manhood, the Lord says, "When Israel was a child, then I loved him, and called my son out of Egypt." He had manifested a very special interest in the fathers of the nation, Abraham, Isaac, and Jacob; he had shown his care for their children during their oppressions under the Pharaohs. It was precisely by means of the *call* of God that Moses was trained, commissioned, and led on to become, under God, the deliverer of the people from Egyptian bondage.——The citation of this passage by Matthew (2: 14, 15), as being fulfilled in the case of the young child Jesus, called up from Egypt, raises the question, Does Hosea in this passage refer in any sense to the Messiah?——The context decides this question in the negative. The entire course of thought, both in what precedes and in what follows, relates to the nation of Israel.——Hence Matthew must mean "fulfilled" only in the sense of an analogous event—an event which *filled out* the natural sense of the words "out of Egypt have I called my son." The nation of Israel was God's child, and might be called his son. So was Jesus. God loved and cared for Israel; so and more for the child Jesus. God brought the former out of Egypt; and the latter also. The same language, therefore, fitly describes each event, and the second becomes in a sort a fulfilment *of the words* which describe the first. It is not a case of the fulfilment of *prophecy*, but only of the *words* of a certain history. The great value of the case lies in its moral bearings as illustrating the unchanging and oft-shown love and care of God for his sons.

2. *As* they called them, so they went from them: they sacrificed unto Baalim, and burned incense to graven images.

God's calling of his son Israel, especially by the agency of Moses, suggested his continued agencies of calling the people by later prophets, and of this he proceeds to speak: "As they"—these later prophets—"called them, so they went away from their presence"—(so the Hebrew):—the more the Lord's servants called, the more the people turned away; "they sacrificed to Baalim," &c., as *e. g.* under Ahab and onward. Indeed, the worship of Baal appears as far back as Num. 25: 3, 5, and Judg. 2: 11–13, and 6: 25–32.——The tense of the verbs "sacrifice" and "burn incense," implies not only that they *had*, but *would still*—of set purpose and fixed habit.

3. I taught Ephraim also to go, taking them by their arms; but they knew not that I healed them.

"Ephraim," here as elsewhere, must be the kingdom of the ten tribes. There was no nationality known as Ephraim till the revolt under Jeroboam. Hence the Lord speaks of his parental care of this new-born nation in its infancy. "I taught Ephraim to walk," as a little child is taught, supported and helped along—"taking them by the arms." But they did not recognize the Lord's hand in their healing and help. He does not imply that they *could* not know; and does not say "they knew not" as lessening, but rather as increasing, their guilt.

4. I drew them with cords of a man, with bands of love: and I was to them as they that take off the yoke on their jaws, and I laid meat unto them.

The description of God's tender care and gentle loving ways with his people continues. "I drew" (not drove) "them—with cords of a man," not cords of a bullock, untamed, headstrong, and wild. These cords are explained fully in the words "with bands of love," by the sweet attractions which manifested love naturally creates.——The next figure also is taken from the ways of the kind husbandman: "I was to them as they that lift up the yoke which presses on their cheek;"—for the rude yokes of oriental countries are heavy and ill-adapted to the comfort of animals while eating.—The description continues: "I brought food to them and caused them to eat." The Hebrew has two verbs here, of which the literal sense is given in this translation. The tense of these verbs implies that God is willing still to feed them, as of old. This showing of God's loving care and gentleness toward his people is at once beautiful and strong. The facts of the case justify more even than this.

5. He shall not return into the land of Egypt, but the Assyrian shall be his king, because they refused to return.

Ephraim as a nation is spoken of as one person.—He shall not be suffered to turn back to the Egypt of his fathers, though the people often manifested a strong desire to do so. God had another and a more fearful doom for them; "the Assyrian shall be his king" The reason—because the people refused to return in penitence to God.——Hosea is remarkable for his play on the various senses of the same word—as here, between "returning to Egypt" in the first clause, and "refusing to return" in the second—the latter return being moral,—that of real repentance. Because they would not repent, the Lord put them under the Assyrian king which they abhorred, and forbade their returning to Egypt, which they sought.

6. And the sword shall abide on his cities, and shall consume his branches, and devour *them*, because of their own counsels.

The word "abide" does not give the full force of the Hebrew, which means, to whirl, to be moved in a circle, brandished. Here, the sword is said to be hurled down upon his cities—as if seen by the prophet, uplifted and waving high in the hand of the Almighty. ——Through the aid of progressive criticism, the word rendered "branch" obtains a modified and better sense. Primarily, the Hebrew word means a *part* of a thing; then a branch as being part of a tree; then from branch, the word comes to mean poles and bars—the latter fastening the gates and becoming in a sort the strength and protection of a city; and finally, by another change, it is used for princes and chieftains, considered as the strength of the city. So here, from the cities on which the sword falls, the prophet passes, not to "branches," for these have no natural connection with the city, but to the chiefs and rulers, and says of them—The sword shall consume and devour them, because of their vicious counsels in departing from God. This last circumstance forbids us to interpret the previous clause as being said of "branches."

7. And my people are bent to backsliding from me: though they called them to the Most High, none at all would exalt *him*.

Though they are *my* people, yet despite of all my love and of all my discipline, they are "bent"—fully purposed, committed—to turning back and away from me.——Though my prophets called them to return to the Most High, yet with one accord they "would not exalt him"—"exalt," in the sense of honoring him as the supreme God—to be adored instead of senseless idols.

8. How shall I give thee up, Ephraim? *how* shall I deliver thee, Israel? how shall I make thee as Admah? *how* shall I set thee as Zeboim? mine heart is turned within me, my repentings are kindled together.

The sense of this verse is plain. The "giving up," is to hopeless ruin and desolation. So the parallel word—"deliver thee"—means to give over to the fell destroyer.——"Admah and Zeboim" are associated with Sodom and Gomorrah as lying near in Gen. 14: 8, and in Deut. 29: 23, as involved in the same terrible doom.—— "Mine heart is turned within me"—with feelings of pity, and grief, and tender compassion. "My repentings are kindled together," implies that in this great conflict of emotions between the high demands of justice and the pleadings of compassion, his relentings were enkindled, and his very heart seemed to burn under the intense yearnings of sympathy.——The reader will notice the striking contrast between his people, "bent to backsliding" from him, and his own heart so tenderly *bent* to love and pity. How wonderful that the last words before this outburst of tenderness, and the last antecedent thoughts, are concerning the cruel waywardness and persistent rebellion of his people!——But no words of comment can heighten the beauty and force of this inimitable passage. The very heart of the God of love stands forth revealed in its glowing and expressive words.

The general strain of the message, sent of God by Hosea, had been of necessity stringent and stern with rebukes for sin, and oftentimes terrible in revelations of impending judgment—all right because absolutely necessary. Yet this strain, alone and exclusive, would not do full justice to the tenderness and the loving pity of Israel's God. These messages therefore cannot close without a most emphatic testimony to the loving-kindness of Jehovah.——What do these testimonies concerning God prove?

(1.) That he has no pleasure in bringing ruin on even the guiltiest sinner.——(2.) That he does not punish in the spirit of vindictiveness.——(3.) That he would always spare the sinner, and forbear to punish, or even chastise, if he could do so wisely and safely.——(4.) That he takes supreme delight in conferring good, and longs to bless all his sentient creatures.——(5.) That it is only with the deepest grief that he ever brings pain and woe upon his creatures.——(6.) Hence, that he will never punish any sinner beyond his real deserts —never beyond what the good of the universe imperatively demands.——(7.) That no sinner, however severely punished, can ever blame God.——(8.) That all sinners are bound to do justice to the divine love and pity, and should never impute to God feelings and motives which his own heart-utterances unmistakably preclude and forbid.——(9.) Finally, that the character and government of such a God should command our unbounded and eternal confidence and love.

9. I will not execute the fierceness of mine anger, I will not return to destroy Ephraim: for I *am* God, and not man; the Holy One in the midst of thee: and I will not enter into the city.

Speaking very much after the manner of men, God represents himself as having more "fierceness of anger" than he executes on the guilty. Often we need to make allowance for the necessity resting upon God, if he would be understood by men, of adopting their modes of expression, so as to speak of himself as men have reason to speak of themselves. In such cases, we must qualify the statements by reference to the known attributes of Jehovah. In the passage before us, we must not suppose that the anger of God had become unreasonably fierce, and that, becoming himself aware of this, he resolved not to execute it in full. It is in accommodation to finite minds that he represents a conflict in his own between his indignation against sin and his pity for the sinner. Such representations can scarcely mislead any except the captious and uncandid. ——In the phrase "I will not *return* to destroy," the first verb is used adverbially, the sense being—"I will not *again* destroy."—— The reason given—"for I am God and not man," reminds us of those beautiful words of Isaiah (55 : 8, 9): "For my thoughts are not your thoughts, neither are your ways, my ways, saith the Lord. For, as the heavens are higher than the earth, so are my ways higher than your ways, and my thoughts than your thoughts."

The last clause should read—not, "I will not enter into the city," but, "I will not come *in wrath*." The former makes no pertinent sense in this connection. The latter is entirely admissible on the score of usage, and is perfectly in harmony with the scope of the passage.

10. They shall walk after the LORD: he shall roar like a lion: when he shall roar, then the children shall tremble from the west.

11. They shall tremble as a bird out of Egypt, and as a dove out of the land of Assyria: and I will place them in their houses, saith the LORD.

Better things are here. The people, once more, "follow after the Lord"—a phrase which always means true obedience.——The Lord is compared to the lion and his voice to the lion's roar with reference to those fearful, awe-inspiring agencies of God in providence which startle and convulse the nations. It was such agencies that overwhelmed the old Assyrian and Chaldean empires, and raised up Cyrus of Persia to befriend the restoration of God's people. ——"The children" here must be the people of God. They "tremble"—*i. e., come* with trembling "from the west," as not unaffected with awe under the majestic presence of Jehovah. Yet they come with ease and rapidity, as is indicated by the flight of the sparrow and the dove. They come from every quarter—from Egypt on the south; Assyria on the north and east; and the west is specially named. Only for the sake of the idea of universality could we expect the west to be mentioned, since there lay the sea. ——God will place them in their habitations, for dwelling again in peace and security.——These verses give promise of a successful result, to some extent, and at some time, to the compassionate labors of the God of Israel to reclaim and restore his people.

12. Ephraim compasseth me about with lies, and the house of Israel with deceit: but Judah yet ruleth with God, and is faithful with the saints.

The Hebrew attaches this verse to the next chapter. In the course of thought it belongs there, and not at the close of this, since it reverts again to the perverseness, treachery, and hypocrisy of Ephraim and Israel; and when justly understood, makes Judah only less treacherous and apostate.——What is said here of Ephraim and Israel is plain; the last clause which respects Judah has been interpreted variously. The sense turns primarily on the Hebrew word rendered "ruleth." * The translators of our version derived it from another root, which means to tread down, and then to bear rule. But the sense above given is far more in harmony with the preceding context, and also with 12 : 2, which indeed quite forbids our taking this passage in a good sense. The best modern critics derive this verb from a root which means, to run wildly and at large, as animals that, after long restraint, have broken loose. So Judah has broken away from the Lord's yoke and runs wanton at her will. The same word occurs (Jer. 2 : 31), "Wherefor say my people—We *are lords;* we will come no more unto thee." *We are lords*, gives the idea; we have broken loose from all authority and restraint.——The entire last clause may be translated—"But Judah runs loose and wild as to God and as to the holy and faithful one"—where God's purity and faithfulness are put in contrast with the infidelity and moral pollution of Judah. The word for "holy" is indeed in the plural here. So are some of the names of God. The marginal reading properly gives it, "the most Holy."

CHAPTER XII.

In this chapter the prophet, besides bringing out yet more fully the sins of Ephraim and of Judah, seeks to encourage repentance and trust in God by referring to events in the early history of the patriarch Jacob—his taking the precedence of his brother Esau (v. 3); his prevailing prayer at Peniel, and his meeting with God at Bethel (vs. 3–5).

1. Ephraim feedeth on wind, and followeth after the east wind: he daily increaseth lies and desolation; and they do make a covenant with the Assyrians, and oil is carried into Egypt.

"Feedeth on wind," literally, pastureth himself on wind as shepherds pasture their flocks on grass, which represents his reliance on the merest vanities, on that which can avail him nothing. "Chasing after the east wind" has the same significance. "Every day he multiplieth lies," and consequently "desolation"—the desolation being manifestly spoken of here as the fruit of his lies. The

* ירוד—*rood,* expressed in English letters.

prophet's eye seems to have been on the historic events narrated (2 Kings 17 : 3, 4), where it is stated that the king of Assyria came against Hoshea, the last king of Israel; that Hoshea became his servant and paid him tribute; that subsequently the king of Assyria "found conspiracy in Hoshea because he sent messengers to So, king of Egypt, and brought no present to the king of Assyria, as he had done year by year; therefore the king of Assyria shut him up and bound him in prison," came up and besieged his capital, subdued his kingdom, and took his people captive. His lies did not *pay*, but brought on him and his kingdom ruin.——"They made a covenant with the Assyrians," but broke it; "they carried oil into Egypt" as a present or tribute, but Egypt could not save them from the Assyrian power. The last three verbs of this verse —rendered "increaseth," "do make," "is carried"—are all in the *incomplete* tense, which implies not only that they have done so, but have the heart to do so still.

2. The Lord hath also a controversy with Judah, and will punish Jacob according to his ways; according to his doings will he recompense him.

"Controversy," in the same sense as in 4 : 1—ground of grievous complaint. "And will visit upon Jacob" (literally rendered), in the sense of retribution for his sins.——"Jacob" in this passage must mean Ephraim, the kingdom of the ten tribes.

3. He took his brother by the heel in the womb, and by his strength he had power with God:

The name "Jacob," applied to the northern kingdom, helps the prophet to pass by an easy transition to the early history of the patriarch who bore this name.——"He took his brother by the heel in the womb," indicating that he would supplant him in the matter of the birthright and of priority. See the history (Gen. 25 : 26). The verb from which the name Jacob is derived means "to take by the heel," to supplant.——No bad intention or purpose on Jacob's part should attach to this supplanting as here spoken of. It simply indicated the purpose of God to put Jacob before Esau, although born last. This preference is alluded to in this passage to encourage the people to return to their own God.——The next clause carries us to the celebrated scene of Peniel, where Jacob wrestled with the angel of the covenant in struggling prayer all night, and finally prevailed, "had power with God," and became a prince through his perseverance and success. The Lord gave him the name Israel, meaning a *prince with God*, at this very time, both to indicate and to honor his prevalence in prayer. (See Gen. 32 : 28.) "Thy name shall be called no more Jacob, but Israel; for as a prince hast thou power with God and with men, and hast prevailed."

4. Yea, he had power over the angel, and prevailed:

he wept, and made supplication unto him: he found him *in* Beth-el, and there he spake with us;

To give the nicer shades of thought from the original, and to present the relations of the different persons brought to view, the verse might be rendered somewhat freely, thus: "And then he had power with the angel and prevailed; he wept and made supplication to him. Also God met him (Jacob) at Bethel, and there spake with him and through him with us." The angel referred to is called God (Elohim) in v. 3, and can be no other than the uncreated angel of the covenant, who appears not unfrequently in the history of ancient Israel, manifesting divine attributes, and obviously being the very Messiah, then, as ever, the Head of the Church on earth.——In the record of the scenes of Peniel (Gen. 32 : 24–30), the historian does not call him "the angel," but says, "there wrestled *a man* with him until the breaking of the day." This gives his external appearance. But Jacob, when the scene had passed, called the name of the place Peniel, the face of God, "for he said, I have seen God face to face." Much to our point are God's words to Moses (Ex. 23 : 20, 21): "Behold, I send an angel before thee to keep thee in the way and to bring thee into the place which I have prepared. Beware of him and obey his voice; provoke him not; for he will not pardon your transgressions; for *my name is in him.*" The power to pardon sin, implied to exist in him, and especially the last words, "my name" (in the sense of nature and attributes) "is in him," must be considered as amply identifying him to be the second person in the Godhead.——With him Jacob wrestled in agonizing prayer—the external struggle being only an index of the inward, which was the vital thing. Jacob was in most imminent peril from his enraged and powerful brother, and therefore must seek help from God. His long agony of struggling prayer suggests that he may have had an unsettled account with the "angel of the covenant," some of the items of which may have been his complicity with his mother in the deception practised by her to get from Isaac the paternal blessing; and not improbably some lack of faithful reproof of his favorite Rachel in the matter of her proclivities toward idol-worship—things to be repented of and adjusted as to God before any signal testimony of his favor could be safely given. It need not surprise us, therefore, that "he wept and made supplication." The full history of his heart might show how bitterly he repented of his sins, and how earnestly he plead that God would remember his covenant, and not account the great faults of his servant as a forfeiture of his claims upon God for protection and help.——In all its parts this was a wonderful case of persevering and prevailing prayer—one that might well be suggested to the whole Hebrew people in the times of Hosea as an assurance that such prayer might yet save them, while nothing less or other than this could.——Abruptly the prophet passes to the third scene in the life of Jacob—that which transpired at Bethel. There the Lord God met the youthful Jacob, reminded him of his own covenant with Abraham and Isaac; renewed this covenant with Jacob, and left him. Then Jacob awoke from this blessed vision and said, "Surely the Lord is in this place, and I knew it not." "How dreadful is this place! This is none other but the house of God, and this is the gate of heaven!" See Gen. 28 : 11–22.——Some difference of opinion exists as to the significance of the last word of this verse, "*us*." In what sense did the Lord speak with *us* in Bethel? Hosea says, "There the Lord found Jacob, and there he spake with not Jacob only, but us."——Some have said, the prophet included with Jacob, himself, and perhaps others also, on the score of a common sympathy, as writers sometimes unconsciously suppose themselves to be participating in scenes that awaken in their hearts deep interest.——Others, noticing that the verb rendered "spake" is in the future, have given it this turn: There the Lord *will* speak with us; *did* speak with Jacob, and will no less with us if we seek him as earnestly.——The latter idea—that God will truly speak with us and with all who wait earnestly on him—is no doubt implied; the Bible usually implies this, though it is rarely deemed necessary to express it.——The first of the two views above given is preferable, expanded with this further idea, that the things God said there belong to the whole future family of Jacob, viz.: the promise of Canaan; a countless seed; a blessing on all the families of the earth through his offspring, and the Lord Jehovah for his God and their God. In view of the broad application of the things said then and there to all the Hebrew race, Hosea might well say, "There the Lord spake *with us*"—with us none the less because through Jacob. In this sense the future *incomplete* tense of the Hebrew is specially apposite.——There was peculiar fitness in this allusion to *Bethel*—the place made so sacred in those ancient times by the presence of God and by his renewed covenant, but, during many generations recently past, most horribly desecrated by giving to a calf the worship due to God alone.

5. Even the LORD God of hosts; the LORD *is* his memorial.

This verse is a close continuation of the preceding. "There *he* spake with us, even the Lord God of hosts."——In most English Bibles the name "*Lord*" is printed in small capitals when it translates the Hebrew word Jehovah. In this verse the Hebrew reads, "Even Jehovah, God of hosts—Jehovah is his memorial." By this is meant that the name Jehovah is that by which he would be specially known, or, more precisely, is that one of his various names whose significance he would have his people evermore remember, as to be fulfilled all along onward in the lapse of the ages. All the names given to the Supreme Being are significant, *e. g.*, "God of Hosts," or of the celestial armies; "El-Shaddai," the Omnipotent or Almighty; "El" alone, the exalted and the mighty one; and in like manner "Jehovah," the immutable, "he that was and is and is to come," forever living and forever the same, the real and the great "*I am.*" See Ex. 3:13–15, and 6:3, where it is said, "This is my name forever, and this is my memorial unto all generations;" and where also God said to Moses, "I am Jehovah; and I appeared unto Abraham, Isaac, and Jacob, by the name of God Almighty, but by my name Jehovah was I not known unto them." This cannot mean that they had never known and used the name Jehovah, for they had. It must therefore mean that God had not fulfilled to them the true significance of this name, *i. e.*, one faithful to his promises. The idea is that this faithfulness results from his immutability, and that his people do not fully *know* this attribute of God till they have tested and proved it in their experience of his faithfulness in fulfilling his promises. In this sense the name Jehovah stands through all time as his memorial name—its significance to be remembered by his people, and perpetually developed and fulfilled more and more in the lapse of ages. The significance of his other names may be verified and fulfilled at once; his omnipotence is seen in the creation of worlds and in every real miracle; but his name Jehovah is verified only *by the aid of time*, through the occurrence of events transpiring all along down the world's history. In this most expressive sense it is his memorial name, and is adduced by Hosea most fitly in this connection to encourage the people to put their trust in him.

6. Therefore, turn thou to thy God: keep mercy and judgment, and wait on thy God continually.

Hence the application here made—"Therefore," since God is forever faithful and true, since he ever has been and ever will be the God of his people Israel, "therefore, turn thou to thy God." "Keep mercy and judgment"—duties toward man; "and wait on thy God continually," living in dependence upon him, and expecting all needful good from him alone. Morality toward man and piety toward God make up the sum of human duty—loving God with all thy heart and thy neighbor as thyself.

7. *He is* a merchant, the balances of deceit *are* in his hand: he loveth to oppress.

The discourse here turns abruptly to another sin of the people of Ephraim—covetousness and consequent oppression. "The Canaanite—balances of deceit are in his hand:" he loves to take advantage in trade, and to drive a gainful bargain to the extent of real oppression. The word "Canaanite" is used for merchant, that people being the traffickers of Western Asia. The Phœnicians, long celebrated for commerce and navigation, were part of the original people of Canaan. The word Canaanite means in Hebrew one who acquires, accumulates. To this also the present use of the word may refer.——"Balances of deceit" were made to cheat with—one weight for buying and another for selling. Thus (Prov.

20 : 23), "An abomination to the Lord is a stone and a stone" (one to buy with and one to sell with); "and balances of deceit are not good," *i. e.*, are utterly bad.——This allusion to the trading usages of Canaan was shaped to take hold of the people of Ephraim, the more so because the latter, while in general holding the Canaanites in contempt, were yet trading, defrauding, and oppressing in the same way. As if the prophet would say: See the Canaanite; you think meanly of him for his low tricks of trade; what do you think of yourselves?

8. And Ephraim said, Yet I am become rich, I have found me out substance: *in* all my labours they shall find none iniquity in me that *were* sin.

"Also Ephraim said: Surely I am rich; I have found wealth for myself; in all the fruits of my business they shall find in me no acts of extortion that are sinful." The last word is from the verb which means to miss the mark, to overdo, to overstep due bounds. Ephraim quietly implies that *in trade* some little crookedness and deception are quite admissible; (probably he would have said, Who can *live* by trade otherwise?) But on the other hand there are things so flagrant that all the world will call them sin. He hopes, indeed he is quite sure, they will not find any of this bad sort of sin in his business life.——So human nature and the usages and moralities of trade were much the same B. C. 750, when Hosea was writing, as they are to-day!

9. And I *that am* the LORD thy God from the land of Egypt will yet make thee to dwell in tabernacles, as in the days of the solemn feast.

Once more the prophet turns abruptly, as is his wont, to promises, yet again to try the power of persuasion and love on the people. "Yet I, the Lord thy God ever since Egypt" (*i. e.*, since the exodus from Egypt), "will yet make thee to dwell in tents," &c., with reference to the feast of tabernacles, the great national thanksgiving. This was always a joyful occasion. Hence this verse must be interpreted as a promise of good, and not a threatening of evil.

10. I have also spoken by the prophets, and I have multiplied visions, and used similitudes, by the ministry of the prophets.

Literally, "I have spoken *to* the prophets"—that they might speak for me to the people. During the great apostasy in the latter years of the kingdom of Ephraim, the Lord greatly multiplied prophets and visions.——"Similitudes" include poetic figures, and also symbols, which latter comprise both illustrative acts done by the prophets, and also things seen in vision.

11. *Is there* iniquity *in* Gilead? surely they are van-

ity: they sacrifice bullocks in Gilgal; yea, their altars *are* as heaps in the furrows of the fields.

Literally, "Lo! Gilead is wickedness!" The next clause is parallel: "surely they are vanity."——Gilead, one of the cities of refuge, where many priests dwelt, has been named for its great wickedness above (6:8).——Gilgal also was notorious for its idol worship. The Hebrew word "heaps" is a play on the word Gilgal, which means a rolled-up heap of stones. Idol altars were thick there as the heaps of stones in a ploughed field.

12. And Jacob fled into the country of Syria, and Israel served for a wife, and for a wife he kept *sheep*.

This brief and abrupt allusion to Jacob was designed to suggest God's watchful care through his providence over his trustful children. This familiar history is found, Gen. chapters 29–33.

13. And by a prophet the LORD brought Israel out of Egypt, and by a prophet was he preserved.

By this prophet, Moses, the Lord brought up his people from Egypt, and can do like things again; by this prophet Israel was *kept*—the same word which is rendered *kept* in v. 12. As Jacob *kept* sheep—a faithful shepherd—so the Lord by Moses *kept* his people, and, as Hosea would have the people infer, *can again.*

14. Ephraim provoked *him* to anger most bitterly: therefore shall he leave his blood upon him, and his reproach shall his Lord return unto him.

But Ephraim has long provoked him most bitterly; therefore shall his Lord leave his blood upon him, unpardoned, and not washed away, and shall turn back his reproach upon himself. The blood referred to is probably that of children sacrificed to Moloch; his reproach is that which he had cast upon the true God by discarding his law and worship, and putting idols before him. God would requite this reproach by consigning Ephraim to public contempt among the nations of the earth.

CHAPTER XIII.

THE main drift of this chapter is to set forth the sins of Ephraim and their certain consequences in his ruin—intermingled with some rich assurances of God's love and promises of mercy and help to the penitent.

1. When Ephraim spake trembling, he exalted himself in Israel; but when he offended in Baal, he died.

Our translators seem to have supposed the first clause to refer to a time when Ephraim was penitent and humble. More recent investigations in the language show that this sense and construction are scarcely admissible, and by no means probable. The word on which the interpretation hinges, occurs in this precise form nowhere else in our Bible. But a cognate word, without much doubt of the same meaning, occurs, Jer. 49 : 24, where it means terror. This word in our passage is a noun, not, as in the English translation, a participial adjective. I translate: "When Ephraim spake, there was trembling; he stood high in Israel; but when he sinned in the matter of Baal, he died." Ephraim, as here used, is the one tribe only, not the whole ten. In the early days of the kingdom the influence of this tribe was very great; the word of Ephraim was law, and was heard with trembling. His sin in the matter of Baal proved the ruin of his influence and of himself.

2. And now they sin more and more, and have made them molten images of their silver, *and* idols according to their own understanding, all of it the work of the craftsmen: they say of them, Let the men that sacrifice kiss the calves.

The word used here for idols, as above remarked, in 4 : 17, is itself significant of toil and labor in their construction.——"According to their own understanding" means with their skill, with the best art and tact they have.——"Wholly the work of the craftsmen," is yet further expressive of the leading idea that these idols are nothing whatever beyond what men make them. There is nothing else about them, in them, or of them. The prophet means to deny that there is any invisible God dwelling in them. In the phrase "they say of them," the pronoun *they* is expressed in the Hebrew, and hence is made prominent in the thought—referring here to the priests, who had the management of idol worship. They gave the order that the men who offered sacrifice should kiss the calves. This ceremony was one form of expressing their reverence, confidence, and affection for these calves.

3. Therefore they shall be as the morning cloud, and as the early dew that passeth away, as the chaff *that* is driven with the whirlwind out of the floor, and as the smoke out of the chimney.

"Therefore," as the fruit of such senseless and guilty worship, their glory shall be evanescent; the whole nation shall soon disappear from the face of the earth, and hold no longer any place among the nations. The threshing floors were fitted up on high hills, and in open, exposed situations, to get the benefit of the wind in cleaning grain. But when an oriental whirlwind fell suddenly upon this operation, the chaff was driven off fearfully.

4. Yet I *am* the LORD thy God from the land of Egypt, and thou shalt know no God but me: for *there is* no saviour beside me.

Yet fearful as their doom must be, and great as their guilt had been, the Lord reminds them that he has been their God ever since the nation came out from Egypt. He evinced this relationship to them then, and had done nothing on his part since to change it.

5. I did know thee in the wilderness, in the land of great drought.

"I did know thee in the wilderness," means more than a mere knowledge of what they were. It implies that he had manifested his knowledge of their case by his sympathy, love, and care. He let nothing pertaining to their case or wants escape his notice. The word rendered "drought" means properly, *thirst*—a land celebrated for the thirst of the weary traveller—one where no water is. In that land, God brought forth water for them from the rock.

6. According to their pasture, so were they filled; and their heart was exalted: therefore have they forgotten me.

The better God made their condition, or, in the prophet's figure, the better pasture he put them into, the more they were sated; this fulness begat pride; and in their pride, they forgat Jehovah.—— Alas, that this should be the history of so many myriads of sinners! God blesses them (must we say) too much; they become too full; then proud; then they forget God, and become awfully strong in their wickedness!

7. Therefore I will be unto them as a lion: as a leopard by the way will I observe *them*.

8. I will meet them as a bear *that is* bereaved *of her whelps*, and will rend the caul of their heart, and there will I devour them like a lion: the wild beast shall tear them.

The figures to represent swift destruction are multiplied.——To "observe," as the leopard, is to lie in wait and watch as for prey. ——God represents himself as doing what is done instrumentally by the Assyrian arms.

9. O Israel, thou hast destroyed thyself; but in me *is* thine help.

The received translation expresses rich truths with great force. Thou art thine own destroyer; thy God thine only deliverer. The destruction is wholly thine; the salvation altogether mine.

But although both these propositions are true, and although

their beauty and force are much enhanced by this vivid juxtaposition and contrast, yet a close and careful study of the original raises a serious doubt in my mind whether this is precisely its sense.

The first clause is all right. "*Thine* is this destruction;" but the last clause, having in Hebrew three words, is more closely and perfectly rendered thus: "Because (thou art) against me, against thy help." The strong objection to our received translation is the proposition *against* before the last word, "thy help." The English translation makes no account of it; but Hosea does not put in words for nothing. Then also the connecting particle more naturally means *because* than *but*.

In this construction we miss the strong antithesis, but we get a pertinent sense, and one in harmony with the previous and following context;—thus v. 8, The Assyrian power shall devour thee: v. 9, This destruction is all of thine own procuring, because thou wast against me, against thy only help: v. 10, Where is thy king now, or any one that can save thee? &c.

10. I will be thy king: where *is any other* that may save thee in all thy cities? and thy judges of whom thou saidst, Give me a king and princes?

The most approved translation is that in the margin: "Where is thy king now—that he may save thee in all thy cities?" In this case the Hebrew marginal reading is followed, not the received text. The difference between the two is that the marginal reading transposes the last two radicals.*

The remark is pertinently made in our English margin, that Hoshea, the last king, was at this time in prison, as is stated 2 Kings 17: 4.

11. I gave thee a king in mine anger, and took *him* away in my wrath.

This statement probably has reference to this very king Hoshea. It was true of Saul, and no less so of many of the kings in the kingdom of the ten tribes. But if we ask for the particular king thought

* The real question for the critic here is whether he shall read אֱהִי "I will be;" or אַיֵּה "Where?" The only difference is in the transposition of the last two radicals. The critical authorities for the two readings in Hebrew are conflicting. I prefer the latter (אַיֵּה) "Where?" (1.) Because as compared with the other, which is followed in our received version, this flows easily, following the natural order of the Hebrew words; while that one labors and almost does violence to the word rendered "where," in the clause, "where is any other," &c. (2.) This last-named word (אֵפוֹא) strongly indicates that the sentence in which it occurs commenced with an interrogative. This is its common use—an enclitic or post-positive particle, after an interrogative. Our received translation makes this word itself an interrogative, which is scarcely admissible. (3.) The sense is indefinitely more pertinent and forcible—a consideration which, superadded to the preceding, is conclusive.

of by the author, no one meets the conditions so well as the last, Hoshea.

12. The iniquity of Ephraim *is* bound up; his sin *is* hid.

This refers to what God, not Ephraim, has done with his sin. It is *not* implied that Ephraim has been able to hide his sin from either man or God. The figures are taken from a man's tieing up and hiding his money or other valuables for safe-keeping. So God has laid away the sin of Ephraim, to be brought forth another day for terrible retribution! Of this coming retribution, the prophet proceeds to speak.

13. The sorrows of a travailing woman shall come upon him: he *is* an unwise son; for he should not stay long in *the place of* the breaking forth of children.

The received translation of this verse can scarcely be improved. The figure in the first clause suddenly changes. Ephraim is first a mother in her travail pains; then an infant voluntarily retarding his own birth, and thus fearfully imperilling both his own life and the mother's.——No figures drawn from human experience can be more forcible than this—the peril that ensues when "children come to the birth and there is not strength to bring forth." If, now, to get the full force of this passage as applied to Ephraim, we suppose the son to bring on this danger by his own voluntary, intelligent agency, we shall see the infatuation and very madness which Hosea so temperately describes as being "unwise." Ephraim is going to the judgment with God in charge of all his sins, and he still lingers under the call to repent, and will not make peace with his offended judge.——The primary reference here is to judgments on earth, and very near; yet the principle is even more pertinent and forcible as applied to every sinner going to the final judgment.

14. I will ransom them from the power of the grave; I will redeem them from death: O death, I will be thy plagues, O grave, I will be thy destruction: repentance shall be hid from mine eyes.

Ephraim is seen ruining himself by his madness. The figure in the prophet's mind suggests death in some of its most painful forms; but God interposes, saying, "I will ransom thee from Sheol; I will redeem thee from death." Sheol, the grave, and death are, of course, personified here, and supposed to be living agents of terrific power over frail mortals.——The clauses translated—"O death, I will be thy plagues;" "O grave, I will be thy destruction—" raise the same critical question which came up in v. 10—the choice between the interrogative and the indicative form—with, however, less reason for the interrogative here than there. The general sense is the same either way; the interrogative form is the more bold and triumphant, and has yet this further fact in its favor, viz.: that Paul (1 Cor. 15: 55) quotes interrogatively—"O death, where is thy sting? O grave, where is thy victory?" ——In regard to this quotation by Paul, it should be said further, that the words as they stand here do not refer to the resurrection, but to salvation from the ruin then impending over Israel; but Paul's quotation applies them to the resurrection—the final triumph of our frail mortality over death and the grave, under the power of a resurrection to unfading life and immortality. The words are beautifully applicable to the latter event, and are, therefore, fitly used.——"Repentance shall be hid from mine eyes," must here be taken as God's own declaration concerning his purpose just before expressed: "I will redeem my people and be the destroyer of their worst foes, even of death and the grave, and *there shall be no reversal of this purpose.*"——This has no reference to God's hiding his eyes from man's repentance in this world or any other. Whatever may be true as to this, the passage before us has nothing to say about it. All language should be construed and applied with reference to the subject in hand.——In this verse the Lord thinks of Ephraim as bringing down on himself remediless ruin; but he interposes one more promise: I will yet redeem them even from this awful death *if they will repent;* or as the future might be rendered—*I would*, on my part, redeem them, if only they would consent!

15. Though he be fruitful among *his* brethren, an east wind shall come, the wind of the LORD shall come up from the wilderness, and his spring shall become dry, and his fountain shall be dried up: he shall spoil the treasure of all pleasant vessels.

Promise of help avails not; so, again, the prophet predicts for Ephraim near impending judgments. Though he may have been eminently fruitful, *i. e.*, populous and prosperous among his brother tribes (said with reference to the significance of his name—Ephraim, the prolific, and with reference also to the facts of his history), yet "an east wind"—often the simoom coming in upon Palestine from the eastern quarter—"the wind of the Lord," *i. e.* sent by him especially, "from the desert"—this shall "dry up his fountain and spring," and be the ruin of his land. In oriental countries the great scourge of the land is drought. Cut off from water, the land becomes one wide waste of desolation. So of Ephraim.——This language has special reference to the Assyrian power, which was God's great instrument for laying waste the kingdom of Ephraim. To this Assyrian king the pronoun "*he*" must be referred; "he shall spoil the treasures of all desirable, valuable things."

16. Samaria shall become desolate; for she hath rebelled against her God: they shall fall by the sword:

their infants shall be dashed in pieces, and their women with child shall be ripped up.

This clear, definite announcement of the ruin to come on the kingdom of the ten tribes for their great sins, was obviously made but a short time before the event. Hosea lived and prophesied in the midst of these very scenes. Thus closes what he has to say in the line of rebuking the sins of the people and announcing their coming doom.

CHAPTER XIV.

This short chapter is a fit and striking sequel to the book of Hosea, almost the entire strain of which sets forth the sins—the ingratitude, incorrigibleness, and the coming doom of the apostate children of Israel. But the Lord cannot let this stern message of rebuke and threatening close without one more call to repentance. If the nation must go down, like a sinking ship into the angry billows, with its vast freight of human souls, they shall at least go with the sounds of offered mercy still ringing in their ears; and further, the Lord would not leave a shade of apology for the inference that his heart is vindictive. After so much said of judgment and wrath, a wrong impression as to these points might be left if the book were to close without yet another testimony to his merciful compassion. How tenderly careful not to crush out hope from even the guiltiest bosom, saying, "I will not contend forever, neither will I be always wroth, for the spirit should fail before me and the souls which I have made." (Isa. 57: 16.)——Yet again: the strain of this closing chapter really *glows* with the beauty and joy of God's restored people when they repose under his shadow and drink at his fountain of bliss—all in charming contrast with the utter blight that falls on the wicked who pasture themselves on wind and chase after the east wind, and whose best delights turn to ashes on their lips. The joyous prosperity of God's penitent people is one of the strong recommendations of true piety.——And finally, the strain of this chapter is doubtless intended as an answer to the question oftener thought than expressed, What will become of the cause and kingdom of God on earth? If his people prove so hopelessly apostate, despite of such loving and persistent labor to save them, what is the hope for God's kingdom? Here we have the answer. It will yet be seen that this kingdom has the infinite God for its king. The interests of truth and righteousness in the earth may seem to go down in darkness; but they can at worst only pass under an eclipse, to shine out the more gloriously in their own appointed time. In this point of view, this closing chapter must be taken as a prophecy of the ultimate triumph of the cause and kingdom of God on earth.

1. O Israel, return unto the LORD thy God; for thou hast fallen by thine iniquity.

"To the Lord *thy* God"—thine own God still—a precious reason for hope and encouragement in your return.

2. Take with you words, and turn to the LORD: say unto him, Take away all iniquity, and receive *us* graciously: so will we render the calves of our lips.

"Take words"—avail yourself of the aid which the expression of your feelings in fit language will give you; and, moreover, do this, not merely alone, each in his solitude; but *socially*, the great body of the people uniting as the heart of one man.——To "render the calves of our lips," means to respond to God's forgiving mercy with oral expressions of gratitude and praise—offering our lips instead of bullocks. The word rendered "calves" means *bullocks*, and is almost without exception used of bullocks *offered in sacrifice*. The construction in Hebrew is not—the calves of our lips; but this—so will we give back our lips (as) bullocks—after the manner in which bullocks are brought forth for offerings in sacrifice to God.

3. Asshur shall not save us; we will not ride upon horses: neither will we say any more to the work of our hands, *Ye are* our gods: for in thee the fatherless findeth mercy.

The returning penitents pledge themselves specifically against three sins: seeking help from Assyria; from the use of horses in war, usually brought from Egypt; and saying any more to what is only the work of their own hands, "Ye are our gods." The reason given is ample—"In God, the fatherless find mercy;"—the helpless and forlorn, like ourselves, find compassion in him. The word used carries us back to "Ruhamah," as in chapters 1 and 2—this being the same.

4. I will heal their backsliding, I will love them freely: for mine anger is turned away from him.

The Lord himself now speaks in response to their vows and prayers. "Heal them *of* their backslidings" means restore them both in heart and in the external life.——"Will love them *freely*"—the last most expressive word having the sense of *spontaneous*—with warm and full heart, even as the blessed God of love is wont to love the truly penitent soul.

5. I will be as the dew unto Israel: he shall grow as the lily, and cast forth his roots as Lebanon.

The dews of Palestine were very heavy, and when in their fulness, went far to supply the want of rain.——The "lily" is noted for its beauty. Our Saviour's reference to it will be readily recalled—" Consider the lilies of the field," &c. (Matt. 6 : 28, 29).——" He," Israel, " shall shoot forth his roots as Lebanon "—referring to its lofty cedars which thrust their roots far out and deep down among the ancient foundations of the mountains, and so withstand the tempests of ages."

6. His branches shall spread, and his beauty shall be as the olive-tree, and his smell as Lebanon.

The olive-tree with its lovely green, furnishes another image of God's people under his faithful culture. Some of the trees and shrubs of Lebanon were fragrant, and perfumed the atmosphere of the mountain, as is indicated here, " the smell of Lebanon."

7. They that dwell under his shadow shall return; they shall revive *as* the corn, and grow as the vine: the scent thereof *shall be* as the wine of Lebanon.

"*His* shadow " is that of God—perhaps suggested by the tacit allusion to the cedars of Lebanon, whose shade is magnificent.——The word rendered scent, in the last clause, is *memorial*—the same used 12 : 5—meaning, they shall be renowned in fame, as the wine of Lebanon which has to this day the highest repute.

8. Ephraim *shall say*, What have I to do any more with idols? I have heard *him*, and observed him: I *am* like a green fir-tree. From me is thy fruit found.

Ephraim renounces idols for ever. The Lord takes note of this, and will observe—watch over him with a loving father's care.——The fir-tree is an evergreen,—setting forth here that God's love and care are ever enduring—green through all the year. And if the thought should arise, "But it yields no fruit"—the Lord at once forestalls that objection. " From me is thy fruit found;" all fruit comes, not from creatures, even the best and surest of them, but from myself.

9. Who *is* wise, and he shall understand these *things?* prudent, and he shall know them? for the ways of the LORD *are* right, and the just shall walk in them: but the transgressors shall fall therein.

The interrogatives here call the reader's special attention. The subject-matter of this book—God's ways of judgment and of mercy toward his people, wayward or penitent—are here set before you; whoever is wise shall understand them and learn their lessons of great truth and of practical life.——For God's ways are altogether right; the just, in the sense of upright, honest, and sincere, shall walk in them with peace and gladness through usefulness and honor here to a blissful end hereafter; but transgressors, whom no truth can reach to bless, shall stumble and fall under the very influences that bring salvation to the just.

Such are the lessons of this richly instructive book of Hosea. We shall need to go far to find other writings more forcible, more tersely written, more beautiful in their poetic imagery, more burning in their rebukes of sin, and more glowing in their testimonies to the deep compassion and yearning love of God toward sinful man.

JOEL.

INTRODUCTION.

THE precise date and duration of the prophetic life of Joel may be conjectured, but cannot be certainly known. He is not named elsewhere in the Old Testament Scriptures. His prophecy seems to be quoted both by Amos (compare Amos 1 : 2 with Joel 3 : 16) and by Isaiah (compare Isaiah 13 : 6 with Joel 1 : 15). Amos prophesied at some period within the long reigns of Uzziah of Judah, B. C. 811–759, and of Jeroboam II. of Israel, B. C. 825–784. Hence, if the writings of Joel were in the hands of Amos, he cannot have prophesied *later* than the reign of Uzziah; he may have been many years earlier. His book shows that he prophesied in Judah, and that the temple worship was then kept up. Remarkably, the book does not notice the kingdom of the ten tribes nor the sin of idolatry. The people are exhorted to repentance, to fasting, weeping, and rending of the heart. It may be inferred that in such a book idolatry would have been rebuked if it had been then prevalent. Some have argued, from his silence respecting the Syrian power, while he mentions Tyre and Sidon (3 : 4) as enemies, that he must have lived before their first invasion of Judah in the time of Ahab (reigned B. C. 918–897). See 1 Kings, chapters 20–22. But this cannot be conclusive, since he might know the Syrian kingdom as an enemy, and yet not mention it. Some weight is rightly given to the fact that the compilers of these sacred books have placed Joel between Hosea and Amos. In general, they observed the order of time, and it is safe to assume that, living so near the age of those prophets, they must have known with a fair measure of accuracy when Joel lived and wrote. This compilation is usually ascribed to Ezra and his associates—perhaps we should rather say, Ezra and his successors. The earliest historical notice of a collection known as "the Twelve Minor Prophets," is in the book of "Ecclesiasticus," or "Wisdom of Jesus, Son of Sirach" (49 : 10), in these words: "And of the Twelve Prophets let the memorial be blessed, and let their bones flourish again out of their place, for they comforted Jacob and delivered them by assured hope." The original of this book bears date 180 B. C. But there is good reason to suppose this compilation to be not much if any later than Malachi, about 420 B. C. Joel may have been somewhat earlier than Hosea, and yet be placed after him in order because shorter or for other reasons. I incline to assign him an earlier date than Hosea. Possibly (not probably) the famine which he portrays so vividly was that terrible one of seven years referred to (2 Kings 8 : 1) in the reign of Jehosaphat in Judah (reigned B. C. 914–891) and of Jehoram, son of Ahab, in Israel (reigned B. C. 896–884). With these only approximate results I pass the question of *date*.

Another question, at once more difficult and more important, respects the principles of interpretation which shall rule throughout the first two chapters. On this depends the determination of the primary and proper sense. On this point very able commentators disagree. It is admitted by all that the language *seems* to describe a fearful visitation of locusts, coupled with drought and consequent famine. But some, with Dr. Hengstenberg, hold that there were no real locusts. Foreign enemies "present themselves to the inward contemplation of the prophet as an all-devouring swarm of locusts."—(Vol. 3 : 103.) That is, Joel saw the locusts only in vision; the only real visitation was that of armed men—the real scourge was war.——Others, with Dr. Henderson, find real locusts, desolating the land, throughout chapter 1. In chapter 2, armed bands are the real thing, but they are compared to locusts. The locust bands, then recent, furnish the imagery by which they are described.——Others still suppose that real locusts are definitely described throughout chapter 1, and also 2 : 1–27. Yet this being a most fearful visitation, a striking and even appalling proof of God's power to inflict judgments on guilty men and guilty nations, it became naturally *suggestive* of what the wicked have to fear in some other and more terrible "great day of the Lord." Without admitting the doctrine of a double sense, *i. e.*, two distinct and coördinate senses of the same words and phrases, it may yet be reasonably held that a fearful devastation by locusts may suggest the ruin brought on a country by war, or by those unknown agencies of destruction which God has in store for the guilty in his magazines of wrath.——This latter view I accept, constrained in general by the fact that this seems to be the obvious sense of the passage.

My plan of commentary precludes any extended discussion of opinions from which I dissent, yet briefly I must reject the first theory above named as too foreign from the obvious sense of the language. There is no hint that the locusts are seen in vision only, and stand merely as symbols and figures of armed men. Hengstenberg speaks of it as an "allegory," but the manner and air of an allegory are wanting. Every allegory should furnish clear evidence of its being such. Besides this, an allegory should not give a minute natural history of the locust.——The second theory fails to harmonize with the drift of the description, for the second chapter gives us locusts as clearly as the first. In vs. 4–9 these locusts are compared to armed men—not armed men to locusts—a distinction which Dr. Henderson seems to ignore or at least overlook.——Other remarks bearing on the true interpretation may be suggested in the notes on particular passages.

In this book there will be very little occasion to comment on the meaning of particular words and clauses. The received translation in most cases is excellent, and gives the sense of the original with accuracy. The point of chief difficulty and of greatest moment is, to arrive at the ultimate sense and instruction—the mind of the Spirit of truth.

CHAPTER I.

A PLAGUE of locusts comes upon the land, unparalleled in its kind; they are described, vs. 6, 7, their devastations, vs. 9–12, 16–20, and various classes of the people are summoned to mourning, vs. 5, 8, 9, 13, and to fasting, v. 14.

1. The word of the LORD that came to Joel the son of Pethuel.

With the greatest brevity we are simply told that this book is the word of God that came to Joel.

2. Hear this, ye old men, and give ear, all ye inhab-

itants of the land. Hath this been in your days, or even in the days of your fathers?

3. Tell ye your children of it, and *let* your children *tell* their children, and their children another generation.

"Hath this been in your days?" must mean, Hath any *such* thing as this been—any visitation so fearful and so desolating? He appeals to the oldest men to say if, either in their days or in the days of their fathers, so great a judgment in its kind has befallen the land. V. 4 opens the description.

4. That which the palmer-worm hath left hath the locust eaten; and that which the locust hath left hath the canker-worm eaten; and that which the canker-worm hath left hath the caterpiller eaten.

Successive armies of locusts come upon the land, each, according to the strong language of this description, devouring all that the next preceding had left.——Great labor has been expended on the natural history of the locusts spoken of in the Bible. They appear under about ten different names, but whether these names represent ten distinct species remains in doubt. This point has no very great practical importance.——It is important, however, to the full impression of these chapters, that the power of these locusts for devastation should be understood. One author says: "Man can conquer the tiger and the lion; can turn the course of mighty rivers, and chain the winds to his car, and can play with the lightnings of heaven, but he is nothing before an army of locusts." Another says: "In some regions of the East the whole earth is at times covered with locusts for the space of several leagues, often to the depth of four, sometimes of six or seven inches. Their approach, with a noise like the rushing of a torrent, darkens the horizon, hides the light of the sun, and casts an awful gloom like that of an eclipse over the fields." Major Moore, when at Poonah, had an opportunity of seeing an immense army of locusts which ravaged the Mahratta country, and was supposed to have come from Arabia. Their column extended five hundred miles, and so compact was it when on the wing, that, like an eclipse, it completely hid the sun. Pliny calls them "a scourge in the hand of an incensed Deity." Before them all verdure disappears; the whole country puts on the appearance of being burnt. Fire itself devours not so fast. Not a vestige of vegetation is left behind them. In a few hours they eat up every green thing, and consign the miserable inhabitants to inevitable famine. "The husbandmen make every effort possible to stay or turn aside these foes or destroy them; they build fires or raise a dense smoke to withstand them, or dig trenches and fill them with water, but all to no purpose; for the trenches are soon filled and the fires extinguished by infinite swarms succeeding one another, and forming a bed on their fields of six or seven inches in thickness. When they die the effluvia becomes intolerable, and often has occasioned a pestilence fearfully destructive to human life." These few facts will suffice to show that the locust is one of the most terrible agents for destruction in the hands of the Almighty.

5. Awake, ye drunkards, and weep; and howl, all ye drinkers of wine, because of the new wine; for it is cut off from your mouth.

Wine-drinkers are called to weep and howl, because their new wine, called "must," fails them.

6. For a nation is come up upon my land, strong, and without number, whose teeth *are* the teeth of a lion, and he hath the cheek teeth of a great lion.

7. He hath laid my vine waste, and barked my fig tree: he hath made it clean bare, and cast *it* away; the branches thereof are made white.

The word here rendered "nation" is usually applied to heathen nations, considered as the enemies of God and of his people. In this case it implies that they are public enemies, a scourge sent of God upon his land. They are strong by reason of their great numbers; their teeth are terrible because of the devastations they can make. Stripping off all the foliage and even the bark, they leave only a mass of ruins and bare white branches.——The grasshopper of our country bears a close resemblance to the oriental locust. The latter, however, appear in immensely greater numbers, and make their desolations absolutely complete and universal.

8. Lament like a virgin girded with sackcloth for the husband of her youth.

9. The meat-offering and the drink-offering is cut off from the house of the Lord; the priests, the Lord's ministers, mourn.

10. The field is wasted, the land mourneth; for the corn is wasted: the new wine is dried up, the oil languisheth.

By a change in the usage of our English word "meat," within the last two hundred years, it has come to mean the flesh of animals. Anciently it was used in the general sense of food, and sometimes in the specific sense of *vegetable* food. Thus (Gen. 1:29, 30) God said, "I have given to you," *i. e.* to man, "every herb, and the fruit of trees, for *meat*;" and "to every beast," &c., "have I given every green herb for *meat*."——So here, this "meat-offering" consisted of flour, meal, or cakes, with oil, frankincense, but not a particle of flesh. Hence the locusts swept it all away.——Those who loved the service of the Lord were specially afflicted, because they were no longer able to bring to his temple the accustomed and required offerings.

11. Be ye ashamed, O ye husbandmen; howl, O ye vine-dressers, for the wheat and for the barley; because the harvest of the field is perished.

Confounded expresses the exact sense, rather than "ashamed," since shame properly implies some sense of guilt. Here the idea is that they were at their wit's end—all their labor had come to naught.

12. The vine is dried up and the fig-tree languisheth; the pomegranate-tree, the palm-tree also, and the apple-tree, *even* all the trees of the field, are withered: because joy is withered away from the sons of men.

13. Gird yourselves, and lament, ye priests: howl, ye ministers of the altar: come, lie all night in sackcloth, ye ministers of my God: for the meat-offering and the drink-offering is withholden from the house of your God.

14. Sanctify ye a fast, call a solemn assembly, gather the elders *and* all the inhabitants of the land *into* the house of the LORD your God, and cry unto the LORD.

The evil was by far the more serious, since not only the vegetables—annual plants—but trees of many years' growth, withered and died under this fearful scourge, so that joy—the joy men feel in these sources of earthly good—withered away.——Here is another call to mourning over these calamities, and especially and most pertinently to fasting, and to a general gathering in the house of God to lift up their prayer to him. Nothing can be more appropriate in seasons of calamity than to humble our hearts before the Lord, and seek his face with deep humility for our great sins.

15. Alas for the day! for the day of the LORD *is* at hand, and as a destruction from the Almighty shall it come.

The locusts being spoken of as present and this "day of the Lord" as being only "*near*," grave questions arise here; viz.: What *is* this "day of the Lord" which is near, but not (as it would seem) yet present? Is it the visitation of locusts, and nothing beyond and greater? If something beyond and greater, then *what* precisely is it? Does the prophet intend to make his description of it definite, as of some special event; or rather to leave it indefinite, designing only to impress the thought of the awfulness and terror of God's retributive judgments, however and whenever sent?

If there were nothing else in Joel but this (v. 15), looking toward another great day of the Lord, there would be no special difficulty in interpreting this of the locusts exclusively. For it might be urged that the locusts were even then scarcely present, and the terribleness of this scourge was still in the nearer future; that the tenses in Hebrew and especially in prophecy are not used with such definite precision as in most other languages; also, that the next verses continue the subject of locusts and the drought as if no other thought had been before the writer's mind.——But this verse does *not* stand alone in reference to the question now before us. The passage (2:1) repeats—"For the day of the Lord cometh, for it is nigh at hand;" and, of more weight still (in 2:31) we read: "The sun shall be turned into darkness, and the moon into blood, before the great and terrible day of the Lord come." This plainly shows that the prophet has some thought of another great and fearful, but somewhat remote, "day of the Lord," besides this in which locusts are the manifestation of his retributive vengeance.——Here, then, are various allusions to a "great day of the Lord," to be explained and accounted for. Do we not find the key to their exposition in those laws of mental association which, under the awe-inspiring power of a present judgment, like this of locusts, carry the mind over to the more awful future—to the great power of Almighty God to bring forth from the storehouse of his plagues far more terrible, annihilating judgments, and which make every mind feel that God's judgments are near at hand? This law of mind is well known. The effect of any present judgment is to make all future judgments seem near. It leads the mind to anticipate them with confidence, to take this present one as itself a prophecy and pledge of more and other in the future, and to lose sight of whatever time may intervene before they come. Thus, a single death-bed scene makes death seem near to ourselves. Sudden deaths by hundreds, as in the awful cholera pestilence, make stout hearts quail under a sense of God's power and justice, so that it shall seem that death and judgment are at the door. Moreover, a guilty conscience fearfully heightens this sense of the great day of the Lord as near at hand.——Thus powerfully suggestive was this fearful day of visitation by locusts. It brought fresh to the prophet's mind a sense of the awful guilt of his people, and of the certainty and nearness of God's sorer judgments. And, moreover, as he wrote *for moral impression*, and as the divine Spirit had this main if not sole purpose, it need not surprise us that he deems it of no special importance to speak more definitely of the *time* or *manner* of these yet future visitations of judgment. Suffice it if he can impress on the souls of wicked men the solemn thought that God's great day of judgment *to them* cannot be long delayed!

Yet further, as bearing on the sense of this verse, let it be noted that the most fearful thing in any form of judgment is that it *comes from God*, and is a proof of his stern displeasure. The conscious sense of his wrath burning against us is of all things most awful.

This becomes fitly the all-absorbing thought. Any form of judgment may suffice to awaken this feeling. Once awakened in a consciously guilty bosom, the man knows and feels that more and greater demonstrations of God's displeasure must be near.

In view of these laws of mind and of their relations to the question in hand, I see in this verse, and also in 2 : 1, no evidence of allusion to any other *specific* day, as *e. g.* the invasion of the Assyrian army. To suppose this, seems foreign from the general drift of the prophet's thought. Besides, if he had wished to predict that invasion, it is marvellous that he should not have made his statements more definite.——The original words rendered "destruction" and "almighty" are from kindred roots—as if we should say, "a *mighty* ruin from the *Almighty* hand."

16. Is not the meat cut off before our eyes, *yea*, joy and gladness from the house of our God?

The same idea as in v. 9, resumed and reiterated interrogatively —*Is* it not so? The prophet reverts to the subject in hand (vs. 2–14) as if no thought of any other day had come in to divert it. This fact shows that v. 15 is no new and foreign subject, but only something naturally suggested by his main theme.

17. The seed is rotten under their clods, the garners are laid desolate, the barns are broken down; for the corn is withered.

The effects of extreme drought, coupled with the work of the locusts. No seed vegetates; all harvests fail.

18. How do the beasts groan! the herds of cattle are perplexed, because they have no pasture; yea, the flocks of sheep are made desolate.

The "cattle are perplexed"—the original word, looking, however, not so much to a state of mind as to its manifestations. They wander up and down as if bewildered and at their wit's end.

19. O LORD, to thee will I cry: for the fire hath devoured the pastures of the wilderness, and the flame hath burned all the trees of the field.

20. The beasts of the field cry also unto thee: for the rivers of waters are dried up, and the fire hath devoured the pastures of the wilderness.

The prophet declares his purpose to cry unto the Lord for help and mercy, for the twofold reason that his heart feels so, and that he would lead the people also to prayer for help.

Thus closes this chapter—a most graphic, life-like description of a fearful devastation by drought and locusts—so severe and so terrible as to impress the mind with a sense of the weakness of man before the great and dreadful God, and of his guilt before One too holy to pass over sin without manifesting his sore displeasure.

CHAPTER II.

THE great alarm is sounded forth from the temple as usual in the presence of some dire calamity (v. 1); a more full description of the locusts is given—in part personal (vs. 4–9, and in part general and in the line of their effects (vs. 2, 3, 10, 11): the Lord exhorts the people to return to him (vs. 12–14). A solemn assembly is called for fasting and prayer (vs. 15–17); the Lord answers graciously (vs. 18–20), and passes over to rich promises of mercy, including rain and abundant harvests (vs. 21–27); and finally to the fuller promise of his Spirit in the latter time (vs. 23, 28–32).

1. Blow ye the trumpet in Zion, and sound an alarm in my holy mountain: let all the inhabitants of the land tremble: for the day of the LORD cometh, for *it is* nigh at hand;

"Blowing the trumpet and sounding an alarm" from the temple was of divine appointment in the law given through Moses. (See Num. 10: 1–10.) It convened the people to consider and act upon any case of general calamity, and had the promise—" Ye shall be remembered before the Lord your God, and ye shall be saved from your enemies."——The near " coming of the day of the Lord " is analogous to chap. 1: 15, and must be explained in the same way.

2. A day of darkness and of gloominess, a day of clouds and of thick darkness, as the morning spread upon the mountains: a great people and a strong; there hath not been ever the like, neither shall be any more after it, *even* to the years of many generations.

Darkness is often, with the Hebrew poets especially, a symbol of calamity. In this verse, however, there is no occasion to interpret it as a symbol. It is rather actual—the darkness produced by immense clouds of locusts, obscuring the light of day. This darkness came on and passed over the land " as the light of morning spread over the mountains;" where the point of the comparison is not in any supposed resemblance between darkness and light, for there is none; but in the *manner* of its coming on over the face of the earth. As the morning light sweeps up from the east, first gilding the mountain-tops, and then quietly pervading the whole face of the earth, so this darkness swept on as an avalanche of cloud, and rested like a dark pall of gloom and terror on the whole land.——That this visitation should be described as surpassing any ever known before, and even any that should come after for many generations, need not surprise us. It may have been strictly true of it *while it lasted*, and *in reference to judgments of this sort.* Moreover, men suffering under any fearful infliction, naturally express themselves in such strong terms.

3. A fire devoureth before them; and behind them a flame burneth: the land *is* as the garden of Eden before them, and behind them a desolate wilderness; yea, and nothing shall escape them.

"Fire" and "flame" are probably figurative; the desolation they wrought being like that of fire on the prairies, as if fire swept on before them, and again behind them, leaving absolutely nothing more to be destroyed. Exquisitely forcible and touching is this—the land seen in all the beauty of Eden before them, but behind them only a desolate wilderness.

4. The appearance of them *is* as the appearance of horses; and as horsemen so shall they run.

5. Like the noise of chariots on the tops of mountains shall they leap, like the noise of a flame of fire that devoureth the stubble, as a strong people set in battle array.

Locusts have been often compared to horses, as in Rev. 9: 7:—"The shapes of the locusts were like unto horses prepared for battle." They are fleet like horsemen, moving rapidly with the wind.——The figure of an army moving in solid phalanx and fearful array, is constantly present to the mind. Yet the thing described is an army, not of men, but of locusts. The locusts are *like* armed horsemen. He does not say that armed horsemen are coming on, and are like locusts.

6. Before their face the people shall be much pained: all faces shall gather blackness.

The word rendered "blackness" means rather a glow or flush of anxiety. The sense is—the people become intensely agitated with fear and alarm.

7. They shall run like mighty men; they shall climb the wall like men of war; and they shall march every one on his ways, and they shall not break their ranks:

8. Neither shall one thrust another; they shall walk every one in his path: and *when* they fall upon the sword, they shall not be wounded.

9. They shall run to and fro in the city; they shall

run upon the wall, they shall climb up upon the houses; they shall enter in at the windows like a thief.

It cannot be reasonably doubted that this is, and is intended to be, a closely accurate description of locusts, as they sweep along in their onward march for devastation. Every feature is in its place, made true to the reality by a master's hand. That the sword avails nothing against them goes to confirm this view, and to shut off the possibility of applying the description to the Assyrian army.

10. The earth shall quake before them; the heavens shall tremble: the sun and the moon shall be dark, and the stars shall withdraw their shining:

Strong poetic imagery should not be pressed to an extremely literal sense. In this passage, we need not insist that the locusts produced an earthquake, or any real concussion of the heavens. Jerome says pertinently on this passage: "Not that the locusts have so much power that they can move the heavens and shake the earth; but to those who are in great suffering and extreme terror, it *will seem* that the heavens are falling and the earth tossing under their feet."——Strong feeling naturally expresses itself in strong language. The darkening of the sun, moon, and stars, is a common figure for a great calamity; as, on the other hand, sun-rising and the joyous light of day are symbols of prosperity. The reader may find scriptural examples in abundance, *e. g.*, of the former class—Jer. 4: 28; Ezek. 32: 7, 8; Isa. 13: 10; Matt. 24: 29.

The consternation commonly felt for many ages when an eclipse occurred, shows how forcible this figure must have been in ancient times. Moreover, there may be here a tacit allusion to the actual darkening of the heavens, occasioned by the flight of countless myriads of locusts.

11. And the LORD shall utter his voice before his army: for his camp *is* very great: for *he is* strong that executeth his word: for the day of the LORD *is* great and very terrible; and who can abide it?

That "his army" is none other than the locusts, is put beyond a doubt by the Lord himself (v. 25), where he says of the locust, caterpillar, etc., "my great army which I sent among you." The words in Hebrew as well as in the English version are the same in both passages. This locust army is strong to execute the mandate of Jehovah. Sent by him, they are terribly efficient in devastating the land.——This "day of the Lord" can look to nothing else primarily save the visitation of locusts.——"Abide" is here used in the sense of endure.

12. Therefore also now, saith the LORD, turn ye *even* to me with all your heart, and with fasting, and with weeping, and with mourning:

13. And rend your heart, and not your garments, and turn unto the LORD your God: for he *is* gracious and merciful, slow to anger, and of great kindness, and repenteth him of the evil.

14. Who knoweth *if* he will return and repent, and leave a blessing behind him, *even* a meat-offering and a drink-offering unto the LORD your God?

This is the only appropriate thing to be done—the only source of hope for deliverance—to return and seek the Lord in penitence, for he is gracious and delights in mercy. Who knows but he may turn from scourging to blessing, and leave us at least so much that we can bring meat and drink offerings before him at his temple? ——This moral lesson is for all time, and for all sorts of affliction and calamity befalling men in this world. Everywhere and always, be the scourge what it may, it behooves men to turn to God, confessing sin, imploring mercy, daring to hope, since they may, that the Lord will yet turn from judgment to mercy.

15. Blow the trumpet in Zion, sanctify a fast, call a solemn assembly:

16. Gather the people, sanctify the congregation, assemble the elders, gather the children, and those that suck the breasts: let the bridegroom go forth of his chamber, and the bride out of her closet.

17. Let the priests, the ministers of the LORD, weep between the porch and the altar, and let them say, Spare thy people, O LORD, and give not thine heritage to reproach, that the heathen should rule over them: wherefore should they say among the people, Where *is* their God?

This summons to a great convocation for fasting and humiliation before God, differs from that in chap. 1: 14, in being more specific as to the classes of people to be convened, and also in giving the form of prayer appropriate for the occasion.——In this prayer, the phrase, "that the heathen should rule over them"—has been thought by some to be conclusive proof that the judgment described in this chapter (or, as others think, in the first as well) is not locusts, but armed men—a foreign invasion.——But a single circumstance like this cannot legitimately outweigh the continued tenor of the description throughout these two entire chapters. Besides, the thing chiefly feared from the heathen is reproach, not subjugation —the reproach of having a God unable to save, and bent on scourging and devastation. This is the thought in v. 17—"Give not thine heritage to reproach;" and also in v. 19 (the Lord's reply) —"I will no more make you a reproach among the heathen." It is also seen in the taunt, supposed to be in their mouth, "Where is their God?" It is therefore only in harmony with the drift of thought to interpret the words rendered "rule over them," as in the margin, "use a byword against them." While it must be admitted that in most cases this verb means *to rule*, yet the noun formed from it has the sense of byword, reproach, in many passages, and the verb is used in this sense in Job, 17: 6.——Or, it might be said that giving this phrase the sense of *ruling*, it may still be thought of as an evil to be feared in the future, not as one suffered in the present. If the land were to remain long so desolate and breadless, the people would become an easy prey to any foreign enemy, for such famine at once cuts the sinews of war and leaves the people no power of self-defence. In this view, therefore, they might fitly pray that God would remove this scourge of locusts, lest otherwise the whole nation, being powerless, should fall before its foreign enemies.

18. Then will the LORD be jealous for his land, and pity his people.

19. Yea, the LORD will answer and say unto his people, Behold, I will send you corn, and wine, and oil, and ye shall be satisfied therewith: and I will no more make you a reproach among the heathen:

"Then," *i. e.*, when his people humble themselves, and with one heart and voice implore his mercy.——Expressly the Lord is said to be "jealous for *his* land," for that land which had long borne his name before the nations, and with which his honor was so deeply involved. The Lord's answer promises blessings that lie over against the previous curse. He will gloriously reverse the calamities with corresponding mercies.——It may be noted that all along through verses 19–26, these blessings point to the devastations of locusts, the destruction of all the fruits of the earth, as *the* evils under which the nation had suffered, with no clearly defined allusion to foreign invasion. This fact goes far to disprove any distinct reference in these chapters to such invasion.

20. But I will remove far off from you the northern *army*, and will drive him into a land barren and desolate, with his face toward the east sea, and his hinder part toward the utmost sea; and his stink shall come up, and his ill savour shall come up, because he hath done great things.

The phrase "northern army" is urged by some as decisive proof of reference throughout this chapter to the Assyrians or Chaldeans, and not to locusts.

Against this it may be said: (1.) The manner and the consequences of the destruction of this army, as given in this verse, show that they are locusts, not men. In destroying this army, the Lord sends a strong wind and drives them into the sea; then they are thrown (this is implied) by the waves upon the shore, and their stench becomes intolerable. Not so would he destroy an army of men.——(2.) It is still a contested question, with authorities conflicting on either side, whether the locust armies do not sometimes enter Palestine from the north or northeast, so that this army might be called "northern" for this reason.——Or, (3.) It may be suggested whether, inasmuch as all the great powers, hostile to Israel in the latter period of their history, lay on the north, viz., Syria and Assyria, this term "northern" might not be a synonym for powerful, so that an army so terrible as this locust horde might be called northern for this reason.

In the last clause, "because he hath done great things," some critics suppose they find voluntary and morally responsible agency, and hence they infer that it can apply only to a *human* foe. But the indications of moral agency in this phrase are by no means decisive.

21. Fear not, O land; be glad and rejoice: for the LORD will do great things.

22. Be not afraid, ye beasts of the field: for the pastures of the wilderness do spring, for the tree beareth her fruit, the fig-tree and the vine do yield their strength.

By a bold personification the "land" and the "beasts" are exhorted not to fear any more, for God will remove his fearful scourge. ——"The Lord will do great things," is here finely contrasted with the locusts "doing great things," as in v. 20. However great their devastations, the Lord can make his ensuing blessings far greater. He delights to set his mercies over against the mischiefs and miseries that sin brings on men, and to show in this way how exceedingly he can surpass them in the greatness and glory of his grace.

23. Be glad then, ye children of Zion, and rejoice in the LORD your God: for he hath given you the former rain moderately, and he will cause to come down for you the rain, the former rain, and the latter rain in the first *month*.

In the interpretation of this verse, the main question, one really of great interest, is this: *Whether the passage is a promise of rain only, or whether it comprises a far richer promise and prophecy of spiritual blessings?*——This question turns mainly on the sense given to the original words rendered in our English text, "the former rain moderately," but in the margin, "a teacher of righteousness." If the latter be the true sense, the passage will be found far more rich in promised blessings than has been commonly supposed. The point is worthy of careful attention, and no apology need be made for a thorough, though it be a somewhat protracted examination.

The evidence in favor of translating "the teacher of righteousness," is in my view fully conclusive. It may be arranged thus:

(1.) This construction becomes antecedently probable in view of the common prophetic usage of engrafting Messianic prophecies upon analogous events of then current history. Some great present mercy suggests the far greater mercies of gospel times. This usage is so common that it may be considered one of the laws of Messianic prophecy. Thus in the passage Isa. 10: 24–34, with chap. 11 and 12, the deliverance wrought for Israel by the destruction of the Assyrian army, suggested the greater deliverance wrought for Zion by her King Messiah. In Zech. 9: 8–10, the protection afforded against Alexander the Great suggested the richer protection coming from the meek and peaceful King, whose empire shall be wider as well as more benign than ever was Alexander's.——There is therefore not only no objection to the gospel idea in this connection, but there is a measure of antecedent probability in its favor, inasmuch as the circumstances are of that very sort in which prophecies of the Messiah so often occur.——I adduce this point, however, especially to rebut the only objection made against the Messianic interpretation, viz.: that it is out of place here in a strain of remark about rain and fertility after famine. Henderson, Rosemueller, Gesenius, and others, seem to think this objection conclusive against the reference of these words to gospel times.——The facts of prophetic usage bear in precisely the opposite direction, and show that Messianic reference is here precisely *in place*, opportune, natural, probable.

(2.) The second argument is of the same sort with the foregoing, heightening the antecedent probability of a reference to gospel blessings. It lies in the fact that the prophet gives special notice that he has great blessings to promise, by calling on "the children of Zion to be glad and rejoice in the Lord their God." This notice very commonly and very naturally precedes a prophecy of gospel blessings, as a preintimation that they are to be brought forward. Thus Zech. 9: 9, "Rejoice greatly, O daughter of Zion; shout, O daughter of Jerusalem; behold, thy King cometh unto thee," &c. And Zech. 2: 10, "Sing and rejoice, O daughter of Zion, for lo, I come, and I will dwell in the midst of thee, saith the Lord." Or, Isa. 49: 13, "Sing, O heavens, and be joyful, O earth, and break forth into singing, O mountains, for the Lord hath comforted his people," &c.——This list might be extended almost indefinitely, sometimes indeed with only the special call of attention, "Behold!" as in Isa. 52: 13, and Jer. 23: 5. This may be set down, therefore, as one of the laws of the Messianic passages, all the more strong in proof of Messianic reference here, because the prophet had already announced the coming fulness of bread instead of emptiness, plenty in place of famine; so that there was really no occasion to call for special joy in the prospect of mere rain. In fact, rain was already presupposed in the verse preceding—"the pastures of the wilderness do spring; the fig-tree and the vine yield their strength."——Hence there are the best of reasons to look for a promise of gospel blessings here. Let us now examine the words themselves:

(3.) The specially essential word, rendered "the former rain," is in Hebrew, moreh,* a participle (Hiphil) from the verb † which means, first, to throw or cast; then to throw javelins, spears, arrows; to throw drops of water, *i. e.*, to rain; and to throw out the hand in pointing out objects to another, and hence, to *teach*. Thus, from this root we in fact get words both for *rain* and for *teacher*. Indeed, the participle in one conjugation (Kal), is used to a limited extent for rain, *e. g.*, Deut. 11:14 and Jer. 5:24, &c.; while in another conjugation (Hiphil)—the one used here—it denotes *teacher*. ——Of course this is a question of usage. Moreh, in precisely this form, occurs in the Hebrew Bible, outside of the passage before us, seven times, and in its plural three times—and in each case in the sense of *teacher* only. The passages are 2 Kings 17:28, "he became their teacher;" 2 Chron. 15:3, "without a teacher, a priest;" Job 36:22—said of God—"who is a teacher like him?" Prov. 6:13, "he is a teacher with his fingers"—(with an eye to the etymology); Isa. 9:14, "the prophet, teacher of lies," &c.; Hab. 2:18, "teacher of lies."——Ps. 84:7 may be considered doubtful. Our English Bible has it—"The rain also filleth the pools;" but Dr. Alexander, better, thus: "The teacher is clothed with blessings:" —one of the good things about the house of God—this being the subject-matter of the psalm.——Besides these, are three instances of the plural in the same sense of teacher; viz., Prov. 5:13, and Isa. 30:20 twice.——Hence the usage in the sense of *teacher* is substantially universal, there being no clear case of the use of this word in this form for *rain*, outside of this passage in Joel. The case Ps. 84:7 is the only one claimed.——Yet further, the usage of the finite verb (Hiphil conjugation), in the sense of *teach*, is most abundant. Taylor's Concordance gives forty-three cases, but not one in the sense to rain. Hence, it would seem that the facts on the point of usage must be conclusive, in proof that the original word *moreh* means here *teacher*.

(4.) The argument is heightened by the use of the article—*the* teacher—the celebrated, distinguished teacher. The article appears in none of the other ten cases where this word means teacher. This then must be *the* teacher, in the highest, noblest sense. But if the word is held to mean *rain*, no reason can be given for the use of the article.

(5.) By a sort of attraction, the word in the last clause of the verse, rendered "former rain," takes this form *moreh* instead of the usual one yoreh,‡ but is without the article. In other respects the form is the same as before, where I render it "*teacher*." If this

* הַמּוֹרֶה † יָרָה ‡ יוֹרֶה

were a case of "renewed mention," as grammarians call it, *i. e.*, if it were used in the same sense here as before, and referred to that use, it should have the article. If that was former rain, this should be *the* former rain, before spoken of. But this is not *the* rain; therefore that was not rain at all.

(6.) The word I render "righteousness" (in our English Bible, "moderately") demands the Messianic sense. This word * is always used in the moral sense—never in the physical. It occurs scores of times in the Scriptures; never in the sense of "moderately," as of rain in due measure, but always in the moral sense of morally right doctrine, and a morally right life.

(7.) Another argument comes from the tenses of the two verbs in this passage, rendered "hath given," and "will cause to come down." This argument perhaps will not be very clear to a merely English reader, yet it has essential weight.——The first verb is indeed in the preter tense—a fact which may seem to preclude its being a prophecy of distant future blessings. But almost all the prophecies are in this very tense—so that this is often called "the prophetic preter."——The tense of the second verb is quite peculiar—known by Hebrew grammarians as the future with vav conversive. It indicates a connection with the preceding verb, which means more than "*and*," *i. e.*, more than simply that one event comes after the other. The connection may be expressed thus—"And *then* or *so*, will he bring down rain," denoting what results as a consequence, or inference, from what has been just said. In the present case the relation of ideas involved in the tense of the second verb may be twofold: (*a.*) That having promised the Teacher of righteousness whose very name is associated with *rain*, he will much more give literal rain in its time; and (*b.*) That having thus made provision for teaching the people righteousness, the reason for withholding rain for discipline or in judgment, will cease, and the Lord will now give rain without stint, since he safely can, without moral harm. The latter I incline to make specially prominent.

(8.) If, with our English Bible, we render "the former rain moderately," then the last part of the verse is tame repetition, and makes no progress in the thought: thus—"He gives you the former rain moderately, and he causes to come down the rain, the former and the latter rain." It is scarcely supposable that this can be the true rendering.——This objection cannot be relieved by the difference in *tense*, presented in our common version—"he *hath* given;" and "he *will* cause to come down;" for the Hebrew tenses do not sustain this distinction.

(9.) Giving this clause the sense—"the Teacher of righteousness" with reference to spiritual blessings, and somewhat to gospel times, there is a striking antithesis between this verse and v. 28; v. 23 promises "the Teacher of righteousness, in the first place." (Our translators found nothing for their word "month.") The Hebrew

* צְדָקָה

means—"in the first place," the first instalment of blessings. Then v. 28 promises that "*afterwards*" another instalment shall be given. As the latter is *not* rain, so neither is the former. As the latter *is* the Spirit, so is the former.——I suggest yet another antithesis: v. 23, addressing specially "the children of Zion," says—"He gives to *you* the Teacher of righteousness;" v. 28, over against this, has it—"I will pour out my Spirit *on all flesh*." In verse 23, the pronoun *you* is fully expressed, and for this reason, by Hebrew law, is slightly emphatic, or at least distinctly prominent. Hence the evidence of designed antithesis is the stronger.

(10.) This antithesis becomes yet somewhat more direct, if by "the Teacher of righteousness" we understand the Holy Spirit—the same blessing promised in v. 28, given first to the children of Zion, and "afterwards poured out on all flesh."——"All flesh," by current usage as well as by the legitimate sense of the words, should mean the whole human family, and in this antithesis, the Gentile world. (See Gen. 6 : 12 ; Ps. 65 : 2 and 145 : 21 ; Isa. 40 : 5, 6, &c.) ——True, the specifications that immediately follow lead the mind rather to the idea of *all classes of society*—"sons and daughters," "old men and young," "servants and handmaids"—this wide range of classes being perhaps in antithesis with the former limitations to the priestly and prophetic orders, to which latter the promise (v. 23), may have special reference. That is, the promise of "the Teacher of righteousness," referring primarily to the Holy Spirit, would contemplate the Spirit as working upon the people *through* his priests and prophets, and thus turning them to righteousness.——The next instalment of these blessings would greatly increase the number of his immediate agents. The New Testament seems to assume that, ordinarily, the Spirit reaches the ungodly through the media of Christians, working and praying "in the Spirit," while he comes down upon Christians *directly*, both to anoint them for their Christian labor for the ungodly, and to secure their own sanctification. This second instalment (v. 28) therefore looks toward the unlimited extension of the Spirit's agencies by multiplying the number and enlarging the circle of his immediate agents.——The arguments then *against* restricting the effusion of the Spirit, promised vs. 28, 29, to the Hebrew line, and *for* its unlimited extension, stand briefly thus: (*a.*) "All flesh" legitimately means all mankind. (*b.*) The specifications only show that the circle of special agents through whom the Spirit works will be vastly enlarged—indeed, will comprise all classes of society—and thus will provide the instrumentalities for diffusing the Spirit's influence over all the world. (*c.*) Peter applies "all flesh" in this large, unlimited sense (Acts 2 : 21, 39) : "*Whosoever* shall call on the name of the Lord shall be saved," (which is his version of Joel 2 : 32), and—"For the promise is unto you and to your children, and *to all that are afar off*, even as many as the Lord our God shall call." This argument from Peter's exposition of Joel is the stronger, because it is preeminently the Spirit's exposition, and not Peter's—the latter not having yet really understood the sense of these words. Acts 10 shows both *when* and *how* his mind was opened to the grand idea that "of a truth God is no respecter of persons;" but gives gospel blessings to Gentile as to Jew.

(11.) That *Moreh*, the Teacher, refers to the Holy Spirit rather than specially to the Messiah, is certainly favored by the strong analogy, everywhere apparent throughout the Old Testament, between the Spirit and the gift of rain—between the agencies of the Spirit, and reviving, cleansing water. This analogy does not hold between rain and the Messiah. That rain is a symbol of the Spirit, probably both in manner of coming and in consequent effects, is apparent even here in v. 28: "I will *pour out* my Spirit." The very form of expression shows that this analogy is before the prophet's mind. So also Isa. 44:3, "I will pour water upon him that is thirsty, and floods upon the dry ground: I will pour my Spirit upon thy seed, and my blessing upon their offspring." Or Ezek. 36:25, "Then will I sprinkle clean water upon you, and ye shall be clean .... from your filthiness:"—"I will put my Spirit within you and cause you to walk in my statutes." The parallelisms here furnish all the evidence needed to show that in these passages water is thought of only as a figure for the Spirit.——Many other passages might be cited from the Old Testament in which the close analogy between the Spirit and water is boldly prominent. Ezekiel, in his last recorded vision, saw living waters flow from under the sanctuary and soon become a mighty river—manifestly looking onward to that blessed age when the fulness of the Spirit shall be shed forth to make pure and effective all the forms of social and moral influences in human society. Let us note also that this passage (Ezek. 47) is the more in point here because it was manifestly suggested by the passage Joel 3:18, and is strictly an expansion of Joel's thought:—"All the rivers of Judah shall flow with water, and *a fountain shall come forth of the house of the Lord*, and shall water the valley of Shittim."

(12.) It is plausibly objected to the rendering, "Teacher of righteousness," that, admitting it, the thought is dropped too soon, and that the current of remark (vs. 24–27) seems to ignore it, as it could not if the gospel idea were really there in the words which I render "The Teacher of righteousness;" in other words, that room enough is not allowed for a thought so great and so important as this.——A closer examination will obviate this objection. First, the greatest joy is invoked in view of the gift of the Teacher of righteousness. Then this teacher is to be a *present* as well as a future blessing, inasmuch as he will manifest his power through his anointed servants—the priests and the prophets of the old dispensation. See Zech. 4 throughout, and especially vs. 11–14. Hence the prosperity of the people will hopefully become both great and permanent, since, when they are radically turned to righteousness, nothing will restrain the rich gifts of God's providence.——Moreover, these views and these only give their full force to verses 26,

27—"Ye shall eat in plenty and be satisfied, and praise the name of the Lord your God who hath dealt wondrously with you; and my people shall never be ashamed; and ye shall know that I am in the midst of Israel, and that I am the Lord your God and none else; and my people shall never be ashamed."——That they should praise God who had "wrought wondrously" in scourging them for their sins, and in thus drawing them back to humiliation, repentance, and a godly life; that they should know that the Lord is their God and is verily in the midst of them—know it by his discipline and by its "peaceable fruits of righteousness;" that they should never be put to shame before their foes, but always live so that the Lord should be their trust and salvation; all these things imply more than a present supply of rain. Their meaning cannot be exhausted short of a living fountain of spiritual truth and life, flowing from the great Teacher of righteousness through his inspired prophets.

(13.) Still another objection will strike many minds against the assumed antithesis between the clauses "Teacher of righteousness," v. 23, and "I will pour out my Spirit," v. 28, viz., Why are the names and statements so diverse if they mean the same thing? If v. 23 means the Holy Spirit, why did not the language say so?

I reply (*a.*) As I have already hinted, there may be some regard to these facts, viz., that rain is before the mind; that the ideas of rain and of teacher are associated in the same Hebrew verb; and yet more, that there is a close and constant analogy in the Hebrew mind between water and rain on the one hand, and the Holy Spirit on the other.——(*b.*) But probably more weight still in determining the *form* of the expression "Teacher of righteousness," is due to the nature of the case in hand, the special sort of blessing needed by the people, as seen in the light of events then present. Great sin had brought upon them a great scourge of locusts, drought and famine. Repentance and divine mercy had driven off the locusts and brought them rain and bread, but yet the people were not half saved without a permanent Teacher of righteousness. A divine teacher, himself teaching their teachers, and holding the people permanently to righteousness, was precisely the greatest blessing possible in their case; was the very blessing they needed; was the only thing requisite to fill their cup full.——These now are not only reasons why God should give the people his Spirit, but were also reasons why He should designate him thus: "The Teacher of righteousness." This name indicated the work most essential then, in the light of the recent calamities and their causes. Hence the name. It is shaped by the surroundings, by the facts then specially present to the mind. Why should it not be?

Finally, since this special interpretation which refers the phrase "Teacher of righteousness" rather to the Spirit than to the Son, is mainly if not wholly new, I choose to present it as a suggestion. I do not press it as a point of vital importance. That the passage promises spiritual and not temporal blessings, the teaching of righteousness and not merely the gift of rain, I think is entirely clear and withal a point of practical value.——Theologically there can be no prejudice against it, for while teaching was one office of the Messiah, it was not the only or the chief one, but it *is* the chief and characteristic function of the Spirit. Jesus himself said of the Spirit, "He shall teach you all things;" and yet more, if possible, to the point in hand, "When he is come, he will reprove the world of sin and *of righteousness*."

24. And the floors shall be full of wheat, and the fats shall overflow with wine and oil.

25. And I will restore to you the years that the locust hath eaten, the canker-worm, and the caterpillar, and the palmer-worm, my great army which I sent among you.

In the clause "The years that the locust hath eaten," the plural "years" indicates that this scourge was not transient nor limited even to one year, but continued through several, a most terrific visitation of divine judgment. But the Lord would make good to his people all the losses and sufferings of those long-remembered years. He seems to refer primarily to restoration *in kind*, i. e., in corn, and wine, and oil; but if he would restore those things of less value, how much more will he make up their losses in the earthly line by superabounding mercies in the spiritual line! This is the wise and ever precious way of the Lord to restore to his penitent people earthly good in *just* measure, but heavenly, in all the plenitude of his grace.

26. And ye shall eat in plenty, and be satisfied, and praise the name of the LORD your God, that hath dealt wondrously with you: and my people shall never be ashamed.

27. And ye shall know that I *am* in the midst of Israel, and *that* I *am* the LORD your God, and none else: and my people shall never be ashamed.

A thanksgiving festival over these mercies would be eminently fitting, especially the thanksgiving and the praise.——*This* repetition is designed to give special force to two ideas: (1) that God's people should *know* by their precious experience that their own God is in the midst of them, a Power and a Refuge, and an only God, there being no other; and (2) that his people, confiding in his love and help, shall never be put to shame. This confidence in their God can never prove abortive. It is always safe to trust in his name. So trusting, his people never have been confounded and never can be.——Knowing by personal experience that God is in the midst of us through scenes of sore affliction, until deliverance and restoring mercy appear, implies that we apprehend the great idea of God's use of earthly discipline, viz., to make all things work together for good to those who love him. When Israel came out from under the scourge of locusts and famine, penitent and humbled, drawn thereby the nearer to God, and made fully aware that his hand had been afflicting them in mercy for their spiritual good, they might well be said to know that God had been in the midst of them all the time as their own Lord God.

28. And it shall come to pass afterward, *that* I will pour out my Spirit upon all flesh; and your sons and your daughters shall prophesy, your old men shall dream dreams, your young men shall see visions:

29. And also upon the servants and upon the handmaids in those days will I pour out my Spirit.

There can be no doubt that this passage predicts the effusion of the Spirit in the gospel sense, and particularly, though not exclusively, in gospel times. That the specifications should point to the extraordinary rather than the ordinary operations of the Spirit, *i. e.*, to visions, dreams, and prophetic functions, rather than to his more common, now more useful but less palpable ministries of convicting, converting, and sanctifying grace—has the same reason in prophecy that it had in the fact itself on the day of Pentecost, viz., the importance of having the Spirit's earlier manifestations made so tangible as to convince gainsayers and demonstrate his presence and power.——"All flesh" must mean the whole race, without distinction of Jew or Gentile. This usage is fully established. In addition to the passages referred to in notes on v. 23, see Gen. 9 : 17; Num. 16 : 22; Isaiah 66 : 23; Luke 3 : 6; and John 17 : 2. The specifications given here, "your sons and your daughters," "your old men and your young men," "the servants and the handmaids," go to show that there shall also be no distinction of sex or age, of rank or station. As the gospel was to be preached to the poor, so the Spirit should come down upon servants and handmaids, as well as upon their employers, however rich and noble. It may also be intended that this spiritual illumination shall not be restricted to the orders of priests and prophets, but diffused through all grades and classes.——The question *When?* must not be overlooked. The only designation of time given here, "afterwards," in future time, was purposely left thus indefinite. The period before Christ and subsequent to Joel, is not necessarily excluded; the early years of the Christian age are certainly included, as Peter shows (Acts 2 : 16–21) in his citation of this passage as then having its fulfilment; nor can the yet future periods of the gospel age be shut out. Indeed, numerous prophecies show that in the times yet future there shall be far richer manifestations of the Spirit's power than the world has yet seen. Nothing in prophecy, nothing in Peter's reference to Joel on the day of Pentecost, forbids this belief.——The connection of thought in which this prophecy stands has been already noticed. The great deliverance wrought for the covenant people on their repentance, by driving away the fearful locust army and by giving instead copious rains and superabundant harvests, suggested the far richer mercies of the divine Spirit. The underlying cause of both is the same—God's loving-kindness and great mercy. It is only in accordance with well-known laws of mind that one great blessing should suggest another yet greater.——Finally, let us notice the favor shown by the Lord to the saints of that early age, in setting before them such glimpses of the better gospel days yet to come, and particularly such revelations of the future effusions of the Spirit. It must have ministered greatly to their faith in God and to their hope and joy in his kingdom among men.

30. And I will show wonders in the heavens and in the earth, blood, and fire, and pillars of smoke.

31. The sun shall be turned into darkness, and the moon into blood, before the great and the terrible day of the LORD come.

Striking portents and prodigies shall precede the coming of "the great and terrible day of the Lord." The two main questions here are (1) Whether this language respecting the sun and moon shall be taken in a strictly literal or a figurative sense? and (2) Whether the reference is to some one great day only, and if so to what? or whether the passage teaches or implies a general truth, viz., that portents shall appear prior to all the really great and signal manifestations of the Lord's judgments on the wicked?——As to the first question, what is said of the sun and moon must be understood of their appearance, and not of their reality. On the question whether these extraordinary things pertain to the realm of nature or the realm of society, I incline to decide for the former, and so far forth to give them a literal construction. That is, I do *not* favor the mode of interpretation which makes the sun and moon represent the greater and lesser kingdoms or princes of the world. The plagues on Egypt, prior to the great deliverance wrought for God's people, seem to have been before the prophet's mind as the case to furnish his illustrative terms. And further, there seems to be a general expectation in the minds of men, in all ages, that God will give preintimations in the natural world of his special comings for judgment. To this point pagan writings furnish ample proof.——As to the question whether this prophecy looks to one particular day alone, or rather announces a general doctrine, I suggest that the phraseology "*the* great and *the* terrible day" leads the mind specially to some one day, and yet the fact that this day shall be heralded by portents in nature may be only one striking case under a general law.——If I am to look for *the* definite day, I cannot place it earlier than the destruction of Jerusalem by the Romans, as to which day the evidence of portents and prodigies seems very strong. Beyond that I fix on no definite day. The future may reveal it. It may have its final and most startling fulfilment shortly prior to the last great judgment day.

32. And it shall come to pass, *that* whosoever shall call on the name of the LORD shall be delivered: for in Mount Zion and in Jerusalem shall be deliverance, as the LORD hath said, and in the remnant whom the LORD shall call.

In these times of terrible judgment on the incorrigibly guilty, some shall escape altogether. This verse informs us very definitely who they are, viz., those who "call on the name of the Lord," and those whom "the Lord shall call." Moreover, the deliverance shall be "in Mount Zion and in Jerusalem," *i. e.*, for their inhabitants, for those who are the Lord's true people.——"Calling on the name of the Lord" must be of and from the heart, since such salvation can be promised to no other.——The primitive Christians were distinguished as those who called on the name of Christ their Lord, *as God;* and to this fact there may be here a prophetic allusion. The common mode of reaching the sense, however, is preferable; all those who heartily cry unto God for mercy and who cast themselves wholly on his grace.——"The remnant whom the Lord shall call," are the same people, for they whom the Lord calls are brought to call on the Lord. In this very thing consists the efficiency of God's call to them. It moves their hearts to call upon him in sincerity.——Thus, in the severest judgments of the Lord on the wicked, salvation is sure to those who take hold of his promised mercy and grace, and call on him in sincere and humble prayer. His people find a sure and everlasting refuge beneath the wing of the same Power, whose uplifted arm comes down in vengeance on his foes.

CHAPTER III.

THE most vital and therefore the first step toward the exposition of this chapter is, to determine the general principles of its interpretation. The choice lies between two methods. One of these is ably carried out by Dr. Henderson, who always leans strongly to a literal and specific construction. He holds that the passage 2: 28–32, is parenthetic, interposed between passages preceding and succeeding, both of which were fulfilled at least a century or more before Christ; while this parenthetic clause carries us forward (for the moment only) to the times of Peter and the Pentecost; that this third chapter returns again to the restoration from captivity in Babylon and to the destruction of Tyre, Zidon, &c., during the two or three centuries next subsequent to that restoration. He accounts it the main drift of the chapter to predict the retributive judgments of God on those particular nations, and then to portray the consequent peace and prosperity of the Jews—all in the period prior to the Christian era.——The other method makes the main drift and purpose of the chapter far more general and less specific in regard to the nations specially named in it; finds here the general doctrine of God's retributive judgments in this world on nations and powers arrayed against his people and kingdom, and accounts the reference to Tyre, Zidon, and Philistia (vs. 4–8), as rather parenthetic and illustrative of the general principle, than as constituting the main subject of the chapter.——On this system it is not supposed that more is said of Tyre and Zidon than was true, not more than has been punctually fulfilled; but it is held that the chapter looks far beyond the case of those nations, and teaches that the retribution which blighted them falls under the general law, serves to illustrate that law, and finds a place in this chapter for this reason, and not as being the leading theme.——I adopt this last-named method of interpretation, and shall feel at liberty to present it without turning aside specially to controvert the other scheme.

The relation of this chapter to the first and second should be noticed.——The locust army, and its attendant drought and consequent famine and distress, gave occasion to prayer, fasting, and penitence, and so opened the way for the signal extermination of that army, and for timely rains and superabundant harvests. These lesser gifts suggested the far greater gifts of the Spirit, the prediction of which constitutes the glory of the closing verses of the second chapter.——But there remains yet another great lesson of moral truth, suggested by the extermination of the locust horde—a lesson hinted at (2: 30, 31) in the allusion to "the great and terrible day of the Lord," but laid over for its special presentation in the third chapter, viz., the fearful and exterminating retribution which God will bring on all those nations and powers which persistently array themselves in arms against his kingdom and people. Hence this is the great theme of the chapter before us. It naturally closes with the resulting peace, prosperity, and purity of the rescued and saved people of God.

1. For behold, in those days, and in that time, when I shall bring again the captivity of Judah and Jerusalem,

The first word, "For," indicates a close connection of thought between this chapter and the preceding. The prophet had said there should be "a great and terrible day of the Lord," so sweeping in the ruin it brings that none shall escape it but those who call upon the name of the Lord. Here, resuming this subject, he begins to give the reason, "*For* I will gather all nations," *i. e.*, for trial and retribution.——"Behold" calls special attention as to truths of momentous import.——The *time when*, is indicated next, viz., when he shall interpose to redeem his people and bring them out of all their affliction. The phrase, "bring again the captivity of Judah and Jerusalem," admits this general sense, as may be seen in Job 42: 10, where it is said that "the Lord turned the captivity of Job"—of course, not in the specific sense of bringing him back from some captivity in a foreign land, but in the general one of bringing him out of a state of great affliction. So, also, Ezekiel (16: 53–55) speaks hypothetically of bringing again the captivity of Sodom and Samaria, but explains the sense by saying, "when Sodom and Samaria shall return to their former estate." We are not, therefore, shut up to find the fulfilment of this chapter at the precise time of some actual restoration of Judah from a real captivity under some hostile nation. The general sense is indeed more probable—When I shall turn my hand from afflicting to restoring and blessing my people, then will I visit retribution on all their foes.

2. I will also gather all nations, and will bring them down into the valley of Jehoshaphat, and will plead with them there for my people and *for* my heritage Israel, whom they have scattered among the nations, and parted my land.

On this verse, the leading question is, whether this gathering of all nations is to be understood literally, or only as a figure for a general retribution? Under this arises the question, whether the valley of Jehoshaphat, as thought of by Joel, was real, or only ideal?——In my opinion ideal only, for there is no proof that any actual valley was then known by this name. The name occurs nowhere else in the Scriptures, applied to any valley. In later times (*i. e.*, since the middle of the fourth century), the name has been given to the valley of the Kidron (in N. T., Cedron), which skirts Jerusalem on the east. With this modern application of the name is connected the current belief among Jews, Catholics, and Mohammedans, that the last judgment will be held in this valley. This fact goes far to show that the name Jehoshaphat was applied to this valley upon the mere supposition that Joel referred to it, and hence is modern only and not ancient, and therefore affording no proof that Joel referred to this valley.——On the other hand, the name is chosen because of its Hebrew significance—*Jehovah judges*—and a "valley" is thought of because in this hilly country valleys afford the only fit locations for convening a vast multitude.——That the writer's mind is specially on the significance of the word Jehoshaphat (Jehovah judges), is more obvious in the Hebrew than in our English, since the verb rendered, "plead with," is from the same root. "I will bring them into the valley of the *Lord's judgment*, and there will I *judge* them," *i. e.*, hold court for their trial on the charge of scattering my people and dividing their land.——The reader should also notice in this connection v. 12: "Let the heathen be wakened and come up to the valley of Jehoshaphat; for there will I sit to judge all the heathen round about." The idea is that of a grand assize, a sublime court, held for the trial and condemnation of the whole heathen world, so far as they have been guilty of wrong and abuse against the known people of God.

The description of this scene is continued, vs. 11, 13–16.——The conception is very similar to that of the final judgment, as it appears in the New Testament; yet this day of Joel cannot be identical with that, because here we have nations on trial; there individuals: here only those nations which have been known as enemies of the covenant people; there all people of all time—the entire population of our earth. This takes place *in* time; that only at the *end of time*, as measured for this world by the great lights God has set in our heavens.——Let it be considered yet further:—No valley, certainly not the one now called the valley of Jehoshaphat, could suffice for convening all the nations specially named in this chapter—to say nothing of the untold myriads really included under this general description.*

I am brought, then, by this mass of concurrent evidence, to adopt the ideal sense of "the valley of Jehoshaphat"—meaning *any* valley—any circumstances in which Jehovah judges guilty nations. The fact that *he does judge them, and visit upon them retribution in time*, is the thing taught;—the place where, and its surroundings, are only the ideal drapery of the scene, designed to make the fact more tangible to the imagination.

3. And they have cast lots for my people; and have given a boy for a harlot, and sold a girl for wine, that they might drink.

Here are more specifications in the indictment against these nations. They have not only scattered the chosen people among the nations and parted their land, but have cast lots over the captives (see traces of this usage in ancient times, Obadiah, v. 11, and Nahum 3:10); and as showing both the wickedness of these conquerors, and the contempt they felt for their captives, they gave a boy for the temporary hire of a harlot, and sold a girl for one drink of wine.——Is it strange that the heart of the great Father should take fire against such abominations?

4. Yea, and what have ye to do with me, O Tyre, and Zidon, and all the coasts of Palestine? will ye render me a recompense? and if ye recompense me, swiftly *and* speedily will I return your recompense upon your own head;

* Still further; the Hebrews had one general term for a broad valley[1] used here; applied also to the broad valley of Esdraelon, and to several others; but never to the valley of the Kidron. They had another term,[2] more specific, for a narrow gorge, the bed of a winter torrent, which is commonly, if not universally, used for the gorge of the Kidron; *e. g.* 2 Sam. 15:23, and 1 Kings 2:37 and 15:13; Jer. 31:40. Thus Hebrew usage seems to forbid the reference of Joel to the gorge of the Kidron.

[1] עֵמֶק [2] נַחַל

"What have ye to do with me?" fails to express quite clearly the exact sense. Better, and strictly literal is this: "What are ye to me, O Tyre?" etc. What account do I make of you? What reason have I to fear your petty wrath? As the context goes on to say—Will ye think to rise against my scourging hand and wreak your vengeance on me, or on my people? Will ye retaliate on me? If ye attempt it, very speedily and swiftly will I hurl back your retaliation upon your own heads.——Of course, in this lofty strain, the Lord speaks after the manner of men, but as one conscious of infinite power to punish his foes, and fully purposed to visit on them most ample and righteous retribution.——As already intimated in the introductory remarks upon this chapter, these nations, Tyre, Zidon, and Philistia, are named here, not as being the only nations involved in this great judgment, but as present to the minds of the prophet and of his first readers, and as fitting illustrations, therefore, of the great truths he would impress.

5. Because ye have taken my silver and my gold, and have carried into your temples my goodly pleasant things.

The silver and the gold which they had taken from Israel by robbery, the Lord calls his own—"*my* silver." Whatever of most costly value they could find they had borne into their own idol temples, as a trophy of conquest over the people of God, and the Lord remembers this against them!

6. The children also of Judah and the children of Jerusalem have ye sold unto the Grecians, that ye might remove them far from their border.

The captives they had taken from his people they had sold to the Grecians, in order to remove them far as possible from their homes, that they might never return.

7. Behold, I will raise them out of the place whither ye have sold them, and will return your recompense upon your own head.

God will recover them notwithstanding, and will bring retribution on their captors, who had held, or had sold them as slaves.

8. And I will sell your sons and your daughters into the land of the children of Judah, and they shall sell them to the Sabeans, to a people far off: for the Lord hath spoken *it*.

This retaliation in kind should perhaps be taken as a case of speaking after the manner of men, and not by any means as implying that God can ever sanction the selling of men into slavery, or can authorize his people to do it, even in retaliation for like offence and abuse.——It should, however, be considered that God, in retributive justice and judgment on wicked nations, may, through his providential agencies, suffer other wicked nations to enslave them, without at all sanctioning as morally right their free acts in enslaving men. This distinction is one of vital moment in regard to God's providential agencies in his government over nations, and, indeed, over individuals no less. When the Lord sends the scourge of war on a nation it will not follow that he accepts as morally right the ambition or the cruelty that instigated the aggressive power, nor does he make himself responsible for their moral acts, however he may permit their existence and providentially direct their blow.

9. Proclaim ye this among the Gentiles; Prepare war, wake up the mighty men, let all the men of war draw near; let them come up;

10. Beat your ploughshares into swords, and your pruning-hooks into spears: let the weak say, I *am* strong.

Having finished the digression in respect to Tyre, etc., and the form of retribution destined for them, the prophet now, speaking in behalf of the Almighty, daringly challenges the Gentile hosts to muster for the mighty conflict.——The first word of the challenge, rendered "prepare" war, carries with it the idea of proclaiming war in the most solemn manner with religious rites. It is the common word for "sanctify," and means here—make this war a sacred thing; bind yourselves to it by solemn oaths, and invoke all your gods to your help.——Beating ploughshares into swords reverses the long prayed for consummation when swords shall be beaten into ploughshares. The sense is—prepare for universal war. The implements on hand might suffice for any ordinary war, but not for this; now you must needs arm every man, and hence you must convert even the tools of agriculture into weapons of war.——Let the conscription be absolutely universal. Let no invalid plead exemption; "let even the weak say, I am strong."

11. Assemble yourselves, and come, all ye heathen, and gather yourselves together round about: thither cause thy mighty ones to come down, O LORD.

Then with striking beauty and force the prophet suddenly turns to the other party in the conflict: "Thither bring down thy mighty ones, Jehovah!"——How fearful is this great battle of earth now coming on!

12. Let the heathen be wakened, and come up to the valley of Jehoshaphat: for there will I sit to judge all the heathen round about.

See notes on v. 2. Observe also how quietly the strain of the passage assumes that this dread array of armed nations, vast as numbers without number, and girded all for bloody war, results in no war at all. Their weapons amount to nothing; they are there only for judgment—culprits before the King and Judge of the universe! They suddenly find themselves on no battle-ground, but summoned to the valley where Jehovah judges; and he comes down to take his lofty judgment throne, and "sit to judge all these nations round about."——What quiet, unostentatious majesty! How does such real greatness eclipse all the assembled littleness of the gathered myriads of the heathen!

13. Put ye in the sickle, for the harvest is ripe: come, get you down; for the press is full, the fats overflow; for their wickedness *is* great.

Here are symbols of terrific slaughter—the sickle laying low the ripened grain, and the wine-vats full and trodden till they overflow with wine—which in such a connection represents human blood.——Dropping all figure, the reason is given in plain language —"For *their* wickedness is great"—not "*the* wickedness," indefinitely, but *theirs*, the wickedness of these hostile nations.

14. Multitudes, multitudes in the valley of decision: for the day of the LORD *is* near in the valley of decision.

Their vast number strikes the prophet's mind, and prompts the exclamation, "O, the multitudes! the multitudes in this valley of judgment!"——The word rendered "decision" means judgment in the sense of a final verdict which decides the criminal's destiny, past all reversal. See the usage of the original word, 1 Kings 29:40, and Isa. 10:22.——This is "*the day of the Lord;*" it comes exceedingly near in this valley of judgment. The word "near" should not carry the mind onward to any other day beyond this. God is here, and his great day has come!

15. The sun and the moon shall be darkened, and the stars shall withdraw their shining.

These figures must here take their usual sense—extreme calamity —casting the deep shades of night over all the hopes of the wicked —engulfing them in deep, impenetrable darkness. So in all languages, of every land or nation, darkness is the symbol of whatever is most fearful to rational beings.

16. The LORD shall also roar out of Zion, and utter his voice from Jerusalem; and the heavens and the earth shall shake: but the LORD *will be* the hope of his people, and the strength of the children of Israel.

In this strain of the boldest poetic imagery, the Lord becomes a lion, and his roar shakes the heavens and the earth. See the same figure under analogous circumstances, Jer. 25:30; Isa. 42:13.

——This roar comes forth "*out of Zion*," because there, in the deep recesses of the temple, Jehovah dwelt. This was not only current and accepted Jewish opinion; it was *fact*. His manifested presence *was there;* and he was careful to impress this upon the hearts of the people.——The "voice of the Lord," in such a connection as this, is thunder, as throughout Ps. 29.——These figures, combined, give the climax of the dreadful scene, in which blended terror and majesty, justice and wrath, encircle and gird the throne of the Almighty round about, as, with the guilty nations, the op pressors of his people, assembled before him, he sits for judgment and final decision.——Then, with inimitable beauty and force, turning to those on his right hand (may we not borrow from that other analogous scene?) he says: "But the Lord will be the hope of his people, and the strength of the children of Israel." They may trust their God forever. He is their strength in every hour of their weakness. He stands for their deliverance, and for retribution on their foes.——"Children of Israel" is here parallel to "his people," the latter, and consequently the former, including far more than the lineal seed of Abraham.

17. So shall ye know that I *am* the LORD your God dwelling in Zion, my holy mountain: then shall Jerusalem be holy, and there shall no strangers pass through her any more.

"So shall ye *know*"—know in your own case and by your own full experience of his saving power and loving heart, that he is *Jehovah*—forever the same; that he "dwells in Zion," manifesting his presence, care, and love among his people forever; and, what is more, making it his holy mountain by purifying his people there. ——"Then shall Jerusalem be holy"—a statement which clearly identifies these events in their general character with those which close the second chapter of this prophet—the outpouring of the Spirit on the children of Zion first, and then on all flesh; for certainly, Jerusalem never becomes holy save under this great sanctifying agency.——"Strangers," foreign and alien in spirit, heathen, wicked men—shall not traverse the holy city any more—shall not come and go as if of her and having rights in her sanctuaries and palaces. No more shall such intruders defile the church of God.—— This betokens an eminent degree of real purity and holiness among God's people.

18. And it shall come to pass in that day, *that* the mountains shall drop down new wine, and the hills shall flow with milk, and all the rivers of Judah shall flow with waters, and a fountain shall come forth of the house of the LORD, and shall water the valley of Shittim.

This description, looking somewhat to that ancient one of the goodly land as flowing with milk and honey, names earthly good, but manifestly means heavenly. Jewish costume and imagery are to be translated so as to give us the fulness of gospel significance—the language of the material Canaan into the language of the spiritual, which is far better.——The last clause strongly implies and demands this significance. "A fountain comes forth from the house of the Lord," where the institutions of religious instruction and worship are in power—"and it waters all the valley of *Acacias*," this being the sense of the word "Shittim." And inasmuch as the oriental acacia enjoys the sterile valley, and puts forth its redeeming beauty and fragrance there where nothing else does, we find here the idea that the gospel turns barrenness to plenty, sterility to verdure, sin to holiness, and woe to bliss, all over this sin-wasted earth. Ezekiel's living waters (chap. 47), starting from the same source, flow into similar desolations, and produce a like result of health, beauty, and glory.

19. Egypt shall be a desolation, and Edom shall be a desolate wilderness, for the violence *against* the children of Judah, because they have shed innocent blood in their land.

Prophecies that are alike millennial in their import differ in one respect among themselves, really falling into two classes. One class represents the whole world as radiant with light and glory, peace and love—the earth full of the knowledge of the Lord as the waters cover the sea (Isa. 11 : 9) :—"in every place incense offered to my name, and a pure offering" (Mal. 1 : 11) ; &c., &c. ; while another class (like the passage before us) still leaves on the picture some traces of the awful mischiefs sin has wrought. "Egypt is a desolation, and Edom a desolate wilderness," as if to heighten by contrast the beauty and glory of the people and kingdom of the Lord. Pressed to its literal sense, it could only mean that some districts, most notoriously representing the persistent and sworn enemies of God's people, shall lie desolate, while all around them, even all else on the face of the earth, blooms in beauty and fertility. Those desolations lie in their ruins—like hell among the myriads of holy worlds—a swift and perpetual witness to the fearfulness of sinning against God, and to the certainty of woe to all sinners who will not repent.——Egypt and Edom were the oldest national enemies of the covenant people. They are doomed because of their violence against Judah and the innocent blood they have shed in the Lord's land.

20. But Judah shall dwell for ever, and Jerusalem from generation to generation.

21. For I will cleanse their blood *that* I have not cleansed: for the Lord dwelleth in Zion.

Judah shall be inhabited forever, dwelling in her places. This perpetuity affirmed of Judah and Jerusalem, must certainly apply only to the real Judah—the true people of God. The Judah that was after the flesh and was of the flesh only, never can fill the sense of these precious words. See Notes on Hos. 1 : 10, 11, and also Dissertation II. in the Appendix.——The word rendered "cleanse" means, to regard as innocent, and therefore to treat accordingly. This might imply either that God, at length, freely and fully forgives their sin and puts it forever away; or that he avenges it upon her foes; probably the former, at least; possibly the latter also. Both ideas are fully brought out in this chapter.——It might well have been remarked ere this, that very much the same course of thought as appears in this chapter of Joel may be seen also in Isa. 66 : 14–24, and in Jer. 25 : 12–38; in Zech. 14; and in Ezekiel, chapters 37–48.—The passage in Joel, coupled with these just above noted, suggest this grave and truly momentous question—Whether the final conquest of the world by the Messiah will or will not be effected in large measure by the destruction of incorrigible enemies. Are we authorized to expect a mingling of judgment and mercy among the agencies in this great conquest; and if so, can we infer with any considerable accuracy the relative measure of each? or to put the case more precisely, the relative numbers of earth's population at that time, destroyed by judgments on the one hand, and saved by mercy on the other. This is not the place for an extended discussion of this question.——Let it suffice then to say that the tenor of prophecy as well as the genius of the gospel system, authorize us to expect the conversion of the world by means of those very gospel agencies which were employed and consecrated by Christ himself—the preaching of the gospel, the faithful testimony of his people, and the gift of his Spirit; that the Lord has always carried along a coördinate work of retributive justice and judgment on the wicked in this world, sometimes more and sometimes less prominent; that he may, to cut short the reign of Satan, intensify these agencies of retribution in the latter days; that universally the underlying principle is, bow or break—repent, or be broken in pieces, so that the finally incorrigible may always know their certain doom. Hence we should not expect a definite revelation of the relative numbers of the saved on the one hand, or of the hardened and destroyed on the other. It is God's way to leave the principles of his moral government and his policy in its administration in such shape as will bring the most solemn and effective moral pressure to bear toward repentance and consequent salvation. His problem is—judgment and mercy being given—so to arrange and mingle them as to persuade the greatest number to flee from the judgment and take hold of the mercy. Could he do better?

Thus ends this grand, sublime, and glorious chapter! We might fitly apply these epithets to the whole book, for few more sublime compositions can anywhere be found, distinguished for conceptions so lofty, a style so pure, truths so vast, so far reaching, so vital to the moral government of God over nations, and so fraught with instruction to mankind.——May the reader catch the inspiration of this admirable book, and drink deeply of its pure and healing waters!

AMOS.

INTRODUCTION.

Of the previous life of Amos before he became a prophet we learn, from chapter 1 : 1, that he "was among the herdmen of Tekoa, and from 7 : 14, 15, that he was not born in the line of the prophets, but was "an herdman and a gatherer of sycamore fruit," and that "the Lord took him as he was following the flock, and said to him, "Go, prophesy unto my people Israel." What the book itself thus states, its style, its choice of words and figures, and its numerous indications of familiarity with the scenes of husbandry, most abundantly confirm. His case, therefore, shows that the old dispensation as well as the new, honored the humble and laboring classes, and drew some at least of its most effective helpers from among "the poor of this world."——Though a native and early resident of Judah, ("Tekoa" being within this kingdom), his prophetic mission was to the northern kingdom exclusively. In chapter 7 : 10–17 it appears that he was then in Bethel, and had made that city his residence. More than this is not known.——His first verse fixes the *date* of his prophetic life within the reigns of Uzziah, king of Judah (B. C. 811–759), and of Jeroboam, son of Joash, king of Israel (B. C. 825–784). How large a part of the sixty-six years, from the accession of Jeroboam to the death of Uzziah, he was engaged in his prophetic work, is not said, nor whether his time lay nearer the close or the beginning of this period. There are good reasons for supposing that he was somewhat later than Joel, but contemporary, during at least a part of his prophetic life, with Hosea, very probably earlier than the active years of Isaiah and Micah. He finds the same sins prevalent and calling for rebuke that Hosea found.——His language is less terse than that of Hosea, less sublime than that of Joel, but yet by no means unworthy of a place among the noblest writings the world ever saw. His style is clear, forcible, and in some passages grand, particularly in his descriptions of the majesty and power of Jehovah.——Commissioned especially to rebuke the sins of Israel, he yet in the first and second chapters denounces judgments on six other contiguous powers outside of Judah and Israel, and then upon these two in like general terms. Then in chapters 3-6 he exposes and reproves in detail the sins of Israel, and threatens judgments therefor.——The last three chapters differ from this middle portion by the introduction of visions for purposes of more vivid illustration, and by the blending of promise with the general strain of threatening. The book closes with predictions of peace and prosperity to the kingdom of God on earth.

CHAPTER I.

After a very brief introduction, which gives us the name of the author and the date of his prophecies, the chapter proceeds at once to name the crowning sin of five adjacent nations, and to announce the judgments of God upon them. They are Syria, the Philistines, Tyre, Edom, and Ammon. His main object in this is to make the stronger impression upon Israel. If for their sins God must scourge and even exterminate heathen powers sitting in the dimness of the light of nature, how much more must he for your sins scourge you to whom his word has come!

1. The words of Amos, who was among the herdmen of Tekoa, which he saw concerning Israel in the days of Uzziah king of Judah, in the days of Jeroboam the son of Joash king of Israel, two years before the earthquake.

Most of the points named here came before us in the general introduction.——This "earthquake" is commonly supposed to be that of which Zechariah speaks (14:5), "Ye shall flee like as ye fled from before the earthquake in the days of Uzziah, king of Judah." Since Amos prophesied during Uzziah's reign, and since they both refer to an earthquake of great power and prominence, it may be safely assumed that they speak of the same. But at what point during the fifty-two years of Uzziah's reign this occurred is not said.

2. And he said, The Lord will roar from Zion, and

utter his voice from Jerusalem; and the habitations of the shepherds shall mourn, and the top of Carmel shall wither.

The first half of this verse seems to be borrowed from Joel 3:16. In Joel the passage makes so close connection with what precedes, that it must be admitted to stand "*in place*," as the geologists say of specimens found in their original rock. Not so in Amos. If we supply "as another prophet has said," we shall not at all disturb the flow of thought. Moreover, Joel prophesied *before* Amos, according to the closest estimate, about seventy-five years.——The last half of the verse is characteristic of Amos. A man who came up among herdmen would naturally think of these rather than other effects of the Lord's sore judgments. Carmel was ordinarily clothed with verdure even to its summit; hence the fitness of saying "the top of Carmel shall wither." This mountain lay in the northwest part of the kingdom of the ten tribes. The word Carmel means a fruitful field, a fact which makes this allusion the more forcible.——In the passage "The Lord will roar from Zion," the original word "roar" is used commonly of the lion, and denotes here that the Lord has aroused himself like the lion of the forest, to assert his rule among the nations, and especially to visit retribution on those which had filled up the measure of their sins. Such a roaring, foreshowing terrible visitations of judgment, would thrill the nations with terror, much as the beasts of the forest tremble when the earth quakes, and the depths of their solitudes reëcho to the lion's roar.

3. Thus saith the LORD; For three transgressions of Damascus, and for four, I will not turn away *the punishment* thereof; because they have threshed Gilead with threshing instruments of iron:

4. But I will send a fire into the house of Hazael, which shall devour the palaces of Ben-hadad.

5. I will break also the bar of Damascus, and cut off the inhabitant from the plain of Aven, and him that holdeth the sceptre from the house of Eden: and the people of Syria shall go into captivity unto Kir, saith the LORD.

In the passage commencing here and extending to chap. 2:6, eight kingdoms are brought up in succession, with Judah and Israel last. Each receives its message, beginning, "Thus saith the Lord;" in each is the phraseology—"For three transgressions, and for four, I will not reverse it;" each specifies the last and most heinous crime, for which, especially (it would seem), the judgment named is sent; and each closes with naming the judgment. This remarkable uniformity in style no doubt had its object. It naturally implied that the same God of nations was taking them all successively in hand to administer justice and judgment upon each and on the same principles, common to all. It was well adapted to confirm the impression that Jehovah is indeed the ruler of nations, and holds them to a solemn responsibility, *here in time*, to bear themselves justly and not oppressively toward each other.——Moreover, as already intimated, these nations contiguous to Judah and Israel are mentioned first, to prepare the minds of the men of Judah and Israel to hear their own sin and doom—first to stir up their sense of justice and draw out their approval of God's righteous ways, and then to say to them—"Thou art the man!" Further, the argument is *à fortiori:* "If those things be done in the green tree"—to those heathen benighted kingdoms,—"what shall be done in the dry"—to a people chosen and long blessed of God, but now shamefully apostate and incorrigible?——And yet further, as if to insure the more certainly a righteous judgment in the minds of Judah and Israel against their heathen neighbors, the sins selected and named are chiefly those committed against Judah and Israel. Everybody sees, feels, and condemns a wrong done against himself. Under this law of even depraved human nature, God first secured from his professed people their indignant condemnation of other peoples' sins, and then lifted the curtain to show them their own!——"For three transgressions and for four," as to the form of expression, may be compared with numerous other passages of Scripture of a like proverbial character; *e. g.* Ex. 20:5—"Visiting the iniquity of the fathers upon the children unto the third and fourth generation of them that hate me;" Job 5:19—"He shall deliver thee in six troubles; yea, in seven shall no evil touch thee;" Eccles. 11:2—"Give a portion to seven, and also to eight; for thou knowest not what evil shall be upon the earth;" Mic. 5:5—"When the Assyrian shall come into our land, then shall we raise against him seven shepherds and eight principal men."——These cases establish a current usage of definite numbers to express the indefinite idea of several.——But the thought is more to us than the drapery that clothes or adorns it. This thought is that these nations had been adding sin to sin, running up a long unsettled account, until at last some one sin, perhaps more aggravated than any preceding, filled up the measure of their iniquities, and *demanded* of their righteous Ruler his visitation of terrible judgment. The fourth and crowning crime is specified in each case. For three sins they have deserved punishment, and the decree has gone out—for the fourth "I will not reverse it," saith the Lord, but (as is implied) will proceed without delay to execute it.——It is noticeable that the original has no word for punishment. The little word "*it*," suffixed to the verb—I will not reverse *it*—leaves us to find its antecedent in the never-failing law of connection between sin and punishment. The Lord assumes that men ought to know *what* he will not reverse, after his allusion to such sins as these. This tacit assumption that judgment *must* follow sin has in itself appalling force.——"Damascus" represents Syria, a strong and flourishing kingdom on the north and northeast of Israel. It was the capital.

Their last sin was that of "threshing Gilead"—putting its inhabitants to torture and death under the huge threshing-wain, armed with savage iron teeth, and drawn by animals over the grain. See a case of such treatment, 2 Sam. 12 : 31, and also 2 Kings 13 : 7 —the last being done by this same Hazael.——The name Gilead covers the territory of the two and a half tribes east of Jordan. Lying contiguous to Syria, it suffered fearfully from that kingdom. ——The judgment was a devouring fire sent on the royal house of Hazael, and of his son and successor, Ben-hadad. (Both his father and his son bore this name, Ben-hadad; but Amos must allude to the son. See 2 Kings 13 : 3, 24.)——"The bar of Damascus" represents its means of defence and protection in war. "The inhabitant"—literally he who *sits*, *i. e.*, on a throne—is parallel to "him that holdeth the sceptre." The sense is that their government should be utterly broken down, and their nationality cease.——The word "Aven" is probably changed from *On*, the Syrian name of a beautiful valley, the country-seat, it may be, of their king. The Hebrews, changing its vowels, called it Aven, to represent the contemptible idolatry of the Syrians. See the same word, Aven, wrought into the name Beth-*el* (Beth-Aven), for a similar reason, Hos. 4 : 15, and 10 : 5, 8.——"House of Eden," equal to Paradise, is another delightful locality, and was called in ancient authors, Paradise.——Tiglath-Pileser, king of Assyria, fulfilled this prediction. He took the people into captivity to Kir, the river and region known as Cyrus, in Iberia. See this fact in history, 2 Kings 16 : 9. "The king of Assyria went up against Damascus and took it, and carried the people of it captive to Kir, and slew Rezin."

6. Thus saith the LORD; For three transgressions of Gaza, and for four, I will not turn away *the punishment* thereof: because they carried away captive the whole captivity, to deliver *them* up to Edom:

7. But I will send a fire on the wall of Gaza, which shall devour the palaces thereof:

8. And I will cut off the inhabitant from Ashdod, and him that holdeth the sceptre from Ashkelon, and I will turn mine hand against Ekron: and the remnant of the Philistines shall perish, saith the Lord GOD.

Gaza, the northern of the five chief cities of the Philistines, represents here the whole cluster. Gath, the only one of the five not named here, is omitted, probably because it was already laid waste, *i. e.*, during the reign of Uzziah (2 Chronicles 26 : 6, 7). This was within the personal knowledge of Amos.——Their crowning sin was that they carried the entire body of their captives to Edom and sold them for slaves. The phrase, "the whole captivity," affirms nothing in respect to the number, as being great or small; it means all they had. Edom, further advanced in wealth and the arts than most of the nations adjacent to Palestine, seems to have been a notorious slave mart. The Lord accounted it the damning sin of the Philistines, that they sent thither all their prisoners of war and sold them into slavery! Who, after this testimony, can deny that God abhors slavery, and will preëminently scourge and destroy the nation that makes itself preëminent for the enslaving of men?——The "fire sent on the wall of Gaza" is the desolation of war, visited on them by Uzziah, as above noted, and by Hezekiah (see 2 Kings 18: 8), and later by various Eastern conquerors.——"The inhabitant" must be understood here as in v. 5. See a striking prophecy of the final fall of the Philistines, in Jer. 47.

9. Thus saith the LORD; For three transgressions of Tyrus, and for four, I will not turn away *the punishment* thereof; because they delivered up the whole captivity to Edom, and remembered not the brotherly covenant:

10. But I will send a fire on the wall of Tyrus, which shall devour the palaces thereof.

Tyre, the city renowned for its commerce and wealth, on the Mediterranean and very near the northwest corner of the land of Canaan, had sinned, in common with the Philistines, by sending the entire body of their captives of war to Edom for slaves —a sin in their case aggravated by the friendly and even covenant relation existing of old between them and the ancient kingdom of Israel. This was indeed a "brotherly covenant," binding each party to mutual friendship and protection. It commenced between Hiram, King of Tyre, and David; the former making the first advances. (2 Sam. 5: 11), "Hiram, King of Tyre, sent messengers to David, and cedar-trees," &c. It was ratified again between the same Hiram and Solomon (1 Kings, 5: 12), "Hiram sent his servants to Solomon [for Hiram was ever a lover of David], and they two made a league together."——It is obvious that the captives, which Tyre sent *en masse* to Edom, were Hebrews, else the Lord could not have deemed it a breach of *that* "brotherly covenant."——Tyre suffered fearfully from the arms of both Nebuchadnezzar and Alexander the Great. They were the fire of Jehovah's vengeance upon her, specially for her sin of selling all her captives into the horrible slave marts of Edom.

11. Thus saith the LORD; For three transgressions of Edom, and for four, I will not turn away *the punishment* thereof: because he did pursue his brother with the sword, and did cast off all pity, and his anger did tear perpetually, and he kept his wrath for ever:

12. But I will send a fire upon Teman, which shall devour the palaces of Bozrah.

Edom himself comes next—an ancient kingdom southeast from Palestine, strong in arms, and very considerably advanced in culture at the time when Israel, forbidden by him to travel through his territory, journeyed round it to reach the Jordan and pass into Canaan, B. C. 1451. His crowning sin lay in his animosity against his brother Jacob. Intensely jealous of the greatness of the Hebrew nation, Edom had almost never neglected any opportunity to let loose his wrath upon them. As stated here, he had "pursued his brother with the sword," and had "cast off all pity." The original more precisely says he "*corrupted*," in the sense of suppressing and smothering the natural dictates of sympathy and compassion. "His anger did *tear*"—the common word used when savage beasts of prey tear in pieces their victims, and he "kept his wrath forever," not suffering even the lapse of time to abate its ferocity. ——Teman and Bozrah were principal cities in Edom, and here represent the nation.

13. Thus saith the LORD; For three transgressions of the children of Ammon, and for four, I will not turn away *the punishment* thereof: because they have ripped up the women with child, of Gilead, that they might enlarge their border:

14. But I will kindle a fire in the wall of Rabbah, and it shall devour the palaces thereof, with shouting in the day of battle, with a tempest in the day of the whirlwind:

15. And their king shall go into captivity, he and his princes together, saith the LORD.

Ammon and Moab, nations taking their name and descent from the two sons of Lot, were ancient kingdoms on the east of Jordan, and of course contiguous to the country of the two and a half tribes here called Gilead.——The last and fatal sin of Ammon was their horrid cruelty upon the pregnant mothers of Gilead, as if it were their purpose to exterminate not only the living population, but the unborn no less. God holds nations solemnly responsible for the sin of cruelty. It was an insignificant apology for such cruelty that they wanted more territory.——The indignation of the Lord against them for such cruelty stands out in the grouping of fire, the war-cry of battle, the tempest and whirlwind, among the figures that set forth the vengeance due and about to fall on Ammon. Oh, how sublimely grand is such vengeance on a nation guilty of such horrid sin!——Let us not fail to note the solemn lesson, which all people of every age should learn from this recital of Jehovah's judgments on nations for violating the plain dictates of common justice and humanity in their treatment of each other.——And let us revert again to the fact that most of these last and damning sins were committed against the Hebrews, a secondary object with Amos being to draw out *their* verdict against these sins as perpetrated by their enemies, and bring them to admit and endorse the principles of God's administration as infinitely right and just, before he shall come to say, "Thus saith the Lord; For three transgressions of *Judah* and of *Israel*, and for four, I will not reverse it." There was no difficulty in getting them to condemn with burning indignation the sins under which themselves had suffered. This done, it only remained to add, Thus saith the Lord; *thou art the man!* Condemning others, thou hast confessed thine own desert and foreshadowed thine own doom!

CHAPTER II.

THIS chapter continues the unfinished series of kingdoms doomed for their national sins—Moab, the last outside of the chosen people; then Judah and Israel. Israel once reached, becomes the subject of rebuke, expostulation, and threatened doom throughout this chapter and the four next following.

1. Thus saith the LORD; For three transgressions of Moab, and for four, I will not turn away *the punishment* thereof, because he burned the bones of the king of Edom into lime:

2. But I will send a fire upon Moab, and it shall devour the palaces of Kirioth: and Moab shall die with tumult, with shouting, *and* with the sound of the trumpet:

3. And I will cut off the judge from the midst thereof, and will slay all the princes thereof with him, saith the LORD.

Moab closes the list of Gentile nations. In his crime—burning the bones of the king of Edom into lime—his vindictive spirit followed his enemy even beyond death, into the grave. It may be supposed that he came into possession of the body of his old enemy by some of the vicissitudes of war. Of the fact we have no history. But this horribly vindictive spirit, and this savage act, called forth the special curse of the Lord.

4. Thus saith the LORD; For three transgressions of Judah, and for four, I will not turn away *the punishment* thereof: because they have despised the law of the

LORD, and have not kept his commandments, and their lies caused them to err, after the which their fathers have walked:

5. But I will send a fire upon Judah, and it shall devour the palaces of Jerusalem.

The crying sin of Judah, corresponding to the enslaving of their captives by Gaza and Tyre, to the barbarities of Damascus and of Ammon, and to the perpetual resentments of Edom, lay in her disowning God, spurning his authority, and turning her heart to idols. The "law of the Lord" is the moral law; "the commandments" are specially the statutes, religious and civil; while their "lies which had led them astray," were their idol gods. Those were lies in the most emphatic sense—lies *in act*, every idol god being a lie acted out, a living falsehood, representing nothing true and real, but only a delusion; or, in the shortest, best phrase, a *lie*. This crime of Judah was all the greater because it was committed against so much light. "To him that knoweth to do good and doeth it not, to him it is sin" (James 4:17). "If I had not come and spoken to them"—so said Christ of the Jews—"they had not had sin; but now they have no cloak for their sin" (John 15:22). Judah had no doubt sinned in other ways; doubtless she had been cruel toward other nations, oppressive toward her own poor, but none of these sins were to be named in comparison with this mother sin, this crowning sin of all—her reproach and dishonor cast upon God in rejecting his authority, renouncing his worship, and giving her heart publicly to lying vanities.——This passage reads to us the guilt and the doom of thousands of ungodly men in Christian lands. They know God and his gospel but too well—too well to have their sin and damnation measured by even the savage barbarities of heathen nations. Of the city where Christ wrought many miracles he said, "It shall be more tolerable in the day of judgment for Sodom than for thee" (Matt. 11:24).——The Chaldean was the first terrible executioner of this threatened doom. (See 2 Chron. 36:19; Jer. 52:13; Lam. 2:1–10.)

6. Thus saith the LORD; For three transgressions of Israel, and for four, I will not turn away *the punishment* thereof: because they sold the righteous for silver, and the poor for a pair of shoes;

7. That pant after the dust of the earth on the head of the poor, and turn aside the way of the meek: and a man and his father will go in unto the *same* maid, to profane my holy name:

8. And they lay *themselves* down upon clothes laid to pledge by every altar, and they drink the wine of the condemned *in* the house of their god.

Last of all is Israel, the northern kingdom, to whom especially the prophet Amos was sent. It is remarkable that their chief sins, as here developed, lay in the line of immoralities against their fellow-men: the violation of natural rights, the oppression of the poor, and dishonoring the law of chastity. This book of Amos discloses startling facts in respect to the luxury of the wealthy, and their oppression of the poor. Note the particulars given here. "They sold the righteous for silver;" good men, bearing God's image, and beloved of him for their moral integrity, they sold for paltry silver! Ought not the righteous Father of all to abhor this crime, and hurl his bolts of vengeance on the heads of such criminals?——They "sold the poor for a pair of shoes," so cheap did they hold personal liberty and the rights of manhood! These "shoes" were only sandals, nothing but *soles* of leather or wood, fastened to the foot with straps; of course very cheap.——"That pant after the dust of the earth on the head of the poor:" so grasping, so avaricious, so bent on extorting every thing the poor man had, if they saw a particle of dust settled upon his hatless head, they are represented as panting after it, as if they could have no rest till they had got it by extortion or by violence! A pretty strong figure truly—but human depravity sometimes comes fully up to the sense of it! Avarice not unfrequently becomes the ruling master passion of a man's soul, and then no sin is more likely to take on a development perfectly monstrous. It behooves men of avaricious tendencies to beware!——Some interpreters suppose the case thought of here is that of a poor man, robbed of all, throwing dust on his head in his grief over his loss, while his rapacious oppressor grudges him even this poor dust!——To "turn aside the way of the meek" is to subvert justice in their case, and bar them from redress for their wrongs through the courts of law.——The case of a man, his father, and the same maid, refers probably to the public prostitutes kept in the idol temples, such abominations being part of that system of unutterable pollution. The prophet says this was done to profane God's holy name, as if it were their set purpose to dishonor God and trample under their feet his blessed law of chastity.——Retaining over night the garments of the poor taken in pledge, was very expressly forbidden, Ex. 22 : 26, 27: "If thou at all take thy neighbor's raiment to pledge, thou shalt deliver it to him by that the sun goeth down, for it is his covering only; it is his raiment for his skin. Wherein shall he sleep? And it shall come to pass when he crieth unto me, that I will hear, for I am gracious." The poor in those countries had no bed-covering other than their outer garments. The Lord would not let the grip of avarice deprive the poor of their bed-covering. But these degenerate Israelites, instead of returning this bed-covering for the owner to sleep under, "laid themselves down upon clothes laid to pledge" (*i. e.*, as security for debts), and this "*by every altar*" in the very presence of their gods, and in their places of religious worship. Plainly their religion bore no testimony against outrageous inhumanity. Any form of religion is practically rotten which bears no testimony or protest against hard-hearted cruelty to man. There is never a stronger proof of religious corruption than a cool and heartless mixing up of professed worship of God with remorseless crime toward man.——"To drink the wine of the condemned in the house of their God," is another sin of the same sort. Literally rendered, it is the wine of the amerced or taxed—the wine they had assessed upon their tenants or other poor, and by fraud or force compelled them unjustly to pay. This they have the impiety to drink "in the house of their god," their religion having no testimony to bear to the conscience against crime toward fellow-men.

9. Yet destroyed I the Amorite before them, whose height *was* like the height of the cedars, and he *was* strong as the oaks; yet I destroyed his fruit from above, and his roots from beneath.

Here the prophet turns to speak in the next three verses of what God had wrought for his people, that in the light of these great works of mercy they may see their more aggravated guilt. ——The Amorites, living of old on both sides of the Jordan, represent the nations of Canaan. Physically, they were a gigantic race, and being proficient in the arts of war, they were exceedingly strong. So they appeared to the twelve spies whom Moses sent up from the wilderness of Paran. They reported: "The people be strong that dwell in the land, and the cities are walled and very great, and moreover we saw the children of Anak there." "All the people that we saw in it are men of great stature; there we saw the giants; and we were in our own sight as grasshoppers, and so we were in their sight" (Num. 13 : 28, 32, 33).——The history shows that God's interposition to drive out this powerful race before Israel, then altogether unused to war, was special. He promised early (Ex. 23 : 27–29), "I will send my fear before thee, and will destroy all the people unto whom thou shalt come. . . I will send *hornets* before thee who shall drive out the Canaanites," &c. See also Deut. 7 : 20, and Josh. 24 : 12. This hornet (so rendered) seems to have been some form of scourge, perhaps a pestilence, as Hab. 3 : 5 would naturally imply. It was at least God's hand, manifested either in some physical scourge, or in mental panic, or in both, and designed to palsy their power and make them an easy conquest to God's chosen people. This Amos beautifully sets forth: "The Amorite, though in his early prowess as the height of the cedars and the strength of the oaks, yet God's hand destroyed his fruit above and his roots beneath."

10. Also I brought you up from the land of Egypt, and led you forty years through the wilderness, to possess the land of the Amorite.

The scenes of the Exodus and of those forty years in the wilderness were full of divine care and love. Every day had its miracles of mercy.

11. And I raised up of your sons for prophets, and of your young men for Nazarites. *Is it* not even thus, O ye children of Israel? saith the LORD.

The order of prophets seems not to have been specially provided for in the Mosaic institutes, but sprang up under the law of *demand*—the exigencies of later times. For the order of Nazarites, however, special provision was made. (See Num. 6.) The persons composing this order were often set apart from their birth, *e. g.*, Samson and Samuel. They were to abstain sacredly and specially from wine and from every thing else that could intoxicate, standing as living witnesses to the value of temperance and a perpetual protest against self-indulgence.——It was truly a favor to the people that the Lord took his prophets and Nazarites from their own sons. We can suppose the case that the men for these orders should have been called in from other nations. This supposition would show at a glance how much better the social and general influence must be to take them from Hebrew families.——Our translators and many commentators interpret the question at the close of the verse as the Lord's appeal to Israel to admit the fact that he had taken his prophets and Nazarites from among them. In my view, such an appeal can scarcely be deemed necessary, and is therefore very improbable. I prefer to read, "And is there nothing of this, O ye children of Israel?" Is this a thing of no account?—implying that it *is* a matter of great account.

12. But ye gave the Nazarites wine to drink; and commanded the prophets, saying, Prophesy not.

This fact evinces the daring impiety of the people. They sought to frustrate the benevolent aims of God in establishing both these classes of reformers. "Ye gave the Nazarites wine to drink"—seducing them into the violation of their vows, and thus paralyzing their influence. "Ye forbid the prophets to prophesy." In some cases, they persecuted, imprisoned, and murdered God's prophets, to suppress their testimony.——Such a people must be fast filling up the measure of their iniquities.

13. Behold, I am pressed under you, as a cart is pressed *that is* full of sheaves.

14. Therefore the flight shall perish from the swift, and the strong shall not strengthen his force, neither shall the mighty deliver himself:

15. Neither shall he stand that handleth the bow; and *he that is* swift of foot shall not deliver *himself*: neither shall he that rideth the horse deliver himself.

16. And *he that is* courageous among the mighty shall flee away naked in that day, saith the LORD.

Here the prophet announces divine judgments for these sins of the people.——The received version—"I am pressed under you," &c., represents the Lord as the cart pressed by its burden of sheaves —with reference to the demand made upon him for vengeance—which demand his justice could not resist, nor could his mercy yield to it without strong pressure and keen anguish. This sentiment may be very true, but it is probably not the truth taught here. The passage should rather be read—"Behold, I am pressing you down as a cart full of sheaves presseth down," *i. e.*, whatever it passes over. The points in favor of this construction are (1.) That the verbs are not passive—"I am pressed," &c., but are strongly active, and even causative—"I am pressing you down"—causing you to be pressed down. (2.) That the word "Behold," more naturally calls attention to the punishment God will inflict than to the state of his feelings in view of the necessity of inflicting it. (3.) And it makes the logic of the following verse far more forcible: —a people so pressed down as with a loaded cart upon them must lose all power of flight, even the swiftest of them; the strong could have no force available under such a weight, &c. This logical connection of thought, expressed by "therefore" (v. 14), is more than lost by the rendering which assumes that the weight and burden of this pressure come down upon God rather than upon his sinning people.——The idea that none can escape is reiterated with great force. The bowmen shall not stand; the swift-footed shall not save even himself, nor he who has a fleet horse at command; and finally, he who unites the utmost courage and the utmost strength shall only escape (if at all) naked, saving nothing but his person.——The reader will readily notice that the figure belongs to husbandry, and is such as we might look for in one who was from boyhood "among the herdmen of Tekoa."

CHAPTER III.

THIS chapter continues the same strain, exposing the sins of the people, showing that the Almighty awakes to judgment against them, and calls his prophet to reveal the fearful truth. Foreign nations are summoned to witness the sins of Samaria, and again her doom is announced.

1. Hear this word that the Lord hath spoken against you, O children of Israel, against the whole family which I brought up from the land of Egypt, saying,

2. You only have I known of all the families of the earth: therefore I will punish you for all your iniquities.

It was the peculiar aggravation of the sins of Israel that God had *known* them as his own, and had blessed them only among all the nations, with abundant revelations of his will; and that, notwithstanding all, they had persistently rebelled against him. Therefore, he would surely punish them for all their iniquities. The sins of other nations God might wink at and pass over with comparatively little notice; the sins of Israel could not be passed over!

3. Can two walk together, except they be agreed?
4. Will a lion roar in the forest when he hath no
prey? will a young lion cry out of his den, if he have
taken nothing?
5. Can a bird fall in a snare upon the earth, where
no gin *is* for him? shall *one* take up a snare from the
earth, and have taken nothing at all?
6. Shall a trumpet be blown in the city, and the
people not be afraid? shall there be evil in a city, and
the LORD hath not done *it?*

These spirited interrogatives imply that God can go on no longer with his covenant people; that the hour of his desolating judgments hastens on; that for these judgments there is abundant cause in their sins; and that the Lord has summoned his prophet to become his oracle of solemn warning to the guilty people.——More particularly, I paraphrase thus: Can God and Israel walk together unless agreed in sympathy of purpose and character, as they are not now?—Will the Lord roar out of Zion in premonitory foreshadowings of coming vengeance, when there is no prey to fall upon?——Can the people fall under war and captivity where no war is, and no captivity, and there is no wrath of God to fear? Are these threatened judgments really nothing?——Are not people wont to be afraid when they hear the clarion blast of war? And shall they not fear as much now, before the awful blast of Jehovah's trumpet, calling out the nations to bring war on his land? Shall we not recognize God's agency as including and working all the inflictions of calamity that fall on guilty cities?——This "evil in the city" which v. 6 assumes that the Lord has done, must be natural, not moral—calamity, not sin. The original Hebrew is used frequently for natural evil, *e. g.*, Gen. 19 : 19: "Lest some evil take me and I die;" and Gen. 44: 34: "Lest peradventure I see the evil that shall come on my father;" also Ex. 32 : 14.——Besides, the strain of the whole passage is of natural evil—the judgments about to come from God on apostate and guilty Israel. To construe this evil, therefore, as being sin, and not calamity, is to ignore the whole current of thought, and to outrage the soundest, most vital laws of interpretation. Moreover, common justice toward God forbids this construction—"Shall there be *sin* in the city, and the Lord hath not done it?" This would assume that God is the doer of *all the sin in our world!*

7. Surely the Lord GOD will do nothing, but he revealeth his secret unto his servants the prophets.

8. The lion hath roared, who will not fear? the Lord GOD hath spoken, who can but prophesy?

The Lord is wont to forewarn his people by his prophets before he smites them with desolating judgments. This forewarning the prophet now gives, as v. 8 implies: "The lion hath roared." God has uttered his fearful note of warning as one about to smite; who can refuse to prophesy when thus called to it of God? The prophet means to say that in the presence of such demonstrations of coming judgments, he should be not only false to God, but false to his countrymen, if he did not solemnly announce God's message, and call them to repentance.

9. Publish in the palaces at Ashdod, and in the palaces in the land of Egypt, and say, Assemble yourselves upon the mountains of Samaria, and behold the great tumults in the midst thereof, and the oppressed in the midst thereof.

This is a call to the people of Ashdod and Egypt, and, by implication, to all the nations named and doomed in the first two chapters, to convene upon the mountains that overlook Samaria, and be witnesses to her great tumults, disorders, and crimes, and to the oppressions done in the midst of her. Guilty as those nations are, they will see deeper guilt and more outrageous crime in Samaria. They are to be witnesses of her doom: let them first witness her sins.——The word "oppressed" in the text, should be "oppressions," as in the margin.

10. For they know not to do right, saith the LORD, who store up violence and robbery in their palaces.

These are the people of Samaria. Despite of all the light of nature and the superadded light of divine revelation, they yet *act* as if they knew not how to do right. The trouble is not their ignorance, but their moral perverseness. Knowledge of duty does them no good: they will go on in sin *as if* they had no moral sense —no knowledge of right.——"They store up in their palaces" the fruits of their "violence and robbery"—the cause, violence, being put for the result—the property they wrest from the poor and innocent.——The frequent allusions to "palaces" imply that the wealthy classes lived in luxury on the fruits of extortion and oppression.

11. Therefore thus saith the Lord GOD; An adversary *there shall be* even round about the land; and he shall bring down thy strength from thee, and thy palaces shall be spoiled.

There shall come an enemy—one who shall pervade the whole land. He shall bring down thy strength, and shall spoil thy palaces. ——The Assyrians were this enemy. The desolation they wrought was complete, as the reader may see in 2 Kings 17.

12. Thus saith the LORD: As the shepherd taketh out of the mouth of the lion two legs, or a piece of an ear: so shall the children of Israel be taken out that dwell in Samaria in the corner of a bed, and in Damascus *in* a couch.

This figure, altogether natural for a shepherd-author, shows that nothing but the merest wrecks and fragments of that great and wealthy people would remain—only some of the aged, bed-ridden, or sick, overlooked in the general slaughter and deportation of captives—here one in the corner of a bed; there another on a couch. ——Some of the people might have fled to Damascus for refuge; hence this reference to the few left there. The devastation would be most terrific and complete.

13. Hear ye, and testify in the house of Jacob, saith the Lord GOD, the God of hosts,

14. That, in the day that I shall visit the transgressions of Israel upon him; I will also visit the altars of Beth-el: and the horns of the altar shall be cut off, and fall to the ground.

15. And I will smite the winter-house with the summer-house; and the houses of ivory shall perish, and the great houses shall have an end, saith the LORD.

Yet another message indicates the point on which especially the judgments of the Almighty would fall, viz., on the idol altars of Bethel, and on the luxurious palaces of rich oppressors. God would direct his judgments so in the line of the sins scourged as to indicate those sins. He would show that his wrath burned especially against those idol altars, and those palaces built with the fruits of violence and wrong.——"The horns of the altar;" its projecting points at each of the four corners, were highly ornamented; hence these especially should be smitten, to rebuke the pride of the people. ——"The houses of ivory" were those in which ivory was used for ornament. Only the wealthy could have one house for summer and another for winter. The curse of extermination fell on Samaria mainly because her wealth was ill-gotten, and represented her cruel, iniquitous oppression of the poor and innocent.

CHAPTER IV.

The prophet still addresses the proud, oppressive, but effeminate people of Samaria, describing them (v. 1); predicting their captivity (vs. 2, 3); in irony, bidding them go on in their sins (vs. 4, 5); reciting successive judgments from God—famine, drought, blasting, pestilence, and the overthrow of some of them even as Sodom—all, however, failing to bring them back to God (vs. 6–11); therefore the Almighty bids them prepare to meet him in his desolating judgments (vs. 12, 13).

1. Hear this word, ye kine of Bashan, that *are* in the mountain of Samaria, which oppress the poor, which crush the needy, which say to their masters, Bring, and let us drink.

2. The Lord God hath sworn by his holiness, that, lo, the days shall come upon you, that he will take you away with hooks, and your posterity with fish-hooks.

3. And ye shall go out at the breaches, every *cow at that which is* before her; and ye shall cast *them* into the palace, saith the Lord.

By the word "kine" (the nearly obsolete plural of cow) some suppose the luxurious and corrupt *women* of Samaria are meant. It is better to apply it to the same class hitherto spoken of, *e. g.*, 2: 6–8, 11–16, and 3: 9–15, *i. e.*, the wealthy, proud, oppressive rulers and leaders in civil and social life, with no special reference to the female sex: (1.) Because the description given of them here identifies them as the same; they oppress the poor, crush the needy, love strong drink, &c. (2.) Because these *cows* of Bashan are spoken of in the Hebrew, now in the feminine and now in the masculine gender, as if the figure drew the writer to the feminine, but the fact to the masculine; and (3.) Because he had special reasons for calling the men "cows of Bashan," as we shall see.——Concerning this figure—Bashan, a region on the east of Jordan, was renowned for its rich pastures and breeds of cattle, fine, fat, and strong. (See Deut. 32: 14; Ps. 22: 12; Ezek. 39: 18.) Especially the "bulls of Bashan," as in David's reference (Ps. 22: 12), were fat, strong, fearless, ferocious: "Strong bulls of Bashan have beset me round." Perhaps with a tacit but cutting allusion to them, Amos meant to say—"Ye cows (not bulls) of Bashan, fat enough indeed and well-fed; fierce and cruel enough toward your helpless poor; but shamefully effeminate and *cowardly* where real danger lies;—hear ye these words! The Lord is about to put his hook in your nose, and take you away to a hopeless captivity. Ye shall be driven out through the breaches made in your city walls, as a man drives out his cows through a gap in their fence—each cow straightforward, *i. e.*, with no option to turn to the right hand or to the left."——This is the general course of thought in the first three verses.——Specially—(v. 1), "*in* the mountain" would be better *on* the mountain, with the figure in view—cows of Bashan, pasturing on the mountains of Samaria.——"Who say to their masters," the king—the plural being probably what is called "*pluralis excellentiæ*,"—a plural form appropriated to one individual—(here a king) as a distinguished honor.——"The Lord hath sworn by his holiness"—as if declaring solemnly—*If* I am holy; *if* I abhor sin; *by* all my abhorrence of such outrages upon the innocent—ye shall be swept from your land!——"Taking them away with fish-hooks," should not lead our thought to fishing for small game, but to the harpooning of sea-monsters, or rather, to the hook in the jaws of leviathan, or in the nose of fierce bullocks, as where the Lord said of the Assyrian king (Isa. 37: 29), "I will put my hook in thy nose and turn thee back by the way by which thou camest;" or of Pharaoh (Ezek. 29: 4), "I will put hooks in thy jaws," &c., "and will bring thee up out of the midst of thy rivers;" or (Job. 41: 1, 2), "Canst *thou* draw out leviathan with a hook?" *Thou* canst not; but God can!——In v. 3, the clause—"Ye shall cast them into the palace"—should rather be read—"They"—the cows, *alias* the rich, proud oppressors of Samaria—"shall be *cast out of* the palace," driven rudely from the ivory mansions, made so splendid by the fruits of robbery and wrong.——Thus the entire passage is keenly ironical and stinging.

4. Come to Beth-el and transgress: at Gilgal multiply transgression; and bring your sacrifices every morning, *and* your tithes after three years:

5. And offer a sacrifice of thanksgiving with leaven, and proclaim *and* publish the free offerings: for this liketh you, O ye children of Israel, saith the Lord GOD.

These verses continue and even intensify the strain of irony. "Come to Bethel, and sin on, since so you like; try it, if you will!"——Bethel and Gilgal were places noted for idol worship.——The Mosaic law required a sacrifice each morning; tithes for the poor at the end of each third year (Deut. 14: 28, 29, and 26: 12), thank-offerings, and free-will offerings also;—but the people of Samaria mixed up these required ritual services with horrible idolatry and not less horrid immoralities—oppression, slavery, outrages on all the rights of the poor and the weak. Hence God abhorred them none the less for their religious rites.——"This liketh you"—means in the original, this you like or love.

6. And I also have given you cleanness of teeth in all your cities, and want of bread in all your places: yet have ye not returned unto me, saith the LORD.

7. And also I have withholden the rain from you,

when *there were* yet three months to the harvest: and I caused it to rain upon one city, and caused it not to rain upon another city: one piece was rained upon, and the piece whereupon it rained not withered.

8. So two *or* three cities wandered unto one city, to drink water; but they were not satisfied: yet have ye not returned unto me, saith the LORD.

9. I have smitten you with blasting and mildew: when your gardens and your vineyards and your fig-trees and your olive-trees increased, the palmer-worm devoured *them:* yet have ye not returned unto me, saith the LORD.

10. I have sent among you the pestilence after the manner of Egypt: your young men have I slain with the sword, and have taken away your horses; and I have made the stink of your camps to come up unto your nostrils: yet have ye not returned unto me, saith the LORD.

Here is a series of milder chastisements which the Lord had tried upon the people, but all in vain. The statement of each form of infliction closes with the same sad result—"Yet have ye not returned unto me, saith the Lord." They are enumerated in this way to show the people how long, how patiently, how sincerely, and with what varied appliances the Lord had labored to reclaim them, that they might themselves see the necessity laid on him to proceed to measures far more stern and fearful.——"Cleanness of teeth" is identical with want of bread, famine. He had withheld rain, long before the maturing of the harvests, so that the harvest must have utterly failed.——The middle clause of v. 9 might be read: "The multitude of your gardens and of your vineyards, also your fig-trees and olive-trees, the locust hath devoured."——V. 10 seems to imply that when the young men were slain by the sword, their horses, left riderless, fell into the hands of the enemy and were taken captive—fit retribution for their vain trust in horses.——A great slaughter had left many bodies unburied, to aggravate the pestilence; but even this fearful scourge did not bring them back to God.

11. I have overthrown *some* of you, as God overthrew Sodom and Gomorrah, and ye were as a fire-brand plucked out of the burning: yet have ye not returned unto me, saith the LORD.

Some of their cities had been laid desolate, even as Sodom and Gomorrah;—by what precise agency is not said; but the rest of the nation might fitly regard themselves as a brand plucked from the flames. These figures occur, Zech. 3: 2, and 1 Cor. 2: 15. Yet this most fearful scourge of all, which seemed almost to kindle the very fires of perdition upon them, failed to secure repentance.

12. Therefore, thus will I do unto thee, O Israel: *and* because I will do this unto thee, prepare to meet thy God, O Israel.

"Therefore" implies that by the very necessities of his moral government, since all discipline and chastisement fail, exterminating judgments *must come!*——The word "thus," which here raises the question, *How* will God deal with them? refers to the previous verses. The answer therefore is—As I have exterminated some of your cities, root and branch, even as Sodom and Gomorrah, so will I do to the whole nation.——*Because* I have purposed to do this, I now give thee warning—"Prepare to meet thy God!" Ye must meet him, coming with exterminating judgments; there is no escape; therefore be in readiness!——The spirit of this announcement seems to be that the decree of judgment had gone forth, and its execution was fixed in the counsels of Heaven; and yet this fact is declared, not with the expectation that the masses will hear and repent, but rather in the hope that some individuals might; and that it might stand as a warning to all other guilty nations in later times. ——It will be noticed that the primary sense of the passage relates to Israel as a nation, and had its fulfilment in the final desolation and captivity effected by the Assyrian power as stated 2 Kings 17. But in principle it applies with even augmented force to all the incorrigibly wicked, summoned to meet God in the final judgment-day. It warns them to be ready to meet him then and there, by turning at once to become his friends and people. O might the wicked only be wise in time, and make the Great Judge their friend while they may, so freely and with such welcome!

13. For, lo, he that formeth the mountains, and createth the wind, and declareth unto man what *is* his thought, that maketh the morning darkness, and treadeth upon the high places of the earth, The Lord, The God of hosts, *is* his name.

To give his readers some just sense of the majesty of that Being whom sinners of that and of every age must meet in judgment, he names a few of his mighty acts. The passage has scarcely a parallel for its beauty and sublimity.——The Creator must be indefinitely greater than his works;—but look at *them*—the mountains and the winds; note how he can tell man all his thoughts; how he can change the glory of the morning into darkness; and with the majestic march of a God, tread upon the high places of the earth—Jehovah, God of the armies of heaven, his name:—then say—Is it well for thee to rouse his wrath to flame and then to fall before it?

Can thy heart endure and thy hands be strong in so dread a conflict? Wilt thou persist in having this Almighty God thine enemy? ——It is remarkable that though this chapter begins with caustic irony, yet it ends with the most tender, solemn warnings. Hence the irony is not malign, but is benevolent—used only for the better moral effect—not for any satisfaction to be found in inflicting a keen and cutting castigation.

CHAPTER V.

In this chapter the prophet laments the fall of Israel; exhorts the people to seek the Lord; portrays the glory and power of Jehovah, as reasons why he should be both feared and sought; rebukes the sins of the people, and affirms God's abhorrence of the mere *forms* of worship without the heart and without justice and righteousness toward fellow-men.

1. Hear ye this word which I take up against you, *even* a lamentation, O house of Israel.

2. The virgin of Israel is fallen; she shall no more rise: she is forsaken upon her land: *there is* none to raise her up.

This lamentation or elegy—a plaintive wail of grief—assumes forcibly that Israel is seen as one fallen, and her nationality extinct. She is compared to a maiden, now gone down to rise no more. "Forsaken upon her land" should rather be "*prostrate* upon her own land," with none to help her rise.

3. For thus saith the Lord God; The city that went out *by* a thousand shall leave an hundred, and that which went forth *by* an hundred shall leave ten, to the house of Israel.

The glory of cities was graduated by the number of men they could send out for war. The passage shows how fearfully their strength had departed. The city that once sent forth a thousand had now but a hundred left; so that the house of Israel was shorn of its military strength.

4. For thus saith the Lord unto the house of Israel, Seek ye me, and ye shall live:

5. But seek not Beth-el, nor enter into Gilgal, and pass not to Beer-sheba: for Gilgal shall surely go into captivity, and Beth-el shall come to nought.

"Seeking the Lord" is returning to him in penitence and imploring his mercy. The promise—"thou shalt live"—usually covers something more and other than natural life, and, in the case of Israel, more than a prolonged nationality; it means the richest blessings. *Life* is one of the most comprehensive and expressive terms in human language to denote blessedness—substantial good. ——"Seek not Bethel;" *i. e.*, the idol gods of Bethel. So Gilgal and Beersheba are not to be sought, considered as seats of idol-worship. In the last clause the prophet fastens the thought in the mind of his Hebrew readers by a play upon his words. Gilgal, meaning the place of rolled-up heaps, shall be rolled away into captivity; Bethel shall become Aven, nothing, void of any living thing. The word rendered "*nought*" is Aven. Bethel came to be frequently called Beth-aven, because it was desecrated by its idols. Here the sense is even stronger—house of nonentities, empty of even its senseless, powerless idols. Even they have gone and perished!

6. Seek the LORD, and ye shall live; lest he break out like fire in the house of Joseph, and devour *it*, and *there be* none to quench *it* in Beth-el.

A further reason for seeking Jehovah is, "lest he break forth like fire on the house of Joseph"—Joseph being another name for the northern kingdom.——The last clause, literally rendered, is expressive: "And there be no quencher for Bethel"—no one to extinguish the fires the Lord kindles upon her.

7. Ye who turn judgment to wormwood, and leave off righteousness in the earth,

"Wormwood" is one of the most bitter of herbs—significantly put here for the grief felt by those who get only wrong and injury where they should have right and good. The passage describes those who wrest the cause of the innocent and pervert justice.—— The clause "leave off righteousness in the earth" is better rendered, "who cast righteousness to the ground." The words imply also that they make it lie there—make that its resting-place— and allow it no practical sway in human affairs.

8. *Seek him* that maketh the seven stars and Orion, and turneth the shadow of death into the morning, and maketh the day dark with night: that calleth for the waters of the sea, and poureth them out upon the face of the earth: The LORD *is* his name:

Men should seek God because he is so great and so glorious— has such power to turn our day to night, and our night to day—to bring up the waters of ocean by his call, and pour them forth as of old, in the deluge. The beauty and sublimity of this passage are exquisite. Job has a similar allusion to those brilliant constel lations (9:9).

9. That strengtheneth the spoiled against the strong, so that the spoiled shall come against the fortress.

This magnificent description of the power of Jehovah closes with a word designed to make it more practical to the Samaritans who relied on the military strength of their capital—"Who makes dèstruction flash out upon the mighty, and desolation shall come upon the strong city." The first verb, which I have rendered "flash out," takes its figure from the breaking forth of the dawn upon the darkness of the night—a figure which has most force in countries near the equator, where the twilight is short. The received translation fails to give the exact sense.

10. They hate him that rebuketh in the gate, and they abhor him that speaketh uprightly.

Again the prophet reverts to the reigning sin of the people. They love darkness and hate light, because their deeds are evil, and they are committed to wrong-doing. The "gate" was in that age the court-house—the place where justice should reign, and sin be always rebuked. The people of Samaria hated the upright, honest judge, and whoever else should speak for righteousness.

11. Forasmuch therefore as your treading *is* upon the poor, and ye take from him burdens of wheat: ye have built houses of hewn stone, but ye shall not dwell in them; ye have planted pleasant vineyards, but ye shall not drink wine of them.

These "burdens of wheat" were cruel exactions in the form of rents or taxes, yet oppressive and unrighteous. For these sins of oppressing the poor, God will tear them away from their houses and vineyards. However much they may build the one and plant the other, he can frustrate their hope of enjoying them. It is hard fighting against God. No wisdom and no strength can withstand him.

12. For I know your manifold transgressions and your mighty sins: they afflict the just, they take a bribe, and they turn aside the poor in the gate *from their right.*

"For I know that your transgressions are many, and your sins great."——"The poor in the gate" are before the courts of justice.

13. Therefore the prudent shall keep silence in that time; for it *is* an evil time.

"The prudent" are the wise and good. They keep silence and forbear to rebuke the sins of the age, because they see no hope of doing good thereby. They recognize God's awful presence to scourge the people, and they bow before his manifestly righteous ways.

14. Seek good, and not evil, that ye may live: and so the LORD, the God of hosts, shall be with you, as ye have spoken.

"As ye have spoken" refers to their professions of being the people of the Lord, and, as such, safe against harm from a heathen foe. The prophet says to them—"Seek good, and not evil;" so the Lord of hosts shall be with you truly—as ye have been saying when it was not true.

15. Hate the evil, and love the good, and establish judgment in the gate: it may be that the LORD God of hosts will be gracious unto the remnant of Joseph.

The phrase "remnant of Joseph" implies that the population was already greatly reduced in numbers, of which fact there is proof in 2 Kings 10: 32, 33: "In those days the Lord began to cut Israel short, and Hazael smote them in all the coasts of Israel."

16. Therefore, the LORD, the God of hosts, the Lord, saith thus; Wailing *shall be* in all streets; and they shall say in all the highways, Alas! alas! and they shall call the husbandmen to mourning, and such as are skilful of lamentation to wailing.

17. And in all vineyards *shall be* wailing: for I will pass through thee, saith the LORD.

The prophet Amos is remarkable for the fulness and solemnity with which he uses the significant *names* of God. Here is an instance: "Jehovah, the God of hosts" (or celestial armies), "the Lord, saith thus," &c. The people at that time had a very imperfect sense of the glory and majesty of the Lord their God. This grouping of his majestic names was therefore entirely appropriate, and had a most worthy object.——In this passage the Lord seeks to impress the certainty of their impending doom by declaring that soon there shall be wailing through all the populous cities and the country. The "skilful of lamentation" were persons who made it their profession to sing or chant mournful dirges at funerals, or on other occasions of public sorrow. Eccles. 12: 5 speaks of this class of persons as "going about the streets." Jer. 9: 17–19 seems to show that women were specially employed in this service. This usage prevailed not only among the Hebrews, but among the ancient Greeks, Romans, Egyptians, and other nations also.——God "will pass through" the land and among the people in such a way that they shall feel his presence and be made fearfully conscious of his wrath.

18. Woe unto you that desire the day of the LORD! to what end *is* it for you? the day of the LORD *is* darkness, and not light.

19. As if a man did flee from a lion, and a bear met him; or went into the house, and leaned his hand on the wall, and a serpent bit him.

20. *Shall* not the day of the LORD *be* darkness, and not light? even very dark, and no brightness in it?

In their foolhardiness some had expressed their desire that this day of the Lord might come, madly daring Jehovah to do his worst. Upon them God denounces special woe. He asks—What will this day of the Lord be to you? and answers—Only darkness, and not light; no rays of light in it; no mitigation to its horrors. Then, by two expressive figures, of a class natural to the mind of one trained in fields and deserts where wild beasts have their homes, he shows that to attempt to flee from God in any direction would be only to meet him there in a more fearful form.——What else can any sane mind think of the daring impiety that challenges God to show his power to curse and punish, save that it is the veriest madness? Do such men suppose they can cope with Omnipotence? Do they assume that God's resources for making them feel the bitterness of his strokes, are likely to be soon exhausted? Or do they glory in rousing their puny souls to bravery and daring, as if it were noble to measure strength with the Almighty? Alas for the folly and the madness that sin begets!

21. I hate, I despise your feast days, and I will not smell in your solemn assemblies.

22. Though ye offer me burnt-offerings and your meat-offerings, I will not accept *them*; neither will I regard the peace-offerings of your fat beasts.

23. Take thou away from me the noise of thy songs; for I will not hear the melody of thy viols.

The people were deluding themselves with the notion that they were high in favor with God, because they kept up the forms of the Mosaic worship. To dispel this delusion, the Lord solemnly protests to them that He not only takes no pleasure in their worship, but thoroughly abhors it: "I hate, I loathe your feast days." The practice of burning incense in worship for the sake of its sweet odors, led to the use of the verb to *smell* in this connection. It may perhaps be as well to translate so as to give only the ultimate sense—I have no pleasure in your solemn assemblies.——The "peace-offerings" are often called "thank-offerings," a term which better expresses their significance—offerings of gratitude and thanksgiving.——The word "*noise*" (v. 23) is highly expressive, showing that music with no heart in it is only *noise*, and never melody to the ear of God, a thought worthy of consideration in reference to the "service of sacred song" in our own times. If the Lord had a prophet Amos to send now into modern congregations, would he not (sometimes) give him this very message?——The sentiment of these verses appears in several other prophets—in Hosea, as we have seen, 6 : 6, and 8 : 13, and 9 : 4; and Isa. 1 : 11–15.

24. But let judgment run down as waters, and righteousness as a mighty stream.

The Lord asks them to reform, not their modes of worship, but their *morals*, their monstrous wrongs and oppressions of their fellow-men. Let judgment (in the sense of justice) flow freely, rolling on as water, smoothly and without obstruction; and let righteousness be as a perennial stream. Some critics say perennial; others say strong, powerful. Either is good sense, and the original bears either. A stream never dry, and never abating its flow, seems most in harmony with the scope of thought.——How strongly does the word of God affirm and reiterate the doctrine that God repels the forms of worship, unless they are accompanied with an honest regard for our fellow-men! He will never accept of worship professedly offered to himself, in place of duties due to man.——This is truly like a father, to insist that we shall treat all his children well, as a condition of his accepting our worship of himself. No worship can be so costly or so imposing that it can supply the place of "loving our neighbor as ourself."

25. Have ye offered unto me sacrifices and offerings in the wilderness forty years, O house of Israel?

26. But ye have borne the tabernacle of your Moloch and Chiun your images, the star of your god, which ye made to yourselves.

27. Therefore will I cause you to go into captivity beyond Damascus, saith the LORD, whose name *is* The God of hosts.

This question assumes that the answer is affirmative. Ye did, indeed, *i. e.*, your fathers, then living, did offer sacrifices in the wilderness; *but*, ye also carried along your little idol images secretly, stealthily, all that time. The same spirit of idolatry has become far more rampant, open, Heaven-daring, in these later times, for which I shall send you into captivity beyond Damascus. This is the general scope.——The particular explanation of v. 26 has been found somewhat difficult. The quotation of it by Stephen (Acts 7 : 42, 43), made from the Septuagint version, shows some of these various opinions. The original words have been spelled and read differently; *e. g.*, the Hebrew reading is Melek, which means king; the Septuagint is Moloch, an ancient idol. Some make Chiun a proper, others a common noun. None of these points of difference materially affect the general sense of the passage, which, beyond all doubt, means that the Israelites in the wilderness bore along with them little shrines and images of idol gods, or of some of the planets.——The Hebrew text might be rendered, "But ye bore the shrine of your king (meaning, your idol) and the little images of your idols, the star of your god, which ye made for yourselves." The last clause implies that the images represented a star, and involved the worship of the planet Saturn. They supposed the planets to be animated, conscious and powerful, wielding a vast influence over human destiny. These ideas and usages they found and embraced in Egypt. Of their perpetual tendency to idol worship while in the wilderness, the history gives painful evidence, especially in the case of the golden calf (Ex. 32). In our passage it is assumed that, like Rachel in Jacob's family, some of the Hebrews, during those forty years, bore along their little idol shrines and worshipped them.——The Jews were never thoroughly cured of their proclivities toward idols until their seventy years' captivity. The captivity of the ten tribes practically destroyed their nationality, and sunk them into oblivion, so that it cannot be known whether they ever abandoned their idol worship.

CHAPTER VI.

Woes on cities and their chief men who can be at ease in their great sins, and in the very face of fearful judgments from the Almighty; further specifications of their sins of luxury, intemperance, and oppression; followed by announcements of yet more desolating judgments, fill up this chapter.

1. Woe to them *that are* at ease in Zion, and trust in the mountain of Samaria, *which are* named chief of the nations, to whom the house of Israel came!

The word Zion embraces Jerusalem and her leading minds, as, on the other hand, Samaria carries us to the chief city of the northern kingdom. The people of Samaria trusted in the natural strength of their position—on the mountains.——"Judah and Israel were renowned as chief among the nations" of Western Asia. The clause "to whom the house of Israel came," refers to the leading men—princes, judges, and religious teachers, to whom the people came for justice in the courts, and to whom they looked for influence and direction.——This woe came on them because of their great guilt, especially the guilt of being reckless in the midst of awful sin, and under God's revealed threatenings of exterminating judgments. For the responsible leading men to say practically in the face of such threatenings, *What do we care?* was fearfully provoking to the Most High, and must inevitably seal their doom. In every age sinners who scorn the warnings of Jehovah, and would fain be at ease in Zion despite of them, are near the point where judgments break forth and "there is no remedy!"

2. Pass ye unto Calneh, and see; and from thence go ye to Hamath the great: then go down to Gath of the Philistines: *be they* better than these kingdoms? or their border greater than your border?

This verse connects itself in thought with the clause "which are named chief of the nations" (v. 1). The thought is—Judah and Israel have stood high among the nations of their time, in military power, in richness of country, and in the light of a true religion: their responsibilities are therefore the greater, and so much the more is their guilt in disowning and abusing the great Giver of their blessings.——That they were truly renowned as first among the nations, any one may see by going (in thought) to those nations with whom the comparison should naturally be made. Pass thus over the Euphrates to Calneh (called Calno, Isaiah 10:9), on the east bank of the Tigris, and see; from thence go to Hamath the great, on the Orontes, one of the great cities of Syria; then go down to Gath of the Philistines: were they better than these two kingdoms, Judah and Israel? or had they a larger and better territory?

3. Ye that put far away the evil day, and cause the seat of violence to come near;

4. That lie upon beds of ivory, and stretch themselves upon their couches, and eat the lambs out of the flock, and the calves out of the midst of the stall;

5. That chant to the sound of the viol, *and* invent to themselves instruments of music, like David;

6. That drink wine in bowls, and anoint themselves with the chief ointments: but they are not grieved for the affliction of Joseph.

Here is a rapid description of the social and moral life of the classes in question—the leading minds, especially in the kingdom of Israel. They "put far away the evil day," *i. e.*, in thought, they assume it to be far distant, and they *act* as if it were; but the throne of violence—the bench of justice whence righteousness should proceed and violence never should—they cause to come near;—the form of expression being antithetic to that in the first clause. They thrust the fear of danger from sin far away, and welcome near the worst forms of wrong, even legalized oppression, rolling in luxury, lounging in idleness, feasting on fatlings from flock and stall, chattering to the sound of the viol (where the word used by the prophet has a spice of irony and contempt); but they are fain to give themselves to music, as if nothing in their great guilt and near approaching doom should be allowed to trench on their hilarity; and to crown all, they drink wine by the bowlful, and, anointing themselves with the richest oils, they think only of personal self-indulgence and never "grieve for the affliction of

Joseph." Their country and the cause of their nation's God have no place in their hearts.——This last clause, "they grieve not for the affliction of Joseph," is analogous to "being at ease in Zion," and shows why the woes of God came down on Israel. They had no true sympathy with God or with his people.——The name "Joseph" represents the kingdom of Israel considered especially as being the chosen people of God, and bearing his name before the nations; yet may there not be, in the choice of this name, a tacit allusion to the original Joseph among his envious, heartless brethren, when they "saw the anguish of his soul, and he besought them, and they would not hear." Little did they heed the affliction of Joseph then; alike heedless are the people of Samaria in the days of this prophet. Hence the righteous woe, so soon to fall upon them.

7. Therefore, now shall they go captive with the first that go captive, and the banquet of them that stretched themselves shall be removed.

As the men of wealth and high standing have been foremost in oppressing the poor and wresting the cause of the meek; foremost also in luxury, self-indulgence, and recklessness of the cause of God: so they shall be first among the captives, heading the sad procession; and the banquet of those who lay stretched out around (in beastly drunkenness, we must suppose), shall be quite broken up. (The Lord has no special tenderness toward this beastly sin!)

8. The Lord God hath sworn by himself, saith the Lord the God of hosts, I abhor the excellency of Jacob, and hate his palaces: therefore will I deliver up the city with all that is therein.

Note the solemn reiteration of the names of God in this case, in which, since "he can swear by no greater, he swears by himself." The things so solemnly affirmed are two: (1.) That "God abhors the excellency of Jacob," &c.; (2.) That he will abandon the city and all its inhabitants to destruction.——The "excellency of Jacob" has been alluded to in this chapter; see v. 1, "chief of the nations," and v. 2, "better than other adjacent kingdoms;"—this excellency being mainly thought of as lying in its natural advantages. The same sense must be the primary one here, the more so because connected with "his palaces;" but the reason why God has come to abhor and hate a noble country, once flowing with milk and honey, and the glory of all lands, lies in the guilt, and especially the pride of its people. To this there seems to be a tacit allusion in the very phrase, "the excellency of Jacob," since this word in Hebrew is used for *pride*, as well as for naturally excellent qualities. The sense then, here, is that the pride and moral corruption of the people were so monstrous and so intrinsically hateful to God, that he abhorred the very country for their sake, and must spoil its fair beauty and consign it to long and blank desolation. And there the land of Palestine lies to-day—as yet, not half recovered from this fearful curse!

9. And it shall come to pass, if there remain ten men in one house, that they shall die.

10. And a man's uncle shall take him up, and he that burneth him, to bring out the bones out of the house, and shall say unto him that *is* by the sides of the house, *Is there* yet *any* with thee? and he shall say, No. Then shall he say, Hold thy tongue: for we may not make mention of the name of the LORD.

To show how utter would be the destruction of its inhabitants, the prophet gives some particulars for illustration. If only a small number, say ten (a definite number for an indefinite), remain in one house, even they shall *all* die. And when a man's uncle (or other friend), together with him whose office it shall be to burn the corpse, bring out a dead body, and finding one poor invalid in some corner or closet of the house, shall ask him, "Is there another dead man here?" he shall say, "No more;" and then shall add, "Hush! for we may not make mention of the name of the Lord."——This last phrase—"make mention of the name of the Lord"—usually signifies, to speak of God in grateful, appropriate acknowledgment, and due honor. See Josh. 23:7, where this is forbidden in reference to false gods; also Ps. 20:7, and Isa. 62:6. Precisely what this prohibition meant in this case is not certain; perhaps it indicates such a sense of the awfulness of God's presence in this scourge upon the land that guilty men could not endure to hear his name!

11. For, behold, the LORD commandeth, and he will smite the great house with breaches, and the little house with clefts.

All the houses, great or little, shall be smitten; the great shattered to pieces, as the Hebrew word implies; the little ones rent with clefts. Oppressors, enriched by wrong, are remembered before God in this day of judgment.

12. Shall horses run upon the rock? will *one* plough *there* with oxen? for ye have turned judgment into gall, and the fruit of righteousness into hemlock:

These questions put cases, not of extreme difficulty so much as of practical impossibility, and aim to illustrate the futility and absurdity of those vain reliances which have kept up the spirits of the people. They had been hoping to repel their foreign enemies and withstand the threatened judgments of the Almighty. He hints to them that they might as well plough the rock with oxen, or run horses upon the precipitous cliffs of their mountain glens.——*Why* could they not escape? *Why* could they not resist Jehovah's wrath? Because they "had turned judgment into gall"—that which is always sweet to good men into the most bitter draught—"and the fruit of righteousness"—righteous judicial decisions—"into the poison hemlock." Such perversions of justice had insured Jehovah's wrath.——What a lesson of warning against American slaveholding!——See a like form of expression, Hos. 10 : 4, and Amos 5 : 7.

13. Ye which rejoice in a thing of nought, which say, Have we not taken to us horns by our own strength?

They had trusted joyfully in what could avail them nought, but must prove a thing of no power to save—a mere nothing. They had said, "Have we not taken to ourselves horns (always an emblem of power) by our own strength?" Not the least recognition of God as their strength appears, but, on the contrary, every word indicates the purest self-conceit, and the pride of self-made help. Such "pride goeth before destruction," just a little way only, before!

14. But behold, I will raise up against you a nation, O house of Israel, saith the LORD the God of hosts; and they shall afflict you from the entering in of Hamath unto the river of the wilderness.

This prediction almost names the Assyrian power—manifestly means it. God raised them up; they came, and did indeed lay the land desolate "from the entering in of Hamath"—a very common phrase for their northern border, and a natural thoroughfare outward to Hamath—"unto the river of the wilderness." This name, "*the* wilderness"—in Hebrew, Arabah—with the article, is applied in the Scriptures to the great valley of the Jordan, the Lake Genessaret (in Heb. Cinneroth), and the Dead Sea. In later times, the name Arabah has been specially given to the extension of this valley southward, from the Dead Sea to the Elanitic Gulf. But in the earlier ages, it was currently given to the portion north of the Dead Sea, and usually translated in our English version, "the plain." The exceptions are Deut. 11 : 30, "champaign," and Josh. 18 : 18, "Arabah." See other passages—"the plain," Deut. 3 : 17, and 4 : 49; Josh. 3 : 16, and 8 : 14, and 11 : 2, 16, and 12 : 1, 3; 2 Kings 14 : 25, and 25 : 4, 5, &c. This wonderful valley was one of the natural boundaries of the kingdom.

CHAPTER VII.

THIS chapter records three successive visions, shown to the prophet, each indicating the judgments impending over the land (vs. 1–9); then an attempt made by Amaziah, an idol priest of Bethel, to prevent Amos from prophesying more in Bethel, and to send him back into Judah; with the defence made by Amos, and the response made by the Lord (vs. 10–17).

1. Thus hath the Lord GOD shewed unto me; and behold, he formed grasshoppers in the beginning of the shooting up of the latter growth; and lo, *it was* the latter growth after the king's mowings.

That this is a *vision* presented to the spiritual eye of the prophet, is indicated by the language—"Thus did the Lord God show me," *i. e.*, cause me to see. He saw the Lord forming grasshoppers. They were young, but fast coming forward for their work of destruction; and he saw God's hand in them. The time was just when the meadows were putting forward their second growth—the after-math. The phrase, "the king's mowings," is supposed to allude to a claim of the king to have a part, at least, of the first growth of the meadows.

2. And it came to pass, *that* when they had made an end of eating the grass of the land, then I said, O Lord GOD, forgive, I beseech thee: by whom shall Jacob arise? for he *is* small.

After he had seen them eat the last of the grass of the land, he prayed that the Lord would forgive the sin for which this scourge was sent, and used this plea: "By whom else shall Jacob arise," *i. e.*, stand, live; "for he is weak" and without strength against God, and against such agents of destruction as these.

3. The LORD repented for this: It shall not be, saith the LORD.

The Lord heard his prayer and changed his purpose, sparing the land the judgments which this vision portended. A clear and striking case of prevailing prayer, even when God's purpose to destroy was not only formed, but made known.——What the precise form of this judgment would have been, is not certain. The grasshoppers, being seen only in vision, may have been symbolic of some other form of judgment, even as the fire in the next verse manifestly must have been. Amos does not say here, as Joel did, that actual grasshoppers came up over the land, visible to all the people, and thrilling all hearts with fear and dread.

4. Thus hath the Lord GOD shewed unto me: and,

behold, the Lord God called to contend by fire, and it devoured the great deep, and did eat up a part.

5. Then said I, O Lord God, cease, I beseech thee: by whom shall Jacob arise? for he *is* small.

6. The Lord repented for this: This also shall not be, saith the Lord God.

In the second vision he heard the Lord calling for the action of fire. The original words imply a controversy, or legal judicial issue by fire, probably only in the general sense of a judgment on the people for their sins. Appalling to behold, this fire seemed to devour the great deep, and to eat up the dry land also. The original word rendered "*a part*" is supposed to have here this sense—not that it ate up a part of the great deep, but ate up the dry land. The previous clause, using the same verb, affirms that it had eaten up the great deep already. Of course I construe this as a vision, and symbolic of some all-consuming desolation, doubtless by war and conquest.——Again the prophet prays, but not in this case as before—"forgive"—which, if answered, would have averted the judgment; but, "*desist;*" cut short this judgment; let it be arrested midway. He uses the same plea as before, in the same words; and the Lord answered to the precise extent of his request. He desisted, after the judgment had run a part of its course. The scourge of war and indeed of captivity came, but probably with the less severity because of the prophet's prevailing prayer.——These cases, as thus recorded, must have been designed of God to encourage his people to come before him with most importunate prayer that he would avert, either in part or wholly, the judgments which he seemed about to inflict on a guilty people.

7. Thus he shewed me: and behold, the Lord stood upon a wall *made* by a plumb-line, with a plumb-line in his hand.

8. And the Lord said unto me, Amos, what seest thou? And I said, A plumb-line. Then said the Lord, Behold, I will set a plumb-line in the midst of my people Israel: I will not again pass by them any more:

9. And the high places of Isaac shall be desolate, and the sanctuaries of Israel shall be laid waste: and I will rise against the house of Jeroboam with the sword.

The third vision will be better understood if we consider that the prophets speak of a measuring line as marking off for destroying as well as for creating; for casting down, no less than for building up. (See 2 Kings 21:13, and Isa. 34:11, and Lam. 2:8.) So here, this plumb-line evinces the moral obliquity of the people and their consequent fitness for destruction. God will not any more *pass by* them, but will take them in hand for scourging and for ruin.

——The "high places of Isaac" were those elevated sites so constantly chosen for idol temples and idol worship. The "sanctuaries of Israel" were their idol temples and shrines. These were doomed to utter destruction, and at least by implication the whole land as well. The "house of Jeroboam" the Lord would cut off by the sword. He did so; Shallum (2 Kings 15 : 10) conspired against Zachariah, son and successor of Jeroboam, and thus ended the royal line of his house.——It should be noted that in this third vision nothing is said of the prophet's interceding by prayer for the removal or even the mitigation of this judgment. He saw that it was most righteously deserved, and fully fixed in the counsels of Jehovah, and therefore he forebore to press any plea for its reversal. Essentially the same answer must be given to the question—Why did he pray "*forgive*" in reference to the first threatened judgment, and only "*desist*" upon the second? "The secret of the Lord is with them that fear him." The conditions of acceptable prayer being fully met on our part, the Lord, on his part, will *lead* our minds in prayer, aiding us thus to ask for those things, and only those, which he is pleased to grant.

10. Then Amaziah the priest of Beth-el sent to Jeroboam king of Israel, saying, Amos has conspired against thee in the midst of the house of Israel: the land is not able to bear all his words.

11. For thus Amos saith, Jeroboam shall die by the sword, and Israel shall surely be led away captive out of their own land.

12. Also, Amaziah said unto Amos, O thou seer, go flee thee away into the land of Judah, and there eat bread, and prophesy there:

13. But prophesy not again any more at Beth-el: for it *is* the king's chapel, and it *is* the king's court.

This historical sketch (vs. 10–17) presents no difficulties that require exposition. Amaziah, "*the* priest of Bethel," was probably the high priest before the golden calf located there, for there must have been other priests as well. The history of Elijah (1 Kings 18) gives us some facts respecting the number of idol priests.——The charge of treason against the king and the state was often brought against the Lord's faithful prophets, and constituted one of their serious embarrassments and trials. It seems that Jeroboam did not think best to interfere with the Lord's prophet. Amaziah therefore resorted to a private effort (vs. 12, 13) to get Amos out of the kingdom. Judah, said he, is a better place for you; the prophets of the Lord get a good living there; there you can be quiet and fulfil your prophetic function, if so you choose: but be off and away from Bethel, for these idol temples are the king's sanctuary—the place where he worships, and the house of his kingdom (so the

Hebrew reads), and it implies that, in their notion, these heathen gods were the patrons of the kingdom, and their favor vital to its permanence and prosperity. Hence they would very naturally arraign the Lord's true prophets for high treason, whenever they dared.

14. Then answered Amos, and said to Amaziah, I
was no prophet, neither *was* I a prophet's son; but I
was an herdman, and a gatherer of sycamore fruit:
15. And the LORD took me as I followed the flock,
and the LORD said unto me, Go, prophesy unto my people Israel.

Amos first gives his own personal defence. With beautiful simplicity he replies: "I was no prophet; I did not come up unto this profession because my father was a prophet before me; but I was earning my bread by honest labor when the Lord took me from following the flock, and said—'Go, prophesy unto my people Israel'—not *Judah*, as you propose, but *Israel*. How could I do otherwise than obey this divine mandate?"

16. Now, therefore, hear thou the word of the LORD:
Thou sayest, Prophesy not against Israel, and drop not *thy word* against the house of Isaac.
17. Therefore thus saith the LORD; Thy wife shall
be an harlot in the city, and thy sons and thy daughters shall fall by the sword, and thy land shall be divided by line; and thou shalt die in a polluted land: and Israel shall surely go into captivity forth of his land.

The rest of his reply comes directly from the Lord himself. Thou hast forbidden me to prophesy against Israel; for this impiety the Lord reveals to thee thy doom—thy wife a harlot in the city; thy sons and daughters falling by the sword; thy landed estates divided by line to others; thou thyself shall die in a foreign and so in a polluted land, and the nation shall be carried away into captivity—a fearful warning against interfering with the divine mission of God's faithful prophets!——The Hebrews regarded all other lands compared with their own as polluted. Hence they naturally desired to make their graves in the holy land.——This captivity was to Assyria, effected by Tiglath-Pileser B. C. 722, or sixty-two years after the death of this Jeroboam.

CHAPTER VIII.

THIS chapter opens with the last vision in this series of four (vs. 1, 2), which is followed by further details of the great and damning sins of the people, and of the terrible judgments then impending.

1. Thus hath the Lord GOD shewed unto me: and behold a basket of summer fruit.

2. And he said, Amos, what seest thou? And I said, A basket of summer fruit. Then said the LORD unto me, The end is come upon my people of Israel; I will not again pass by them any more.

Summer fruit ripens quick and soon decays. The people had ripened for ruin, and their ruin was near at hand. The latter of these two ideas seems rather more prominent than the former; perhaps both are implied. The special idea is that the end is come to the nation of Israel. God can pass by them, sparing them and deferring his judgments, no longer.

3. And the songs of the temple shall be howlings in that day, saith the Lord GOD: *there shall be* many dead bodies in every place; they shall cast *them* forth with silence.

Since the time of David, songs had formed a part of the temple worship. In the dark and sad day just at hand, those songs should become howlings—the wails of agony. The original is concise: "The songs of the temple shall wail in that day."——The last half of the verse Dr. Henderson translates with graphic power:

"The carcasses are many!
Throw them out anywhere!
Hush!"

This is a close translation of the Hebrew, except that the verb *throw* is not imperative, but indicative—"men do throw them out anywhere." The last word "hush" should be compared with Amos 6: 10, where the word is the same, and the sentiment also, doubtless, the same. Some suppose this injunction to silence looks toward their danger from the invading foe, it being such that they could not bury their beloved and honored dead with safety, save in secrecy and silence. Perhaps so; but the passage (6: 10) favors another view, viz., that an appalling sense of the presence and wrath of God awed every heart into silence.

4. Hear this, O ye that swallow up the needy, even to make the poor of the land to fail,

5. Saying, When will the new moon be gone, that we may sell corn? and the sabbath, that we may set forth wheat, making the ephah small, and the shekel great, and falsifying the balances by deceit?

6. That we may buy the poor for silver, and the needy for a pair of shoes; *yea*, and sell the refuse of the wheat?

The guilty people are once more exhorted to hear the threatened judgments of the Almighty, and the recital of those judgments is prefaced by a further description of their oppressions of the poor. In this passage, as in 2: 6–8, these oppressions stand as the crowning, damning sin—that which filled to the brim the cup of their iniquity.——"Swallow up the needy," exhibits the same verb that is rendered (chap. 2: 7) "that *pant after* the dust of the earth on the head of the poor." It might more precisely be rendered here—"that pant after the poor," even to make the needy of the land cease altogether, *i. e.*, to annihilate them so that none should remain.——So eager are they to drive hard bargains, and wrest from the poor the last pittance of their earnings, they cannot wait for the new moon and for the Sabbath to pass over—so would they hurry off their religious duties to get back again to their extortion and fraud. Their religion stood in the way of their sin in no other respect than that it demanded a few hours' suspension of trade and business. It utterly failed of its proper influence, viz., to make their heart thoroughly benevolent, and, consequently, their business-life just.——It would seem that these tradesmen bought by the shekel and sold by the ephah. So they perverted their measures and weights to subserve the ends of fraud. They made false balances *for* deceit.——Yet further, they drive their fraudulent trade to get money in order to buy the poor for slaves, cheapening even *their* price, so that they could get a poor man or a poor boy for a pair of sandals, which are of much less value than American shoes.——And one thing more, they sell as merchantable the refuse of the wheat—the light, half-filled grains.——What a depth of corruption in morals do such sketches of the ways of business and trade reveal! The reader will be careful to note how sharply the Lord rebukes and exposes such outrages on human rights and on commercial justice, and how fearfully he punishes the guilty.

7. The LORD hath sworn by the excellency of Jacob, Surely I will never forget any of their works.

Here begins the message which (in v. 4.) the people were exhorted to hear. It opens with a most solemn asseveration, the oath of the Almighty. "The excellency of Jacob" cannot well mean here any quality or thing that Jacob possessed—not his moral qualities, not his goodly land—but it must refer to and describe Jehovah himself. He was "the excellency of Jacob" in the sense of being his most glorious "portion," his richest treasure; that in which Jacob should more exult and rejoice than in all things else. ——Comparing this passage with Amos 6:8, where the Lord says, "I abhor the excellency of Jacob," the difference is that *there* the phrase refers to the glorious land and country of Jacob which the people *did* account their chief glory, as they should not; *here*, to their covenant-keeping God whom they *ought* to have accounted their chief glory, but did not. The object in using this one phrase in these two different senses may have been to make this contrast palpable.——It is by no means uncommon for Jehovah to swear by himself. Paul (Heb. 6:13) intimates the reason to be that he can swear by none greater—by nothing else so solemn. ——As to the form of this oath, it is very common in Hebrew, but not often retained in our English translation: "If I shall ever forget any of their works"—where the full force would be expressed by filling out the sentence—*then I am not God.* A very strong emphasis on the word *if* suffices, however, to express the sense. God will not lose from his memory one of the least of all their doings. All shall come up again for judgment.

8. Shall not the land tremble for this, and every one mourn that dwelleth therein? and it shall rise up wholly as a flood; and it shall be cast out and drowned, as *by* the flood of Egypt.

The tone of awful earnestness, manifest in this oath of Jehovah, should lead us to expect appalling judgments, in hearing which, all ears should tingle. The prophet compares the convulsions that shall shake the land to an earthquake, and represents this earthquake as heaving up the land, even as the Nile lifts up its waters in its annual inundations. The verse might be paraphrased thus: "For this, shall not the land tremble as in an earthquake, and every dweller therein mourn, when the whole land rises up as the Nile, and rolls to and fro, and then subsides like the river of Egypt after its mighty inundations?"——Of the two words rendered "cast out," and "drowned," the first must mean, *driven and tossed*, as impelled by mighty forces; and the second, *subsiding again*, when the moving force is spent. The ultimate thought is, that convulsions shake and rock the kingdom of Israel, and finally sweep it away into the gulf of ruin.

9. And it shall come to pass in that day, saith the Lord God, that I will cause the sun to go down at noon, and I will darken the earth in the clear day:

This is the usual figure for great calamity. The last clause reads literally—"I will darken the light to the earth in the daytime." The actual thing indicated by these figures should not be looked for in the natural but in the political and moral world. (See Joel 3:15 and 2:31.)

10. And I will turn your feasts into mourning, and all your songs into lamentation; and I will bring up sackcloth upon all loins, and baldness upon every head; and I will make it as the mourning of an only *son*, and the end thereof as a bitter day.

These are the tokens of grief common among the people of the East in all ages.

11. Behold, the days come, saith the Lord God, that I will send a famine in the land, not a famine of bread, nor a thirst for water, but of hearing the words of the Lord:

12. And they shall wander from sea to sea, and from the north even to the east; they shall run to and fro to seek the word of the Lord, and shall not find *it*.

13. In that day shall the fair virgins and young men faint for thirst.

In their deep calamity, their ideas and feelings in regard to messages from the Lord by his servants, will utterly change. Whereas they had made light of these messages when they had them—even scorning the word of God and misusing his prophets—now, the Lord having withdrawn and trouble having come on, they are in the horrors of a great famine of the words of the Lord. They long for some word from him, and wander over the whole land in vain to find a prophet. Like Saul after the Lord had forsaken him, they say—"I am sore distressed; God is departed from me, and answereth me no more, neither by prophet nor by dreams" (1 Sam. 28 : 15).——This was one of the prophet's last appeals to the people to give heed to the words of the Lord while they had them.

14. They that swear by the sin of Samaria, and say, Thy god, O Dan, liveth; and, The manner of Beer-sheba liveth; even they shall fall, and never rise up again.

The "sin of Samaria" is here idol gods. One of Jeroboam's calves was put up in Dan, the extreme northern limit of the kingdom.——The "*manner* of Beersheba" means first the ways of idol worship practised there, and next, the idol gods themselves, which is the sense here.——The form of the oath might be better expressed—"As thy God, O Dan, liveth;" or, "By the life of thy god, O Dan;" and so of the god Beersheba.——All who have had such reverence for these infamous gods as to swear by them shall fall, never to rise again.

CHAPTER IX.

This chapter opens with the fifth and last special vision shown the prophet: affirms the complete destruction of the guilty, apostate people of Israel; denies in vivid forms all possibility of their escape (vs. 1–7, 10), yet promises the rescue of a small remnant (vs. 8, 9); predicts the raising up of the fallen tent of David, and the saving of the true Israel for an era of extraordinary and long-continued prosperity.

1. I saw the Lord standing upon the altar: and he said, Smite the lintel of the door, that the posts may shake: and cut them in the head all of them; and I will slay the last of them with the sword: he that fleeth of them shall not flee away, and he that escapeth of them shall not be delivered.

In the outset, a question arises respecting *the* altar referred to here, the decision of which affects the interpretation of the chapter fundamentally.——Some, with Dr. Henderson, take it to be the idol altar at Bethel, and adduce the following reasons for this view: (1.) The reference (8:14), immediately preceding, to the utter and final fall of the worshippers of those idols, showing that this subject was in mind; (2.) That Amos (3:14) affirms this very thing—"In the day that I shall visit the transgressions of Israel upon him, I will also visit the altars of Bethel, and the horns of the altar shall be cut off and fall to the ground;" (3.) The fitness of this fact in itself, and in all its relations; (4.) That Hosea, under the same circumstances, distinctly predicts that God will break down those altars and spoil their images (Hos. 10: 2, 5, 8).——Others, including Dr. Hengstenberg, Rosenmuller, and Calvin, take it to mean the altar of burnt-offering at Jerusalem. I adopt this opinion decidedly, for the following reasons: (1.) This, and this only, is *the* altar—the one to be thought of when we have nothing else to determine the sense except this emphatic definite article. (2.) The idol altar was not, to the same extent, the prominent thing at Bethel. The calf, the god himself, was much more prominent. (3.) The scope of this chapter, and more especially from v. 8 to the close, contemplates Judah and Jerusalem, as well as Samaria, Bethel, and the northern kingdom; *e. g.*, v. 7, "brought up Israel out of the land of Egypt;" v. 8, "the house of Jacob," and v. 9, "the house of Israel," who are spoken of as "my people," v. 10; "the tent of David," v. 11; "my people of Israel," v. 14. (4.) The allusions, v. 11, and especially the use of the plural number, are thought to refer to both kingdoms: "In that day will I raise up the tent of David that is fallen (looking, perhaps, in part to the crushing down of the temple, as in this v. 1), and will wall up *their* (not *its*) breaches"—the breaches of both kingdoms, and "I will raise up *his* ruins," those of David, and "I will build *it*"—the tent—"as in days of old."——The two points of argument last made (Nos. 3 and 4) offset the consideration that most of the book of Amos relates to the northern kingdom. That is freely admitted, yet when the Lord reaches, in this last chapter, the revelations of mercy, the phraseology embraces the southern as well as the northern kingdom; or rather that temporary distinction is lost sight of, and we have the earlier Israel of the times of the Exodus and of David. In this point of view we go back also to the great altar at Jerusalem. (5.) But more than all is the argument from the scope and course of thought. To see this in its full force, we must look first at the fact that the people of the northern kingdom, though fearfully apostate from God into idol-worship, yet kept up some of the forms of the Mosaic system, and manifestly depended upon God's protection and favor on this account. See the evidence, chap. 4:4, 5: "Bring your sacrifices every morning, your tithes after three years, your thank-offerings and your free-offerings"—where the sense is, Bring them if you will, and rely on them for salvation if you will; they can avail you nothing. Also 5:14, 18–26: "Seek good and not evil; so the Lord shall be with you *as ye have said;*" *i. e.*, they had said the Lord would be with them, because of their religious worship. The prophet replies, "God will be with you then, and only then, when you seek good and do right." V. 18 shows that they did not fear but even dared the coming of the day of the Lord—manifestly through their vain confidence in his favor. Hence he solemnly affirms, "I hate, I despise your feast-days; I will not accept your burnt-offerings," &c. The whole connection here shows that the Lord would fain annul their vain reliance on the mere forms of ceremonial worship for the salvation of their country.

With this fact in mind, let us come to our verse (9:1). I paraphrase it thus: "I saw the Lord standing beside the great altar of burnt-offering in Jerusalem, and he said, 'Smite the capitals of the columns, and make the very thresholds tremble, and dash them in pieces upon the heads of all the people within, and the remnant of them I will slay with the sword; whoever flees shall not escape, and he that gets away shall not be finally delivered.'"——In this vision the people are supposed to be assembled in the temple for safety against the judgments of God, but he comes down with his destroying angel and orders the whole temple to be crushed down from pinnacle to basement, that it may fall crashing upon the heads of the assembled throng. Then, whom the falling temple does not crush, the sword shall slay, and none shall escape.——The context in the next three verses confirms this view of the general course of thought in this passage, as we shall see.

This vision of the temple crushed down upon the heads of those who had fled to it for refuge against the judgments of God, is altogether in harmony with Amos 6:8:—"The Lord hath sworn by himself, I abhor the excellency of Jacob, and hate his palaces." See Notes on the passage. The whole heart of the Holy One revolts at the idea that his temple should be made a hiding-place and sanctuary of refuge for hypocrites so foul, apostates so guilty and so Heaven-provoking; and as he abhors their goodly land because of the sins of the people, and will not spare it for its natural beauty, so neither will he spare its goodly temple.

2. Though they dig into hell, thence shall mine hand take them; though they climb up to heaven, thence will I bring them down:

3. And though they hide themselves in the top of Carmel, I will search and take them out thence; and though they be hid from my sight in the bottom of the sea, thence will I command the serpent, and he shall bite them:

4. And though they go into captivity before their enemies, thence will I command the sword, and it shall slay them: and I will set mine eyes upon them for evil, and not for good.

The aim throughout these verses is to deny all possibility of escape.——It is not essential to the fitness or the force of these supposed cases that they should be actually possible. The affirmation is that *if* they were so, and *if* men should hide there, it should avail them nothing. There is no escape from the Almighty by any expedient, possible or even supposable. "The top of Carmel" is suggested as a place to hide one's self, both because of its numerous caves and thick undergrowths, and because, lying adjacent to the Mediterranean, it naturally stood in contrast with the bottom of the sea.——"Going into captivity" presupposes that their lives are at first spared; but even the rights of prisoners of war should not save them from death.

5. And the Lord God of hosts *is* he that toucheth the land, and it shall melt, and all that dwell therein shall mourn: and it shall rise up wholly like a flood; and be drowned, as *by* the flood of Egypt.

6. *It is* he that buildeth his stories in the heaven, and hath founded his troop in the earth; he that calleth for the waters of the sea, and poureth them out upon the face of the earth: the LORD *is* his name.

These bold descriptions of Jehovah's power over the material world are adduced here in the same line of thought with the preceding—to show how hopelessly futile must be every attempt of guilty men to evade his scourge or escape his retributions. The manner of the original is graphic: "And the Lord Jehovah of Hosts—he is touching the earth, and then it melts, and all the dwellers in it mourn; its whole surface is lifted up like the rising Nile, and then subsides as the river of Egypt (the effects of an earthquake, as in Amos 8:8). He builds his chambers in the heavens; he has founded his arched vault upon the earth (*i. e.* the blue concave firmament). He calls for the waters of the sea, and then pours them out upon the face of the earth—Jehovah, his name."——What our translators meant by "troop" is not clear. The original word refers to the apparently arched concave above us, which the Hebrews thought and spoke of as solid, "the firmament," and its pillars or lower edges as resting upon the earth.

7. *Are* ye not as children of the Ethiopians unto me, O children of Israel? saith the LORD. Have I not brought up Israel out of the land of Egypt? and the Philistines from Caphtor, and the Syrians from Kir?

This verse aims to confront and demolish another delusive reliance of the apostate people, viz., that, being the seed of Abraham and children of the covenant, brought by a series of miracles into the land of promise, they were invincible against any heathen power, since their God would surely protect them.——The Lord replies to their thought—"What are ye to me more than the Cushites and Ethiopians? I did indeed bring you up out of Egypt; so I also brought the Philistines from Caphtor (Crete), and the Syrians from Kir"—the region of the river Cyrus. Does such a removal insure the perpetual prosperity of any people? Can it save you from being removed again, far beyond Damascus? (See Amos 5:27.)——The Ethiopians, or Cushites, originally holding central Arabia, were removed to the interior of Africa.

8. Behold the eyes of the Lord GOD *are* upon the sinful kingdom, and I will destroy it from off the face face of the earth; saving that I will not utterly destroy the house of Jacob, saith the LORD.

The phrase "sinful kingdom" leads the mind to the kingdom of the ten tribes, that being at this period far more corrupt than Judah. The sentence "I will destroy it from the face of the earth," had special reference to the ten tribes. The excepting clause, "saving that I will not utterly destroy the house of Jacob," raises the question whether the saved were of the ten tribes, or of Judah only. On this point, the statements in this verse are not altogether explicit: v. 9 favors the hope that some from the ten tribes were plucked from utter ruin; v. 10 shows that all the *sinners*—all who were past repentance and reform—would be cut off by the sword.

9. For, lo, I will command, and I will sift the house

of Israel among all nations, like as *corn* is sifted in a sieve, yet shall not the least grain fall upon the earth.

It would seem that "the house of Israel," as used in this verse, must be a different class from "the sinful kingdom," named in v. 8, and from "the sinners of my people," spoken of in v. 10. The latter, he says, "shall be destroyed" (v.8); "shall die by the sword" (v. 10); but the former, though sifted fine and far among the nations, shall none of them be lost. They are the precious grain, and God's eye is on them to save them and to use them for his own purpose, as his eye is also on the sinful kingdom to destroy it from the face of the earth. The "house of Israel," therefore, must include here only the real people of God, "faithful found among the faithless;" the same whom, considered as captives, he will restore, as said below.——The word rendered "the least grain" is thought by Hengstenberg to mean a bundle, or any thing bound up. This is the almost universal sense of the word. Its meaning here would be essentially as in 1 Sam. 25 : 29 : "Men rise up to persecute and to seek thy soul; but the soul of my Lord is bound in the bundle of the living by the Lord thy God." So in our passage with this sense of the word, the house of Israel are bound up in the bundle of life by the Lord himself, and cannot be lost in the sifting process of discipline by dispersion among the nations. ——If we might give the word the sense—a small grain—the ultimate meaning would be much the same.

10. All the sinners of my people shall die by the sword, which say, The evil shall not overtake or prevent us.

The sense here must be—"All the sinners *out of* or *among* my people"—the sinners being one class and God's people another. The sinners shall die—the judgment of God being the fearfully sifting process.——The description given of them evinces their vain self-confidence. The evils threatened by the prophets of the Lord, they are sure, will neither overtake them from behind, nor come in ahead of them from before. "Prevent" has usually in our Bible that ancient, now obsolete sense, of getting in advance, coming in ahead to intercept and confront an adversary.——Vain self-confidence never saves; it only hastens and aggravates destruction.

11. In that day will I raise up the tabernacle of David that is fallen, and close up the breaches thereof; and I will raise up his ruins, and I will build it as in the days of old:

The point of time indicated by "in that day," is not definite. It looks into that future period when discipline shall have wrought its desired result and the fulness of the Lord's time of mercy shall have come.——The "tent" or booth "of David"—not his royal palace, which would indicate prosperity and strength—but his reduced and humble dwelling, a booth of tree-boughs, and even this fallen down, God will now raise up. The reigning family of David had been sadly broken down by the revolt under Jeroboam; far more so still by their apostasy into idol-worship, oppression, and other immoralities, for all which God had doomed the sinners of his people to be utterly cut off; but the day will come for rearing up again this royal line and its kingdom. He will wall up the breaches of the "double house," the two kingdoms (for so the plural pronoun, rendered "thereof," should naturally mean): "I will raise up David's ruins and build his tent as in days of old." These promises suggest the original covenant with David's line (2 Sam. 7 : 16). "And thy house and thy kingdom shall be established forever before thee; thy throne shall be established forever." King Messiah is to come in this royal line, and, according to the strain of this prophecy, events ripen for his coming. Only in him can this prophecy find an adequate fulfilment.

12. That they may possess the remnant of Edom, and of all the heathen which are called by my name, saith the LORD that doeth this.

The "remnant of Edom" reminds us that in chap. 1 : 11, 12, we saw Edom doomed to sore judgments, almost exterminating, because of his relentless hostility to his brother Jacob's race. Now the revived and rebuilt house of David shall possess what is left of Edom. There may also be a tacit allusion to the fact that the literal David himself subdued the Edomites and made them tributary, and that they took advantage of the breaches in David's tents—in other words, the weakness induced by the revolt and by the great sins of the covenant people—to throw off this yoke. David's line, having returned to God and to consequent prosperity and power, shall again possess what remains of Edom. And not of Edom alone, but of all the heathen over whom God's name is called, for so saith the Lord who bringeth to pass these promised events.—— The calling of God's name over a person or people is not an empty ceremony, but a most significant fact. It implies their consecration to his love and service. Thus it was said concerning Israel—Deut. 28 : 9, 10 : "The Lord shall establish thee an holy people unto himself," &c., "and all people of the earth shall see that thou art called by the name of the Lord," literally rendered, "that the name of the Lord hath been called over or upon thee," and consequently that thou art the people of God, and the object of his protecting care and love. To the same purport is Dan. 9 : 18, 19, "O Lord, behold the city over which thy name is called"—"for thy city and thy people are called by thy name."——In this most interesting sense God's name has been called over the gentile nations. This is the great fact affirmed in this passage. May it not be that Isaiah, in nearly the same words, means the same thing (54 : 5)? "The God of the whole earth shall he be called," *i. e.*, "his name shall be called over or upon it all."——Another mode of expressing essentially the same thing is this—"They"—the royal seed of David —"shall possess" (inherit) "the remnant of Edom and of all the heathen." Precisely this Isaiah affirms—"Thy seed shall inherit the Gentiles" (54 : 3).——Yet further, let us not lose sight of the idea that this calling of the name of God over these heathen nations, and this inheriting or possession of the Gentiles by the royal seed of David, must all be understood, not in the worldly but in the gospel sense. Israel takes possession of the gentile nations, only in the name of her King Messiah; only by preaching to them his gospel, revealing to them his love, and taking their hearts captive for him by the power of his cross. We must think of no other conquest, no other form of possession, but this.——Finally, let us revert to the quotation of these verses (11, 12) by the Apostle James (Acts 15 : 14–17) in his speech before the great council at Jerusalem. He began with saying, "Simon Peter has been relating to you how God has visited the Gentiles to convert some of them to himself; and to this agree the words of the prophet Amos;" and then he quotes substantially from the Septuagint version these two verses. His quotations differ from the Hebrew chiefly in reading "the residue of men," instead of "the remnant of Edom." The Hebrew reader will readily see the resemblance between "Edom" and "Adam"—which was specially close when the Hebrew was written without the vowels. Yet James gives the general sense with entire accuracy, viz., that God had of set purpose called the Gentiles within the pale of his church, to inherit in it among his people.

13. Behold, the days come, saith the LORD, that the ploughman shall overtake the reaper, and the treader of grapes him that soweth seed; and the mountains shall drop sweet wine, and all the hills shall melt.

14. And I will bring again the captivity of my people of Israel, and they shall build the waste cities, and inhabit *them;* and they shall plant vineyards, and drink the wine thereof; they shall also make gardens, and eat the fruit of them.

15. And I will plant them upon their land, and they shall no more be pulled up out of their land which I have given them, saith the LORD thy God.

Here let us first note the sense of particular words and phrases. ——"Days come," looks forward to the remote and indefinite future. The manner of calling attention to the matters revealed in these last three verses, "*Behold,*" coupled with the change from "in that day" (v. 11), to "days come" (v. 13), imply that these latter events lie onward in the future, beyond those recorded (vs. 11, 12).——"The ploughman overtaking the reaper," &c., implies great prosperity and abundance. The reaper will have so much to do, and the ploughman withal is so eager to get in readiness a large field, that he treads on the heels of the reaper. The mountains terraced and cultivated in grapes to their summits shall seem to distil new wine. It flows down their declivities as if the mountains themselves were becoming liquid. To "bring again their captivity" always implies good and not evil—promised blessings and not threatened calamities. It is also used in a broader and more general sense than that of bringing captives home to their own land. How this came to pass may be seen in the history of the Hebrews as related to Canaan. In all those ages of promise, prior to their possession of Canaan under Joshua, "to inherit the land," to possess the land of promise, was the consummation of hope, the thing of most earnest desire. "The meek shall inherit the land," shows the significance of this phraseology.——In later times, after captivity in foreign lands had been their sad experience, the phrases "bring again their captivity," and "plant them again in their own land," superseded the former phrase in a like sense of general prosperity. Cases that both illustrate and prove this figurative use of the phrase "to bring or turn again the captivity," may be seen (Job 42 : 10), "And the Lord turned the captivity of Job," but Job had been in no captivity in the literal sense. The Lord changed his state by a change analogous to that from bondage to freedom. Also Ezek. 16 : 53, 55, "When I shall bring again the captivity of Sodom and her daughters," &c., but the trouble with Sodom was not a real *captivity*. This term is used here figuratively for another calamity worse than that. The precise sense of the phrase is given in a clause explanatory (v. 55), "When thy sister Sodom and her daughters shall return to their former estate." These cases will suffice to establish the usage which I have assumed.——Let us beware lest we stop in the letter and miss the spirit of this prophecy. So doing, we shall find in it only a Mohammedan paradise, and God surely intended something far richer and better than that. We shall greatly err if in reading this passage we think only of great harvests, hills running down with wine, and the people of Israel restored again and forevermore to Palestine. The construction we are compelled to put on the two verses next preceding forbids this. The sense given to those verses by the Apostle James, viz., the calling of the Gentiles into the gospel faith, forbids it. It would be a sad falling off if, borne along by the whole current of thought in this ninth chapter, and especially in verses 11, 12, we should begin to rejoice in the glory of gospel salvation, spreading widely over all the Gentile world, and then, in these last three verses, should reach the climax by dropping down to Judaism, and find none but sensual ideas, luxurious harvests, plenty of good wine, and the land of Palestine held forever by the Jews. The current strain of all the gospel prophecies forbids this construction. Amos himself would rebuke us! He would say, How could you forget that, being myself a husbandman from my youth, I ought to be allowed to draw my figures and illustrations from things with which I had been all my life familiar? Had you not noticed this same thing throughout my book? And could you not learn to distinguish between the drapery and the person clothed in it—between the costume and the inward reality?——Yes, thou lovely, venerable prophet of the Lord, we will not torture thy figures of speech into sensualities that never came into thy mind! We will try to see in this rich imagery of nature the glorious and munificent things of gospel times. We will not impute to thee the inconsistency of denouncing the woes of God on men "at ease in Zion," because they "drink wine in bowls" (6: 6), and then representing the saints of God as finding their highest spiritual life and glory in vineyards, grapes, and wine!

I cannot close this book of Amos without a passing tribute to his clear, forcible, and earnest style; to the richness of his figures, drawn chiefly from the familiar but often sublimely grand fields of nature, and from the scenes of husbandry; to the sublime and solemn grandeur with which he recites the significant names of Jehovah, God of hosts; and not least, to his warm sympathy with the wronged and outraged poor, and to his intense abhorrence of the luxury, pride, ostentation, and especially the *oppression* which manifestly was the crowning and damning sin of the leading men in the kingdom of Israel. We shall need to go far to find keener invectives against these Heaven-provoking sins, or a more earnest wielding of Jehovah's thunders against the oppression of the poor, the perversions of justice, and the enslaving of men.——Well, indeed, had it been, if during the past hundred years, our American churches had drank deeply of the spirit of Amos, the herdman-prophet, and had given heed to the burning words against oppression which God spake through his lips! Then had our American Christianity never stricken hands with the oppressor! American systematized oppression would have been throttled in its cradle, and the woes of the great war of rebellion under which the nation has bled and groaned need never have been!——It may be noted that Amos, like Hosea and Joel, closes with an outlook from the lofty heights of the mount of Vision into that goodly land of Promise, yet mostly future, when "the earth shall be full of the knowledge of the Lord," when his kingdom and people shall possess the world, and all its tribes and kingdoms shall become the kingdom of our Lord and of his Christ that he may reign forever and ever.

OBADIAH.

INTRODUCTION.

Of the author of this shortest book in the Bible, we have the briefest possible account. His name was Obadiah—there the record ends. The book contains historical (not prophetic) allusions to the capture and destruction of Jerusalem by the Chaldeans and the consequent captivity, and therefore must have been written subsequent to that event, yet how long after cannot be certainly determined by any evidence external or internal. The tone of the passage (vs. 11–14) implies that those events connected with the fall of Jerusalem were then recent.——The name, Obadiah, meaning "servant of the Lord," occurs frequently in the Hebrew genealogies, and several times in Bible history. The author of this book was not the Obadiah who stood up so nobly for the Lord under that wicked Ahab (1 Kings 18 : 3, 4, 7, 16), nor that other Obadiah who was employed by Jehoshaphat to teach religious duty (2 Chron. 17 : 7).——We must be content to know but little of his personal history.

His subject is one—a prophecy concerning Edom. The posterity of Esau, otherwise called Edom, founded this kingdom at a very early period. They manifestly had their land under cultivation before the Hebrews entered Canaan. They appear repeatedly in the scenes of Jewish history during the reign of David, and more especially after the revolt. The early antipathy which brought Esau out with four hundred armed men to intercept Jacob on his return from Padanaram to Canaan, though sometimes kept down under the pressure of conscious inability to do his brother harm, yet seems never to have been fully suppressed. As said by Amos (1:11), "he cast off all pity, and his anger did tear perpetually, and he nursed his wrath forever." This enduring hatred seized its opportunity when Jerusalem fell before the Chaldean power, and broke forth, not only in most unfraternal words, but in most cruel deeds. This was the special occasion of the prophecy here recorded. ——Other prophets have predicted the fall of Edom, some of earlier date, *e. g.*, Isaiah and Joel, and some contemporary, or of later date, *e. g.*, Jeremiah, Ezekiel, Malachi, and the writer of Psalm 137. (See Isaiah 21:11; and 34: and Joel 3:19, and Jeremiah 49:7–22 (closely parallel), and Ezek. 25:12–14, and Mal. 1:3, 4.)

CHAPTER I.

1. THE vision of Obadiah. Thus saith the Lord GOD concerning Edom; We have heard a rumor from the LORD, and an ambassador is sent among the heathen, Arise ye, and let us rise up against her in battle.

The Lord commissions his servant Obadiah to proclaim, We have heard from the Lord a message, *i. e.*, a thing to be announced (not a "rumor" in the sense of an uncertain, flying report), to the effect that his providential agencies have summoned the heathen forth, calling on them to arise and come up for battle against Edom.

2. Behold, I have made thee small among the heathen: thou art greatly despised.

3. The pride of thine heart hath deceived thee, thou that dwellest in the clefts of the rock, whose habitation *is* high; that saith in his heart, Who shall bring me down to the ground?

4. Though thou exalt *thyself* as the eagle, and though thou set thy nest among the stars, thence will I bring thee down, saith the LORD.

The great men of Edom had been proud (we may suppose) of the high antiquity of their nation; of their great wealth, their country having been for ages the thoroughfare of commerce between Egypt and North Africa on their southwest, and the rich countries of Mesopotamia and India on the east and northeast; of their eminent progress in the arts, of which the ruins yet remaining are ample proof; and of their early knowledge of letters, of which the Book of Job (native to this country) is good testimony. Sir Isaac Newton came to the conclusion that Edom was the nursery of the arts and sciences for all the world, and that even the Egyptians received from them their earliest knowledge of astronomy and of its use in navigation. Men of the world think and speak of pride on such grounds as honest and honorable; but, however this may be, it surely cannot atone for moral obliquities, for national animosity, jealousy, revenge, and perpetual hatred. And when, as in this case, national pride deceives a people so greatly as to make them think they have nothing to fear from the just judgments of God, the mistake is fearful. This was the sin and ruin of ancient Edom.

The phrase "Thou that dwellest in the clefts of the rock, whose habitation is high," has in modern times received a very striking confirmation from the personal visits and examination made by a large number of travellers—Burckhardt among the earliest; Dr. Edward Robinson among the most accurate and reliable. They and others have found on the site of ancient Petra a vast amount of ruins of the homes of both the living and the dead, especially along the face of an immense gorge or chasm, where the perpendicular rock, several hundred feet in height, was improved for temples, sepulchres, and private residences, chiselled from the rock itself. The massive grandeur of these ruins aids us to appreciate the description, "Thou that dwellest in the clefts of the rock, whose habitation is high." It also accounts for the pride and vain confidence felt by the men of Edom in the military strength of their fastnesses, and evinces the pertinence of the divine word, "Though thou lift thyself high as the eagle, and set thy nest among the stars, thence will I bring thee down." How vain it must ever be for even the loftiest and mightiest of men to defy the Almighty, or count themselves above the reach of his retributions!

5. If thieves came to thee, if robbers by night (how art thou cut off!) would they not have stolen till they had enough? if the grape-gatherers came to thee, would they not leave *some* grapes?

6. How are *the things* of Esau searched out! *how* are his hidden things sought up!

These supposed cases—the thieves, the night-robbers, and the grape-gatherers—all have the same object, viz., to show that the spoiling of Esau would be unsparing. The interjected exclamation —"How art thou cut off!"—implies that the desolation of Esau would be more dire than that wrought by thieves and night-robbers. The latter, compelled by fear to make short work, are wont to seize what comes first to hand till they have enough for present want, or, as the case may be, all they can carry away; and so may leave some valuables behind. Grape-gatherers leave gleanings. But Esau's wealth will be carefully searched out. Those who shall come to spoil him will find all his hidden stores.——The exclamation in v. 6 corresponds in form of statement precisely to that thrown into the middle of v. 5—"How art thou cut off!" The prophet's eye and heart were full of the sad fate of so much wealth, beauty, and glory, doomed to utter desolation.

7. All the men of thy confederacy have brought thee *even* to the border: the men that were at peace with thee have deceived thee, *and* prevailed against thee; *they that eat* thy bread have laid a wound under thee: *there is* none understanding in him.

When the Lord's time comes to cast a mighty nation down, he causes all their friends to turn against them. So this verse affirms of the kingdom of Edom. First, all his allies ("men of thy confederacy"), bound by treaty to stand or fall with him, cast him out of their country, chasing him even to their border, as one turns a villain out of his doors. Next, those who were on terms of peace and friendship turn to deceive him, and prevail against him; and last, even his dependents, who ate at his table, put a snare under his feet to entrap him. Snare (not "wound") is the sense of the original word used here.——Finally, this utter failure of all his reliances suggests the remark, "There is no understanding in him." He should not have trusted such helpers, and rejected the Almighty God!

8. Shall I not in that day, saith the LORD, even destroy the wise *men* out of Edom, and understanding out of the mount of Esau?

The closing thought of the verse preceding suggests these questions. Edom was celebrated for her wise men, and was proud of them. Would not the Lord in that day destroy those great men, and cause wisdom to cease from the mount of Esau?

9. And thy mighty *men*, O Teman, shall be dismayed, to the end that every one of the mount of Esau may be cut off by slaughter.

Her warriors also should be smitten with panic, in order that the slaughter of the people might be complete.——"Teman" was the name of a city and region in the eastern part of Idumea. Perhaps it was celebrated for its courage and prowess in war.

10. For *thy* violence against thy brother Jacob, shame shall come over thee, and thou shalt be cut off for ever.

The discourse turns here from the destruction of Edom to those sins which were its special cause. These sins were their violence and outrages against the posterity of Jacob, their brother. For this they should be ashamed and confounded; and for this the nation should ultimately be cut off forever. These two inflictions would be distinct, and might be somewhat widely separated in time. The form of the prophetic statement admits this distinction; the facts of history fulfilled it. The shameful defeat came from the hand of Nebuchadnezzar; the final overthrow was postponed into the early ages of the Christian era.

11. In the day that thou stoodest on the other side, in the day that the strangers carried away captive his forces, and foreigners entered into his gates, and cast lots upon Jerusalem, even thou *wast* as one of them.

12. But thou shouldest not have looked on the day of thy brother in the day that he became a stranger; neither shouldest thou have rejoiced over the children of Judah in the day of their destruction; neither shouldest thou have spoken proudly in the day of distress.

13. Thou shouldest not have entered into the gate of my people in the day of their calamity; yea, thou shouldest not have looked on their affliction in the day of their calamity, nor have laid *hands* on their substance in the day of their calamity;

14. Neither shouldest thou have stood in the crossway, to cut off those of his that did escape; neither shouldest thou have delivered up those of his that did remain in the day of distress.

These specifications of what Esau had done in the line of violence and wrong toward his brother Jacob are put in the form of pointed rebuke, after the fact.——In the day when the Chaldeans took his (Jacob's) armed men captive, entered his gates, and cast lots upon whatever was fair and precious in the holy city, thou wast hostile and violent as they.——"Thou stoodest on the other side" means more than simply standing aloof and distant; it implies the attitude of an adversary. The original words have this sense (2 Sam. 18:13): "Thou wouldest have set thyself against them."——"Thou wast as one of them" might possibly, if taken by itself, mean only that the men of Edom sympathized fully with the Chaldeans and against the Jews; but it more naturally implies that they participated heartily in the assault and pillage of the hated city. V. 14 certainly means all this. "Thou shouldest not have looked on (exultingly) in the day when he was treated as an alien." V. 12 shows that they were present in the sack and ruin of the city, seizing the opportunity to rush within those gates and lay hands on her spoil.——The middle clause of this verse (12) is made specially emphatic—"Thou shouldest not," of all the nations, "*thou* shouldest not have been looking on, to gloat thine envious and cruel eye with the sight of their calamities." V. 14 represents that they most cruelly stood in the road-crossings to waylay the fleeing Jews, to cut off their escape, and to deliver them up as captives to their cruel captors. They should have done none of these things. God—the righteous God of nations—is now holding them to a strict and stern responsibility for those cruel violations of fraternal sympathy which should have bound them to the posterity of their father's brother.——The writer of Ps. 137 felt the spirit of this just retribution—"Remember, O Lord, the children of Edom in the day of avenging Jerusalem, who said: Rase it, rase it, even to the foundation thereof" (v. 7).

15. For the day of the LORD *is* near upon all the heathen: as thou hast done, it shall be done unto thee: thy reward shall return upon thine own head.

"The day of the Lord" is his time for retribution, declared here to be "near upon all the heathen." It came soon by the hand of Nebuchadnezzar. "As thou" (Edom) "hast done to Jerusalem, so shall it be done unto thee; thy reward" (the sort of treatment thou hast shown to others) "shall come back upon thine own head."

16. For as ye have drunk upon my holy mountain, *so* shall all the heathen drink continually, yea, they shall drink, and they shall swallow down, and they shall be as though they had not been.

These allusions to drinking are explained by the usage of the prophets. When they bore predictions of dire calamity, they were said to carry a cup filled with a mixture which represented the wrath and vengeance of the Almighty. The ground passage is Ps. 75 : 7, 8: "But God is the judge; he putteth down one, and setteth up another; for in the hand of the Lord there is a cup, and the wine is red; it is full of mixture: but the dregs thereof—all the wicked of the earth shall wring them out and drink them." To Jerusalem Isaiah said (51 : 17): "Stand up, thou who hast drunk at the hand of the Lord the cup of his fury." In Jer. 25 : 15-33, this figure is carried out fully: "Take the wine-cup of this fury at mine hand, and cause all the nations to whom I send thee to drink it." So also Jer. 49 : 12, in a passage very closely parallel to this of Obadiah. ——With this view of the sense of this figure, it seems necessary to refer the first clause—"ye who have drunk on my holy mountain"—to the Jews themselves. They had taken their turn in drinking from this cup of retributive justice; now all the heathen—Edom among them—must follow.——These guilty heathen nations must drink copiously, for the word rendered "swallow down" is strong—shall guzzle down, as men who love it, and suck out the very dregs with keenest relish. And this shall be the end of them—their cup of national annihilation.

17. But upon mount Zion shall be deliverance, and

there thall be holiness; and the house of Jacob shall possess their possessions.

Over against the final fate of those oppressive and wicked nations, Mount Zion stands in the strongest contrast. Turning now to promises for the people of God, the prophet portrays the victory given to Zion's side. Mount Zion shall be delivered, and, best of all, "shall become *holy*." This will secure her forever against such fearful calamities, for these come only as needful discipline to cleanse her from her sins. That "the house of Jacob shall possess their possessions" will either mean that they repossess their former land, or that they gain possession of the country of the heathen—one or the other, according as the pronoun "*their*" is reflexive, meaning their own, or refers to heathen nations. The former is most probable. The latter fact is taught specially in vs. 19, 20.

18. And the house of Jacob shall be a fire, and the house of Joseph a flame, and the house of Esau for stubble, and they shall kindle in them, and devour them; and there shall not be *any* remaining of the house of Esau; for the LORD hath spoken *it*.

Fire is one of the oriental images for war and its devastations. Thus, Num. 21:28: "For a fire is gone out of Heshbon, a flame from the city of Sihon; it hath consumed Ar of Moab," &c. Isaiah (10:17), setting forth how God's consuming wrath fell on the Assyrian host, says, "The light of Israel shall be for a fire, and his Holy One for a flame, and it shall burn and devour his thorns and briers in one day." So here, the house of Jacob shall be a fire, &c., and Esau stubble. This must imply that Jacob should be the executioner of the Lord's vengeance upon Esau. A signal fulfilment of this prophecy took place under John Hyrcanus, B. C. 125.

19. And *they of* the south shall possess the mount of Esau; and *they of* the plain the Philistines: and they shall possess the fields of Ephraim, and the fields of Samaria: and Benjamin *shall possess* Gilead.

The people of the southern part of Palestine should possess the mount of Esau, that being contiguous to their homes. They of the plain country, the southwest portion of Palestine, should have the country of the Philistines, adjacent to them, &c.

20. And the captivity of this host of the children of Israel *shall possess* that of the Canaanites, *even* unto Zarephath; and the captivity of Jerusalem, which *is* in Sepharad, shall possess the cities of the south.

"The captives of this host" are the captives returning from Babylon. They shall possess the country long held by the Canaanites, even to Zarephath, a city near Zidon (see 1 Kings 17 : 9), and called "Sarepta," Luke 4: 26.——The geography of "Sepharad" is not fully settled. It was a place whither some captives from Jerusalem were sent by the Chaldeans. Recent critics locate it in Western Asia, near the Bosphorus.

21. And saviours shall come up on mount Zion to judge the mount of Esau; and the kingdom shall be the LORD'S.

"Saviours" must be used here in the sense in which God raised up saviours to deliver the people in the days of the Judges that succeeded Joshua. The passage teaches that the princes reigning on Mount Zion shall rule over Mount Esau: "the elder shall serve the younger," or rather, in the much broader sense, the people who *stand with God* shall bear sway over all the realms and peoples of the earth. The wicked shall no more bear rule: "the kingdom is the Lord's and he is Governor among the nations." This is the great truth in which the whole Book of Obadiah culminates– a glorious truth indeed!

JONAH.

INTRODUCTION.

THIS book, more than any other in the Bible, has been assailed with ridicule by infidels, and tortured from its simplicity by neological critics. Whereas its air is that of a simple narrative of facts, immense efforts have been made to show that its statements are not fact, but fiction. Some of these critics would make it a vision; some an allegory; some a parable; others a tale of ancient tradition, believed by people of weak minds, perhaps, but by such only, and never reliable.——It would scarcely pay to follow out these critical fancies in detail. Let it suffice that the narrative bears not the least trace of being a vision, or an allegory, or a parable, or a tale of old-time tradition. From beginning to end it is simple, straightforward, nobly honest and self-condemning, especially considered as written by Jonah of himself; in short, in every respect bearing the best internal evidence of truth.——Then further, the book has worthy moral objects; *e. g.*, to set forth the peril of fleeing from the path of duty, however rough or even dangerous that path may be; also, the ways of God's discipline to bring his wandering servants back, and the tenderness of his pity and forgiving love toward them despite of their sins; and yet further, the principles on which God deals with nations, even the heathen, whether in judgment when they sin, or in sparing mercy when they repent. Such objects as these are great and good enough to entitle the book of Jonah to a place in the sacred canon; or we might go farther back and say, sufficiently important to justify God in making those arrangements of his providence which constitute *his part* in these scenes of Jonah's history.——But more than all, Jonah is distinctly recognized, in both the Old Testament and the New, as an historical and not a fictitious person. In Old Testament history, 2 Kings 14: 25 distinctly refers to this Jonah, the son of Amittai, in these words: "He (Jeroboam II.) restored the coast of Israel from the entering of Hamath unto the sea of the plain, according to the word of the Lord God of Israel, which he spake by the hand of his servant Jonah, the son of Amittai, who was of Gath-Hepher." This city was assigned to the tribe of Zebulon (Josh. 19:13), so that Jonah's residence was within the kingdom of the ten tribes. He is thus located, precisely as to *place*, and proximately as to *time*, not later than the early part of the reign of Jeroboam II. (reigned B. C. 825–784).——In the New Testament, the proof to the point that Jonah was a real and not a fictitious character, is complete. (See Matt. 12: 39–41, and 16: 4.) The Lord Jesus most distinctly refers to Jonah as the subject of a sign—*i. e.*, of a miracle—as having been three days and three nights in the whale's belly, and as having preached to the people of Nineveh, under which preaching they repented; and finally, he definitely compares himself with Jonah: "Behold, a greater than Jonah is here."——Now, if, despite of these testimonies to the contrary, men insist that Jonah is to be accounted a fictitious character, they may say the same with equal reason of the queen of Sheba and of the wise Solomon. Will it be claimed that the Lord Jesus did not *know* whether the history of Jonah were truth or fiction? or that, knowing it to be fiction, he did not care how strongly his allusions to it implied its truth and misled the people? Neither of these positions will ever be taken by those who intelligently accept and honor Jesus Christ as a teacher sent from God, and the very impersonation of truth.

Yet further, the apocryphal Book of Tobit (14: 4, 8) recognizes Jonah as an historical and not a fictitious character, a fact which at least testifies to current Jewish opinion at its date. Josephus is yet another witness to the same point (Ant. 9: 10, 12).

The case of Jonah suggests that the Hebrew prophets, though brought into very near relations to God, were yet only human—men of like passions with the race at large, and subject to the temptations incident to human frailties. His course in fleeing to Tarshish and his spirit while at Nineveh, are at once surprising and painful. In view of the fact that he was one of the earliest of the Hebrew prophets whose writings have come down to us, it is at least supposable that the Lord intended this example to be a lesson of special admonition to all subsequent prophets. Let us hope that it was blessed to them as a warning against being unfaithful to their mission, and against assuming to dictate or question the policy of the Most High God.

CHAPTER I.

JONAH is commissioned to go to Nineveh and forewarn them of their destruction (vs. 1, 2). He attempts to flee away to Spain instead (v. 3); a tempest from the Lord arrests the ship (vs. 4–11); he is thrown overboard and caught up by a great fish (vs. 11–17).

1. Now the word of the LORD came unto Jonah the son of Amittai, saying,

2. Arise, go to Nineveh, that great city, and cry against it; for their wickedness is come up before me.

Nineveh, on the eastern bank of the Tigris, opposite the site of the modern Mosul, for many ages past in ruins, has been discovered and its ruins somewhat thoroughly explored in the present century. It was the capital of ancient Assyria, one of the oldest cities since the flood (Gen. 10: 11, 12), long celebrated for its size, wealth, and magnificence. At this time its wickedness had come up before God, and he mercifully sent to them a prophet from Israel to forewarn them of impending ruin and exhort them to repent.——The Hebrew prophets were somewhat frequently commissioned to utter predictions of judgment on Gentile nations, but seem to have been very rarely sent in person to bear these predictions to those nations. In Jer. 27 may be seen a proximate case. The prophet was directed to send his prophetic message by the hand of foreign ambassadors present at the Jewish capital.

3. But Jonah rose up to flee unto Tarshish from the presence of the LORD, and went down to Joppa; and he found a ship going to Tarshish: so he paid the fare thereof, and went down into it, to go with them unto Tarshish from the presence of the LORD.

It is now quite settled among critics that "Tarshish" was the city Tartessus, in Spain, with which the Phœnicians kept up an active trade by sea. Jonah thought to escape the responsibility of his unwelcome commission to Nineveh by taking ship at once to Tarshish. The narrative is particular to state repeatedly that this was "fleeing from the presence of the Lord"—as if there would be no God in Tarshish to make him trouble! or at least, as if God could not object to his laying down his prophetic office, and going abroad to foreign lands.——We naturally ask—What could have been his motive and what his temptation to a course so wicked and so foolish? Fear for his personal safety is the cause we most naturally think of, yet of this it might well be asked—Did not he know that if the Lord sent him into danger, he could protect him through it? and that it is always safe for a child of God to go where he knows his Father sends him?——Another motive, even less worthy than this of fear, is indicated by his own strange expostulation with God (4:1, 2), because He retracted his threat to destroy Nineveh and turned from punishment to pardon. This change on the part of God "displeased Jonah exceedingly, and he was very angry!" (Alas for poor human nature!) "And he prayed unto the Lord and said—I pray thee, O Lord, was not this my saying when I was yet in my country? Therefore I fled before to Tarshish; for I knew that thou art a gracious God and merciful, slow to anger, and of great kindness, and repentest thee of the evil."——Ah, indeed! then Jonah did not like to go to Nineveh, through fear that they would repent, and then the Lord would forgive them and not destroy the city, as he was about to proclaim. And was he concerned lest his reputation should suffer, and he be thought a false prophet? Alas, again we must say, for the follies and sins of man!——In some points of view it seems wonderful that God should employ such a man at all as a prophet—only that in the sins of Jonah many a man might see his own, if he would.——The Lord has great moral lessons to teach us from these sins of Jonah. Let none of us be too blind to see them, nor too much in love with sin to accept the rebuke they read to us, and repent.

4. But the LORD sent out a great wind into the sea, and there was a mighty tempest in the sea, so that the ship was like to be broken.

The verb rendered "sent out" is strikingly expressive. He hurled down upon the sea a great wind. The same word is used in the next verse for *casting out* the wares from the ship. So easily does God cast forth his tempest blasts and lash the sea into fury.

5. Then the mariners were afraid, and cried every man unto his god, and cast forth the wares that *were* in the ship into the sea, to lighten *it* of them. But Jonah was gone down into the sides of the ship; and he lay, and was fast asleep.

Those heathen men—for such they doubtless were—had each his god. In his danger each of those men prayed to the god he was wont to worship. Who does not pray in the hour of peril? Certainly the heathen are usually no exception. Probably there are no people on earth further removed from confidence in some superhuman power able to befriend and save, than the irreligious and profane class in Christian lands.

Some have thought that the statement respecting Jonah as fast asleep under such circumstances, is violently improbable.——But who knows how far he had walked during the previous day to reach Joppa, or how much he may have suffered in his mind throughout his journey, and for days previous? The ways of sin are not wont to be ways of pleasantness, nor her paths those of peace.

6. So the shipmaster came to him, and said unto him, What meanest thou, O sleeper? arise, call upon thy God, if so be that God will think upon us, that we perish not.

This rousing call must have stung the sleeper, especially when, having fully awakened, he saw that God had met him in his guilty way, and had brought such peril upon others for his sake.——It is noticeable that the word God in the last clause has the article: "It may be that *the* great and the true God will think upon us," &c. Had he not some just conception of the one only true God?

7. And they said every one to his fellow, Come, and let us cast lots, that we may know for whose cause this evil *is* upon us. So they cast lots, and the lot fell upon Jonah.

The "lot" was practically an appeal to God to decide a pending question by his providence. In this case the Lord took the disposal of the lot, according to Prov. 16: 33: "The lot is cast into the lap; but the whole disposing thereof is of the Lord." It put the finger of God upon Jonah.

8. Then said they unto him, Tell us, we pray thee, for whose cause this evil *is* upon us; What *is* thine occupation? and whence comest thou? what *is* thy country? and of what people *art* thou?

9. And he said unto them, I *am* an Hebrew; and I fear the LORD, the God of heaven, which hath made the sea and the dry *land*.

10. Then were the men exceedingly afraid, and said unto him, Why hast thou done this? For the men knew that he fled from the presence of the LORD, because he had told them.

The alarm felt by those sailors was greatly increased when Jonah told them that the God whom he feared and worshipped was that great God of heaven who made the sea and the dry land. They could not help rebuking him. How couldest thou offend *such a God?* See what comes of it! Didst thou think to escape the wrath and the reach of so great a God?

11. Then said they unto him, What shall we do unto thee, that the sea may be calm unto us? for the sea wrought and was tempestuous.

They see plainly that they must do something with Jonah. He is the Achan in their camp. So they frankly ask him what they shall do with him.——The last clause manifestly means that the sea was becoming more and more tempestuous.

12. And he said unto them, Take me up, and cast me forth into the sea; so shall the sea be calm unto you: for I know that for my sake this great tempest *is* upon you.

Here is one redeeming quality in the character of Jonah. It is pleasant to see a man, when found in sin, so frank, so honest, so consciously sensible of his fault, and so ready to suffer the whole fruit of his own misdoings, and relieve his companions.

13. Nevertheless the men rowed hard to bring *it* to the land; but they could not: for the sea wrought, and was tempestuous against them.

The spirit which Jonah manifested awakened the sympathy of the captain and crew in his behalf, and again they dug into the sea with their oars (so the Hebrew means), to bring their ship to land; but all in vain. The sea only became the more furious.

14. Wherefore they cried unto the LORD, and said, We beseech thee, O LORD, we beseech thee, let us not perish for this man's life, and lay not upon us innocent blood: for thou, O LORD, hast done as it pleased thee.

It was a solemn thing to take this human life; and like men who appreciate this, they once more implore the mercy of God, and beseech him to note the necessity that lies upon them, which they refer distinctly to his manifest hand in providence, so that they may not be held guilty of innocent blood.

15. So they took up Jonah, and cast him forth into the sea: and the sea ceased from her raging.

16. Then the men feared the LORD exceedingly, and offered a sacrifice unto the LORD, and made vows.

17. Now the LORD had prepared a great fish to swallow up Jonah. And Jonah was in the belly of the fish three days and three nights.

The original word rendered "prepared" means appointed, assigned, *i. e.*, to this service. This fish was providentially ready. ——The fact here stated is the great stone of stumbling and rock of offence to that class of critics who deny the existence of miracles.

We need have no special sympathy with their perplexities or their stumbling; for there can be no good reason for rejecting miracles. Besides, in this case, our divine Lord distinctly recognizes the presence of miracles by saying that Jonah was "a *sign*," *i. e.*, a man in whom miracles were manifested.——It is not necessarily a miracle that a great fish should swallow a man. There are several varieties that are capable of swallowing a man whole, for they have done it. But that a man should live three days and three nights, or, indeed, one hour, in the belly of a fish, must be a miracle.

CHAPTER II.

In this short chapter, Jonah has put on record the prayers he poured out unto God from his heart of anguish while imprisoned three days in the stomach of a sea-monster.

1. Then Jonah prayed unto the Lord his God out
of the fish's belly,
2. And said, I cried by reason of mine affliction unto
the Lord, and he heard me; out of the belly of hell cried
I, *and* thou heardest my voice.

The phrase—"out of the belly of hell"—should not carry our minds to the place of final torment for the wicked, but to the pit or grave, where the bodies of men are laid at death. He felt like one buried alive—his consciousness still active and keen as ever, but himself shut up in darkness; imprisoned, apparently past hope of ever seeing the light of this fair world again, save as he knew and felt that his God might mercifully restore him.——The Hebrew word used here (Sheol) often has this sense—the grave.

3. For thou hast cast me into the deep, in the midst
of the seas; and the floods compassed me about: all thy
billows and thy waves passed over me.

Many of the expressions in this prayer of Jonah occur in the Psalms, with only slight variations, if any. The reader may find it interesting to compare v. 2 with Ps. 120:1; v. 3 with 42:7; v. 4 with 31:22; v. 5 with 69:1; v. 7 with 142:3; v. 8 with 31:6; and v. 9 with 3:8. This comparison goes far to establish two interesting facts: (1.) That these psalms were extant in Jonah's time; (2.) That he had read them often, had become familiar with their phraseology, especially that which was used in prayer, and was therefore accustomed to use their language in his own devotions. He did as Christians now do who are familiar with the devotional portions of God's word—use those forms of expression in their daily and hourly intercessions before God.

4. Then I said, I am cast out of thy sight; yet I will look again toward thy holy temple.

It cannot surprise us that Jonah both said and felt, "I am cast out of thy sight." When his fellow-passengers on shipboard took him up and cast him overboard, it must have seemed to him that God was casting him forth out of his sight forever.——But Jonah had once known the loving-kindness of his God. Hence, the thought of possible mercy came now to his relief, and he said, "Yet I will look once more toward thy holy temple." Did he not appreciate in that hour how much the mercy of God is worth to a soul consciously lost?

5. The waters compassed me about, *even* to the soul: the depth closed me round about, the weeds were wrapped about my head.

He seemed to himself to lie on the bottom of tne sea—its weeds wrapped as his winding-sheet about him.

6. I went down to the bottoms of the mountains; the earth with her bars *was* about me for ever: yet hast thou brought up my life from corruption, O LORD my God.

The word "bars," in the clause "the earth with her bars was about me forever," Gesenius supposes to refer to the bars of Sheol—the under world—as closed now upon him forever. But the prominent position of the word "*earth*" in the sentence favors another construction, viz., that the earth, in the sense of land as opposed to sea, had cast him out, and closed its bars upon him, so that he could not hope ever to see its light and beauty again. If he had meant the bars of Sheol, he might readily have said so in unambiguous terms.——Yet, notwithstanding he was so imprisoned in the depths of the sea, he lifts up his grateful eye and his voice of acknowledgment to God above—"Thou hast brought up my life from the pit, O Lord my God.

7. When my soul fainted within me I remembered the LORD: and my prayer came in unto thee, into thine holy temple.

8. They that observe lying vanities, forsake their own mercy.

"They that observe lying vanities" are the worshippers of idol gods which are always false and vain. They do indeed "*forsake*" in the sense of rejecting and losing their own mercies. They miserably forego the blessedness that is in store for them in the true God, if only they will seek it there. So of all sinners who seek their good elsewhere than in the living God. They "forsake their own mercies."

9. But I will sacrifice unto thee with the voice of thanksgiving; I will pay *that* that I have vowed. Salvation *is* of the LORD.

Precisely what his vows were in his trouble he has not said. Doubtless he promised the Lord never again to try to flee from his presence to avoid an unwelcome duty.——He closes with this most expressive, glorious testimony: "*Salvation is of the Lord.*" He and he only can save in times of trouble.

10. And the LORD spake unto the fish, and it vomited out Jonah upon the dry *land.*

With infinite ease the Lord spake—only *spake* to the fish—and it vomited Jonah forth upon the dry land, doubtless on the shore of his native country, Palestine. It would seem that the ship had not gone far from its starting-point, Joppa, when the storm headed and beat it back.

CHAPTER III.

COMMANDED a second time, Jonah goes to Nineveh, and proclaims its approaching ruin. The people and their king humble themselves and repent before God; he turns from his purpose and spares the city.

1. And the word of the LORD came unto Jonah the second time, saying,

2. Arise, go unto Nineveh, that great city, and preach unto it the preaching that I bid thee.

Jonah was not only to *go* as commanded, but he is specially charged to preach to that great and proud city what God should bid him preach—a charge very probably significant of some apprehension lest Jonah might trip at this point, and certainly full of suggestions to all who are ever called of God to preach in his name. What have they to do to preach out of their own heart, to subserve some supposed interest of their own, other than that for which God sends them? They might as well flee to Tarshish, to escape the duty of preaching the ruin of the wicked, as to withhold God's threatenings, or preach something else and other than what God bids them, when they reach the Nineveh whither he sends them.

3. So Jonah arose, and went unto Nineveh, according to the word of the LORD. Now Nineveh was an exceeding great city of three days' journey.

Now Jonah obeys. He is a wiser and a better man for the discipline God has given him. "Before I was afflicted, I went astray;

but now have I kept thy word."——The phrase "an exceeding great city," stands in the Hebrew, "a city great *to God*," *i. e.*, great before him—great as to him, in his estimation. The Hebrews were accustomed to express their highest ideas of the superlative degree by using the name of God, *e. g.*, "mountains of God," &c. The sense of this passage may be somewhat more specific, representing the city as great in its relations to God, and not merely as very great apart from those relations.——In estimating an oriental day's journey, we must think of a caravan, heavy laden, many on foot, in a hot climate. Twenty miles would be the maximum. The statement "a city of three days' journey" should probably be applied to its circumference, and not to its diameter; because sixty miles in diameter would make the city incredibly large; because one of the most reliable ancient historians, Diodorus Siculus (II., 3) represents it as sixty miles in circuit; and because Jonah's beginning to enter it one day's journey (v. 4) may have been on a tortuous course, and not on a right line through its centre.

4. And Jonah began to enter into the city a day's journey, and he cried, and said, Yet forty days, and Nineveh shall be overthrown.

Jonah seems to have begun his preaching as he entered the city, and to have made his proclamation in the streets and public places, wherever he found people to hear him.

5. So the people of Nineveh believed God, and proclaimed a fast, and put on sackcloth, from the greatest of them even to the least of them.

The first step toward their repentance and salvation lay *in their believing God.* They accepted the message of this solitary stranger as one sent them by the Most High God.——To those who have noted the strange incredulity of millions under the light of the gospel, this fact appears surprising. We must suppose that Jonah spake as one who felt the solemnity of his mission and carried the air of a deeply honest man, and we must also suppose that he had their conscience on his side, and that the power of God was in and with his words.

6. For word came unto the king of Nineveh, and he arose from his throne, and he laid his robe from him, and covered *him* with sackcloth, and sat in ashes.

It does not appear that the king heard from Jonah's own lips; but the word came to him through his servants. They testified to the deep, pervading conviction of the people, and the king at once believed God as his people had done.——The name of this king is not given or known. This record of him may well rebuke many an ungodly monarch who plants his foot upon the very idea of "a higher law of God," and scornfully repels all authority higher than the mandates of his own will.

7. And he caused *it* to be proclaimed and published through Nineveh by decree of the king and his nobles, saying, Let neither man nor beast, herd nor flock, taste any thing: let them not feed, nor drink water:

8. But let man and beast be covered with sackcloth, and cry mightily unto God: yea, let them turn every one from his evil way, and from the violence that *is* in their hands.

It is specially noticeable that this proclamation calls not only for humiliation, fasting, and all the customary oriental tokens of sorrow and penitence, and for prayer also—crying mightily to God—but also specially enjoins on all men to "turn every one from his evil way and from the violence that is in their hands." So manifest is it that the law of justice and right is everywhere in the human mind, and that no heathen can be so blind as not to see it.——This also is a stinging rebuke to men, who, under far clearer light than theirs, yet labor to extinguish this light, or, in the more fit and expressive words of revelation, "put darkness for light and light for darkness."

9. Who can tell *if* God will turn and repent, and turn away from his fierce anger, that we perish not?

The form of this question suggests that the king of Nineveh did not *know* that God would always forgive a penitent people. He had heard less of God than we have. But he could say, "Who can tell (literally, "who knows") whether he will turn and repent, that we perish not?" On this assumed possibility he bases his call to humiliation, fasting, prayer, and reform.

10. And God saw their works, that they turned from their evil way; and God repented of the evil that he had said that he would do unto them; and he did *it* not.

"God saw," not their professions, nor merely their prayers, but "their works, that they turned from their evil way." Of course, when they changed their moral attitude before him, he changed his plan; turned from his purpose, and spared the city. So he always deals with the nations of the earth. Works meet for repentance will infallibly secure the reversal of threatened and impending doom. God's immutability is that of principle—not of plan and action. He immutably hates and punishes sin: hence, when a sinner becomes a penitent, God turns from threatened vengeance to free pardon.

CHAPTER IV.

This chapter is a mournful record of the moral frailties of a good man, and a glorious testimony to the pity, forbearance, and love of the blessed God. Jonah is greatly displeased because the Lord reversed the predicted fall of Nineveh: he waits outside the city to see what the Lord would do to it; he put up a rude tent for shelter from the heat; and the Lord brought up a gourd over him for his further relief; but a worm destroys the gourd. Jonah is again fretful, impatient, and angry, and the Lord very gently rebukes him, and gives reasons for sparing Nineveh.

1. But it displeased Jonah exceedingly, and he was very angry.

Some critics give the word rendered in this passage "displeased," the sense of *grieved*. It would be a great relief to my feelings of sorrow and shame, if the words and the circumstances would bear this construction. But as an interpreter of God's word, I must honor the truth rather than humor the feelings of the heart. So this passage must stand, "displeased," "angry exceedingly."

2. And he prayed unto the LORD, and said, I pray thee, O LORD, *was* not this my saying, when I was yet in my country? Therefore I fled before unto Tarshish: for I knew that thou *art* a gracious God, and merciful, slow to anger, and of great kindness, and repentest thee of the evil.

In the clause, "Therefore I fled before unto Tarshish," the sense is not that I fled *at a former time*, but that I fled *before* I came into such an emergency as this; I anticipated precisely such a result as this, and I fled *beforehand*, to avoid it. I did not wish to declare to them from the mouth of the Lord that the city should fall within forty days, and then have my words prove false.——To this construction, the reasons he assigns correspond: "For I knew that thou art a gracious God, and wouldest probably repent so as not to inflict this evil."——The last clause which groups his testimony to God's mercy is in the very words of Joel (2 : 13), and almost identical with Ex. 34 : 6, 7. Probably both passages were familiar to his mind. This boldness before God, while so grievously in the wrong withal, is appalling. It is awful that a sinner, plucked himself as a brand from the burning, and living on mere mercy alone, should object to God's showing the same mercy to his fellow-sinners. Why did he not rather rejoice and shout for joy when he saw the king and people of Nineveh on their faces before God—his warnings pressing them effectually to repentance, and the clouds of gathering vengeance swept away by the hand of love?

3. Therefore now, O LORD, take, I beseech thee, my life from me; for *it is* better for me to die than to live.

And now he is so much vexed and so angry, that he prays God to take his life! How could he think himself prepared to die in such a temper?

4. Then said the LORD, Doest thou well to be angry?

Some interpreters render this verse—"Then said the Lord, Art thou *much* vexed?"——There are two fatal objections to this rendering: (1.) The question so put is needless, since Jonah had shown his extreme anger but too plainly; and (2.) The original words cannot, legitimately, bear this construction. They mean—Does thine anger burn justly, rightly? Hast thou any good reason for such anger? Is it doing well, that thou shouldest let such passions rise?—A very gentle rebuke indeed, for sins so great and so provoking to God!

5. So Jonah went out of the city, and sat on the east side of the city, and there made him a booth, and sat under it in the shadow, till he might see what would become of the city.

"Till he might see what would become of the city"—as if this question were still in suspense. Can it be supposed that he thought—Possibly the Lord will hear my prayer and my expostulation, and will turn again to execute his first sentence of destruction?

6. And the LORD God prepared a gourd, and made *it* to come up over Jonah, that it might be a shadow over his head, to deliver him from his grief. So Jonah was exceeding glad of the gourd.

Still the Lord is mindful of the little comforts of his servant Jonah, and brings up over him very suddenly the shade of a rapidly growing plant, to "relieve his sufferings"—for so, more accurately, I render the words translated "to deliver him from his grief." This "gourd" is supposed to be the shrub known by the name of "Palma Christi."

7. But God prepared a worm when the morning rose the next day, and it smote the gourd that it withered.

8. And it came to pass, when the sun did arise, that God prepared a vehement east wind; and the sun beat upon the head of Jonah, that he fainted, and wished in himself to die, and said, *It is* better for me to die than to live.

This east wind, which the text reads "vehement," the margin, nearer the truth, has "silent." It was not a violent but a *sultry* wind, such as comes up from the desert on the southeast, like the breath of a great furnace. Jonah sinks under this great heat, and again wishes that he may die!

9. And God said to Jonah, Doest thou well to be angry for the gourd? And he said, I do well to be angry, *even* unto death.

The same question, in the same words as in v. 6, and with the same meaning, only that this respects his recent anger because of the withered gourd. Strange to say, Jonah justifies himself, and by implication, complains of God for suffering the worm to kill his gourd!

10. Then said the LORD, Thou hast had pity on the gourd, for the which thou hast not labored, neither madest it grow; which came up in a night, and perished in a night:

11. And should not I spare Nineveh, that great city, wherein are more than sixscore thousand persons that cannot discern between their right hand and their left hand, and *also* much cattle?

The verb which expresses Jonah's feeling for the gourd is the same which expresses the Lord's feeling for Ninevah, yet our translators render the former "hast *had pity*," and the latter "Should I not *spare?*" This is unfortunate. Pity for the gourd was not precisely the feeling of Jonah; he rather pitied *himself*. The gourd was not a sentient being—was not a sufferer. Yet Jonah deplored the loss of the gourd, and in this point of view the antithesis bears. The scope of the antithesis is essentially this:—Thou, Jonah, wast pained at the ruin of that gourd, though it had cost thee nothing, and thou hadst done nothing to interest thy heart in its welfare, and it is a short-lived thing at best: should not I, much more, deprecate the ruin of that great city, Nineveh, in which are more than one hundred and twenty thousand *human beings* (so the Hebrew specially denotes) who have not yet reached the period of moral accountability, and also many cattle who never reach it? These are all sentient beings; their happiness is a positive good to them, and therefore to me. They have not sinned against me; shall I not, therefore, spare the city if I can do so safely and wisely; spare it especially for the sake of the unsinning beings who are in it and who must be involved in its doom if it falls?——Thus it is vegetable life on the one hand against animal life on the other; a shrub against a babe or a lamb. For the shrub Jonah had done nothing to enlist his sympathies, but God implies that he has been watching over these infants and the lambs too, with a Father's tender care, and has good reason, therefore, to be deeply interested in their happiness.

The passage makes useful and rich revelations in respect to the feelings of the great God as to those fearful judgments which fall on the wicked, but which, as the world is, must involve some innocent beings—a part of them innocent as having not yet reached sufficient intelligence to make them morally accountable, and others as not having by nature any moral attributes. In the light of this passage it becomes altogether plain that God always takes into account the case of these sinless sufferers, and regards their presence as itself a plea for sparing the guilty. Of course he will give this plea all the consideration which the nature of the case will allow. He will punish, in forms that necessarily involve the unsinning in the general ruin, only when the ends of a moral system imperatively demand it. Who can estimate the amount of sparing mercy which the guilty of our world owe, in this life, to God's pity for infants and for the sentient but unsinning animal races?

MICAH.

INTRODUCTION.

MICAH, a name abbreviated from Micaiah, which signifies—Who is like God? was of Moresheth-gath, a city near Eleutheropolis, and not far from the country of the Philistines. His introductory verse states that he prophesied in the reigns of Jotham, Ahaz, and Hezekiah, kings of Judah. As the two former reigned each sixteen years and the latter twenty-nine, the entire duration of his ministry possible within this statement is sixty-one years. He was contemporary with Isaiah, who dates one vision "in the year that king Uzziah, the father of Jotham," "died" (6 : 1), and who was certainly in active service as a prophet under Hezekiah. Interesting collateral evidence that Micah prophesied in the reign of Hezekiah is found in Jer. 26 : 17–19. While some of the priests, princes, and false prophets demanded that Jeremiah should die for the alleged crime of speaking against the royal city, certain of the elders rose up to defend him with this plea: "Micah, the Morasthite, prophesied in the days of Hezekiah king of Judah, and spake to all the people of Judah (very publicly), saying: 'Thus saith the Lord of hosts, Zion shall be ploughed like a field, and Jerusalem shall become heaps, and the mountain of the house as the high places of the forest.' Did Hezekiah king of Judah and all Judah put him at all to death?" &c. See the original passage (Micah 3 : 12).

This Micah was not that noble Micaiah, son of Imlah, whom Ahab did not love because he told him too much unwelcome truth. (See 1 Kings 22). Ahab died one hundred and thirty-eight years before Jotham came to the throne.——Micah, the author, also spake bold and fearless words for God and righteousness. He spake concerning both Samaria and Jerusalem, mostly the latter, exposing and rebuking their sins. He predicted the destruction of both cities. He expatiated on the final glory of Zion, the real kingdom of the Messiah, in words of great beauty and power.

It is important to a full understanding of the work of these prophets that we think of their relations to the throne, stemming the tide of wickedness under such reigns as that of Ahaz; powerfully aiding the work of reform under such good kings as Hezekiah. Contemporary with these two kings were Micah, Hosea, Isaiah, and Nahum.

CHAPTER I.

The sin and doom of Samaria, embracing of course the kingdom of which it was the capital, constitute the leading themes in this chapter. Vs. 10–16 describe the effects of the Assyrian invasion as it swept along over a line of cities that lay in his path.

1. The word of the Lord that came to Micah the Morasthite in the days of Jotham, Ahaz, *and* Hezekiah, kings of Judah, which he saw concerning Samaria and Jerusalem.

2. Hear, all ye people; hearken, O earth, and all that therein is: and let the Lord God be witness against you, the Lord from his holy temple.

3. For behold, the Lord cometh forth out of his place, and will come down, and tread upon the high places of the earth.

4. And the mountains shall be molten under him, and the valleys shall be cleft, as wax before the fire, *and* as the waters *that are* poured down a steep place.

The prophet summons all the nations of the earth to hear. Practically, they are supposed to be convened for a great judgment scene, and the Almighty God comes down from his throne in heaven to appear as a witness against them for their sins. His coming down is portrayed with wonderful grandeur. "See! the Lord comes out of his place: he comes down: he treads on the high places of the earth," as if his glorious footsteps rested only on the mountain tops; and "the mountains are molten" under the touch of his feet; new valleys are cleft; the solid hills melt as wax before the fire, and flow as water leaping down a precipice. Such convulsions of nature betoken the majesty of nature's God!

5. For the transgression of Jacob *is* all this, and for the sins of the house of Israel. What *is* the transgression of Jacob? *is it* not Samaria? and what *are* the high places of Judah? *are they* not Jerusalem?

Why is all this? "For the transgression of Jacob, and the sins of the house of Israel." God comes down to take account of the great sins of his covenant people, and to bring on them retribution therefor. This great judgment to which all the nations are convened is, for the present, that of the covenant people only; but the Gentile nations may well ask—"If judgment begin at the house of God, what shall the end be of them that obey not the gospel of God? And if the righteous scarcely be saved, where shall the ungodly and the sinner appear?"——Indeed, this judgment of Judah and Israel is of most vital concern to all the nations of the earth, since in it and from it they may learn the ways of God's reign over all nations, and the doom which awaits them unless they repent. ——"What is the transgression of Jacob? Is it not Samaria?" That is, is it not found *in* Samaria, concentrated, embodied, developed there, viz., in her idolatry, her violence, injustice, pride, and general corruption of morals? So also Jerusalem had taken the lead in the idolatries and corruptions of Judah.——The phrase "house of Israel," in the second clause of this verse, refers specially to Judah, as is shown by the last clauses of the verse.——From this point forward through the chapter, the doom of Samaria and her kingdom is the main subject.

6. Therefore, I will make Samaria as an heap of the field, *and* as plantings of a vineyard: and I will pour down the stones thereof into the valley, and I will discover the foundations thereof.

This is a picture of utter desolation. "Heaps of the field," said of a city, shows a surprising contrast to what it was. Once full of noble buildings, now only piles of ruins, heaps of stones and furrows cast up by the plough. So Samaria returns back to the status of a plantation with its ploughed fields and vineyards. Its stones are tumbled down the hill on which the city stood to fill the valley below, and the very foundations on which it stood are laid bare. Modern travellers testify to the precisely literal fulfilment of these words, saying that the valley adjacent to the hill of Samaria is full of the stones which once had a place in her houses and idol temples. So the words of the Lord never fail.

7. And all the graven images thereof shall be beaten to pieces, and all the hires thereof shall be burned with the fire, and all the idols thereof will I lay desolate: for she gathered *it* of the hire of an harlot, and they shall return to the hire of an harlot.

As is usual and altogether right, God's judgments follow and point out the great sins they come to punish. Hence, the altar and all that pertains to idolatry come up in remembrance before God in the day of his visitation, as appears in this verse.——The original word rendered "the *hires*" thereof, carries the mind to the income derived to the city from its idol altars, temples, and worship. The word refers primarily to harlot-hire—the wages of prostitution—and is applied to the money profits of idolatry, under that current prophetic usage which speaks of idolatry as itself harlotry. The last clause of the verse says that, as Samaria had accumulated her wealth and splendor by this sort of harlot-hire, idolatry, and its wages, her people shall return to harlot-hire in the literal sense—to that lowest of all pursuits for a living—the life of a common prostitute. If not to this precisely and literally, yet to a sort of life analogous to this and fitly represented by it.——How inexpressibly appalling is such a doom!

8. Therefore, I will wail and howl; I will go stripped and naked: I will make a wailing like the dragons, and mourning as the owls.

It cannot appear strange that the prophet should pause over such a doom and say—"*Therefore,*" *for this* "I will wail and howl."——"Dragons," in the sense of sea-monsters, are not the animals here intended, but probably jackals or wolves. Either of these, in oriental countries, make night hideous with their howling. The best modern critics concur in rendering the last word not "owl," but ostrich. The latter were distinguished for their plaintive cry far out on the desert.

9. For her wound *is* incurable; for it is come unto Judah; he is come unto the gate of my people, *even* to Jerusalem.

The blow that fell on Samaria and the ten-tribe kingdom was fatal. It swept the nation into a hopeless captivity, and laid the whole land utterly desolate. It also alarmed Judah. Under Sennacherib and Rabshakeh, this same Assyrian power even came within sight of Jerusalem, and might be said to have reached her gates.

10. Declare ye *it* not at Gath, weep ye not at all: in the house of Aphrah roll thyself in the dust.

The remaining part of this chapter is a graphic painting of the first results of the Assyrian invasion, as they were felt in one city after another along the line of his march. In most of the cases the things said of each city are a play upon the significant name of that city—a method of writing well adapted to impress the idea upon the memory. Sometimes there is simply a resemblance in sound between the prominent word spoken of a city and the *name* of that city. Both of these cases fall under the figure of speech technically called a *paronomasia.* The latter form of it—resemblance in sounds—is of course untranslatable. The other form—a play upon the *significance* of the name of a city—is as if one should exclaim: What! is there quarrelling in Concord; war in Salem [Peace]; family feuds in Philadelphia [Brotherly Love]; slavery in Freetown? *

"Tell it not in Gath," comes from David's lament over Saul and Jonathan. The idea is—Let not the enemies of Zion hear of her sad fall.——Modern critics read the next clause, "weep not in Ako," with which the Hebrew word for "weep" (baka) gives us a case of *paranomasia*, better seen when the Hebrew preposition (b) is put before ako, as in the original, making it *bako.* This city fell within the sweep of this march of the desolating army. So did Aphrah, which means dust. "In the '*dust*' city, roll thyself in the '*dust.*'" Weeping is too feeble an expression for a ruin so terrible. To roll thyself in the dust is befitting, and therefore enjoined.

11. Pass ye away, thou inhabitant of Saphir, having thy shame naked: the inhabitant of Zaanan came not forth in the mourning of Beth-ezel; he shall receive of you his standing.

12. For the inhabitants of Maroth waited carefully for good: but evil came down from the LORD unto the gate of Jerusalem.

13. O thou inhabitant of Lachish, bind the chariot to the swift beast: she *is* the beginning of the sin to the daughter of Zion: for the transgressions of Israel were found in thee.

14. Therefore shalt thou give presents to Moresheth-gath: the houses of Achzib *shall be* a lie to the kings of Israel.

15. Yet will I bring an heir unto thee, O inhabitant of Mareshah: he shall come unto Adullam the glory of Israel.

I translate these verses rather freely, in order to give as fully as possible the same play upon the words—by paranomasia—that I

* Isaiah, contemporary with Micah, is equally remarkable for his free use of paronomasia. A beautiful example is in Isa. 5: 7—"He looked for judgment, but behold bloodshed; for righteousness, but behold an outcry." That is, he looked for מִשְׁפָּט, and lo, מִשְׂפָּח; for צְדָקָה and lo, צְעָקָה. The Hebrew reader will notice that the prominent antithetic words are as like as possible in sound, but as unlike as possible in sense. Herein lie the beauty and force of this figure of speech. It is as if an English writer should say—He looked for the law of *right*, but lo, the law of *might;* he looked for *good*, but behold, *blood.*

find in the original, and also to give the ultimate sense. To aid the reader yet more, I put the correlated words in italics. "Pass ye on, ye dwellers in *Saphir* (the *beautiful* city), in utter nakedness" (as those who flee, stripped by the ravages of war); "the dwellers in Zaanan" (the city of *flocks*), "do not *flock out* to the mourning of Beth-ezel:" "from you" (*i. e.*, of *Beth-ezel*, city of *firm root*), "will he, the conqueror take his camping-ground;" *i. e.*, he will make his camp—his place of halting and stay there (hence their mourning—to which the people of Zaanan do not flock out to sympathize with them, though neighbors—having sorrow and fear enough at home).——"For the dwellers in *Maroth*" (the city of *bitterness*) "are in anguish for some good" (all good being lost to them); "but evil comes down from the Lord, even to the gates of Jerusalem." How, then, can one of the lesser feeble cities, like Maroth, hope for any good? It is only natural that a "Maroth," city of bitterness, should be in bitter grief and destruction.——This "evil came *to the gate* of Jerusalem"—no farther. The Assyrian invader never sacked Jerusalem. The blow that smote the kingdom of the ten tribes fatally, may have alarmed Jerusalem; it left her untouched. The invasion of Sennacherib a few years later proved the ruin of himself, not of Jerusalem.——"Bind the chariot to the fleet steed" (for rapid flight)—"thou dweller of *Lachish*" (the *smitten* city), "the first cause of sin was she" (Lachish), "to the daughter of Zion, for in thee were found the sins of Israel." Lachish lay on the southern border of the ten tribes, and being not far from Jerusalem, became the channel through which the temptations to idolatry passed over from Israel, after the revolt, into Jerusalem. Hence this special judgment on Lachish.——In the first clause Micah has a paranomasia which is untranslatable between "Lachish" and "Rekesh," the word for fleet steed.

"Therefore shalt thou" (Israel) "give divorce papers to Moresheth-gath;"—though her name signifies *city of possession*, thou must forego all *possession* of her and let her go before the destroyer. ——"The houses of *Achzib*" (*city of lies*) shall be for a *lie* to the kings of Israel"—no dependence in their need.——"Yet will I bring an heir" (one who shall possess) "to thee, O dweller of Mareshah"—which name seems here to mean *city of possession*. This heir is the conqueror.——"He," this conqueror, shall come even to *Adullam*, which means *justice of the people*—and this significance, if realized, would be "*the glory of Israel.*"

This passage (vs. 10–15) is admitted to be extremely difficult. No doubt it was intelligible in the age of Micah, though somewhat enigmatical. But such nice, delicate allusions to cities and their significant names must inevitably become obscure by the lapse of ages, and the oblivion of those associations of thought with cities and their names which are in their nature incidental and temporary.

16. Make thee bald, and poll thee for thy delicate

children; enlarge thy baldness as the eagle; for they are gone into captivity from thee.

The eagle is referred to as an illustration of baldness. Tearing out the hair, or even cutting it off, were usual signs of extreme grief. Hence the prophet exhorts Israel, considered as the mother of her people, to go into mourning for her children, because they are gone away into captivity, to return no more.——Except in the use of the paranomasia, the passage (Isa. 10 : 28–32) is strikingly analogous to this (Mic. 1 : 10–16). There Isaiah sketches the advance of Sennacherib's host toward Jerusalem, by noting its effects of panic, mourning, or flight, on various cities as he approached. Here Micah describes a similar march of *an* Assyrian army to destroy the northern kingdom, and to alarm the southern.

CHAPTER II.

This chapter presents the sins of the people (vs. 1, 2); God's threatenings (v. 3); lamentations over her doom (vs. 4, 5); the gainsaying of a wicked people against God and his prophets (v. 6); the prophet's indignant reply (v. 7); a further description of their sins (vs. 8, 9); the sort of prophets the people choose (v. 11); and promises of good (vs. 12, 13).

1. Woe to them that devise iniquity, and work evil upon their beds! When the morning is light, they practise it, because it is in the power of their hand.

This woe fitly comes down, not on those who sin inadvertently, or only under the impulse of sudden temptation, but on those who coolly and with the clear-headed thought of the night-watches, frame plans of mischief and work out schemes for wrong, to be executed in the morning; and who are wicked enough for all the mischief their hands have the power to do.

2. And they covet fields, and take *them* by violence; and houses, and take *them* away: so they oppress a man and his house, even a man and his heritage.

"Oppressing a man and *his house*," means robbing not him alone, but his family as well. They take away property in which his wife and children have their living. This is the same class of sins which Amos and Isaiah rebuke so sharply.

3. Therefore thus saith the Lord; Behold, against this family do I devise an evil, from which ye shall not remove your necks; neither shall ye go haughtily: for this time *is* evil.

The idea of retaliation and of just retribution stands out clearly in the very form of the prophet's expressions: *They devise* iniquity; *God devises* calamity to punish it. They devise it *upon* their *beds;* God devises it *upon* this whole *family*—the prophet choosing a word for *family* which has the leading radicals of the word for *bed.* ——God's calamities shall be on them as a yoke which they cannot throw off, and under which they can no longer walk proudly, carrying their heads high—for the prophet's words have this sense.

4. In that day shall *one* take up a parable against you, and lament with a doleful lamentation, *and* say, We be utterly spoiled: he hath changed the portion of my people: how hath he removed *it* from me! turning away he hath divided our fields.

The best lexicographers would read the second clause—not, "lament with a doleful lamentation," but thus—"And wail in a dirge of wailing, *It is done!*" *i. e.*, all is over! "and say, we are utterly spoiled!"——"Changing the portion of my people" means here changing the title to their landed estates, and hence implies that they lose possession of their country.——The last clause better —"He hath apportioned our fields to one who takes them all away from us"—*i. e.*, God has given them all to the conqueror of our country.

5. Therefore thou shalt have none that shall cast a cord by lot in the congregation of the Lord.

Consequently there shall be none to set off their land to them by lot in the public congregation. "Cord" is used here for a measuring line for land. The soil has passed into the hands of a foreign power. This is one of their bitter plaints.

6. Prophesy ye not, *say they to them that* prophesy: they shall not prophesy to them, *that* they shall not take shame.

7. O *thou that art* named the house of Jacob, is the Spirit of the Lord straitened? *are* these his doings? do not my words do good to him that walketh uprightly?

At this point, the ungodly people interpose to gainsay the prophet, forbidding him to prophesy, and suggesting the sort of prophet they would have. The passage is quite obscure, the transitions being abrupt, and the point where the objector's language closes and the prophet's reply begins, being a matter of some doubt. Thus, among the ablest critics now before me, Rosenmuller assigns to the objector less than half of v. 6; Henderson precisely v. 6, and no more; Hengstenberg apparently, vs. 6 and 7. I find the best point of transition from the objector to the prophet at the close of v. 6, and translate thus: "Prophesy not; let those prophesy who will not prophesy as to such things; reproaches will never cease."

This is their demand and this their complaint. They say—We can't hear any more such prophesying; let us have another sort of men who will not say such hard things;—there is no end to your faul-finding.——Then the prophet resumes in v. 7, "Shall this be said in the house of Jacob?" "Is the Spirit of the Lord to be straitened?"—*i. e.*, to be dictated to by mortal man? "Are these *his* doings?" *i. e.*, is it his fault that he must predict calamity? Is it not rather your sins that bring down the wrath and curse of God? "Do not my words always bless him who walketh uprightly?"——This is the beginning of the prophet's reply.——I dissent from the English version—"O thou that art named the house of Jacob:" (1.) Because this verb without any preposition following, seems not to be used in the sense *to name;* (2.) And mainly, because, beyond all question, this first clause is interrogative and not vocative. There are four distinct questions asked in this verse, each indicated by its interrogative particle. There is, therefore, as much reason for making this first clause a question as either of the three that follows. Beyond a doubt, each of the four is an interrogative clause. The first expresses the surprise and horror felt by the prophet that men should arise *in the house of Jacob* to say such things in the way of dictation to the Almighty!——The construction of v. 6 is exceedingly obscure. The sense I have given is a choice among difficulties.

8. Even of late my people is risen up as an enemy: ye pull off the robe with the garment from them that pass by securely as men averse from war.

9. The women of my people have ye cast out from their pleasant houses; from their children have ye taken away my glory for ever.

These verses are interposed here to show that the objectors who cavil against the prophets of the Lord do not themselves "walk uprightly." Then v. 10 warns them out of the land; and v. 11 returns to tell them what sort of a prophet they choose, and shall have.——The words "Even of late" do not necessarily imply that the event is very recent.——The horrible thing is that "*my people*," God's own people, "should have risen up," *i. e.*, in their full strength, "to become an enemy" to every man's rights and interests—a public enemy to all. For instance, "they strip off both the outer robe and the inner from men passing along securely" with no thought of danger, "returning from war." Their worn and weary soldiers, returning from hard service for their country, they fall upon, and rob and strip even to the skin; for the common oriental dress included only these two garments, the outer robe and the inner.——"The wives among my people ye expel from their pleasant houses, and from their children ye take away *my* ornaments" (the good clothing I have given them), and never return it —"take it away *for ever*." These are named as instances and illustrations of their rapacity and wickedness, to show what is meant by their "rising up as an enemy." Bad as any foreign enemy were they even toward the soldiers of their country returning from war, and toward wives and children who, being dependent and defenceless, are specially under God's protection.

10. Arise ye, and depart; for this *is* not *your* rest: because it is polluted, it shall destroy *you*, even with a sore destruction.

"Up, and away"—be out of this land; "for this is not your rest." God gave Canaan as a land of rest to his people, but never to such apostates as you! They had so polluted the land by their sins that it should itself destroy them. The very land is thought of as instinct with life, and fired with holy indignation to devour these guilty inhabitants!

11. If a man walking in the spirit and falsehood do lie, *saying*, I will prophesy unto thee of wine and of strong drink; he shall even be the prophet of this people.

Having shown (vs. 8, 9) that these cavillers against the Lord's prophets do not "walk uprightly," and having (v. 10) warned them out of the land as their fit doom, he comes now to describe the sort of prophet they would like and shall have.——"If a man walking in wind and falsehood will lie for them, and will prophesy to them (not *of*, but) *for* wine and strong drink"—taking his pay in those articles as meeting his chief want—"he shall be the prophet of this people." The middle clause is in the first person, as in our English Bible, giving us the very words of his proposal—"I will prophesy for you if you will give me all the wine and strong drink I want." Fit showing of the depth of degradation into which wicked men would sink the prophetic office, if they could!——The first point in this description is richly graphic:—"If a man walking in wind and lies will lie for them all they wish," &c. Men who are *windy*, gassy, full of talk but void of sense and thought, and utterly reckless of truth—such are commonly in every age the high priests of error and falsehood, the champions of religious delusion.——For this use of the word "*wind*" to denote what is empty, light as air and worthless, see Isa. 41:29, "Their molten images are *wind* and confusion;" and Job 16:3, "Is there any end to words of *wind?*"

12. I will surely assemble, O Jacob, all of thee; I will surely gather the remnant of Israel; I will put them together as the sheep of Bozrah, as the flock in the midst of their fold: they shall make great noise by reason of *the multitude of* men.

13. The breaker is come up before them: they have

broken up, and have passed through the gate, and are gone out by it; and their king shall pass before them, and the LORD on the head of them.

This sudden transition to the richest promises of restoration and salvation is indeed remarkable. It would seem that the divine Spirit, fired with indignation in view of such depths of moral pollution and guilt, rallies himself to the defence of his own cause of truth: "I will surely save my people, and restore my crumbling kingdom." Glorious turn of thought this—rebounding from the greatness of man's sin to the richness of God's mercy!——The promise is that God will surely gather together all of Jacob, and all who survive of Israel; will become their shepherd; and that there shall be "*a hum*" (so the Hebrew) as of bees in swarm —a loud noise by reason of the great number of men. They are thought of as having been imprisoned within high walls; hence "the breaker" who makes great breaches in this wall goes out before them. They break through; they pass out through the gate; they go forth by it; and their king marches before them, and Jehovah at their head.——This deliverance is wholly of the Lord. His providential agencies are omnipresent, and his Spirit inspires the movement.——The allusion in this passage to the Exodus from Egypt should be noticed. Here, as there, the people are first gathered together; the Lord takes charge of them as his flock; then he sends Moses to break down the prison walls. The Exodus, or going forth, is made prominent here by repeated reiterations, as it was there in the historic facts; and, finally, Jehovah puts himself here at the head of his ransomed people, as then and there in the pillar of fire and of cloud.

As to the ultimate significance of these verses, it will be noted that they speak both of Jacob and Israel; but these terms are not distinctive as between the two rival kingdoms. Neither of them is the usual name to designate the kingdom of Judah. It would seem to be no part of the prophet's intention to regard the distinction of kingdoms which was made by the revolt. The names Jacob and Israel have rather the general sense—the covenant people of God.——So also, as to time and circumstances of fulfilment, the passage is altogether general and indefinite. Beyond a doubt it must imply that God will at some future day gather his scattered people of Israel, and put himself at their head as their Deliverer and King. He will make his earthly kingdom great and glorious. As to the question whether Gentiles form a part of it, or whether Jews alone are thought of, no more should be sought in any given passage than it contains. Not every passage can say every thing. This prophecy does not name the Gentiles, nor does it exclude them. One instalment—a small one—of this broadly comprehensive promise was paid in the restoration from Babylon. Vastly more remains unpaid yet.

CHAPTER III.

The prophet returns to speak against the sins of the people, dwelling specially in this chapter on the sins of the princes and judges (vs. 1–4, 9–11); giving the sin and doom of the false prophets (vs. 5–7); and closing with predictions of the desolation of the holy city and of the temple mountain (v. 12).

1. And I said, Hear, I pray you, O heads of Jacob, and ye princes of the house of Israel: *Is it* not for you to know judgment?

"And *then* I said," &c., connecting this in thought with what he had said before. In the previous chapter he had sharply rebuked and terribly doomed those who devise iniquity on their beds (2: 1–5); now he asks, Why are not such sins forestalled by the faithful administation of justice and law? Does it not behoove princes and judges—men at the head of their "thousands"—(see Ex. 18: 21) "to know judgment?" He implies by this more than merely knowing the *theory* of law and justice. Ought they not to know it in *practice*, and to see it administered all the more faithfully and earnestly by how much the greater the reigning corruption?

2. Who hate the good, and love the evil; who pluck off their skin from off them, and their flesh from off their bones;

3. Who also eat the flesh of my people, and flay their skin from off them; and they break their bones, and chop them in pieces, as for the pot, and as flesh within the caldron.

So far are they from knowing judgment in the practical sense that they even hate good and love evil, and they show this by their deeds.——This description of rapacity and robbery is fearfully strong. They not only fleece but flay their victims; not only flay but tear off the flesh and eat it; then go on to the bones; chop them fine for the pot, as if they would boil and eat up the last thing in the poor body of their victims. So with insatiable extortion, they strip men of their last right, of their last acre, and of their last farthing.

4. Then shall they cry unto the Lord, but he will not hear them: he will even hide his face from them at that time, as they have behaved themselves ill in their doings.

Yet these men, of such outrageous extortion, set themselves to pray to God; but of course he will not hear. "The prayer of the wicked is abomination to the Lord." "If I regard iniquity in my *heart* even, the Lord will not hear me;" how much more when such iniquities are found in men's hand! "He will hide his face from them at that time according as they haye made their doings vile," *i. e.*, inasmuch as they have done so wickedly, and according to the wickedness of those doings, God will hide his face from them.

5. Thus saith the Lord concerning the prophets that make my people err, that bite with their teeth, and cry, Peace; and he that putteth not into their mouths, they even prepare war against him.

Turning from civil to religious leaders, vs. 5–7 speak of the corrupt prophets of that age.——The clause, "that bite with their teeth," &c., may be construed in either of two ways: (1.) As indicating extortion, following out the idea in vs. 3: "Who eat the flesh of my people;" or (2.) As indicating gross and supreme sensuality; who live *only* to eat, and prophesy only for the sake of good eating. In the former construction, the remainder of the verse might be put thus: "Who bite savagely with their teeth, yet cry 'all's well;' and if one resist their extortion, they even declare war on him." But the latter construction is preferable: "Who are mere sensualists, and for good feeding will prophesy peace to the most wicked of men; but if one refuse to fill their mouths well, they are up in arms against him."——Such shamefully low impulses and low sensual natures, ought to be anywhere else rather than in the sacred office! Alas for the people when those who minister to them in holy things make a god of their belly, and live only for good eating!

6. Therefore, night *shall be* unto you, that ye shall not have a vision; and it shall be dark unto you, that ye shall not divine; and the sun shall go down over the prophets, and the day shall be dark over them.

7. Then shall the seers be ashamed, and the diviners confounded: yea, they shall all cover their lips; for *there is* no answer of God.

This is the doom of these false, ungodly prophets: "There shall be night to you so that there can be no vision; it shall be too dark for you to divine; the sun shall go down upon the prophets," &c. ——"They shall cover their lips"—as those who have nothing to say, and with the further idea of intense shame and sorrow, inasmuch as the beard—always prominent in oriental life—was to the male sex the seat of beauty and honor. The leper (Lev. 13 : 45) was to put a cover on his upper lip. Ezekiel (24 : 17, 22) was forbidden to cover his lips in mourning for his deceased wife.——The cause of this intense shame and confusion is that they not only get no answer from God, but that he frustrates their predictions, confounds their machinations, and exposes the groundlessness of their claims to be prophets of the Lord. The darkness God brings over them is that of calamity and judgment where they were predicting only good.

8. But truly I am full of power by the Spirit of the LORD, and of judgment, and of might, to declare unto Jacob his transgression, and to Israel his sin.

With a strong and full consciousness of honesty, and of being filled with the Spirit of God, Micah puts himself in contrast with those false prophets. His soul is deeply stirred within him by his abhorrence of their spirit and life, so that his holy indignation overleaps the restraints of false modesty, and he speaks out fearlessly what so fills his indignant soul that he cannot but say it. He must and will rebuke the sins of the people and of their leaders even; for no regard to rank and station shall soften the just severity of his reproofs.

9. Hear this, I pray you, ye heads of the house of Jacob, and princes of the house of Israel, that abhor judgment, and pervert all equity.

10. They build up Zion with blood, and Jerusalem with iniquity.

11. The heads thereof judge for reward, and the priests thereof teach for hire, and the prophets thereof divine for money: yet will they lean upon the LORD, and say, *Is* not the LORD among us? none evil can come upon us.

Once more, as in v. 1, he inveighs against the horrible corruption of the princes and judges of the land. With Judah specially in his eye, he charges them with abhorring not sin and wrong, as they should, but judgment and justice as men never should; and with distorting and perverting equity. "They build up Zion with blood" by devoting the fruits of their robbery and murder to splendid buildings and gorgeous display. They judge for bribes in open contempt of the law given through Moses (see Ex. 23 : 8, and Deut. 16 : 19); and yet they lean upon the Lord and vainly think that, being called the people of God and keeping up the forms of his worship, they are safe against calamity. Jeremiah rebukes the same wretched folly (7 : 4): "Trust ye not in lying words, saying, The temple of the Lord, the temple of the Lord, the temple of the Lord, are these." So in later times, the self-righteous, extortious Pharisees said, "We have Abraham to our father;"—"Lord, Lord, have we not prophesied in thy name?" &c.

12. Therefore shall Zion for your sake be ploughed *as* a field, and Jerusalem shall become heaps, and the mountain of the house as the high places of the forest.

Retribution for such sins must come. "Zion"—the hill of David in the south part of the city—"the mountain of the house" (temple) *i. e.*, Mount Moriah, the temple-mountain on the north, and Jerusalem in general—shall become desolate: Zion to be ploughed as a field; Jerusalem to be heaps of desolate ruins; and the temple-mountain "as the high places of a forest," thickly covered with an undergrowth of shrubs. This has special reference to the destruction of the city by the Chaldeans when, for seventy years, even Jerusalem lay in utter desolation.

CHAPTER IV.

THE first eight verses are a graphic prediction of God's restoring mercy to his real Zion; vs. 9, 10 resume the subject of the captivity to Babylon; vs. 11–13 note the events of a later period—the Syrian invasion, and the heroic deeds of the Maccabees.

1. But in the last days it shall come to pass, *that* the mountain of the house of the LORD shall be established in the top of the mountains, and it shall be exalted above the hills; and people shall flow unto it.

2. And many nations shall come, and say, Come, and let us go up to the mountain of the LORD, and to the house of the God of Jacob; and he will teach us of his ways, and we will walk in his paths: for the law shall go forth of Zion, and the word of the LORD from Jerusalem.

3. And he shall judge among many people, and rebuke strong nations afar off; and they shall beat their swords into plough-shares, and their spears into pruning-hooks: nation shall not lift up a sword against nation, neither shall they learn war any more.

These words occur substantially in Isa. 2: 2–4, but appear to be original with Micah. At least it must be admitted that here they fit nicely to the previous context (3: 12), and also to the following context. In Isaiah, the passage has no such close connection with the preceding context.——In this passage, the relation of thought to what precedes is the first thing to be noted. Zion is seen in ruins; the temple-mountain dishonored and waste—all for the sins of the covenant people. Must it hence be inferred that the kingdom of God among men is crushed down, never to rise? By no means. In the last days this kingdom shall rise in far greater glory than ever before. The temple-mountain—called here "the mountain of the house *of the Lord*," though in 3: 12 it is only "the mountain of the house"—shall be lifted high and firmly set on the tops of the other mountains, and high above all the hills in glory and esteem. Such I understand to be the sense of this striking poetic conception—the temple-mountain (Moriah) lifted up and set on the top of all other mountains. In honor it shall surpass and overtop them all. In Ps. 68:16, the Psalmist, supposing the other mountains to envy Mount Moriah this distinction, says—"The hill of God is as the hill of Bashan; an high hill," &c. "Why do ye look invidiously, ye high hills? This is the hill which God hath desired to dwell in." Zech. 14:10 carries the figure one step further. All the rest of the world becomes a plain; its mountains subside altogether, and then the temple-mountain stands out solitary and alone, the one great and only mountain of the world! The sense here is the same as in Micah—this mountain, the one place of surpassing honor, dignity, and glory.——Next, "peoples, even all the nations of men, shall flow unto it." That they shall *flow* thither implies, not that they are dragged or driven into this worship, but that they come spontaneously, as water moves with the utmost ease under the power of gravitation. Many nations shall come of their free accord. They shall exhort one another to go up to the house of the God of Jacob, to learn of the true God and of all moral duty there. God's will, as revealed in Zion, they recognize to be the fountain of all law, and they joyfully place themselves under his supreme dominion. Then his peaceful reign over the nations of men begins; they need sword and spear no longer; the culture of the soil supersedes the arts of war, and nation no more lifts up sword against its brother nation. For the law of God is the law of supreme, impartial love, administered under the sway of the Prince of Peace: how then can the result be other than universal tranquillity? Obeyed, it must supplant war forever. Men can no longer "hurt or destroy in all God's holy mountain, for the earth shall be full of the knowledge of the Lord as the waters cover the sea." Glorious scene! Blissful consummation! And this is no visionary dream. It shall yet be. The days of battles and carnage, the days of fell animosity, satanic ambition, demoniac hate, must cease, and give place to days of blessed peace and good-will among men. *Let the love of the Great Father have the praise for all this!* ——Micah sees it in the distant future. Briefly and in general, he locates it "in the last days." They are future yet; but they will surely come and (may we not hope and pray?) will not long tarry!

4. But they shall sit every man under his vine and under his fig-tree; and none shall make *them* afraid: for the mouth of the Lord of hosts hath spoken *it*.

Over against the scenes of war lie the pursuits of peace and the quiet enjoyment of God's good gifts of nature and providence, and of the fruits of human labor. Each man sits under his own vine and fig-tree;—none shall make them afraid. These are the usual oriental symbols of a state of paradise on earth.

5 For all people will walk every one in the name of his god, and we will walk in the name of the LORD our God for ever and ever.

This verse shows how the people in that good day are to feel and act. These are their supposed words. They recognize the common law of human life, that men follow the God they acknowledge and trust, and then they avow their own full purpose to walk in the name of their God for ever and ever. They are altogether satisfied with his worship and service. In the love of his name and in the full strength of their convictions they pledge themselves to his ways and worship for all time.

6. In that day, saith the LORD, will I assemble her that halteth, and I will gather her that is driven out, and her that I have afflicted;

7. And I will make her that halted a remnant, and her that was cast far off a strong nation: and the LORD shall reign over them in Mount Zion from henceforth, even for ever.

At that time the Lord will gather to himself the halting, *i. e.*, the lame, the smitten, scathed, and long-rejected remnant of his people, and will make them a strong nation, reigning over them himself in Mount Zion forever. As vs. 1–4 by their very terms expressly include the Gentiles, so these verses have special reference to the long-dispersed Jews. When the fulness of the Gentiles shall have come in, then shall all Israel be saved; her partial blindness shall pass away, and the Lord's great plan of redeeming, saving mercy shall grasp the world, and bring the nations of every race and clime beneath Immanuel's sceptre. (See Rom. 11:15, 23–27).

8. And thou, O tower of the flock, the strong hold of the daughter of Zion, unto thee shall it come, even the first dominion; the kingdom shall come to the daughter of Jerusalem.

In this passage God is thought of as the shepherd, and his people as his flock. Hence the "tower of the flock" is Jerusalem. Towers were built in or near the sheepfold for defence.——The original dominion, as under David, shall return again. That prosperous era of the Hebrew people in which they subdued all their enemies round about, and greatly improved the modes of public worship, is a common illustration of Messiah's reign. The kingdom of Immanuel shall have this Mount Zion for its centre and capital forever.——But let us give this scripture its gospel sense. Let us not fall into the error of the Pharisees, as seen in the New Testament, who could find in the Scriptures nothing but a "kingdom of this world" for the outward Israel and her earthly king. We need to distinguish the clothing of ideas from the ideas themselves. That the great truths of gospel times and of Christ's millennial reign, should be clothed in Jewish imagery and costume, ought not to surprise or stumble us. The human mind being what it is, this mode of writing *for Jews and among Jews* is unavoidable, is natural, is indeed the only language that could have been at that time understood.

9. Now why dost thou cry out aloud? *is there* no king in thee? is thy counsellor perished? for pangs have taken thee as a woman in travail.

10. Be in pain, and labour to bring forth, O daughter of Zion, like a woman in travail: for now shalt thou go forth out of the city, and thou shalt dwell in the field, and thou shalt go *even* to Babylon; there shalt thou be delivered; there the LORD shall redeem thee from the hand of thine enemies.

With v. 9 commences a remarkably regular series of prophecies, forecasting great events that were specially to affect the welfare of the Jews down to the coming of Christ, and of the church of God thenceforward. It is very noticeable that the beginning of each is indicated in our English Bible by the word "*now*," which has its corresponding Hebrew word. It stands at the head of vs. 9, 11, and 5 : 1. Consequently, the distinct predictions are (1.) vs. 9, 10; (2.) vs. 11–13; (3.) chapter 5 : 1, and onward substantially through the chapter. No. 1 speaks of the captivity to Babylon and the restoration from it. No. 2, of the gathering of the great Syrian armies, together with those of some other adjacent powers, against the Jews in the times of the Maccabees, with their heroic defence and final victory. No. 3, of the siege and fall of Jerusalem, when the sceptre finally departed from Judah; of the Messiah's birth at Bethlehem, and then of his peaceful, triumphant reign, its policy and results.——With this summary of the points before us to the end of chapter 5, we may the better understand each separate prophecy.

In the first prediction of this series (vs. 9, 10) the people are seen in extreme agony: the prophet hears their sharp outcry of anguish, and asks the cause of it. "And where are thy reliances for help? Hast thou no king? no counsellor?" The trouble is, that the city is falling before the fierce Chaldean, and their honored temple and loved homes are in ruins. How much they rested on their king is indicated (Lam. 4 : 20), where they say of him: "The breath of our nostrils, the anointed of the Lord, was taken in their pits, of whom we had said, Under his shadow we shall live among the heathen." Zedekiah was both weak and wicked, yet he was the Lord's anointed king, and the people, long accustomed to reverence royalty, and to expect good from the Lord through his anointed ones, bemoaned his fall into the enemy's power. The prophet foresaw these events with entire historic accuracy.——A woman in her travail pains is the next figure, used here to represent only the painful side of the case—not the joy over a happy birth. In the clause, "there shalt thou be delivered," the original forbids us to think of any reference to the bright side of this figure. It means merely that they should be brought out of this captivity at some future time.——The "dwelling in the field" lies intermediate between their expulsion from Jerusalem and their residence in or near Babylon, and seems to allude to their exposure in the open country during their long and weary journey to Babylon.—— The twice repeated "*there*"—"*there* shalt thou be delivered," "*there* shall the Lord redeem thee," &c., was equivalent to saying, Do not dread this going to Babylon, as if it must be the tomb of all your hopes, for *there* your God will meet you for your deliverance. So in fact it came to pass. Precisely *there* God raised up Cyrus; precisely at Babylon he gave him those victories which paved the way for the restoration of his people. So true is it that the people of God never need fear to pass under any cloud which the Lord their God may bring up over them. What seems to them their ruin, God can make their salvation.

11. Now also many nations are gathered against thee, that say, Let her be defiled, and let our eye look upon Zion.

12. But they know not the thoughts of the Lord: neither understand they his counsel: for he shall gather them as the sheaves into the floor.

13. Arise and thresh, O daughter of Zion: for I will make thy horn iron, and I will make thy hoofs brass: and thou shall beat in pieces many people: and I will consecrate their gain unto the Lord, and their substance unto the Lord of the whole earth.

Here the course of thought makes another stage onward, and reaches the second distinct prophecy in this series. Many nations gather together against Zion in bitter malignity and haughty scorn, and with set purpose to defile her sanctuary. Manifestly a real hatred of their religion gives the impulse to this onslaught upon Zion. "Let her be defiled," say they, "and let us have the joy of looking on to see her anguish."——No language could more accurately describe the spirit of Antiochus Epiphanes and of his allies, in their fell, demoniac attempts to uproot and overwhelm the holy city, its temple, and all the true worshippers of Jehovah. The reader will find a most thrilling history of these events in the first and second books of Maccabees. It specially appears there that the wrath of these enemies of God was aimed at the temple, its worship, and all worshippers of the true God, since, when at one time the temple fell into their hands, they polluted it in every way they could devise, even offering swine's flesh on the sacred altar. Hence "the cleansing of the sanctuary" finds a prominent place in Daniel's prophecy of these events, and in Jewish history.——"But," says our prophet, "they do not understand God's thoughts and counsels." No, indeed; for God thought, first, to discipline, prove, and purify his people; next, to scourge and terribly punish his enemies; the latter only being made prominent here in the prophecy. He gathered them as sheaves into the floor, preparatory to bringing the threshing power of his people down upon them. Then the prophet calls on the "daughter of Zion to arise and thresh." The mixing of metaphors here need not surprise us, for we have strength, even if we have not the most finished concinnity and fitness in the points of the illustration. That a virgin should thresh with the feet of cattle, and that with threshing should be blended the use of horns of iron, is all strong and full of meaning, however it may lack the nicer beauties. It should be said, however, that in the phrase "daughter of Zion," the idea of a female is lost in the general conception of the military force of the city. There was a terrible significance in these figures when the things they denoted became actual history, when God fired the souls of the heroic, lion-hearted Maccabees, and made "one of them chase a thousand, and two put ten thousand to flight," grinding to powder one after another the huge armies sent upon them by the enraged Syrian king.——Remarkably, the Lord promised to turn the spoils of these wars to account toward the wealth of his own kingdom. Perhaps this is an historic allusion to David, who turned the spoils of his many victories to account for building and adorning the first temple.

So it is evermore the Lord's purpose to make the wicked lay up treasures for the just, and coin money, to be consecrated under his providence, though against their intent, unto the Lord of the whole earth.

CHAPTER V.

As already indicated, this chapter records the third in the connected series of consecutive prophecies. It begins with the siege of Jerusalem and the dishonor done to her Judge; advances to the birth of the Messiah, and then to the character and results of his glorious reign on earth.

1. Now gather thyself in troops, O daughter of troops: he hath laid siege against us: they shall smite the judge of Israel with a rod upon the cheek.

The descriptive points in this verse are few; the thronging of her own troops within the city, the siege, the extreme insult offered to the Judge of Israel. The Lord summons the armed hosts of Jerusalem together for battle, and probably of Judah as well;

some hostile power besieges the city and inflicts utter disgrace on the head man of the nation, at that time embodying and representing the government, and called "the Judge of Israel," with allusion to the Judges who fell between Joshua and Saul, and were inferior to their kings—showing that already royalty had greatly declined. After this decline came ruin, for, to smite the chieftain of the nation with a rod upon the cheek must imply extreme indignity and utter impotence—not only that all influence and authority had gone from this particular Judge, but, since he is a representative man, that the sceptre had passed away from Judah herself.

In what special event was this prophecy fulfilled?——Some (with Hengstenberg) have said, in the fall of Jerusalem, before the arms of Titus, A. D. 70.——The objections to this view are: (1.) It involves a serious anachronism, since, as this verse immediately precedes the account of the birth of King Messiah, so its events should precede that event. But the fall of the city, instead of coming before his birth, was seventy years after.

(2.) On this theory the last and main point of the description does not appositely fit the historic facts. In the prophecy, the main thing is the utter dishonor done to the supreme authority; but in the final destruction of the city by the Romans, the terrible thing was the slaughter of more than a million of her people, the horrors of famine and pestilence, and appalling judgments on the whole nation. It was not the loss of their sceptre, for this had practically gone long before.

(3.) There are clear indications throughout this chapter that the prophet had his eye on that striking prophecy (Gen. 49 : 10): "The sceptre shall not depart from Judah, nor a Lawgiver from between his feet, until Shiloh come; and unto him shall the gathering of the people be." Note the coming forth of the Ruler of Israel (v. 2); the gathering of the people to him (v. 3); even of all nations to the ends of the earth (v. 4); that he shall be "*the Peace*"—the real Shiloh—the Prince of Peace (v. 5), &c., &c.

These considerations go far to show that the passage does *not* look specifically to the fall of Jerusalem before the Roman arms under Titus, A. D. 70.

Another interpretation is already indicated by the leading points made in this description, viz., the siege and fall of Jerusalem, B. C. 34, when King Antigonus, the last monarch of the Asmonean dynasty (Jewish), fell before Herod the Great, who was aided by eleven Roman legions. Herod was an Idumean. In him the Jews came under a foreign dynasty, and never again had a king of their own race, save King Messiah. This siege was an obstinate contest of one year's duration. History * notes especially that "King Antigonus surrendered himself in a most cowardly manner, and was accordingly treated with the greatest indignity. He threw himself at

* See Jahn's "Hebrew Commonwealth," p. 375, and Taylor's "Manual of History," p. 176.

the feet of the Roman general, who repelled him with contempt, and scornfully called him *Antigona*, as if he were unworthy the name of a man. The deposed king was loaded with chains, carried to Antioch, and there beheaded like a common malefactor."

Thus signally was the Judge of Israel "smitten with a rod upon the cheek:" thus did the "sceptre depart from Judah." The order of time is complete, for it was during the reign of this very Herod who thus supplanted Antigonus that the Prince of Peace was born and the Shiloh of ancient prophecy came; and thenceforward the true Israel never lacked a glorious King.

2. But thou Beth-lehem Ephratah, *though* thou be little among the thousands of Judah, *yet* out of thee shall he come forth unto me *that is* to be ruler in Israel; whose goings forth *have been* from of old, from everlasting.

"The Judge of Israel"—all his dignity and power gone—has passed away, and with him that earthly kingdom and dispensation which so long embosomed or imprisoned the germ of the true kingdom of God. Now a new "Ruler in Israel" appears who is truly King and Lord of all.——The first point presented is his birthplace. On the side of his human nature, he comes forth from Beth-lehem Ephratah—that little city, too small to have a place among the thousands of Judah—for this is precisely the sense of the Hebrew; not that Bethlehem was a small one *among* the thousands, yet being one of them, but *too* small to be one of them. The expression refers to a classification of the people of each tribe into thousands which commenced during their sojourn in the wilderness, each thousand having its head officer, who combined both civil and judicial authority. The rise of this system may be seen Ex. 18: 21, 25. Saul recognizes its existence long after the settlement of Canaan, when he said of David (1 Sam. 23: 23), "If he be in the land, I will search him out throughout all the thousands of Judah." In the transition from nomadic life in the wilderness to fixed residence in Canaan, this system of division into thousands, with each its head-man, "captain," or "judge," took this modification. Those cities that numbered one thousand people rose to the rank of being among the thousands, and had one such officer. The smaller villages must needs unite two or more together to constitute a family of a thousand. Bethlehem had less than a thousand people, and was therefore among the smaller cities—only a village in Judah. It lay six miles southwest of Jerusalem, in a fertile region, as its name, "house of bread," denotes. Ephratah also means "fruitful." It was the birthplace of David, and partly for this reason, we may suppose, was the birthplace of his greater Son. Royalty in the house of David had fallen low at the period contemplated in this prophecy. Indeed, there are indications here that it was seen by Micah to be practically extinct, so that David is thought of as having returned back from the place of his throne on Mount Zion, to the place of his humble birth and shepherd life, Bethlehem. Its being a small city was really no disqualification for a birthplace of King Messiah, since David himself was born here and not in any of the greater cities of the land, and also because it was no part of God's plan, in determining the birthplace of his incarnate Son, to make him famous by its greatness or renown.——The appended name "Ephratah" carries us back to Gen. 35 : 16–19, where this place was distinguished by yet another birth.——Though thou art so small, O Bethlehem, "yet out of thee shall he come forth who is to be *for me* ruler in Israel." *For* me, rather than "unto me" —the idea being, not that the Messiah comes from Bethlehem *unto God*, but that he is to be ruler *for God*, acting under God and in his behalf in the great mediatorial scheme. The word "ruler" means chief ruler, king.——On the last clause of the verse, opinions differ. There can be no doubt that the noun rendered "goings forth" is correlated with the verb just before it, rendered "*shall come forth*," *i. e.*, from Bethlehem—the noun being from the same root. In one point of view, he shall go forth out of Bethlehem; but in another, his goings forth have been from of old, from everlasting. The last point in this correlation, the precise sense in which his goings forth have been from of old, is that on which critics have differed. Some say that, as in his human nature he came out of Bethlehem, so in his divine nature he came forth from eternity. Others, urging that eternity is no *place*, and therefore cannot be antithetic to Bethlehem which is a place, find a reference to his repeated manifestations through his divine nature and before his proper incarnation, *e. g.*, to the patriarchs, to Moses, Joshua, Samuel, and others.——I adopt the latter view, as constituting the most natural antithesis, as avoiding the rather harsh conception of coming out of eternity, as involving a reference to a series of facts of the highest moment in identifying this glorious Ruler of Israel, and finally as well accounting for the use of the plural, "his *goings* forth," which implies that there had been *many*. But the construction first stated above, provides for only one coming forth, viz., from eternity.——The prophet, then, means to say that this was not his first manifestation among men. During all the earlier ages, he had often come forth and made his presence manifest. In the wilderness he was the angel of Jehovah's presence (Ex. 23 : 20–23, and 33 : 14); to Joshua (5 : 13–15) he appeared as captain of the Lord's host, and to Manoah (Judg. 13 : 17, 18) as one whose name is "Wonderful." So the Hebrew, which occurs again in Isa. 9 : 6. And these are only a few out of many.——It was manifestly pertinent that Micah, in predicting his human birth in Bethlehem, should indicate the fact of his preëxistence and of his frequent previous manifestations to his people in the earlier ages. ——It only remains to note that the Jews of the Saviour's time so far understood this prophecy as to apply it to the Messiah, and to learn from it that he should be born in Bethlehem. Matthew informs us (2 : 4–6) that Herod gathered the chief priests and scribes together and demanded of them where Christ should be born. They at once answered, "In Bethlehem of Judea," and appealed to this prophecy for the proof.

3. Therefore will he give them up until the time *that* she which travaileth hath brought forth: then the remnant of his brethren shall return unto the children of Israel.

He (Jehovah) gives up them (his covenant people), in the sense of leaving them to be scourged for their sins and purified under this discipline, until this great Ruler, the Messiah, should be born. The verb rendered "give up," has this sense in 1 Kings 14: 16, and 2 Chron. 30: 7, "Be not as your fathers who transgressed against the God of your fathers; therefore he *gave them up* to desolation."——"She that travaileth" must refer to the thought in the previous verse, the human birth of the Messiah in Bethlehem. Micah may have had before his mind what Isaiah wrote (7: 14), "Behold, a virgin shall conceive and bear a son, and shall call his name Immanuel." ——The giving up to temporary calamities is referred to in verse 1. The divine policy seems to have been to let his apostate Israel sink very low as to its outward estate, and then by this means bring out the more prominently before all the world the Great Deliverer.—— "The remnant of his brethren" should naturally be those of the Jewish communion who were scattered abroad. They were to return to the main body.

4. And he shall stand and feed in the strength of the LORD, in the majesty of the name of the LORD his God; and they shall abide: for now shall he be great unto the ends of the earth.

The Hebrew verb "feed" belongs to shepherd life, and includes both feeding and ruling, supplying the want of food and the want of protection and government as well. The attitude of a shepherd is a *standing* one, hence "he shall *stand* and feed." He shall fulfil this office, not in any merely human might and majesty, but in the strength and majesty of the very God.——"And they," his people, his flock, "shall *abide*," in the sense of permanence and security, not driven about and away into captivity, as they then would have been so recently. May there not be a quiet antithesis between the shepherd *standing* over them, and themselves *sitting* securely and at ease under his guardian eye and overshadowing presence? ——One reason why they sit so securely is that their king is "great unto the very ends of the earth." The range of his power sweeps far beyond Judea. It fills the wide world, and leaves no place for nations and armies hostile to the people of the Messiah.

5. And this *man* shall be the peace, when the Assyrian shall come into our land: and when he shall tread

in our palaces, then shall we raise against him seven shepherds, and eight principal men.

"This man," the Messiah, "shall be *peace*," the fountain and author of peace, and of peace in a sense involving not only the absence of war but the presence of all the best earthly good and even heavenly good besides. Yet the special sense is that of peace as opposed to war. The course of thought throughout this passage contemplates the people as in a militant state, often assailed by outward, active enemies. Under such circumstances, "peace" is a word fraught with intense and precious significance.——The brevity of this expression, "this man shall be peace," favors the opinion that Micah had before his mind, and assumed that his readers would have before theirs, those other prophecies which he had almost quoted: "The sceptre shall not depart from Judah, nor a lawgiver from between his feet, until Shiloh (Prince of Peace) shall come; him shall the people obey" (Gen. 49: 10); and that of Isaiah (9: 6): "For unto us a child is born; unto us a son is given; and the government shall be upon his shoulders; and his name shall be called Wonderful, Counsellor, The Mighty God, The Everlasting Father, The *Prince of Peace*." As if he would say, You will understand my brief allusion to this man as "peace;" you will remember those prophecies so very similar to what I have been saying. ——The Assyrian foe is named because he was then far more formidable than any other. This does not imply that precisely this enemy would be on hand in the days of the Messiah's advent or thenceforward. He expects that help from God against foreign enemies will come in the way of supplying competent leaders. That these military leaders are called "shepherds," may have a tacit reference to Moses, the shepherd leader, and to David, the shepherd king. It may also imply that if the people are taught and fed in the ways of God, they will be invincible against outward enemies.——"Principal men" is in Hebrew, *anointed men*, set apart, anointed and qualified of God. "Seven" and "eight" are definite numbers used as indefinite, in the sense of an adequate number for leaders against the foe. See notes on Amos 1: 3.

6. And they shall waste the land of Assyria with the sword, and the land of Nimrod in the entrances thereof: thus shall he deliver *us* from the Assyrian, when he cometh into our land, and when he treadeth within our borders.

The verb rendered "waste" is the same rendered "feed" in v. 4, and is probably a play on the possible senses of that word. While King Messiah shall feed his own people like a shepherd, they, made brave in war by his might within them, shall *feed down* the land of Assyria by the sword—of course in the sense of consuming and laying desolate.——The Assyrian stands here to represent the enemies of God's people, and is selected because when Micah wrote, he was *the* enemy chiefly to be feared. With this view I see no necessity of looking after a literal fulfilment on *that* Assyria. *Any* powerful foe is Assyria.

7. And the remnant of Jacob shall be in the midst of many people as a dew from the LORD, as the showers upon the grass, that tarrieth not for man, nor waiteth for the sons of men.

8. And the remnant of Jacob shall be among the Gentiles in the midst of many people as a lion among the beasts of the forest, as a young lion among the flocks of sheep: who, if he go through, both treadeth down, and teareth in pieces, and none can deliver.

9. Thine hand shall be lifted up upon thine adversaries, and all thine enemies shall be cut off.

"The remnant of Jacob" comprises those who survive the wars and desolations sent of God to scourge and purify his people. It is of course implied that these have been purified by the afflictions which they have survived, and are now prepared for effective usefulness in the service of their King Messiah. First, they shall "be among Gentile nations like the dew and like showers from the Lord"—figures suggestive of munificent blessings—blessings that come before men ask for them, "on the just and on the unjust;" anticipating the wants of vegetation.——The next figure also locates them among Gentile nations, where they are as a lion among beasts, or a young lion among the flock—everywhere a power to be respected and even feared. The idea of destructiveness is (we may hope) less prominent than that of efficiency, or at least we are to think of destructiveness only as relating to the real and incorrigible enemies of God, and even then of their agency as incidental and passive rather than direct and active. "Vengeance belongeth unto God," and when his providence employs his people in the destruction of guilty nations, it is commonly not by any direct agency, but rather by indirect.

10. And it shall come to pass in that day, saith the LORD, that I will cut off thy horses out of the midst of thee, and I will destroy thy chariots:

11. And I will cut off the cities of thy land, and throw down all thy strong holds:

These statements show that God's people are not thought of here as fighting with carnal weapons, for if they were, then horses and chariots would come into use. "Cities" must be here thought of in the military sense, parallel to "strongholds." The idea is that the Lord will be himself their Refuge and Strength, and will take away their confidence in human sources of help. The Psalmist gives the spirit of this passage, saying—"Some trust in chariots and some in horses; but we, in the name of the Lord our God" (Ps. 20:7).

12. And I will cut off witchcrafts out of thine hand; and thou shalt have no *more* sooth-sayers:

13. Thy graven images also will I cut off, and thy standing images out of the midst of thee; and thou shalt no more worship the work of thy hands.

14. And I will pluck up thy groves out of the midst of thee: so will I destroy thy cities.

Witchcraft and soothsaying are twin sisters to idol gods; all unite in a common sympathy with Satan and his kingdom against God and his truth and worship. What he here promises is therefore a blessing to his church and kingdom. Indeed, we might say, He can give no greater blessing to his people than to take away their sins, by mild measures and influences, if he can; by stern and painful agencies, if he must. The destruction of "cities" here also, as in v. 11, must contemplate them, not as mere residences of a dense population, but rather as the corrupt centres and fountains of idolatry and vile superstition.

15. And I will execute vengeance in anger and fury upon the heathen, such as they have not heard.

The church being purified, it remains to execute vengeance on the heathen who are still incorrigible. Then and so will the world be redeemed from its sins, and the reign of Messiah be omnipotent in all the earth. What we should expect from the nature of the case is rendered certain by the sure word of prophecy, viz., that this subjugation of the world to King Messiah will be effected by a twofold agency: (1.) The power of truth and of the Spirit of God to whatever extent they may become effectual. (2.) Desolating and exterminating judgments on all who are incorrigible under the best appliances for their salvation that God can wisely employ.

Thus closes this most instructive Messianic chapter. Some have said that the portion of this chapter which promises prosperity closes with v. 8, the remaining part denoting adversity. Such interpreters seem to forget that God can give his people no richer blessing than to cut off and remove their sins. Aye, let his name be praised for this, even though it be by stern excision, the cutting off of right hands, or the plucking out of right eyes!

CHAPTER VI.

A GRAND public hearing of the case made by Jehovah against his covenant people is called for (v. 1); the mountains are summoned to be present (vs. 1 and 2); the Lord presents his complaint and appeals to his past mercies (vs. 3–5); the people ask what they shall do to please God (vs. 6, 7); the prophet replies (v. 8), and continues still to expose their sins, and to speak of the judgments inflicted therefor.

1. Hear ye now what the LORD saith; Arise, contend thou before the mountains, and let the hills hear thy voice.

2. Hear ye, O mountains, the LORD's controversy, and ye strong foundations of the earth: for the LORD hath a controversy with his people, and he will plead with Israel.

The first verse is the Lord's word to his prophet. "Contend" is used here in the sense of a legal contending—a pleading before a court. This complaint made by Jehovah against his people, the prophet is to bring before the "mountains and the strong foundations of the earth," as if inanimate nature could not fail of having moral sense enough to appreciate the merits of so very plain a case. The scene is sublimely grand—this holding court before the mountains and the strong pillars of the earth, giving them to understand that the Lord has a controversy with his people, and summoning them to hear and pass upon the case.

3. O my people, what have I done unto thee? and wherein have I wearied thee? testify against me.

The case now opens. The Lord says, "O my people, what have I done that could in any possible degree justify thee in such apostasy against thy God?" If they have ought to reply, the court is open; "testify," saith the Lord, "against me."

4. For I brought thee up out of the land of Egypt, and redeemed thee out of the house of servants; and I sent before thee Moses, Aaron, and Miriam.

5. O my people, remember now what Balak king of Moab consulted, and what Balaam the son of Beor answered him from Shittim unto Gilgal; that ye may know the righteousness of the LORD.

Miriam became prominent in the song of triumph on the hither side of the Red Sea, Ex. 15.——The striking narrative respecting Balak and Balaam may be seen, Num. chap. 22–24. Balak thought to prevail against this new and formidable people by means of divination and the cursing power of one widely known and honored as a master in the mysteries of magic; but the Lord headed Balaam, and would not let him go to sell his conscience and his soul for the wages of unrighteousness, and make capital for Balak against the Lord's people. The Lord's control over Balaam evinced his power on the hearts of even wicked men, for Balaam still continued to be a bad man, and met his death at last among God's enemies (Num. 31: 8).——"Shittim" was a valley in Moab. Gilgal was the place, close on the west side of the Jordan, where the Hebrew people pitched their first camp in Canaan, and raised their monument of stones.——"From Shittim unto Gilgal" cannot be directly connected with Balaam's answer to Balak, as if this answer was kept up throughout this entire journey. We must supply the ellipsis: "Remember all that occurred from Shittim till ye were across the Jordan in Gilgal."——"That ye may know the righteousness of the Lord" cannot here refer to *justice*, but must rather mean the favors and mercies of the Lord. The word "righteousness" has this sense in quite a number of passages. One clear case occurs 1 Sam. 12: 7, where Samuel says, "Let me reason with you of all the righteous acts of the Lord (righteousnesses), which he did to you and to your fathers;" whereupon he proceeds to recite a long catalogue of divine benefits, *mercies*—not by any means acts of mere justice.

6. Wherewith shall I come before the LORD, *and* bow myself before the high God? shall I come before him with burnt-offerings, with calves of a year old?

7. Will the LORD be pleased with thousands of rams, *or* with ten thousands of rivers of oil? shall I give my first-born *for* my transgression, the fruit of my body *for* the sin of my soul?

These are questions put by the people to the prophet. They respond to his rebukes and expostulations with the inquiry, What will meet the demands of the Lord our God? What does he require us to do?——Two things are worthy of note in the general cast of these inquiries: (1.) That they are deeply shaded with the current thought of the heathen nations round about them, rather than by the tone of the Institutes of Moses; and (2.) That they seem to imply that the Deity demands offerings of the most costly sort, and penance the most severe—overlooking all the weightier matters of the law—justice and love.

8. He hath shewed thee, O man, what *is* good; and what doth the LORD require of thee, but to do justly, and to love mercy, and to walk humbly with thy God?

This is the prophet's brief but exceedingly comprehensive reply. "Do justice" first of all, everywhere, and always; then, yet further, toward your fellow-men "show mercy;" do acts of kindness and favor where no merit creates a claim of justice; and finally, as toward God, walk with him humbly, in constant communion and fellowship. Recognize his surrounding, all-pervading presence, and adjust thy spirit and thy life to a due sense of that presence. In the last clause the Hebrew is specially expressive: "*Bow low to walk with God*," as if only so could sinning mortals hope to come near to the Holy One.——Thus, in fewest, briefest words, does the prophet reply, giving us precisely the great duties which man owes both to his fellow-man and to his God.

9. The LORD's voice crieth unto the city, and *the man of* wisdom shall see thy name: hear ye the rod, and who hath appointed it.

Again the prophet returns to expose and reprove the sins of the people, and to announce the judgments that the Lord must needs send.——The "city" to which the Lord's voice crieth is Jerusalem, prominent for her responsibilities, prominent in her sins. It was therefore every way fitting that the Lord should cry unto her.——In the next clause the Hebrew margin presents a slightly different reading, which would give this sense: "Those who fear thy name will have wisdom." But this reading has no claims for precedence before the one in our Hebrew text and in our English text—"The wise will regard thy name"—whatever fools may do or may not. The prophet assumes that the unwise will not regard the name of Jehovah.——The exhortation is, "Hear ye the rod"—the lessons taught by the Lord's rod of discipline—and so learn to know him who has appointed it, and who directs its mission in a sinning world.

10. Are there yet the treasures of wickedness in the house of the wicked, and the scant measure *that is* abominable?

As if surprised as well as grieved, the Lord asks, Are there yet in wicked men's houses the treasures they have gotten by wickedness and the scant measure, or "ephah?" This form of question strongly implies that there are.——The Hebrew people seem to have been strangely addicted to falsifying by unjust weights and measures, although their statute law most expressly forbade it. See Lev. 19:35, 36, and Deut. 25:13–16. Other passages note the prevalence of this sin, and strongly condemn it: Prov. 11:1 and 20:10; Hos. 12:7; and Amos 8:5.

11. Shall I count *them* pure with the wicked balances, and with the bag of deceitful weights?

The use of the first person creates the only difficulty of exposition. The verb properly means "Shall I be pure?"—not, Shall I count others as pure? Read thus, we must suppose the prophet to put the question as of himself, that the people may in like manner each ask it of himself, "Shall I be pure with" (*i. e.*, while using) "wicked balances and a bag of deceitful weights?" literally, *stones to deceive with.*

12. For the rich men thereof are full of violence, and the inhabitants thereof have spoken lies, and their tongue *is* deceitful in their mouth.

"For the rich men thereof," *i. e.*, of the city of Jerusalem, referred to v. 9.

13. Therefore also will I make *thee* sick in smiting thee, in making *thee* desolate because of thy sins.

14. Thou shalt eat, but not be satisfied; and thy casting down *shall be* in the midst of thee; and thou shalt take hold, but shalt not deliver; and *that* which thou deliverest will I give up to the sword.

15. Thou shalt sow, but thou shalt not reap; thou shalt tread the olives, but thou shalt not anoint thee with oil; and sweet wine, but shalt not drink wine.

Here are the judgments to be sent on the people for these sins. In the clause "I will make thy wound incurable," the words imply that this wound comes of the Lord's smiting.——V. 14 I translate closely, thus: "Thou shalt eat and not be satisfied, for thy hunger shall still be within thee; thou shalt remove away (*i. e.*, thy goods for safety), but thou shalt not save them; and whatever thou shalt save I will give up to the sword."

16. For the statutes of Omri are kept, and all the works of the house of Ahab, and ye walk in their counsels; that I should make thee a desolation, and the inhabitants thereof an hissing: therefore ye shall bear the reproach of my people.

Omri, the father, and Ahab, the son, were leaders in the idolatry of Israel. Their example and influence were intensely pernicious over Judah.——"The reproach of my people" is not reproach cast *by* my people, but such reproach as is *due to* my people, considering that they were mine by covenant, under the highest obligations, but violated all.

CHAPTER VII.

THE course of thought in this chapter embraces the prophet's distress (v. 1); its causes in the extreme wickedness of the people (vs. 2–4); so great that no confidence can be reposed in man, not even in best friends (vs. 5, 6); but should be in God (v. 7). Trusting in her God, Zion exults over her enemies (vs. 8, 9), who are covered with shame (v. 10); enlargement for Zion (vs. 11, 12), albeit judgments have come and must come for her sins; the prophet's prayer (v. 14); and the Lord's answer (vs. 15–17); the prophet testifies in sublime strains to God's pardoning mercy, and the people respond (vs. 18–20).

1. Woe is me! for I am as when they have gathered the summer fruits, as the grape-gleanings of the vintage: *there is* no cluster to eat: my soul desired the first ripe fruit.

The prophet gives expression to his sadness, grief, and disappointment, by comparing his case to that of a man longing for the first ripe fruits, but who finds the summer fruits all gathered, the grapes all gleaned, and not a cluster left for his hunger. The state of things among the people which causes him such grief and disappointment, he proceeds to describe.

2. The good *man* is perished out of the earth: and *there is* none upright among men: they all lie in wait for blood; they hunt every man his brother with a net.

3. That they may do evil with both hands earnestly, the prince asketh, and the judge *asketh* for a reward; and the great *man*, he uttereth his mischievous desire: so they wrap it up.

4. The best of them *is* as a brier: the most upright *is sharper* than a thorn-hedge: the day of thy watchmen *and* thy visitation cometh; now shall be their perplexity.

The received translation gives the sense, in the main, well. The verb rendered "*wrap it up*" implies not merely covering over, but tying up—interlacing, and making all secure by artful planning.—— The "watchmen" (v. 4) are prophets, and "the day of thy watchmen" is the day thy prophets have foretold as one of destruction, and of God's visitation in judgment. Now shall the wicked who fall under these judgments be perplexed and confounded in their plans of wickedness, so that they shall not know what they can do.

5. Trust ye not in a friend, put ye not confidence in a guide: keep the doors of thy mouth from her that lieth in thy bosom.

6. For the son dishonoreth the father, the daughter riseth up against her mother, the daughter-in-law against her mother-in-law; a man's enemies *are* the men of his own house.

This entire description, beginning with v. 2, reveals a state of appalling corruption of morals, and gives the soundings of the great depths of human depravity as seen where the light of God's word is withdrawn, and idol worship with its surroundings comes into its place. As Christianity sanctifies and makes benign all the sweet relationships of home and family, so does human depravity, finding free scope, and ever-quickening impulse under the reign of idolatry, desecrate and render fiendish those same precious relationships. It is terrible that homes of love should become "habitations of cruelty;" but human depravity, unrestrained, has precisely this tendency, and sometimes reaches this result.

7. Therefore I will look unto the LORD; I will wait for the God of my salvation; my God will hear me.

No conclusion from such premises as these could be more fitting than this. When all our dearest earthly friends fail, let it be our joy that God is true and faithful—a doubly precious friend.

8. Rejoice not against me, O mine enemy: when I fall, I shall arise; when I sit in darkness, the LORD *shall be* a light unto me.

The special thing to be noticed in the Hebrew of this verse is that the verb rendered "rejoice," and the noun, "mine enemy," are both *feminine*, showing that the prophet addresses some city or political power, present to his thought; and consequently does not speak in his own person exclusively, but in behalf of his people; the sense being this: Speaking for Judah and Jerusalem, I say to Edom or to Babylon—"Rejoice not over me, thou insulting and exulting enemy; though I fall in war, and my sons and daughters go into captivity, I shall arise through the strength of my Redeemer God; though I sit in the darkness of a fallen kingdom, my people in a strange land, yet the Lord shall be a light unto me." ——It should be carefully noticed that the prophet's mind is projected forward from the awful sins of the land to the consequent curse—the captivity in Babylon, and to the deliverance ultimately wrought there for the covenant people when they became humbled, reformed, and penitent. It is with those scenes in view that he addresses Edom and Babylon so triumphantly in these verses.

9. I will bear the indignation of the LORD, because I have sinned against him, until he plead my cause, and execute judgment for me: he will bring me forth to the light, *and* I shall behold his righteousness.

10. Then *she that is* mine enemy shall see *it*, and shame shall cover her which said unto me, Where is the LORD thy God? mine eyes shall behold her: now shall she be trodden down as the mire of the streets.

In these verses also, Micah speaks in behalf of the covenant people. V. 9 gives utterance to the feelings appropriate under such sore chastisements from the Lord—a moral lesson for all in affliction, be the form of it what it may.——"Righteousness," in such a connection, does not mean simple justice, but beneficence, goodness, God's interposition in redeeming and saving mercy. This specific sense is in some passages entirely essential; I, therefore, confirm it: (1.) By the fact that in many passages "righteousness" is parallel to "salvation," and therefore synonymous with it, *e. g.*, Isa. 51: 5, 6, 8: "My righteousness is near; my salvation is gone forth," &c.—"but my salvation shall be forever, and my righteousness shall not be abolished"—"but my righteousness shall be forever, and my salvation from generation to generation; (2.) In other passages, the strain of the context and the nature of the case demand this sense, *e. g.*, Isa. 54: 17; which means—God will save his Zion from all her foes, "and their righteousness" (*i. e.*, this salvation) "is of me, saith the Lord." Also Ps. 51: 14: "Deliver me from blood-guiltiness, thou God of my salvation, and my tongue shall sing aloud of thy righteousness."—See notes on Micah 6: 5.

In v. 10, the English translators have given the gender of the party spoken of—manifestly the same that is addressed in v. 8. The sense is—The great enemy of Zion (probably Edom or Babylon) shall see the salvation wrought of God for us. She who had said tauntingly, "Where is the Lord thy God?" shall now be overwhelmed with shame, and be herself trodden under foot as mire in the streets. Whereas she looked exultingly on me in my fall, now mine eye shall behold her under God's righteous retributions.

11. *In* the day that thy walls are to be built, *in* that day shall the decree be far removed.

12. *In* that day *also* he shall come even to thee from Assyria, and *from* the fortified cities, and from the fortress even to the river, and from sea to sea, and *from* mountain to mountain.

These verses obviously speak of blessings upon Zion in the day when the Lord, having turned again her captivity, shall rebuild her walls, bring home her captives from afar, and with them also "the forces of the Gentiles."——Critics have differed greatly as to the precise sense of the words rendered "shall the decree be far removed." What our translators meant by "the decree," or by its being "far removed," is by no means clear. It is plain to one who reads the original, that Micah chooses his words, the verb * and the noun,† for the sake in part of a paranomasia, the two last radicals of the verb and the two which compose the noun being the same, and therefore the sounds of each are similar. For the

* רָחַק. † חֹק.

sake of this result, he may, perhaps, have used one or both of these words in a somewhat unusual sense. This may occasion some of the difficulties found by critics in the interpretation of the passage.

The following construction is suggested as fully in harmony both with the context and with the original and normal use of both these words: "In the day for rebuilding thy walls, in that day shall *limit be far away*"—*i. e.*, the city bounds shall be far off; the city indefinitely extended.——This use of the noun is amply justified by Job 14: 5, "Thou hast appointed his *bounds* that he cannot pass" (here, of *time*); and Job 26: 10, "He hath compassed the waters with *bounds*" (here limits in space, as in our passage), and 28: 26, "He made a decree (bound) for the rain" (determining its locality, and, perhaps, quantity). Isa. 5: 14, "Hell hath opened her mouth without *measure;*" literally, "and there is no limit."

The primary sense of the verb is--to be far off, far removed. ——Parallel in general meaning is Zech. 2: 1–4, where the first thought is—Go, measure the length and breadth of the city walls, as if to rebuild on the old foundations; but this direction is withdrawn, and God promises—Jerusalem shall be inhabited without walls for the multitude, &c.——So here the purpose of God is to enlarge her borders so that she may receive great accessions, as the next verse proceeds to say.——The verb used here occurs Isa. 33: 17: "Thine eyes shall see the King in his beauty; with joy shall they behold the land greatly *extended*," enlarged—their king in his glory, with a subject territory greatly increased on every side.—— In sentiment Isa. 54: 2, 3, is parallel: "Enlarge the place of thy tent, and let them stretch forth the curtains of thy habitations; spare not; lengthen thy cords, and strengthen thy stakes, for thou shalt break forth on the right hand and on the left, and thy seed shall inherit the Gentiles, and make the desolate cities to be inhabited." Remembering that Micah was contemporary with Isaiah, and that there are abundant proofs of their acquaintance with each other's writings, we shall readily account for their saying the same things, in much the same language, as to the day when the fallen walls of Zion shall be rebuilt. Taught by one and the same Spirit, and writing of the same things in the same age, why should not their views and their language be essentially the same?——Gesenius gives these words here this sense—"The set time is greatly extended." But it does not clearly appear from the context what this "set time" is, nor is any good reason apparent for restricting the enlargement to the one element of *time*. I prefer the broader sense as given above, which may indeed comprise enlargement in *territory*, in *capacity* for receiving great accessions to the church, and in the *period* of this prosperity—*enlargement* in the most general sense. Hence, the broad, indefinite form of the statement. ——In v. 12, the first verb is impersonal, and therefore means, not that "*he*," some one man, shall come from Assyria, but that *men*, peoples, it may be in vast numbers, shall come. The word rendered "fortified," * I prefer to render *Egypt*, thus—"In that day shall men come to thee from Assyria and from the cities of Egypt; and from Egypt even to the great river (Euphrates); from sea to sea and from mountain to mountain;" *i. e.*, from all the intervening regions, which indeed comprise all that vast country lying contiguous to Palestine, and stretching out to the remotest bounds of Egypt on the southwest, and to Assyria on the north and east. From these remote lands shall the exiles return, and, as above intimated, perhaps Gentiles as well, for the promise may look far on beyond the restoration from Babylon, although its primary reference is probably to that event.

13. Notwithstanding the land shall be desolate because of them that dwell therein, for the fruit of their doings.

The sense is—Notwithstanding these glorious promises of future enlargement, every way adapted to inspire high and brilliant anticipations, yet bear in mind "that for the great sins of the people, an age of judgment and desolation will surely intervene. Before those better days shall come, the land will lie a long time desolate as the fruit of the people's sins." A caution against abusing these promises.

14. Feed thy people with thy rod, the flock of thine heritage, which dwell solitarily *in* the wood, in the midst of Carmel: let them feed *in* Bashan and Gilead, as in the days of old.

The word rendered "*feed*" is pastoral—the usual term to describe the service of the shepherd. It, therefore, combines the two ideas—feeding, and ruling, or guiding. Hence to the Hebrews there would be no incongruity in supposing this feeding to be done with the "rod"—which is here the shepherd's crook; not a rod for scourging. The sense of the verse is—Take charge of thy people as a shepherd of his flock; they are thine heritage, now solitary in the forest; let them feed in the rich pastures of Bashan and Gilead, as of old. This is the prayer of the prophet. He expects the people to join in it.

15. According to the days of thy coming out of the land of Egypt will I show unto him marvellous *things*.

This verse may fitly be considered as the answer of the Lord to the prayer in the verse preceding. It pledges miraculous interposition and effective help, as in the Exodus from Egypt—the standing historic case to signify a glorious salvation.

* מָצוֹר

16. The nations shall see and be confounded at all their might: they shall lay *their* hand upon *their* mouth, their ears shall be deaf.

17. They shall lick the dust like a serpent, they shall move out of their holes like worms of the earth: they shall be afraid of the LORD our God, and shall fear because of thee.

Here are the effects on the Gentile nations of God's marvellous deliverances to be wrought for his people. They shall see and shall be ashamed of their own insignificant prowess. They may be supposed to say—"We have no power to cope with that; all our strength vanishes away before such marvellous works." They shall be dumb and deaf, as men astonished and stupefied with amazement. They shall lick the dust, humbling themselves low before the glorious majesty of Jehovah. They shall crawl out of their holes in the ground—a strong figure, to denote the change that has come over their glory and greatness.——The last clause should read thus: "They shall approach with humble fear and reverence *unto* the Lord our God"—this shade of meaning being required by the preposition rendered "*unto*." See notes on Hos. 3 : 5. Thus those thrilling impressions of awe and fear are to avail for the conversion of the Gentile nations.

18. Who *is* a God like unto thee, that pardoneth iniquity, and passeth by the transgression of the remnant of his heritage? he retaineth not his anger for ever, because he delighteth *in* mercy.

That sins so great should be so entirely forgiven, so fully passed over, to be noticed and known no more—and that God should so fully turn from his righteous anger, and give scope only to his great mercy—is most wonderful! As the prophet thinks of these qualities of the divine mercy in the case of his forgiving his covenant people and restoring them again to favors so great, his heart is overwhelmed within him. And why not? What can be more wonderful?——This language is full of beauty and of strength as well. "Who is a God like Thee, taking away sin" (to be seen and noted no more), "passing over the transgressions of the remnant of his chosen" (as a traveller *passes by* what he does not wish to notice); "and he does not make his wrath strong forever" (implying that he does the very opposite—makes it subside and give place to loving-kindness.) And all this "because he delighteth in mercy"), finding his real bliss, even the highest joy of his heart in forgiving the chief of sinners.) Is not all this most precious and most wonderful? Who, having once seen his own guilt in all its appalling blackness and vileness, and then felt the sweet sense of pardon, as if God himself were whispering peace and love to his heart, will not appreciate this inimitable description of the pardoning love of the Lord?

19. He will turn again, he will have compassion upon us; he will subdue our iniquities; and thou wilt cast all their sins into the depths of the sea.

This verse may, without violence, be construed as a sort of refrain or response, taken up by the people themselves, who enter into the spirit of the prophet's words, and respond in terms scarcely less pertinent and affecting. Or it may very fitly be considered as the prophet's own application of the previous verse to the case of God's covenant people. Either way the general sentiment is the same. God will turn from scourging to blessing, when his smitten people *turn* from their sins to righteousness. "He will have compassion upon us." Ah, yes, indeed he will! Such a God, so full of loving pity, how can it be otherwise?——"He will subdue our iniquities," the original word for "subdue" implying that he will tread them down under his feet—as an apostle said, "He will tread Satan under your feet shortly." Sin, personified, commanding its forces of temptation, is thought of as a powerful foe of man, as his arch enemy, perpetually ensnaring, assailing, crushing down and piercing through with bitter pangs; but God subdues this enemy; he withstands his efforts; sets himself to counteract his temptations, and becomes himself a strong tower of refuge, whither his people may fly and into which they may run and be safe! O how inexpressibly precious!——"Thou wilt cast all their sins into the depths of the sea," and they go down like a millstone, to rise no more! The idea is, that they come up no more to remembrance—as the Lord has said, "Their sins and their iniquities will I remember no more!" (Heb. 8:12). Considering that the Infinite Mind of the Universe never has lost from its thought and knowledge one fact, however minute, and never can, this statement seems most wonderful of all. God would have us feel that he does not remember against us the sin which we have fully repented of and heartily forsaken, and which therefore he has altogether forgiven and put away. He would almost lead us to think that he can forget them and has forgotten them, so that they shall come before his mind even in memory no more!——O how divinely kind and gracious is this! How like a tender Father! That he should labor to dispel from our mind those painful feelings of shame and grief over our sins, and should seem to say, "Come near to me and be my free-hearted, loving child, as welcome to my smiles and confidence and favor as if you had never sinned against me!"——Let this infinite Friend, so kind and so gracious, be loved, trusted, and adored by us all, for ever and ever!

20. Thou wilt perform the truth to Jacob, *and* the mercy to Abraham, which thou hast sworn unto our fathers from the days of old.

Here the book closes, affirming that such a God will surely perform all the good things, the truth and the mercy promised to the fathers long years ago. No doubt he will! Zacharias, filled with the Holy Ghost, caught the spirit as well as the leading words of this passage: "To perform the mercy promised to our fathers, and to remember his holy covenant," &c. (Luke 1 : 72).

NAHUM.

INTRODUCTION.

The introduction to this short book gives us only the general subject—a prediction of sore calamity on Nineveh; the name of the author and the place of his residence, or perhaps nativity. The latter point, being of small importance, I dispose of it briefly.—— Two places bear the name of Elkosh, and claim the honor of this prophet's birth;—one, beyond the Tigris; the other, in Galilee—the latter with the greater plausibility. Some think that Caper-*naum*—village of Naum—bears the name of this prophet.

The date of the book is a greater question. It can, however, be answered only proximately. The location of the book in the series of minor prophets probably had some reference to its date; but the internal evidence in the line of historic allusion is our main reliance. This goes to place him a little after Micah.——His great theme being the fall of Nineveh, there can be no reasonable doubt that he wrote soon after the famous invasion of Judah by Sennacherib and the utter overthrow of his army. That this event had thrilled the nation may be seen in numerous passages of Isaiah, *e. g.*, 10 : 24–34, and 14 : 24–27, and 17 : 12–14, and 33 ; and 36–39 chap. It could not be otherwise. Hence, naturally and properly, the Lord by his prophets sought to turn these signal events to the best moral account. Isaiah, though alluding to these transactions so often, had yet mostly passed over the retribution which the Lord would one day bring on Nineveh. This was left for Nahum. It was important, for the best moral impression on the people, that this should be revealed, and indeed that it should be written and made public soon after the invasion by Sennacherib and the defeat of his army

—at least, before the first impressions made by those events ha.l passed away.——Now, this great invasion was in the fourteenth year of Hezekiah (2 Kings 18: 13), whose reign of twenty-nine years fell B. C. 728–699—consequently, about B. C. 714, and Nahum would be located in time during the latter part of Hezekiah's reign. ——This book furnishes one other historic point—a reference (3 : 8–10) to the fall of "No-Amon," otherwise called Thebes and Diospolis, the famous capital of Upper Egypt. The manner of the prophet's allusion to this event implies that it was then past, yet probably recent and fresh in the minds of his first readers. But no extant history chronicles precisely the date of her fall. What Isaiah says (20 : 1–6) of Sargon, king of Assyria, and of his general Tartan, almost without doubt refers to this event, the more surely so, because both Isaiah and Nahum represent the Ethiopians as being the allies of the Egyptians, and involved in the ruin of their great city. The location of this narrative in the book of Isaiah favors its date somewhat earlier than the march of Sennacherib upon Jerusalem. Sargon is known to have reigned next before Sennacherib.——These facts and suppositions go to confirm the views above presented respecting the date of this book, as falling in the latter part of the reign of Hezekiah, *i. e.*, B. C. 710–700.——The fall of Nineveh, which Nahum so vividly describes, chapters 2 and 3, took place from seventy-five to eighty years after the date assumed for this prophecy. It fell before the allied forces of the Medes under Cyaxares and the Chaldeans under Nabopolassar, the precise date being assigned by the most reliable historians to B. C. 625

All the critics accord to Nahum a style of lofty sublimity and a power of graphic painting rarely surpassed. He wrote as one whose very soul was permeated and thrilled by the great events of his time, and who saw God's hand in them—a present and glorious *power* for salvation to his people, and for vengeance on their foes. To see the beauty and feel the force of his book, we shall need to imbue our hearts deeply with the true spirit and significance of those momentous facts of history.

CHAPTER I.

After the briefest possible introduction, the prophet breaks into the midst of his theme, his starting-point being most fitly those great qualities of the divine character which both the recent events of history and the burden of his prophecy conspire to illustrate—especially his retributive vengeance upon his enemies, coupled with his merciful protection and deliverance of his people. Hence we have mainly God's judgments on his foes (vs. 2–6); God a refuge for his people (v. 7); the overthrow of Sennacherib's army before Jerusalem (vs. 8–14); and the ensuing peace and joy (v. 15).

1. The burden of Nineveh. The book of the vision of Nahum the Elkoshite.

A "burden" in prophecy, here as elsewhere, is a message of calamity, predicting judgment and desolation.

2. God *is* jealous, and the Lord revengeth; the Lord revengeth, and *is* furious; the Lord will take vengeance on his adversaries, and he reserveth *wrath* for his enemies.

It should be borne in mind that these attributes of Jehovah are suggested by his retributive justice on Assyria, first, in destroying her great army when it came proudly and defiantly to lay waste the holy city; and next, in the future desolations of Nineveh, their great and proud capital. These historic facts may serve as illustrations of the sense in which Jehovah is "jealous," "revengeth," and "taketh vengeance."——The word "*furious*" in the English version should not be taken in the bad sense which has in modern times become predominant—as when spoken of wild beasts enraged, or men half frantic. The original is innocent of this special significance, and simply implies that the Lord is moved with indignation against his proud, determined enemies.

3. The Lord *is* slow to anger, and great in power, and will not at all acquit *the wicked:* the Lord *hath* his way in the whirlwind and in the storm, and the clouds *are* the dust of his feet.

The first clause continues the glowing description of Jehovah's attributes, most of the expressions being taken from the classic passage (Ex. 34: 6, 7) where the Lord proclaimed his name to Moses as one slow to anger, yet who will not at all acquit the guilty.——The last clause opens one of the grandest portrayings of the majesty of Jehovah ever drawn by human pen: "Jehovah—his way is in the whirlwind and in the storm, and the clouds are the dust about his feet." Across the deserts of the East a moving caravan is seen farthest by the dust they raise. So the clouds are the dust rising beneath his feet and marking the pathway of his glorious presence.

4. He rebuketh the sea, and maketh it dry, and drieth up all the rivers: Bashan languisheth, and Carmel, and the flower of Lebanon languisheth.

With an eye perhaps on the Red sea and the Jordan, the prophet proceeds: "He rebuketh the sea and so dries it up," *i. e.*, by his mere word of rebuke. Also, through his power of withholding rain, all vegetation, even in the most fertile regions, withers.

5. The mountains quake at him, and the hills melt, and the earth is burned at his presence, yea, the world, and all that dwell therein.

In the phrase "the earth is burnt at his presence," the original verb gives no sanction to the sense *to burn*, but must mean *is lifted up*, with reference to the upheaval of its crust by volcanic agents. The whole verse refers to this class of agencies.——"The mountains tremble before him," or "because of him" (not properly "*at him*"), "the hills melt," liquid lava gushing forth from their bowels and pouring down their sides—and the solid crust of the earth's surface is upheaved with its cities and all their vast population.

6. Who can stand before his indignation? and who can abide in the fierceness of his anger? his fury is poured out like fire, and the rocks are thrown down by him.

With the terrible agencies of the volcano and the earthquake still in mind, the prophet fitly asks—"Who can stand before Jehovah's indignation?" "Who can rise up against his burning wrath?" "Rise up," and not "*abide*," is the sense of the Hebrew. His fury is poured forth like rivers of lava from the craters of Vesuvius. How, then, can the wicked endure before him when once he ariseth in his wrath?

7. The Lord *is* good, a strong hold in the day of trouble; and he knoweth them that trust in him.

By a sudden, yet most expressive transition, this same God is a glorious refuge for his people. He is none the less good because he feels such indignation against incorrigible sin. He will defend his trustful children none the less because his wrath is so terrible against his and their foes. Indeed, his wrath against their foes is the pledge and guaranty of his love for them, and of his purpose to defend them forever.——This side of his character had its present illustration in the deliverance wrought for Judah when just about to fall before the armed hordes of Assyria. In the phrase "he *knoweth* them that trust in him," "*knoweth*" takes the strong sense of a peculiar and most tender *regard*.

8. But with an overrunning flood he will make an utter end of the place thereof, and darkness shall pursue his enemies.

From this point onward through the chapter, Sennacherib's army is before the mind, and the prophet alludes to their mischievous plottings against the people of God, and to his consequent retribution upon them in their complete destruction. A question of some importance arises here, upon which interpreters differ, viz., Whether the prophet's allusions to the invasion of Judah by Sennacherib (vs. 8–15) are prophecy or history. Was this passage written *before* or *after* the invasion?——My mind inclines strongly to the latter view, on the following grounds: (1.) The tenses of the verbs used at least admit this construction. Owing to a striking peculiarity in the use of the Hebrew tenses in prophecy, or rather, perhaps, to the mental stand-point of the prophet when visions of the future are brought before him, it becomes very difficult to determine, *from the tenses alone*, what is prophecy and what is history. In this passage it would be hard to show absolutely from the tenses alone, that either theory is impossible. There is plainly nothing in the tenses to forbid the construction of what relates to Sennacherib's invasion as recently past.——Thus the verbs in v. 8 are future, but they refer to the future fall of Nineveh—about B. C. 625. (V. 9), thus (literally): "What will ye devise against Jehovah?" The sense is—How can ye devise any thing to purpose against such an one as Jehovah?—which has augmented force, considered as spoken *after* the fall of Sennacherib's host. The reasons given are, "He makes" (not "will make") "ruin complete." "Affliction shall not rise again"—from you, or from any whom the Lord has once undertaken to destroy. These reasons are all fully in point, considered as said *after* the invasion and its defeat.——In v. 10 the sense is—"Though compacted like tangled thorns and soaked with strong drink, they *were devoured*" (the Hebrew is in the past tense) "like dry stubble." In v. 11 read "From thee *came out*" (past tense) "one who plotted mischief"—alluding to the past purpose and deed of Sennacherib. The twelfth verse has past tenses throughout; not "*shall* they be cut down," but they *were* cut.——"Though I have afflicted thee, I will afflict thee no more," is literal, and properly assume that the invasion is past.——The thirteenth verse means that now and henceforth, I will break off his yoke from upon thee. Thou shalt have nothing to fear more from the Assyrian power.——In v. 14, the infamy and disgraceful death of Sennacherib assume that the invasion is past.——In v. 15, the messengers with tidings of their fall—the call to Judah to resume her solemn feasts for her Belial shall never come near even to alarm her again —all is specially pertinent and life-like on the assumption that the deed is done.——There can, therefore, be no objection to its construction as history on the score of the Hebrew tenses, nor in the strain of the passage.——(2.) The passage (1 : 2–7) is especially pertinent and forcible on the supposition that the fall of Sennacherib's host is in the recent past, and fresh before all minds.——(3.) There is great pertinence in going forward from these events of recent history to predict the final ruin of Assyria, in righteous retribution for her bold and impious defiance of the Most High God.——(4.) The history of the event as given (Isa. 37) goes far to show that no prophecy of Nahum, predicting the fall of this Assyrian host, was extant *before* that fall. The king and even the pious portion of the people were in deep agitation, not to say consternation; they come to Isaiah for some light from the Lord, and he gives it. Then their fears are allayed and their faith confirmed.——The whole tenor of these transactions implies that nothing is known of any prediction from Nahum of the failure of this invasion and the consequent ruin of its author.——(5.) The Book of Nahum must be taken as one whole, written at one time. But it is scarcely supposable that the whole, including the prediction of the final fall of Nineveh, dates *before* this great invasion of Judah.——These considerations seem decisive.

There is a sudden transition from v. 7, where God is a refuge to his people, to v. 8, where he is a sweeping flood, overwhelming Nineveh and obliterating even its ancient foundations. The ideas, however, are kindred, for God is such a refuge to his people *because* he is such a power of destruction upon her enemies.——The figure—"with a flood sweeping over the land"—is probably borrowed from Isaiah 8 : 7, 8, where it describes the desolating march of the vast Assyrian army over the land of Judah. By a fit and most palpable retribution, armies, equally vast and desolating, shall yet come down on Nineveh, and shall make an utter end of even the site where she stood so long in her glory. The darkness of oblivion shall chase down these enemies of God, and they shall sink from the knowledge of coming generations.

9. What do ye imagine against the LORD? he will make an utter end: affliction shall not rise up the second time.

The prophet puts this bold question to the proud Assyrian invader: "What would ye plot against Jehovah?" "He will make an utter end" of his foes and of *you*. "Trouble to many people shall not arise from you a second time." Once smitten, you will never return to harass them again.

10. For while *they be* folden together *as* thorns, and while they are drunken *as* drunkards, they shall be devoured as stubble fully dry.

For though your armies move in phalanx, closely interlaced as thorns in their wild growth, and though they reel under their intoxication, they shall be devoured as stubble burns when perfectly dry.——That they are said to be drunken as with wine, and hence to reel in their intoxication, may allude to a striking fact in God's agency over nations doomed to judgment, and also to a very striking figure to represent this fact—the fact being that God gives such nations over to infatuation; and the figure to express it being this (as appears in Jer. 25 : 15–29). God sends round to the nations the wine-cup of his fury, and they drink till they are "moved" and "mad." Hence they are easily destroyed. They more than half destroy themselves. The slaveholding power of this American nation is a case quite in point, evincing this same mad infatuation which is both a natural and a governmental forerunner of destruction. The wine-cup of Jehovah's fury has been to their lips!

11. There is *one* come out of thee, that imagineth evil against the LORD, a wicked counsellor.

Sennacherib or Rabshakeh. He comes forth out of Assyria, or perhaps, specially from Nineveh, devising evil against Jehovah as the king of his covenant people.

12. Thus saith the LORD; Though *they be* quiet, and likewise many, yet thus shall they be cut down, when he shall pass through. Though I have afflicted thee, I will afflict thee no more.

The Lord sees this heathen king deliberately plotting the destruction of Judah, and therefore declares his purpose to destroy him and his army.——The first prominent word, rendered "quiet," more properly means *complete*, furnished with every appliance for success in their proposed object. Though they are fully equipped, and withal so very many, yet shall they be cut down (as the figure in v. 10 had expressed it) when he, the destroying angel, shall pass through their camp.——Isaiah records this event in these brief words: "Then the angel of the Lord went forth and smote in the camp of the Assyrians an hundred and fourscore and five thousand, and when they arose early in the morning, behold, they were all dead corpses" (Isa. 37 : 36).——Byron has put this scene in his best style:

"Like the leaves of the forest when summer is green,
That host with their banners at sunset were seen;
Like the leaves of the forest when autumn hath blown,
That host on the morrow lay withered and strown.
For the angel of death spread his wings on the blast,
And breathed on the face of the foe as he passed,
And the eyes of the sleepers waxed deadly and chill,
And their hearts but once heaved, and forever were still."

The last clause—"though I have afflicted thee," &c., refers to Judah, now relieved from danger, and no more to be afflicted by this long dangerous enemy.

13. For now will I break his yoke from off thee, and will burst thy bonds in sunder.

This verse expands the thought just before expressed.

14. And the LORD hath given a commandment concerning thee, *that* no more of thy name be sown: out of the house of thy gods will I cut off the graven image and the molten image: I will make thy grave; for thou art vile.

The person spoken of must be the Assyrian king. No scion of his family should again take root; no child come to the honor of his father's throne. This would seem to be the most natural sense of these words.——But according to the dim light of the history of those times, its precise fulfilment is not readily made out. The king should be Sennacherib who headed the famous invasion of Judah and Jerusalem. All the latter part of this verse 14 finds an accurate fulfilment in him. He made his grave in the house of his gods—a vile, "*light*" man, of no particular account. "*Light*" is the sense of the Hebrew word. But Isaiah records (37:38), "and Esarhaddon, his son, reigned in his stead." History assigns to this Esarhaddon a reign of thirty-five years. How, then, could it be said, no son of Sennacherib should come to the throne?——To avoid this difficulty, Dr. Henderson holds that the threatening was not to take effect at his death, but only at the final destruction of Nineveh—which he locates B. C. 625—almost a century in the future. *Then*, his dynasty should become extinct. He says, "It does not mean that none of his sons should succeed him in the government." But this is just what it seems to say, if we give the language a sense which affirms the extinction of his dynasty. If the words affirm extinction at all, they affirm it to take effect at once.——Others, with better success, give the words this turn—that his *name*, in the sense of fame, reputation, should be diffused abroad—sown *broadcast*, no more. He should die in dishonor as a vile man, and his name go down to posterity only in disgrace. In this sense of the prophecy, its fulfilment presents no difficulty.

15. Behold upon the mountains the feet of him that bringeth good tidings, that publisheth peace! O Judah, keep thy solemn feasts, perform thy vows: for the wicked shall no more pass through thee: he is utterly cut off.

War telegrams were borne in those days by swift runners (see 2 Sam. 18:19 ff.). When they brought tidings of victory and peace, their approach might well be hailed with joy. So now of these messengers with tidings of the utter ruin that befell Assyria's proud hosts in that one fatal night. The prophet's graphic touch of this scene is masterly. He gives no long and tedious details: his mind flashes over and past them all, to light on one or two most significant and expressive results. "Go, Judah, now, and keep thy solemn feasts: perform thy vows made in the hour of thy peril: this Belial shall pass through thy land no more: he is utterly cut off!"

As to keeping those solemn feasts, Judah *could*, for no enemy remained in her land to prevent: she *should*, for never before were there such themes for praise, such reasons for coming to the house of God with her thank-offerings to pay her solemn vows.

CHAPTER II.

This chapter brings us at once to the prophet's great theme—the burden of Nineveh. The mad and proud invasion of Judah by Sennacherib must first be noticed, that being the antecedent occasion of this final overthrow—the great sin of which this fall was the signal retribution. That consequently is spoken of in the first chapter. This chapter and the third give us the assault on ancient Nineveh, and her final fall.

1. He that dasheth in pieces is come up before thy face: keep the munition, watch the way, make *thy* loins strong, fortify *thy* power mightily.

Instead of finding in this first verse a summons to Hezekiah to prepare his capital for defence against Sennacherib (as some have done), I prefer to apply it (as manifestly vs. 3–13 must be applied) to the Assyrian king Chynilidan, in whose reign the combined forces of the Medes and Chaldeans came up against great Nineveh, and laid it in ruins. With this construction, v. 2 is interposed as a reason for God's overthrowing Nineveh—good, although the event occurred more than half a century before. Then v. 3 resumes and carries forward the thought of v. 1.——Moreover, Sennacherib has been effectually disposed of in chapter 1, tumbled into his dishonored grave, and his name given over to contempt and oblivion. It is not meet to raise him from his grave, to appear again on the face of this chapter.——Nineveh and her kings are addressed. Nineveh had been in her day a conquering power, dashing nations and their strong cities to atoms. Now, another great "hammer of the nations" is raised up of God, and appears at her gates, and the prophet tauntingly admonishes her to look well to her fortifications; to set watchmen along the ways leading to the city; to gird her loins for strife, and fortify to the utmost.

2. For the Lord hath turned away the excellency of Jacob, as the excellency of Israel: for the emptiers have emptied them out, and marred their vine-branches.

Why? "Because the Lord hath" (not turned *away*, but) "restored the glory of Jacob as the glory of Israel, although the 'emptiers' (her foreign enemies) had (almost) emptied the land of her population, and marred their vine-branches." This language implies that Judah had suffered sorely from her enemies, both in the waste of precious life, and in the damage done her vines, and of course other vegetable growths as well. The same facts are indicated by Isaiah of this very time: "And the remnant that is escaped of the house of Judah shall again take root downward," &c. "From out of Jerusalem shall go forth a remnant," &c., showing that many must have perished (see Isa. 37: 31, 32). V. 30 shows that cultivation had been entirely neglected during two full years. ——The word rendered "excellency" is sometimes (*e. g.*, Amos 6: 8 and Ps. 47: 4) applied to the land of Palestine, as being the "glory of all lands." So here, with the accessory idea of the land in its state of prosperity and glory. Jacob and Israel are here, not each the name of a distinct people, but both the name of one. With tacit allusion to the change of Jacob's name to Israel (Gen. 32 : 27, 28), the Lord is said to restore the glory of Jacob as being the people who have a princely power with God, and are recognized by him as his covenant people. Jacob and Israel are never the distinctive names of the two kingdoms. Here God blesses Jacob, as if in remembrance of what his other name, Israel, implies.

3. The shield of his mighty men is made red, the valiant men *are* in scarlet: the chariots *shall be* with flaming torches in the day of his preparation, and the fir-trees shall be terribly shaken.

4. The chariots shall rage in the streets, they shall justle one against another in the broad ways: they shall seem like torches, they shall run like the lightnings.

This description, given by the prophet, of the approaching hosts of Media and Chaldea, is, like all his descriptive paragraphs, full of fire, painting to the eye most vividly.——"The shields of his mighty men are reddened; his heroes are in scarlet; his chariots flash with the brightness of their iron scythes, as in the day of their preparation (*i. e.*, when new); the spears of cypress also wave on high. The chariots dash madly in the streets; they run to and fro in the open grounds; they look like lamps of fire; they dart like the lightning."

5. He shall recount his worthies: they shall stumble in their walk; they shall make haste to the wall thereof, and the defence shall be prepared.

Here the king of Nineveh is seen starting up as from a reverie or a sleep, to begin to appreciate his danger. He sees the fearful onslaught of converging hosts upon his capital. Now, "he thinks of his generals," and summons them to their work; they start off in haste, or in panic, and "stumble in their goings;" they make haste to the city wall," where their soldiers and military defences were located for the protection of the city, "and the breastworks are made firm." Breastworks is rather the modern phrase. This was a mantlet, apparently of interwoven boughs, to protect their heads as well as breasts from the missiles of ancient warfare.——According to Diodorus Siculus, Nineveh had fifteen hundred towers, distributed around on her city walls. These mantlets may have been located in the intervening spaces.

6. The gates of the rivers shall be opened, and the palace shall be dissolved.

7. And Huzzab shall be led away captive, she shall be brought up, and her maids shall lead *her* as with the voice of doves, tabering upon their breasts.

"The gates of her water-courses are burst open, and the palace is swept away." Nineveh stood upon the Tigris, on low ground. These "rivers" were her artificial canals for letting in their supply of water for irrigation and for other uses. Now, burst open by the besiegers, the palace, and consequently much of the city, was inundated.——The word rendered "Huzzab" has been variously interpreted, as the margin indicates. All modern critics agree in making the word a verb, and not, as in the English version, a proper noun.——The reader may choose among the following constructions, the first of which disregards the usual division of verses:

(1.) (v. 6). "The palace is dissolved, though firmly established." (v. 7). "She is made bare; she is carried up," &c.

(2.) (v. 7). "It is settled! (*i. e.*, decreed and done!) she is led off into captivity," &c.

(3.) (v. 6). "And the palace is dissolved. (v. 7.) "Though it (the palace) was firmly founded, yet is she (the city) led into captivity; she is borne away (as a captive queen); her maids are leading her as with the voice of doves, smiting (drumming) upon their breasts." ——This choice between various constructions involves no doctrinal truth of special importance. The last interpretation, requiring no change in the Hebrew accents, and otherwise meeting both the exigencies of the context and the established usage of the individual words, has slightly my preference.

8. But Nineveh *is* of old like a pool of water: yet they shall flee away. Stand, stand, *shall they cry*, but none shall look back.

"Though Nineveh has been since her early days as a reservoir of waters"—a point for the confluence of people from every clime and kingdom, "yet now are they fleeing." "Stand! stand! but there is no turning them back." This translation imitates the terseness and gives the sense of the original.——All great commercial centres, like the London and New York of our times, will have a population gathered from the whole civilized world. The exigencies of business and trade produce this result.——Our passage touches graphically the effect of a panic on such a population. The masses have but one impulse—to run. The authorities, who would fain save the city, shout, "Stand! stand!" but the call is powerless; it turns no one back.

9. Take ye the spoil of silver, take the spoil of gold; for *there is* none end of the store *and* glory out of all the pleasant furniture.

The prophet turns for a word to the conquerors, who are thought of now as within the city. "Seize the silver; seize the gold; there is no end to her stores" (*i. e.*, of carefully prepared and curiously wrought furniture, equipage, &c.)—a huge mass of all beautiful things." There is no other word but "things" so nearly equivalent to the Hebrew in comprehensiveness.——The great wealth of Nineveh now lies at the mercy of her conquerors.

10. She is empty and void, and waste: and the heart melteth, and the knees smite together, and much pain *is* in all loins, and the faces of them all gather blackness.

The first three adjectives aim to intensify the idea of utter emptiness, as if Nineveh had been a huge and full bottle, now inverted, and the contents gurgle and gush out to the last drop.——"Hearts melt; there is shaking of knees and keen pangs in all loins; all faces lose their cheerful glow"—contract and seem to draw in their brightness. This seems to be the exact sense of the Hebrew.

11. Where *is* the dwelling of the lions, and the feeding-place of the young lions, where the lion, *even* the old lion, walked, *and* the lion's whelp, and none made *them* afraid?

12. The lion did tear in pieces enough for his whelps, and strangled for his lionesses, and filled his holes with prey, and his dens with ravin.

13. Behold, I *am* against thee, saith the LORD of hosts, and I will burn her chariots in the smoke, and the sword shall devour thy young lions: and I will cut off thy prey from the earth, and the voice of thy messengers shall no more be heard.

Nineveh is here thought of as an old lion's den. This figure is the more pertinent because the ancient Assyrians (like the modern British) chose the lion for their national symbol. This figure consequently is prominent in the ruins of ancient Nineveh (see Layard's "Nineveh," pp. 32, 47, 85, 88, &c.) Hence the prophet exultingly asks, Where is the old den now?——In the last verse the figure is half dropped and half retained. "Burning her chariots in the smoke," drops the figure; "the sword devouring her young lions, and cutting off his prey from the earth," mostly retains it.——"The voice of her messengers" is that of her ambassadors, who represented her power in distant countries, with perhaps a tacit allusion to the taunting speech of her Rabshakeh to the Jewish people on the walls of Jerusalem, as in Isa. 36 : 4–20. Such a voice as this shall be heard no more.——The immediate cause of her ruin is presented forcibly: "Behold, I am against thee, saith Jehovah of hosts."——Not the proudest or the mightest of cities can stand when the great Jehovah is against her.

CHAPTER III.

THE same subject—the fall of Nineveh—is resumed and concluded.

1. Woe to the bloody city! it *is* all full of lies *and* robbery; the prey departeth not;

First come the moral causes of this fearful desolation. It is a city of blood; "all full of lies"—no truth between man and man; and thence come, by natural result, violence and robbery. The seizing of prey, by the strong from the weaker, never ceases. The original words suggest that men, created rational and moral, have become fierce and savage as beasts of prey.

2. The noise of a whip, and the noise of the rattling of the wheels, and of the prancing horses, and of the jumping chariots.

3. The horseman lifteth up both the bright sword and the glittering spear: and *there is* a multitude of slain, and a great number of carcasses; and *there is* none end of *their* corpses; they stumble upon their corpses:

These verses resume the account of the siege and assault, continued from 2 : 3–5, 9, 10: "The crack of the whip; the noise of rattling wheels, prancing horses, bounding chariots. There are horsemen mounting; flashing swords, the lightnings of the spear; heaps of slain, masses of the dead, and no end to the corpses; men stumble over their dead bodies." Think of it, and note how it looks —this onslaught of warriors through the crowded streets of helpless Nineveh, leaving traces of their work in the heaps of her mangled dead!——One of the marvels is, that the pen of prophecy should paint such a life-scene with no less vividness and force than the ablest historic pen. Surely we must see in this the impress of God's own finger!

4. Because of the multitude of the whoredoms of the well-favored harlot, the mistress of witchcrafts, that

selleth nations through her whoredoms, and families through her witchcrafts.

Again the prophet recurs to the moral causes of this appalling slaughter. There had been sin no less appalling!——If these terms that usually denote lewdness, referred to Israel and Judah, it would be legitimate to give them the sense of idolatry—this usage being well established with reference to the covenant people. In this passage the same usage may be inferred from the connection of whoredom with witchcraft. Hence, under this figure of a lewd harlot, the prophet really means idolatry and its monstrous brood of superstitions, witchcrafts, and doubtless licentiousness as well. Through the influence wielded by her world-wide commerce, Nineveh had corrupted all the nations round about. It was, therefore, only a fit retribution that her fall should be a public disgrace before them all.

5. Behold, I *am* against thee, saith the LORD of hosts; and I will discover thy skirts upon thy face, and I will shew the nations thy nakedness, and the kingdoms thy shame.

6. And I will cast abominable filth upon thee, and make thee vile, and will set thee as a gazing-stock.

This is her doom of shame. The figure of a harlot is kept up throughout these two verses.——"Discover"—not in the modern sense, to *find by search*, but in the ancient one, to *expose* to public view, and here to public scorn. God will expose her nakedness before all the nations; and then, to make her shame the greater, will cast abominable filth upon her naked person.

7. And it shall come to pass, *that* all they that look upon thee shall flee from thee, and say, Nineveh is laid waste: who will bemoan her? whence shall I seek comforters for thee?

None can bear the horrid sight. Her old associates flee away, and no one cares to pause, to bewail her doom.

8. Art thou better than populous No, that was situate among the rivers, *that had* the waters round about it, whose rampart *was* the sea, *and* her wall *was* from the sea?

9. Ethiopia and Egypt *were* her strength, and *it was* infinite; Put and Lubim were thy helpers.

When Nahum wrote, Nineveh was still in her glory. Her people felt as secure from this or any other destruction as the people of London, Paris, or New York, to-day. It was to meet such a feeling of security that the prophet calls their attention to *No*, the great city known as Thebes and Diospolis, the capital of Upper Egypt—which, from a state of unrivalled splendor, wealth, and greatness, had been suddenly laid in ruins.——"Art thou better," *i. e.*, stronger and more safe, "than No-Amon?" The word rendered "populous" should be taken as part of the proper name of the city. "No-Amon," called only "*No*," Ezek. 30: 14–16, and Jer. 46: 25, but more often in Egyptian history, "Thebes," stood on both sides of the Nile—a most magnificent city, the ruins of whose temples and tombs are at this day one of the wonders of the world. This city is supposed to have fallen under the assault of Sargon, king of Assyria, of whom Isaiah 20 speaks.—See introduction to Nahum.——Thebes had powerful allies. Being the centre of trade, business, and religion for all Upper Egypt, and probably for Ethiopia also, she had their aid, and the prophet says this was *without limit.* Lubim was the Hebrew form of the name Libyans, and Put is supposed to have been part of their extensive country—the whole lying on the west of Egypt.

10. Yet *was* she carried away, she went into captivity: her young children also were dashed in pieces at the top of all the streets: and they cast lots for her honorable men, and all her great men were bound in chains.

"Yet she became an exile," &c. The verse sketches the usual fate of a conquered people in that almost savage state of the world.——If such had become the doom of Thebes, ought not Nineveh also to fear?

11. Thou also shalt be drunken: thou shalt be hid, thou also shalt seek strength because of the enemy.

Nineveh also as well as Thebes should "be drunken"—should take the wine-cup of Jehovah's wrath and drink her death-doom. See notes on Nahum, 1: 10.——"Thou shalt be hid," means shall be lost to public view—obliterated and forgotten; dropped from the knowledge of the human race.——How wonderfully has this been true of old Nineveh for twenty-five centuries! Until the present generation, ages have passed over her ruins, and no living man knew the site where once she sat so proudly and sinned so fearfully! The Arab rode his steed high above her fallen towers and crumbled walls, all unconscious how much human greatness lay dead and forgotten beneath his feet!——"Shall seek strength." The Hebrew properly means a *stronghold*—a place of safety against the enemy. To this they should be subjected, despite of their lofty walls and almost countless towers. So understood, the course of thought is continued into the next verse.

12. All thy strong holds *shall be like* fig-trees with the first ripe figs: if they be shaken, they shall even fall into the mouth of the eater.

13. Behold, thy people in the midst of thee *are* women: the gates of thy land shall be set wide open unto thine enemies: the fire shall devour thy bars.

By a most significant figure, the prophet shows that her military strength was of small account—rather a temptation to an assault than a defence against it. Nineveh had become too rich, and too luxurious and effeminate, to stand against the plundering robber-hordes of younger and more vigorous races. Her warriors had become as women.——The "bars" which the fire shall devour, are those of her gates.

14. Draw the waters for the siege, fortify thy strong holds: go into clay, and tread the mortar, make strong the brick-kiln.

Tauntingly the prophet commends to her a little more labor on her fortifications—advice the more in point, because Nineveh had already expended an untold amount of wealth and labor upon this very thing, and also because she was so sure her walls were impregnable, and because they were, after all, of so very small account as against her enemies. The irony was put on for an edge, to make the truth cut.

15. There shall the fire devour thee; the sword shall cut thee off, it shall eat thee up like the canker-worm: make thyself many as the canker-worm, make thyself many as the locusts.

Even there in thy brick-kilns and mortar-beds, the fire of Jehovah's retribution will find thee out and devour thee. It shall eat thee, as the canker worm (a species of locust) eats the herbage of the land.——Then the locust having been suggested to his mind as a figure of devastation, he seizes it as a figure for a multitude, and says—"Make thyself a countless host like the locusts, yet shall the fire and sword of the Almighty consume thee."

16. Thou hast multiplied thy merchants above the stars of heaven: the canker-worm spoileth, and flieth away.

She had enjoyed an immense commerce with India on the east, and with all western Asia and northeastern Africa on the west. The wealth of those valleys of the Euphrates and the Tigris was also immense; but the prophet quietly suggests that the locust pillages and then flies away. So would her great wealth vanish before the hosts of her foes.

17. Thy crowned *are* as the locusts, and thy captains as the great grasshoppers, which camp in the hedges in the cold day, *but* when the sun ariseth they flee away, and their place is not known where they *are*.

"Thy crowned" are her princes, of whom Sennacherib said, "Are not my princes altogether kings?"——The original rendered "captains" is an Assyrian word, meaning satraps, governors. They will disappear as the grasshoppers, who lie close under the wall during the cool of the day, but when the sun rises flee away, and their very place is unknown. So these high officers on whom he had so much relied, would fail him and disappoint his expectations. Nahum 2:5 represents the king, when first aroused to his danger, as thinking of these officers—to how little purpose may be seen here.

18. Thy shepherds slumber, O king of Assyria: thy nobles shall dwell *in the dust:* thy people is scattered upon the mountains, and no man gathereth *them.*

"Thy shepherds" must mean, in this connection, his viceroys—officers in charge of his provinces. They are in a deep sleep, inactive, overcome with sloth—as a real shepherd might be. "Thy nobles have sat down"—as if in utter unconcern for the peril of Nineveh. Thus, nobles and people alike fail him in the hour of his extremity.

19. *There is* no healing of thy bruise; thy wound is grievous: all that hear the bruit of thee shall clap the hands over thee: for upon whom hath not thy wickedness passed continually?

The nearly obsolete word "*bruit*" means *report* concerning thee—the news of thy fall. The world was ready to rejoice over her righteous doom; for where could a tribe be found that had not felt the galling of her yoke—the infliction of some wrong from her overbearing power?——So the prophet leaves proud Nineveh to her righteous yet fearful doom! Considering this prophecy as written and sent forth to the world almost a century before the final catastrophe, it was a standing admonition to the king and people of Nineveh to prepare tc meet God in the judgments of his wrath. Considered in its relations to God's people in the reign of Hezekiah, it was admirably adapted to secure a right moral impression from the overthrow of Sennacherib's army, and to make the people feel that, with God on their side, they need not fear the mightiest or proudest of their foes.

HABAKKUK.

INTRODUCTION.

The introduction to this short book gives nothing but the writer's name. He leaves the reader to ascertain from the book itself the time when, the place where, and the theme of which he wrote. These points may be ascertained with a good degree of definiteness and certainty in the first chapter, especially vs. 5–11. These verses show that the Chaldean power is now for the first time coming up to view as a desolating scourge on Judah. They were to do a work which men would not readily believe (v. 5), indicating that they had scarcely been known as a dangerous power before. The minute description of their character and ways (vs. 6–11) bears toward the same result, showing that previously they had been but little known.——Hence this must have been their first invasion. It was very near at hand when Habakkuk wrote. The invasion occurred in the fourth year of Jehoiakim, whose reign of eleven years was B. C. 611–600. It has been usual to date this invasion B. C. 606. Habakkuk's writing must be located somewhat (perhaps a few years) earlier. The desolation and famine which he contemplates (3 : 17) and which his exalted faith enabled him to triumph over, came with this sweep of a conquering, cruel enemy, probably not long after the publication of this wonderful book.——Habakkuk was contemporary with Jeremiah, who began to prophesy in the thirteenth year of Josiah, and continued down to the destruction of the city and the last deportation of captives in the eleventh year of Zedekiah, a range of some forty years. Near the middle of this period fell the first invasion by the Chaldeans in the fourth year of Jehoiakim. From Jeremiah, therefore, we may learn much respecting the general and moral condition of the people when Habakkuk wrote.——One leading course of thought runs through the entire book: the sins of the covenant people; God's raising up the Chaldeans to scourge them therefor; the prophet's expostulation with the Lord against permitting a people so cruel and wicked as they to afflict and destroy Judah; the Lord's answer touching the Chaldeans; closing with the prophet's prayer that God would reënact the glorious scenes of deliverance that appear on so many pages of the nation's early history; and God's virtual reply, by causing his glory to pass before the prophet's eye, thus impressing his soul with a sense of his power to save, and of his faithfulness and love as well. In view of these manifestations, the prophet exults in Jehovah alone, satisfied that under the wing and in the love of such a God he has nothing to fear, but every reason for joyful trust and triumph.——In point of style, Habakkuk stands unrivalled. Who can name the writer that excels him in the best qualities of a poetic imagination, and especially in his grand and sublime conceptions of Jehovah?

CHAPTER I.

The prophet, distressed by the appalling prevalence of wickedness among his people, cries to God for help (vs. 2–4); the Lord replies that he is raising up the Chaldeans to scourge them, and describes that people (vs. 5–11), against which the prophet expostulates with God (vs. 12–17).

1. The burden which Habakkuk the prophet did see.

"Burden" is here, as usual, a prophetic message of such sort as bears heavily on the prophet's heart.

2. O Lord, how long shall I cry, and thou wilt not hear! *even* cry out unto thee *of* violence, and thou wilt not save!

3. Why dost thou shew me iniquity, and cause *me* to behold grievance? for spoiling and violence *are* before me: and there are *that* raise up strife and contention.

4. Therefore, the law is slacked, and judgment doth never go forth: for the wicked doth compass about the righteous; therefore wrong judgment proceedeth.

A preliminary question arises here as to the general scope of these verses. Some suppose they describe the effects of the Chaldean invasion—the demoralization and oppression which they produced; others, that they present the state of morals and of the public life of the Jewish nation shortly before that invasion. I hold the latter view decidedly, for the following reasons: (1.) Because the prophets were accustomed to record the sins for which God judges and punishes his people, before they record the punishment itself. This is their established usage, and is, moreover, demanded by moral considerations, it being necessary for the best moral results that not only the punished but the world should know *why* God punishes.——(2.) In v. 5 the prophet manifestly introduces the Chaldean power for the first time to the reader's notice. It was obviously unthought of before. That this must be true will be readily seen by supposing the other theory (the first above named) to be true. On this supposition the prophet (vs. 2–4) would be made to say—O Lord, how long shall I cry out to thee of the mischiefs wrought by those Chaldean savages, and thou wilt not hear? See how they have broken down the public morals, and made justice between man and man a mockery!——To which (by the supposition) the Lord replies: "Let all the heathen take notice of it and marvel exceedingly, for I am about to do a strange and almost incredible thing." And what is it? "I am raising up the Chaldeans!"——"Ah, Lord God," the prophet might reply, "we have had them upon us a long time! They are the very mischief that I complain of," &c.——Such a construction of the passage is utterly inadmissible.——(3.) The description (vs. 2–4) corresponds to the moral and social state of Judah under the reign of Jehoiakim, and also of Zedekiah. See Jer. 22, and 2 Chron. 36. The public morals were utterly prostrate, and wickedness in all forms was rampant. (4.) On the other hand, the state of the country does *not* correspond with the results of the Chaldean invasion. The latter are indicated in 3 : 17.——Hence in vs. 2–4 I understand the prophet to speak of the state of society in Judah before the Chaldeans were thought of.——V. 2 seems to imply that the prophet had been for some time in his prophetic work, laboring among a degenerate people, battling against sin, and almost impatient that the Lord did not interpose to convert, or chastise, or exterminate. Jer. 22 shows that the people were then horribly corrupt, and that their king Jehoiakim was the weakest, meanest, and wickedest king that had ever disgraced their throne.——V. 3 is literally rendered thus: "Why dost thou cause me to behold iniquity, and why dost thou look (unconcerned) upon human misery? Destruction and violence are before me; there is strife, and men excite contention." The second clause does not well admit the sense—Why dost thou *make me behold?* The implied expostulation with God is stronger—Why dost thou thyself look on this woe with no effort to relieve or prevent? The sense of v. 4 is not obscure: "Therefore," under the influence of almost universal violence and strife, law becomes frigid, cold as if near death; right judgment is never issued by the courts of law; the wicked circumvent the righteous, and always secure unjust decisions.

5. Behold ye among the heathen, and regard, and wonder marvellously: for *I* will work a work in your days, *which* ye will not believe though it be told *you*.

Here the Chaldeans are brought first to our notice. Indeed, it would seem that they were brought by this prophecy to the notice of the Jews *as a dangerous power*, they having previously neglected to observe the sudden rise and rapid growth of this new power among the nations. The Lord says, "Look abroad, consider attentively, and you will have occasion to wonder exceedingly," the last imperative in a series of two or more being usually in sense a future. God will do a work which will seem incredible, even though sustained by good testimony.

6. For lo, I raise up the Chaldeans, *that* bitter and hasty nation, which shall march through the breadth of the land, to possess the dwelling-places *that are* not theirs.

This is the work, the raising up of a new first-class power, the Chaldeans. By taking notice of recent events, the Jews might see the rise of this power. The Chaldean king Nabopolassar, aided by the Medes, had overthrown Nineveh (B. C. 625), as Nahum had foretold. The Egyptians, alarmed at their growth, came against them, but were badly beaten at Carchemish, on the Euphrates. Thenceforward no nation was able to stay their progress. The Jews, moreover, were probably the less alarmed at this because they were in sympathy with the Chaldean, while he was devastating Nineveh, and were certainly in league with him when Josiah felt bound in honor to march out against Necho, king of Egypt, as a common enemy to himself and to his ally, the Chaldean. But relations of friendship with such a power are evanescent. The Jews soon had reason to fear this new enemy.——The Lord describes them, "bitter and rapid," "who march upon broad regions," vast countries of the earth, *i. e.*, who fear nothing, and strike for vast conquests.

7. They *are* terrible and dreadful: their judgment and their dignity shall proceed of themselves.

8. Their horses also are swifter than the leopards, and are more fierce than the evening wolves: and their horsemen shall spread themselves, and their horsemen shall come from far; they shall fly as the eagle *that* hasteth to eat.

Sad proof that they were "terrible and dreadful" appears in the history (2 Chron. 36:17): "He brought upon them the king of the Chaldees, who slew their young men with the sword in the house of their sanctuary, and had no compassion upon young man or maiden, old man or him that stooped for age."——"Their judgment and their dignity proceeding from themselves," seems to mean that they are an independent, self-made people. Literally, it reads—"Their decision" (plans) "and their lofty bearing are self-originated."——In the clause, "their horsemen spread themselves," the verb rendered "*spread*" means they "leap fiercely and proudly," their horses being probably like the Arabian stock of more modern times. The flight of the eagle when roused by hunger is a vivid figure for the most rapid motion then known.

9. They shall come all for violence: their faces shall sup up *as* the east wind, and they shall gather the captivity as the sand.

In the clause, "their faces shall sup up as the east wind," the obscurity of this translation suggests a doubt of its correctness. The various marginal readings confirm the opinion that our translators were much perplexed with the passage. Later commentators also doubt and differ. It *is* difficult. The principal word * is little known in our extant Hebrew. Henderson renders—"The aspect of their faces is like the east wind." Gesenius—"The gathering of their faces is forward." The latter I approve, with only a slight modification, so as to signify not the *act* of gathering, but their faces already gathered, *i. e.*, "the set or phalanx of their faces is forward;" all as one in solid phalanx and complete array, they set their faces forward, turning never to the right hand nor to the left, and turning back for none. This construction answers to the individual words, and to the demands of the context. Such an army will, of course, gather up captives as the sand.

10. And they shall scoff at the kings, and the princes *shall be* a scorn unto them: they shall deride every stronghold; for they shall heap dust, and take it.

More than fearless of kings and of strongholds, they scoff at the one and deride the other. It is only their sport to strike terror through them all.——The last clause alludes to the usual method in that age of capturing walled towns—heaping up huge embankments of earth that even overtopped the enemy's walls, whence they hurled their missiles into the city.

11. Then shall *his* mind change, and he shall pass over, and offend, *imputing* this his power unto his god.

The sentiment of this verse is, that constant success has made the Chaldean another man. The moderation and modesty of his

* מְגַמַּת

early years have given place to unbounded aspirations. He assumes that the gods are on his side, and ascribes his victories to their favor and help.——The first verb, rendered in our version "change," means more definitely "to *pass over*"—to pass beyond former bounds. The next verb, which the English version renders "shall pass over," usually means to go beyond due bounds, in the sense to *transgress*.——The verse therefore means to say that success has excited his ambition, and also given stimulus to his trust in his idol gods; and for both reasons will bring down on him the wrath of the Almighty.

Vs. 9–11 may be translated thus: "They shall all come for violence; the serried host of their faces is forward, and so they shall gather captives as the sand. They shall scoff at kings; princes shall be their derision; they laugh at all strongholds, and forthwith cast up embankments, and so shall take them. Then his spirit is changed; he transgresses and sins, ascribing this power of his to his god."

12. *Art* thou not from everlasting, O LORD my God, mine Holy One? we shall not die. O LORD, thou hast ordained them for judgment; and, O mighty God, thou hast established them for correction.

Here the prophet interposes. The remainder of this chapter must be expounded as his expostulation or debate with God, the spirit of which is: "O Lord, spare thy heritage, and give it not over to utter devastation. Thy people doubtless need correction, and thou hast ordained the Chaldean power for this purpose; but do not let them ruin our nation utterly and forever. They are more wicked than we, and they hold human life cruelly cheap, as the fishermen do the lives of the little fishes brought up by their huge drag-nets." ——It will be noted that the prophet seizes the best point for introducing his plea—just where the Chaldean's sins of ambition and trust in idols are brought before the mind.——The phrase "we shall not die," might be more fitly rendered, "Let us not die," *i. e.*, "let not thy chosen people be utterly destroyed." He sees that they need discipline, and recognizes God's purpose to use the Chaldean power for this end.

13. *Thou art* of purer eyes than to behold evil, and canst not look on iniquity: wherefore lookest thou upon them that deal treacherously, *and* holdest thy tongue when the wicked devoureth *the man that is* more righteous than he?

14. And makest men as the fishes of the sea, as the creeping things, *that have* no ruler over them?

The verb rendered "look," occurring here twice—"look on iniquity," and "look on them that deal treacherously"—is the same with the second verb in v. 3, there rendered (improperly) "cause me to behold." The sense here, as there, I take to be, "Thou canst not look calmly and unconcerned upon iniquity, or rather, upon *misery* —the woe that sin begets; it is not in thy nature. Wherefore, then, dost thou look quietly on the perfidious—those faithless Chaldeans—and wherefore art thou silent," &c. One point in the prophet's plea is, that the Chaldeans are greater sinners than the Jews; therefore the Lord should not allow the greater sinners to devour the less.

The connection with the previous verse is close. That wicked Chaldean not only devours his more righteous brother nation, but eats up men as if they were little fishes before him, or the tiny insects which have no protector.

15. They take up all of them with the angle, they catch them in their net, and gather them in their drag: therefore they rejoice and are glad.

16. Therefore they sacrifice unto their net, and burn incense unto their drag; because by them their portion *is* fat, and their meat plenteous.

The figure of speech which compares the seizing and consuming of nations of men to the taking of fishes in a net, runs through this verse. "Drag" is really a *drag-net*, drawn along the bottom to scoop up small and great together.——Their idolatrous hearts and habits must not be omitted in this argument with Jehovah. "These impious Chaldeans have no regard for thee, O Lord. They ascribe all their success to their nets, and worship them as their gods, honoring their own martial prowess, and not the ever-living God."

17. Shall they therefore empty their net, and not spare continually to slay the nations?

Will God allow them to go on, emptying and then filling their nets, and having no compassion in their souls toward sparing the nations from perpetual slaughter? Such is the prophet's plea in behalf of his people.

CHAPTER II.

In this chapter the prophet is seen on his watch-tower, waiting for an answer from the Lord to his expostulations (v. 1.) The remainder of the chapter contains this answer in its various parts, directing the prophet first to write out the vision plainly (v. 2); assuring him it was soon to be fulfilled (v. 3); indicating how the proud and unbelieving would abuse it, but the believing be blessed thereby (v. 4); and then (vs. 5–20) depicting the sins of the Chaldeans, and showing that both general justice and the special agencies of God's providence would surely overtake them with fearful retribution.

1. I will stand upon my watch, and set me upon the tower, and will watch to see what he will say unto me, and what I shall answer when I am reproved.

Considered as a seer, the prophet must needs *look* two ways: first, to God, for his message; and then down into the future, and abroad into the realms of divine providence, to see those coming events which no human vision, unaided, could reach. This verse strikingly presents the prophet looking the first way—*toward God.* He says: "I will take my stand on my watch-tower, and place myself on the fortress, and will watch to see what God will say to me, and what I shall bring back (from Him)" concerning my expostulation. "The message I shall bring back from God, and what God will say to me," are essentially parallel clauses with the same idea. The word here rendered "shall answer,"* much more naturally means to bring back, *i. e.*, from God, than to answer to God.——In the first chapter, some of the prophet's expostulations amounted very nearly to rebuke and chiding; and this idea is frequently embraced in the noun here used, † rendered in our English version, "when I am reproved," but better, "concerning my expostulation," *i. e.*, with God. The preposition before the noun fits this construction, having the sense, concerning, in reference to. The prophet having said what is recorded (chap. 1:12–17), should of course watch to see how the Lord received it, and what he would say in reply. He acted for the people of Judah, representing their case before God, and could not but feel deeply solicitous to get the answer both for himself and for them.

2. And the LORD answered me, and said, Write the vision, and make *it* plain upon tables, that he may run that readeth it.

Here the answer begins. "Write the vision"—all I reveal—"engrave it on tablets, so that the reader of it may run," *i. e*, with it, reading from it as he runs. "He that readeth in it," is possibly here a public reader for an assembly; but in this case, since he is expected to *run*, he is more probably a public crier for the streets and public grounds. Some interpret thus: That he may run his eye over it easily and rapidly, as sermon-readers over their manuscripts. But though the word for reader may mean either a reader before an audience, or a herald in public grounds, yet no Hebrew usage sustains the sense of *fluent reading* for the verb *to run.*

* אָשִׁיב † תּוֹכַחְתִּי

3. For the vision *is* yet for an appointed time, but at the end it shall speak, and not lie: though it tarry, wait for it; because it will surely come, it will not tarry.

There seems to be no absolute demand for restricting the vision here spoken of to any particular part of what God revealed to Habakkuk. Of the whole, the main events yet future were: (1.) The Chaldean invasion of Judah (recorded 1:5–11); and (2.) The ultimate destruction of the Chaldean power, and of Babylon, in righteous retribution for their sins (2:5–21).——Yet, inasmuch as the latter was then about to be announced to the prophet (the former having been so already), and especially, inasmuch as this latter was the hopeful part to the Jewish mind, toward which they might look with comfort, as being a proof of God's mercy toward themselves and of his regard for intrinsic justice and righteousness, we may well assume that in this verse the latter is specially in mind. Both parts were fixed in the divine counsels, each had its definite time to wait, yet neither would tarry long. The former came probably within a few months; the latter at the end of about seventy years, Cyrus being the instrument of Jehovah's vengeance in its execution.——In the second clause, the word rendered "shall speak," is supposed by Gesenius to mean here "shall hasten." This word, however, meaning primarily to breathe out, to breathe hard, to throw out the breath, has much more often the secondary sense to *speak* than to *hasten*. The former is also more naturally correlated with "shall not lie." Sense—At the end it shall testify for itself without mistake as to its fulfilment. Ye shall know the fulfilment when it comes.——In the last two clauses the English version seems first to imply that it will "tarry," and then to affirm that it will *not* "tarry." The Hebrew has no such apparent contradiction, for it uses two different verbs, and does not, as the English does, repeat the same. "Though it linger, yet wait for it, for it will surely come; it will not be *behind the time*," *i. e.*, will not be too late, so as to *come in afterwards*. This is the exact sense of the second verb.

4. Behold, his soul *which* is lifted up is not upright in him: but the just shall live by his faith.

In these times that try men's souls, involving the invasion by the terrible Chaldeans, just coming upon the people as announced above (1:5–10), and the retribution to come at some future day on them—a thing of faith, forming the chief burden of chapter 2—some would be intensely agitated, having practically no faith in God's promises, or in his threatened retributive judgments on the wicked Chaldean. Others would repose calmly upon God through their faith. These two classes are before us in this verse. I paraphrase it thus: "Behold the proud, disquieted man. His soul within him is not placid; but as for the righteous man, he shall live by his faith."——The verb "*live*" must be taken in its very common moral sense of true blessings—the calm repose of a true faith in God.——The Hebrew accents connect very closely the words rendered "*the just*" and "*by his faith*," showing that the earlier Jews read the clause, "He who is all right in respect to his faith shall live." This construction also makes a natural antithesis between the proud man of the first clause and the sincerely believing man of the second. The former is never placid; the latter enjoys in the rest of faith that true *life* which is real blessedness. ——The construction given first above disregards the authority of the accents.——Some take the proud, disquieted man of this verse to be the Chaldean. I prefer to find in him the unbelieving Jew, and assume that the discourse turns to the Chaldean in v. 5.

5. Yea, also, because he transgresseth by wine, *he is* a proud man, neither keepeth at home, who enlargeth his desire as hell, and *is* as death, and cannot be satisfied, but gathereth unto him all nations, and heapeth unto him all people:

At this point the strain of discourse turns to the Chaldean power, considered as a unit, and continues to speak of him through the chapter.——Starting with the thought in the first clause of v. 4—the case of the proud, unbelieving, and therefore disquieted Jew—the prophet proceeds to say: "How much more of this one (the Chaldean) because he errs the more by reason of wine, is a proud man, and never rests quietly at home; who enlarges his desire as Sheol (*i. e.*, the grave) does its mouth, and he is like Death and is never satisfied; and consequently he gathers unto him all the nations and annexes to himself all the peoples." This represents the ambition of a young conquering power, grasping the dominion of the world, and, like Alexander, pained to tears when he finds no other world to conquer. Such is the Chaldean.——The reader will note, here and onward through the chapter, how the Lord does in fact answer the expostulations of his prophet, recorded 1:12–17. The prophet had virtually said: "O Lord, thou art ever righteous and just; thou canst not look quietly on wrong and its resulting miseries; how, then, canst thou see the Chaldean exterminate another nation more righteous than he? How canst thou let him go on unpunished, sweeping the nations into his drag-net, and slaughtering myriads of men to satiate his mad ambition?"——The Lord replies: Be at rest; the Chaldean is indeed guilty, he shall have his just doom not far hence. There shall never be just occasion to say or to think that I can look down upon wrong-doing and its consequent misery with indifference, or that justice has forsaken my throne.——This is what the prophet brings back from God concerning his expostulation (2:1).

6. Shall not all these take up a parable against him, and a taunting proverb against him, and say, Woe to

him that increaseth *that which is* not his! how long? and to him that ladeth himself with thick clay!

The great sin of the Chaldean having been indicated, retribution comes next. The moral sense of mankind is against him, condemning his grasping, cruel ambition, and demanding vengeance. Of course, it is implied that the voice of universal humanity is also the voice of God.——The special mode of giving utterance to this voice of mankind is that of pronouncing a *woe* on the Chaldean, superadding to the solemnity of the woe the keen retort which carries with it the idea of deserved and righteous retribution—the sort of taunt expressed when men say, "You have only your deserts." A similar taunt, done in the loftiest strain of irony, may be seen in Isa. 14, over the foreseen fall of this same Babylon.——"Shall not all these nations whom he has warred against, subdued, or imperilled, take up this taunting strain against him and say: Woe to him who grasps and accumulates what is not his own! How long must this be?"—implying that in the Chaldean's purpose there would be no end to it, but in the retributions of justice it could not last long. ——"Woe to him that ladeth himself" (not with "thick clay," but) "with goods taken in pledge"—such as the Hebrew law forbade men to keep over night if taken from the poor—the sense being, with sins against mankind which demand and shall have their just retribution. The Chaldean was loading himself quite too heavily with sins that would bring upon him the vengeance of justice.—— This taunting strain is methodically arranged—its successive stanzas beginning with "*Woe*"—as the reader may see (vs. 6, 9, 12, 15, 19).

7. Shall they not rise up suddenly that shall bite thee, and awake that shall vex thee, and thou shalt be for booties unto them?

Those who ultimately came down on Babylon to "bite" and to "vex" her—God's instruments for vengeance upon her, viz., the Medo-Persian power—did start up suddenly, and spring upon her in an unexpected hour, and she became their spoil.

8. Because thou hast spoiled many nations, all the remnant of the people shall spoil thee; because of men's blood, and *for* the violence of the land, of the city, and of all that dwell therein.

"Because thou hast spoiled many nations, all the remaining nations" (not utterly crushed) "shall make common cause, and shall spoil thee,—because of the blood of men" (shed in wanton profusion), and for the violence wrought in the earth, in the city, and upon all that dwell therein."

9. Woe to him that coveteth an evil covetousness to his house, that he may set his nest on high, that he may be delivered from the power of evil!

The Chaldeans employed the wealth and the muscle of the nations they subdued, in building their immense walls, towers, and castles—hoping thereby to make their city impregnable, and thus deliver themselves from the fear of future harm from foreign enemies. They did indeed set their nest on high, as the eagle in the lofty crags of the rock.

10. Thou hast consulted shame to thy house by cutting off many people, and hast sinned *against* thy soul!

Thy counsels in this thing have brought shame (implying not only dishonor but ruin) to thy house, destroying so many nations to enrich thyself. So doing, thou hast sinned against thine own life. ——Other instances of the phrase—"to sin against one's own sou or life"—may be seen, Prov. 8:36 and 20:2.

11. For the stone shall cry out of the wall, and the beam out of the timber shall answer it.

The sense of wrong and the demand for retribution, so universal in all human hearts, is, by a bold but most beautiful conception, thought of here as pervading the very stones and timbers of the house built by injustice. Jesus Christ once said—"If these should hold their peace, the stones would immediately cry out." So the stone in this wall cries out against the wrong done—against the bloody fingers laid upon it—and the cross-beam among the timbers responds to reëcho the complaint.

12. Woe to him that buildeth a town with blood, and establisheth a city by iniquity!

13. Behold, *is it* not of the Lord of hosts that the people shall labor in the very fire, and the people shall weary themselves for very vanity?

This woe looks to the city of Babylon. She obtained her laborers for her immense walls by taking them captive in war, and then coercing them into slaves under her military power. So they wrought with their bloody fingers. Babylon laid up her walls in blood and planted their foundations in wrong: so the woes of God and of universal justice abode upon her!——"Behold," calls special attention to the fact that it came from the Lord of hosts that this great work was done, not "*in* the fire," but "*for* the fire," to be consumed ere long, both utterly and forever. So also in the parallel clause—"*for* mere vanity"—for no enduring benefit. The original is expressive—"*for fire in plenty*," for abundance of fire—that it may become the sport of whirlwinds of flame. Surely this is of the Lord: let all men see his hand and his righteous retribution in all this!——Essentially the same language is used by Jeremiah (51:58): "Thus saith the Lord of hosts; The broad walls of Babylon shall be utterly broken, and her high gates shall be burned with fire, and the people shall labor in vain and the folk *for* the fire; and they shall be weary;" but though laboring to weariness, yet all in vain.

14. For the earth shall be filled with the knowledge of the glory of the LORD, as the waters cover the sea.

The general scope of the context must determine the specific sense of this passage. This shows that the prophet thinks of God as glorifying himself by the retributions of justice on nations guilty of great oppression and wrong. Hence our verse assumes it to be a great principle in the government of God over nations as such that he will not only glorify himself by the retributions of justice upon them, but will fill the whole earth with the knowledge of this glory, even as the waters cover the bed of the sea. He will manifest himself so abundantly as the avenger of the oppressed and as one who takes vengeance on oppressors, that no man in all the earth can fail to know it—none be too blind to see it.——The same sentiment is in Num. 14:21—referring there, however, to retribution on the unbelieving Hebrews who gave credit to the unbelieving spies more than to the God of all the promises: "But as truly as I live, all the earth shall be filled with the glory of the Lord"—which was revealed then in forty years of wandering in the desert, through privations and plagues which swept to their early graves the last man of that unbelieving host.——The very analogous promise (Isa. 11:9) looks towards the visitations of mercy and the triumphs of love:—"They shall not hurt nor destroy in all my holy mountain; for the earth shall be full of the knowledge of the Lord as the waters cover the sea;" and this knowledge shall mould human hearts into the spirit of heavenly love and blessed peace.——So it is clearly in God's plan to manifest his glory in both ways—in the retributions of justice, and in the visitations of mercy.

15. Woe unto him that giveth his neighbor drink, that puttest thy bottle to *him*, and makest *him* drunken also, that thou mayest look on their nakedness!

16. Thou art filled with shame for glory: drink thou also, and let thy foreskin be uncovered: the cup of the LORD'S right hand shall be turned unto thee, and shameful spewing *shall be* on thy glory.

Translated thus: "Woe to him who causeth his neighbor to drink" (*i. e.*, whatever can intoxicate)—"who pourest out thy hot wine that inflames, and even makest him drunken—that thou mayest look (exultingly) on their nakedness!" "Thou shalt have thy fill of shame instead of glory; drink thou too and expose thine own nakedness. The cup of the Lord's right hand shall come round to thee, and shame shall come over all thy glory. The rendering "shameful spewing," though pertinent sense, is not well sustained by the original text.——The "cup of the Lord's right hand" carries the mind to the fuller statement by Jeremiah (25:15:) "Take the wine-cup of this fury at my hand, and cause all the nations to whom I send thee to drink it. And they shall drink and be moved and be mad, because of the sword that I shall send among them." See Notes on Nahum 1:10.——The Babylonians were notorious for their excesses in wine and strong drink, for which God remembered them in the day of his visitation. Much in point here are the facts of her history when on the very night of her final fall, Belshazzar and his lords drank wine from the sacred vessels of Jehovah's temple, and in the height of their drunken revelry the thunder-bolts of ruin fell! (Dan. 5:1–4, 30, and Jer. 51:39).

17. For the violence of Lebanon shall cover thee, and the spoil of beasts, *which* made them afraid, because of men's blood, and for the violence of the land, of the city, and of all that dwell therein.

"The violence of Lebanon" is not that done *by* Lebanon (this would be entirely aside from the course of thought); but done *to* Lebanon. "Lebanon" here is probably Jerusalem and her temple—so named partly because the cedars of Lebanon were in her temple—partly in reference to the lofty grandeur of that mountain which fitly symbolized the glory of the holy city.——The violence done by Babylon to Jerusalem shall return in retribution to overwhelm herself. So also shall an onslaught like that on a herd of wild beasts which terrifies them, fall on thee—implying that they would be in like manner frightened and panic-smitten. ——In this translation, I supply the needed verb from the next preceding clause. Two things cover Babylon, in the sense of overwhelming her in the day of her ruin, viz., the violence she has brought on Lebanon (Jerusalem), and an onslaught like that on wild beasts, who furnish a striking example of a panic-smitten host.——The last clause has occurred verbatim (v. 8).

18. What profiteth the graven image that the maker thereof hath graven it; the molten image, and a teacher of lies, that the maker of his work trusteth therein, to make dumb idols?

Exegetically, the only question in this verse turns on the precise relation between the first clause and those that follow, indicated in our English Bible by "*that* the maker," &c. Some take the connecting particle* as a relative, thus: "What's the use of the graven image *which* its maker graveth?" I prefer to make this particle indicate a reason why idol images are profitless, viz., *because* they are made by human fingers, thus—"What can be the use of a graven image, *for* its human maker hath wrought it," &c. "What

* כִּי

is the use of a molten image and a teacher of lies (an idol priest), *for* the maker of it trusts in his own work, in a thing himself has made?"

19. Woe unto him that saith to the wood, Awake; to the dumb stone, Arise, it shall teach! Behold, it *is* laid over with gold and silver, and *there is* no breath at all in the midst of it.

All this is plain, and sets forth vividly the intense folly of idol-making, idol-worship, and of all trust in idols.

20. But the LORD *is* in his holy temple: let all the earth keep silence before him.

All unlike the whole idol system are the power, the majesty, and the all-pervading reign of the dread Jehovah! That he should be thought of *by a Jew* as *in his holy temple* at Jerusalem, was both natural and truthful; for his manifested presence *was there* in the Holy of Holies, reposing above the mercy-seat and beneath the wings of the cherubim. All the idol temples were godless. Not so the temple of the Lord of hosts in Mount Zion!——His rule is both supreme and universal. Let all the earth stand in awe before him—all the more so, as they note how the proud and conquering nations of the earth, like old Babylon, meet their righteous doom from the retributive justice of his throne!

CHAPTER III.

THIS chapter, said in the preface to be a "prayer," is not exclusively or even chiefly prayer in its strict sense; though it begins with prayer and closes with most wonderful utterances of simple faith and exulting joy in God.——The chapter is chiefly *song*, embodying as the immediate answer to his prayer what is technically called a "*theophany*"—*i. e.*, a manifestation of God to his prophet—to his mental, not bodily eye, we must suppose; bringing up before him in vivid review the glorious things God had wrought for his people in ancient days. The special aim was to reveal God as seen in his glorious power, and in his loving faithfulness to his chosen people, so that the prophet should see that Jehovah is verily great and glorious, and especially worthy to be *trusted* as the enduring protector of his own people. It was under the influence of this sublimely grand manifestation of Jehovah, that the prophet makes at the close such an utterance of his simple faith and of his unbounded joy and triumph in the God of his salvation.

The publication of this song, in connection with the revelation of such calamities, was designed to inspire the same faith and joy in the believing portion of the people as it had done in the prophet's own soul, despite of the fall of their beloved city and land before the terrible Chaldean power.

1. A prayer of Habakkuk the prophet upon Shigionoth.

"Upon Shigionoth," refers to the music in which this song was to be sung—no doubt lofty, bold, triumphal, in keeping with the strain of the sentiment.

2. O LORD, I have heard thy speech *and* was afraid: O LORD, revive thy work in the midst of the years, in the midst of the years make known; in wrath remember mercy.

"O Lord, I have heard thy *message*"—verbal prediction, *i. e.*, concerning the invasion by the Chaldeans (as recorded chap. 1: 5–11), "and I was afraid." "O Lord, re-enact thy work" (of deliverance for thy people) "in the midst of these years; even now make known"—*i. e.*, thyself and thy power to save; in this manifestation of thy wrath against us for our sins, "remember mercy."——The word rendered "revive," means literally to *make alive.* In this connection it must be in the sense of reproducing, performing once more those great works of salvation for Israel with which their early history is filled.——The language of this prayer, "O Lord revive thy work," may be used fitly by all Christians in the way of accommodation, as a prayer for a revival of true religion in the hearts of men. Yet this passage must be interpreted according to the nature of the subject as shown in the context; and this requires us here to apply the words to God's work of saving his people from being utterly ruined by the Chaldean invasion, then close at hand.

3. God came from Teman, and the Holy One from mount Paran. Selah. His glory covered the heavens, and the earth was full of his praise.

The theophany proper commences here. Bearing in mind that the prophet had besought God to reproduce those glorious works of saving power wrought of old for his people, we shall readily see the fitness of this peculiar manifestation. The Lord seems, practically, to reply to his servant—Thou hast prayed me to *do again* what I did in ancient days for my people. Rather let it suffice thee that I make all my glory pass before thee in displays of my power and faithful love to my people. Thou shalt see the uplifted glorious arm of Jehovah, as in former times, made bare for his people, and thou shalt know that I am still and evermore the God of thy salvation.——It is plain that God forbore to do precisely the thing for which Habakkuk prayed—*i. e.*, come down to save Judea and Jerusalem just as he had long before saved his people out of Egypt, and made them victorious in Canaan;—but he does a second thing, not less effective for the repose and even joy of the prophet's heart: he makes such revelations of himself by the aid of those historic scenes as avail to inspire unbounded faith and even triumphant joy in the God of his salvation.——Probably we can get no better conception of this theophany, as it appeared to Habakkuk, than to conceive of it as a *panorama*, passing before the prophet's mental eye—the divine Spirit causing him in the light of those ancient historic scenes to *behold a present God*, marching before the hosts of his chosen, or standing on the confines of Canaan, or lifting up his voice in awful thunder, shaking the mountains and filling rivers and seas with consternation. The prophet's mental state was such, we may suppose, as Elisha prayed for in behalf of his servant—"Lord, open his eyes that he may see. And the Lord opened the eyes of the young man, and he saw; and behold, the mountain was full of horses and chariots of fire round about Elisha" (2 Kings 6: 17). So the eyes of Habakkuk were opened and *he saw God*;—the groundwork of this manifestation of God being his former deeds of power in delivering his people from their enemies, and planting them in their promised land. These scenes are made to pass before him in a sort of panoramic vision, while God opened his eyes to see things in their true relations to the ever-present agency of Him who worketh all in all, and worketh none the less really because for the most part invisibly to mortal eyes.

Similar conceptions and representations of God are not uncommon in Hebrew poetry. Thus (Deut. 33: 2, 26, 27) Moses, in his last words of blessing upon the tribes, said: "The Lord came from Sinai, and rose up (like the rising of a sun) from Seir unto them; he shone forth from Mount Paran, and he came with ten thousands of saints—from his right hand went a fiery law for them."——Also, "There is none like unto the God of Jesurun, who rideth upon the heavens in thy help and in his excellency on the sky."——This is as if his very eye saw without a veil the unclouded majesty of the Infinite One! Such was his poetic conception of the scenes of Sinai; or, as we might say—This was Sinai *seen in panoramic vision.*——Of the same character is a passage in the Song of Deborah—(Judg. 5: 4, 5), "Lord, when thou wentest out of Seir, when thou marchedst out of the field of Edom, the earth trembled, and the heavens dropped; the clouds also dropped water. The mountains quaked (so the Heb.) before the Lord, even that Sinai before the Lord God of Israel." Of the same sort is Ps. 68: 7, 8, 33: "O God, when thou wentest forth before thy people, when thou didst march through the wilderness, the earth shook, the heavens also dropped at the presence of God, the God of Israel."—"Sing praises to him that rideth upon the heavens of heavens that were of old; lo, he doth *send* out his voice, and that a mighty voice."——Very similar in the line of poetic conception are many expressions in Ps. 77: 10–20 and 114: 1–8, and Isa. 63: 11–14., *e. g.*, "The waters saw thee, O God; the waters saw thee, they were afraid; the depths also were troubled." "The sea saw it and fled; Jordan was driven back. What ailed thee, O thou sea, that thou fleddest?" &c. As if the great deep were waked into intelligence and consciousness by those august and thrilling manifestations of the majesty of her King! ——Such conceptions of dead nature quickened to life, thought, and feeling before a present God, give wonderful power to these panoramic scenes, of which the one intent is to set the all-working and energizing God before the mind.——Some Christians in later ages have testified to manifestations of God to their souls, under which their sense of his attributes and works has been not less impressive than supernatural presentations of divine power to the senses would be. Not without reason, they ascribe these manifestations of God to the divine Spirit's agency. In this manifestation to Habakkuk, the hand of the same Divine Teacher must be assumed.——It is remarkable how much these conceptions of God working upon Nature, and of Nature responding to the agencies of God, blend themselves with the genuine spirit of poetry, exemplifying the fact that genuine poetry, so far from being necessarily unreal and untruthful, may be the veriest reality and the purest truth. Most certain it is that the poetic conceptions of God and of Nature in this theophany in nowise over-paint the actual verities of things.

Before I proceed to comment on particular terms or clauses, a few words are due in respect to the use of the tenses in this theophany.——If the views advanced above are just, it is obvious that the tenses throughout should be *present*. A panorama made up of a series of historic paintings must naturally represent each scene as present. The events which constitute the groundwork, and to which the paintings perpetually refer, may have transpired long ago. Others like them may occur again; but the painting has for its object to give the observer a view of them as then passing.—— So here, all is made present by the impressions wrought upon the prophet's mind by the teaching Spirit.*——These preliminary remarks will sufficiently prepare the way for the study of the passage.——"God comes up from Teman," the South, this being both the etymological significance of the name, and the geographical position of the place. Mount Paran is well known as often associated with Sinai. God comes up from those regions as one who had revealed himself there in forms of surpassing majesty and glory in the giving of the law.——It will be recollected that Moses (in Deut. 33) and the author of Ps. 68 both speak of God as coming up from Mount Sinai, the land of the south.——The best critics mostly agree that "Selah" is a musical term, meaning *pause*, and perhaps a direc-

* The Hebrew student will readily notice that in this passage (vs. 3–15) both of the two normal Hebrew tenses are used, the perfect and the imperfect (often called the future), some of the verbs being in one tense and some in the other. The explanation of this remarkable fact seems to be that these two tenses meet at a common centre in the present, and in a case of this sort, may be used almost indiscriminately for the present, yet not altogether so, since still the perfect will imply that the event *was* as well as *is*; and the imperfect not only that it *is*, but *will be* yet again.

tion to the singers to rest while the instruments filled out an interlude. In some cases (not in all) the thought just expressed renders a pause for reflection appropriate.——His visible glory seems to illumine the whole concave heavens above. The earth is full of manifestations of God that are proper themes of praise. The sense is not that he sees the world full of men actually praising God, but rather that the very earth itself seems vocal with praises. Mountains, rivers, and the pestilence, all seem to be doing God's work so perfectly, though unconsciously, as to fill all the earth with voices of praise.

4. And *his* brightness was as the light; he had horns *coming* out of his hand; and there *was* the hiding of his power.

The word rendered "light,"* modern critics suppose here to mean the *sun.* Also that "horns coming out of his hand" are *rays of light* streaming forth and bearing to the eye the appearance of horns. The Arabic (a cognate language) shows that this usage of "horn" is oriental. It is also Hebraistic, as appears in the use of the same word as a verb (Ex. 34: 29, 30, 35), where three times over it is said that the skin of Moses' face was *horny, i. e.,* emitted horn-like rays of light; in the English version, "*shone.*"——The whole verse may be freely translated—"His brightness was as the sun in his strength; rays of light streamed from his hand; there lay concealed his unknown power."

5. Before him went the pestilence, and burning coals went forth at his feet.

Jehovah is still coming up from the land of the south, the region of Sinai and the wilderness, marching at the head of the thousands of Israel, to give them possession of Canaan. This is the conception of God throughout this theophany (vs. 3–15).——Before him moves onward the pestilence, and fevers seem to go forth from his presence on their mission of death. The word rendered "burning coals" has but two well-established senses: (1) lightnings; (2) fevers—both having the common idea of intense heat. The general sense is that God sent "the hornet" (see Ex. 23: 28; Deut. 7: 20, and Josh. 24: 12), *i. e.,* plagues, judgments, and, no doubt, the pestilence, to cut off the strong and warlike Canaanites, and make them a more easy conquest to the then unwarlike children of Israel. It is very obvious, from a comparison of the Canaanites as seen by the spies, with the Canaanites as found by Joshua, that by some means a great change had come over them. Their military prowess was far less formidable.

6. He stood, and measured the earth: he beheld, and drove asunder the nations; and the everlasting

* אוֹר

mountains were scattered, the perpetual hills did bow: his ways *are* everlasting.

The sense is, I see him stand (as in the days of Joshua he stood) on the confines of Canaan, a mighty conqueror and the rightful Lord of all; "he measures off the land" for his people with the sweep of his eye, according to the purposes of his wisdom. "He *looks*," and the terror of that look "drives asunder the nations" of Canaan, and dispossesses them of their land, that his people may take possession. In the presence of such majesty "the everlasting mountains are scattered;" "the enduring hills bow low" as in awe before him; "his ways are of old," *i. e.*, they were manifested in those ancient days.

7. I saw the tents of Cushan in affliction: *and* the curtains of the land of Midian did tremble.

The best authorities agree in finding one branch of the Cushites in eastern Arabia, and the Midianites in western.——That their "tents are in affliction" means that the people themselves, dwelling in tents, are troubled by the glorious things Jehovah is achieving for his people. The "curtains of Midian" are their tent-curtains, trembling in sympathy with the trembling hearts of their occupants. The two clauses are essentially parallel, and show that the fear and the dread of Israel, while Jehovah is so manifestly marching at their head, fell on even remote nations, so that they stand appalled by what they hear and see of his power. The policy of the Gibeonites (Josh. 9) is in proof of this. (See vs. 24, 25).

8. Was the LORD displeased against the rivers? *was* thine anger against the rivers? *was* thy wrath against the sea, that thou didst ride upon thine horses, *and* thy chariots of salvation?

This verse contemplates the passage of the Red Sea and of the Jordan. A bold imagination in the strains of lofty song does not stop to narrate the facts and detail the circumstances. On the contrary, assuming these, and speaking of events as they appear to the eye, the prophet exclaims: "What aileth thee, O thou Jordan?" Is it because the Lord is angry against the rivers? is it that his wrath is on the sea that he drives their waters back, and seems to rebuke them for obtruding themselves in the pathway he has marked out for the hosts of his chosen?——"Rivers," twice in the plural, contemplate the Red Sea as one, the Jordan another. Though it was more properly an arm of the sea, yet its tides are said to rise seven feet, and consequently must make an active current. But a strong imagination is not wont to be precise as to number. Indeed, the startling *fact* is the main thing, and not the number of rivers in question. The last clause shows that the Red Sea is in his mind.——"That thy chariots are salvation" is the precise rendering, the full construction being that thy chariots are chariots of salvation, *i. e.*, that riding in royal state as a conquering hero on thy horses and chariots of war thou dost save thy people from the grasp of Pharaoh, and bring them forth in triumph.

9. Thy bow was made quite naked, *according* to the oaths of the tribes, *even thy* word. Selah. Thou didst cleave the earth with rivers.

This verse should close with "Selah." The first clause presents no difficulty. The second has perplexed commentators, and scattered their opinions more than almost any other passage in the Bible. Dr. Henderson remarks that one hundred different expositions of it have been given.——"Thy bow is made quite naked" conceives of Jehovah as still a warrior chieftain at the head of his martial hosts, coming down in battle upon the nations of Canaan. To "make the bow naked" is to draw it out from its sheath or case, which was a protection necessary to preserve the string from dampness, and keep it in order for service. Drawn out and made quite naked, it was ready for use.——The next clause, interpreted so variously, has in Hebrew three words,* all of them words of very frequent occurrence, especially the first two, and of well-established meaning. The first word may be a noun in the sense of oaths, possibly sevens, or a participle, meaning sworn. The second is a noun, meaning originally a rod, something stretched out; then a shoot or twig; but in use most often, the tribes of Israel. The third means a word, a word of command or of threatening; in rare instances, a watchword or a song.——Here follow some interpretations by the ablest commentators.——Dr. Henderson—"Sevens of spears was the word!" *i. e.*, let there be a full complement of spears for the war. This is the divine mandate.——Gesenius—"Sworn are the rods of his word," *i. e.*, the promised chastisements; he has sworn the overthrow of his enemies. But Gesenius favors a slight change in the first letter of the first word, by which it would come from a different root, meaning to be *sated*, to be *full*, and then would render—"Sated are the spears, *i. e.*, with blood! A song!"——After a somewhat extended examination, I prefer the rendering of our received translation, on the following grounds:

(1.) It gives each word its most common meaning. The usage of the words rendered "oaths" and "tribes" is very strong. It is not easy for one who has examined it to see how a Hebrew reader could understand these words to mean any thing else in this connection.

(2.) This sense is in harmony with truth, and the truth is one which the Lord has often taken special pains to reassert and impress, viz., that the conquest of Canaan for the tribes of Israel was in fulfilment of his oft-sworn promise to their fathers. (See Deut. 7: 7, 8, 12; Ps. 105: 8–11; Jer. 11: 4, 5).——The great theme of

* שְׁבֻעוֹת מַטּוֹת אֹמֶר

this theophany is this very conquest. Hence the fitness of this reference to the oath of Jehovah to give Canaan to the tribes.

(3.) In this construction the oldest authorities all agree, *e. g.*, the Chaldee Paraphrast: "Thou didst marvellously reveal thyself in thy great power on account of thy covenant which thy word had made with the tribes for the ages to come."——Also Jerome: "Ascending thy chariot and seizing thy bow, thou wilt give salvation to thy people, and wilt fulfil for all time the oaths which thou hast sworn to our fathers and the tribes."

(4.) No other interpretation is so well supported, or is obnoxious to so few objections.——"Selah" calls for a pause, appropiate here for reflection.——"Thou didst cleave the earth with rivers" looks toward those fearful convulsions occasioned by earthquakes, which often open new fountains and plough out new watercourses.

10. The mountains saw thee, *and* they trembled: the overflowing of the water passed by: the deep uttered his voice, *and* lifted up his hands on high.

A strong imagination gives to inanimate objects life, thought, and emotion. So here—The "mountains see" Jehovah as he stands forth at the head of his hosts in Canaan, "and they *tremble*." The verb here used means to move in a circle, to dance; then to be in pain, to writhe; also to shake, as here, with the accessory idea of being in anguish.——The great floods of water swept past and along, with reference perhaps to the Jordan, long dammed up while the people were passing through its bed, and then rushing with augmented volume and force; or possibly to great storms of hail and rain which the Lord sent down in some of the great battles fought with the Canaanites.——In the phrase "the deep uttered his voice," lies one of the grandest conceptions found in any language. The conscious spirit of the Great Deep, affrighted before the majesty of Nature's King and Lord, throws up his hands and utters screams of awe and terror! How can he endure such a Presence? How can he be placid when the great and dreadful God comes so near!

11. The sun *and* moon stood still in their habitation; at the light of thine arrows they went, *and* at the shining of thy glittering spear.

Not only are the mountains and the great deep agitated at the presence of Jehovah: "The sun and the moon stand back toward their dwelling-places"—literally, stand toward, in the sense in which it is said of a ship at sea, she stands toward a given point. They made for the dwelling-places where they were thought to repose when withdrawn from human view. Ah! they, too, cannot bear the dread presence of Jehovah in his majesty!——They retire to their hiding-places "at the light of thine arrows which flew—at the brightness of the lightning of thy spear." So conscious are they of their inferiority, so ashamed to put their feeble light in contrast with the blaze of Jehovah's splendor, they shrink away to their recesses.——Orientals are accustomed to speak of the heavenly bodies as having their homes, mansions, abodes.*——The word "*they*" before "went" refers, not to the sun or moon, nor to the Hebrew soldiers, but to God's arrows, the lightnings. These are said not merely to *go*, but to *fly*—a very intensive form of the verb *go*.

12. Thou didst march through the land in indignation, thou didst thresh the heathen in anger.

Putting the emphatic words first in order, the Hebrew would run—

"In wrath thou didst march through the land;
In fury thou didst thresh the nations"—

sweeping away the guilty and doomed nations of Canaan from before thy people.

13. Thou wentest forth for the salvation of thy people, *even* for salvation with thine anointed; thou woundedst the head out of the house of the wicked, by discovering the foundation unto the neck. Selah.

The first clause is plain; the last is specially difficult.——"Thy anointed" must, by the demands of the parallelism, be the same with "thy people." The sentiment is simply that God marched thus through the land to save his people, considered as his chosen and anointed, to give them victory over their enemies and possession of Canaan.——Upon the last clause few words must suffice, presenting only the construction which I on the whole prefer.——By "house" (*i. e.* of the wicked) may be meant the family, the class of people; or the structure, the building, conceived of as embodying their interests and strength. I prefer the latter.——By "head" may be meant the head-men, the princes of the family or clique of the wicked; or the *highest part* of the structure. I adopt the latter, and therefore translate: "Thou dashest to pieces the head" (and dost strike it off) "from the house of the wicked, laying bare the foundation even to the neck"—*i. e.* as deep as water would be that came up to the neck—of course, utterly destroying the entire structure which represents the strength and cause of the wicked. A similar case of smiting the head and dashing the whole structure to atoms appears Amos 9:1. This may have been in the prophet's mind. The phrase "even to the neck" was proverbial, at first to indicate a depth of water nearly sufficient to drown a man. See Isa. 8:8 and 30:28. Probably it came thence to be used for about the same depth, five feet, more or less, in other relations.

* I render "*toward* their habitation," on the strength of what grammarians call "*He* local" which is appended to the word for habitation, giving the sense, "*toward* their habitation."

This would be deep enough to tear up the foundations of a building, and effect its utter ruin. If we adhere to the Hebrew text, and suppose any connection of thought between these two clauses now under consideration, this must be the construction. If it were ever allowable to admit that a slight error of one letter has crept into the text, for which the manuscripts give no authority, I should favor such a solution here, and then read *rock* in place of *neck*.* But I hold it to be the work of a commentator to interpret his text rather than to amend it, and therefore abstain on principle from tampering with such conjectures. To decide between conflicting testimonies of manuscripts and other authorities is another matter, sometimes quite inevitable, and quite allowable.

14. Thou didst strike through with his staves the head of his villages: they came out as a whirlwind to scatter me: their rejoicing *was* as to devour the poor secretly.

"Thou didst strike through (pierce) with his own spears the head of his princes." The word "head" is the same as in the first clause of v. 13, but means here a man's head, and not either the head-men (princes), or the head (summit) of a building. The passage may allude to the case of Jael smiting a nail through the head of Sisera. In general, it means that God turned their own weapons upon themselves, panic-smiting their hosts and setting them to slaughter one another. See Judges 7:20–22, and 1 Sam. 14:15, 16—Gideon and his three hundred against the countless Midianites; Jonathan and his armor-bearer against the Philistines.——"They, the Canaanites, came forth like a whirlwind to scatter me"—where "*me*," through the prophet's sympathy with the people of God, represents that whole people.——The Canaanites rejoiced in their work of destruction, as wicked men rejoice when they can devour the poor defenceless ones secretly, without exposure and consequent punishment. David, in several passages, refers to this joy of the wicked in maltreating the defenceless, without exposing themselves to retribution. See Ps. 10:8–11.

15. Thou didst walk through the sea with thine horses, *through* the heap of great waters.

The word rendered "heap" means here the foaming—in this case, the foaming of the mighty waters. "Thou, Jehovah, didst march through the sea with thy horses," &c., with a tacit reference to the passage of the Red Sea for the figure, but probably, as to the thing intended, referring to Jehovah's marching with his victorious hosts among the mad and raging nations of Canaan. This was the last scene in this august panorama. Thus closes this magnificent

* צוּר instead of צַוָּאר

portrayal of Jehovah's great achievements for his ancient people. Never were nobler conceptions wrought up with bolder and yet so chaste imagination, or in loftier strains of triumphal song.

16. When I heard, my belly trembled; my lips quivered at the voice: rottenness entered into my bones, and I trembled in myself, that I might rest in the day of trouble: when he cometh up unto the people, he will invade them with his troops.

Here the prophet falls back to the point from which he started (v. 2)—to the fear which agitated him so deeply when he first heard from the Lord that the fierce and terrible Chaldeans were surely coming to overwhelm the nation, to lay the land desolate, and the loved and holy city with its sacred temple in ruins.——With all the oriental nations, the belly is the seat of the emotions, especially of grief. Thus Habbakuk: "My bowels were strangely agitated; my lips quivered at the voice," *i. e.*, that uttered those words about the Chaldeans; "rottenness entered into my bones" and all my strength perished—the bones being the pillars and framework of the animal system; "I trembled," not precisely "in myself," but *under me*, my knees shaking and refusing their office—so strong was my agony of desire "that I might have rest in the day of trouble, in the coming up of the people who shall invade us." The last clause must be connected with the preceding more closely than in our English Bible. I have given a very literal and (as I suppose) an accurate translation.——The period around which his anxieties clustered was the hour of the anticipated invasion by the Chaldeans. His prayer and his solicitude looked toward rest for his spirit in that day of trouble when this fierce and savage people should come up against Jerusalem.——The word rendered "invade," means to press upon and besiege with troops.

17. Although the fig-tree shall not blossom, neither *shall* fruit *be* in the vines; the labor of the olive shall fail, and the fields shall yield no meat; the flock shall be cut off from the fold, and *there shall be* no herd in the stalls:

18. Yet I will rejoice in the LORD, I will joy in the God of my salvation.

19. The Lord GOD *is* my strength, and he will make my feet like hinds' *feet*, and he will make me to walk upon mine high places. To the chief singer on my stringed instruments.

The prophet's prayer was most abundantly answered. The Lord gave him "peace like a river;"—nay, more than merely peace—joy and exultation in the Lord his God, and in him alone and only. The sentiment of the seventeenth verse is that though every thing else should fail, the fig-tree, the vine, the olive, the fields, the flocks and the herds, yet the everlasting God would still live and never could fail or be cut off, or be any the less a faithful and glorious God for all the storms of earth, or for the invasion and desolating sweep of the most savage robber hosts. The last verse heightens the showing of his joy. Elastic and buoyant, his feet like the feet of the hind who bounds over the cliffs and never makes a mis-step on the crags of the mountain—so he moves along the high places of the earth, all undisturbed by the storms and troubles that harass the dwellers in the vales below.——It seems plain that the prophet was brought to this sublime height and placid rest of faith by means of those vivid, soul-thrilling views of God presented in this chapter, in which God is seen in his great works of mercy and of power in behalf of his people. Herein lie the special instruction and the great value of this wonderful chapter. In point of literary merit, its beauty and sublimity are of the highest order, and challenge our intense admiration; but far above and better than all those beauties is the sublime moral lesson it teaches, viz., that if any "good man would fix his hand upon the skies and bid earth roll, nor feel her idle whirl," the rational mode of reaching this sublime repose of faith is to study the great works of God's power and mercy as found in the historic pages of his word, and as first revealed from heaven in the ways of his providence and miracle-working power toward his people in the days of old. This study of God, deep, appreciative, prayerful, with the aid of his teaching Spirit, must be the one great condition on our part—a trustful, believing study, with a loving and appropriating faith. Such a study of God, with such help from his Spirit, give their utmost vividness and power to those great truths respecting God which we need to see and feel as realities. Oh, it is beyond measure blessed to have the soul thus filled with the practical impression of those truths! Then what was only as a dream before, becomes reality, clearly seen and deeply felt, and then it becomes natural and easy to adjust one's heart and life to the demands of those truths. They call for implicit faith in God; impressed by such views of God, and drawn by his Spirit, we seem spontaneously to yield it. So Habakkuk found his heart full of the simplest, sweetest trust in God, and in God alone—in God, though every thing else should fail.

It should have been more distinctly noted that the fig-tree and the vine stand here to represent, not themselves alone, but every other earthly good. They stand for home and dear ones, for country and sanctuary, for safety of person and for dear life. Although all these should fail, yet, said the prophet, will I rejoice in the Lord; I will joy in the God of my salvation. In the same spirit, a psalmist said: "My flesh and my heart faileth; but God is the strength of my heart, and my portion forever" (Ps. 73:26). ——The reader will scarcely need to be reminded that any and every one who cometh to the knowledge of this sublime example of faith may reach it for himself personally by the same steps. There is no exclusiveness in this gift of faith; it cometh alike to the simple-hearted child and to the wisest philosopher—to each and to all who heartily receive God as their supreme portion, and fully open their souls to his teaching, moulding Spirit.——And who will not prize this simple yet mighty faith? To whom would it not be a blessing high above all other blessings possible? It is like possessing and inheriting the Infinite God! This prophet foresaw that soon he should own no vine or fig-tree, no herd or flock; but he was more than satisfied, for he had (it might almost be said, he *owned*)—he had, *as* his own to trust in and enjoy, the Infinite and ever-blessed God!——When flesh and heart shall fail us, and all of earth shall be fading fast away from our mortal vision, there will be at least one hour in which it will be more to us than all the universe besides to have this God as our own!

ZEPHANIAH.

INTRODUCTION.

Of this prophet, his own introduction gives us the names of his immediate ancestors through four generations, of whom, however, nothing is known to us certainly except their names. It gives also the much more important statement that this word of the Lord came to him in the days of Josiah, king of Judah. Josiah's reign of thirty-one years fell, B. C. 642–611. A careful comparison of this Book of Zephaniah, with the history of Josiah's reign, as found, 2 Kings chapters 22 and 23, and yet more fully 2 Chron., chapters 34 and 35, will throw yet more light upon the precise date of his writings, and upon the much more important point of its definite aim and purpose.——Let it be borne in mind that after the great reformation wrought by Hezekiah with the aid of Isaiah and other prophets during his reign of twenty-nine years, a fearful relapse followed during Manasseh's long reign of fifty-five years; that the brief history sets forth in very strong terms the horrible influence of this wicked king who "made Jerusalem and Judah do worse than the heathen" (2 Chron. 33: 9); that his repentance occurring late in life, while it may have saved his own soul in answer to a godly father's prayers, yet seems scarcely to have at all arrested the strong currents of national wickedness; that his son Amon, reigning two years most wickedly, and then losing his life by conspiracy among his own servants, must have left the nation yet waxing worse and worse; and then that Josiah, coming to the throne at the tender age of eight years, began to seek after the God of his fathers at the age of sixteen, commenced a vigorous reform yet four years later, *i. e.*, at the age of twenty, which was the twelfth year of his reign, and had gone over the work with commendable thoroughness at the end of six years' labor, *i. e.*, in the eighteenth year of his reign. That was the era of a remarkable passover, kept with great solemnity and with hopeful results. But the roots of wickedness had gone deep into the national life. Hence this reform, as to the mass of the nation, could not have penetrated much beneath the surface. ——This reign of the good Josiah was the Lord's last call of the nation to repentance. Toward this result, Zephaniah and Jeremiah lent their aid—the latter beginning to prophesy in the thirteenth year of Josiah, and the former probably about the same time. Zephaniah (1 : 4) predicts—"I will cut off the remnant of Baal from this place," &c., and the history states (2 Chron. 34: 3, 4) that Josiah began this very work in his twelfth year, and closed it in his eighteenth. It may also be noted that Zephaniah (2 : 13–15) predicts the fall of Nineveh, which occurred B. C. 625—*i. e.*, in the seventeenth year of Josiah.——It was to aid King Josiah in his great work of reforming the nation and of saving it from ruin under the long-accumulating wrath of God, that Zephaniah was commissioned to reiterate the solemn declarations of Jehovah—"I will utterly consume this whole land"—especially every vestige of its idolatry, and not sparing its fearfully corrupt and wicked people. This is the one great thought throughout the first chapter. The next chapter heightens the force of this dread decree by assuring the people that the adjacent nations sunk low in general corruption and idol worship, were also doomed to fearful devastations—the Philistines, Moab, Ammon, Ethiopia, and Assyria, with her proud capital, Nineveh. In this general sweep of desolating judgments, Judah could by no means hope to escape, save by earnest and thorough repentance before God.——Chapter 3 sets forth yet more fully the extreme corruption of her prophets, priests, and princes, but closes with merciful promises of salvation in a future day for the remnant of his people.

CHAPTER I.

FOR the general scope of this chapter, the reader is referred to 2 Kings 23 : 26, 27. Closely following a very full account of the great reformation effected by Josiah, the historian says: "Notwithstanding, the Lord turned not from the fierceness of his great wrath wherewith his anger was kindled against Judah, because of all the provocations that Manasseh had provoked him withal. And the Lord said, "I will remove Judah also out of my sight, as I have removed Israel, and will cast off this city Jerusalem which I have chosen, and the house of which I said, My name shall be there."

1. The word of the LORD which came unto Zephaniah the son of Cushi, the son of Gedaliah, the son of Amariah, the son of Hizkiah, in the days of Josiah the son of Amon, king of Judah.

2. I will utterly consume all *things* from off the land, saith the LORD.

3. I will consume man and beast; I will consume the fowls of the heaven, and the fishes of the sea, and the stumbling-blocks with the wicked; and I will cut off man from off the land, saith the LORD.

See the general introduction. The stumbling-blocks are here, the idol-gods which had proved such a stumbling-block of ruin to the people. This shows that the reformation under Josiah entirely failed to save the land from its sins, and hence, from its deserved and fearful doom.

4. I will also stretch out mine hand upon Judah and upon all the inhabitants of Jerusalem; and I will cut off the remnant of Baal from this place, *and* the name of the Chemarims with the priests;

God would utterly finish the destruction of Baal, including the idols, their priests, and their worshippers, and would exterminate the very "name of the Chemarims." This word—meaning priest, as one who goes about in black or mourning, an ascetic—came from Syria, and was always applied by the Jews to the priests of idols.—— The history (2 Kings 23: 5) states that Josiah put down the Chemarims, whom the kings of Judah had ordained to burn incense in the high places," &c.; but ultimately, the Lord, by the long captivity in Babylon, made much more thorough work in rooting them out from among his people and burying their very name in oblivion. ——The last words of the verse, "with the priests," refers to Jewish priests—probably such as professed to serve the true God, but had apostatized into idol-worship.

5. And them that worship the host of heaven upon the house-tops; and them that worship *and* that swear by the LORD, and that swear by Malcham;

6. And them that are turned back from the LORD; and *those* that have not sought the LORD, nor inquired for him.

"The host of heaven" were the heavenly bodies, the sun, moon, stars, and planets. This form of idolatry, Sabianism (from Saba *) (used for the host of heaven), was very ancient, and widely extended throughout the East. The worship was offered on the house-tops, possibly for secrecy, but more probably for the sake of a better view of the objects of their worship.——The next class of worshippers, "worship, swearing by the Lord and swearing by *their king*"—a term here supposed to refer to Moloch. That is, they mix together the ostensible worship of Jehovah with the real worship of Moloch, whom they practically recognized as their king.——To swear by Jehovah is to recognize his supreme divinity, at least professedly. They rendered the same recognition to Moloch also. Of course such men render no true worship to Jehovah, and he dooms them to fall with the guiltiest idolaters.——V. 6 describes them in more general terms—all who have turned back, having once professed to serve him, and those who have not sought him—in every age a great and fearfully guilty class.

7. Hold thy peace at the presence of the Lord God: for the day of the Lord *is* at hand: for the Lord hath prepared a sacrifice, he hath bid his guests.

"Hold thy peace before the face of the Lord God" enjoins silence in the spirit of profound reverence and solemn awe. See a similar sentiment, Amos 6: 10. The reason assigned is, "because the day of the Lord is near," a day of judgment on the people. "The Lord hath prepared a sacrifice"—here in the sense of a great slaughter, as in Isa. 34: 6: "The Lord hath a sacrifice in Bozrah, and a great slaughter in the land of Idumea." The original word rendered "bid," † means to sanctify, but here in the sense in which war was declared with religious solemnities, and the warriors practically sworn in and consecrated to their work.——The Lord's "guests"—his *called ones*, as the original word means—are here, not men invited to dine at a festival, but those whom he had called in his providence to be the executioners of his vengeance on the wicked in this great slaughter—in the case, the Chaldeans.

8. And it shall come to pass in the day of the Lord's sacrifice, that I will punish the princes, and the king's children, and all such as are clothed with strange apparel.

Royalty in Judah had been deep in guilt and should be first in punishment.——In the phrase, "strange apparel," strange does not mean uncouth or surprising, but *foreign*. Indeed, the words "strange" and "stranger" in our Bible always means foreign, pertaining to Gentiles and not to Jews. The idea here is that the adoption and use of the foreign costume in dress indicated apostasy

* צָבָא. † הִקְדִּישׁ.

from God and a love for the institutions and customs of the heathen. Hence it marked men out for special plagues from the Lord.

9. In the same day also will I punish all those that leap on the threshold, which fill their masters' houses with violence and deceit.

The phrase, "those that leap on the threshold," is explained variously by commentators. Some suppose an allusion to the worshippers of Dagon (1 Sam. 5: 4, 5), who, because their helpless idol fell before the ark of God, and broke his neck over the threshold, took care forever after not to step *on* the threshold but *over* it. I see no analogy between this case and that. Here are persons who leap, not *over*, but *upon* the threshold. The parallel clause—"who fill their masters' houses with violence and deceit"—*i. e.*, with goods, property, obtained by violence and deceit, shows that robbers are thought of. Hence the probable sense of leaping upon the threshold is, invading the sanctity of other men's houses; violently leaping upon and over their thresholds, to enter their houses for robbery and spoil.

10. And it shall come to pass in that day, saith the LORD, *that there shall be* the noise of a cry from the fish gate, and an howling from the second, and a great crashing from the hills.

The city is here thought of as attacked by Nebuchadnezzar. The panic and the outcries of terror mark the progress of the conqueror through the city. First, "the noise of a cry from the fish gate." To this gate we find allusions in 2 Chron. 33 : 14, and Neh. 3: 3, and 12: 39. Doubtless it was the gate through which fish were brought into the city for market, and probably its direction was toward the lake of Tiberias and the Jordan, where fishing was certainly common in the New Testament age. At this point the Chaldean army would most naturally strike the city.——"A howling or wailing from the second"—not the second gate, but the second city, *i. e.*, a later addition to the city (see Neh. 11: 9), very probably the one built by Manasseh, as recorded, 2 Chron. 33 : 14: "He built a wall without the city of David, on the west side of Gihon, in the valley, even to the entering in at the fish gate, and compassed about Ophel (a hill so called), and raised it up a very great height," &c. The location of this new or second city shows that the Chaldean army would strike it next in order after entering at the fish gate.——"A great crashing from the hills" refers to hills *within* the city; Zion, Moriah, Ophel, &c. The echoes of crash after crash of ruin from these hills would be, to Jewish ears, terrific.

11. Howl, ye inhabitants of Maktesh, for all the merchant people are cut down; all they that bear silver are cut off.

"Maktesh" means *the* mortar, the article being prefixed, which shows that it is not a proper name generally known. It is plausibly supposed to refer to some valley, mortar-shaped, and probably the Tyropoeon, a valley within the city, occupied largely by merchants. —The reason for their wailing is that "all the merchants are cut off" —"all who are heavy laden with silver," for this is the sense of the Hebrew word. Those who were not only rich, but rich in silver, would suffer most severely in the sack of the city.——It is tacitly implied that these merchants are men of not the best repute; "people of Canaan" is their designation here. Hos. 12 : 7, 8, shows that the merchants of that day were not held in the highest esteem by the Lord. Their fraudulent habits are repeatedly rebuked by the prophets.

12. And it shall come to pass at that time, *that* I will search Jerusalem with candles, and punish the men that are settled on their lees: that say in their hearts, The LORD will not do good, neither will he do evil.

"Searching Jerusalem with candles" is an expressive figure, to show that none could secrete themselves in recesses so dark as to escape the vigilance and vengeance of Jehovah.——"Settled on their lees," alludes to wine standing long on its sediment, and not racked off into another vessel. The primary sense of the verb is to settle down in the oriental manner of sitting upon one's ankles, with the feet bent under the person (see Jer. 48 : 11). It describes those who have repelled all fear of retribution from God for their sins, and have gone on quietly in their great iniquities, as if there were no God above; who say in their hearts, "The Lord will do neither good nor evil, will neither reward the righteous nor punish the wicked." This is the cherished feeling of myriads of heathen minds; witness the Budhists of the East, who think of God only as reposing in eternal sleep in some indefinitely remote region of the universe, never concerning himself with the moral conduct of his creatures.

13. Therefore, their goods shall become a booty, and their houses a desolation: they shall also build houses, but not inhabit *them;* and they shall plant vineyards, but not drink the wine thereof.

The allusion to their "goods" shows that the prophet still has in view the wealthy classes who have grown rich through fraud or violence.

14. The great day of the LORD *is* near, *it is* near, and hasteth greatly, *even* the voice of the day of the LORD: the mighty man shall cry there bitterly.

15. That day *is* a day of wrath, a day of trouble and

distress, a day of wasteness and desolation, a day of darkness and gloominess, a day of clouds and thick darkness,

16. A day of the trumpet and alarm against the fenced cities, and against the high towers.

This great and awful day of the Lord, so graphically described, is the period of the Chaldean invasion. The "mighty man who shall cry there bitterly," is the warrior to whom the city intrusts its defence, but who will find himself utterly inadequate to the task. He can only wail in the anguish of his soul over his complete overthrow.

17. And I will bring distress upon men, that they shall walk like blind men, because they have sinned against the LORD: and their blood shall be poured out as dust, and their flesh as the dung.

18. Neither their silver nor their gold shall be able to deliver them in the day of the LORD's wrath; but the whole land shall be devoured by the fire of his jealousy: for he shall make even a speedy riddance of all them that dwell in the land.

Under the great and universal distress, men shall act as if bewildered, groping about as blind men, equally void of wisdom and of power for the emergency.——The conclusion of this fearful denunciation of doom is, that God will make a sweeping destruction, even a hastened one, of all the inhabitants of the land. So it came to pass.

CHAPTER II.

THE scope of this chapter was spoken of in the general introduction to this book. It aims to enforce repentance: (1.) By the shortness of time yet remaining before otherwise the shafts of vengeance must fall. (2.) By the fact that desolating judgments were coming upon other nations contiguous. This fact should assure them that the Lord was about to take in hand the work of retribution upon guilty nations on a broad scale; that he had his agencies in readiness; and that Judah and Jerusalem could by no means hope to escape.

1. Gather yourselves together, yea, gather together, O nation not desired;

The connection shows that this verse, and the two that follow it, were addressed to Judah, exhorting her to immediate repentance and righteousness as her last hope. With this view of the course of thought, I find no appropriate sense in the rendering of the first verb, "gather yourselves together." The question must be met, For what purpose? What would be the use of merely "gathering together?" Better than this rendering is that of Gesenius: "Collect your thoughts; consider your ways;" examine yourselves and think of your sins.——Still better is Henderson's derivation of the verb from another though a cognate root,* in the sense *to bend, to bow low before God*, in repentance and profound humiliation for your sins.——"O nation not desired," Gesenius renders, "nations never pale with shame," and the sense of conscious guilt. But the sense of longing after and greatly desiring is much better sustained by usage. I therefore adopt this rendering, according to our English Bible, only giving its strongest negative power to "*not*," so that it shall imply that so far from loving and longing for this nation in its present moral state, God altogether loathed them. He could have no other feeling toward them but that of loathing while they were so intensely corrupt. Hence the urgency of the call to humiliation and to a new heart and life.

2. Before the decree bring forth, *before* the day pass as the chaff, before the fierce anger of the Lord come upon you, before the day of the Lord's anger come upon you.

The decree, *i. e.*, the purpose of God to destroy, is thought of here as pregnant with a sure execution, and soon to "bring forth." *Before* this execution of the Lord's wrath, so near at hand, there was a short moment for repentance. The prophet exhorts the people to seize and improve it.——In the clause "before the day pass as the chaff," Henderson explains "day," not as the period of judgment, but as the short space for repentance lying yet before it. But the uniform usage of the word "day," fourteen times repeated in a connection like this, within the first chapter, and again in this verse, in every instance in the sense of *the period of the judgment*, seems to forbid his construction. I prefer to explain it: "Before that day of judgment shall sweep along as the chaff flies"—swiftly and waiting for none.

3. Seek ye the Lord, all ye meek of the earth, which have wrought his judgment; seek righteousness, seek meekness: it may be ye shall be hid in the day of the Lord's anger.

Here is the point of the exhortation, the duty to which they are exhorted. All the meek, the humble ones of the land, the only hopeful class—all those who have obeyed the Lord's revealed will ("judgments" here in the sense of revealed statutes), are implored to seek the Lord, and also to seek righteousness

* קוש instead of קָשַׁשׁ.

and a deeper humiliation ("meekness"), in the hope that so they may be hidden from danger in the day of the Lord's anger. It could not be regarded as certain that they would be exempt from all harm, even though penitent, for sometimes the righteous must suffer (in this world, not the next) with the wicked. Hence the qualified form of the statement, "it *may be*, that ye shall be hid."

4. For Gaza shall be forsaken, and Ashkelon a desolation: they shall drive out Ashdod at the noon-day, and Ekron shall be rooted up.

With this prediction of desolation on the cities of the Philistines, compare Amos 1: 6–8.——The Hebrew verbs which express the doom of Gaza and Ekron form a paranomasia with those names. If the word *gazee* meant forsaken, we might imitate the Hebrew by saying Gaza shall be *gazeed*.——These paranomasias are not merely beauties of style; they are utilities as well, for the doom of a city so expressed could not be forgotten. It would be riveted in the mind with the name itself.

5. Woe unto the inhabitants of the sea coast, the nation of the Cherethites! the word of the LORD *is* against you; O Canaan, the land of the Philistines, I will even destroy thee, that there shall be no inhabitant.

6. And the sea coast shall be dwellings *and* cottages for shepherds, and folds for flocks.

This "sea coast" is the eastern shore of the Mediterranean, and the western border of Canaan, along which the Philistines (Cherethites)—to some extent a maritime people—were located. All that region would fall before the Chaldean power. It did.——The sea coast shall be not "dwellings and cottages," but "pastures with shepherds' *cisterns*, and folds for flocks."

7. And the coast shall be for the remnant of the house of Judah; they shall feed thereupon: in the houses of Ashkelon shall they lie down in the evening: for the LORD their God shall visit them, and turn away their captivity.

This looks forward to the better days, when the Lord should restore his captive people, and they, returning, should find their old enemies, the Philistines, no longer there, but should themselves enjoy quietly the country of the sea coast.

8. I have heard the reproach of Moab, and the revilings of the children of Ammon, whereby they have reproached my people, and magnified *themselves* against their border.

God had heard what Moab and Ammon had said in contempt of Israel and of Israel's God, and would now remember it and visit them with retribution.——"Magnified themselves against their border," has the sense of carrying themselves proudly and in an overbearing way along and over their border—with reference, doubtless, to hostile encroachments upon Jewish territory.

9. Therefore, *as* I live, saith the LORD of hosts, the God of Israel, Surely Moab shall be as Sodom, and the children of Ammon as Gomorrah, *even* the breeding of nettles and salt-pits, and a perpetual desolation: the residue of my people shall spoil them, and the remnant of my people shall possess them.

This is the doom of Moab and Ammon. How fearfully it has been put in execution! For the past twenty-four centuries, the world has scarcely known where those nations once stood!——In the phrase "the breeding of nettles," the Hebrew gives the sense, the *possession of nettles*—a place which nettles shall occupy as all their own.

10. This shall they have for their pride, because they have reproached and magnified *themselves* against the people of the LORD of hosts.

So God will avenge himself on those who reproach *him* through their reproach of his people.

11. The LORD *will be* terrible unto them; for he will famish all the gods of the earth; and *men* shall worship him, every one from his place, *even* all the isles of the heathen.

The course of thought here should be noted. God becomes terrible to idolatrous nations when he famishes, *i. e.*, wastes away and destroys their gods; for when a nation's gods are gone, what have they more?——On the other hand, and as a result of destroying both the idol gods of those nations and their incorrigible worshippers as well, men everywhere, over all the isles of the Gentiles, shall worship the true God. "The isles of the nations" embrace all remote countries lying beyond the sea.

12. Ye Ethiopians also, ye *shall be* slain by my sword.

These Ethiopians are those of Africa—probably including the Egyptians. They were destined to fall before the same all-devouring Chaldean sword.

13. And he will stretch out his hand against the north, and destroy Assyria; and will make Nineveh a desolation, *and* dry like a wilderness.

See Nineveh, doomed in like manner (Nahum, chap. 2 and 3).

14. And flocks shall lie down in the midst of her, all the beasts of the nations: both the cormorant and the bittern shall lodge in the upper lintels of it; *their* voice shall sing in the windows; desolation *shall be* in the thresholds: for he shall uncover the cedar work.

The word rendered "cormorant" means "the vomiter," and is supposed to designate the pelican. The "bittern" is the porcupine or hedge-hog, so called from his rolling himself up.——These shall "lie among the capitals"—the tops of the columns—which of course are now fallen to the ground. The columns are those of her ruined temples and palaces.

15. This *is* the rejoicing city that dwelt carelessly, that said in her heart, I *am*, and *there is* none beside me: how is she become a desolation, a place for beasts to lie down in! every one that passeth by her shall hiss, *and* wag his hand.

Thus great Nineveh, once proud and joyous, is doomed to lie an utter waste, the scorn of passers-by. She was doubtless standing in her strength and glory when this servant and seer of the Lord uttered and penned these terrible words. The nations of the earth have had ample occasion to verify their truth during more than two thousand years.

CHAPTER III.

This chapter opens with further statements of the guilt and doom of Jerusalem (vs. 1–4); of God's justice in her punishment (v. 5); of his judgments on other nations (vs. 6–8); then turning to words of mercy, the Lord promises to convert the nations (vs. 9–10), and to restore and bless most abundantly the remnant of his people (vs. 11–20).

1. Woe to her that is filthy and polluted, to the oppressing city!

2. She obeyed not the voice; she received not correction; she trusted not in the Lord; she drew not near to her God.

The entire strain of remark shows that this passage speaks of Jerusalem; *e. g.*, that she had heard the voice of God; had been instructed and corrected, yet in vain; and that Jehovah is spoken of as "*her* God."——The word rendered "filthy," means rebellious: she had polluted herself by her sins, especially by idolatry, and had outraged justice by her oppressions of her own poor and defenceless people. Hence the wrath of God upon her.——She had also been taught her duty by the servants of the Lord, especially in later times by his prophets; yet she would neither obey God nor trust him.

3. Her princes within her *are* roaring lions; her judges *are* evening wolves; they gnaw not the bones till the morrow.

Her princes and judges had been fearfully corrupt. Those who should have withstood the influx of vice had been themselves examples and ministers of all wickedness.——"Roaring lions," in the sense of being mighty in sin, bold and rampant in their iniquity. ——"Evening wolves," who in oriental countries go about in the darkness, making night hideous with their howl and perilous by their ferocity, stand here to represent those judges who make an utter wreck of justice and peace, prostrating beneath their feet the very interests they are sworn to sustain.——These (human) wolves are voracious; "they do *not* gnaw the bones in the morning;" so the Hebrew reads, and implies, not that they leave *all*, but that they leave *nothing* till the morrow. Their voracity saves not even the bones till morning.

4. Her prophets *are* light *and* treacherous persons: her priests have polluted the sanctuary, they have done violence to the law.

"Her prophets are light," in the sense of vain-glorious, proud, and boastful—bearing on their hearts no sense of their responsibility. The priests seem for the most part to have gone down in degeneracy and sin with the people by at least an equal pace. The Lord had some prophets that were thoroughly faithful and bold in rebuking sin; yet the history shows that under the wicked kings, false prophets were never wanting who claimed to speak for God, but who really prostituted the whole influence of the prophetic name, and of God's name too, so far as they could, to the cause of vice and idolatry.

5. The just Lord *is* in the midst thereof; he will not do iniquity: every morning doth he bring his judgment to light, he faileth not; but the unjust knoweth no shame.

Note the designed antithesis between the flagrantly unjust judges, false prophets, and degenerate priests on the one hand; and on the other, the just Lord, never doing iniquity, bringing forth his just decisions every morning without fail.——Courts were held in the morning hour.——Those unjust, wicked men are shameless—lost to all compunction of conscience for wrong-doing. This fact shows that the moral tone of public sentiment was deplorably low.

6. I have cut off the nations: their towers are desolate; I made their streets waste, that none passeth by: their cities are destroyed, so that there is no man, that there is none inhabitant.

This is thought, with good reason, to have special reference to the calamities brought by a great Scythian invasion upon most of the nations of Western Asia during the reign of Josiah. From these evils, Judah, under his wise and righteous reign, was exempt.—— In seasons of great public danger, travel must cease, and none would pass along the highways. (See Judg. 5:6.)

7. I said, Surely thou wilt fear me, thou wilt receive instruction; so their dwelling should not be cut off, howsoever I punished them: but they rose early, *and* corrupted all their doings.

At this time the Lord said: "My people" will appreciate this merciful protection afforded to them: they "will fear me and receive instruction." In case they did so, "their dwelling" (in the sense of place of rest and safety) "should not be cut off, according as I have visited all others with judgments." The English, "howsoever I punished them," fails to give the true sense, which is this: that if his kind protection of them against the Scythians had moved them to gratitude, obedience and trust, he would not now punish them as he had done other nations. I prefer to adhere to the usual sense of the verb here used, viz., to visit with judgment, rather than to give it (with Dr. Henderson) the new and doubtful sense of appointing for punishment.——"But they rose early and corrupted all their doings"—as men who work with their might and with earnest heart, are up betimes in the morning. It is noticeable that God represents his own earnestness in efforts to save them by the same impressive figure (2 Chron. 36:15): "The Lord God of their fathers sent to them by his messengers, *rising up early in the morning* and sending, because he had compassion on his people and on his dwelling-place." The contrast gives a sad impression of *their* horrible depravity, but a rich and exalted one of *his* unutterably tender compassion and loving-kindness! They, up early in the morning, working with might and main, to do a long and hard day's work in sin; God, up betimes to press his agencies mightily to save them!

8. Therefore, wait ye upon me, saith the LORD, until the day that I rise up to the prey: for my determination *is* to gather the nations, that I may assemble the kingdoms, to pour upon them mine indignation, *even* all my fierce anger: for all the earth shall be devoured with the fire of my jealousy.

"Therefore" (in view of all these things) "wait ye for me" (*i. e.*, to fulfil my threatenings) "until the day of my rising up for the prey, to spoil the nations, for this is my purpose."——Great and widely extended judgments are in the plan of God, to fall on all the guilty nations of the earth. Let his people expect them in their time.

9. For then will I turn to the people a pure language, that they may all call upon the name of the LORD, to serve him with one consent.

Here is a reason for awaiting those judgments, because then, in close connection, the Lord will convert the remnant of the nations to himself. His great judgments will prepare the way for mercies no less great.——"I will turn to the nations (Gentiles) a pure language"—freed from the very names of idols (see Hos. 2:17), and from all those terms that are suggestive of the pollutions and corruptions of human depravity. God will give them a new vocabulary; the language of Zion will be all new when all men shall call upon the name of the Lord.——"To serve him with one shoulder," is the striking expression of the Hebrew—as we might say, moving on in military phalanx, shoulder to shoulder, for soldiers dress to a line by the shoulder. Or the phrase may allude to two or more men bearing the same burden on their shoulders, in which case they must move accurately together. So in Zion should order and harmony be perfect, resting on the basis of having one heart and one soul.

10. From beyond the rivers of Ethiopia my suppliants, *even* the daughter of my dispersed, shall bring mine offering.

This must be the African Ethiopia, south of Egypt, embosoming the head-waters of the Nile. Thence should suppliants from the Lord's scattered people come with their offerings to Jerusalem. The reader will readily recall the case of an "eunuch of great authority under Candace, queen of Ethiopia, who came to Jerusalem to worship" (Acts 8:27 ff.), and who went home with more of the gospel than he had ever known before. The case proves that there were some dispersed people there, probably Jews, who remembered Zion, and that a purer knowledge of God went among them after the Christian era. It would seem that there have been nominal Christians in Abyssinia ever since. They were found there by Bruce in his travels, early in the present century.

11. In that day shalt thou not be ashamed for all thy doings, wherein thou hast transgressed against me: for then I will take away out of the midst of thee them that rejoice in thy pride, and thou shalt no more be haughty because of my holy mountain.

This cannot mean that they shall have no sense of shame for the sins of which they are or have been guilty. The Scriptures and Christian experience combine to teach that pardoned sinners have the very keenest sense of sorrow and shame for their sins. (See Ezek. 16 : 61–63 and 36 : 31.)——The meaning here is therefore only this: that they shall not be confounded before the nations by God's judgments upon them for their sins. They will not sin as they had done; and moreover, God will forgive and forbear to punish. That their sin itself should mostly cease—at least, their specially provoking, heaven-defying sins—is expressly said: "For then I will take away out of thee thy proud, exulting ones, and man shall no more be haughty in my holy mountain." The Hebrew has it "*in*," not "because of."

12. I will also leave in the midst of thee an afflicted and poor people, and they shall trust in the name of the LORD.

The few spared and surviving, after the many had fallen under sore judgments, are blessed by what they have suffered, and by what they have seen others suffer; and these return to the Lord their God. Of this promise there have been many fulfilments.

13. The remnant of Israel shall not do iniquity, nor speak lies; neither shall a deceitful tongue be found in their mouth: for they shall feed and lie down, and none shall make *them* afraid.

This applies readily to the remnant restored from Babylon, and affirms their general purity of character, greatly reformed as compared with the morals of the nation before the captivity. It may apply also to subsequent periods.

14. Sing, O daughter of Zion; shout, O Israel; be glad and rejoice with all the heart, O daughter of Jerusalem.

This call to great joy indicates that precious blessings are to be revealed.

15. The LORD hath taken away thy judgments, he hath cast out thine enemy: the king of Israel, *even* the LORD, *is* in the midst of thee: thou shalt not see evil any more.

"Hath taken away thy judgments," not in the sense of removing from them the administration of justice or the jurisdiction of his law, but of terminating his inflictions of calamity and his retributions for their sin. The days of her sore scourging had passed.——"He hath cleared away thine enemies from before thee"—perhaps with historical allusion to their early days in Canaan, when the Lord did *not* fully clear away the Canaanites and Philistines. Now he will, and they shall repose in quiet—less tempted to sin, and less annoyed with thorns in their side—enemies within their own borders.——Their king, Messiah, the real Jehovah, being in the midst of them as Immanuel (God with us), verily, "they shall see evil no more," as compared with former evils.

16. In that day it shall be said to Jerusalem, Fear thou not: *and to* Zion, Let not thine hands be slack.

"Let not thy hands be slack" is said in the sense of not waxing feeble through despondency and unbelief.

17. The LORD thy God in the midst of thee *is* mighty; he will save, he will rejoice over thee with joy; he will rest in his love, he will joy over thee with singing.

Her Lord is not in the midst of her—his Zion—as a terror or a scourge, but as a mighty one for help, rejoicing in her purity and blessedness.——The phrase "he will rest in his love" seems to mean in the original, "will be silent in his love," in the sense of freely forgiving her sin, and henceforth forbearing to speak of it in words of threatening, and to act against it in retributive judgments. His love is silent from upbraiding and chastising, in contrast with the continual strain of rebuke which had been the common manifestation of his presence in their former apostasy. Now, they being no longer apostate, but walking humbly and softly before God, he takes the purest delight in abiding among them, and silently enjoys their worship and their responsive love. It is indeed a precious thought, but is most fully authorized, that God rejoices in the sincere love and worship of his people. It is a source of ineffable delight to his benevolent heart. This doctrine is reiterated with great force in this passage.

18. I will gather *them that are* sorrowful for the solemn assembly, *who* are of thee, *to whom* the reproach of it *was* a burden.

"Those who are grieved" (because of their exclusion) "from thy solemn festivals, I will gather home (they were of thee), who have borne reproach for her" (Zion's) "sake;" or the last clause might be read, "to whom reproach for her sake was a burden." The sentiment is that God will gather home to Zion those dispersed ones who had been sad because of their long exclusion from her solemn feasts, and who had borne reproach for their God.

19. Behold, at that time I will undo all that afflict thee: and I will save her that halteth, and gather her that was driven out; and I will get them praise and fame in every land where they have been put to shame.

20. At that time will I bring you *again*, even in the time that I gather you: for I will make you a name and

a praise among all people of the earth, when I turn back your captivity before your eyes, saith the LORD.

The original, rendered "I will undo," means I will deal with—take them in hand for justice and judgment. This would doubtless involve their *undoing*. Sentiment—God will reverse the state of her long-depressed and scattered people. The feeble shall be saved with strength; the exiled brought home in triumph; the long-dishonored and disowned shall have praise and fame in the very place where they had been put to shame. The public sentiment of the world is changed, and the real friends of God are now held, not in contempt, but in honor.——It can scarcely be supposed that the restoration from Babylon exhausted the significance of these promises. Then the restored people were few and feeble. Though honored and favored by Cyrus, yet they were by no means greatly honored by their nearest neighbors, the Samaritans, nor by other contiguous nations. Something more and better than that must lie yet treasured up for Zion in these promises. Yet further, the clear indications in this chapter (vs. 9, 10) of the conversion of the Gentiles also, must carry the great body of these predictions over into the gospel era, and some portion of them down into those times described by Paul (Rom. 11), when, almost simultaneously, the Jews will be grafted back into their former stock, and the Gentile world be converted to the same ever-blessed God.——O come, that glorious day!

HAGGAI.

INTRODUCTION

Both the date and the occasion of this book are given very distinctly. Its date is subsequent to the restoration from captivity in Babylon by sixteen years. Its occasion was the fact that the Jews were sinfully neglecting to complete the building of their temple. Consequently the Lord sent Haggai to rebuke them for this sin, and to exhort them to resume the work and complete it.——It should be borne in mind that Cyrus, on his accession to the Medo-Persian throne, two years after it had absorbed the Chaldean empire and made Babylon its capital, issued an edict, strongly inviting the Jews to return to their own land, and rebuild both their holy city and their temple. Fifty thousand responded to this call, and under Zerubbabel as governor, and Joshua as high priest, returned to the land of their fathers, and commenced rebuilding the city, and in process of time the temple also. The Book of Ezra gives the Jewish history of these events. It there appears that in the second year of Cyrus (B. C. 535), and in the second month, they began to rebuild the temple; that soon the Samaritans began to oppose and retard their work, and kept up this opposition during the remaining five years of the reign of Cyrus (Ez. 4: 5), and yet more vigorously and successfully, under his vile son and successor Cambyses (called, Ez. 4: 6, "Ahasuerus"), who reigned seven years and five months. At length, from his successor, Smerdis (called, Ez. 4: 7, 8, 11, 23, Artaxerxes), they obtained an order that the work should absolutely cease. This Smerdis reigned but seven months. A better king succeeded, in the person of Darius Hystaspes. As Smerdis was at best only an usurper, and as the decree of Cyrus was therefore still the law of the realm, there was no legal obstacle in the way of resuming this work the first moment after the pressure of violent prevention was removed. When, throughout the first year of Darius, it was seen that the people did not resume this work, but occupied themselves in fitting up and even embellishing their own houses, the Lord sent his prophet Haggai, and two months later Zechariah, to rebuke them for this neglect, and to encourage them to resume and complete the building of the temple. The work was completed in the sixth year of Darius (Ezra 6 : 15).——These are briefly the historic facts which, being intimately connected with the subject matter of this book, are essential to its intelligent exposition.

CHAPTER I.

The Lord rebukes the neglect of the people to build his house; calls their attention to their lean and meagre harvests, and to his blighting curses upon their land and labor because of this neglect; and when the people shall have returned to this duty, pledges them his favoring presence.

1. In the second year of Darius the king, in the sixth month, in the first day of the month, came the word of the Lord by Haggai the prophet unto Zerubbabel the son of Shealtiel, governor of Judah, and to Joshua the son of Josedech, the high priest, saying,

2. Thus speaketh the Lord of hosts, saying, This people say, The time is not come, the time that the Lord's house should be built.

The people excused their delay in finishing the temple, on the alleged ground that the time for it had not yet come.——It has been supposed that they bolstered up this lame apology by their own construction of Jeremiah's prophecy (25 : 12), which had named seventy years as the duration of the captivity. As the temple was not destroyed until eighteen years after the first captives were taken away, and as only about fifteen years had passed, up to the first year of Darius, since the first captives returned, they perhaps persuaded themselves to think that the temple must lie desolate yet some three years longer, to complete its full period of seventy years. ——Men sometimes put constructions upon Scripture which God has neither put nor authorized, the ultimate cause being that they are but too well pleased to have it so. This may have been a case of the same sort.

3. Then came the word of the LORD by Haggai the prophet, saying,

4. *Is it* time for you, O ye, to dwell in your ceiled houses, and this house *lie* waste ;

In the question, "Is it *time* for you," &c., the Lord uses the word "*time*" because the people had used it, saying, "The *time* has not come to build the Lord's house." Thus ye say, "The time has not come to build my house;" has the time come for you to build yours, and finish them off with comfort and even elegance, while you let my house lie waste? Is this a proper expression of gratitude to Jehovah for condescending to dwell in the midst of you, and for redeeming you from your long captivity? The word "*you*" in the Hebrew is made specially emphatic. It is for *you*, for such as *you*, for *you*, in view of all your circumstances, &c. This emphasis is indicated by repeating the pronoun you.——"Ceiled houses," from the Hebrew word meaning covered, refers to the inside covering of the walls with more or less of ornament—in modern phrase, called "finishing"—for both comfort and beauty.

5. Now, therefore, thus saith the LORD of hosts ; Consider your ways.

6. Ye have sown much, and bring in little ; ye eat, but ye have not enough ; ye drink, but ye are not filled with drink ; ye clothe you, but there is none warm ; and he that earneth wages, earneth wages *to put it* into a bag with holes.

The expressive form of the original is, "Set your heart on your ways," *i. e.*, look on your ways, not only thoughtfully but solemnly, appreciating and realizing the significance of your course toward God, and of God's toward you. Since they had dishonored God by neglecting his temple, he had scourged them by suspending his usual gifts of timely rain and sun. He appeals to them to note the facts of their own case, how they had prospered in nothing, and had toiled to small purpose.

7. Thus saith the LORD of hosts ; Consider your ways.

8. Go up to the mountain, and bring wood, and build the house ; and I will take pleasure in it, and I will be glorified, saith the LORD.

This second exhortation to consider their ways may have a look forward, as the first (v. 5) looked back, as if the Lord would say: "Take note of what shall be hereafter, as well as of what has been heretofore. Go to the mountain; get wood; finish my house; then see what a change shall come over your labor, and the fruits thereof."

9. Ye looked for much, and, lo *it came* to little ; and

when ye brought *it* home, I did blow upon it. Why? saith the LORD of hosts. Because of mine house that *is* waste, and ye run every man unto his own house.

10. Therefore, the heaven over you is stayed from dew, and the earth is stayed *from* her fruit.

11. And I called for a drought upon the land, and upon the mountains, and upon the corn, and upon the new wine, and upon the oil, and upon *that* which the ground bringeth forth, and upon men, and upon cattle, and upon all the labor of the hands.

The phrase "blow upon it," some interpreters render (as the margin has it) blow it away. The preposition rendered *upon*, strongly favors our received translation. The sense will then be—Even after you had gathered your harvests home, I blighted them as by the breath of my mouth.——The word "*run*," "ye *run* every man to his own house," indicates that their hearts were not in God's house, nor toward it, but toward their own.——It was specially characteristic of the entire age before the coming of Christ that God's moral government over men in this world was made manifest by *present retribution.* It was never intended that those present retributions should be perfect, or should supersede the necessity of a future state in which all deficiencies would be made up; but it was the design of God to make his government palpable, so that all men should have tangible, visible evidence of its reality. Obviously there was indefinitely more need of present retribution then than now. It was a sort of compensation to offset their inferior light respecting God, duty, and salvation.——The genius of that whole dispensation in regard to the point now in hand—present retribution for right and wrong doing, visited on the people in blessings or in curses—is set forth strongly in the latter chapters of Deuteronomy, especially chapter 28. These verses of Haggai presuppose this type of God's moral government over men in this world.

12. Then Zerubbabel the son of Shealtiel, and Joshua the son of Josedech, the high priest, with all the remnant of the people, obeyed the voice of the LORD their God, and the words of Haggai the prophet, as the LORD their God had sent him, and the people did fear before the LORD.

13. Then spake Haggai the LORD's messenger in the LORD's message unto the people, saying, I *am* with you, saith the LORD.

14. And the LORD stirred up the spirit of Zerubbabel the son of Shealtiel, governor of Judah, and the spirit of Joshua the son of Josedech, the high priest, and the

spirit of all the remnant of the people; and they came and did work in the house of the LORD of hosts, their God,

15. In the four and twentieth day of the sixth month, in the second year of Darius the king.

It is pleasant to note that these messages from the Lord produced the desired result. The Lord stirred up the spirit of both rulers and people, and they took hold earnestly of the neglected work of rebuilding the temple. Twenty-four days sufficed to arouse them and to make the necessary preparations.——The masses of the people were far more obedient to the voice of God than before the captivity—furnishing yet another case of blessings coming through sore chastisement. "Before I was afflicted, I went astray, but now have I kept thy word."

CHAPTER II.

THE distinct portions of this chapter are strongly marked: (1.) The portion (vs. 1–9) which speaks to those hearts that were sad and depressed by the greatly inferior glory of this temple compared with that built by Solomon. (2.) Vs. 10–19, designed to show that their late neglect to build the house of God had vitiated all their labors, and brought a blight from the Lord upon all their fruits; and (3.) Vs. 20–23, encouraging their rulers, and confirming the great promise made (vs. 6–9).

1. In the seventh *month*, in the one and twentieth *day* of the month, came the word of the LORD by the prophet Haggai, saying,

The reader will note that this date is one month, less three days, after they began upon the work of rebuilding. (See 1:15.) With what had been done in the former effort, commenced some fourteen years before, the work of this month sufficed to show that this temple must be greatly inferior in splendor and in all its appointments, to that which had stood from the time of Solomon down to the captivity.

2. Speak now to Zerubbabel the son of Shealtiel, governor of Judah, and to Joshua the son of Josedech the high priest, and to the residue of the people, saying,

3. Who *is* left among you that saw this house in her first glory? and how do ye see it now? *is it* not in your eyes in comparison of it as nothing?

A few patriarchs of venerable age remained to remember the glory of that first temple which had now lain desolate about sixty-eight years. The Lord calls their attention to the contrast between that and this. "How do ye see this now? Is not this in your eyes, compared with that, as nothing?"——Ezra. 3:12, 13, gives us a touching allusion to this scene, blending the joy of the young people with the grief of their fathers—the shoutings of the one class and the sad wailings of the other—each swelling up, and perhaps each exciting the other, until the noise was heard afar, and men could not distinguish the shouts of joy from the outcries of grief—a scene not soon forgotten by either the joyous or the sad ones of that day.——The Lord calls attention to the wide contrast between this latter house and the former because he had something to say about it, as we shall see.

4. Yet now be strong, O Zerubabbel, saith the LORD; and be strong, O Joshua, son of Josedech the high priest; and be strong, all ye people of the land, saith the LORD, and work: for I *am* with you, saith the LORD of hosts:

The first thing he would say is, Be strong of heart, and never yield to depression; "be strong and work," for I am with you, and my presence ought to outweigh greater and more discouraging contrasts than this which saddens your hearts to-day. Shall it not be enough for you that I am with you?

5. *According to* the word that I covenanted with you when ye came out of Egypt, so my Spirit remaineth among you; fear ye not.

The proper construction of the term "word," in the phrase rendered "according to the word that I covenanted," &c., presents difficulties. There seems to be no authority in the original for the words "according to," or for the idea that the continued presence of the Spirit is in accordance with that original covenant made when the nation came forth from Egypt. This may or not be true: it is not expressed clearly and beyond a doubt here.——On the contrary, this passage, almost beyond a doubt, affirms (1.) That the covenant made at Sinai is still in force, no less *since* the captivity than before; and (2.) That God's Spirit also still abides with the people; so that for both reasons the people ought not to fear, but be strong and of good courage. With such a covenant of promise, and such a present, indwelling Spirit, why should they bewail the lack of those external splendors which pertained to the temple of Solomon?

6. For thus saith the LORD of hosts; Yet once, it *is* a little while, and I will shake the heavens, and the earth, and the sea, and the dry *land;*

Exegetically, the chief difficulty in this verse turns on the word rendered "*once.*" The choice seems to me to lie between these two constructions: (1.) "Yet once more, and that very soon, I will shake," &c.; or (2). "It is yet but one short period, and I will shake," &c. In the latter case, the word *one* (this is the usual sense of the Hebrew) is only equivalent to the article. Of this usage there are some examples. The choice between these two constructions is a matter of no great importance as to the ultimate sense. The first construction may be thought to imply once more, and once *only*.

The "shaking of the heavens, the earth, the sea, and the dry land," must be taken in the figurative and not the literal sense, to indicate, not an earthquake, reaching far out through boundless space, but convulsions among the great nationalities of the world—Assyrian, Chaldean, Medo-Persian, and Grecian—to pave the way for the coming of Messiah's kingdom. They dash one against another, each in succession overwhelming its immediate predecessor, but each revolution ripening the world for the coming of Messiah. In a similar strain Ezekiel says (21:27): "I will overturn, overturn, overturn, and it shall be no more, until he come whose right it is, and I will give it him."——In this view of the sense, the next verse will be explanatory—"Yea, I will shake all nations," &c.

7. And I will shake all nations, and the desire of all nations shall come: and I will fill this house with glory, saith the LORD of hosts.

8. The silver *is* mine, and the gold *is* mine, saith the LORD of hosts.

The test word in verse 7 is "*desire*." Is this a synonym for the Messiah? Is it only another name for the same exalted *man*, thought and spoken of here as one "desired by all nations"? So the current sentiment of the Church and so its sacred songs have for the most part assumed. This has been a pleasant and cherished interpretation. I must confess that I have felt its strong attractions. But I have been compelled by the force of grammatical and exegetical reasons to modify somewhat this interpretation, yet not so as ultimately to lessen but rather to augment the richness of its spiritual significance.——The usual construction, which interprets the word "desire" as meaning precisely the Messiah, must be rejected:

(1.) First and mainly, because the verb is plural—"*they* come, even the desire of all the nations." The word "desire" must therefore be a noun of multitude, *i. e.*, a noun embracing in its meaning not one object alone, but many. There seems to be no way to get over this difficulty so long as we make "desire" synonymous with Messiah.

(2.) The scope of thought is not congenial to its strict application to the Messiah, especially as seen in the declaration, "The silver is mine, and the gold is mine, saith the Lord of hosts." Silver and gold were eminently absent, not present, in the personal life of the man of Nazareth. Yet in this prophecy silver and gold must stand in a close relation to the sense of the clause "the Desire of all nations shall come."——A better construction is possible, and indeed unobjectionable. Let it be borne in mind that this entire passage grows out of the contrast between the meagreness of the new temple and the wealth and splendor of the old, and out of the consequent discouragement and depression of the Lord's people. He calls their special attention to this wide contrast (v. 3). He proceeds to intimate (vs. 4, 5) that the absence of gold and silver, and of material splendor in this new temple, may be abundantly compensated by his spiritual blessings; by the fact that "*I am with you*," and the further fact that the covenant and the Spirit are still remaining. He advances yet in the same line of thought—I am about to convulse the nations—to revolutionize the state of the world, and thus, as the ultimate outcome, *the desirable things* of all nations—their wealth, beauty, and glory—shall come to Zion; and "I will fill this temple with glory, saith the Lord of hosts." The silver and the gold of all the world are mine, saith the Lord of hosts, and by the might of my power over the hearts of men and over all human society, it shall be consecrated to Immanuel's kingdom.——Special stress must be accorded to this frequent repetition of the phrase, "saith the Lord of hosts," closing each of three successive verses, 7, 8, 9.——Let it also be borne in mind that, according to this construction, the Lord speaks precisely *to* that which constituted the chief solicitude of the pious Jews. They were saying in their heart: How much we do miss the riches—the silver, the gold, the cedars, the tapestry—of that ancient temple! When and how can we ever rear a temple worthy of the God of our fathers? We are very poor; shall we ever be rich enough to build and adorn a temple worthy of our God?——To this the Lord very kindly and pertinently replies: Give yourselves no solicitudes in that line. I am the Lord God of hosts; I rule this wide world, and I can command all its silver and gold when I will for my kingdom. And *I shall do it!*——In support of this construction may be urged (1.) It gives the ordinary and established sense to the word rendered "*desire*." This word is used mainly for those things which worldly men desire. (2.) It meets the exigencies of the plural verb, since it embraces in its idea many things, not one only. (3.) It is, as we have seen, fully in keeping with the previous context—the train of thought which occasioned this prophecy, and which introduced this passage. (4.) It is equally in harmony with the subsequent context—filling this house with glory, and God's claiming the silver and the gold of the world as his own. (5.) It is also entirely in harmony with other and more ancient prophecies, *e. g.*, Isa. 60. To set this in its full light would demand the whole chapter, in which we read: "The abundance of the sea shall be converted unto thee"—"all they from Sheba shall come, bringing gold and incense"—"the isles shall wait for me, and the ships of Tarshish first, to bring thy sons from far, their silver and their gold

13

with them, unto the name of the Lord thy God"—"the glory of Lebanon shall come unto thee to beautify the place of my sanctuary, and I will make the place of my feet glorious," &c., &c.—— The same strain runs through the seventy-second Psalm: "The kings of Tarshish and of the isles shall bring presents; the kings of Sheba and Seba shall offer gifts."——Let it be said very distinctly that in this construction of the passage, I do not exclude but include the Messiah. One advantage of this construction is that under it we get, not the Messiah alone, but much more besides. It is only under his reign and after the power of his cross over human hearts has been gloriously developed among the great and distant nations of the earth, that all the silver and gold of the world shall be brought and laid at his feet for use in the purposes of his spiritual kingdom. Even yet, how little of the real wealth of nominally Christian nations—nay, more, how little of the wealth of the visible Church is truly consecrated to the Saviour of men! It shall yet be far otherwise than this! Prophecy cannot receive its entire fulfilment until the wealth of the world shall press forward voluntarily (so to speak) to lay itself at Immanuel's feet, to be used so that he may soonest and best see of the travail of his soul, and may have most of that "joy set before him," in the conversion of myriads to his love and service.——It may be asked: Do you expect, in the good time yet coming, to see a temple built with cedars from Lebanon, and beautified with the silver and the gold of all the earth?——I answer, Nothing can be further from my thought than the going back of Christianity to real Judaism. The New Testament "temple of God" is the loving and pure heart wherein God dwells (2 Cor. 6:16). In this temple, by another figure, Christians are themselves "living stones" (1 Pet. 2:5), and in this temple "the sacrifices of God are a broken heart and a contrite spirit."——Of course, Jewish prophets *must* think and write in Jewish symbols and terms. Good Christian sense must find the spiritual meaning of those terms and symbols—the New Testament and its teaching Spirit furnishing the key.

9. The glory of this latter house shall be greater than of the former, saith the LORD of hosts: and in this place will I give peace, saith the LORD of hosts.

To the first clause, two different interpretations have been given; (1.) That the "latter house" is that of Zerubbabel, the former that of Solomon; and the thing affirmed, that the glory of this built under Zerubbabel, shall be greater than the glory of that built by Solomon; (2.) That the temple of Solomon is out of mind, and that the antithesis really lies between the former and the latter glory of this same temple then in building—its "former glory" being what it had under Zerubbabel, and onward down through what remained of the age before Christ; and the latter, that which it shall attain when the desirable things of all nations shall come into it; when the wealth and beauty of the world shall be consecrated to Immanuel, and the Prince of Peace shall reign in his own spiritual temple, filling it with the glory of his own presence.——The latter is doubtless the true construction: (1.) Because it is precisely what the words in their order mean, and *must* mean. They stand thus: "Great shall be the glory of this house—the latter more than the former, saith Jehovah of hosts." (2.) Because this construction alone answers to the drift of the context, the very thing that the Lord is saying in this passage being this—The meagre glory of this temple, as ye now see it, shall give place to a glory vastly greater when the wealth and beauty of all the nations shall be brought into it. That is, the era of spiritual power, beauty, and glory, shall immensely surpass all the external splendors of Judaism; the spirit shall eclipse the letter; the inward be more and better than the outward; the homage of countless warm and living hearts shall more adorn and glorify God's temple than all the gold of Ophir, the smoke of incense and the blood of thousands of bullocks and of rams.——"In this place will I give peace"—can have but one interpretation;—not tranquillity as opposed to the disturbances of war; not peace of mind as opposed to agitation and distress: but including all these and much more, the abstract word peace, used for the concrete, it means the great *Peacemaker*, the great author and Prince of Peace, the world's pacificator as toward its abused, offended Maker;—the Shiloh of earlier prophecy, repeatedly foretold under precisely this appellation. (See Micah 5: 5 and Isa. 9: 6, 7.) ——This naturally completes the evidence in proof that this entire passage refers to the then future times of the Messiah.

10. In the four and twentieth *day* of the ninth *month*, in the second year of Darius, came the word of the LORD by Haggai the prophet, saying,

11. Thus saith the LORD of hosts, Ask now the priests *concerning* the law, saying,

12. If one bear holy flesh in the skirt of his garment, and with his skirt do touch bread, or pottage, or wine, or oil, or any meat, shall it be holy? And the priests answered and said, No.

13. Then said Haggai, If *one that is* unclean by a dead body touch any of these, shall it be unclean? And the priests answered and said, It shall be unclean.

14. Then answered Haggai, and said, So *is* this people, and so *is* this nation before me, saith the LORD; and so *is* every work of their hands; and that which they offer here *is* unclean.

The priests being the authorized expounders of the ceremonial law, the Lord directs the people to propound to them two questions: (1.) In case a priest, bearing holy flesh in his garment, brings it in contact with any thing else, does it impart its own sacredness to whatsoever it touches?——To this, they answer, No. Ceremonial holiness is not imparted by the touch.——(2.) Over against this is the second question: Does a man, who has been made unclean by contact with a dead body, impart his own uncleanness by the touch? They answer, Yes. Ceremonial uncleanness *is* imparted by the touch.——This doctrine of the ceremonial law, the Lord applies to the people. They had sinned in neglecting to build the Lord's temple. By reason of this sin, their moral state became analogous to that of the man ceremonially unclean. This sin imparted its moral character to all they did. The Lord could not take pleasure in the labors of their hands; it all became unclean.——On the other hand, if they should do any good thing, it could not carry its good quality over to any thing else they might do. Under the law of God, works of supererogation are unknown.

15. And now, I pray you, consider from this day and upwards, from before a stone was laid upon a stone in the temple of the LORD:

16. Since those *days* were, when *one* came to an heap of twenty *measures*, there were *but* ten: when *one* came to the press-fat for to draw out fifty *vessels* out of the press, there were *but* twenty.

17. I smote you with blasting and with mildew and with hail in all the labors of your hands; yet ye *turned* not to me, saith the LORD.

The Lord would have them review the period from that day backward to the point where the building of the temple commenced, and so from that day onward to the present, and observe how fearfully their harvests had been blighted. "I smote you with blasting and blight, yet ye moved not toward me"—literally, "there was nothing of you to me." Up to this point his chastisements had proved altogether unavailing.

18. Consider now from this day and upward, from the four and twentieth day of the ninth *month*, *even* from the day that the foundation of the LORD's temple was laid, consider *it*.

19. Is the seed yet in the barn? yea, as yet the vine, and the fig-tree, and the pomegranate, and the olive-tree, hath not brought forth: from this day will I bless *you*.

Here is another call to examine the course of the Lord's providence toward them throughout the interval from the day when they commenced laying the foundations of the Lord's house to that hour.——Is the seed yet in the barn? No. Planting-time is past, and you have planted; but have you any harvests of any sort? Not any.——But now that ye have resumed this labor upon the temple, from this day I will bless you. Note and see.

20. And again the word of the LORD came unto Haggai in the four and twentieth *day* of the month, saying,

21. Speak to Zerubbabel, governor of Judah, saying, I will shake the heavens and the earth;

22. And I will overthrow the throne of kingdoms, and I will destroy the strength of the kingdoms of the heathen; and I will overthrow the chariots, and those that ride in them; and the horses and their riders shall come down, every one by the sword of his brother.

This message, sent especially to Zerubbabel, bears the same date with that immediately preceding, and seems intended to supplement and reaffirm the prophecy recorded (vs. 6–9). It is quite plain here that the "shaking of the heavens and the earth" is the same thing as "overthrowing the throne of the kingdoms," and has no application other than this. God will cast down vast armies, overthrowing chariots and their riders, horses and horsemen, and turning a man against his brother, so that God's enemies should give their strength to mutual slaughter. Thus those vast, ungodly kingdoms of the earth are doomed to fall.

23. In that day saith the LORD of hosts, will I take thee, O Zerubbabel, my servant, the son of Shealtiel, saith the LORD, and will make thee as a signet; for I have chosen thee, saith the LORD of hosts.

But throughout this slaughter of his foes, God will protect his friends. He indicates this by saying that their governor shall be as his signet-ring upon his finger. This implies care, love, and protection. No doubt the Lord intended this promise should be good to the successors of Zerubbabel;—good for his people so long as they put their trust in him, whoever their Zerubbabel may be.

ZECHARIAH.

INTRODUCTION.

THE usual preliminary questions of personal history—date, occasion, and special object—are readily settled in the case of the prophet Zechariah. He began to prophesy in the eighth month of the second year of Darius Hystaspes, B. C. 520, contemporary with Haggai, when Zerubbabel was governor of Judah, and Joshua was high priest. At this period, the great matters of interest in the visible kingdom of God were the rebuilding of Jerusalem, the resettlement of the returned and still-returning captives from Chaldea, and yet more especially, the rebuilding of the temple, and the culture of the faith and religious life of the people composing the new community. In many respects it was a time of laying again the foundations of religion and morals, and of planting anew those institutions which were to be the fountains of their future religious life, and hence of their abiding prosperity. Consequently, there was abundant work for the prophets of the Lord.——It is pleasant to note that their work was more hopeful and less discouraging than that of their predecessors for many generations. The people were more impressible; the word of the Lord was effective; the spirit of obedience, and not of rebellion, was in the main predominant. Hence, most of the messages sent from the Lord by Zechariah were of cheerful tone, breathing far more of promise than of threatening.

The reader will notice in this prophet (relatively to the whole amount of his writings) more predictions of the Messiah than in any other.——The people were at first a small and feeble band, estimated in comparison with other tribes and sovereignties about them. They could scarcely have stood their ground against these hostile powers, save under the protection of the Persian throne. In this throne, God had remarkably provided for their security. Hence, they had great reason to feel that in this respect their salvation and national life were from the Lord. In the same line of thought, the Lord often revealed to them that Greater Patron and more glorious Refuge, ere long to appear in the person of Immanuel, the real King of Zion.

The first six chapters are distinguished from the rest of the book, and indeed from most of the other prophetical writings of the Old Testament, by the blending of symbol and vision. The things presented to the prophet in vision were highly symbolic. Most of these symbols were so far explained to the prophet as to give us an adequate clue to their significance.——Some critics have assumed that the diversity in the point of symbolic vision, between the first six chapters and the remaining eight, is sufficient proof that the latter portion was not written by the same Zechariah. The only valid ground for this assumption must be another further back, viz. that, if God reveals any truth to a given prophet by symbolic visions, he must pursue this precise method and no other without variation throughout that prophet's life. But what authority can be found for such an assumption? Does it obtain in the case of the prophet Amos, or Daniel, or Ezekiel, or Jeremiah? I look upon this assumption as one of the follies, not to say absurdities, of hyper-criticism.——The book throughout is richly instructive, fraught with spiritual life and power, and consolatory to the feeble but trusting children of God.

CHAPTER I.

This chapter contains three distinct portions: vs. 1–6 derive admonition for the people from the case of their fathers whom the Lord sent into captivity for their sins; vs. 8–17 is the first symbolic vision, viz., of horses and their riders, and vs. 17–21 the second, of four horns, and of smiths to break those horns in pieces and destroy their power for harm.

1. In the eighth month, in the second year of Darius, came the word of the Lord unto Zechariah, the son of Barachiah, the son of Iddo the prophet, saying,

Zechariah is said (Ezra 5:1) to be the son of Iddo the prophet. We must suppose that "son" is used there in its less rigid sense, for grandson. Iddo is perhaps made prominent there as his ancestor, because he was a prophet.

2. The LORD hath been sore displeased with your fathers.

The statements of the history respecting this sore displeasure of God against their fathers are abundant and very strong. (See 2 Chron. 36 : 11–16, and 2 Chron. 33, and 2 Kings 21 : 2–16.)

3. Therefore, say thou unto them, Thus saith the LORD of hosts; Turn ye unto me, saith the LORD of hosts, and I will turn unto you, saith the LORD of hosts.

In view of God's wrath against their fathers and its results in the desolation of their city and land, the Lord commissions Zechariah to say to the people then present: "Turn unto me in penitence, and I will turn unto you in forgiving love and mercy." This is the standing law of God's moral kingdom in this world of probation.——The reader will notice the frequent yet not "vain repetition" of the divine title, "the Lord of hosts," the Great Ruler of the celestial armies, the King of the universe.

4. Be ye not as your fathers, unto whom the former prophets have cried, saying, Thus saith the LORD of hosts; Turn ye now from your evil ways, and *from* your evil doings: but they did not hear, nor hearken unto me, saith the LORD.

5. Your fathers, *where are* they? and the prophets, do they live for ever?

6. But, my words and my statutes which I commanded my servants the prophets, did they not take hold of your fathers? And they returned and said, Like as the LORD of hosts thought to do unto us, according to our ways and according to our doings, so hath he dealt with us.

With great pertinence and force the Lord exhorts them not to be as their fathers, stiff-necked, obdurate, reckless of the warnings and entreaties sent them of God by the former prophets. *Where are those fathers now?* Gone from the world where they became so fearfully hardened in their sins; gone from the land they polluted by their abominations and cursed by their persistence in rebellion; gone to their righteous but most fearful doom! It were well for the children to think often of those fathers and ask, Where are they?——The prophets, too, having served their generation amid sore trials and heart-griefs unutterable, had gone to their blissful reward. Let the people consider!——Did not the words which God sent by those former prophets "*take hold* of your fathers?" Did they slip off as things of loose grasp, and prove void of result? Did not those awful threatenings *hold on*, and have not you yourselves seen and felt the terrible judgments which those words portended?——They themselves were forced to admit this. They returned and said, *i. e.*, they took a new and better view of the case under the pressure of appalling facts, and then they said—All that God thought and threatened to do unto us as a nation, he has done! Let their children take warning!

7. Upon the four and twentieth day of the eleventh month, which *is* the month Sebat, in the second year of Darius, came the word of the LORD unto Zechariah, the son of Barachiah, the son of Iddo the prophet, saying,

8. I saw by night, and behold a man riding upon a red horse, and he stood among the myrtle-trees that *were* in the bottom; and behind him *were there* red horses, speckled, and white.

9. Then said I, O my lord, what *are* these? And the angel that talked with me said unto me, I will shew thee what these *be*.

10. And the man that stood among the myrtle-trees answered and said, These *are they* whom the LORD hath sent to walk to and fro through the earth.

11. And they answered the angel of the LORD that stood among the myrtle-trees, and said, We have walked to and fro through the earth, and behold, all the earth sitteth still, and is at rest.

12. Then the angel of the LORD answered and said, O LORD of hosts, how long wilt thou not have mercy on Jerusalem and on the cities of Judah, against which thou hast had indignation these threescore and ten years?

13. And the LORD answered the angel that talked with me *with* good words *and* comfortable words.

14. So the angel that communed with me said unto me, Cry thou, saying, Thus saith the LORD of hosts; I am jealous for Jerusalem and for Zion with a great jealousy.

15. And I am very sore displeased with the heathen *that are* at ease: for I was but a little displeased, and they helped forward the affliction.

16. Therefore thus saith the LORD; I am returned to Jerusalem with mercies: mine house shall be built in it, saith the LORD of hosts, and a line shall be stretched forth upon Jerusalem.

17. Cry yet, saying, Thus saith the LORD of hosts, My cities through prosperity shall yet be spread abroad; and the LORD shall yet comfort Zion, and shall yet choose Jerusalem.

These verses comprise one entire and distinct vision, the first in a series, and of symbolic character. The symbols represent the executive forces by which the Lord administers his providential government over the nations. The special aim here is—(1.) To assure the Hebrew people that God had more judgments to send on the nations that had oppressed them; and (2.) That he would greatly augment the growth and prosperity of Zion. So much for the general scope of the passage.——As to the particulars, let us note that this is a night-vision, presented to the mind's eye of the prophet by special divine agencies.——That men riding on horses are used to represent the executive forces of God's reign over the nations is due (we may suppose) to the use of post-horses as vehicles of the royal mandates, as the nerves of communication (so to speak) from the working brain on the throne to the remotest organs of his will in all his distant provinces. They seem to be thought of here rather as explorers to observe and report, than as executioners. ——The reader will better understand this representation if he will be at the pains to classify the personages of the scene—what are sometimes called "the dramatis personæ"—thus: (1.) The man riding upon a red horse (v. 8), who stood (on horseback) among the myrtle-trees in the shaded vale, at the head of others, also on horses of various colors; the same who (v. 10) explained and said, "These are they whom the Lord hath sent," &c., to whom the other horsemen report (v. 11); and to whom prayer is offered as "the Lord of hosts" (v. 12); and who answers so kindly (v. 13). This can be no other than the uncreated angel—the very Son of God, so often if not always the God revealed and made manifest in all the ages before his incarnation. (2.) Next are his attendants, on horses, representing angels proper; those "ministers of his who do his pleasure," and whom he continually employs in the administration of his providential government on earth. They appear (v. 8) where it must be assumed that the horses have riders upon them; also (v. 11), they report what they have seen in their mission to and fro through the earth. (3.) The revealing angel, specially attendant upon the prophet as his interpreter, usually called "the angel that talked with me," *e. g.*, v. 9, 13, and also in v. 14, where our translators have given the same Hebrew word another rendering, "that communed with me." It is the same angel who offers the prayer (v. 12), since the answer (v. 13) is given to him. That *he* offers this prayer is due to his strong sympathy with the prophet, to whom he was a sort of guardian angel.——This grouping of the characters of this scene will help the reader to understand its significance. The horses and their riders are seen among the myrtle-trees in a shady vale—both the myrtles and the vale indicating the low and humble condition of God's people and kingdom, especially at that time, yet showing us plainly that however low and humble in human estimation, *God was in the midst of them*, and did not disdain to reveal precisely there his glorious Son, and under him the angels clothed in might as the executive servants of his reign among the nations.——No other speciality of meaning can be safely assigned to the color of these horses, except that red commonly indicates war-scenes of blood, and that the variety may suggest that God's agency embraces all varieties of manifestation—curses and blessings, war and peace.——The prophet asks his attendant angel what those horses and their riders mean. He promises to show him, but the statement is given by the personage first seen and standing in the foreground of the picture—the Great Uncreated Angel of Jehovah—"These are they whom the Lord sends to traverse the whole earth." Then they themselves come forward and make their report in the hearing of the prophet: "We have traversed the earth, and lo, all the nations are still and at rest." Even those great powers which had so cruelly oppressed the Jews were not receiving their deserved retribution. This is the main point of their report.——Upon this, the revealing angel, warming in sympathy with the prophet and his people, cries—"How long, O Lord, ere thou wilt have mercy on Jerusalem and on Judah, upon which thou hast manifested thine indignation now seventy years?" ——To this the Lord answers with words of comfort and cheer. He has purposed to scourge and soon to destroy that fierce Chaldean power, and he will surely lift up Jerusalem.——V. 15 may be paraphrased thus: "I am very sore displeased with Chaldea and Edom: I was comparatively a little displeased with my people, Judah and Jerusalem, and therefore I suffered those powers to come down on the holy city and land; but they augmented that infliction; they gave vent to their cruel and vindictive spirit, and have quite overdone the work which I commissioned them to do. For this, they are to have a fearful doom."——In v. 16, the Lord promises to return in mercy and to help onward the rebuilding of the city; and in v. 17, that the population should overpass the city walls and fill the adjacent country.——"Will yet choose Jerusalem"—means, will yet *manifest* his loving choice of her by appropriate mercies.

18. Then lifted I up mine eyes, and saw, and behold four horns.

19. And I said unto the angel that talked with me, What *be* these? And he answered me, These *are* the horns which have scattered Judah, Israel, and Jerusalem.

20. And the LORD shewed me four carpenters.

21. Then said I, What come these to do? And he spake, saying, These *are* the horns which have scattered Judah, so that no man did lift up his head: but these

are come to fray them, to cast out the horns of the Gen tiles, which lifted up *their* horn over the land of Judah to scatter it.

This second vision is closely connected in significance with the first, looking especially to the destruction of those heathen powers which "had scattered Judah and Jerusalem." The "horn" is a natural emblem of power. The number, four, does not count so many hostile nations, but rather means all, in every quarter of the earth, toward every cardinal point of the compass, who have been pushing and scattering the saints of God.——The word rendered "carpenters," should be "smiths," workers in iron or other metals, and therefore armed with suitable instruments for breaking horns. The word "fray," mostly obsolete as a verb, means to frighten. The next verb, rendered "cast out," has a stronger sense —*cast down to the ground*, so as altogether to paralyze their power for harm.——This prediction was fulfilled shortly after. Chaldea revolted against its late Medo-Persian conquerors during the reign of this same Darius. He consequently attacked and subdued them, and then greatly marred the military strength and glory of Babylon. Thenceforward Chaldea was no more felt or feared as a power among the nations.

CHAPTER II.

THIS chapter introduces one vision and has but a single theme. The vision presents a man going forth to measure Jerusalem; but he is soon stopped, and it is announced that Jerusalem shall be so prosperous and populous that her people shall overpass her former limits and fill the adjacent country with unwalled villages (vs. 1–4). God will dwell in the midst of her, revealing his glory there; her captive children are exhorted to flee out of Babylon and hasten home. In the greatness of her future prosperity, many other nations shall join themselves unto the Lord (vs. 5–13).

1. I lifted up mine eyes again, and looked, and behold a man with a measuring line in his hand.

2. Then said I, Whither goest thou? And he said unto me, To measure Jerusalem, to see what *is* the breadth thereof, and what *is* the length thereof.

3. And behold, the angel that talked with me went forth, and another angel went out to meet him,

4. And said unto him, Run, speak to this young man, saying, Jerusalem shall be inhabited *as* towns without walls for the multitude of men and cattle therein:

In this vision a man is seen with a measuring line, going forth to measure Jerusalem—probably its dimensions before its recent destruction—as if preparing to rebuild it on the same foundations. ——The angel that talked with the prophet went forth (*i. e.*, *from* the prophet) and another angel came forth (it may be supposed) from the Lord, to meet him and to say to him: Hasten to that young man who has the measuring line, and tell him there is no occasion to measure the old limits of the city; the new one shall spread out beyond her former walls, and her people shall live in the surrounding country without walls, because of the multitude of men and of cattle.——In this passage, the point most in dispute among critics is the question—Who is this "young man"? (v. 4). Some say he is the prophet Zechariah; others, that he is the "man with a measuring line" of v. 1—an appropriate work for an active young man. I incline to the latter view, especially because v. 4 implies that the measurement of the city is arrested for reasons there given. The whole scene was designed to impress vividly upon the prophet and his people the great promise of God respecting the growth, prosperity, and glory of the new city, and ultimately of that spiritual Zion of which this was the outward symbol.

5. For I, saith the LORD, will be unto her a wall of fire round about, and will be the glory in the midst of her.

The connection of thought here is admirable: Think no more of walls to be rebuilt for the new city, nor of costly outlays to beautify and adorn it; "for I, saith the Lord, will be myself her wall," even "a wall of fire round about her;" and I will be her adornment also—even "a glory in the midst of her." This magnificent promise we cannot suppose to have been exhausted in the days of Zechariah, nor in the entire period before the incarnation of the Son of God; but preëminently then when He, the great Incarnation of God, became manifest in human flesh in the midst of his Zion. Yet its fulfilment began in those days of Zion's reformation and rebuilding. Our divine Lord reasserted essentially the same thing and made it a promise of perpetual love to his Church, when he said, "Lo, I am with you alway, even to the end of the world."

6. Ho, ho, *come forth*, and flee from the land of the north, saith the LORD: for I have spread you abroad as the four winds of the heaven, saith the LORD.

7. Deliver thyself, O Zion, that dwellest *with* the daughter of Babylon.

This call summons all Jews still remaining in Chaldea to return, especially to escape from the judgments God was soon to bring on Babylon. Babylon is "the land of the north." (See Jer. 6:1–22, and 16:15.)——This call to escape contemplates (probably) that impending devastation of Babylon referred to in the notes on Zech. 1 : 21.——The Lord had scattered them abroad as if the winds from every quarter of the heavens had been combined for this work. This is the most natural sense of the words "*as* the four winds of heaven"—*i. e.*, would do it. So, in Isa. 64 : 6, and Job 30 : 15. A different phrase is used to express the sense—*into* or *toward* the four quarters of the heavens; as in Jer. 49 : 32–36.

8. For thus saith the LORD of hosts: After the glory hath he sent me unto the nations which spoiled you: for he that toucheth you toucheth the apple of his eye.

Here two points may need each a word of explanation, viz., the sense of the phrase "after the glory," and the identification of the persons "he" and "me," in the clause "he hath sent me," &c.—— "After the glory" is an elliptical, shortened phrase, looking to v. 5, and meaning that *after having become the glory of Zion* by revealing himself as her king, her refuge, and protector, it followed naturally that he should be sent to scourge the nations that had spoiled Jerusalem, *i. e.*, the Chaldeans, and perhaps the Edomites also.——As to the persons "he" and "me," in the phrase "he hath sent me," &c., the language implies that the speaker who calls himself the "Lord of hosts," has been sent by some one referred to as "he;" "*he* hath sent *me*," &c. The one thus "sent" can be no other than the leading personage in the vision (1 : 8–13), there seen on a red horse (v. 8); to whom the other horsemen report (v. 11); to whom the angel interpreter offers prayer (v. 12); and moreover the same personage who in 2 : 5 says, "I will be a glory in the midst of her," *i. e.*, the Son of God.——The antecedent of "*he*" is implied in thought, rather than expressed in word; yet can be no other than the infinite Father—often represented in the Scriptures as sending the Son—here on a mission of providential judgments on the guilty nations that had desolated Jerusalem.——The reason assigned is beautifully significant of the tenderness of even the Father's love toward his people. We often see manifestations of tenderness in Jesus Christ while wearing our nature in its human weaknesses; but here Jesus says of his Father—"He that toucheth you, toucheth the apple of *his* eye." "Toucheth"—in the sense of doing harm. The apple is the pupil of the eye, which the Hebrews call the *little man* of the eye, or as here, the little boy of the eye, both terms coming probably from the fact that, looking into the eye, you see a *miniature* picture of yourself.——Can we realize the precious truth taught here—that God feels every injury done to his people, as we feel a wound in the apple of our eye? Then let us forever dismiss and discard the cruel assumption that the Infinite God has little or no sympathy with our spiritual life, with the real welfare of his people, the interests of his truth, and the cause of human salvation!

9. For, behold, I will shake my hand upon them,

and they shall be a spoil to their servants: and ye shall know that the LORD of hosts hath sent me.

Immanuel, as the God of universal providence, sent to the nations that had wasted Zion, here declares what he will do, and calls special attention to it: "I will shake or wave my hand over them" —so much only being necessary to indicate to the executioners of his will what they were to do; and "they shall become a spoil to those who have heretofore been their servants;" *i. e.*, the nations some time in servitude under Chaldea now rise up, overcome, and spoil her.——Ye shall know by your experience of divine blessings that my commission is truly divine.——It is remarkable that the phrase "the Lord of hosts" is used interchangeably of the Father and the Son: of the Father here; of the Son in v. 8, and elsewhere in this and the previous chapter. No other explanation of this is needed save the fact that this name is equally applicable to either, and that the Scriptures in some cases represent the Father and in some cases the Son, as administering the government of this world.

10. Sing and rejoice, O daughter of Zion: for lo, I come, and I will dwell in the midst of thee, saith the LORD.

Closely parallel with this is Zech. 9: 9: *There*—"Rejoice greatly, O daughter of Zion; shout, O daughter of Jerusalem; behold, thy king cometh unto thee," &c. *Here*, as the reader will see, "Sing and rejoice," for lo, I come and I will dwell in the midst of thee, saith the Lord, *i. e.*, Jehovah. This close similarity strengthens the evidence that the speaker here is the promised Messiah, and that this promised coming can be exhausted in nothing less than his appearance in human flesh, and indeed in nothing less than his abiding presence (spiritually) with his people "to the end of the world." This abiding presence, in somewhat lower forms, he manifested from the time of Zechariah onward to his incarnation.—— All this is indeed occasion for exultant joy.

11. And many nations shall be joined to the LORD in that day, and shall be my people: and I will dwell in the midst of thee, and thou shalt know that the LORD of hosts hath sent me unto thee.

Christ's coming to dwell incarnate and subsequently by his Spirit, the Comforter, would result in the calling of the Gentiles into his Church, and ultimately in the gathering of *many nations*, and in their becoming joined in the relationships of love and trust to their redeeming Saviour and king.——Here recurs again that expressive phrase—"Thou shalt know" (in thine own blest experience) that I am sent of the Eternal Father, that the work is not mine alone, but his as well—evermore sustained by the common sympathy and the coöperative agency of each and of both.

12. And the LORD shall inherit Judah his portion in the holy land, and shall choose Jerusalem again.

"Inherit," in the sense of having them as indeed his own peculiar people, with their most hearty concurrence and true devotion to his service. This verse manifestly had its special fulfilment in the nearer future—already apparent in the time of this prophet.

13. Be silent, O all flesh, before the LORD: for he is raised up out of his holy habitation.

So glorious are these promises, so magnificent and momentous these achievements, that the prophet gives utterance to his sense of the impressive presence of Jehovah, who works them all, by saying —"Be silent, O all flesh, before" such a God, so present in this guilty world, "for he hath roused himself up from his holy habitation," and is about to gird himself for solemn and mighty issues!

CHAPTER III.

THIS chapter records another distinct and entire vision, in which Joshua, the high priest, is the prominent personage. He appears, not in his own person, but as representing the priesthood, and particularly in their depressed condition at that time. The vision aims to show that God does not reject but forgives and restores the priesthood, and indeed will at length make it perpetual in the person of his Messiah.

1. And he shewed me Joshua the high priest standing before the angel of the LORD, and Satan standing at his right hand to resist him.

The tense of the Hebrew verb connects this verb closely with the preceding: "And *then* he caused me to see Joshua the high priest standing," engaged in his official ministrations before the uncreated angel Immanuel; and Satan, *the* well-known adversary of God's people, standing at his right hand to act the Satan against him—literally to "*Satan*" him— the Hebrew for Satan meaning to persecute, oppose, resist. Bearing in mind, that the high priest was by virtue of his office a representative man, officiating for the people before the Lord, and remembering the low estate of their entire religious system at this time, it need not surprise us that the people should be sinfully despondent and weak of faith. Probably this was the great sin which is here represented by the filthy garments of the priest. It is fully in character for Satan to take advantage of their unbelief, and thrust forward his plea against their being forgiven or in any wise accepted before God. He dreaded the present and prospective revival in their religious state, and roused himself (as is his wont) to head it off at the outset. *Is* not he a very devil?

2. And the LORD said unto Satan, The LORD rebuke thee, O Satan; even the LORD that hath chosen Jerusalem rebuke thee: *is* not this a brand plucked out of the fire?

He who in v. 1 is called "the angel of the Lord," is here "the *Lord*," "Jehovah." So also in the phrase "The Lord rebuke thee," "Jehovah" is the word for "Lord," showing that this term is applied interchangeably to both the Father and the Son.——The clause, "The Lord rebuke thee," is repeated, both for the greater emphasis, and in order to connect with it the consolatory words—he, the same that has chosen Jerusalem, rebukes thee. The term "choose" here, as in 1: 17 and 2: 12, implies God's special love for Jerusalem as representing his own people.——"Is not this a brand plucked out of the fire?" implies that after the fires of utter destruction were already kindled upon her, the Lord plucked her out and extinguished the fires. Having done so much to save her and at such personal risk, would the Lord give her up to Satan now?——This language is used by Amos (4: 10), and may be borrowed from him.——Commenting on these verses, Dr. Henderson raises the question as to the ground of Satan's opposition, and remarks that the passage does not inform us; but that he finds a clue to it in Jude 9, in which passage he adopts the construction which resolves "the body of Moses" into the Jewish church, and assumes a reference there to this passage in Zechariah. But in that dispute it was Michael the archangel who contended with the devil; in this, it is the Lord Jehovah, not to say also that Jude's language, "the body of Moses," should by no means be made to mean any thing else but his physical, veritable body, without good reason. The literal sense, if admissible, as it is here, has the prior claim.

3. Now Joshua was clothed with filthy garments, and stood before the angel.

4. And he answered and spake unto those that stood before him, saying, Take away the filthy garments from him. And unto him he said, Behold, I have caused thine iniquity to pass from thee, and I will clothe thee with change of raiment.

The Mosaic law prescribed the priest's garments very minutely, and made great account of them as indicative of the moral purity requisite in those who came before God. Here the filthy garments represent the sins of the people, probably (as suggested above) their unbelief and despondency at that time, and their long and guilty wanderings from God into idolatry in past time, from which they were only now returning.——He stood before the divine angel who, in v. 4, pardons sin. This divine personage says to his attendant angels: "Take those filthy garments away;" and to Joshua, "See, I have caused thine iniquity to pass from thee, and I will clothe thee with festive garments," such as the priests should wear on holy days. This removing of his sin is a representative thing, its import being, not that the Lord forgives his personal sin, but rather the sins of the people, and practically reinaugurates the long disused functions of the priesthood. As if he would say to all the people: "Return to the modes of worship enjoined upon your fathers in the wilderness; your own covenant-keeping God will hear your prayers and accept your offerings through the High Priest of his own appointment. The great sins of your nation before and during the captivity are forgiven, and again the way is open to you for acceptable worship before him and for confidence in his love."——V. 4 commences: "He" (the angel Jehovah) "*answered.*" But the narrative has nothing that called for an answer. Frequently, in both the Old Testament and the New, the word "answer" refers to something thought but not expressed; in the present case, to the silent prayer of Joshua standing before the Lord as a sinner, that God would forgive him. To this unuttered prayer the answer comes.

5. And I said, Let them set a fair mitre upon his head. So they set a fair mitre upon his head, and clothed him with garments. And the angel of the LORD stood by.

The original word, rendered "I said," Dr. Henderson thinks should have its vowels changed so as to read, "And he" (the Lord) "said." He pleads for this change on the ground that it would be impertinent for the prophet to speak here. I do not see force enough in this objection to justify a change of the text. The prophet's request I attribute to his deep sympathy with the transaction—a sympathy upon which his Lord would not frown, and which in his eye would readily atone for any seeming impertinence.——The prophet saying in his heart as he saw the filthy garments taken away, "*That is good,*" begged that his head-dress might be changed as well. His request was at once complied with.——In the last clause, some suppose that the angel of the Lord *stood by*, as supervising the transaction till all was complete, thus expressing his deep personal interest; while others render it simply *stood*, as if he rose up preparatory to the solemn asseveration recorded in the next verse. I prefer the former construction, with our English version.

6. And the angel of the LORD protested unto Joshua, saying,

7. Thus saith the LORD of hosts; If thou wilt walk in my ways, and if thou wilt keep my charge, then thou shalt also judge my house, and shalt also keep my courts,

and I will give thee places to walk among these that stand by.

The word rendered "protest" means to affirm with special solemnity, to asseverate.——In the word "charge," the margin is more true to the original, "ordinance." Our translators seem to have misapprehended the word rendered "places to walk."* It is a participle, with the sense of *guides*, attendants, who shall aid you to walk—cause you to walk safely. They are to come from among "these that stand by"—his own attendant, ministering angels. It is a plain promise of the aid of ministering angels. The essential meaning of the verse is clear: "If thou art both obedient and faithful, thou shalt be established in the priesthood, thy services shall be accepted before me, and thou shalt have ministering angels to lead and aid thee in thy work."

8. Hear now, O Joshua the high priest, thou and thy fellows that sit before thee: for they *are* men wondered at: for behold, I will bring forth my servant The BRANCH.

This call of Joshua's special attention implies that statements are to be made of things highly important. The word rendered "thy fellows," means thy associates in the priesthood, the subordinate priests who served under the general direction of the high priest. ——In the rendering "they are men wondered at," few readers would be likely to see the true idea, which is—they are men of typical character, men who are significant signs or representatives of the great intercession, performed for God's people by Jesus Christ, their Great High Priest. The most literal rendering is "men of wonder." See the same use of the word, Isa. 8:18 and 20:3; Ezek. 12:6, 11, and 24:24, 27. In this line of thought the prophet gives a striking prediction of the Messiah. The course of thought is: "Hear and give special heed, O Joshua, thou high priest, and thy attendant priests also, for ye are all typical men; for lo, I shall soon cause to appear among men my servant the Branch!"——The original for "bring forth" does not refer specifically to his human birth of a virgin, but to his being caused to come down to our world, and so to appear among men.——The word "branch" should not carry our thought to a branch in the sense of *limb*, as one among many on the same tree, but to the one shoot which springs up from the root, and which, though small at first, becomes a tree of wonderful qualities. The word seems to be chosen because it well expresses the humble origin of the Messiah, and the small beginnings of his work, and also his descent from the stock of David as to his human nature. It occurs as a name for the Messiah in Isa. 4:2; Jer. 23:5 and 33:15; and Zech. 6:12. "My servant" is also a well-known designation of the Messiah, occurring Isa. 42:1, and 49:3, 5, 6, and 52:13, and 53:11. The earliest Jewish expositors known to us in-

* מַהְלְכִים

terpret this passage of the Messiah. The Chaldean Paraphrase (older than the Christian era) reads it: "Behold, I bring my servant the Messiah, who will be revealed."

9. For behold the stone that I have laid before Joshua; upon one stone *shall be* seven eyes: behold, I will engrave the graving thereof, saith the LORD of hosts, and I will remove the iniquity of that land in one day.

This verse brings forward another great truth, manifestly regarded as one of high importance, since special attention is called to it. The first and main inquiry is, What *is* this "stone"?——Note what is said of it. It is laid before the high priest Joshua, manifestly to be under his care; the seven eyes of God—his perfect eye—are upon it; it is not a stone to be built on, but to be engraved—wrought with the chisel into forms of beauty; and finally, the real thing signified by it must have some natural connection with the great work of Christ's atonement, in which, by one offering, "in one day," he bore away the sins of men. All these conditions cannot be fulfilled in the foundation stone of the temple, although not improbably the stones of the temple suggested this figure of a stone. They are, however, all fulfilled in the *living Church of God*, and in nothing else. God's Church was then "laid before Joshua," in the sense of being put under his charge; then, as ever, the perfect eye of God was upon it; its engraving into forms of spiritual beauty is eminently God's work by the chisel of his providence, and by the agency of his Spirit; and finally, the sins of this Church Christ took away by that one offering of himself on Calvary.——By a figure somewhat analogous to this, Christians are said to be "the temple of the living God" (2 Cor. 6:16), and "his building" (1 Cor. 3:9), and "living stones, built up a spiritual house" (1 Peter 2:5).——The passage Zech. 4:10 definitely alludes to this verse, and asserts that "they are the eyes of the Lord, which run to and fro through the whole earth." The usage of accounting seven as the perfect number seems to have been oriental, and not merely Jewish—pervading the literature of the East, and not restricted to Palestine.——These truths were well adapted to inspire the people with fresh confidence in God as their present Friend and Guardian, interested evermore in the spiritual culture of his people, and purposing to use the priesthood again, as in early days, as his instrument in the spiritual training of his people; and at the same time signifying that a more perfect atonement would be made—finished and complete—"in one day," and not needing, therefore, perpetual sacrifices, year by year, which never could do their work perfectly. (See Heb. 7:27, 9:9, 25, 26, and 10:1–4.)

10. In that day, saith the LORD of hosts, shall ye call

every man his neighbor under the vine and under the fig-tree.

In that future day, when the Messiah shall be revealed, "the iniquity of his people be taken away in one day," and their spiritual discipline be made effective to their sanctification, there will be superabounding joy and blessedness, beautifully represented here by the common Jewish conception of reposing in peace and in love under the vine and the fig-tree.——The last words of the verse —"under the vine and under the fig-tree"—are given here as the very language of the call. Every man shall cry to his neighbor, "Ho! under the vine and under the fig-tree;" come and let us have peace and rest, enjoying the gifts of our bountiful God!

CHAPTER IV.

This chapter is another complete vision, having one set of symbols, illustrating one leading truth, viz., that the only perpetual fountain of power for spiritual life and labor is in God, and reaches man through his Spirit.

1. And the angel that talked with me came again, and waked me, as a man that is wakened out of his sleep,

This verse has special interest, because of the analogy it gives us to illustrate the mental state of the prophet while enjoying prophetic visions. His angel interpreter came and "*waked* him," arousing his mind into a new state of activity, corresponding to the ordinary change from sleeping to waking. Of course, it is only by experience that any one can know every thing pertaining to this prophetic state. Its powers must be quite analogous to those of a new *sense*, and we do not need to be told that each of our five senses must give its own sensations and impressions. No one of them can perform this service for another; the eye cannot give us sounds, nor the ear colors. We must have the prophetic *sense* before we can hope to have the prophetic sensations or impressions, or to *know* them perfectly.

2. And said unto me, What seest thou? And I said, I have looked, and behold a candlestick all *of* gold, with a bowl upon the top of it, and his seven lamps thereon, and seven pipes to the seven lamps, which *are* upon the top thereof:

3. And two olive-trees by it, one upon the right *side* of the bowl, and the other upon the left *side* thereof.

In this vision the symbols and their meaning are plain. Christians are the lights of the world. Churches are candlesticks, and their members luminous bodies, candles or lamps, revealing light concerning God in this otherwise very dark world.——Here, then, are one golden candlestick; a bowl or reservoir on the top of it, to contain oil; two olive-trees, one on each side, for supplying the oil; and pipes or tubes (v. 2 seems to say seven in number, and v. 12 two), to carry the oil from the tree to the reservoir. This is essentially the apparatus for supplying light. That the candlestick is all of gold indicates its excellence—the value, in God's sight, of the Church, and of living, shining Christians.

4. So I answered and spake to the angel that talked with me, saying, What *are* these, my lord?

5. Then the angel that talked with me answered and said unto me, Knowest thou not what these be? And I said, No, my lord.

6. Then he answered and spake unto me, saying, This *is* the word of the LORD unto Zerubbabel, saying, Not by might, nor by power, but by my Spirit, saith the LORD of hosts.

These symbols, interpreted into literal language, amount to this word which the Lord sends to Zerubbabel, then the governor of Judah, and in charge of the great work then present and pressing—the rebuilding of the temple: "Not by might, nor by power, but by my Spirit, saith the Lord." The work upon which you labor seems to you very difficult—often, perhaps, too great for your resources; but know that success is not by any human power alone, but by the Spirit of God. This Spirit supplies the oil that feeds the lamps. Christian souls and religious institutions correspond to the lamps and to the machinery which supplies them; but the living fountain of oil is of the Lord alone by his Spirit. This is the precious doctrine of the New Testament as well as of the Old. Paul loved to say, man may labor, "God alone giveth the increase." (See 1 Cor. 3:5–9.)

7. Who *art* thou, O great mountain? before Zerubbabel *thou shalt become* a plain: and he shall bring forth the headstone *thereof with* shoutings, *crying*, Grace, grace, unto it.

Obstacles, high and strong as great mountains, may seem to block the prosecution of this work; but say in the hearing of your governor, "Who art thou, great mountain," that thou shouldst think to withstand this work of God? "Before Zerubbabel become thou a plain!"—a summons to the great mountain of difficulty and opposition to lie low before the Lord's servant, and cease to retard his efforts.——The "headstone" seems most naturally to mean the crowning topstone, put on at the completion of the temple. This would be put on with loud ascriptions of praise to divine grace for the effective power which had carried the work through to its final consummation.

8. Moreover the word of the LORD came unto me, saying,

9. The hands of Zerubbabel have laid the foundation of this house; his hands shall also finish it; and thou shalt know that the LORD of hosts hath sent me unto you.

This message translates into literal language the symbols of the vision (vs. 2, 3, 11–14), and the strong poetic imagery of v. 7. Through mercy and help from God, Zerubbabel shall finish the building of the temple, and the people shall know, when they experience this fulfilment, that the Lord has truly sent his prophet to them.

10. For who hath despised the day of small things? for they shall rejoice, and shall see the plummet in the hand of Zerubbabel *with* those seven; they *are* the eyes of the LORD, which run to and fro through the whole earth.

Here is an additional word to those who have been greatly discouraged in the rebuilding of the temple and painfully impressed by its insignificance, compared with the greatness and splendor of the former one. I translate—"For who have despised the day of small things? Let them rejoice when they see the plumb-lead in the hands of Zerubbabel; those seven—the eyes of the Lord are they, ranging through all the earth."——The words "those seven" are somewhat abrupt, but manifestly refer to the passage (3 : 9), "Upon one stone are seven eyes;" and they are immediately explained to be the eyes of the Lord, which never fail to see any of the least possible things in all the earth. They traverse the universe, and take cognizance of every thing. Let the disheartened dismiss their despondency when they see the plumb-line in the hands of Zerubbabel for laying out this temple work, and especially when they consider that the perfect eye of the All-seeing One is upon him, and that his universal, almighty agency guarantees the execution of this work.——Dr. Henderson, by severely inverting the order of the words, translates thus: "Who hath despised the day of small things? For those seven eyes of Jehovah, which run to and fro through the whole earth, rejoiced when they saw the plummet in the hand of Zerubbabel." He would make this the sense: Let no man think lightly of that over which God rejoices. ——But I very much prefer the construction given first in order above, not only because it follows the order of the words without any violent inversion, but because it avoids the harshness of saying that "the eyes of God rejoiced;" and, yet further, because the eyes of God are introduced here, not as themselves rejoicing, but as a reason why his people should rejoice, and why they should trust implicitly in his promise to carry the work through. This most vital idea is missed and lost in Dr. Henderson's translation.

11. Then answered I, and said unto him, What *are* these two olive-trees upon the right *side* of the candlestick and upon the left *side* thereof?

12. And I answered again, and said unto him, What *be these* two olive branches which through the two golden pipes empty the golden *oil* out of themselves?

13. And he answered me and said, Knowest thou not what these *be?* And I said, No, my lord.

14. Then said he, These *are* the two anointed ones, that stand by the Lord of the whole earth.

The prophet still seeks a fuller explanation of the two olive-trees and of the olive clusters in the symbolic vision, and at last obtains it. They represent the two anointed ones (Heb. "sons of oil"), by which I understand the two anointed orders—the civil rulers and the priests. Both of these classes were inaugurated into their work by being anointed with oil—the significance being the same in each case, viz., that God imparts the graces of his Spirit to qualify them for the functions of their office.——I prefer to apply the phrase, "the two anointed ones," to the two orders, kings and priests, rather than to the two individuals then filling those offices, Zerubbabel and Joshua, because this provision for oil through these conducting tubes was not transient, limited to the lifetime of these two men, but permanent—to continue so long as God should give them kings and priests; and especially because permanence was a cardinal idea in the symbol. Its special intent was to show that the God of Israel still honored his own institutions as of old, and would do so onward into the distant future.——These anointed kings and priests stand *before* rather than "*by*" the Lord of the whole earth—standing being the appropriate attitude for servants in the presence of their masters, preëminently so for the servants of the Most High God.

CHAPTER V.

This chapter comprises two visions—a flying roll, and a woman sitting in an ephah—both denoting the judgments of God on his chosen people, considered as having filled up the measure of their iniquities.

1. Then I turned, and lifted up mine eyes, and looked, and behold a flying roll.

2. And he said unto me, What seest thou? And I

answered, I see a flying roll; the length thereof *is* twenty cubits, and the breadth thereof ten cubits.

This roll is to be thought of as being the ancient form of book or *volume*, made of parchment or prepared skins; but immensely large, the dimensions being those of the porch in front of Solomon's temple. (See 1 Kings 6 : 3.) This correspondence cannot be supposed to be accidental. Hence we must conclude it was intended to intimate that this "fiery law" and its judgments come forth from their God, who dwelt in the temple.——That it was seen "flying," showed that it hastened to its work. Ezekiel's roll (2 : 8–10) probably suggested this symbol.

3. Then said he unto me, This *is* the curse that goeth forth over the face of the whole earth: for every one that stealeth shall be cut off *as* on this side, according to it; and every one that sweareth shall be cut off *as* on that side, according to it.

This further explanation shows that this flying roll symbolizes the curse of the Almighty going forth over the earth for execution upon the guilty. The roll, like Ezekiel's, was written on both sides, and it would seem that the first table of the law was written on one side—the second on the other. The case of the false swearer represents all sins against the precepts of the first table; the case of the thief, all sins against the second. According to the high behest of this law of God, now going forth to punish violations against itself, the thief is cut off according to the law written on one side; the swearer, according to the law written on the other.

4. I will bring it forth, said the Lord of hosts, and it shall enter into the house of the thief, and into the house of him that sweareth falsely by my name: and it shall remain in the midst of his house, and shall consume it with the timber thereof and the stones thereof.

The Lord brings forth this flying roll, and causes it to enter the house of every sinner against the law of God. It abides there, and utterly consumes every vestige of his habitation—a terribly vivid representation of God's judgments upon all unpardoned sin! To think of the law itself as written out, and its written record then armed with power to search out every sinner, enter into his house and there consume every thing—all his ill-gotten wealth, the last crumb of his accumulated comforts, and finally himself—this surely must imply a ruin for the guilty from which there can be no escape, and in which there can be no alleviation.

5. Then the angel that talked with me went forth, and said unto me, Lift up now thine eyes, and see what *is* this that goeth forth.

6. And I said, What *is* it? And he said, This *is* an ephah that goeth forth. He said moreover, This *is* their resemblance through all the earth.

7. And behold, there was lifted up a talent of lead: and this *is* a woman that sitteth in the midst of the ephah.

8. And he said, This *is* wickedness. And he cast it into the midst of the ephah; and he cast the weight of lead upon the mouth thereof.

A new scene opens. The first apparent object is an ephah, the largest Hebrew dry measure, corresponding to the common corn-basket of our country, containing by one computation one and one-ninth bushels, and by another one and one-half. This is seen "going forth," as if this also, like the flying roll, was hastening to execute its mission. We shall probably best reach the sense of this symbol if we remember that the Scripture speaks of sinners as "filling up the measure" of their iniquities (Matt. 23: 32, and 1 Thess. 2: 16). Here is the largest-sized measure. A woman sits in it, who is explained to represent or symbolize "*wickedness*"—the sins, or, yet more precisely, the *sinners* of the covenant people. The female person is a common symbol in the Scriptures for a city with its masses of people, *e. g.*, Babylon (Jer. 50 and 51; Rev. 16: 19 and 18: 2–11), Jerusalem (Lam. 1: 1 ff). This woman, therefore, represents strictly the Jewish people apostate from God, having filled the measure of their iniquities, and now about to receive due retribution.——She is first seen (v. 7) sitting in the midst of this large measure. Then he throws her down ("*he*" is God's minister of vengeance) into the midst or bottom of the vessel, and casts a weight of lead upon the mouth of the vessel, manifestly to hold her down and prevent her escape.——The word rendered "talent," *i. e.*, of lead, means a large round lump, probably large enough for its purpose, *i. e.*, to fill the mouth of the vessel.——The clause "This is their resemblance through all the earth," is interpreted variously. The original word is the common one for *eye*. Some manuscripts, however, and other authorities, make a slight change in the word itself, by which it would mean *sin*. Not improbably this change began with the attempt of some critic to make a difficult text more easy.——The reading *eye* some explain to mean their *intent*, the thing they have their eye upon, viz., to sin on without restraint, and fill up the measure of their iniquities. Others render, as our received version does, "their resemblance" or appearance, what they look like everywhere. In this sense of the word the clause would mean that all over the land the moral condition of the people who have filled up the measure of their sins is well represented by a large vessel, and a woman, personifying the whole sinning people, thrown down and confined in it, and awaiting her doom. The ultimate meaning of the vision is much the same, whichever of these two senses shall be given to the word in question. The latter certainly gives a good sense; the former is not bad

9. Then lifted I up mine eyes, and looked, and behold, there came out two women, and the wind *was* in their wings; for they had wings like the wings of a stork: and they lifted up the ephah between the earth and the heaven.

10. Then said I to the angel that talked with me, Whither do these bear the ephah?

11. And he said unto me, To build it an house in the land of Shinar: and it shall be established, and set there upon her own base.

Two women (are they not angelic forms?)—two, because so large a burden required one on each side—come forth, the wind in their wings to indicate the most rapid motion; and they bear the ephah containing this woman far away into the land of Shinar (Babylon), to fix for it there a permanent abode.——The main question here is, whether this is retrospective, looking back to the recent captivity in Babylon; or prospective, predicting some future judgment on the covenant people.——The latter view I accept: (1.) Because the other visions throughout this series are prophetic, not historic.——(2.) Because the late captivity in Babylon was transient; this is at least very long.——(3.) Because *that* always contemplated a restoration: this gives no hint of any restoration, but the contrary.——(4.) Because in v. 4 the "curse that goeth forth" inflicts judgments more severe and exterminating than those in the captivity to Babylon. This vision of the ephah should correspond to that of the roll.——There is no particular difficulty in applying this entire chapter to the judgments that fell on the Jewish nation for their rejection of their Messiah, according to their own imprecation—"His blood be on us and on our children!" The first instalment of this doom came from the Roman arms; the rest in the almost universal persecution, dispersion, and reproach under which they have suffered for ages. In this view of its prophetic significance, "Shinar" is used by way of historic allusion—a second Shinar—another captivity like that of Babylon, only more terrible, more protracted, and (so far as appears here) not alleviated by the promise of restoration. "Shinar" was the country in which Babylon lay (Gen. 11: 2, 9). Both these visions were intended as solemn warnings to the people, at that time and onward, against violating the law of God, and filling up again the measure of their national sins. Such warnings were in their nature wholesome, and through the divine mercy might long postpone that depth of depravity which should be ultimately reached, and then be so terribly punished.

CHAPTER VI.

This chapter is in two quite distinct parts; the first a vision, and the second a symbolic transaction. The vision (vs. 1–8) presents four chariots, and shows their mission. The symbolic transaction (vs. 9–15) is the making of crowns and setting them on the head of Joshua the high priest, who becomes the type of the Messiah.

1. And I turned, and lifted up mine eyes, and looked, and behold, there came four chariots out from between two mountains; and the mountains *were* mountains of brass.

2. In the first chariot *were* red horses; and in the second chariot black horses;

3. And in the third chariot white horses; and in the fourth chariot grizzled and bay horses.

4. Then I answered and said unto the angel that talked with me, What *are* these, my lord?

5. And the angel answered and said unto me, These *are* the four spirits of the heavens, which go forth from standing before the Lord of all the earth.

6. The black horses which *are* therein go forth into the north country; and the white go forth after them; and the grizzled go forth toward the south country.

7. And the bay went forth, and sought to go that they might walk to and fro through the earth: and he said, Get ye hence, walk to and fro through the earth. So they walked to and fro through the earth.

8. Then cried he upon me, and spake unto me, saying, Behold, these that go toward the north country have quieted my spirit in the north country.

As the fifth chapter predicted judgments on the covenant people for their sins, this last vision (6 : 1–8) predicts corresponding judgments on the enemies of God's people.

The leading objects of vision here are four chariots drawn by diverse-colored horses, red, black, white, and gray. They "come forth from between two mountains of brass," to denote the amazing strength of that power of which they were the representative agents, and, as some suppose, with a tacit reference to the geographical position of Jerusalem, it being but natural that these chariots, symbolizing God's providential agencies among the nations of the earth, should seem to proceed *from* him in his own place of abode at Jerusalem. Like the horses seen in the first vision (1 : 8–13), these chariots must be understood to represent, in pertinent symbols, those varied agencies of God's providential rule over nations, by which he puts down one and sets up another, and in general administers the retributions of an actual government. The principal shade of difference between the horses and their riders of the first vision, and the chariots with their horses in this last, is that the horses with their riders serve rather as scouts; the chariots as executioners: the riders on horses explore the state of the nations; the chariots put in execution the mandates of Jehovah; or (nearer to the expressive language of the text) they convey the very *animus* of Jehovah—his spirit of indignation and retributive justice—and cause it to fall on those guilty nations. As was remarked in the notes on chapter 1, the use of post-horses in those vast oriental kingdoms (Esth. 3 : 13 and 8 : 10) suggested their use in that vision, so here we may find a good reason for this symbolic use of the chariot in the prominent place held by chariots of war in the armies of that day.——The explanation of the chariots (v. 5), "These are the four spirits or winds of the heavens," should not suggest to us the literal *winds*, nor any literal sense of the word *spirit*, but, as already hinted, those invisible agencies of the divine hand in providence which act upon the nations of the earth, in judgments especially, but in blessings also, as the case may be, constituting the working forces of an actual administration of the government of God over nations as such in the present world.——These chariots "go forth from standing before the Lord of all the earth," the usual attitude of servants awaiting their orders, and going forth, when bidden, to their execution.——It will be noted that two of these chariots, that with black and that with white horses, go forth toward the north country, Babylon, where the enemies specially contemplated here were located. One chariot (v. 7) seems to have had a very general commission "to traverse the whole earth," implying that these agencies of God's reign over the nations are not restricted to any special district or to any one human kingdom, but embrace them all.——In v. 8 we read—"Behold, these that go toward the north country have quieted my spirit in the north country," which translation can be understood rightly in no other sense than that of *quieting* the spirit of God by executing his righteous indignation and giving scope to the retributions of justice. A less ambiguous rendering would be—"have brought my anger down upon the north country." This is doubtless the sense of the passage. The judgments of God fell on Babylon for her too cruel oppression of the covenant people. Darius, heading the Persian armies, was the first executioner of this wrath; the time, not long after this prophecy was revealed.——The various color of the horses may have been slightly significant, yet some interpreters incline to make too much of it. It is manifestly one of the very subordinate and less important things in the vision. Plainly the revealing angel, or it may perhaps be said, the recording mind, made little account of this feature, else we should find more accuracy in the references to the different chariots. Thus we have at first four, designated by their horses, but the last span has a twofold description; they are gray, and also active, fleet, this being the only sense of the Hebrew word rendered "bay" (vs. 3, 7). When they are named again, the red-colored disappear, and the chariot commissioned to traverse the whole earth is indicated (very appropriately) as that drawn by the active, fleet span. (The span that had the wide world for their range should be preëminently *fleet.*) Thus the red are dropped from view, and what was the fourth in the first description now becomes two. The twofold description given of its horses is divided, and we have two spans and two chariots out of the one. ——This criticism may be thought of small importance. It is chiefly valuable as showing that the color of the horses and the distinction of chariots is really in the eye of the revealing Spirit a small and not important matter. The vital points are more cared for, and are put with more accuracy.——Some critics suppose that the two mountains are the kingdoms of Media and Persia. This view is wide of their real significance. The material—"brass" or copper—denotes the strength, not of any heathen nation whose power God might use by overruling it, but of *God himself*, in reference specially to the deep, immovable foundations of his throne. The location should be the supposed and indeed actual dwelling-place of God, *i. e.*, among his people, in his temple at Jerusalem. As the chariots represent his providential agencies, going forth on their mission, so their head-quarters and starting-point should be the place of his abode.——That they come forth from between two mountains is due simply to the necessities of chariot-driving in a mountainous country. They cannot run on the tops or sides of rugged mountains, but only in the valley, which will be between two mountains.

9. And the word of the LORD came unto me, saying,
10. Take of *them of* the captivity, *even* of Heldai,
of Tobijah, of Jedaiah, which are come from Babylon,
and come thou the same day, and go into the house of
Josiah the son of Zephaniah;
11. Then take silver and gold, and make crowns,
and set *them* upon the head of Joshua the son of Josedech, the high priest;
12. And speak unto him, saying, Thus speaketh the
LORD of hosts, saying, Behold the man whose name *is*
The BRANCH; and he shall grow up out of his place,
and he shall build the temple of the LORD:
13. Even he shall build the temple of the LORD; and
he shall bear the glory, and shall sit and rule upon his

throne: and he shall be a priest upon his throne: and the counsel of peace shall be between them both.

14. And the crowns shall be to Helem, and to Tobijah, and to Jedaiah, and to Hen the son of Zephaniah, for a memorial in the temple of the LORD.

15. And they *that are* far off shall come and build in the temple of the LORD; and ye shall know that the LORD of hosts hath sent me unto you. And *this* shall come to pass, if ye will diligently obey the voice of the LORD your God.

The series of visions is now closed, and we have here an actual transaction of a symbolical character. That this is not a vision, but is a real transaction, appears on the face of the record. It does not open with "I saw by night" (as 1:8); nor "I lifted up mine eyes and saw" (as 1:18); nor "I lifted up mine eyes again" (as 2:1); nor "he showed me" (as 3:1); nor as 4:1 and 4:5; nor as 6:1—all which statements testify that the scenes that follow respectively were witnessed in prophetic vision. On the contrary, this is simply "The word of the Lord came unto me," as in 1:1, and 7:1, and 8:1, &c., where verbal communications are made.——Moreover, here is not a presentation of things to be *seen* by the prophet, but a command respecting things to be *done*. And finally, these crowns, after being made and solemnly placed on the head of the high priest, were to be "laid up for a memorial in the temple of the Lord," all indicating an actuality, things done in real life.——The leading points are the preparation of crowns; the solemn coronation of the high priest; the accompanying announcement and explanations, showing that the purport of the transaction was to make Joshua a special type of the Messiah, and to reveal vastly important truths respecting his person and relations to men; and finally, to indicate that Gentile nations were to participate in the services and the glories of his coming kingdom.——This seems to have been a double crown, the word for crown being plural, the verb (v. 14) being in the singular; and manifestly but one head, that of Joshua, is crowned in the transaction.——To obtain the silver and the gold for its construction, the prophet is directed to go to certain men here named, who are recently from Babylon, captive Jews, who remained behind when the first company of their brethren left, and who seem to have come to Jerusalem now with a contribution from their brethren still behind, to aid in building the temple. Josiah, son of Zephaniah, may have been the treasurer of this fund; hence the direction to go with the other three without delay to his house to draw the money. The original brings in the phrase, "who are come from Babylon," at the end of the verse, showing that Josiah, as well as the other three, was in the delegation from the captive Jews there.——Having made the crowns, he sets them upon the head of Joshua the high priest, and then solemnly announces from the Lord, "Behold the man—Branch is his name; he shall branch" (shoot) "up from underneath himself" (from his own humble root), "and he shall build the temple of the Lord."——As already indicated, the sense of the word rendered "Branch" is shoot, the single stock that springs from the root and becomes the one trunk of the tree. In the original the verb rendered "shall grow," is the same—shall *shoot up*.——The specially emphatic declaration here is that this man—the Branch—"*shall build the temple of the Lord.*" Hence this is solemnly repeated (v. 13): "Even *he*" (he alone, and he in distinction from all others) "shall build the temple of the Lord." This cannot refer to the temple then being built by Zerubbabel, for of this the Lord had explicitly declared (4 : 9), "The hands of Zerubbabel have laid the foundations of this house, and *his hands shall also finish it.*" We must therefore look to another temple, which can be none other than that so often referred to in the New Testament, built by Jesus, the Messiah, of which it is said, "ye" (Christians) "are the temple of the living God" (2 Cor. 6 : 16). "For the temple of God is holy, *which temple ye are*" (1 Cor. 3 : 16, 17). "Ye also, as living stones, are built up a spiritual house," &c. (1 Peter 2 : 5).——The comprehensive idea embraces the spiritual kingdom of the Messiah, of which the Jewish temple was an apposite symbol. In that ancient temple Jehovah dwelt, revealing his presence. So in this, the presence of the Holy Ghost reclaims men's hearts to God, and makes them pure before him.——Yet further: "He shall bear *the* glory," *i. e.*, preëminent glory, becoming the "head of all things to his church," "King of kings" "moreover, and "Lord of lords." "He shall sit and rule upon his throne," truly a king, not in Zion alone, but over all the earth, or rather all the earth shall ultimately become his Zion, since his kingdom shall in the latter days embosom and absorb into itself all other kingdoms and all other love, obedience, and homage, so that it can be said truly, "The kingdoms of this world have become the kingdoms of our Lord and of his Christ, and he (alone) shall reign for ever and ever."——He shall also "be a priest upon his throne," uniting these two functions in his own person, and never ceasing to mediate for his people, and be their great atoning sacrifice because of his exaltation to so great power and glory on his throne.——The phrase "the counsel of peace shall be between them both," does not refer to some second person other than the Messiah, coöperating with him; nor does it mean merely that Messiah as king and Messiah as priest shall be harmonious and not conflicting, but rather that both as King and as Priest, Messiah shall consult for and shall secure the peace, the highest spiritual good of his people. The full energy of both relations shall be made subservient to the spiritual life and consequent peace and blessedness of his children.——After these crowns had served their temporary purpose in this typical inauguration of Joshua the high priest, they were to be laid up in the temple of the Lord, as a memorial for those four delegates who came up from afar with those offerings of silver and gold for the temple. They are now representative men, to indicate that people from afar, even the Gentile nations, "shall come and build in the temple of the Lord," *i. e.*, shall come into the Christian Church, bringing into it their wealth, their personal service, and the full homage of their willing hearts.——That they should come and build in the temple, is Jewish costume, like that of Isaiah (ch. 60), to show that in the latter day, Gentile nations from all the ends of the earth shall swell the hosts of the people of God and contribute their wealth and their hearts to the greatness and glory of his kingdom on earth. ——As usual with Zechariah, the final seal is put upon this glorious prophecy: "Ye shall know by your own precious experience that the Lord hath sent me to you to say these things." They cannot fail.——The names of those four representative men are given differently, yet too much should not be made of this. Heldai, the first one named (v. 10), becomes in v. 14 Helem, a word of nearly the same significance; while Josiah, son of Zephaniah (v. 16), becomes in v. 14 Hen, the son of Zephaniah, which is also of kindred meaning. There are no certain data upon which to account for these changes of names. These two men may have had each two names, or there may be a play upon their first name by giving another of similar significance; or the intent of it may have been to call attention to the meaning of their names. The case is scarcely of sufficient importance to justify or call for much speculation.——The last clause has the appearance of being broken off abruptly, leaving the corresponding part to be supplied. "And it shall come to pass if ye will diligently obey the voice of the Lord your God" . . . . (supply) all these promised blessings shall come to you most abundantly. You shall have them on condition of obeying the Lord diligently, but on no other.——So all the great blessings of the gospel are, as to each of us, suspended on this condition of honest diligence and faithful obedience to the Lord our God. Perhaps it was with the intention of making this condition the more impressive, that the sentence breaks off thus abruptly, leaving the reader to inquire the more carefully into the force of this great condition, and the wealth of blessings suspended upon it.

CHAPTER VII.

This chapter and the next were both occasioned by one special circumstance. For seventy years the people had been observing certain days of fasting, in remembrance of prominent events connected with the fall of their beloved city and temple. Now, they had returned from their captivity; the city was rebuilt; the work on the temple was far advanced toward completion. It was now the fourth year of Darius, and the temple was finished in his sixth year. The community was decidedly prosperous; hence the question arose—Shall we continue to observe those days of fasting Would it not be more appropriate to observe days of praise and thanksgiving?——The Lord sends his answer by his prophet Zechariah. It is twofold.——(1.) It rebukes the hypocrisy and selfishness manifested by some of the people in those very fasts which should have been seasons of special humiliation and honest confession of sin before the Lord; admonishes them that God's eye is on their moral conduct as well as on their hearts, and exhorts them to justice and righteousness, especially by the sad case of their fathers, whom the Lord had scourged so severely by a long and terrible captivity. This part of the reply fills out the seventh chapter (vs. 4–14).——(2.) The second part fills the eighth chapter, and is rich in promised blessings to the obedient, closing with a direct answer to their inquiry.

1. And it came to pass in the fourth year of king Darius, *that* the word of the LORD came unto Zechariah in the fourth *day* of the ninth month, *even* in Chisleu;

2. When they had sent unto the house of God, Sherezer and Regem-melech, and their men, to pray before the LORD,

3. *And* to speak unto the priests which *were* in the house of the LORD of hosts, and to the prophets, saying, Should I weep in the fifth month, separating myself, as I have done these so many years?

The date is given precisely, this being a matter of historic importance. From the arrival of the first caravan of returning Jews in the first year of Cyrus (B. C. 536) to the second year of Darius (about B. C. 520), the people had been harassed by their Samaritan enemies; the work on the temple for a time dragged heavily, and was finally quite suspended. At length, under special messages from God by Haggai and Zechariah, it was resumed in the second year of Darius. With this resumption commenced an era of great prosperity. Their foreign enemies ceased to annoy them; the smiles of God rested on all their labors. After two years of such prosperity, the question naturally arose, whether they should continue to observe certain days of fasting, as they had done then some seventy years. The most prominent of these days are specially referred to here; that in the fifth month (v. 3), and that also in the seventh month (v. 5). Chap. 8:19 refers to two others, viz., one in the fourth month and another in the tenth. The history indicates the special reason of fasting on these days. In the fifth month the temple was burnt (Jer. 52:12). In the seventh, Gedaliah was slain, and the small remnant that remained with him were scattered and destroyed (Jer. 41:1 ff). In the fourth month the city was taken (Jer. 52:6, 7). In the tenth it was invested by the armed hosts of Nebuchadnezzar (Jer. 52:4).——V. 2 should be translated—"When

Bethel" (the household of God, in the sense of the congregation of the Lord) "sent Sherezer," &c., *i. e.*, the people in the capacity of a worshipping congregation, sent this commission to their priests and prophets with this inquiry.——V. 3. "Separating myself," *i. e.*, from my accustomed secular labors—making it a holy and solemn day.

4. Then came the word of the LORD of hosts unto me, saying,

5. Speak unto all the people of the land, and to the priests, saying, When ye fasted and mourned in the fifth and seventh *month*, even those seventy years, did ye at all fast unto me, *even* to me?

6. And when ye did eat, and when ye did drink, did not ye eat *for yourselves*, and drink *for yourselves*?

This rebuke manifestly applied to some of those who united in this inquiry. The Lord asks—Did your fasting have any regard to *me?* Did you think of your sins *against me?* Did you humble yourselves before me? So, when ye ate and when ye drank, was it not *ye* that ate, and *ye* that drank? This is the literal rendering, and implies that they thought of nothing but their own sensual gratification, ate and drank merely to enjoy themselves, and as if there were no God to thank, no great Giver to recognize as the fountain of all blessings.

7. *Should ye* not *hear* the words which the LORD hath cried by the former prophets when Jerusalem was inhabited and in prosperity, and the cities thereof round about her, when *men* inhabited the south and the plain?

The original omits the verb before "words" in the beginning of the verse, apparently assuming that the sense would be clear without it. In supplying it, the choice lies between our English text and the marginal reading, the former giving the sense most in harmony with the strain of the passage.——The verse suggests the substance of the next special message (vs. 8–14), the admonitions sent from God by the prophets to their fathers, their rejection of them, and the consequences.

8. And the word of the LORD came unto Zechariah, saying,

9. Thus speaketh the LORD of hosts, saying, Execute true judgment, and shew mercy and compassions every man to his brother:

10. And oppress not the widow, nor the fatherless,

the stranger, nor the poor; and let none of you imagine evil against his brother in your heart.

11. But they refused to hearken, and pulled away the shoulder, and stopped their ears, that they should not hear.

12. Yea, they made their hearts *as* an adamant stone, lest they should hear the law, and the words which the LORD of hosts hath sent in his Spirit by the former prophets: therefore came a great wrath from the LORD of hosts.

13. Therefore it is come to pass, *that* as he cried, and they would not hear; so they cried, and I would not hear, saith the LORD of hosts:

14. But I scattered them with a whirlwind among all the nations whom they knew not. Thus the land was desolate after them, that no man passed through nor returned: for they laid the pleasant land desolate.

Here the Lord gives to his servant Zechariah a summary of the message he sent by many of his prophets shortly before the captivity. V. 9 should therefore read—"Thus the Lord did speak," *i. e.*, to your fathers, by Jeremiah and Zephaniah in the days of Josiah; and somewhat earlier by Hosea, Amos, Isaiah, and Micah. ——In v. 11, "pulled away the shoulder," is in Hebrew, "They gave a refractory shoulder," *i. e.*, they made their shoulder refractory—with allusion to the bullock who refuses to be broken into patient labor.——V. 12 most fully recognizes the inspiration of the prophets. The Lord sent His words to the people *by his Spirit*, by the hand, *i. e.*, the ministration of the former prophets.——*By* his Spirit, rather than "*in*," is the sense of the original, the preposition being the same as that before the "*hand* of the prophets."——V. 13, "Hence it is come to pass"—referring still to the history of what occurred shortly before the captivity.——V. 14 fully confirms this general course of interpretation, as referring to the ways of God toward the people, and of the people toward God, in the age next preceding the time of Zechariah. That history was exceedingly full of most pertinent and valuable instruction.

CHAPTER VIII.

As already remarked in the introduction to chap. 7, this continues and concludes the subject opened in that chapter. It gives the brighter side—the message of the Lord to the truly humbled, penitent, and believing portion of the people. Hence it abounds in cheering promises.

1. Again the word of the LORD of hosts came *to me*, saying,

2. Thus saith the LORD of hosts; I was jealous for Zion with great jealousy, and I was jealous for her with great fury.

"Jealous for Zion." The same sentiment is even yet more expanded (chap. 1 : 14–16). This revived jealousy for Zion implies that the Lord's love for her was enkindled afresh; his pity, too, became active; his apprehensions also for the honor of his name before the nations; and not least, his indignation toward the people that had so cruelly oppressed Zion. All these feelings conspired toward his purpose to return in mercy to Zion, as the next verse states.

3. Thus saith the LORD; I am returned unto Zion, and will dwell in the midst of Jerusalem: and Jerusalem shall be called, a city of truth; and the mountain of the LORD of hosts, the holy mountain.

These are the blessings. It is noticeable that moral purity stands specially prominent. "Jerusalem shall be called" (because she shall *really be*) "the city of truth," distinguished above all other cities for substantial integrity of character; and the temple-mountain where the Lord dwells shall be "the holy mountain"—holy, by reason of the regeneration and sanctification of those who worship the Lord there.——Such should be the results of the Lord's returning to Zion, to dwell there by his spiritual presence. These are the legitimate criteria of his real presence by his Spirit anywhere.

4. Thus saith the LORD of hosts; There shall yet old men and old women dwell in the streets of Jerusalem, and every man with his staff in his hand for very age.

5. And the streets of the city shall be full of boys and girls playing in the streets thereof.

A beautiful scene of peace and prosperity, indicated by the groups of the aged, still living as witnesses to the long-continued exemption from desolating wars, and the yet more numerous throng of little boys and girls playing and happy in the streets. Evermore, through all the ages before Christ, such external prosperity is accounted as evidence of God's favor and approval. "Length of days is in her right hand; in her left, riches and honor." The genius of God's providential government in that age involved a high degree of present retribution.

6. Thus saith the LORD of hosts; If it be marvellous in the eyes of the remnant of this people in these days,

should it also be marvellous in mine eyes? saith the LORD of hosts.

Though it should seem marvellous and almost incredible in your eyes, that I should bestow so great blessings, yet must it be marvellous in mine? Is any thing too hard for the Lord? Is any measure of blessings so great as to be marvellous in view of the great depths of divine love?

7. Thus saith the LORD of hosts; Behold, I will save my people from the east country, and from the west country;

8. And I will bring them, and they shall dwell in the midst of Jerusalem: and they shall be my people, and I will be their God, in truth and in righteousness.

This is a promise to save his people wherever they were, and to gather them in from their dispersions—two quarters of the heavens, the land toward the sun-rising and the land toward the sun-setting being named—a part for the whole.——Its fulfilment in the literal sense took place while yet that economy continued, which required the residence of the Jews in their own land.

9. Thus saith the LORD of hosts; Let your hands be strong, ye that hear in these days these words by the mouth of the prophets, which *were* in the day *that* the foundation of the house of the LORD of hosts was laid, that the temple might be built.

10. For before these days there was no hire for man, nor any hire for beast; neither *was there any* peace to him that went out or came in because of the affliction: for I set all men every one against his neighbor.

11. But now I *will* not *be* unto the residue of this people as in the former days, saith the LORD of hosts.

12. For the seed *shall be* prosperous; the vine shall give her fruit, and the ground shall give her increase, and the heavens shall give their dew; and I will cause the remnant of this people to possess all these *things*.

These words exhort the people to courage, fearlessness, and vigor, in the prosecution of the temple-building, and in whatever labor the Lord might impose. While the temple lay neglected all things went awry; enemies pressed them from abroad; dissension, stagnation, and starvation distressed them at home.——When the Lord says, "I set all men each one against his neighbor," he refers to what he let men do, in the sense of *not preventing it*—as a judgment on them for their sins.

13. And it shall come to pass, *that* as ye were a curse among the heathen, O house of Judah and house of Israel; so will I save you, and ye shall be a blessing: fear not, *but* let your hands be strong.

The expression, "ye were a curse among the heathen," &c., might in itself mean either that they *brought curses* upon the heathen, or that they were themselves *cursed among* the heathen. The latter I take to be the sense here.——So of blessings: the sense is, ye shall be blessed.

14. For thus saith the LORD of hosts; As I thought to punish you, when your fathers provoked me to wrath, saith the LORD of hosts, and I repented not:
15. So again have I thought in these days to do well unto Jerusalem and to the house of Judah: fear ye not.

The antithesis here is this: As I thought to punish your fathers for their great provocations, and did not swerve from my thought, but carried it into execution; so have I now thought to bless Jerusalem, and *I shall not fail to do it!* Fear not!

16. These *are* the things that ye shall do; Speak ye every man the truth to his neighbor; execute the judgment of truth and peace in your gates:
17. And let none of you imagine evil in your hearts against his neighbor; and love no false oath: for all these *are things* that I hate, saith the LORD.

The usual and always pertinent exhortations to practise righteousness and truth. The last clause of v. 16 enjoins upon them to administer law in the courts according to justice and truth. This would promote real peace and prosperity. Such decisions are decisions of peace.

18. And the word of the LORD of hosts came unto me, saying,
19. Thus saith the LORD of hosts; The fast of the fourth *month*, and the fast of the fifth, and the fast of the seventh, and the fast of the tenth, shall be to the house of Judah joy and gladness, and cheerful feasts; therefore love the truth and peace.

Here we find the explicit answer to the question sent up from the people by the hand of Sherezer and Regem-melech. Those fasts shall be changed to seasons of joy and gladness, and to cheerful feasts—only the Lord still enforces that which is evermore essential to their abiding prosperity—"*Love the truth and peace.*"

20. Thus saith the Lord of hosts: *It shall* yet *come to pass*, that there shall come people, and the inhabitants of many cities:

21. And the inhabitants of one *city* shall go to another, saying, Let us go speedily to pray before the Lord, and to seek the Lord of hosts: I will go also.

22. Yea, many people and strong nations shall come to seek the Lord of hosts in Jerusalem, and to pray before the Lord.

23. Thus saith the Lord of hosts; In those days *it shall come to pass*, that ten men shall take hold, out of all languages of the nations, even shall take hold of the skirt of him that is a Jew, saying, We will go with you: for we have heard *that* God *is* with you.

The renewed vitality of the religious life in these times of Zechariah, suggested the yet far more glorious revival and consequent extension of pure religion in the latter days. The transition from the gloom and grief of the captivity to the peace and joy indicated thus far throughout this chapter, becomes suggestive and significant of another advance—perhaps I might say a similar transition from the narrow limitations of the kingdom of God then, to that wondrous expansion when "many people and strong nations shall come to seek the Lord of hosts in Jerusalem and to pray before the Lord."——Such seems to be the mental law of association under which these predictions of the Messiah's enlarged and glorious kingdom are brought to mind.——I can find no adequate fulfilment of these promises short of the millennial days. Nothing at all equivalent has yet transpired. Let us look a moment at their significance. ——In v. 21, "Let us go speedily," is the usual intensive repetition of the infinitive with the finite verb, and might as well be rendered "Let us go with all our heart"—earnestly. This would imply going speedily; but it would also mean much more than that. The last clause also is strong: "I, too, will surely go;" or "Let me go too."——"Ten men" is a definite number for an indefinite, as many as could well get hold of one man's skirt—and obviously means that *many* men shall follow one Jew as their guide; *as* many as one man can teach. This throng of pupils represents far more than a single nation. Indeed, each of the ten representative men stands for one nation, since they are each of different language, and taken together represent "all languages of the nations"—indicating that people of every tongue and clime shall come to Zion for the law and the light of God.——That they are said to come to Jerusalem is due to the necessary modes of Jewish thought. That was the only way in which the Jews before Christ could conceive of real conversions—the only language descriptive of conversion which they could understand. They had not yet reached the idea that God can be worshipped acceptably and spiritually, just as well anywhere else as in Jerusalem. Hence those glorious conversions of Gentile nations, which are to take place far down in the ages of the gospel dispensation, if foretold at all by Jewish prophets and for Jewish readers, must be presented in thoroughly Jewish language and in harmony with Jewish conceptions. So we ought to expect to find it throughout the Old Testament prophets; so we do find it. On this principle, the "Jew" is *any one* with whom *God is.* Under the gospel system "he is not a Jew who is one *outwardly*" (Rom. 2 : 28, 29). ——This passage, therefore, is a prediction that "the inhabitants of many cities"—"yea, many people and strong nations"—yea, nations so diverse that they speak all the languages of the earth—shall come to those who have the gospel and beg to be led to the Lamb of God. They shall come with great earnestness and zeal, manifesting the utmost readiness to go themselves, and exhorting others likewise—the people of one city pressing the people of another city to join the great company of those who shall go to pray before the Lord and to seek the Lord of hosts.——Such is the import of this wonderful prophecy. We can scarcely wish it were greater and better in the breadth and richness of its promises. Who can find it in his heart to wish it were less?

CHAPTER IX.

Vs. 1–8 sketch the sweep of the conquering hosts of Alexander the Great in western Asia, and along the eastern coast of the Mediterranean, and refer to the special protection afforded by the Lord to his people in the midst of that scene of danger; then the prophet (vs. 9, 10) passes over to the greater protection and salvation wrought out by King Messiah for his people; and then (vs. 10–17) on the same analogy predicts the protection of the Jews against the Greco-Syrian power in the age of the Maccabees.

1. The burden of the word of the LORD in the land of Hadrach, and Damascus *shall be* the rest thereof: when the eyes of man, as of all the tribes of Israel, *shall be* toward the LORD.

"Burden," as usual, is a prediction of calamity, here destined to fall, not on God's people, but on their enemies.——"Hadrach" has given critics ample occasion for research, ingenuity, and diversity of opinion. It would seem, from the connection, to be a country; yet geographically this name for a country is unknown. The vague reports of some obscure city bearing this name, are, in the first place, very unreliable at the best; and then the position which this name occupies in the first eight verses among Damascus, Tyre, Zidon, &c., and at the head of them all, quite forbids that it should be an insignificant, almost unknown city.——The best solution yet suggested is that of Hengstenberg, who thinks it is purposely enigmatical, and refers to *Persia;* and that etymologically, it is made up from two Hebrew verbs,* the former meaning *to be strong*, and the latter *to be weak*, giving the significance—*The strong-weak;*—thus intimating that she is at one time strong; at another, weak;—strong under a Cyrus; weak under her last Darius.——The reason for an enigmatical name lay in the delicate relations which the Jews of his time sustained to the Persian throne. The Books of Ezra and Nehemiah make the delicacy of those relations very palpable. See especially Ezra, chap. 4–6. It could not be wise for a Hebrew prophet to utter such predictions against Persia as might be caught up and construed into proof of unfriendliness toward that power. ——Enigmatical names are not entirely without precedent among the Hebrew prophets. Jeremiah has Sheshach for Babylon (25 : 26 and 51 : 41).——It is remarkable that though Hadrach (Persia) is named as the first to feel the sweep of this conquering devastator, Alexander, and though precisely this is the order of the historic facts, yet the prophet passes her with only her enigmatical name. A burden of the word of the Lord is upon her land; that is all he thinks proper to say. Damascus is the place upon which this burden rests down. The predicted ruin should smite and crush her.

To the last clause, interpreters have given two different constructions: one thus—"Because the Lord's eye is upon men, even upon all the tribes of Israel;" the other thus: "Because the eyes of men, even of all the tribes of Israel, are toward and unto the Lord." The latter is much better sustained by the grammatical relations of the words, and has also this in its favor, that it practically involves the former. When the eyes of men, even of all God's people, are toward him for help, then his eye is surely upon them in love, care, and succor. It was in answer to the humble uplifted eye and prayer of God's people that this conquering sweep of Alexander crushed down so many of those ancient powers hostile to the covenant people, but spared them.

2. And Hamath also shall border thereby; Tyrus and Zidon, though it be very wise.

Hamath, a country lying north of Palestine, bordered on Damascus, and therefore fell within the range of this great conqueror, and came down beneath the force of his arms. So did Tyre, with Zidon, because she had taken great pride in her wisdom, and had so utterly renounced all reliance on the true God.——In this passage Tyre leads the thought, as also in the historic facts she had quite eclipsed Zidon. Hence, the verb rendered "be very wise," is in the singular, and refers primarily to Tyre. The word rendered "though" should be read "because," this being its usual and best established meaning. The full thought is brought out by Ezekiel in 28 : 2, 3, 6, 17: "Say to the prince of Tyrus, Thus saith the Lord God, *Be-*

* רָכַךְ חָדַד.

cause thine heart is lifted up and thou hast said—I am God; I sit in the seat of God, in the midst of the seas; yet thou art a man and not God, though thou set thy heart as the heart of God; therefore, because thou hast set thy heart as the heart of God, behold therefore I will bring strangers upon thee, the terrible of the nations, &c., &c.

3. And Tyrus did build herself a strong hold, and heaped up silver as the dust, and fine gold as the mire of the streets.

4. Behold, the Lord will cast her out, and he will smite her power in the sea; and she shall be devoured with fire.

Further and special notice is taken of Tyre. After having been once fearfully desolated by Nebuchadnezzar, she had fortified herself on an island with immense strength, and, by means of her extensive commerce, had amassed great wealth. But the Lord would *dispossess* her of all this wealth. So the original signifies, and not merely "cast her out." He would also smite her bulwarks, built up and standing in the sea, and she should be at length devoured utterly by fire.——After a siege of seven months, Alexander took the city, B. C. 332, and every feature of this prophecy was fulfilled.

5. Ashkelon shall see *it*, and fear; Gaza also *shall see it*, and be very sorrowful, and Ekron; for her expectation shall be ashamed; and the king shall perish from Gaza, and Ashkelon shall not be inhabited.

From Phœnicia the conqueror swept on to Philistia. The prophet's course of thought is the same. The fall of Tyre sent a panic through those cities of far inferior strength. How could they stand before a power with which Tyre, in all her glory and prowess, could not cope? See the same thoughts in Isa. 23.——Tyre held Alexander's army at bay seven months; the cities of Philistia scarcely retarded the conquering march of his army at all.——The verse may be read thus: "Ashkelon shall see and be afraid; Gaza, too, and she shall be in great anguish; and Ekron, because she shall be ashamed of her trust (*i. e.*, in Tyre); kings perish from Gaza, and Ashkelon shall no longer fill her throne"—literally, "shall not sit on a throne." Both shall cease to be nationalities ruled by kings.

6. And a bastard shall dwell in Ashdod, and I will cut off the pride of the Philistines.

7. And I will take away his blood out of his mouth, and his abominations from between his teeth; but he that remaineth, even he *shall be* for our God, and he shall be as a governor in Judah, and Ekron as a Jebusite.

The first clause I prefer to read—"A foreigner shall rule in Ashdod." The sense, however, may be only that foreigners shall *dwell* there. The verbs will bear either interpretation. Probably the meaning is, that the civil power has passed forever from the hands of the original Philistines to foreigners. Of course, the population would be in good part changed as well.——The pride of Philistia would be effectually humbled. And furthermore, the Lord would thoroughly cure them of their idolatry. The prophet, in representing this fact, thinks of them as eating things offered to idols, or as feasting in honor of their idols, and then the Lord plucks out the flesh from between their teeth and cleanses out the blood from their mouth. Then the remnant are converted—"shall be for our God"—are honored as a captain of a thousand in Judah; and they of Ekron shall come to be as near to God as the Jebusites —the primitive inhabitants of Jerusalem—after that city became the holy and the chosen one of God. (See Josh. 15: 63, and Judg. 19: 10, 11, and 2 Sam. 24: 16.)——This prophecy had its special fulfilment when the gospel was preached with great success by the apostles in those cities. It has its general fulfilment under the broad doctrine that all the great revolutions which the Lord brings about by war shall culminate at last in the wider range and sweep of his converting grace. Hence so many prophecies terminate like this. (See Isa. 19: 18–25 and 23: 15–18, and Jer. 12: 15, 16.)

8. And I will encamp about mine house because of the army, because of him that passeth by, and because of him that returneth: and no oppressor shall pass through them any more: for now have I seen with mine eyes.

The strain of the chapter thus far is that the Lord will let the great conqueror, Alexander, overwhelm the nations that had so often oppressed Israel. Here, on the other hand, he protects his own chosen people: "I will encamp about them and myself be a wall of fire around them for their sure defence." The special reason now thought of is the danger from the army of Alexander, "going and returning," moving to and fro, to Egypt and back, through or very near Judea. "No oppressor," in the precise sense of exactor of service or tribute, "shall pass over them any more," because henceforth the eye of God's love and care is upon them, in the same sense, a watchful eye, as in Zech. 3: 9 and 4: 10.——The fulfilment of this promise began with the nearer future, and was specially developed in the time of Alexander, when it was indeed striking and almost miraculous. If we may credit Josephus, Alexander sent to the Jews his usual demand for tribute as a token of submission, and was answered that they were in allegiance to the Persian throne. Offended by this reply, he soon after came in person; met Jaddua, the high priest, in his robes of office, attended by other priests; was solemnly impressed by their appearance; treated them with extraordinary deference, and ever after accounted the Jews his special friends. In explanation of this extraordinary conduct, he referred to a dream in which a personage attired like this high priest, met him while yet at home and pondering the question of invading Persia, encouraged him to go forward, assuring him of victory and success. Consequently, he recognized this high priest as the minister of the invisible gods, and all the more so when the Jews showed him the prophecies of Daniel respecting himself.——Of the general fact of Alexander's special favor to the Jews, there can be no doubt. This favor fulfilled the prophecy before us (v. 8). God's hand was in the agencies that secured it. Whether those agencies are given with general accuracy by Josephus, has been questioned; but for aught that appears, with more reason for affirming than for denying. In its general significance, this promise is good for the true church of God in every age of time.

9. Rejoice greatly, O daughter of Zion; shout, O daughter of Jerusalem: behold, thy King cometh unto thee: he *is* just, and having salvation; lowly, and riding upon an ass, and upon a colt the foal of an ass.

This striking case of protection against one of the world's greatest and most formidable conquerors—protection which specially shielded Jerusalem when all the adjacent cities and kingdoms were overrun and fearfully desolated—suggested the greater and more glorious protection achieved for the people of God through their incarnate Messiah, at once their great High Priest and their supreme King. Over this Deliverer, let Zion rejoice exceedingly! This summons to exultant joy indicates that Messianic blessings are before the prophet's eye.——His character as *King* is specially prominent here because suggested by the protection he gives his people against their enemies.

"Behold," see! "Thy King shall come to thee," for thy help and refuge. "He is just," the first quality of a good king; and "is *saved*," *i. e.*, protected of God. This word, rendered "having salvation,"* is the passive participle of the common verb, to save, from which our word Jesus is derived. It must, therefore, legitimately be taken in the sense—protected, carried safely through all danger—in this case, with reference to the sustaining hand of the Father, upholding his beloved Son through all the temptations and conflicts incident to his incarnation, sufferings, and death.——Moreover, he is an afflicted one, sorely bruised and suffering, for this is the usual sense of the word rendered "lowly."——The last clause of the verse demands special attention:—"Riding upon an ass, and upon a colt, the foal of an ass."——The primary sense of these words is plain enough. It is also clear that the first and proper meaning of the words is precisely what they seem to say, viz., that

* נוֹשָׁע

he should ride upon an ass, and even upon one yet young. The fact that the Lord Jesus fulfilled this prediction to the very letter; that he seemed to take special pains to fulfil it; and more than all, that this riding was not for the common purpose of a more comfortable conveyance from place to place, but was in manner and form the solemn and joyous procession of his inauguration and coronation as King in his own Jerusalem;—coupled also with the fact that each one of the four evangelists has given with more or less fulness his own account of the transaction*—all combine to show that it must have had some ulterior and extraordinary significance. It cannot by any means be supposed that the transaction has no speciality of meaning. What, then, is this special meaning—the significance of both the prophecy and the fulfilling act?——Very much has been said to show that the ass is everywhere despised, and that riding on an ass indicates whatever is low and scarcely above contempt. That the Lord Jesus rode on an ass has been supposed to denote the position he held among the men of his generation, as one "despised and rejected." This idea has been fostered by the fact that in some Christian countries Jews have been forbidden to ride on horses, or on any other animal but the ass, for the purpose of branding them with national odium. It is well understood among critics that Jewish commentators since the Christian era have been sorely perplexed with this prediction of their Messiah in whom they have expected a conquering hero, and therefore could find no place in their preconceived notions of his character for such a feature and fact as this, especially inasmuch as modern ideas have led them to interpret the fact as a thing of dishonor.——To relieve their King Messiah from this odium, they have taxed their ingenuity upon tradition and fable, *e. g.*, asserting that this ass was the identical one created within the six days of Gen. 1, the *original* ass (!), and the same on which Abraham rode to Mount Moriah to offer his Isaac there, and which Moses rode when he came from Midian into Egypt as their deliverer—thus asserting for him at least the honors of a renowned antiquity!——

But these Jewish commentators, and some not Jewish, have made themselves gratuitous labor in explaining away the supposed disgrace of riding on an ass. It were better first to consider that the notions of modern Europe and America concerning the ass are no rule for the people of Western Asia; and further, that the notions of Arab tribes and Mohammedans who glory in the horse are not to be the standard by which to determine Hebrew ideas. Manifestly the sole question here is, not what Western nations think of the ass, nor what Arabs think of him, nor indeed what is thought of him by any people in any age or country who are accustomed to use his rival, the horse; but what were the current usages and hence the current ideas *of the Jews*, the people among whom Zech-

* The reader will find the history of the fulfilment in Matt. 21:1-16, Mark 11:1-11, Luke 19:29-40, and John 12:12-18.

ariah lived and wrote? That this is the very point to be ascertained seems too plain to need proof, and yet it has been strangely overlooked.——It cannot be deemed necessary to prove that Jewish ideas were substantially the same from Abraham to the Christian era—certainly among all who, like Zechariah, held in high esteem the patriarchs of the nation and their ancient Scriptures.——Let it then be considered that during the entire life of the Jewish nation, the horse had never any footing in Palestine, and therefore had no opportunity to disparage his lowlier rival. It was the divine policy to keep him out, as being uncongenial to the Hebrew state, too aristocratic, and withal dangerous as a temptation into the ways of the idolatrous and corrupt nations in their vicinity; and more than all, *too much associated with war.* These considerations all conspired to retain the ass in service and to secure for him a fairly respectable standing.——But let us look at the historic facts. Abraham, the honored father of the nation, rode an ass. The sons of Jacob, heads of the tribes of Israel, rode every man his ass. Balaam, a great man in his country, rode on an ass. The daughter of Caleb, and Abigail too, among the worthy women of Jewish history, rode each on her ass. All the sons of David rode on mules—an animal of the same general character; Absalom also, when at the head of his army. In the transfer of the kingdom from David to Solomon, great account is made of his riding on David's mule in the royal procession on coronation day.——It is therefore simply impossible that any odium could have been attached to riding on an ass at the time Zechariah wrote, or at the time when Christ fulfilled his prediction.——But there is one idea, already hinted at though not fully developed, which deserves a far more prominent position than it has had. *The ass was not adapted to war; the horse was.* For the most part the ass appears in Jewish history either used by men in peaceful life, or by women who should never be in any other. On the contrary, the horse of scripture history is a war-horse, with either his dragoon or his chariot. The Egyptians on one side; the Assyrians, Chaldeans, and Persians on the other; made great account of horses for war. Hence, when the horse in Jewish history sets foot on Palestine, he is there for war, for aggression.——Nor let us fail to notice in our context that while King Messiah is to ride on an ass, the Lord says: "I will cut off the chariot from Ephraim, and *the horse from Jerusalem;* " and he shall speak peace to the heathen." *Jerusalem* especially, the holy city where Jehovah dwelt, must have no horses. Their very names and their presence are too much associated *with war.*——Zech. 12:4 shows how the horse is commonly thought of as related to the Hebrew state. In the millennial age, horses for once (for the first time?) shall be really consecrated to God (14:20), a most remarkable fact, and indicating a stupendous change! The ass then is here an emblem of peace—of peaceful pursuits, of a peaceful king, and of his peaceful reign, showing that Messiah's kingdom should not be of this world, and should not make its conquests with carnal weapons. This significant act, riding on an ass, is a symbol of Christ's peaceful reign, inaugurating him for the sort of work which the next verse describes.

10. And I will cut off the chariot from Ephraim, and the horse from Jerusalem, and the battle-bow shall be cut off: and he shall speak peace unto the heathen: and his dominion *shall be* from sea *even* to sea, and from the river *even* to the ends of the earth.

This verse is closely connected with verse 9—a part of the same grand prophecy of the Messiah and of his reign on earth—set here in a fine antithesis with the conquering, world-wide kingdom of Alexander.——The chariot and the horse must be discarded and abolished as *war-institutions*, and therefore wholly out of place under this peaceful reign. They can bear no part in the great conquests which Zion's King is to make. He has no fighting to do with carnal weapons. On the contrary, he "*speaks*" peace to the nations. The gospel of his word carries with it peace and love to the very hearts of men.——The reader will notice how fully this view of Messiah's reign harmonizes with that given by Micah 4: 1-4; Isa. 11 and Ps. 72, &c., &c.——Though the kingdom of Messiah relies on peaceful agencies alone for its diffusion, yet it shall be extended far away to the ends of the world. "His dominion shall be from sea to sea"—from land's end in one direction to land's end in another—"from the great river" (Euphrates) "to the ends of the earth." The prophet is not aiming to fix certain geographical boundaries to this kingdom, as if implying that it lies within these and in no case beyond them, but rather means that it is coextensive with the known world, sweeping away to the very ends of the earth.——That this passage (vs. 9, 10) is a prophecy of Jesus Christ, admits of no rational doubt. (1.) The course of thought which suggests and introduces it, the transition from the protection afforded against Alexander to the greater and better protection afforded by Zion's King against Satan, the world's worst conqueror and tyrant, goes far to prove it Messianic.——(2.) The call for extraordinary joy in this glorious King belongs to the prophecies of the Messiah, and to nothing of less magnitude and value.——(3.) The points made can apply to none but the Messiah.——(4.) They all apply to him easily, accurately, and fully.——(5.) The one most extraordinary point—his riding on an ass—was not only fulfilled *in* him but *by* him, with more appearance of special aim to fulfil this prophecy than is apparent elsewhere in regard to any other. Yet, in view of the exposition above given of the significance of this act, we must suppose that he did it *because* of its significance rather than merely for the sake of fulfilling this prophecy. He *did* fulfil it, however, none the less.——(6.) The testimony of the disciples in their comments on the historic fact is in point. Matthew (21: 4) remarks: "All this was done that it might be fulfilled which was spoken by the prophet," and then cites this passage; while John (12 : 16) remarks that his "disciples did not understand these things at the first, but when Jesus was glorified, then they remembered that these things were written of him, and that they had done these things unto him." When the Spirit had fully come to teach them all things, and to bring all things Christ had said and done to their remembrance, then the significance of this transaction became wonderfully clear to their minds.——All these points of evidence combined make the proof signally complete—indeed, overwhelming.

11. As for thee also, by the blood of thy covenant I have sent forth thy prisoners out of the pit wherein *is* no water.

12. Turn you to the strong hold, ye prisoners of hope: even to-day do I declare *that* I will render double unto thee;

13. When I have bent Judah for me, filled the bow with Ephraim, and raised up thy sons, O Zion, against thy sons, O Greece, and made thee as the sword of a mighty man.

The ninth and tenth verses may be regarded as a digression from the regular course of thought, and embraced in a parenthesis. In v. 11 the prophet returns to speak of events that follow shortly after those predicted (vs. 1–8). The conflict (v. 13) between the sons of Zion and the sons of Greece finds its fulfilment in the furious wars waged during twenty-four years between the Jews and the Syrian Greeks, commencing in the reign of Antiochus Epiphanes. His people are here called Greeks because his kingdom was one of the four into which the great Grecian empire of Alexander was divided, and also because their language and customs were Grecian.——"As for thee also (O daughter of Zion, as in v. 9), because thou art in a covenant with thy God which is sealed with blood, I will send forth thy prisoners out of the pit in which is no water." The covenant of the Lord with the Jewish nation was sealed with sprinkled blood. See Ex. 24 : 8.—"And Moses took the blood and sprinkled it on the people, and said: Behold the blood of the covenant which the Lord had made with you concerning all these words."——A "pit without water" is one from which the water has by some means gone, leaving mud on the bottom, exceedingly offensive and often miasmatic. See the experiences of Joseph and of Jeremiah, Gen. 37 : 24 and Jer. 38 : 6. The Lord's people are thought of as having been imprisoned in such a pit; but the Lord sends them forth. The past tense, rendered "have sent," is doubtless used because the event is so fixed in the counsels of God as to be accounted *done*. Hence this tense (the perfect) is used by the prophets even for events yet as to actual occurrence in the future. This was to occur *after* Zechariah's day.——"Return ye to the *strong hold*"—a high and therefore strong, inaccessible position, and here in contrast with the "deep pit" where they had lain imprisoned. Being the people of Jehovah and in covenant with him, they were evermore "prisoners of hope"—prisoners having just ground of hope in his protecting, delivering grace.——To "render double" is to give them blessings twice as great as their afflictions had been. See the same expression, Isa. 40 : 2 and 61 : 7. It is altogether the way of the Lord to send grief and affliction only in single measure, but joy and blessing in double—weighing out the retributions of justice carefully and the inflictions of his rod very tenderly; but pouring forth the bounties of his mercy as if he could not think of measuring them by any rule less than the impulses of infinite love!——In v. 13—"Because I have trodden Judah for my bow, and filled my bow with Ephraim as mine arrow"—means that the Lord is to use the military strength of Judah and Ephraim in protecting his land against the Syrian armies.——The strong bows of the warrior were bent by using the foot as well as the hand. Hence the phrase "to tread the bow," for bending it to fit its string for use.——Applying the arrow "filled the bow"—this being a necessary complement, without which it was of no account.——"Raised up" should rather be "roused up"—exciting and inspiring to deeds of heroic valor—all which had its precise fulfilment in those inspirations of heroism with which the Lord anointed the souls of the Maccabees against their Syrian foes.

14. And the LORD shall be seen over them, and his arrow shall go forth as the lightning: and the Lord GOD shall blow the trumpet, and shall go with whirlwinds of the south.

The agencies of God's providence in this war shall be as palpable as if Jehovah himself were visible above them as they fought their battles. His own arrows shall go forth like the lightnings; he shall blow the trumpet-blasts of the battle, and shall march upon his foes as in the whirlwinds of the south—those most fearful tornadoes that carry death in their wings. These whirwinds of the south are referred to by Job (37 : 9), and by Isaiah (21 : 1). This grouping of the boldest and most terrible elements of nature represents God's agencies in those wars.

15. The LORD of hosts shall defend them; and they shall devour and subdue with sling-stones; and they shall drink, *and* make a noise as through wine; and they shall be filled like bowls, *and* as the corners of the altar.

"The Lord of hosts" ("God of the celestial armies" is the right name to use here) "shall defend them" (literally, shall throw his shield over them), "and they shall devour" (literally "eat" as it were the flesh of their enemies), "and shall tread down sling-stones"—implying that their enemies are now as powerless as a small sling-stone when lying on the ground, which is dangerous only when hurled and flying from its sling. The sense is not—"subdue with sling-stones," *i. e.*, of their own; but tread under foot their enemy as they would tread upon sling-stones.——"They shall drink," *i. e.*, the blood of their enemies, as men drink wine, and shall shout as men under its stimulus, and be filled with it as the bowls of the altar, and as its corners upon which the blood was daily sprinkled.——These allusions to the bowls and the corners of the altar may refer tacitly to the covenant sealed with blood, under which help came from God for victory.

The reader will be careful to notice the contrast between these verses (13–15) and the Messianic passage (vs. 9, 10) on the point of war with deadly weapons. Under Messiah's peaceful reign there shall be no chariots or horses of war; the battle-bow shall be cut off and unknown: but here, in the age before Messiah came, Judah is the Lord's bow, Ephraim his arrow; the Lord fights at their head, and they too fight with determined and almost furious bravery.——The Lord had his own reasons for making the age before Messiah came so militant. Let us not question their wisdom or their love. But manifestly it is his purpose in this chapter to put the future kingdom of the Messiah in the strongest possible contrast with those militant features of the earlier age, and to assure us that in the good time coming men shall truly "learn war no more." The gospel, having once developed its whole genius and power, shall prove itself thoroughly and only "peace on earth and good will to men."

16. And the LORD their God shall save them in that day as the flock of his people: for *they shall be as* the stones of a crown, lifted up as an ensign upon his land.

"The Lord their God shall save them as the flock of his people"—as if he were indeed their own shepherd. "Because diadem-stones," the jewels of a crown, "are they," borne on the head of a conquering king, and waving high over his land.——A beautiful contrast should be noted here between their Syrian foes—sling-stones under foot—and themselves crown-stones, precious gems, set in a crown, and borne aloft over the land on the head of conquerors.

17. For how great *is* his goodness, and how great *is* his beauty! corn shall make the young men cheerful, and new wine the maids.

There is good reason for this exclamation of surprise and joy in view of the goodness of God to his people, and the beauty of his providential dispensations as seen in the time of those Syrian wars. ——In the last clause, "cheerful" is not precisely the idea, but rather *fruitful*, *prolific*, which, according to well-known Jewish ideas, was one of the most conclusive and joyous proofs of great prosperity. Early marriages, healthful parents, "sons as plants grown up in their youth;" daughters as corner-stones, polished after the similitude of a palace: "happy is that people that is in such a case" (Ps. 144: 12–15). "Happy is the man that hath his quiver full of them" (Ps. 127: 5).——These are the peaceful and prosperous times that succeed those wars.

CHAPTER X.

This chapter is a continuation from the close of chapter 9, and hence has for its ground idea the wars of the Maccabees against the Syrian power. V. 1 stands immediately connected with 9: 17, indicating the external prosperity that succeeded those wars; v. 2 falls back to note the apostasies which brought on this Syrian scourge; v. 3 the zeal and jealousy of the Lord kindled against the corrupt Jewish leaders, and the remedy for their mischiefs; in v. 4 men rise up, capable of filling positions of responsible trust; in v. 5 they fight valiantly, because the Lord is with them, and confounds their foes. In vs. 6–12, on the basis of this great deliverance wrought for his people, the prophet predicts that in times more remote the Lord will work similar but yet more glorious achievements for his Zion.

1. Ask ye of the Lord rain in the time of the latter rain; *so* the Lord shall make bright clouds, and give them showers of rain, to every one grass in the field.

Under the ancient dispensation the Lord gave timely rains and abundant harvests to his people when they were obedient and trustful, and sought him in prayer. He took care to have them understand this from the outset. See Deut. 11: 13, 14:—"And it shall come to pass that if ye shall hearken diligently unto my commandments which I command you this day, to love the Lord your God, and to serve him with all your heart, and with all your soul, that I will give you the rain of your land in his due season, the first rain and the latter rain, that thou mayest gather in thy corn and thy wine and thy oil."——Hence the prophet says here: "Ask of the Lord rain"—it comes for the asking, for the Lord your God hears the prayer of his obedient people. Rain "in the time of the latter rain" was especially useful to perfect the maturing crops.——"So the Lord shall give"—not "bright clouds," but "lightnings," always portending rain.——The Hebrew words translated "showers of rain" imply abundance—"the rain of great rain"—so that not in detached districts alone, but over the whole land, "every one shall have grass in the field."

2. For the idols have spoken vanity, and the diviners have seen a lie, and have told false dreams; they comfort in vain: therefore they went their way as a flock, they were troubled because *there was* no shepherd.

The reason is given here why the Lord comes to the rescue; "*for* the people have been sorely deceived by diviners and by the priests of idol gods, and have been seduced away from me," alluding to the antecedent apostasy which was the occasion and procuring cause of that fearful Syrian scourge. Historical evidence to this apostasy exists in 1 Mac. 1:11–15.——The "idols," is in Hebrew "the teraphim," household gods which appear not unfrequently in Jewish history, *e. g.*, with Rachel (Gen. 31:19, 34); with Michal, Saul's daughter (1 Sam. 19:13, 16); with Micah in Judges 17:5, &c., &c.——All the light that came from these gods and diviners was only darkness; their guidance only misled the people; the hopes they inspired were worse than vain; consequently the whole people were led off in a wrong and ruinous way, going *en masse*, as a flock of sheep follow the lead given them. They were in great affliction (the sense of the word rendered "were troubled"), because there was no competent and real shepherd.

3. Mine anger was kindled against the shepherds, and I punished the goats: for the Lord of hosts hath visited his flock the house of Judah, and hath made them as his goodly horse in the battle.

"My wrath" (saith the Lord) "is kindled against those shepherds" who so mislead the people. "I will punish the he-goats," so called because the he-goat leads the flock.——"For the Lord hath visited his flock," implying that he is the real shepherd of the house of Judah, and hath made them victorious in the conflict against their enemies, crowning them with honor before the nation, as he indicates by comparing them to his own horse, one specially honored by his own use in the day of battle.——In the middle of the verse is a play upon the two meanings of the usual Hebrew word for *visit*,* which, with a preposition following, equivalent to *upon*, means to inflict judgment; but standing alone means to look after in a good sense. God will look after those enemies in the sense of *visiting upon* them his plagues; but will look after his people in the sense of looking into their case with kindness, and redressing their wrongs with his glorious right arm.

4. Out of him came forth the corner, out of him the

* פָּקַד.

nail, out of him the battle-bow, out of him every oppressor together.

When the Lord visits Judah in mercy, he gives her the very blessings she needs—good leaders in place of the bad who had been so sore a curse upon her. Hence out of Judah now come forth the "corner-stone" men, good for bearing the weightiest responsibilities: the "nail" men, to hold things in their right place, or to bear great burdens. "The battle-bow" are the men skilful in the line of war, but the word rendered "oppressor" does not in this passage imply any injustice, but only an active, vigorous, and capable ruler. ——The nail, in oriental use, was rather a spike or tent-pin, sometimes so large that all the kitchen utensils were hung upon it. (See Isa. 22 : 23, 25 and Ezra 9 : 8.)

5. And they shall be as mighty *men*, which tread down *their enemies* in the mire of the streets in the battle: and they shall fight, because the LORD *is* with them, and the riders on horses shall be confounded.

This graphic and vigorous description of the Lord's valiant warriors corresponds admirably with the historic character of the Maccabean brothers, who girded themselves for heroic fight in the name of the Lord God of their fathers. They felt that the Lord was with them. The "riders on horses" were their Syrian invaders. The history makes frequent mention of large bodies of horsemen in their armies, *e. g.*, 1 Mac. 3 : 39: "Seven thousand horsemen," and 4 : 1, "one thousand of the best horsemen," &c. They were confounded to meet such power among those despised Jews.

6. And I will strengthen the house of Judah, and I will save the house of Joseph, and I will bring them again to place them; for I have mercy upon them: and they shall be as though I had not cast them off: for I *am* the LORD their God, and will hear them.

The general conception in this verse is that of reproducing the best days of Israel, *e. g.*, under David and Solomon. Consequently "Joseph," the ten tribes, must be saved; the people all made ready to "*dwell*" in a settled and secure way in their own land, the Lord showing his mercy upon them even as though he had not ever cast them off for their sins.——But this conception carries us onward into the Messianic age, and could have its fulfilment in nothing short or less. The recall of the ten tribes, in any age subsequent to Zechariah, must, of necessity, be regarded as Messianic, and to be fulfilled only in the New Testament sense.——With these principles of interpretation before the mind, this entire passage (vs. 6–12) becomes not only clear and free from its otherwise insurmountable difficulties, but rich in gospel significance and in the fulness of glorious promise for Zion in her latter days.

7. And *they* of Ephraim shall be like a mighty *man*, and their hearts shall rejoice as through wine: yea, the children shall see *it*, and be glad; their hearts shall rejoice in the LORD.

8. I will hiss for them, and gather them; for I have redeemed them: and they shall increase as they have increased.

9. And I will sow them among the people: and they shall remember me in far countries; and they shall live with their children, and turn again.

"Ephraim" contemplates in its literal sense the ten tribes; but in its real prophetic outlook, the ingathering of the nations to Jesus Christ in the gospel age. A Jew in the time of Zechariah could conceive of no state of things more desirable than the reproducing of the good times of David and Solomon. Hence language and figures are drawn from that state to represent the best condition possible for God's earthly kingdom—the sublimely glorious conquests of peace and victories of love in the latter days.——In v. 8 Ephraim comes back with heart full of joy; the Lord lifts up his shrill cry for them, as the keeper of bees whistles for them, and they come to his call. They multiply as of old (Ephraim took his name from the idea of being prolific in population).——In v. 9 God will scatter them abroad among the nations, and there, under the moral influence of this affliction, they shall remember the Lord their God and repent of their great sins.——So the Lord said by Hosea (2:4), "I will allure her into the wilderness and speak to her heart."——"They shall *live* with their children"—*live* in the high spiritual sense, with allusion perhaps to Ezek. 37:9: "Come from the four winds, O breath, and breathe upon these slain, that they may *live*."——"With their children," implies that these blessings go down to future generations—not to themselves alone, but to their children after them as well.

10. I will bring them again also out of the land of Egypt, and gather them out of Assyria; and I will bring them into the land of Gilead and Lebanon; and *place* shall not be found for them.

These words must be understood as historic allusion, and not as specific and literal prediction. The sense is not—I will gather my captives out of Egypt and out of Assyria, but—I will do a similar thing to the great achievement of bringing my people out of Egypt under Moses. I will redeem them from a second Egypt, and save them from a second Assyrian Sennacherib. That only Egypt and Assyria, and not Chaldea, are referred to, is explained by the fact that the kingdom of the ten tribes had disappeared before the Chaldean came into notice; hence, Ephraim never knew Chaldea as an enemy.——Note also that the prophet does not say they shall return to Judah and Jerusalem; but, to show the enlargement of the Lord's kingdom, he names "Gilead," the extensive region on the east of Jordan, and "Lebanon," on the north, which lay outside the usual boundaries of the tribes of Israel; and, indeed, he says, "place large enough shall not be found for them."——But this has never been fulfilled in the lineal descendants of Abraham, nor can it ever be. Their numbers, all told to-day, would not meet the demands of this prophecy, interpreted however moderately. We must, therefore, find Israel and Ephraim in that new era of Messiah's kingdom in which there is no distinction of Jew and Greek, but all are one in Christ Jesus.——Yet another reason for omitting to name Judah and Jerusalem is, that the prophet has in mind the ten tribes specially, and not Judah. The demand for *restoring* mercy lay chiefly in their direction, as seen in the age of Zechariah. Further, the Jews were never carried captive literally into Egypt. If any Jews fled thither for refuge in those seasons when their homes were broken up, they went and were received *as friends*. But v. 11 conceives of their rescue from Egypt as being from the hand of enemies, a fact which shows that Egypt comes in here only by way of historic allusion.——Arguing against the doctrine of a literal restoration of the Jews to Palestine, Dr. Hengstenberg pertinently says: "If it cannot be denied that the lands *out of which* the Israelites were brought back, are to be understood only as types, what objection can be urged if the land *to which* they shall be restored is in like manner to be regarded as a type?" (Christology, ii., 143.)

11. And he shall pass through the sea with affliction, and shall smite the waves in the sea, and all the deeps of the rivers shall dry up: and the pride of Assyria shall be brought down, and the sceptre of Egypt shall depart away.

This verse begins with a change of person from the first, "I," as in vs. 6–10, to the third, "he." But "he" must be understood of the same Lord God.——The "sea" can be no other than the Red Sea, named by way of historic allusion. The Lord passes through it at the head of his people to achieve a like deliverance to that of the Exodus from Egypt.——Not "with affliction," for there is no word corresponding to "with," and nothing out of which to make this sense; but the sea which *is itself* their affliction—which stands in their way, and is the occasion of their trouble—in apposition with the word "sea." Whatever their *affliction* may be, analogous to the Red Sea of the olden time, the Lord will march through it at the head of his people.——"And he will smite the waves" in that sea which represents their affliction, as he is wont to smite his enemies. ——"And all the depths of the Nile shall be dried up"—with historic reference to the Jordan, which, however, being a comparatively small stream, is not itself named here, but the usual word for the

Nile is taken instead. That is, the idea of *drying up* comes from the Jordan; the *magnitude* of the stream from the Nile.——Isaiah (11:15, 16) has a very similar allusion to the passage of the Red Sea. ——"The pride of Assyria" and "the sceptre of Egypt" are also historic allusions to those hostile powers from whom Israel had suffered so much. The sense is—God will humble all the foes of Zion, and will effectually break in pieces their power to harm.

12. And I will strengthen them in the Lord; and they shall walk up and down in his name, saith the Lord.

Finally, they shall be made gloriously strong in the Lord, and through his strength alone. So shall they walk up and down, traverse the land at their will, or in their duty, without fear. No harm can befall them, since they walk with God.——Many parallel passages might be cited from Isaiah, Jeremiah, Hosea, and Micah, serving to confirm the general interpretation here given, and to show that the prophets harmonize remarkably in these views of the general course of events in the great future of Zion; and also to show that they give the same sense to individual and special phrases. It has not seemed necessary to collate and compare these texts, except in passages of special difficulty.——The reader will find in Isaiah 11:11–16 a passage remarkably similar to this in all important respects. It is beyond all question *Messianic;* so must this be also.

CHAPTER XI.

If the Book of Zechariah be divided into two portions, the first six chapters being the first division, and the remaining eight the second, then this eleventh will be a digression from the current strain of promised blessings in the second portion, very analogous to the fifth chapter in the first part. As the fifth was interposed for the purpose of moral warning to the careless, apprising them that the judgments of God awaited the guilty, so here this eleventh chapter is interposed for the same purpose. There can be no doubt that it predicts judgments on the covenant people at some period of their history then future.——The manner of presenting this truth is very peculiar, essentially that of symbolic vision—a case quite unique in the respect that, in vision only, and not in actuality, and as personating, not himself, but others, the prophet is required to perform the functions of a shepherd to the Lord's people, considered as his flock. On this theory of interpreting the chapter the best modern commentators are united. Despite of the unique peculiarities of the case, it is generally agreed that the chapter predicts the overthrow of the Jewish state, and the ruin of their city and temple, effected by the Romans, about A. D. 70, in consequence of their national corruption, and of their blind and mad rejection of their Messiah. The prophet, acting the part of a good shepherd (vs. 4–14), personates the Messiah himself. Acting the part of the foolish shepherd (vs. 15–17), he personates the Scribes and Pharisees of the Saviour's day.——The first three verses, wrought up in high poetic imagery, predict the fall of the nation before the Roman arms; while the remaining part of the chapter gives the antecedent moral causes of that fall. Whereas those morally blinded and hardened Jews had said in the madness of their wrath against the spotless Redeemer, "His blood be on us and on our children," on them and on their children his blood did come, and their blood flowed like rivers of water! The Saviour himself had said, "Behold your house is left unto you desolate." Here is an earlier prediction of those fearful retributions. History endorses its accuracy to the very letter.——The comprehensive thought of this chapter is, therefore, *Judaism, utterly corrupt and apostate, repelling the merciful efforts of her Redeemer to reclaim and save her, and thus bringing on herself dire destruction.*——The divisions of the chapter are already indicated incidentally: vs. 1–3, a comprehensive prediction of ruin upon their city and nation; vs. 4–14, the causes of this ruin shown to lie in the utter corruption of those orders (the priests, scribes, and doctors of the law) who should have been, under God, their good shepherds, and their consequent rejection of their true Shepherd, Jesus, the Messiah. Lastly, vs. 15–17 give the course and doom of those corrupt teachers, specially personated by the prophet, acting the part of a foolish shepherd.

1. Open thy doors, O Lebanon, that the fire may devour thy cedars.

Lebanon and her lofty cedars represent Jerusalem; her doors, the gates of the city. Hence this is a summons to Jerusalem to prepare for approaching ruin. The ground of this poetical conception of Lebanon for Jerusalem may be a tacit analogy between them—Lebanon one of the grandest objects in the realm of nature, Jerusalem in the realm of art; Lebanon among the works of God, Jerusalem among the works of man—with, perhaps, a side-look to the fact that the temple was largely built with cedars from Lebanon.

2. Howl, fir-tree, for the cedar is fallen; because the mighty are spoiled: howl, O ye oaks of Bashan, for the forest of the vintage is come down.

The sentiment is—This destruction shall be complete. The loftiest and strongest fall; how, then, can the feebler hope to stand?——The same strain of poetic conception is carried through the verse, the grandest trees of the forest representing Jerusalem and other strongholds of the nation. "Wail, O cypress, for the cedar has fallen" (*i. e.*, what were most lofty are now destroyed); "wail, ye oaks of Bashan, for the forest of the inaccessible mountain-heights is laid low." "If these things be done in the green tree, what shall be done in the dry?"

3. *There is* a voice of the howling of the shepherds; for their glory is spoiled: a voice of the roaring of young lions; for the pride of Jordan is spoiled.

Here the figures turn from inanimate nature to animate. The ornament and glory of the shepherds are their rich pastures—now laid waste. Compare Jer. 25:36: "A voice of the cry of the shepherds, and an howling of the principal of the flock; for the Lord hath spoiled their pasture."——"The pride of Jordan," in which the young lion made his lair, were the dense thickets along his banks. This phrase was already in use by Jeremiah, whom Zechariah follows remarkably in his terms and phrases. See Jer. 12:5, where the "swelling of Jordan" is the same original phrase here rendered "pride of Jordan." So also, Jer. 49:19, and 50:44—in all cases said of the thick undergrowths along the Jordan, where the lions had their homes.——The sentiment is here the same as above—All classes of people are in distress, for their choicest treasures are wasted; what they most love and value is in ruins. A poetic imagination seizes on the ruin of individual classes, and by a few striking details gives a vivid conception of the universal desolation.

4. Thus saith the Lord my God; Feed the flock of the slaughter;

As already stated, vs. 4–14 are a sort of parable—a dramatic scene, in which the prophet personates the Messiah, and represents in himself what the Messiah was to do for the Jewish nation, considered as the people of God. The figure throughout is that of a shepherd and his flock—a figure often applied to the spiritual relations of the Lord to his people. Those who act under and for him, ministering to the religious life of his people, are also called shepherds, pastors of his people. This figure had become very common in the age of Zechariah, and of the prophets during the captivity. The reader will see, in Ezek. 34 and Jer. 23, how familiar those prophets were with this conception, and how much use they made of it to set forth the relations sustained by the Lord toward his people. It also served with them, as with Zechariah, to represent how fearfully the priests and prophets of that age had degenerated, and were scattering and wasting the sheep of the Lord's pasture.——"The flock of the slaughter" means the flock doomed to slaughter for their sins—the Jewish people, now ripe for the fearful retributive judgments of the Almighty.

5. Whose possessors slay them, and hold themselves not guilty: and they that sell them say, Blessed *be* the Lord; for I am rich: and their own shepherds pity them not.

The persons of the drama in this verse are (1.) *The flock*, who are the Jews during the period A. D. 30–70, conceived of as the flock of the Lord's pastures; (2.) Their *buyers* ("possessors") and their *sellers*, the Romans; and (3.) Their *own shepherds*, the priests, Scribes, and Pharisees, who should have taught them the knowledge of God, but who had no care or pity for their deplorable moral condition.——Their buyers who buy them for slaughter kill them and are not punished as guilty, because it is of the Lord to scourge the nation for its great sins. The verb here used * has only these two well-established senses: (1.) To *sin;* (2.) To suffer punishment for sin. See notes on Hos. 5 : 15. It occurs Jer. 2 : 3 and 50 : 7, both of which passages strikingly illustrate the sense of the clause before us. The former, referring to the time when Israel was holiness to the Lord, says—"All that devour him *offend*," *i. e.*, sin against God, and shall suffer punishment; "evil shall come upon them, saith the Lord." The latter, referring to a time when the Lord would scourge his people, reads—"All that found them have devoured them; their adversaries said, We *offend* not, because they have sinned against the Lord." It is remarkable that foreign enemies whom the Lord made use of to scourge his people, seem to have in some sort understood why the Lord gave them this license. The king of Assyria (Isa. 36 : 10) said: "Am I now come up *without the Lord* against this land to destroy it? The Lord said unto me, Go up against this land to destroy it."——That "they who sell them bless the Lord for their gains," corresponds to the clause, "they are not punished" ("offend not"). They think they are doing God service, and thank him for the personal selfish good they get as if all were morally right.

6. For I will no more pity the inhabitants of the land, saith the LORD: but lo, I will deliver the men every one into his neighbor's hand, and into the hand of his king: and they shall smite the land, and out of their hand I will not deliver *them*.

The reason for the ruin that comes thus terribly on the covenant people is that God has given them over to destruction for their incorrigible sins.——The repetition of the verb rendered "pity" is a play upon the word, thus: As their shepherds have lost all pity for the moral condition of their flock, so will I abjure all pity for them, flock and shepherd both; and will give them over to remediless ruin.——This doom, thus made prophetically specific, is shown by the history to be drawn with entire accuracy. The facts were, that the people had no head; that intestine discord and civil war were scarcely less destructive than the Roman sword. Every one was delivered into the hand of his neighbor and into the hand of the Roman king. The slaughter was terrific, scarcely equalled by

* אָשֵׁם

any other scene recorded in authentic history. Josephus is the chief original authority. His statements are full and reliable. According to his account, the loss of life on the Jewish side, during that horrible siege and capture, could not have been less than eleven hundred thousand!

7. And I will feed the flock of slaughter, *even* you, O poor of the flock. And I took unto me two staves; the one I called Beauty, and the other I called Bands; and I fed the flock.

Not "I *will* feed," for this fails to give the tense of the original; but, "so then I fed the flock doomed to slaughter because of the poor of the flock"—*i. e.*, out of my pity for the poor ones of the flock—a pertinent and beautiful statement of the labor and love of their own Messiah, who was so often "moved with compassion when he saw the people as sheep having no shepherd." For the proud and self-righteous and for those who were rich toward this world but not rich toward God, he manifested no specially tender pity; but for the masses who had no shepherd, and especially for the poor, his heart was tenderly touched. In the line of pure benevolence he rose indefinitely high above all other religious teachers of every age in this—"*he preached the gospel to the poor.*"

These "staves" were the usual well-known shepherd's *crook*, the only special instrument used by the shepherd; useful to him both in the management of the flock, and in repelling its enemies. They represent here those providential agencies by which the Lord aided the pastoral work of the Messiah over his people, as appears from their significant names. The one he called *Grace* (not so properly "Beauty"), but grace in the sense of that divine favor which restrained hostile heathen nations from assaulting the people of the Lord while they faithfully served him.——The other, "Bands," was a crook of cords, significant of those providential agencies which held the people together in peace. With these aids he acted the part of a shepherd to the flock.

8. Three shepherds also I cut off in one month; and my soul loathed them, and their soul also abhorred me.

The prophet, personating the Messiah, is supposed to have subordinate shepherds under him. These three shepherds cannot mean three individuals. The general strain of the subject forbids this. Besides, Zechariah is wont to present individuals as representatives of orders or classes of men. See chap. 3, throughout, where Joshua represents the order of priests; and 4: 14, where the two anointed ones must mean the two orders, the regal and the priestly, which were inducted into office by the ceremony of anointing.——Here we must suppose that the prophet takes the number three from precisely those three established orders upon whom the pastoral responsibility of caring under God for the covenant people devolved—priests, prophets, and civil magistrates. (See Jer. 2: 8, 26 and 18: 18.) Those who represented these classes during our Lord's public ministry must be specially intended here, probably the priests; the scribes in the place of the ancient prophets; and the civil magistrates. The Lord Jesus rejected them from their places of trust, not instantaneously, but very summarily, as "one month" shows. It was the labor of his public life. The history of our Lord's public ministry, in its relation to the scribes, doctors of the law, and Pharisees, shows that he and they had not the least common sympathy. He loathed them, as the Hebrew word implies; he lost all confidence in their moral integrity and even honesty; and on the other hand, their soul rebelled against him because of the purity of his character, and the fidelity and pungency of his rebukes of their sin.

9. Then said I, I will not feed you: that that dieth, let it die; and that that is to be cut off, let it be cut off; and let the rest eat, every one the flesh of another.

The Messiah abandons the flock, the Jewish people, to the sweep of terrible judgments. "I will be your shepherd no longer." A threefold judgment shall be your extermination;—pestilence; the sword from without; the sword from within;—the two last looking toward (1.) the Roman arms; (2.) those horrible conflicts of hostile parties which made the very strength of the nation its essential weakness and ruin.——Let the pestilence sweep away whom it will; let the Roman sword drink the blood of the victims so doomed by the will of the Most High; let every man's teeth be sharpened to devour his neighbor's flesh!——The reality set forth in this prophetic language was fearfully terrific! They had said—"His blood be on us and on our children!" The Lord responded, "So let it be!" Here is the prediction. History verifies it to the letter!

10. And I took my staff, *even* Beauty, and cut it asunder, that I might break my covenant which I had made with all the people.

The first crook, now broken, represented the sundering of the covenant which God is supposed to have made with foreign nations (the sense of "all the people"), to restrain them from harming his chosen. This covenant lay in the divine mind—his purpose to restrain heathen nations from making war on his people. See the same sense in Hos. 2: 18: "In that day I will make a covenant for them with the beasts of the field," &c. Compare Job. 5: 23 and Ezek. 34: 25.

11. And it was broken in that day: and so the poor of the flock that waited upon me knew that it *was* the word of the LORD.

The staff once broken, the Roman arms came down upon the land. "Then the poor of the flock"—Christ's disciples—having been apprised by him (Matt. 24 : 15–21), knew that the hour of judgment for the land had come, and fled for safety to the mountains of Pella, on the east of Jordan. History records the remarkable fact that not one Christian Jew fell in that awful carnage. All who had faith in their divine Lord gave heed to his warnings. The Lord by his special providence gave them ample time to make good their escape before the city was invested by the Roman legions. They fled to Pella in the mountains east of the Jordan, and were all safe.

12. And I said unto them, If ye think good, give *me* my price; and if not, forbear. So they weighed for my price thirty *pieces* of silver.

13. And the LORD said unto me, Cast it unto the potter: a goodly price that I was prized at of them. And I took the thirty *pieces* of silver, and cast them to the potter in the house of the LORD.

The great shepherd, about to close his services, proposes in the business settlement that they, the Jews, should give him the wages due. It is not implied by the original words that he fixed the price himself. "Give me my price," should rather read, "Give me my hire or reward." He manifestly left it with them to fix the price. He only said, Give me what wages you please, and let me go.——They weighed out thirty pieces of silver, the very price for which Judas betrayed him, and the usual price for a slave. (See Ex. 21 : 32.) Maimonides, one of the most reliable ancient Jewish authors, speaks of this as the price of a slave's services, but contemptible for a free man's. The meagreness of it indicates how low they estimated his services. Precisely this is the intended showing of the transaction. ——"A goodly price," &c., is ironical, and shows how keenly the insult was felt. It has, moreover, a prophetic outlook toward the very deed of Judas.——The Lord said, "Cast it to the potter." He did so. This, too, was one of the points of remarkable coincidence between this symbolic prophecy and one of the prominent scenes in the betrayal of his Lord by Judas.——It should be noted that Matthew, having stated that Judas, filled with remorse, returned the price of blood (27 : 3–10), says that the chief priests "bought therewith the potter's field to bury strangers in," which thenceforth bore the name of "the field of blood," and that "then was fulfilled that which was spoken by *Jeremy the prophet*, saying, And they took the thirty pieces of silver, the price of him that was valued, whom they of the children of Israel did value; and gave them for the potter's field as the Lord appointed me."——These words are not found in the Book of Jeremiah, but the general sense and nearly the same words occur in this passage of Zechariah. How came it to pass that Matthew named Jeremiah instead of Zechariah?——It should be considered that Zechariah's words, "the potter," &c., connect his prophecy closely with Jeremiah, chaps. 18 and 19. "The potter" of Jeremiah worked down in the valley of the son of Hinnom, as the expressions "go down" and "went down" (Jer. 18: 2, 3) render probable, and as the passage (19 : 2) proves, for here the "east gate" is (in Heb.) "the entrance to the potter's gate." There Jeremiah was to denounce upon the people most solemn threatenings from the Lord, and then break a potter's vessel before them. The place, already made abominable; the breaking of the vessel, significant of a doom for which there can be no remedy; and the fearful solemnity of the message—all conspired to make the associations connected with this potter's house specially solemn and portentous. These things need to be understood in order to get the full sense of this passage in Zechariah. It may be supposed that Matthew had before his mind the full account of Jeremiah as well as the more brief one of Zechariah, and quoting from memory, assigned to the former what is found as to its precise words most nearly in the latter.——It is by no means necessary to the reliability of the Scriptures that we prove them perfectly accurate in all the minutest literary points. Let it suffice that every thing vital is right and true, and that every doctrine of any importance is revealed without the least admixture of error.

14. Then I cut asunder mine other staff, *even* Bands that I might break the brotherhood between Judah and Israel.

The phrase "the brotherhood between Judah and Israel" is an historic allusion to the case of the two nations after the revolt under Jeroboam. Under their mutual relations, brotherhood was peace; brotherhood broken was civil war. Hence the breaking of this second staff or crook symbolized the withdrawal of those providential agencies which had kept the people together in friendly relations with each other. Those agencies being withdrawn, intestine discord at once broke out, hostile parties arose, and civil war became their most fearful curse. The history of the period, commencing shortly before the invasion by the Romans, and continuing till the city lay in ruins, is a mournful confirmation of this symbolic prophecy.

15. And the LORD said unto me, Take unto thee yet the instruments of a foolish shepherd.

16. For lo, I will raise up a shepherd in the land, *which* shall not visit those that be cut off, neither shall seek the young one, nor heal that that is broken, nor feed that that standeth still: but he shall eat the flesh of the fat, and tear their claws in pieces.

17. Wo to the idol shepherd that leaveth the flock! the sword *shall be* upon his arm, and upon his right eye: his arm shall be clean dried up, and his right eye shall be utterly darkened.

This passage seems to prove conclusively that the person who is commanded here (v. 15) to "take the instruments of a foolish shepherd," and who was ordered (vs. 4–14) to "feed the flock of slaughter," can be no other than the prophet himself; yet not acting in his own person, or rather not prefiguring aught concerning himself; but in vs. 4–14 personating the Messiah during his public ministry; and here (vs. 15–17) personating those priests, scribes, and civil magistrates whom the good shepherd cut off "in one month" (v. 8). The object here is to give a more full view of the character, life, and doom of those faithless shepherds.——The passage is very brief; hence we are not told precisely what the "instruments of a foolish shepherd" are. They were not the two crooks, Grace and Bands, as in the former case; the savage scalpel and butcher-knife would be more appropriate.——"Lo, I will raise up a shepherd in the land," &c., reminds us that God is said to do what he providentially permits to be done. As a judgment on those utterly corrupt Jews, the Lord gave them shepherds of like moral corruption.——That the prophet should say "a shepherd," as if but one, when the sense is a whole class, an entire body of professedly religious teachers, is in accordance with his usage, as we have seen in the notes on v. 8.——The things which this bad shepherd will *not* do come first in order; "he will not visit the perishing; will not seek after the outcasts; will not heal the bruised; will not nourish the halting," who can scarcely walk, *i. e.*, he neglects precisely the very things which a good shepherd should by all means do.——On the other hand, with supreme selfishness, he gets all the good he can for himself. He eats the flesh of the fat ones, and even tears in pieces their hoofs, so eager is he to get the last thing of any value from the carcass.——In the clause "Woe to the *idol* shepherd," the Hebrew word rendered "*idol*" *admits* this sense, but does not *require* it, and therefore should not have it here, there being no allusion in the case to idolatry, and the more general sense of *useless*, *worthless*, *faithless*, being in point, and fully justified by usage.——The judgments on this worthless and wicked shepherd fall on those bodily organs most useful to the shepherd—the arm and the eye. The sense is, that God will utterly paralyze his power for such services, and will moreover send his judgments so in the line of his sins, that they will be a perpetual index and remembrancer of that for which he suffers. As the shepherd *would* not use his arm and his eye in the care of his flock, the Lord withers them utterly and forever. "To him that knoweth to do good, and doeth it not, to him it is sin" (Jam. 4:17). Wasted talents, powers for good unused, bring down from God the most terrible retribution.

CHAPTER XII.

This chapter manifestly opens a new subject. The first leading inquiry should respect its general scope and spirit, and the period of time to which it relates.——In chapter 11, the Jews of our Saviour's time reject him, their offered Messiah, and bring upon their city and nation an avalanche of ruin. Now the question may be supposed to arise, Is the kingdom of the Messiah therefore utterly broken down?——To this inquiry, chapters 12 and 13 reply —By no means. The Lord has yet a "Judah," and a "Jerusalem," and a "House of David:" he will redeem them from their external enemies (see 12 : 2–9); and what is yet more to the purpose, he will pour upon them a spirit of grace, supplication, and penitence, which shall make them in a far higher and nobler sense his people, and shall insure their glorious prosperity as his people and kingdom. ——The exposition of this portion of Zechariah involves the investigation and proof of several points:

I. *The scenes here predicted lie onward in the Christian age subsequent to those predicted in* chapter 11.

(1.) Because, in the absence of proof to the contrary, it should be assumed that our author advances in time. He has been thus advancing in his course of thought throughout chaps. 9, 10, and 11. Why not also yet further in chapter 12?——(2.) Because there is manifestly a close analogy between the order of subjects in the first six chapters (made up of a series of visions) on the one hand, and chaps. 7–14 (not such visions) on the other. As chaps. 1–4 promise good to Zion, so do chaps. 7–10. As chap. 5, on the other hand, predicts the sin and doom of the guilty, so does chap. 11; and then as chap. 6 : 1–8 returns again to God's loving care and protection of his people, and specifically as manifested against hostile nations, so does this chap. 12, and also chap. 14. As the last part of chap. 6 is eminently Messianic, predicting also the ultimate reception of the nations into his kingdom, so we find the same idea in these chapters 12–14, and especially in chap. 14.——(3.) Because manifestly we are in this chapter borne on beyond the date of chap. 9, for there the Lord was protecting his people against Alexander and his Syrian successors; here against "all nations" (vs. 2, 3, 9); and, moreover, here we have passed the crucifixion of Christ (which is essentially involved in chap. 11), for the people bewail their guilt in that act (see v. 10).——The location of these events *in time* must therefore be onward, after the advent of Messiah. So much may be considered as fixed. But other questions remain.

II. It is a question of no trifling importance whether the terms "Israel," "Judah," "Jerusalem," "the house of David," are to be taken here literally or figuratively. Is "Judah" in these chapters (12–14) the very Judah of Zechariah's time; are her people the lineal descendants of Abraham; and does the lineal Jew here, as then and there, represent and embody the earthly kingdom of God? Is

Jerusalem still, as of old, her capital, and the centre and throne of Messiah's kingdom? Do the Gentile hosts besiege her literally, as the Chaldeans had done so recently when Zechariah was writing?——I cannot think so, for these reasons: (1.) With the events predicted (chap. 11), the literal Judah and Jerusalem ceased to be the recognized visible Church and kingdom of God on earth. It is the precise purpose of chap. 11 to affirm this fact. Consequently, ever since the apostolic age, Church history has taken on a new type. No Church historian thinks of looking for the Christian Church in the Jewish line.——(2.) Whatever Old Testament prophecy is clearly shown to refer to the New Testament age must, by all legitimate rules of interpretation, be construed in accordance with New Testament light, with gospel ideas, with the new principles of Messiah's kingdom, then first fully brought out. Hence the Judah and Jerusalem of gospel prophecy, standing as types and symbols of Messiah's kingdom, must be construed, not literally, but figuratively—just as "the temple" is no longer, as of old, the one place of God's dwelling, and of all acceptable worship, but the Christian "temple" is the living pious heart.——(3.) That the Jews shall return again—not to their own land merely, but to *Judaism* restored after the order of Moses; that Jerusalem shall again become the living centre of all visible worship, and of all the true religion of the world—this worship conforming itself, as of old, to the Mosaic ritual; and that, as such, Judah shall be invaded and Jerusalem besieged by all the Gentile nations of the earth, according to the literal construction of chapters 12 and 14, are not things even supposable. If the New Testament is held to be of any account, Judaism, after the order of Moses, is dead, and those ideas must hence be rejected. For, practically, that state of things must ignore all the Christianity of the Gentile world—all the actual Christianity of the whole world as it now is, and as it has been since the death of Christ. Can any sane man believe that all the Gentile Christian churches are at some future period to be annihilated; the religious world be put back to its condition and relations as in the age of Zechariah; bloody sacrifices and passovers and feasts of tabernacles be restored, and Judah and Jerusalem stand as the sole representatives of the Church of God upon the earth? Or can it be believed that all the great nations of the present or of any future age shall gather in one vast crusade against the converted Christian Jews in their own land to besiege Jerusalem, and to exterminate all true religion from the face of the earth?——The literal construction of chapters 12-14 would hold us to such results: therefore the literal construction must be promptly rejected.——(4.) Nor let it be thought that we do violence to the laws of language when we reject the literal and adopt the figurative sense under such circumstances as these. Let the reader ask himself—How *should* a Jewish prophet, writing in the midst of Judaism, with no other history of the Church before him, and no other conception of the Church in his mind but that of Judaism, with no other first readers but Jews, write of the future

Church and kingdom of God in the gospel age? Shall we demand that he write of the Christian Church and of millennial times in New Testament words and phrases, and with fully-developed New Testament ideas? Let us remember that the time had not come for such ideas. Let us recall the striking fact that more than three years' personal communion with Jesus himself, and no small amount of his personal labor, quite failed to convert his disciples from Jewish to Christian ideas; that only the shock given to the old system by his death, aided by the subsequent teaching of the Holy Ghost, availed, and then rather slowly, to effect this great change. How absurd, then, to expect that the Hebrew prophets and their first readers could readily reach those new ideas and take in the sense of Christian as contrasted with Jewish phraseology!—— Plainly, those Jewish prophets and their first readers must think of Christianity only as of Judaism extended and purified; must conceive of a world converted only as a world coming up to Jerusalem to worship; and must conceive of irreligion, infidelity, every form of hostility to Christ, as the gathering of nations for war against Jerusalem and Judah, to crush them from the face of the earth.—— Hence when we speak of Jewish costume and drapery as clothing gospel ideas in these sublimely grand and glorious prophecies, we are not parting company with common sense. We are simply interpreting in harmony with the stern necessities of their condition. Jewish minds, with no other than Jewish training, *must* think so and speak so, by the inevitable laws of human thought.

III. Consequently, it is no longer a question whether, in these remaining prophecies of Zechariah (chap. 12–14), we are to find blessings for the Gentile world; even the extension of the gospel to all the nations of the earth. If these prophecies relate to times subsequent to the death of Christ, they *must* predict the prosperity of the Christian Church, the conversion of the world to Immanuel.——It might be a much more difficult question (were it needful to be settled) whether the lineal Jew is here, and if so, where and by what marks we shall identify him. If he were named here alongside of his brother Gentile, as Paul names them in Rom. 11, it would be easy to make this discrimination. But it is at least supposable that in the greater part of these three chapters there is no intention to discriminate between Jew and Gentile. If so, how can it be expected that a discreet interpreter should make any distinction? Interpreters should not be asked to *make* prophecy, nor to put into it what was not there before; but only to unfold the sense already there.——It may be well to remember also that the change wrought in the transition from Judaism to Christianity, fitly described as a "breaking down of the middle wall of partition between us" (Eph. 2:14), aimed not to thrust the Jew out, but to let the Gentile in; to abolish henceforth all distinction as to Christian rights and privileges, and make both one henceforth in Christ Jesus. Why, then, may not Old Testament prophecy assume precisely this state of the future kingdom of the Messiah?——The thoughtful reader can scarcely fail to appreciate the importance of these points, and if so, will not account this discussion unreasonably full or protracted.

Chapter 12 is naturally in two parts, of which the first (vs. 1–9) represents Judah as invaded and Jerusalem as besieged by the combined powers of all nations; but the Lord delivers them. The second part (vs. 10–14) represents the house of David and the people of Jerusalem as deeply penitent for their sins, especially the sin of crucifying their Messiah.——In my comments on this chapter, I propose first to explain the words and phrases so far as may seem necessary, and then to speak of its general scope and fulfilment as prophecy.

1. The burden of the word of the LORD for Israel, saith the LORD, which stretcheth forth the heavens, and layeth the foundation of the earth, and formeth the spirit of man within him.

This prophecy is a "*burden upon Israel*" only to a limited extent, for the assault of all nations upon her and the siege of Jerusalem were transient, ending soon in complete victory on Zion's side.——That help comes from the Lord alone, who is mighty to save, is indicated by the allusion to his great and glorious works of creation.

2. Behold, I will make Jerusalem a cup of trembling unto all the people round about, when they shall be in the siege both against Judah *and* against Jerusalem.

The phrase rendered "cup of trembling" is read by some, "threshold of shaking"—one upon which a violent assault should be made, but which should react in ruin upon the assailants. There seems, however, to be no good reason for rejecting the usual sense of the words "a cup of reeling, intoxication"—with reference to that very common conception of the wine-cup of the wrath of the Lord which maddens and infatuates nations doomed to ruin. (See Jer. 25 : 15–31, and notes on Nahum 1 : 10).——All the nations are thought of as gathered against Judah and Jerusalem. In the last clause the sense is, that what the Lord had said of Jerusalem should be true of Judah also in the siege of her capital.

3. And in that day will I make Jerusalem a burdensome stone for all people: all that burden themselves with it shall be cut in pieces, though all the people of the earth be gathered together against it.

The reference to a burdensome stone alludes to a custom among the Jewish young men of trying their strength at lifting a very heavy stone as high as possible, in which some were wont to get wounds and bruises. Such a stone, fully equal to one's utmost strength, and often beyond it, should Jerusalem be to the nations. The stone itself is not harmed by the lifting, but the lifters thereof were sure to be lacerated.

4. In that day, saith the LORD, I will smite every horse with astonishment, and his rider with madness: and I will open mine eyes upon the house of Judah, and will smite every horse of the people with blindness.

Remarkably, the Lord accounts *horses* to be a power hostile to Christ's kingdom. This appears throughout Zechariah, and aids us to the true conception of Messiah's riding on an ass (9 : 9). The warring enemies of God's people come on horses, this animal being associated with human pride and rebellion against God.——This astonishment and madness are among the effects of the cup of intoxication, given to God's enemies to drink.——Note the beautiful antithesis. God smites with blindness the warring powers of his foes, but opens his own eyes wide on his people to see their wants and to provide therefor.

5. And the governors of Judah shall say in their heart, The inhabitants of Jerusalem *shall be* my strength in the LORD of hosts their God.

6. In that day will I make the governors of Judah like a hearth of fire among the wood, and like a torch of fire in a sheaf; and they shall devour all the people round about, on the right hand and on the left: and Jerusalem shall be inhabited again in her own place, *even* in Jerusalem.

7. The LORD also shall save the tents of Judah first, that the glory of the house of David and the glory of the inhabitants of Jerusalem do not magnify *themselves* against Judah.

Without saying it openly, yet in their secret thought, the governors of Judah are relying for their own protection under God on the military strength of Jerusalem and the valor of her defenders. But the Lord will make Judah safe and mighty against her foreign foes, as a hearth of fire to its fuel, which itself burns not, but only facilitates the burning of the wood, or as a torch of fire to a sheaf, which consumes it with no danger to itself. So shall they devour the gathered nations who assail them.——And "Jerusalem, too, shall still sit on her throne in her own place," on her own foundations. The Lord saves Judah *first*, that he may forestall the pride of self-reliance on the strength and glory of the city. So vital to true religion is it to crucify all human glorying, to cherish the spirit of absolute dependence on the Lord alone, and to give him for evermore all the glory as the source of all spiritual life and of all power for good to Zion.

8. In that day shall the LORD defend the inhabitants of Jerusalem; and he that is feeble among them at that day shall be as David; and the house of David *shall be* as God, as the angel of the LORD before them.

The Lord defends Jerusalem, yet not without their own concurrent agency. The doctrine that God saves his people must not be abused to human inaction. He saves rather by augmenting and reanimating their strength than by superseding their agency. So here, the feeble shall be as David, who is the type of a most athletic warrior; and the men of David's cast and power shall be now as God, even as the angel of Jehovah—the uncreated one who had so often appeared in forms of majesty and power. This is a strong figure, and must represent a vast augmentation of spiritual force in the people of God.

9. And it shall come to pass in that day, *that* I will seek to destroy all the nations that come against Jerusalem.

Now the Lord sets himself earnestly to destroy all the nations that array themselves in hostile mood against his people and their sacred city.

10. And I will pour upon the house of David, and upon the inhabitants of Jerusalem, the spirit of grace and of supplications: and they shall look upon me whom they have pierced, and they shall mourn for him, as one mourneth for *his* only *son*, and shall be in bitterness for him, as one that is in bitterness for *his* first-born.

These terms are strongly in contrast with those in v. 9. God will seek to *pour out* vengeance and ruin on those hostile nations; but grace, mercy, and blessings on Jerusalem.——To "pour out" is to bestow in large and abundant measure. It is the usual phrase for the effusions of the Holy Spirit, as in Joel 2:28—"I will pour out my Spirit upon all flesh."——In this passage, "the Spirit" is the Holy Spirit of God, and not a quality or grace in man. It is thought of, however, as producing piety and prayer in the hearts of men, and hence is called "the Spirit of grace and of supplications"—meaning that Divine Spirit, whose special work it is to beget as to one's self a tender prayerful frame of mind, and as to others a loving compassion for the souls of men, and earnest prayer for their salvation. "*Grace*" in man stands for that which is specially pleasing to God, and which secures his favor. In the case of sinners, the first buddings of grace are penitence and prayer, a broken and contrite spirit, which inspires prayer both for our own pardon and for mercy on other sinners also. The close connection between the gift of this Spirit, begetting such grace and supplications, and the "looking upon him whom they have pierced," shuts us up to this sense of the passage—its leading thought being the conversion of sinners.——To "look on me whom they have pierced" can mean nothing else than thinking of their guilt in crucifying the Lord of glory. They now look upon the crucified One with bitter penitence and grief for the sin of piercing his heart, and with imploring cries for pardon through his own blood. This sin of piercing the Lord belongs not alone to that Roman soldier who drove the nails into his hands and his feet, nor to him alone whose spear opened his side, but obviously to all who participated then and there in his death, and indeed to that indefinitely greater mass who in all ages have had the same wicked heart as they had, and have abused, insulted, scorned, and rejected Jesus Christ in a spirit like theirs. All such have crucified the Son of God afresh, reënacting the very scenes of Calvary, and its very sins too!——But when, touched by the Spirit of God, they look on the crucified One as pierced by their own hands, and when they think of their own sins as the nails and the spear that gave him his bitterest pangs, and then take also into view the wonderful truth that, despite of such abuse from myself, that murdered Saviour loves me in his pity still, and offers me pardon as it were through the blood my own guilty hands have shed, O then the deep fountains of my grief burst open, and for once, if never before, it is a luxury to weep. Thousands have felt this bitterness of grief for their sins against the crucified One, made doubly keen by the sense of his enduring and forgiving love, despite of guilt so black and ingratitude so vile!——Such I take to be the thought of this passage.——This mourning for sin is as when one mourns over an only son, lost in death; its bitterness is as that over a first-born. Ask the real parent's heart for the depth of anguish in such mourning!

11. In that day there shall be a great mourning in Jerusalem, as the mourning of Hadadrimmon in the valley of Megiddon.

12. And the land shall mourn, every family apart; the family of the house of David apart, and their wives apart; the family of the house of Nathan apart, and their wives apart;

13. The family of the house of Levi apart, and their wives apart; the family of Shimei apart, and their wives apart;

14. All the families that remain, every family apart, and their wives apart.

This mourning for sin against the slain Messiah is not restricted to a few, but is widely extended; it is "a great mourning in Jerusalem," like that over the death of the good King Josiah, who fell in battle against Necho, king of Egypt, in the valley of Megiddon, the long-famed battle-ground of Esdraelon. See the history in 2

Chron. 35 : 23–25 and 2 Kings 23 : 29, 30.——Note here that this mourning for sin is not merely a public thing: public mournings are sometimes a pageant only, with more of display than of heartfelt grief. This is so much a personal matter, lying between each individual soul and his Saviour, that each one is drawn to weep and mourn apart and alone. Every instinct leads the mourner to seek solitude, and to pour out his whole heart there, under no other eye than God's! Who has not felt this impulse toward silent, secret mourning, under such mingled shame and grief, coupled with the conviction that your whole concern is now with that crucified One whose heart you have pierced, and whose possible mercy is now your only hope?——The mode of presenting this thought is by Jewish terms and historic allusions. The house of David and the house of Nathan, one of his sons, in the royal line; then the house of Levi and the house of Shimei, one of his sons, representing the priesthood;—these stand for the whole people, and show that they all mourn apart, and their wives apart.——The first verse of the next chapter belongs with this, showing that such penitence and prayer bring pardon full and free. "In that day a fountain is opened for sin and for uncleanness" "to the house of David and to the inhabitants of Jerusalem"—the same on whom (12 : 10) the spirit of grace and of supplication is poured out. In that blood which their own guilty hands have shed, is pardon found for all the truly penitent.

That this chapter must relate to events subsequent to the death of Christ—that it concerns the Christian Church and the gospel age, and therefore must be interpreted according to New Testament ideas—has been already said, and I trust adequately shown. It still remains to inquire whether its fulfilment can be located yet more definitely, and if so, *where;* and whether now past or yet future.——It may be proper for me to say that during several years past, and until this present reinvestigation, I have been inclined to locate the fulfilment of this portion of Zechariah, chapters 12–14, yet in the future—near or in the millennial age. I must now modify this opinion so far at least as to suggest the strong probability that this chap. 12, looks primarily to a series of events that occurred within the first three centuries of the Christian era. My reasons for this view fall under two different heads: (1). The consecutive order of Zechariah's prophecies throughout chapters 9–11, which, unless some reason appear to the contrary, should continue also through chap. 12. Thus in chap. 9 : 1–8, we have the conquering sweep of Alexander's armies, over Persia, Syria, Tyre, and Philistia, while God protected Judah—all in the fourth century before Christ; then, in 9 : 11–17 and 10 : 1–5, the wars of the Syrians in the age of the Maccabees, in the second century before Christ; then in chap. 11, the very events of Christ's personal ministry, his being rejected by the Jews, and their consequent destruction by the Romans—all in the period A. D. 1–70. This regular order of time suggests with very considerable force whether chap. 12 does not continue on with no great chasm into the Christian age.——(2.) But a second reason, certainly worthy of consideration, is that, adopting the principles of interpretation already presented, we find great events to which these prophetic descriptions very accurately correspond. Thus in 12 : 1–9, the leading idea is that of *persecution*, a fierce and bloody onslaught upon the Church of God. A Jewish prophet could not depict an era of persecution in any other form so definite and decisive as this. Judah invaded, Jerusalem besieged and assailed by heathen nations; this *in the Christian age* can be nothing else but violent persecution.——And who does not know that the history of the Church during the first three centuries is largely the *history of persecutions?* The Church is bitterly and cruelly assailed; but she is like "the bush that burned with fire, yet was not consumed," or in this prophet's own figures, not less pertinent, she is a cup of reeling to all that besiege her; a burdensome stone they cannot lift, however much they essay it, and can by no means harm, but are only themselves harmed thereby; or yet more fitly, she is a hearth of fire, and her enemies the burning fuel; or a torch, and they the sheaf that readily takes fire and is consumed.——So the Church stood the shock of persecution unshaken; bore its fires unscathed; became only the more pure, grew only with the more rapid growth; while on her enemies the wrath of the Lord came down to their uttermost destruction.——Must we not account this series of historic events as fully answering to the drift of these prophetic representations? Taking this natural harmony between the historic facts and the prophetic portrayals, in connection with the probable continued consecution of the prophetic steps along the track of time, is there not at least a very high degree of probability that this is the true interpretation of Zech. 12 : 1–9?

We come next to the closing portion 12 : 10–14 and 13 : 1. Here it should be borne in mind that chap. 11 has virtually assumed the rejection of Messiah by his covenant people and his consequent crucifixion. It is hence but fit that the Lord, through his prophet, should meet the natural inquiry— *What was the result of his violent death?* Did it utterly crush the young germ of the shoot and scion of David? Did it wither the hopes of the world, and the raised expectations of the hierarchies of heaven? Did it ring the death-knell of Zion's promised future glory?——Not at all; nothing of the sort. Indeed, that very death on the cross unsealed the fountains of spiritual power; brought down the glorious effusions of the Spirit of God; made the hearts of even his murderers like water in the tenderness of their contrition and the outflow of their sorrows, and drew the hearts of millions, with a power of attraction never known on earth before, into loving gratitude and all-consuming zeal and labor for the risen Redeemer of men. Is not such the plain teaching of this most wonderful passage?——We scarcely need, therefore, to ask more particularly *when* it was fulfilled. Its fulfilment began, we may say, on the day of Pentecost when God first "poured out the Spirit of grace and of supplications," and when three thousand men "were pricked in their heart" in view of this very fact that they had taken Him of Nazareth, and by wicked hands had crucified and slain him. Its fulfilment continued on through that glorious age of gospel triumphs. It continues still wherever the sense of Christ crucified goes deep to the heart, and, under the Spirit's light, men feel that they have themselves been his betrayers and murderers.——The fountain opened for the penitent people of the house of David is only the great fact of the gospel age, the way of pardon revealed and brought out fully to glorious light through the atonement of the crucified Son of God.——It need not be assumed that these prophecies are exhausted in those events to which they primarily refer. Their truths are for all time, and their fulfilment in this sense cannot be exhausted until the gospel shall cease to be "the power of God unto salvation to every one that believeth." So long, the agencies of outward violent persecution shall never crush the true Church, but only serve to purify her the more; so long, a Saviour crucified shall be the power of God, through the Holy Ghost, unto penitence, and prayer, and pardon, and a new and holy life unto God and the Lamb.

If any objection can be plausibly urged against the explanation above given of this chapter 12, *as already fulfilled prophecy*, it will be on the ground that vs. 10–14 are thus put, in time, *before* vs. 1–9; whereas, according to their order of sequence, they should come *after*.——My answer is twofold: (1.) Claiming a large abatement from the facts as stated in the objection. (2.) Accounting for the relative location of the two passages on other grounds than the order of time.——(1.) The objection assumes that *as to time*, the passage (vs. 10–14) looks to the death of Christ and to the immediate effects of that death upon its authors.——I answer: Such limitation *as to its effects* is by no means necessary or natural. And the *moral effects* of that death, not the death itself as an historic event, are here the subject of remark. These moral effects are thought of as characterizing the gospel dispensation—specially prominent indeed in its opening era, but characteristic of it throughout. V. 10 is not connected with what precedes it as an event that closely follows in time. The Hebrew language would naturally indicate such a connection by the future with *vav* conversive. But here the connective particle might as well be rendered "*but*," indicating an event of an opposite antithetic character.——And the thought that follows is obviously antithetic to what precedes. This relation of the two thoughts determined the location of the latter passage. I will seek to pour out judgments unto their destruction on the nations that come against Jerusalem; but the grace of my Spirit unto salvation on Jerusalem herself. This is manifestly the law of thought that suggested the passage, v. 10–14. That is, vs. 1–9 give the judgments of God against the sworn, violent enemies of his Church; vs. 10–14 the blessings that come through the death of Christ, and the mission of his Spirit upon the Church and people.

CHAPTER XIII.

The first verse, as already intimated, belongs very properly to the previous chapter, since it stands in the closest relations of thought with the penitence of the people for their sins against the Lord Jesus.——The next point made is the *purifying* of the people from their sins, as shown by specifying two most besetting sins of the ancient Hebrews, idolatry and false prophesying, both of which are thoroughly removed from the land (vs. 2–6). Then, by association of ideas, the crucified Messiah is brought to view (v. 7); finally, the ungodly portion are cut off, only one-third part remaining, but these are purified by stern discipline, and come to know Jehovah as their God (vs. 8, 9).

1. In that day there shall be a fountain opened to the house of David and to the inhabitants of Jerusalem for sin and for uncleanness.

2. And it shall come to pass in that day, saith the Lord of hosts, *that* I will cut off the names of the idols out of the land, and they shall no more be remembered: and also I will cause the prophets and the unclean spirit to pass out of the land.

The manner of Zechariah is to affirm a general truth by affirming certain individual facts which are left to imply it. So here, to show that the land is purified from its great sins, he makes no general statements, but simply individualizes two of the prominent and most dangerous sins of the covenant people—idolatry and false prophecy—and represents them to be effectually exterminated.——"Cutting off the very names of idols, so that they should be no more remembered," implies that idolatry is thoroughly expelled from the land. (See Hos. 2:17 and 14:8 and Mic. 5:12–14.)——The "prophets" named here in connection with idols before and "the unclean spirit" after, must be *false* prophets, called prophets only because they falsely and foully assumed this name. The Lord will drive them out of the land, forcibly expel them.——The reference to an "unclean spirit" recognizes Satanic agency.

3. And it shall come to pass, *that* when any shall yet prophesy, that his father and his mother that begat him shall say unto him, Thou shalt not live; for thou speakest lies in the name of the Lord: and his father and his mother that begat him thall thrust him through when he prophesieth.

A supposed case is made: If any one shall yet attempt to prophesy falsely, his own father and mother shall be so zealous for God and for truth that they shall solemnly declare unto him, "Thou shalt not live;" and, moreover, they shall not merely threaten; they shall even thrust him through in his very act of prophesying.—— To make the case stand out the more strongly, stress is laid upon the parental relation: his father that begat and his mother that bare him will not shrink from taking his life. This would be according to the Mosaic law. See the passages, very strong and explicit: Deut. 13:6–10 and 18:20.

4. And it shall come to pass in that day, *that* the prophets shall be ashamed every one of his vision, when he hath prophesied; neither shall they wear a rough garment to deceive:

Public sentiment gives no countenance to the abominable sin of pretending to be the Lord's prophet. Hence, all men of this class should be ashamed of their former pretended visions.——The "rough garment" was one used by mourners, and worn by false prophets to make the people think they were bearing the sins of the nation sorrowfully on their hearts—somewhat in imitation of the true prophets of the Lord.

5. But he shall say, I *am* no prophet, I *am* an husbandman; for man taught me to keep cattle from my youth.

6. And *one* shall say unto him, What *are* these wounds in thy hands? Then he shall answer, *Those* with which I was wounded *in* the house of my friends.

"But one shall say" (a supposed case), "I am an husbandman, for a man sold me from my youth," *i. e.*, as a servant. This is the precise sense of the original, which says nothing specially about "keeping cattle." He means to show that his position in life has been such as should remove all suspicion of his playing the false prophet. He has been held as a servant all his days.——But there are palpable marks on his person that convict him of lying even now; hence, one replies to him—What mean those gashes on your hands? He can only confess the truth: "They were inflicted by my associates according to the custom of idol worshippers, in their temples."——The word rendered "friends" means properly lovers; but is used in the bad sense, and here of his fellow idolaters involved like himself in this harlotry to which the word "lovers" refers.—— Jewish as well as profane history shows clearly that cutting the flesh was common in idol worship. (See 1 Kings 18; Jer. 16:6 and 41:5; Deut. 14:1.) The common idea of penance may be supposed to lie at the bottom of such practices; a consciousness of guilt; the demands of remorse; coupled with the notion that the gods will exact some suffering for such sins, and hence each man had best inflict it upon himself, rather than leave it for the gods to inflict.

7. Awake, O sword, against my shepherd, and against the man *that is* my fellow, saith the LORD of hosts: smite the shepherd, and the sheep shall be scattered; and I will turn mine hand upon the little ones.

This verse refers to the death of Christ by violent hands, and its results as to the flock of which he was the shepherd. An active imagination gives life and will to the *sword*, considered as the instrument in a violent death, and the Lord of hosts commands—"Awake" (as if it had been asleep, at rest), "awake against my shepherd" (the Messiah), described here as being "the man that is my nearest friend"—for such is the sense of the word rendered "my fellow." This word occurs elsewhere only in the Pentateuch, and there in such passages as Lev. 6: 2, and 19: 11, 15, 17, and 25: 15, &c., "Ye shall not lie nor deceive each man his near friend," &c. "If a man lie unto his *neighbor* in that which was delivered him to keep, or hath deceived his neighbor," &c. This usage shows that the word is used for the nearest human relationship, not involving consanguinity. It, therefore, well expresses the relation between the Father and the Son, when he is thought of as incarnate—in his human nature. This human nature of Jesus stood in this close relation to the Father.——The bold metaphor, "Awake, O sword," &c., has its analogy in Jer. 47: 6, 7: "O thou sword of the Lord, how long ere thou wilt be quiet? Put up thyself into thy scabbard; rest and be still."——"How can it be quiet, seeing the Lord hath given it a charge against Ashkelon and against the sea shore? There hath he appointed it."——This sword of the Lord is the Lord's executioner. So in our passage the Lord of hosts commands the sword to its work, remarkably recognizing the divine agency in the atoning death of the Lamb of God. Our Saviour intimated the same agency when he said to Pilate (John 19: 11), "Thou couldest have no power against me except it were given thee from above."——The Lord Jehovah had most important ends to accomplish in his kingdom by this violent death of "the Lamb of God who was to take away the sin of the world," and therefore suffered him to fall into the hands of wicked men, and suffered those wicked hands to take his life. What God suffers to be done, he is sometimes said to do.——The consequences to the flock are depicted: "Smite the shepherd, and the sheep shall be scattered"—the natural result when their protector and guide falls. So in chap. 11: 6, 9–14, where the good shepherd is practically rejected by his flock, and where a tacit allusion to his dishonored death is implied (vs. 12, 13), the consequences are the utter ruin of the corrupt and guilty portion of the covenant people. Those Jews who murdered the Son of God and repented not of their deeds, brought down on their city and their entire nationality a fearful doom.——But the Lord turns back his hand to spare and save his little ones. (The same use of this verb, "turn back," may be seen Isa. 1: 25.) The same hand that was stretched out to destroy the guilty, reversing its action, turned itself back to protect and bless "the poor of the flock that waited on me," as they are described, chap. 11: 11. A few of the Jewish people received Jesus as their Messiah, became his disciples while he lived or converts to his faith after his death, and these became objects of his special care and love.——It remains to consider the connection of this verse with the one immediately preceding. I think this connection falls under the law of association of ideas. The close analogy between the false prophet, whose hands had been gashed and pierced "in the house of his friends," and the Messiah, whose hands were pierced in a death by crucifixion among those who ought to have been his friends, suggested the latter case, and led the prophet to speak of it here. This accounts for its coming in here *out of place* in the sense of being both aside from the general course of thought in this chapter, and out of its chronological order—his violent death having been assumed in chap. 11, and certainly thought of as already past in 12: 10 and 13: 1. This renewed allusion to it is therefore due to the power of this law of suggestion.——In this explanation, it is assumed that in speaking to men, the Spirit of inspiration not only uses human language, but follows human laws of thought in determining the succession of ideas. We may be quite unable to make up a full and perfect answer to the question, *What is* inspiration? but it stands out undeniably on the face of these inspired writings that inspiration does *not* supersede nor override the laws of mental association by which one thought suggests another analogous one.

8. And it shall come to pass, *that* in all the land, saith the LORD, two parts therein shall be cut off *and* die; but the third shall be left therein.

9. And I will bring the third part through the fire, and will refine them as silver is refined, and will try them as gold is tried: they shall call on my name, and I will hear them; I will say, It *is* my people; and they shall say, The LORD *is* my God.

The primary sense of these verses is clear. Over all the land, two parts out of three are cut off and die; the third part remaining, is purified through the fires of earthly discipline. These become far more fully than before the people of the living God.——But while the rendering of these words is plain, and their current usage well established, the question of their application and fulfilment as prophecy is by no means so obvious.——It has been common for interpreters to assume the closest possible connection between these verses and v. 7, and hence to apply them to the case of the lineal Jews immediately subsequent to the crucifixion of Christ, when, as they would say, the greater part—two-thirds—of the people were cut off violently by the Roman arms; the remaining third purified and brought into the Christian Church.——This may *possibly* be the correct view; but there are serious objections to it: (1.) The facts of history do not verify it; the proportion cut off being much more than two parts out of three, and the saved being less than one in three.——(2.) The saved are here thought of as being the entire visible Church of God. But in fact, the Church in the apostolic age was far more of Gentiles than of Jews. (3.) This construction is out of the chronological order which runs not only through chapters 9–11, but also through chapters 12 and 13, up to the digression which takes us back for a moment to the crucifixion in 13: 7.——Chapter 12: 1–9 gives us the Christian Church passing through its first three centures, a period of persecution. Chapter 12: 10 to 13: 1 gives the effect of Messiah's death as through the Holy Ghost a power unto penitence, prayer, and pardon. Chap. 13: 2–6, the great advance made in the Christian Church in real piety, presented by means of Jewish historic allusions, but manifestly meaning that the people of God are, through divine mercy, redeemed from reigning sin, and brought into a far higher state of Christian life than the covenant people had reached during the ages before Christ.——Thus far, then, the reader will notice a somewhat regular chronological order, a progress onward in time in the course of thought. It is reversing this course to go back in this passage (13: 8, 9) to the date of chap. 11. It quite breaks out of the line of historic events in which we were moving in the passage 13: 2–6.——I therefore suggest another construction, viz.: that vs. 8, 9 lie in the same line of thought with vs. 2–6, and looking to a somewhat later period in the Christian age, give us *the corruptions of Christianity*, and indicate that God will sever those corrupt portions, prior to the millennial age.——It is obvious that chap. 14 gives us first the opening scenes and then the full consummation of millennial purity and glory. If we give due heed to the chronological succession of prophetic events in this prophet through chapters 9 to 13: 6, and allow for continued progress on the same grade of advance, we shall find ourselves drawing nigh the millennial age in the closing verses of chap. 13.——It has been already suggested that the main reason for applying vs. 8 and 9 to the lineal Jews at the point where they took sides for Christ or against him in the latter half of the first century, is the assumption that they stand closely connected with v. 7. This class of interpreters would paraphrase thus: "Smite the shepherd, then shall the ancient covenant people be scattered and broken up; two parts of them shall reject Jesus Christ and perish miserably under the Roman arms; the remaining third part shall become the beloved and sanctified people of God."——But instead of this, the connection may be quite different, thus: The manifestation of Jesus Christ in the flesh served to reveal the utter rottenness of the visible Jewish church. When the shepherd was smitten, the mass of that church went to ruin; only a few of the little ones were saved. So, in the advanced ages of the Christian Church, corruption became again fearfully prevalent, and another great sifting process became indispensable before the era of the final conquest and triumph of Christ's kingdom could open. That is, as v. 7 came in under the influence of association of ideas, so it goes out and v. 8 comes in, under the same general law of analogy—v. 7 standing alone as a diversion from the current strain of chronological thought. The analogy between the corrupt Judaism of the Saviour's day on the one hand, and the corrupt Christianity of the mediæval Christian age, onward indeed to the present day, is the law of connection between v. 7 and v. 8.——In support of this view, let it be noted that the prophet does *not* put the eighth verse in close connection *as to time* with verse 7. He does not say, "*in that day*, two parts therein shall be cut off," &c. Let the reader notice how constantly he has used this phrase wherever he meant this thing, as *e. g.*, in 12: 3, 4, 6, 8, 9, 11, and 13: 1, 2, 4—nine times within this and the previous chapters. Hence its omission here should at least suggest a grave doubt whether he could have located these events (vs. 8 and 9) "*in the same day*" with those of v. 7. If he did, why did he not say so?——Yet further, our translators manifestly leaned strongly toward the application of these verses to the Jews exclusively, and therefore rendered "in all the *land;*" but Zechariah wrote it, "in all the *earth.*"* This Hebrew phrase is used more than fifty times (I count fifty-nine) in the sense of *all the earth.* I find but three cases of its use for Judea only, and in these the connection furnishes the limitation. This same phrase is used by our prophet in 14: 9: "And the Lord shall be king *over all the earth;* in that day shall there be one Lord, and his name one."——This usage ought (it would seem) to be accounted decisive proof that Zechariah in vs. 8, 9 speaks of Christianity as a whole all over the world, and not of Judaism in Palestine only.

Such, in brief, are the reasons which compel me to differ widely from the current interpretation of these verses. I am constrained to apply them to the gigantic corruptions of the nominally Christian Church, especially the Roman and the Greek, and not altogether excepting some of those that have been once ostensibly *reformed.* Let it be asked, What does the "American and Foreign Christian Union" find to do? Or let us ask, How large a portion of nominal Christendom to-day comes up to the standard of these words: "They shall call on my name and I will hear them; I will say, It is my people, and they shall say, The Lord is my God"? Who can doubt that the fires of discipline and of judgment must pass over the nominally Christian world, sifting out the precious from the vile, and consuming whatever proves to be only dross?——How large a part of this work shall be wrought by the moral and spiritual agencies of truth, purifying and converting; and how much by the stern agencies of consuming fire, time only can fully show. This language looks toward the latter. Let the people of God press their gospel work to the utmost while they may!

* בְּכָל־הָאָרֶץ

CHAPTER XIV.

The principles of interpretation which should rule in this chapter have been fully discussed and brought out in my remarks introductory to chapter 12. The events which it portrays are all yet in the future. Consequently there is no occasion to try to locate them in history, or to define their *precise* historic character. Their general significance and results may be inferred with reasonable certainty.——The entire costume is Jewish, as we ought to expect. Jerusalem is invested by the combined forces of all nations; the city taken and sacked; half its people go into captivity (vs. 1, 2). The Lord comes forth to fight against those nations (v. 3); he stands on the mount of Olives and cleaves it in twain for his people to pass through (v. 4); they flee, but ultimately the Lord and his holy ones appear for their salvation (v. 5); a most peculiar twilight period follows, breaking forth near evening into the effulgence of full day (vs. 6. 7); living waters flow from Jerusalem perpetually (v. 8); Jehovah alone is King over all the earth (v. 9); the whole world becomes a plain, and the temple-mountain stands alone the only mountain (v. 10); the plague that comes on those who fought against Jerusalem (v. 12)—panic and mutual slaughter consume them (v. 13); Judah aids Jerusalem in this great conflict against their common foes (v. 14); God's judgments reach all the domestic animals used by their enemies, as well as their owners (v. 15); all the surviving people of the world shall go up to Jerusalem to worship (v. 16); the plague on those who will not go up (v. 17), and especially on Egypt (vs. 18, 19); holiness to the Lord in all inanimate things, universal and final (vs. 20, 21).

1. Behold, the day of the Lord cometh, and thy spoil shall be divided in the midst of thee.

"Behold," calls special attention to what follows, as of the deepest interest and greatest importance.——Remarkably, the usual form, "day of the Lord," is materially changed here. It is—"a day comes *for* the Lord"—one day preëminently *for him*, in which he will fully vindicate his name as the God of Zion, his power as one mighty to save, and his faithfulness as one who, having long ago promised, comes forth now in the fulness of time to perform. The other form—simply day of the Lord *—occurs in Joel 1:15 and 2 : 1, 11, 31, and 3 : 14; Amos 5 : 18, 20; Zeph. 1 : 14, and elsewhere; but this is unique and peculiar,† occurring, however, substantially in Jer. 51 : 6, "Flee out of the midst of Babylon; be not cut off in her iniquity; for it is a time of vengeance *for* the Lord." Also in Isa. 2 : 12.——"Thy spoil shall be divided in the midst of thee," is of course said of Jerusalem, and implies that she

* יוֹם יְהֹוָה

† יוֹם בָּא לַיהֹוָה

is in the power of her enemies; "for no man can enter into a strong man's house and spoil his goods, except he first bind the strong man; then shall he spoil his goods."——Sad eclipse must this be for the Church of God, represented as analogous to that of the Jews when the proud Chaldean spoiled her city and temple.

2. For I will gather all nations against Jerusalem to battle; and the city shall be taken, and the houses rifled, and the women ravished; and half of the city shall go forth into captivity, and the residue of the people shall not be cut off from the city.

This verse gives somewhat the details of the case, to show how it comes to pass that the spoil of the city is divided among its captors within her very walls. The Lord, by his providential agencies, brings all the nations up against Jerusalem to battle. In this one prominent feature, this prophecy harmonizes with Ezek. 38 and 39, and with Rev. 20:8, 9.——The city is taken; the horrible scenes usually consequent on such a capture ensue. Finally, half the people go into captivity; the other half remain in the city.——We do not hear from these captives again. They meet the doom of the wicked, and doubtless represent the corrupt and not truly pious portion of the people.——This cleansing of the nominal Church by which one-half is sloughed off, taken in connection with the similar operation predicted (chap. 13 : 8, 9), which cut off two parts out of three, gives us a strong view of the fearful corruption of the Church, and of the amount of winnowing and separation requisite before her great victories over the wide world can be achieved. Like the host of Gideon, her host is to be reduced to the faithful few.

3. Then shall the LORD go forth, and fight against those nations, as when he fought in the day of battle.

"Then shall the Lord *go forth*"—this Hebrew verb being the common one for "going out" to war and battle, *e. g.*, Hab. 3; 13, and Isa. 26 : 21, which latter passage, like the one before us, assumes that the Lord has been at rest, waiting for the fit hour, and now comes forth for special displays of his power against his foes.——"As when he fought in the day of battle," suggests the inquiry, What special day, if any, is referred to. The original repeats the word "day" thus: "as in the day of his fighting in the day of battle." Very probably the prophet alludes to the overthrow of Pharaoh's host in the Red Sea. That conflict stood preëminent above all others yet, and should the more surely be assumed as present in thought here because the parting asunder of the Mount of Olives, as in the next verse, is a tacit allusion to that parting of the Red Sea for a similar purpose, viz., the escape of his people from their pursuing foes.

4. And his feet shall stand in that day upon the mount of Olives, which *is* before Jerusalem on the east, and the mount of Olives shall cleave in the midst thereof toward the east and toward the west, *and there shall be* a very great valley; and half of the mountain shall remove toward the north, and half of it toward the south.

The commander of a vast army takes some elevated position which overlooks the battle-field. So Jehovah takes his stand on the Mount of Olives, which overlooked the city on the east, affording the best commanding view of the city. To give the greater vividness to the scene as a reality, it is said "his feet shall stand there."——The mountain cleaves asunder in the middle, half removing northward and half southward, leaving a wide valley. There can be no doubt of a tacit historical allusion here to the very similar cleaving of the Red Sea for his people to escape from Pharaoh's pursuing host. That was done literally; this, being an historical allusion, means only that a deliverance is now effected *like that*, equally glorious to the power that saved his people, equally effective for their salvation. The analogy will be yet more complete if we may suppose, with Hengstenberg, that the mountain is cleft by an earthquake, which, while it opened the mountain for their easy escape, swallowed up their enemies. As the text does not affirm this, however, it must stand as mere conjecture.——This earthquake alarmed the retreating host and hastened their flight—of which fear and flight the next verse speaks.

5. And ye shall flee *to* the valley of the mountains; for the valley of the mountains shall reach unto Azal: yea, ye shall flee, like as ye fled from before the earthquake in the days of Uzziah king of Judah: and the LORD my God shall come, *and* all the saints with thee.

"And ye flee along the valley of my mountains"—called here the Lord's, because he had cleft and prepared them for his people to pass along the valley between them—"for this valley of the mountains shall reach to Azal"—a city lying east of the Mount of Olives, its name signifying that it is a suitable place for halting in safety.——This earthquake in the days of Uzziah is not noticed in the historical books, but is probably alluded to by Amos (1:1). That, like this, was a time of panic and of earnest flight from the city to the mountains for safety.——"Now there comes the Lord my God, and all the saints with thee." With this the scene changes; Immanuel appears in preëminent splendor, and all the holy in his train. The nearest parallel to this scene as respects his retinue is Deut. 33:2, where Moses said: "The Lord came from Sinai; he shined forth from Mount Paran, and he came with ten thousands of saints," &c. The prophet speaks of this scene as it appeared to him in prophetic vision. The scene was peculiarly and preëminently impressive. He had a vivid sense of Immanuel, "the captain of the Lord's host," *as his own God*, and the God of his own people, and therefore says, "There comes the Lord *my God!*"

The next striking feature he puts in the form of an address to Immanuel: "All the holy ones are with thee."——The great aim of this revelation is to impress the prophet, and through his words all the people of God in every age, with this great truth, that Jesus Immanuel is the Almighty Saviour of his people, and that he employs angelic spiritual beings as his agents in the ministrations of his mediatorial reign, both in the care of his people and in his judgments on the wicked. Hence these agents sometimes appear in the visions of prophecy. Isaiah "saw the Lord sitting upon a throne, high and lifted up, and above him were the seraphim." The same thing was symbolized when (2 Kings 6 : 17) Elisha prayed in behalf of his young servant: "Lord, I pray thee open his eyes, that he may see. And the Lord opened the eyes of the young man, and he saw, and behold, the mountain was full of horses and chariots of fire round about Elisha."——This was only bringing before the prophet's mental eye the actual verities of things—those agencies, full of power, though usually invisible to mortals, by which Jesus Christ administers the providential government of this world. In this view of the passage, the saints (literally the holy ones) are especially the angels, who are all ministering spirits sent of God, either to minister blessings to the heirs of salvation, or judgments on the heirs of perdition.——Some interpreters suppose they find in this passage the visible personal advent of Christ with his risen saints—the pious dead—to reign in this world, in what must be essentially a "kingdom of this world." I find in it no such thing. There is nothing in the language of this verse that demands such a construction, and nothing in the subsequent scenes of the chapter at all suggestive of an order of things so very peculiar, and so entirely unlike what prophecy currently sets forth as the era of the triumphs of gospel truth and love upon earth.

6. And it shall come to pass in that day, *that* the light shall not be clear, *nor* dark:

7. But it shall be one day which shall be known to the Lord, not day, nor night: but it shall come to pass, *that* at evening time it shall be light.

The sixth verse requires a more careful and accurate translation, thus: "And it shall be on that day, there shall be no light; the sources of splendor" (the luminaries of heaven) "shall be shut up, and it shall be one day" (unique and unlike all other days), "known to the Lord" (only); "not day and not night: but it shall come to pass that at evening time it shall be light."——There seems to be a gradation here through three distinct stages: first, utter darkness; then, a dim twilight, like that of an eclipse; then, at the close of the day, when you might expect darkness soon to cover the earth, lo, the effulgence of full and glorious day!——This must be taken as an epitome of the state of the Church, as seen by the prophet somewhere in the then distant future. How long this period, here called "a day," shall be, we have no means of knowing, nor can we know yet the peculiar circumstances which constitute the darkness of its morning, the dim twilight of its mid-day, and the glorious effulgence of its close; which, indeed, instead of being its close, seems rather to be the opening of a long and ineffably glorious day!——It must suffice us that we may learn from such prophecies that the Lord knoweth his thoughts of mercy toward our sinful world, and that he has great and glorious blessings yet to bring forth from the infinite stores of his love!——The prophet proceeds to give us yet further illustrations of the better day that shall follow this darkness and dimness.

8. And it shall be in that day, *that* living waters shall go out from Jerusalem; half of them toward the former sea, and half of them toward the hinder sea: in summer and in winter shall it be.

As we have seen in the notes on Joel 3:18 ("a fountain shall come forth of the house of the Lord, and shall water the valley of Shittim"), water is a natural symbol of God's spiritual blessings, especially those in which the agencies of the Holy Spirit are prominent. Indeed, water is the special symbol of this divine Spirit, as may be seen in the explanatory clauses of Ezek. 36:25, 27, and of Isaiah 44:3. The latter reads, "I will pour water on him that is thirsty"—shown to mean, "I will pour my Spirit upon thy seed, and my blessing upon thy offspring." Ezekiel has it, "Then will I sprinkle clean water upon you, and ye shall be clean," &c.—shown to mean, "I will put my Spirit within you, and cause you to walk in my statutes," &c. Moreover, the very terms which express the manner of giving the Spirit indicate this: "I will *pour* my Spirit upon you," &c.——Strikingly parallel to this passage of Zechariah is Ezek. 47:1–12. There the water flows from under the sanctuary, here from Jerusalem; there in one widening, deepening stream, till it becomes a mighty river, and sweeping through the desert eastward, pours itself into the Dead Sea and heals its waters; here one-half flows into the front sea, which is, of course, the Dead Sea, and the other half into the Mediterranean on the west. That of Ezekiel carries on its bosom health, abundance, undying verdure, and is of course to be considered perennial; this flows during the arid summer as well as the rainy winter, which amounts to saying that it flows all the year, and year after year, never failing.——Now, as Palestine would be rendered almost an earthly Paradise by such living streams as Zechariah and Ezekiel have described, *if they were to be miraculously created by the finger of God*, and become literal verities, so we must take these figures as predictions of blessings of the richest, most abundant, and most enduring kind possible for God to bestow on human souls.——That Zechariah's stream of water flows from Jerusalem and Ezekiel's "from under the sanctuary" indicate plainly that the Spirit of God will yet continue, as ever, to make the institutions of the gospel—the service and worship of the sanctuary—the vehicles and the channels through which he will pour abroad the fulness of his blessings upon men.

9. And the Lord shall be king over all the earth: in that day shall there be one Lord, and his name one.

The precious fact predicted here is that the Lord Jehovah reigns supreme over all the earth, and *is recognized everywhere as the only true God.* The sense is not precisely this—that now and henceforth there shall *really be* but one God, as if to imply that in former times there had been more true Gods than one; but this—that now he is known, acknowledged, honored, obeyed, as the one only God. The very names of other gods are forgotten. No other name than his is recognized as a name for God. Now, therefore, "the kingdoms of this world have become the kingdoms of our Lord, and of his Christ, and he shall reign forever." Now, at length, the long-offered prayer, the burden of pious hearts age after age, is fulfilled: "*Thy kingdom come;* thy will be done on earth as it is in heaven." That good promise by the mouth and pen of David (Ps. 22:27, 28), has now come to pass: "All the ends of the earth shall remember, and turn unto the Lord, all the kindreds of the nations shall worship before thee; for the kingdom is the Lord's, and he is Governor among the nations."

10. All the land shall be turned as a plain from Geba to Rimmon, south of Jerusalem: and it shall be lifted up, and inhabited in her place, from Benjamin's gate unto the place of the first gate, unto the corner gate, and *from* the tower of Hananeel unto the king's winepresses.

"All the land" should read, as it clearly means, *all the earth*, being precisely the same words rendered "all the earth" in the previous verse: "The Lord shall be king over all the earth." "Turned" means *changed*, in its physical conformation, from a mountainous to a plain, level country. The sense is not that all the land from Geba to Rimmon—so much, and no more—shall become *a plain*, but this: that all the earth shall become a plain similar to that from Geba to Rimmon. The Hebrew reads, "All the earth shall be changed and become like to *the* plain from Geba to Rimmon," &c., not *a* plain. "South of Jerusalem" is added to Rimmon to distinguish it from another, known as "the rock Rimmon." (See Judges 20:45, 47, and 21:13.) Geba was on the northern border of Judah (2 Kings 23:8), and Rimmon on the southern (1 Chron. 4:32). ——"*It* shall be lifted up" means that Jerusalem shall rise in lofty, towering grandeur, the only mountain in all the world, and, of course, the chief wonder and admiration of the world, the Chimborazo of the globe, all else being a plain. It shall be crowned on its summit with the glorious temple of the living God. This carries forward the figure used Micah 4:1 and Isaiah 2:2, at least one important step further. Micah and Isaiah speak of the temple-mountain as "established" (firmly set) "on the top of the mountains, and exalted above the hills." Zechariah sees all other mountains and hills sinking down to a plain, and the temple-mountain, or rather Jerusalem herself as a whole, is lifted up and becomes the only mountain of the world. So magnificent, honorable, and glorious is to be the future kingdom of Messiah—the state of Christian faith and life in this world redeemed from its sins and pollutions!——The last clause of the verse states that Jerusalem shall again sit in her queenly majesty, the metropolitan city of this glorious kingdom. "In her place" means upon her former foundations, which is also expressed by the more particular specification of the gates and well-known points of the old city.

11. And *men* shall dwell in it, and there shall be no more utter destruction; but Jerusalem shall be safely inhabited.

As Jerusalem had been repeatedly visited with the fearfully blighting curse of Jehovah for her great sins—once inflicted by the cruel Chaldeans, and again to be, as already predicted, by the stern Romans—it was specially pertinent for the prophet to say that there should be no more such visitations of ruin. Her sins having been washed away and herself taken under the special protection of her Redeemer, there would be no more occasion for such "utter destruction." Henceforth she should be "inhabited safely."

12. And this shall be the plague wherewith the LORD will smite all the people that have fought against Jerusalem; Their flesh shall consume away while they stand upon their feet, and their eyes shall consume away in their holes, and their tongue shall consume away in their mouth.

The prophet left the enemies of Zion at the third verse, to follow the fortunes of Zion herself, and to show us, through vs. 4–11, how signally the Lord appeared for her help, and how gloriously he turned her darkness into day, and then poured out for her living waters and rebuilt her capital in greater and more enduring splendor than ever. Now he returns to inform us of the doom of those old enemies who marshalled their hosts against Zion, as appears vs. 1–3. They are smitten with a living death. Their flesh, touched with some consuming leprosy, perishes while yet they stand upon their feet. Their eyes consume away in their sockets; their tongue in their mouths. The eye and the tongue are specified as being the most valued organs—those of sight and of speech; and probably, too, as having been specially used in their war upon Zion. With their tongue they had spoken proudly, blasphemously, profanely. The type of their spirit had been, "Let her be defiled; let our eye look upon Zion" (Mic. 4:11). "Where is the Lord thy God? Mine eye shall behold her" (Mic. 7:10). The Lord is wont to make his retributive judgments indicate the sin for which they are sent.——This plague wherewith the Lord shall smite the open enemies and actual assailants of his Zion is intended to be terrible. What could be more so than such a wasting and consuming away, if slowly, yet surely, through the horrors of a living death, till the dread reality shall have fully come?

13. And it shall come to pass in that day, *that* a great tumult from the LORD shall be among them; and they shall lay hold every one on the hand of his neighbor, and his hand shall rise up against the hand of his neighbor.

The word "tumult" does not naturally convey the full sense of the original, which rather means a *panic*—the blended terror and confusion which an awful sense of the fact that Almighty God is against them would naturally produce. Analogous cases appear in the pages of Jewish history, as in Judges 7: 22, where "Gideon's three hundred men blew with the trumpet, and the Lord set every man's sword against his fellow throughout all the host;" or the case of Jonathan and his armor-bearer (1 Sam. 14:15, 16), "and there was trembling in the host, in the field, and among all the people"—"the earth quaked, so it was a very great trembling; and behold, the multitude melted away, and they went on beating down one another." Also 2 Chron. 20: 23—"They lay hold every one on the hand of his neighbor," not to help, but to disarm and smite him.——This verse and the preceding should be located in the events of this chapter, immediately after the first three verses. We are not to suppose that this plague of v. 12, and this panic with mutual slaughter of v. 13, come in only long after the scenes of the first three verses, and *after* Jerusalem has become peaceful and glorious. They rather go back to give us in detail the manner in which the Lord disposed of those enemies that fought against Jerusalem, took and divided her spoil, and made captives of half her people. All suddenly, the plagues of Jehovah smite them; their flesh consumes away; this awful form of death serves to panic-smite their hosts, and they fall upon each other in the dread work of mutual slaughter!——"So let all thine enemies perish, O Lord; but let them that love thee be as the sun when he goeth forth in his might!" (Judges 5:31).

14. And Judah also shall fight at Jerusalem; and the wealth of all the heathen round about shall be gath-

ered together, gold, and silver, and apparel, in great abundance.

Judah fights *in* Jerusalem, not as the margin has it, *against* her. The meaning is that, with a mutually good understanding, the people of the country rush to the help of the city, and fight heroically within the city for her defence. The spoil from the enemy is immense.——The ultimate truth taught here is that *real union* shall be the strength and glory of the millennial Church.

15. And so shall be the plague of the horse, of the mule, of the camel, and of the ass, and of all the beasts that shall be in these tents, as this plague.

The same plague that came from the Lord upon incorrigibly wicked men falls also on all their cattle, horses, mules, camels, and asses. They are supposed to be polluted by the horrible corruption of their owners. Moreover, the Lord would make his judgments so terrible as to inspire awe of his majesty and justice. The cattle of a city given to idolatry were to be destroyed. So were the animals in some of those most wicked cities doomed of God to destruction.——The word "tents" should have been "camps," which is the sense of the original—thus removing the incongruity of having these animals in their *tents*.

16. And it shall come to pass, *that* every one that is left of all the nations which came against Jerusalem, shall even go up from year to year to worship the King, the LORD of hosts, and to keep the feast of tabernacles.

The slaughter of the wicked nations, implied in v. 3, and terribly indicated in vs. 12, 13, leaves some yet living; how many relatively to the whole number, or to the number slain, we are not told. But we are told that those who remain shall be converted to God. They now come up to Jerusalem, no longer to fight against her, but to worship the living God in her temple, and to join heart and hand with the Lord's people. They are changed men—changed from sinners to saints.——The Jewish idea of a convert made to the true God in distant Gentile lands must naturally imply that he will come up year by year to Jerusalem to worship God at their great festivals. This idea they could not fail to carry over to the reign of their expected Messiah. Prophecy makes him a second David, the great successor on David's throne, to reign over all the nations from that great central metropolis of his kingdom. It remains for us to translate this Old Testament phraseology into that of the New Testament, and to modify those ideas which were the natural, not to say necessary, outgrowth of the ancient dispensation, and make them correspond to the new type of things established by our Lord and his apostles. So modified, we no longer think of converts in the ends of the earth making their annual pilgrimage to Jerusalem to keep her holy feasts and to worship Jehovah there. We understand that every living Christian heart is God's temple, and that every sincere worshipper is accepted in the New Mediator of the better covenant.——This passage, then, interpreted in harmony with New Testament doctrines and ideas, predicts the conversion of most if not all the ungodly who survive the fearful judgments already referred to.——That out of the three great annual festivals, the feast of tabernacles should be selected, is due to its special adaptation to the times. It was the national thanksgiving for God's favors in the fruits of the year, and was also a grateful memorial of their change from a wilderness life, forty years in tents, to a settled rest in Canaan. Now after Zion has been redeemed from her sins, made victorious over her foes, has received all that survive of them to her bosom as friends, and they are made welcome to her munificent blessings from her King, why should they not bring up their annual offerings of thanksgiving and praise?——Isaiah (66 : 23) names the "new moons and the Sabbaths" as the periods at which all flesh should come up to worship before the Lord—showing, when compared with this statement by Zechariah, that a literal coming is not thought of by the Spirit of inspiration. The essential idea is expressed as well by one form of statement as by the other. This idea is, that all the people of the earth will worship the true God in the modes of his own appointment, as Christ taught the woman of Samaria (John 4 : 20–24), and as the converted Jews were taught (Heb., chapters 7–10).

17. And it shall be, *that* whoso will not come up of *all* the families of the earth unto Jerusalem to worship the King, the LORD of hosts, even upon them shall be no rain.

This curse is entirely in accordance with the principles of the ancient Theocracy which promised rain to the people if obedient, but threatened to withhold it if they turned aside to idols. (See Deut. 11 : 13–17.)——The ancient economy provided for retribution in the present world sufficiently full and sure to make the sense of it effective in those early ages, and to minister to an intelligent faith in God's actual government of the world.——The previous verse speaks of "nations;" this, particularly, of "families," because it was by families that the Hebrew people came up to Jerusalem on their great annual festivals.

18. And if the family of Egypt go not up, and come not, that *have* no *rain;* there shall be the plague, wherewith the LORD will smite the heathen that come not up to keep the feast of tabernacles.

It is not entirely clear why the family of Egypt is specified here. We naturally think the reason to be that no rain ever falls in portions of that country, and therefore, since this plague would not touch them, another of special sort would be provided. But the Hebrew clause, which reads in our version, "that have no rain," is elliptical, and therefore quite indefinite, since it may be supplied either thus: Upon whom rain does not (usually) fall; or thus: Upon them shall be no rain.——The general sense, however, is plain, viz., that Egypt shall be no exception to the general law. If they go not up, the same plagues shall fall on them for this neglect as on other nations. The fact is, that the failure of rain around the head-waters of the Nile is as fatal to Egypt as the failure of rain in other countries.——Let it be noted that these threatened plagues (vs. 17, 18) do not of necessity imply that any families will refuse to go up to worship the Lord of hosts. They may only show that men are still moral agents, acted upon by fear and hope, and made responsible for their free moral acts. The assurance (v. 16) that "every one that is left of all the nations *shall go up*," needs no abatement because of this threatened plague on whomsoever shall not go. Yet it must be admitted that this language may purposely imply that there will be even in that glorious day some still persistent enemies of God upon whom his judgments shall actually fall.

19. This shall be the punishment of Egypt, and the punishment of all nations that come not up to keep the feast of tabernacles.

Sin is the more usual sense of the word here rendered "punishment," but the course of thought seems to demand the sense of punishment. "This" (*i. e.*, the withholding of rain) shall be the punishment of all who do not come up to this feast.——Hengstenberg, giving the word the sense of *sin*, makes the passage mean that the chief sin, the test sin, the one specially noticed and punished, is this of not going up, &c. But to make out this sense, the passage should read—"This not going up to the feast of tabernacles, shall be the test sin of all the nations"—a very different statement from this which the verse does make.

20. In that day shall there be upon the bells of the horses, HOLINESS UNTO THE LORD; and the pots in the LORD's house shall be like the bowls before the altar.

21. Yea, every pot in Jerusalem and in Judah shall be holiness unto the LORD of hosts: and all they that sacrifice shall come and take of them, and seethe therein: and in that day there shall be no more the Canaanite in the house of the LORD of hosts.

That holiness to the Lord shall be not only very pure, but widely extended, is taught here by three distinct statements: (1.) Things that have no special sanctity, *e. g.*, bells on horses, shall be consecrated as altogether holy.——(2.) The less sacred things about the temple shall become as holy as those most sacred were wont to be, *e. g.*, common pots for cooking food shall become no less sacred than the bowls which received the blood of animals slain in sacrifice; the latter being of old accounted most holy, the former least so.——(3.) The Canaanites shall be no more in the Lord's temple.——Canaanite was the common Hebrew word for trafficker, merchant—a business in bad repute among the Hebrews because so much associated with fraud and deceit. See Hos. 12 : 7, 8.——There is special force in the allusion to the bells upon the horses because the Hebrew law and Hebrew sentiment had a prejudice against horses, as associated with pride and vain show; with reliance also on some other power than God, and with *war*. This prejudice was all the stronger because their most powerful enemies came upon them with a strong force of cavalry and chariots; while, on the other hand, their own kings were forbidden to multiply horses. (See Deut. 17 : 16.) The pious Psalmist said, "Some trust in chariots and some in horsemen; we, in the name of the Lord our God." The pious in Hos. 14 : 3, say, "We will not ride upon horses." But now, in the purity of the millennial age, even the bells, mere ornaments on the horses, shall bear the same inscription as the ancient breast-plate worn by the high priest—"*Holiness to the Lord.*" How exceedingly expressive of the absolute and universal consecration of all things to the service and worship of the one all-glorious God!——So also is the last clause rich in its special significance. When we consider how much the love of "filthy lucre" has polluted the sanctuary, both under the Mosaic and throughout the Christian age, it is a relief to feel that in the good time coming, "there shall be no more the Canaanite in the house of the Lord of hosts." No more shall men carry the spirit of gain into the gospel ministry. No more shall dishonesty and overreaching for pelf pollute the Church of God.

Reviewing briefly the course of thought in this entire chapter, I call renewed attention to the following points: (1.) The whole chapter must be taken as figurative, and not literal. The literal sense, implying the actual cleaving of the Mount of Olives, and the escape of half the population of the city through its cleft bowels; two literal rivers flowing from Jerusalem, one east and the other west; all the mountains in the world levelled down to plains, save the one on which Jerusalem and its temple shall stand; all the nations coming up to Jerusalem yearly to the feast of tabernacles; Judaism with its bloody sacrifices enjoined on all the Gentile world, despite of the whole New Testament to the contrary: such things, supposed to take place literally, are simply incredible and absurd. Some of them, if they were to take place literally, would inevitably defeat their own ends. All would defeat and crush out New Testament Christianity. There can be no sufficient reasons for giving this chapter a literal construction.——(2.) I have studiously abstained from the attempt to determine and define the fulfilment of any minute feature in this grouping of Hebrew figures, because I have no faith in such attempts. *When* these things shall be fulfilled; in what precise form the wicked shall assail the Church of God; how many of them shall be cut off by the plagues of the Lord, and how many shall remain to be converted—these points, and such as these, I think it wise to make no attempt to determine. Ungodliness has its group of specific forms to-day; who can tell whether they will change essentially before this general onslaught upon Zion? The world has long since passed the besieging of the literal Jerusalem, *as being herself the Lord's Zion;* probably has passed the era of religious wars, avowedly to destroy Christianity. But stern conflicts with Satan and his human aids await the kingdom of Christ ere its great and final victory.——(3.) In the exposition of this chapter the first main inquiry should be—How would the Jews of Zechariah's time understand it? What would be the general impression made upon them by this grouping of Jewish images and ideas? Would not they hail this chapter as God's word of promise, that the worship of their own Jehovah would one day become universal; that their old enemies would first be greatly reduced in numbers by fearful plagues, and the remnant be converted to the living God, and that then the worship of God would become pure and substantially universal? They could make of it nothing less than this. No other language could express these points more surely or more forcibly than this.——(4.) Then this is the general sense of the chapter. For it was written to be read and to be understood by the Jews of his time. The writer of it was himself a Jew, writing for first readers who were Jews, and therefore he used and could use only Jewish terms and figures.——The general sense of these figures we get from that ancient economy. It only remains (as already said) that we translate Jewish into Christian terms, Jewish symbols into Christian thought and meaning, and we have the truth which the Lord hath taught us with so much clearness, beauty, and force in this chapter.——Let the name of the Lord be praised for such and so much light upon the otherwise unknown future of his earthly Zion! We will bless his name, not only that he has formed such purposes of loving-kindness—not only that he has determined to bring all the nations of men to live joyfully beneath Messiah's sceptre, but that *he has revealed to us this purpose,* and delineated in such forms of beauty and joy the glorious future which awaits Messiah's kingdom among men.

MALACHI.

INTRODUCTION.

Of this prophet we have no personal history. The book gives us only his name, and over even this there hangs a doubt in some minds whether it be a proper name, or whether it designates some unknown person as "my messenger," the original being the same as is translated thus (chap. 3 : 1): "Behold, I send my messenger," &c. I take it, however, to be a proper name, because every other prophetical book gives the real name of its author; because a name and a personal character were essential as credentials; and because the other view ("my messenger") gives us no light whatever as to the author, in the very place where we have a right to expect it. By the universal consent of biblical critics, he was the latest known prophet. The internal evidence leaves scarcely a doubt that he was contemporary with Nehemiah's last visit to Judea, aiding him in his work of correcting the abuses which had gained a footing among the people. A careful comparison of the Book of Malachi with Nehemiah 13 : 7–31 exhibits the same flagrant sins as prevailing in each, *e. g.*, intermarriages with foreigners, even in the case of the priests (Neh. 13 : 28–30 with Mal. 2 : 7–16); neglect of tithes (Neh. 13 : 10–13 with Mal. 3 : 7–10); violation of the Sabbath and of religious worship generally (Neh. 13 : 15–22 with Mal. 1 : 13 and 2 : 8). Hence it appears highly probable that Malachi coöperated with Nehemiah in his last reformation, as Isaiah did with Hezekiah, and Jeremiah with Josiah. The civil ruler would greatly need the aid of some earnest and pure-minded prophet in such a work. The Lord took care to provide it.——The precise date of this last visit of Nehemiah is a question of some historic interest, inasmuch as it is the date of the latest inspired Old Testament history and prophecy. The following brief synopsis of historic dates is supposed to be proximately correct. It may aid the reader to locate these events in time, and fix their connections with profane history. (1.) The first captives returned under Zerubbabel, in the first year of Cyrus, B. C. 536. (2.) Fifty-eight years after, Ezra went up to Jerusalem, in the seventh year of Xerxes (called Artaxerxes, Ezra 7:1, 7), B. C. 478. (3.) Nehemiah's first visit was yet thirty-four years later, viz., in the twentieth year of Artaxerxes Longimanus, B. C. 444. (4.) After twelve years' stay in Judea, Nehemiah returned to Babylon in the thirty-second year of this same king, B. C. 432. (5.) The date of his second visit to Judea is probably twenty-four years subsequent, *i. e.*, in B. C. 408, although it may have been less. Some critics fix it B. C. 423, after an interval of only nine years instead of twenty-four. The interval must have been long enough for the introduction of grievous abuses, for intermarriages with foreigners, and births from those marriages, and children old enough to speak "according to the language of each people." The data do not suffice for a more precise determination of the time. This, however, is near enough for all practical purposes. Not far from four hundred years before Christ, this last in the long series of inspired prophets united his efforts with those of Nehemiah to call back the apostate people to their forsaken God, to rebuke them for their great sins, and to animate the believing portion by some very distinct and precious promises of the conversion of the Gentiles; of the coming of the glorious Lord, "the Messenger of the covenant," to his earthly temple; and also of the coming of John Baptist, here designated as "my messenger who shall prepare the way before me," and as "Elijah the prophet."

CHAPTER I.

To show the people their great guilt, the Lord testifies to his special love for their nation, particularly as compared with the posterity of Esau (vs. 2–5); rebukes the priests for their contempt of his worship (vs. 6–10); assures them that he will find countless sincere worshippers among the heathen (v. 11); exposes and denounces their heinous sins (vs. 12–14).

1. The burden of the word of the LORD to Israel by Malachi.

This prophecy, as a whole, comprises so much rebuke for sin and threatening of judgment, that it may fitly be called a "burden" in the usual sense—sins and judgments, which it is a heart-burden to think of and to reveal.

2. I have loved you, saith the LORD. Yet ye say, Wherein hast thou loved us? *Was* not Esau Jacob's brother? saith the LORD: yet I loved Jacob,

3. And I hated Esau, and laid his mountains and his heritage waste for the dragons of the wilderness.

A view of the love sinned against deepens the sense of guilt. As one who appreciates this law of our moral nature, the Lord begins his endeavors to convict the Jews of sin by setting before them the special love he had borne for their nation ever since Jacob was chosen to be the heir of his promises and Esau was rejected.——This hating of Esau was rather a *not-loving*, and looks especially to the fact that God rejected him from being the heir of the promises made to Abraham and Isaac. The history shows that Esau did not value the inheritance of those promises. The writer of the Epistle to the Hebrews calls him "that profane person," as if to intimate that his rejection was not an arbitrary act of God in the sense of being irrespective of Esau's ill desert.——As to the words "I hated Esau," let it be carefully noted that God's hatred is never malign and never causeless.——The "laying of his mountains and heritage waste" was done soon after the fall of Jerusalem before the Chaldean arms, and by the same power.

4. Whereas Edom saith, We are impoverished, but we will return and build the desolate places; thus saith the LORD of hosts, They shall build, but I will throw down; and they shall call them, The border of wickedness, and, The people against whom the LORD hath indignation for ever.

5. And your eyes shall see, and ye shall say, The LORD will be magnified from the border of Israel.

Edom resolutely determined to rebuild; the Lord as resolutely to cast down. The Lord, and not Edom, triumphed in this conflict. ——Men in general, the voice of the nations, "shall call them the border of wickedness," *i. e.*, the wicked country, the people against whom Jehovah's wrath burns forever. Their sins had been so base and so notorious that all mankind would appreciate the reasons of God's wrath against them.——Ye shall say, "Let the Lord be magnified by all the people of Israel;" let his praise come forth from that whole country. It behooved all the Jews to extol the justice of God in sending such retribution upon Edom.

6. A son honoreth *his* father, and a servant his mas-

ter: if then I *be* a father, where *is* mine honor? and if I *be* a master, where *is* my fear? saith the LORD of hosts unto you, O priests, that despise my name. And ye say, Wherein have we despised thy name?

This reasoning from the honor due and usually accorded to a father, is full of force as applied to the great God. How much more a Father is he than any of these "fathers of our flesh," and how much greater! Most forcibly, therefore, does he demand from us, "Where is my honor?" "Where is my fear?"——This appeal was made with special pertinence to the priests, to whom God had given high responsibilities and ample means of knowing his name and his love.——"Yet ye say, Wherein have we despised thy name?" This is the first case out of many in which the priests retort the charge made against them, daring the prophet or the Lord to the proof! It is the rankest pride and self-justification. It may well amaze us that a priesthood so enlightened should become so fearfully corrupt, so rotten morally, so blind to their own past and present sins!

7. Ye offer polluted bread upon mine altar; and ye say, Wherein have we polluted thee? In that ye say, The table of the LORD *is* contemptible.

8. And if ye offer the blind for sacrifice, *is it* not evil? and if ye offer the lame and sick, *is it* not evil? offer it now unto thy governor; will he be pleased with thee, or accept thy person? saith the LORD of hosts.

The ceremonial law specified, with almost extreme precision, what offerings should be made and how prepared, laying the greatest stress on their being the *very best of their kind.* The significance of this is obvious. No greater insult could be offered to God than to turn him off with the refuse of their flocks and herds, and with polluted bread for his altar! Yet this the priests of that day had done, and moreover seemed still to have no sense of their horrible sin! Forcibly does the Lord say, "Offer such presents to your governor; will he feel himself honored?" Alas! many a human heart ought to be smitten with a sense of its sins against the glorious Jehovah, in having constantly withheld from him the best of its love, homage, and service, and in doling out only the meanest, cheapest offerings, in a way which signifies that the heart does not intend to give the least thing in real love to the good and glorious God!

9. And now, I pray you, beseech God that he will be gracious unto us: this hath been by your means: will he regard your persons? saith the LORD of hosts.

The clause, "this hath been by your means," seems to refer to the deplorably low state of piety and of divine worship, and to charge the cause of it to the priests, and on this ground implore them to repent and conciliate the favor of God.

10. Who *is there* even among you that would shut the doors *for nought?* neither do ye kindle *fire* on mine altar for nought. I have no pleasure in you, saith the LORD of hosts, neither will I accept an offering at your hand.

The service they did render was done in supreme selfishness, for they would not even close the doors of the temple or kindle the fire upon the altar, without special pay for it. So utterly mercenary and heartless had they become in all their religious duties! No wonder the Lord declares to them, "I have no pleasure in you!" The pure, loving heart is above all things else first and highest in his esteem; it might almost be said to be *all* he cares for; without it, all else goes for nothing.

11. For from the rising of the sun even unto the going down of the same, my name *shall be* great among the Gentiles; and in every place incense *shall be* offered unto my name, and a pure offering: for my name *shall be* great among the heathen, saith the LORD of hosts.

The logical connection, indicated by the word "*for*," should be distinctly noted. The Lord would say to those corrupt priests— You have no heart in my worship; you make it contemptible be fore the people; your whole heart is meanly selfish; I cannot accept such worship, and *I have no occasion to do so.* You greatly mistake if you suppose that I am in such need that I shall thankfully accept at your hand such miserably poor service. I have other and far purer service coming in from the Gentile nations, upon whom you are looking down with haughty scorn, "*for* from the rising of the sun even to the going down of the same, my name shall be great among the Gentiles" (not cast out as vile, after the manner of your devotions). "In every place" (not in Jerusalem alone) "incense shall be offered to my name and a pure" (not a polluted) offering; "for my name" (which you have despised, v. 6) "shall be great among the heathen, saith the Lord of Hosts."——Sublimely glorious promise! Its outlook into the Christian age is truly wonderful. That great change wrought out under the apostles, by which the pure worship of God passed from Jewish to Gentile hands and hearts, is here most clearly indicated.——Let it be noted also that more is here than the world has yet seen. The sweep of the gospel has never yet ranged from the rising to the setting sun. "Incense and a pure offering" have not yet been offered "in every place." The glorious name of Jehovah has not yet become "great among all the heathen."——But all these things shall yet be! Let all hearts hail the coming day! And let all hands hasten it onward!

12. But ye have profaned it, in that ye say, The table of the LORD *is* polluted; and the fruit thereof, *even* his meat, *is* contemptible.

13. Ye said also, Behold, what a weariness *is it!* and ye have snuffed at it, saith the LORD of hosts; and ye brought *that which was* torn, and the lame, and the sick; thus ye brought an offering: should I accept this of your hand? saith the LORD.

14. But cursed *be* the deceiver, which hath in his flock a male, and voweth, and sacrificeth unto the LORD a corrupt thing: for I *am* a great King, saith the LORD of hosts, and my name *is* dreadful among the heathen.

The prophet returns again to the sins of the priests, exposing and rebuking them with deserved severity. Who can wonder that the curse of Jehovah falls on such priests and on all such worshippers at his altar? How can he regard it as better than intended insult? ——Verily God is too great, and too holy to be so contemned! Woe to the man who offers such abuse to the Great King whose "name is dreadful among the heathen!"

CHAPTER II.

THE corrupt priests are specially exhorted, rebuked, and threatened (vs. 1–9); the sin of practically divorcing their Jewish wives and marrying heathen women is condemned (vs. 10–16); and finally the priests are rebuked for denying the justice of God in his providential government (v. 17).

1. And now, O ye priests, this commandment *is* for you.

2. If ye will not hear, and if ye will not lay *it* to heart, to give glory unto my name, saith the LORD of hosts, I will even send a curse upon you, and I will curse your blessings; yea, I have cursed them already, because ye do not lay *it* to heart.

The priests had been deeply guilty in the great apostasy of that age. They had not only failed altogether to teach the people faithfully and truly for God, but they had fearfully seduced them into sin by their pernicious example. Hence the prophet gives them to understand very explicitly that this message of command

and rebuke is for them.——The threatening is not merely "I will send *a curse*"—some unknown, indefinite curse—but *the* curse (so the original has it), referring doubtless to Deut. 27 : 14–26, "And the Levites shall say unto all the men of Israel with a loud voice, Cursed be he," &c., "and all the people shall say, Amen!" To this fearful catalogue of twelve curses the prophet must have referred.——To "curse your blessings" is to change them to curses.——The clause rendered "yea, I have cursed them already," &c., should read, "yea, I will curse each one of them." The tense is the same as in the preceding clause. There is no authority for the sense "*already*."

3. Behold I will corrupt your seed, and spread dung upon your faces, *even* the dung of your solemn feasts; and *one* shall take you away with it.

"I will rebuke your seed sown," implies that he will forbid its coming to maturity.——The spreading of dung upon their faces must imply a doom both publicly disgraceful and intrinsically loathsome. Themselves shall be thrown out and borne away with the offal of their sacrifices, in one promiscuous mass.

4. And ye shall know that I have sent this commandment unto you, that my covenant might be with Levi, saith the LORD of hosts.

I take this verse to mean—Ye shall know in your own experience that I make this last effort to save you, in order that my covenant may still be as of old with Levi, and that the priesthood may still abide in honor and usefulness with my blessing upon it; but that this effort *shall be the last!*

5. My covenant was with him of life and peace; and I gave them to him *for* the fear wherewith he feared me, and was afraid before my name.

This seems to refer to some events in the early history of Israel, in which the tribe of Levi manifested a special regard for the name and honor of God, and for this reason was honored with the covenant of the perpetual priesthood. The reference may be either to Ex. 32 : 26–29, or to Num. 25 : 7–13, or to both. In the former case the whole tribe of Levi came forth promptly to the call of Moses, "Who is on the Lord's side?" and girding on each man his sword, they slew the worshippers of the golden calf wherever they were, sparing not even a brother, companion, or neighbor. To this case Moses reverts (Deut. 33 : 9, 10) in his last blessing upon the tribes: "Who said unto his father and to his mother, I have not seen him, neither did he acknowledge his brethren, nor know his own children; for they have observed thy words, and kept thy covenant. They shall teach Jacob thy judgments, and Israel thy law; they shall put incense before thee," &c.——The other case, that of Phineas

(Num. 25), did not pertain so directly to the whole tribe of Levi, and yet has in its favor the fact that for his zeal the Lord said of him: "Behold I give unto him my covenant of peace, and he shall have it, and his seed after him, even the covenant of an everlasting priesthood, because he was zealous for his God, and made an atonement for the children of Israel." The latter also has closer relations with the priesthood, while the former concerned the whole tribe of Levi. Very probably there may be a tacit reference to both cases.

6. The law of truth was in his mouth, and iniquity was not found in his lips: he walked with me in peace and equity, and did turn many away from iniquity.

7. For the priest's lips should keep knowledge, and they should seek the law at his mouth: for he *is* the messenger of the LORD of hosts.

In the outset the tribe of Levi and the family of Aaron were selected because of their fidelity to God and to his truth. In the early times of the nation they were in the main true to their responsibilities, and taught the people the knowledge of the Lord faithfully and successfully.——The passage shows that the priests were by profession the public teachers of religion, and performed that service until they became too corrupt. Then prophets were raised up to supply in some measure their lack of service.

8. But ye are departed out of the way; ye have caused many to stumble at the law; ye have corrupted the covenant of Levi, saith the LORD of hosts.

9. Therefore have I also made you contemptible and base before all the people, according as ye have not kept my ways, but have been partial in the law.

The original puts the antithesis forcibly between "ye" (v. 8), and "I" (v. 9), *ye* departed out of the way; "therefore *I* have made you contemptible and base before all the people." Note here the thing signified by the bold figures in v. 3. The Lord will surely take away all honor from the priest who dishonors God and disgraces himself. "They that despise me shall be lightly esteemed."

10. Have we not all one father? hath not one God created us? why do we deal treacherously every man against his brother, by profaning the covenant of our fathers?

11. Judah hath dealt treacherously, and an abomination is committed in Israel and in Jerusalem; for Judah hath profaned the holiness of the LORD which he loved, and hath married the daughter of a strange god.

12. The LORD will cut off the man that doeth this, the master and the scholar, out of the tabernacles of Jacob, and him that offereth an offering unto the LORD of hosts.

13. And this have ye done again, covering the altar of the LORD with tears, with weeping, and with crying out, insomuch that he regardeth not the offering any more, or receiveth *it* with good will at your hand.

14. Yet ye say, Wherefore? Because the LORD hath been witness between thee and the wife of thy youth, against whom thou hast dealt treacherously: yet *is* she thy companion, and the wife of thy covenant.

15. And did not he make one? Yet had he the residue of the Spirit. And wherefore one? That he might seek a godly seed. Therefore take heed to your spirit, and let none deal treacherously against the wife of his youth.

16. For the LORD, the God of Israel, saith, that he hateth putting away: for *one* covereth violence with his garment, saith the LORD of hosts: therefore take heed to your spirit, that ye deal not treacherously.

This passage is best understood when considered as one distinct and entire subject. It refers to the sin of practically or actually putting away their Hebrew wives, and taking wives from the idolatrous heathen. Even the priests had done this; and, indeed, they seem to have been foremost. (See Neh. 13:23–29.)——With a masterly hand the prophet calls their attention first in order to the very highest moral considerations—to their obligations to God, their common Father, which bind them to deal faithfully and forbid them to deal treacherously against their fellow-beings, children of the same common Father. In the clause "every man against his brother," &c., the thing in mind is the obligation that binds a man to fidelity with his wife. "Brother" is used in the general sense of fellow-creature—one who is a child of the same Creator.——"The covenant of our fathers" is the covenant of marriage, ordained of God, and given first to the common father of our race. In the clause (v. 11) "Judah hath profaned the holiness of the Lord which he loved," I take the sense to be, that the people of Judah had abused and dishonored the sacredness which the Lord had attached to his own people in forbidding intermarriages with the heathen, and requiring them to marry within the pale of the covenant people. The Lord had felt a special interest in this law. It recognized a certain holiness in his own people which he had valued as a distinction vital to the preservation of morals and piety among them. The priests and people had profaned this sacredness by marrying the daughters of strange gods—heathen idolatrous women.——In v. 12 it is said, "The Lord will cut off the man that doeth this," be he who he may. This is the ultimate sense of the original rendered, "the master and the scholar." Its proximate sense, however, is not "master and scholar," but "the waker and the answerer," with reference to the night-watch of the priests or Levites in the temple where the party retiring from their watch aroused their successors, who answered to their call. The two parties taken together might include all. The description should apply to the priests; this does; and, moreover, follows strictly the sense of the original.

In v. 13, "done this again," means ye have a second time relapsed into this great sin; the first time being that great apostasy from which they were reclaimed under Ezra. (See Ezra 9.) This reform seemed for the time to be thorough, but subsequently the people and priests apostatized again.——They "covered the altar of God with tears," inasmuch as the Hebrew wives, supplanted in the affections of their husbands by heathen wives, fled to the altar to lay their case before the God of their fathers there, and to pour out their sorrows into his ear, and their tears upon his altar. Such scenes as these touched the heart of God, and he could no longer accept the offerings brought to this same altar by these adulterous and apostate priests.——The self-justifying priests still say, "Wherefore?" Why should God repel and disown us? Is it for these trivial matters pertaining to our wives?——The prophet answers: Because the Lord became a witness between thee and the wife of thy youth on the day of thine espousals; and he cannot but mark, and marking, abhor thy treachery in the breach of that covenant.——Pursuing this point yet further, the prophet inquires, Did not the Lord create one woman, and one only, to be the wife of the first man? Yet he had the residue of the creative Spirit, and might easily have made for Adam another wife, or even a score of wives, if he had thought it best. Wherefore did he limit Adam to one wife? The reason was, he sought a godly seed. His heart was on securing such family influences as would avail to "train up a child in the way he should go," and he knew full well that polygamy—the presence of two or more wives in the same household—must utterly forbid such moral training. No godly seed can be expected in that family where polygamy is forever begetting discord, jealousy, and every thing immoral, selfish, and ungodly.——"For the Lord saith he hateth divorce," which implies that virtually, if not directly, this taking of foreign wives resulted in putting away their Hebrew wives. Very probably the results might vary somewhat; for some Hebrew wives might consent for a time, longer or shorter, to be crushed down and trodden under foot; while others would not brook such treatment an hour. In the end, the usual result would be the expulsion of the Hebrew wife from the household. ——In the next clause, the word "garment" is thought to mean *wife*. Arabic usage favors this sense. The meaning of the whole passage would then be, "For the Lord, the God of Israel, hateth divorce, in which one heaps violence upon his wife—covers and buries her as it were with accumulated wrongs and violent assaults" —a sad, dark picture of the domestic scenes attendant upon that monster sin of divorcing the wife of one's youth, to wed one's self to a foreign idolatress.——The prophet closes with repeating the exhortation to take heed to their spirits that they no more deal treacherously with the wife of their first sacred covenant.

17. Ye have wearied the LORD with your words. Yet ye say, Wherein have we wearied *him?* When ye say, Every one that doeth evil *is* good in the sight of the LORD, and he delighteth in them; or, Where *is* the God of judgment?

The essence of this crime, which had wearied the Lord of hosts, was a denial of his justice in the administration of his moral government. They said, "Every one that doeth evil is good in the sight of the Lord," who manifests as much delight in them as in well-doers. They also said, with the same implication, "Where is the God of just judgment?"—implying, We know not where he is. Hence it must be inferred that the horrible sins of the priests in contemning the worship of God, offering polluted offerings, and putting away their Hebrew wives to marry heathen idolaters, had at bottom a deep apostasy in principle and theory from the living God. They had ceased to vindicate the ways of God to man; had ceased to think and speak well of his government; had ceased to regard him as holy, just, and good.——But it need not be supposed that they had forsaken his worship and gone thus into sin *because* they had first reached the conclusion intelligently that he was unworthy of their regard. By no means. The reverse order is almost if not quite universal. Sins of the heart and of the life, long cherished, create a demand in the mind, and especially before the conscience, for false notions of God to serve as a quietus to the conscience. Men first have evil deeds; then necessarily love darkness more than light for their convenience and comfort in their evil ways; and then their love of darkness leads them on to any conceivable absurdities of error.——The developments of this Book of Malachi reveal an appalling depth of depravity among the priests and Levites—the very men who should have been true to God and inflexible against all the seductions of popular sins.

CHAPTER III.

THE coming of John Baptist and of Jesus the Messiah is foretold with some of the results (vs. 1–5); then exhortations to repentance and rebukes for sin, especially the sin of robbing the Lord of his tithes and offerings (vs. 6–12). The spirit of the wicked is contrasted with the spirit of the righteous (vs. 13–18).

1. Behold, I will send my messenger, and he shall prepare the way before me: and the LORD, whom ye seek, shall suddenly come to his temple, even the messenger of the covenant, whom ye delight in: behold, he shall come, saith the LORD of hosts.

The most ample proof is found in the New Testament that "my messenger" is John Baptist. Our Lord bore witness to John (Luke 7:27): "This is he of whom it is written, Behold, I send my messenger before thy face, who shall prepare the way before thee." His father, Zacharias, when filled with the Holy Ghost, said—"Thou, child, shalt be called the prophet of the Highest, for thou shalt go before the face of the Lord to prepare his ways," &c. (Luke 1:76.)——Consequently, "the Lord whom ye seek," "the messenger of the covenant," can be no other than Jesus the Messiah. It was of the wisdom and mercy of God that he should be so definitely pointed out both in this and kindred prophecies, and by a messenger so fitted every way for his commission as John. Such indications must have been eminently welcome and satisfactory to all honest minds.——This feature in the description of Messiah, "whom ye seek," was pertinent in the latest prophecy of him, and pertinent at the time of his coming, inasmuch as high expectations concerning him were now raised, and a lively interest in his coming was awakened. The testimony concerning Simeon and Anna, as given by Luke, is in point to illustrate the "seeking" of the pious portion of the people. Plainly their hearts were keenly alive with interest and hope.——That he should be spoken of as "*coming to his temple*," may be due in part to the fact that the temple was *his* by long residence—his visible glory having dwelt there for ages, reposing upon the mercy-seat and beneath the cherubim; partly also to the indications of prophecy, as in Zech. 6:12, 13—"he shall build the temple of the Lord."——But why is he called "the messenger of the covenant"? "Messenger" means angel. It is the word usually translated angel. Jesus is the angel of the covenant in the twofold sense: (1.) Of being the same personage so often called in the Old Testament an "angel," *e. g.*, Ex. 23:20–23, which if the reader will examine, he will see refers to the uncreated angel who pardons sin, in whom is the name of Jehovah, and who is a perpetual Presence with his Church under both the old dispensation and the new; called "the angel of the covenant" also, because so long promised by covenant with the patriarchs and saints of old: and (2.) Of being especially "the Mediator of the new covenant" (Heb. 9:15); and of "the better covenant, established upon better promises" (Heb. 8:6–13).——"Behold" indicates an announcement worthy of particular attention, the more so because repeated —"Behold, he shall surely come, saith the Lord of hosts."——Can we trace any connection of thought between this promise as it stands here, and the preceding context?——If any, it is this: The priesthood is becoming hopelessly corrupt, the people going astray as sheep having no shepherd; the kingdom of God will never rise and become far extended by such agencies alone; the name of God is everywhere dishonored. This course of things will not answer the ends of divine mercy; something more and other than this must be done; I will send my servant John, and close after him, the Lord of all! He will bear up the otherwise sinking cause of God and of righteousness.——The reader will notice the person who speaks in this verse. He is "Jehovah of hosts." Yet he says: "*I* will send one who shall prepare the way before *me*." The testimony of inspiration thus makes the promised Messiah no other than "Jehovah of hosts." This name is given him by divine authority.

2. But who may abide the day of his coming? and who shall stand when he appeareth? for he *is* like a refiner's fire, and like fuller's soap:

"Who shall be able to bear the day of his coming"—the searching ordeal of such moral scrutiny? Not those corrupt priests, so recently before the prophet's mind. Ah! full soon will he scourge them out of his temple, and hurl them down from the high position which they so shamefully desecrate!——"Who shall stand when he appeareth?" Some few—those who "looked for redemption in Jerusalem"—will hail his coming as "the horn of salvation for us in the house of his servant David;" but the sensual, the worldly, the formal,—however carefully they may have covered up their iniquity with the cloak of sanctimonious profession, will be put through such processes of refining and proving as shall surely reveal their dross—"for he is like a refiner's fire, and like fuller's soap,"—physical agents which well illustrate the work of the coming Messiah in purifying his Church. The state of the Church and its leading men at that time strongly suggested the need of this purifying work to be done by "the Messenger of the covenant."

3. And he shall sit as a refiner and purifier of silver: and he shall purify the sons of Levi, and purge them as gold and silver, that they may offer unto the LORD an offering in righteousness.

"Sitting" is the posture of the refiner of silver, chosen as being more convenient for the long, patient, careful watching of the process which is essential to success. Silver is too precious to be wasted by having too much heat; and its purity is too valuable a quality to be missed by having too little.——That "he shall purify the sons of Levi" was suggested by the deeply-felt want of this at that time, and is always vital because of the essential importance of having those who minister in sacred things spotless examples of the godliness which they should commend to others. How can the Lord send blessings to men through instrumentalities that are corrupt and rotten? Having wisely determined to work through human agents, and having designated them, what if they prove faithless, and only hinder and block the progress of the work they should set forward? Hence the first labor of the Messiah when he appears among his people will be "to purify the sons of Levi, that they may offer unto the Lord an offering in righteousness."

4. Then shall the offering of Judah and Jerusalem be pleasant unto the LORD, as in the days of old, and as in former years.

This done, the offerings of Judah and Jerusalem shall be pleasing to the Lord as in the better, purer days of the Hebrew people, when "Israel was holiness to the Lord." (See Jer. 2:3.) The verse has a refreshing look toward that one perfect offering of Jesus, our Great High Priest, in which God was well pleased, and on the ground of which he will joyfully accept the humble offerings of his people.

5. And I will come near to you to judgment: and I will be a swift witness against the sorcerers, and against the adulterers, and against false swearers, and against those that oppress the hireling in *his* wages, the widow, and the fatherless, and that turn aside the stranger *from his right*, and fear not me, saith the LORD of hosts.

"*But*," over against this, "*to you*" and to all such as you (referring to the priests and Levites of that day) "will I come near in judgment, and I will be a swift witness," &c.—*swift*, as affording no more time for such wickedness, and as cutting short their most abused probation. These words refer to the horribly wicked religious leaders of those days.

6. For I *am* the LORD, I change not; therefore ye sons of Jacob are not consumed.

The connection of thought here turns on the special significance of the name *Jehovah*—the ever faithful and unchanging One—the God of the promises, who hath said and will surely fulfil. If he had not made such promises of enduring protection and mercy to the ancient covenant people, he would even now cut them off at once. This only is the reason why they are not consumed. It is only because he is Jehovah that his faithfulness spares "the sons of Jacob." There is a power in that name, "sons of Jacob," that avails to save them yet, on the score of those never-failing promises. See notes on Hos. 12: 4–6.

7. Even from the days of your fathers ye are gone away from mine ordinances, and have not kept *them*. Return unto me, and I will return unto you, saith the LORD of hosts. But ye said, Wherein shall we return?

8. Will a man rob God? Yet ye have robbed me. But ye say, Wherein have we robbed thee? In tithes and offerings.

9. Ye *are* cursed with a curse: for ye have robbed me, *even* this whole nation.

This apostasy had already been of long standing.——The spirit of divine command and promise is tersely and beautifully expressed here—"Return unto me, and I will return unto you." So also is the spirit of man's depravity truthfully expressed in the quick response—Are we not all right now? "Wherein shall we return?" .... Alas for the blindness of sin! Alas for the hardness it brings on human hearts! It is only when conviction of the truth as it is, fastens on the mind through the Spirit of God, that sinners think to any purpose of returning to God.——Strange that a man should rob God! "Yet ye have robbed me," in withholding the stipulated tithes—the tenth part of their annual income. For this withholding, the Lord was visiting the land with the curse of barrenness and famine.

10. Bring ye all the tithes into the storehouse, that there may be meat in mine house, and prove me now herewith, saith the LORD of hosts, if I will not open you the windows of heaven, and pour you out a blessing, that *there shall* not *be room* enough *to receive it.*

This striking passage has the richer interest to Christians because, under the principles of the ancient economy, viz., temporal blessings to the faithfully obedient, it presents to us the great law of his spiritual administration as well, showing that there can really be no limit (short of our utmost capacity) to the spiritual blessings God will give those who, really hungering for righteousness, "open wide their mouth that God may fill it," and hence who honestly use all appropriate means for this result.——God is forever the same, and certainly is no less bountiful of blessings under the Christian than under the Jewish economy.——"Prove me;" put my words to the test; try it and see. If you have doubts, there is a ready way to solve them; do all I say, and bide the issue.——"Pour out," as the margin indicates, is the verb that means to *empty out*, as if God meant to say he would empty forth his vast reservoirs of blessings.——In the last clause, our translators found it necessary to italicise too many words—a common indication that they did not clearly see the primary sense of the passage. The word they rendered "*that*" never has this meaning, but means *until*. The other Hebrew words are "*not*" and "*enough*"—"until not enough," *i. e.*, until my stores shall fail me—a result you never need think of as possible. Since this can never be, the Lord would have his people understand that nothing can limit his blessings short of their capacity to receive. The Hebrew of this clause is the same as in Ps. 72: 7—"Abundance of peace until" (there is) "no moon;" translated, "so long as the moon endureth.

11. And I will rebuke the devourer for your sakes, and he shall not destroy the fruits of your ground; neither shall your vine cast her fruit before the time in the field, saith the LORD of hosts.

12. And all nations shall call you blessed: for ye shall be a delightsome land, saith the LORD of hosts.

These verses still expand the promise commenced in v. 10. If you will truly bring in all the tithes and meet all your obligations to God, then I will rebuke the devourer for your sakes—the locust, put here for all forms of destructive agents. All the nations shall witness to your prosperity.

13. Your words have been stout against me, saith the LORD. Yet ye say, What have we spoken *so much* against thee?

14. Ye have said, It *is* vain to serve God: and what profit *is it* that we have kept his ordinance, and that we have walked mournfully before the LORD of hosts?

15. And now we call the proud happy; yea, they that work wickedness are set up; yea, *they that* tempt God are even delivered.

Once more recurring to those wicked men who have constantly gainsayed the prophet and his Lord, he charges them—"Your words have been *hard*, *strong* against me, saith the Lord." They retort by virtually denying the charge. Then the Lord makes his charge more specific. When I promised, "Bring in all the tithes," so shall your cup be filled with good, ye replied, "It is vain to serve God; what profit have we found in keeping his ordinances, and walking mournfully before the Lord," as those who sorrow for their sins? Thou, Lord, hast said the nations shall call the righteous blessed; on the contrary, *we* call the proud blessed; yea, they that work wickedness are built up in enduring prosperity. They that "prove God" in this way, daring him to do his worst if he will, not those that prove him by bringing in all the tithes, are delivered from evil, and even from the danger of it.——The antithesis between what God had said before (vs. 10–12), and what these wicked gainsayers reply (vs. 14,15), is much more apparent in the original, especially of v. 15 than in the received translation. First, the pronoun "*we*," being expressed in full, is slightly emphatic: you say one thing; *we*, on our part, not admitting what you say, are stoutly maintaining the opposite. Then the verb, "call you *blessed*" (in v. 12), and the corresponding verb, "call the proud *happy*" (v. 15), are precisely the same; as if they would say—You claim that the nations shall call God's obedient people blessed; we, for our part, call the proud blessed. So the word rendered "*prove*" (v. 10) is the same as is here (v. 15) rendered "tempt." You have said, Let my people *prove* me. We have to say in reply, that the wicked *have proved thee* by scoffing at thy words; and yet so far from being punished, they are even delivered from all fear and danger. Their eyes stand out with fatness; they have more than heart could wish.——What a portrayal this of most shocking hardihood in sin!

16. Then they that feared the LORD spake often one to another: and the LORD hearkened and heard *it;* and a book of remembrance was written before him for them that feared the LORD, and that thought upon his name.

17. And they shall be mine, saith the LORD of hosts, in that day when I make up my jewels; and I will spare them, as a man spareth his own son that serveth him.

18. Then shall ye return and discern between the righteous and the wicked, between him that serveth God and him that serveth him not.

Here we turn to the other class, in every respect the moral opposites of the ungodly and the proud.——"Then," *i. e.*, in the very face of such bold, defiant blasphemy against God and righteousness; "then they that feared the Lord"—all unlike the proud who had no fear of God before their eyes—"held free communion one with another." They did not suppress their thoughts because the defiant godless blasphemers were so outspoken, but none the less for that, they talked freely one with another.——There was One who listened, all unawares to them; "*the Lord* hearkened and heard;" and what is more, he made a record for the perpetual remembrance of a thing that touched his heart so tenderly. There he entered the names of those who, at such a time, in the face of such blasphemy, yet feared the Lord, and had thoughts of affection and esteem for his name. "These shall be mine, saith the Lord of hosts, in that day when I make up my treasures;" I will hold them among my choicest, best jewels; and until that future, final gathering of them into my heavenly cabinet, I will manifest my compassion and loving-kindness toward them, as a man does toward his own son that serveth him. Such is the sense of the word rendered "*spare.*" The Lord implies that he has indeed real service for his people—some of it, perhaps, hard and earnest work; but his great and tender love for them will insure the kindest treatment possible, even as a kind father may set his son to earnest service, but will lovingly watch over him to spare him from excessive toil and exposure. No good father makes his son a galley-slave. The kind Lord drops many a loving tear over the hardships to which his needful service may subject his people in these years of their toil and of reproach for his name. Let it be enough for us that he feels toward us such pity and such tender love!——"Then shall ye return," look again, and then ye shall see a broad distinction, nay more, a real contrast, between the destiny of the righteous and the destiny of the wicked. The proud and defiant ones have been saying, "Where is the God of judgment?" "Every one that doeth evil is good in the sight of the Lord;" "it is vain to serve God;" "the proud are blessed;" "they that tempt God with most daring provocation are delivered;"—but *the reckoning day will shortly come!* Let the righteous return after a little space, and they will see a broad line of diverse destiny ranging "between him that serveth God and him that serveth him not."——The beginning of the next chapter is closely connected with this, for there this line of difference becomes a wide and striking contrast.

CHAPTER IV.

WITH no break in the continuous thought, this chapter proceeds to contrast the destiny of the wicked and of the righteous (vs. 1–3); gives a general injunction to observe the law of Moses (v. 4); and a promise of John Baptist under the name of Elijah, with brief hints of the work he should do (vs. 5, 6).

1. For behold, the day cometh, that shall burn as an oven; and all the proud, yea, and all that do wickedly, shall be stubble: and the day that cometh shall burn them up, saith the LORD of hosts, that it shall leave them neither root nor branch.

"For" indicates a close connection with chapter 3. "Behold," calls solemn attention. "The day," in its usual prophetic sense, is a period which is peculiar, "sui generis"—here a time of fearful judgments on the wicked.——The wicked are said in the

Old Testament, as well as the New, to be destroyed by fire. Thus Psalm 11 : 6, "Upon the wicked he shall rain forked lightnings, fire, and brimstone, and an horrible tempest." The prime exemplar is the ruin on Sodom, Gen. 19: 24, "Then the Lord rained upon Sodom brimstone and fire from the Lord out of heaven." See also Ezek. 38 : 22.——The great question here respects the *time*, and hence the sort of judgment referred to. In my view, the primary reference must be to judgments on the wicked *in time*, providential inflictions, like that on Jerusalem by the Romans, like the still earlier judgments that fell on the ungodly portion of the Jews in the fearful Syrian wars during the second century before Christ; indeed, embracing all those forms of special infliction which belong to God's providential government over nations and individuals too in the present world. All these are to be taken as prophecies and pledges of that far more terrific vengeance which shall come down on all the finally wicked in the world to come. I would not apply this passage to either this world or the next, to the entire exclusion of the other, but assume that it refers primarily to judgments in this world; then as a type, a harbinger, prophecy, and pledge, it embraces also those heavier, sorer judgments which execute full and unmitigated justice on the ungodly in the world to come.——The context shows that the primary reference here is to judgments in time; for the righteous are thought of as walking over the ground where the ashes of the perished wicked lie strewn.

2. But unto you that fear my name, shall the Sun of righteousness arise with healing in his wings; and ye shall go forth, and grow up as calves of the stall.

3. And ye shall tread down the wicked; for they shall be ashes under the soles of your feet in the day that I shall do *this*, saith the LORD of hosts.

This is the joyous, far different lot of the righteous. The fearers of God's name are in strong contrast of character as well as destiny with the proud blasphemers.——The rising sun is a glowing and glorious image of hope and joy. "Righteousness" has here the not uncommon sense of deliverance, salvation, blessedness, with no implication of its being strictly *deserved* on the score of simple justice, and by no means excluding mercy. The reference is mainly to the Messiah as the great fountain of light, peace, and joy, to the saints of God. His wings are the beams of his light.——"Ye shall go forth and *leap* as well-fed calves of the stall." Leaping rather than growing is the sense of the Hebrew, indicative of exultant joy.——How solemn and impressive the scene, to walk over the ashes of the wicked and say—Here the wrath of God smote them, and here their ruins lie, an awful monument to the madness of sin and to the justice of Jehovah's most fearful retributions! Such views of their horrid blasphemous wickedness as are given above (3 : 13–15), ought to reconcile every sane mind to the severity of these judgments, and even ought to inspire in all hearts the song of Moses and of the Lamb—"Great and marvellous are thy works, Lord God Almighty; *just and true are thy ways*, thou king of saints."

4. Remember ye the law of Moses my servant, which I commanded unto him in Horeb for all Israel, *with* the statutes and judgments.

Specially pertinent, in view of the shocking abuses and corruptions of the ceremonial law, is this last injunction to observe those statutes and judgments until the better system shall supersede them.

5. Behold, I will send you Elijah the prophet before the coming of the great and dreadful day of the LORD:
6. And he shall turn the heart of the fathers to the children, and the heart of the children to their fathers, lest I come and smite the earth with a curse.

The remarkable thing in this passage is that, without any special explanation, the great forerunner of the Messiah is here called "Elijah the prophet." The New Testament has solved this enigma to us; but how could the Jews of Malachi's time have understood it?——Still the general sense might perhaps have been clear to them, viz., one who should be a second Elijah, who should come with a spirit and power like his, sternly rebuking sin, and earnestly calling all men to repentance. This would be the more apparent by how much the more they regarded Elijah as a representative man, embodying in himself precisely those qualities which fitted him for the prophetic work. The shocking corruption of the priests in the time of Malachi would suggest strongly that the covenant people would need another Elijah, filled with his spirit and power, to do the work which the priesthood were only undoing and counteracting.——Our Lord, in Mark 9 : 11–13, gave a very specific explanation. "They asked him—'Why say the scribes that Elias must first come?'" He answered—"Elias verily cometh first and restoreth all things; but I say unto you that Elias is indeed come, and they have done unto him whatsoever they listed." Or as narrated by Matthew (11 : 14), "If ye will receive it, this is Elias who was to come."——The phrase rendered—"the great and dreadful day of the Lord," is in the original verbatim from Joel 2 : 31, "before the coming of the day of the Lord, the great, and the terrible." Standing here it must refer to the "day that shall burn as an oven" (v. 1), while not unnaturally the language may be borrowed from Joel. ——To warn in mercy before he smites in judgment, is evermore the order of God's throne. Hence the second Elijah should come before the Jewish people and polity should be smitten down by the terrible Roman arms. They were fearfully corrupt already. It was foreseen that they would become yet more so before and during the Messiah's incarnation. Hence the last warnings sent them through John Baptist, in the form of a call to repent, and to welcome their Great Deliverer, soon to appear, came in the hour of their greatest moral extremity.——But what is the pertinence of describing the moral work wrought by John Baptist, as "turning the hearts of the fathers to the children and the hearts of the children to the fathers"?——Perhaps few of us appreciate the loving heart and the social influence of this John. It may have come to us with the notions of our childhood to think of the man of camel's-hair cloak and leathern girdle, making his meals of locusts, and ranging the wilderness of Judea to preach repentance, as only a stern reprover—a battle-axe upon men's sins, and scarcely less savage toward the endearing relationships of society.——If we added the latter inference, we made a great mistake. It never was any part of true religion, never was the function of any true reformer, to ride roughshod over the tenderness of the parental and filial relations. No, it is idolatry that first debases and then crucifies parental affection, and makes the mother that bare him heartless and cruel enough to cast her boy into the burning arms of Moloch. Avarice and lust are doing the same thing in tens of thousands of families in Christian lands to-day. So always and everywhere sin quickens selfishness; and selfishness, grown rampant and rabid, severs parent from child, and child from parent. On the other hand, what do we always see in all genuine revivals of religion? What so universally as a revival of deep, all-absorbing *love for others*, especially within the circle of the domestic relations? How often do we see the hearts of parents borne down with almost crushing solicitude in the tenderness of their love for the souls of their children! What but this turning of the hearts of parents to their children begets such agonizing prayer of Christian parents for ungodly children, and of converted children for yet unconverted parents?——Hence it was the Spirit of the Lord that moved this prophet to touch by one master-stroke the central influence of John Baptist's preaching. When the men whom he called so mightily to repentance, had bowed their hearts to this high behest, their next thought was that of renewed care and love for their children. If we had been present in that revival, we should have found it by no means unlike all the true revivals of our day in this one most precious feature.——Such a revival of the home and household affections is eminently pleasing to God. In such a soil religion thrives. Where the hearts of fathers turn with loving, tender interest toward their children, and the hearts of children in like manner to their fathers, the Saviour finds a congenial home and takes up his abode.——It seems to be implied that if John's preaching had altogether failed of this result, the gospel of salvation from the lips of Jesus might have fallen powerless upon the world, and left to Judea and to the nations of the earth only the remediless "*curse*."——How forcibly, then, comes the appeal to us to cherish the tenderness of mutual love and earnest care for others' souls, especially within the dear circle of family relationships, lest the gospel should fail to bless us, and lest we doom ourselves and those we ought to love, to a moral ruin for which God has no remedy! ——Thus close the admonitions of the last prophet of the Old Testament age, and with them the volume of Scripture as it stood till in the fulness of time the Messiah came.

DISSERTATION I.

ON THE CRITERIA FOR DISTINGUISHING, IN THE PROPHETIC LIFE, BETWEEN THINGS SEEN AND DONE IN VISION ONLY, AND THINGS DONE IN FACT.

The importance of this point seems to justify a more extended examination than could properly be introduced in the notes.

It is clear beyond a doubt that some of the prophets had visions, somewhat analogous to dreams, yet not altogether dreams, in which objects were presented to their mind's eye only; or as the case may be, they were transported, not in body, but in thought, to distant points, and made to see or do things that had no actuality in the external world. It is equally clear that these prophets all lived an actual life in this external world, and that, in the ministry of their prophetic office, they were required of God to *go* and to *do* in the external world things of a symbolic nature, belonging properly to their prophetic work.——Now our first question is, *Are there any criteria by which these two very different things can be distinguished from each other?*

Our second question is, *If so, are they in the records themselves*, in the very forms of the statement, or are they mainly or only in *our own ideas* of the fitness or unfitness of the things to be done in actual life?

The only decisive and satisfactory answer to these questions must be obtained by a careful examination of the cases which belong to one class or the other as they stand in the record. If there are laws of prophetic usage, so well established as to afford us the criteria we seek, they must be sought and found by a thorough induction from particular cases; not otherwise. We are shut up to an examination of the record. Does the record give us the distinctive criteria, or does it commit the decision to the taste and judgment of each reader? The subject will be exhausted only when *all* the cases that belong to either class have been carefully and candidly examined.——Ezekiel abounds in these cases. We will begin with him.——Note a case of mere vision (37: 1–14), the well-known "valley of dry bones." The very introduction shows this to be a vision only. "The hand of the Lord was upon me," indicating some special extraordinary power, "and carried me out in the Spirit of the Lord," not in actuality, but in that peculiar, prophetic state often described as "*in the Spirit;*" and "set me down in the midst of the valley, which was full of bones, and caused me to pass by them round about," &c. Here the form of the statement seems designed to shut off the thought of an actual scene. But vs. 15–22 in the same chapter present an actual scene. "Take thee one stick, and write on it 'For Judah,' and take another stick, and write on it, 'For Ephraim,' &c.; join them one to another into one stick, and they shall become one in thy hand." That this is actual, and not in vision only, appears from the fact that the form of statement gives no intimation of a vision, but has throughout the air of reality. Thus, "When the children of thy people shall ask, Wilt thou not show us what thou meanest by these?" it is plainly implied that they saw the sticks joined, and did not merely hear the prophet report the case as presented to himself alone, and in vision only. Still further, the Lord said: "The sticks whereon thou writest shall be in thine hand *before their eyes*," *i. e.*, as an illustration of great truths to be prophetically announced.——It should be constantly borne in mind that the people are in the external world only—never in the state of prophetic vision. What *they* see and hear, therefore, must be in the external world—in the world of sense, and not in the prophetic world of the "Spirit." Hence this union of the two sticks must have been real, and not visional only.——Yet further, comparing the two portions of the 37th chapter above named—the former a vision, viz., of the dry bones, and the latter an actuality—the union of two sticks in one in the prophet's hand—we may note another distinctive criterion. The former consists mainly of things *seen* by the prophet; the latter of things *done*. So we might expect that in visions the prophet will be mainly an *observer*, but in things made actual for symbolic purposes, mainly a *doer*.——Ezek. 40–48 is declared to be a vision. "The hand of God was upon me, and brought me thither," *i. e.*, to the city of Jerusalem: "in the visions of God brought he me into the land of Israel, and set me on a very high mountain," &c., where he saw the frame of a city, and a man in appearance as brass, &c., with a measuring line in his hand; and he was told to note with special care all he should see and hear, that he might declare it to the house of Israel.——The whole account shows beyond a doubt that this is a vision only. The record is throughout one of things *seen* by the prophet, not of things *done*. The "hand of the Lord," which is "upon him," and by which he is "brought" from one point of the scene to another, is continually referred to, *e. g.*, 40: 2, 3, 17, 24, 35, 48, and 41: 1, and 42: 1, and 43: 1, &c., &c.——Equally clear to the same conclusion is the passage Ezek, chapter 8–11, inclusive. Both the introduction and the close of this passage are decisive. The prophet is sitting in his house; the elders of Judah are sitting before him; "the hand of the Lord falls there upon him;" he sees a strangely glorious form "of the likeness of fire from the loins downward, and of brightness like amber from the loins upward." This personage, says Ezekiel, "put forth the form of a hand, and took me by a lock of mine hair, and the Spirit lifted me up between the earth and the heavens, and brought me in the visions of God to Jerusalem." There he saw scenes significant and most impressive. At the close he records: "Afterward the Spirit took me up and brought me in a vision by the Spirit of God into Chaldea to them of the captivity. So the vision that I had seen went up from me." "Then I spake to them of the captivity, all the things that the Lord had shown me." ——The reader will take note that these chapters are throughout a narration of things *seen* by the prophet—not of things *done*. Indeed, very special care is taken to make it clear that these things are seen and transacted in vision only. The language used is strongly distinctive. "The Spirit lifted me up," "brought me in the visions of God to Jerusalem." "Afterward the Spirit took me up and brought me in a vision by the Spirit of God into Chaldea." "So the vision that I had seen went up from me," as if it had been a great sheet of panoramic representation.——This extreme care to define the precise character of the transaction should be especially noticed, since it manifestly justifies the inference that God would have us distinguish between this class of cases and those of a symbolic character, where external acts are really done. It also shows that he intends to furnish the criteria for this discrimination himself, so as to leave us no responsibility, and no exercise of judgment, save that of interpreting his very plain words.——Over against these visions there lies a class of symbolic transactions, done in real life, in the external world, before the open eyes of the people—their symbolic character having for its aim a deeper impression on the popular mind. In this class stands Ezek. 12 : 1–16. It opens not by saying, "The hand of the Lord was upon me;" "the Spirit took me up;" "I was brought in vision by the Spirit," &c.; but thus, "Son of man, thou dwellest in the midst of a rebellious house, who have eyes to see, and see not," &c., implying the occasion for new and peculiar means of impressing truth on their dull minds and hard hearts. "Therefore, thou son of man, prepare thee stuff for removing, and remove by day in their sight" (not by night, and in dreams only); "it may be they will consider, though they are a rebellious house."——The whole plan of operation is then detailed, and he is especially charged again (v. 6) to "do it *in their sight*," and finally the reason is given: "For I have set thee for a sign (a thing both visible and significant) to the house of Israel." The prophet proceeds to say (v. 7), "I did so as I was commanded," *i. e.*, this was an actual transaction. Furthermore, the end sought was in part at least gained; the people inquired, and the Lord improved their awakened curiosity. "Son of man, hath not the house of Israel, the rebellious house, said unto thee, What doest thou? Say thou unto them, Thus saith the Lord God: This burden (*i. e.*, of predicted calamity) concerneth the prince in Jerusalem, and all the house of Israel that are among them. Say, I am your *sign;* in like manner as I have done, so shall it be done unto *them;* they shall remove and go into captivity." Here we see at every point most decisive indications that this is a symbolic transaction, actually wrought before the eyes of the people. The prophet is here a *doer*, not a *seer;* the people *see*, and therefore the things done must have been in the world of sense before them.——Of the same sort is the transaction recorded Ezek. 4. Here we miss the statements: "The hand of the Lord was upon me;" "the Spirit took me up or brought me;" "I was in vision," &c., &c.; but on the other hand, we find the other class of statements: "Son of man *do*" certain things; "this shall be a sign to the house of Israel." In this case the things to *do* are: "Take thee a tile and lay it before thee, and portray upon it the city—even Jerusalem—and lay siege against it. Set the camp against it, and battering-rams—all the enginery of assault in ancient warfare. Nor may he omit the means of protection to the assailing party: "Take thee an iron pan, and set it for a wall of iron between thee and the city," and so make the siege complete. And then the Lord said: "This shall be a *sign* to the house of Israel"—the usual formula to show that this is a symbolic and real transaction. In this case also we have a long series of details respecting the prophet's lying first on the left side and then on the right side, and the significance of each; the duration of each and *its* significance; then, moreover, his food and drink the while are fully defined. The circumstance of his cooking his own food shows that his lying on one side was not absolutely continuous during the whole twenty-four hours of every day. It was sufficient that it should be *so* continuous, and withal so public, as to avail for a *sign* to Israel. The decisive proof of an actual transaction in this case lies partly in the absence of any hint that this is seen in vision only, and partly in the fact that throughout it is represented as a veritable transaction; but especially in the declaration, "This shall be a *sign* to the house of Israel." For if the whole thing were seen by the prophet in vision only, and not *done* at all, how could it be *seen* by the people and be a "sign unto them?" For it cannot be even supposed that they were in a state of prophetic vision, and so were able to see things presented in vision only. Note here also that the prophet is a *doer*, not a *seer*.——Ezek. 1 is a vision throughout, for so the record states:—v. 1, "The heavens were opened, and I saw visions of God;" and v. 3, "The hand of the Lord was there upon him;" "And I looked and beheld," &c. Ezek. 2 is also a vision. "The Spirit entered into me when he spake unto me, and set me upon my feet, and then I heard him that spake unto me"—the prophetic state, that of one into whom the Spirit had entered, being a prerequisite to his hearing the words spoken to him in the vision.——The "roll" of which we read, 2:8–10, and 3:1–10, should be accounted a thing of vision, this being indicated by the words (2:9), "When I looked, behold an hand was sent unto me, and lo, a roll of a book was therein."——In Ezek. 3: 11–27 some of the transactions seem to have been of the external world, and some only seen or done *in vision.* Of the former sort are his "going to them of the captivity," (vs. 11–15), and "his going forth into the plain" (vs. 22, 23). Of the latter, "the Spirit took me up" (v. 12), "lifted me up and took me away" (v. 14), &c. In the former case, if they of the captivity are spoken of as actual and not visional, then his going to them must have been in the external world, and not in the world of thought only.——Ezek. 5: 1–4, the prophet polling his hair and dividing it into three parts, one part to be burned with fire in the midst of the city, another to be smitten about with a knife, and the last third scattered to the wind; and the application of this to Jerusalem (vs. 5–17) we must obviously interpret as a real transaction, although the forms of statement which specially indicate a symbolic proceeding are not here. On the other hand, the yet more uniformly present indications of a vision are wholly wanting; and moreover, the thing itself is so obviously done *to be seen by the people,* and would have so little force as a thing presented to the prophet only, and in vision, that all doubt is substantially precluded.——In Ezek. 21: 6, 7, we must recognize an actual scene, the tokens of bitter grief, groans, and sighs, must have been heard and seen by the people. This was the intent of the command: "Sigh, therefore, thou son of man, with the breaking of thy loins; and with bitterness, sigh *before their eyes.* V. 7 shows that they saw, and therefore inquired the cause: "It shall be when they say unto thee, wherefore sighest thou?" that thou shalt answer, "For the tidings, because it cometh," &c. This awakened curiosity and attention, the Lord used of set purpose to get into their dull and unbelieving minds the great idea of coming calamity.——In Ezek. 24, we have first a supposed case, for it is definitely named a "parable," and is to be spoken to the people, and not done, in fact, before them. "*Utter* a parable to the rebellious house, and *say* unto them, Thus saith the Lord God; Set on a pot, set it on, pour water into it; gather the pieces, *i. e.*, of a slain animal, and let them seethe the bones therein." And this was to represent the bloody city, Jerusalem, in which flesh, bones, and blood promiscuously, were seething together. This parable forms the text for the discourse, vs. 6–14. Strictly, this case is neither a symbol nor a vision. It is only and precisely what the Lord called it, a "parable," and shows that the Lord is specially careful to define sharply the particular *manner* of his revelations to men by his prophets, so that there shall be the least possible occasion for misapprehension on this point.——Over against this parable, vs. 15–18 describe a real transaction. The prophet is apprised that the Lord will "take away the desire of his eyes with a stroke," and is forbidden to mourn or weep therefor. "So," he adds, "I spake unto the people in the morning, and in the evening my wife died, and I did as I was commanded." This was visible to the people, and therefore an actual death, and a real case of a bereaved husband, refraining from the usual tokens of grief.

The people ask—"Wilt thou not tell us what these things are to us that thou doest so?" showing that they understand this to be a symbol, and therefore significant as to themselves. Further, the narrative repeatedly declares: "Ezekiel is unto you a sign" (v. 24), "and thou shalt be a sign unto them" (v. 27). Thus by the words and forms of statement the line is drawn, and in the main clearly, between things actually done for symbolic or other purposes, and things only seen by the prophet himself in vision. This examination has aimed to touch all the cases of either sort that occur in Ezekiel. An induction of cases that is exhaustive, bringing under consideration, and properly classifying all the passages that relate to the question in hand, must bring out the laws of prophetic usage in this matter. Indeed, this method must furnish the only legitimate and ultimate data for obtaining these laws of prophetic usage. In this matter the Book of Ezekiel is classic ground, furnishing us more data than all the other Old Testament prophets combined. Hence the great length of this examination of Ezekiel.

In Zech. 1 : 7 to 6 : 8 are eight distinct visions, and in 6 : 9–15 is one symbolic transaction in actual life. The broad line of distinction between these two classes in the very forms of statement is worthy of special attention. The visions open thus: "I saw by night, and behold a man riding upon a red horse," &c. (1 : 8); "Then I lifted up mine eyes and saw, and behold four horses," &c. (1 : 18). "I lifted up mine eyes again and looked, and behold a man with a measuring line," &c. (2 : 1); "And he showed me (*i. e.*, caused me to see) Joshua, the high priest, standing before the angel of the Lord, and Satan standing at his right hand to resist him," &c. (3 : 1); "And the angel that talked with me came again and waked me, as a man that is wakened out of his sleep, and said unto me," &c. (4 : 1). This passage is specially valuable as showing that the state of receptivity for prophetic visions was peculiar, *sui generis*. Further, "I turned and lifted up mine eyes and looked, and behold a flying roll," &c. (5 : 1). "The angel that talked with me said, Lift up now thine eyes and see what is this that goeth forth," &c. (5 : 5). "And I turned and lifted up mine eyes and looked, and behold four chariots," &c. (6 : 1). The uniformity and precision of these statements is certainly complete, leaving nothing more for us even to desire.——From this series of prophetic visions let us pass on to the closing portion of this same sixth chapter. The record here is very definite, yet entirely different from what we have seen in the eight visions that immediately precede. Not a word is said about "lifting up his eyes," nor about "being made to see," nor does he say at the commencement, "behold," nor is he "wakened out of his sleep," nor is it "seen by night." But squarely over against these characteristics, "the word of the Lord comes to him," just as it does in the passages 1 : 1–6, and 7 : 1, ff., and 8 : 1, &c., &c. Then the Lord commands him not to *see* something, but to *do* something; in this case, "Take from the captive delegation, late from Babylon, silver and gold and make crowns, and set them on the head of

Joshua the high priest," &c., to make him a symbolic type of the Messiah, as both priest and king. And yet further, to show that this was to be actually *done*, it was ordered that after the coronation is over and has served its present purpose, the crowns shall be deposited in the temple for a memorial to this delegation from the far Eastern land, to show that nations from far were yet to come and build in the temple of the Lord. Thus every special feature in each class, the visions on the one hand and the symbolic actualities of the prophetic life on the other, is distinctly drawn—so distinctly as to leave no apology for misapprehension or mistake.

Daniel, throughout, has visions, and not symbolic acts of his own. His visions embrace more or less objects having a symbolic nature. This, however, does not touch the point of discrimination now before us. We inquire simply after the line between things only *seen* by the prophet, and things actually *done* by him. Daniel, in chap. 2 interprets Nebuchadnezzar's dream. In chap. 7 he is careful to say, "Daniel had a dream and visions of his head upon his bed." In chap. 8, "a vision appeared unto me." In chap 9: 21–27, the man Gabriel came; and in chaps. 10–12 the future is revealed to him by an angel. Thus everywhere the forms of statement are full and definite to the point before us.

In Jeremiah, the great body of communications read simply, "Thus saith the Lord," and the narrative presents neither visions nor symbolic acts. But chap. 24 records a vision, introduced thus: "The Lord showed me," *i. e.*, two baskets of figs; and in chaps. 18 and 19 we must recognize symbolic transactions in real life. Here, too, the proof of this lies in the form of the statement—"Arise and go down to the potter's house, and there will I cause thee to hear my words." Here is something to be done before the revelation proper from the Lord even begins. More still to our argument is the implication (v. 6) that the house of Israel are witnesses of what was done by the potter. "O house of Israel, cannot I do with you as this potter?" This, of course, locates the scene in the external world. So in chap. 19, something is to be actually done in the outer world: "Go and get thee a potter's earthen bottle, and take of the ancients of the people, &c., and go forth unto the valley of the son of Hinnom and proclaim there the words that I shall tell thee."——A part of this message stands (vs. 3–9), and then in v. 10 the Lord said, "Then shalt thou break the bottle in the sight of the men that go with thee and say, Thus saith the Lord, Even so will I break this people and this city, as one breaketh a potter's vessel, that cannot be made whole again."

Here we have the usual criteria of actuality. Things are to be *said* and *done* by the prophet—not merely *seen* in vision; and they are to be said and done before the eyes of the people. There can be no doubt that this is a symbolic transaction. It stands, therefore, as further proof of a constant divine care and purpose to distinguish between visions and things of actual life, done for the greater effect through the power of symbol.——In chap. 13, the girdle which the prophet is to "go to the Euphrates and hide there in a hole of the rock," must be, according to our laws of construction, actual, and not merely visional, although it were a long way to the Euphrates for a place to hide it and let it rot. That very mission to the Euphrates had its object and its special significance. The people were soon to go there, and their nationality should there decay, not to say be marred and rot, like the prophet's girdle.——The language is decisive—"Go, get thee a linen girdle;" "take the girdle and arise, go to Euphrates," &c. There is nothing said of "the hand of the Lord upon him," or of being "in the Spirit," or "being in vision," or of being "brought by the Spirit" to Euphrates, &c. Hence we must interpret it of a real transaction.——In Jer. 27 and 28, the bonds and yokes to be made by the Lord's command for the neck of the prophet, and to be sent to various kings whom the Lord had made subject to Nebuchadnezzar, must be construed as actual, and not visional only. The command was—"Make thee bonds and yokes," &c., "put them upon thy neck, and send them to the king of Edom," &c., by messengers, and "command them to say unto their masters," &c.,—the yoke being symbolic of the main idea of the message. The false prophet Hananiah, who confronted and gainsayed Jeremiah, gave a counter-message, professedly from the mouth of the Lord, and then to symbolize this, took the yoke from off Jeremiah's neck and broke it. For this daring and impious lie, the Lord doomed him to die within the year. He died in the seventh month. These transactions must, beyond a doubt, be interpreted as real, and not of vision only.

Isaiah had a vision (chap. 6) indicated by—"I saw the Lord, sitting upon a throne," &c.; but Isa. 7:3, must be actual: "go forth to meet Ahaz."——In Isa. 20 the Lord commands Isaiah to "loose his sackcloth from his loins and put off his shoes, and he did so, walking naked" (*i. e.*, with no outer garment) "and barefoot." The Lord plainly shows this to be a real transaction when he says—"Like as my servant Isaiah hath walked naked and barefoot three years for a *sign* and a wonder upon Egypt and upon Ethiopia, so shall the king of Assyria lead away the Egyptians prisoners, naked and barefoot." The fact that this was to be a "sign"—a thing attracting wonder—proves it an actuality. Besides, it might be asked—What could be the use of this thing, if done in vision only? The record, however, and not any judgment of our own as to the fitness or propriety of the things for either vision or external symbol, must be our main authority. Everywhere we see that the Lord intended to make the record itself decisive to the point of this discrimination.

Amos had visions (7:1, 7, 8, and 8:1, 2, and 9:1, ff.), always indicated by the usual statements—"The Lord showed me," "I saw the Lord," &c.

The Book of Jonah must be construed as actual life, and not merely prophetic vision. If it be asked, Why? the answer is furnished by this full induction of all the cases of either sort found in the other Old Testament prophets, and may be stated briefly, thus:

(1.) There is not the least indication of a vision in the entire book. (2.) The forms of statement are throughout those of a real transaction—things *done* and suffered by the prophet, and not things *seen*. (3.) The moral aim and instruction of the whole book demand its interpretation as a scene of actual, real life.——Mythical interpreters do indeed avoid some of those things which they are fain to call unnatural and impossible, by explaining this book throughout as a myth, or a thing of vision only. There is no difficulty in supposing a man to *dream* of being swallowed by a great fish. No; but there ought to be great difficulty in overriding the plain, obvious sense of the Book of God. A solemn responsibility rests on every man to study the laws of prophetic interpretation with both care and candor, and with whatever good sense the Lord may give. ——Following these laws of prophetic usage, we must make the locusts in Joel (chap. 1 and 2) literal and real, not ideal and things of vision only. For Joel does not say, "I lifted up mine eyes and saw"—does not say, "The Lord showed me," or that "the hand of the Lord was there upon me." He simply narrates events as matters of fact. The locusts come up in successive swarms, and utterly desolate the land; the people are famished, and turn to fasting and prayer for the divine mercy. This belongs to real life. He further describes them in chap. 2—"They look like horses;" "they run like horsemen" (v. 4); and, again, "they run like mighty men" (v. 7)—which certainly is not saying that they *are* mighty men, and that the real thing was never a locust-host, but only a raid of armed men.——Over against this, Amos saw locusts in vision, for he *says* so: this is the proof. He says: "Thus hath the Lord caused me to see, and behold, he formed locusts" (7:1).——Hence Dr. Hengstenberg, though an excellent, acute, and almost faultless commentator, is manifestly wrong in assuming that the locusts of Joel were never actual, but only ideal—only seen in vision.

We have now gone through the cases (*all*, as I suppose) that occur in the various Old Testament prophets, bearing on the point before us, designedly omitting none; and we find a clear line of distinction drawn between the things seen and shown in vision only, and those which were done in the outward life for symbolic or other purposes. These distinctions lie not mainly—indeed, scarcely at all—in the nature of the things as convenient to be done, or as impossible, but in the very *form* of the statements. In other words, the Lord has been specially careful to leave us in no doubt as to what was actually *done* by his prophets on the one hand, and what was only *seen* by them in vision on the other.

Let us now come to the case of Hosea (chapters 1 and 3). Was his "taking a lewd wife"—lewd either before *and* after marriage, or after only—a real transaction; or was it only a thing seen in vision? Were those three children, and their significant names, things of vision only, or actualities of real life?——The laws of interpretation are already educed from the usage of all the other prophets, with whom such cases occur throughout the Old Testament. It only remains to apply them here.——(1.) There is not the least intimation that these things are in vision only. He does not say—"The Lord showed me," does not say "I saw," does not hint that "the hand of the Lord is upon him," and that he is "in vision" or "in the Spirit," so that he might *see* such things done in the prophetic ecstasy. This essential evidence of a mere vision is altogether wanting.——(2.) On the other hand, the language of command is explicit: "Go, take unto thee a wife of whoredoms," &c. The entire narrative lacks not one of the features of an actual transaction. The children are born in the usual succession of time (see vs. 3, 8), and each has its significant name. So also chap. 3 is the natural description of real life. Let it also be carefully noted that in all this the prophet is a *doer*, not a *seer* only.——(3.) The reason why God requires this of his prophet is specially given, viz., because "the land has committed great whoredom in departing from the Lord." There was therefore a fitness in having this fact symbolized in the prophet's family state, and also in having other important facts symbolized in the significant names of his children. And it may have been a further reason that the Lord would have his prophet sympathize with himself, and appreciate more keenly the feelings of the divine mind under such abuse.

This naturally completes the argument, so far as concerns the principles and laws of prophetic interpretation. That usage which rightly gives law to language is all on one side, and if the authority of this law be admitted at all, can leave no doubt as to the right interpretation in this particular case.——It need only be added that if this law of language—prophetic usage—be discarded in this case, it may be in any and every other, and we are all afloat, with no principles of interpretation to guide us.——It amounts to little to say in abatement or exception to this, that we can fall back upon our own sense of the fitness or unfitness of the things to be done in fact, using our discretion and interpreting that as done in vision only which seems to us unfit to be done in fact. For the vital question is—Does God leave us to this exercise of our own discrimination, giving us no other data for determining the sense of his words? Does prophetic usage show numerous cases, or indeed any one clear case, in which there is only this discretion to guide us? The examination here presented should suffice (it would seem) to prove the negative.——The question might be pressed—Would it be *safe* to leave with men the discretion and responsibility of deciding this question by their own sense of fitness? The care God has taken *not* to leave the question to this umpire should suffice to show that he, at least, has not thought it wise to do so.——Yet, though this may seem clear, yet some excellent men and able interpreters hold the opinion that Hosea took this wife Gomer no otherwise than in vision, and had these children born to him only in the sense of dreaming it—seeing them so born in prophetic vision. Their main reliance in support of this view is in the idea that marrying a "wife of whoredoms" and having "children of whoredoms" *in real life*, must be immoral, and therefore that God could not command Hosea to do it.——I reply, (1.) The force of this objection is mainly obviated by the supposition (entirely admissible in view of the language and history) that Gomer, though of previously lewd habits, had become professedly penitent and reformed, and was accepted by the prophet on these professions of penitence and promises of conjugal fidelity. The marriage covenant would of course in her case involve these promises.——Like Israel, in relation to her covenant God, she too may have lapsed again, and so have symbolized the more forcibly the course of that guilty nation toward God.——(2.) It need not be claimed that Hosea, or any other man, would choose to marry a woman of previously bad life, even upon any professions of amendment, however fair. The special command of the Lord in this case assumes that the thing required was a hardship—a thing that no good man would be likely to do, save under a positive command from God and for a very special purpose.——(3.) In this view of it the transaction cannot be regarded as immoral in the prophet. Hence the moral objection against it as a reality, loses its force.

The application of these principles of interpretation to that system which converts the simple narratives of Scripture into *myths*, will be readily seen. It must suffice here only to suggest it.

DISSERTATION II.

ON TWO MILLENNIAL THEORIES.

The theories here discussed are:

I. That the Old Testament prophecies of the millennium treat of the heavenly as well as of the millennial state; that in giving a general view of the kingdom of the Messiah, they describe first in the order of time, the New Testament age and its peculiarities as contrasted with the Jewish; but that then, in addition to this, they pass over by analogy, or by a natural continuation of the same theme, to give also the eternal blessedness of the saints in heaven after the resurrection and general judgment.

II. The second theory denies all reference of these prophecies to the New Testament age, and locates their fulfilment exclusively, as to *time*, after the resurrection and the judgment day; as to *space*, upon this earth, purified by the fires of the last day, and made the eternal abode of the righteous. This theory excludes all promise of the conversion of the world to Christ.——The principal passages here referred to as millennial are—in the minor prophets—Joel 3: 17–21; Amos 9: 11–15; Mic. 4: 1–8; Zeph. 3: 9–20; Zech. 14: 6–9, 16, 20, 21.——In other prophets, Isa. 4: 2–6, and 9: 1–7, and 11, and 35, and 54, and 60, and 66: 18–24; Jer. 31: 31–40; and Ezek. 36: 25–28, and 37: 21–28, and 47: 1–12.

Taking up first in order the theory first named above, let us note the main arguments adduced in support of it, viz.:——1. These prophecies describe a state *too holy* to be realized in such a world as this, under its present physical laws.——2. The state described is *too long* to be exhausted in this world, inasmuch as it is repeatedly said to continue *forever*.——3. The Old Testament reveals no heaven, unless it be in these prophecies. The results of Messiah's work for our race are exceedingly incomplete without a somewhat full revelation of its great consummation in an eternal heaven for the saints. Hence we have a right to expect a revelation of heaven in these prophecies.——Replying to these arguments in their order, I admit, as to the first, that the language implies a high standard of holiness, very much in advance of the average under the Jewish dispensation, with which it would of necessity be tacitly compared. ——Thus (Joel 3:17)—"Jerusalem shall be holy; and there shall no stranger pass through her any more."——Zeph. 3:9—"For then will I turn to the people a pure language, that they may all call upon the name of the Lord to serve him with one consent." ——Zech. 14:20, 21—"In that day shall there be upon the bells of the horses *holiness unto the Lord*, &c.; and in that day there shall be no more the Canaanite in the house of the Lord of hosts." ——See also Isa. 4:3, 4, and 11:9, and 35:8, and 54:13, and 60:18–21; and Jer. 31:31–34; and Ezek. 37:23.

But this feature of these prophecies does not necessarily carry their fulfilment over to the heavenly state, because——(1.) The gospel system provides for a high degree of holiness in the present life, especially through Christ's intercessions for his people, his manifested presence with them, and the indwelling of his Spirit with power in their hearts. Hence Christ himself says: "I pray that thou wouldest keep them from the evil" (John 17:15). "My grace is sufficient for thee, for my strength is made perfect in weakness" (2 Cor. 12:9). Paul testifies: "I can do all things through Christ who strengtheneth me (Phil. 4:13).——(2.) Those prophecies which give us the largest promises of spiritual life and power indicate their own fulfilment in the present world and in the New Testament age. Some of them are cited by inspired apostles with this understanding, *e. g.* (Joel 2:28–32), the great promise of the effusion of the Spirit which Peter affirmed began to be fulfilled at the opening of the gospel age (Acts 2:16, ff.; also Gen. 22:18), "In thy seed (Jesus Christ) shall all the nations of the earth be blessed." This Peter applies (Acts 3:25, 26): "Unto you first, God having raised up his Son Jesus, sent him to bless you in turning away every one of you from your iniquities." This, then, is a case showing *how* all the nations are to be blessed in Christ.——So the great promise of the new covenant, which stands at the head of the predictions of eminent holiness (Jer. 31:31–34) is cited (Heb. 8:8–13) as being the very genius and soul of the gospel dispensation.——That extraordinary promise of moral cleansing by the Spirit (Ezek. 36:25–28), "I will sprinkle clean water upon you, and ye shall be clean; from all your filthiness will I cleanse you; I will put my Spirit within you and cause you to walk in my statutes," &c., proceeds to say: "And ye shall dwell in the land that I gave to your fathers"—as much as to say—These promises belong to earth and not to heaven; to this world in its present state, and not to the next, after these heavens and this earth shall have passed away.——(3.) While the New Testament descriptions of the heavenly state affirm an absolute perfection, and make it sure by the beatific presence of the Saviour, the prophecies in question fall manifestly short of this, especially so if we may even proximately estimate the holiness they promise by the experience of any period of the gospel age which has thus far transpired.——Thus the New Testament witnesses of the heavenly state: "We know that when he (Christ) shall appear, we shall be like him, for we shall see him as he is" (1 John 2:2).——"Neither can they die any more, for *they are equal to the angels*, and are the children of God, being children of the resurrection" (Luke 20:36).——The Old Testament prophecies fall somewhat short of this.

2. I pass to the second argument, viz., that these prophecies apply not to the earthly state, but to the heavenly, because they represent it as being *eternal*.——To this I answer: (1.) It may be admitted that possibly a few of these passages conceive of the Messiah's reign as holding over beyond this world to the heavenly—an absolutely eternal reign—yet without giving any special account of that heavenly state.——Supposing this to be true, all the specific features of this millennial state, except its absolute eternity, belong to this world and to *time;* so that this admission abstracts nothing from the glories of the millennial state.——And yet it would be somewhat difficult to find the passages that clearly hold over to the future world. If you say they are Dan. 2:44, and 7:14, 18, 27, the negative side of the description, "shall not be left to other people, but shall break in pieces and consume all these kingdoms"—"which shall not pass away" (supplanted by some conquering power); and the fact that *the saints* shall take the kingdom and possess it forever;" also, that it is the kingdom and dominion *under* the whole heaven, not *in heaven*, go far to show that the thought here is specially of this world, and not of the eternal one.——Again, Micah says: "The Lord shall reign over them in Mount Zion from henceforth even forever;" but the reigning *in* Mount Zion, and the previous "assembling of her that halteth and her that was cast far off," hold the mind to this earthly state as the thing specially in view.——(2.) Many of these descriptions forbid us to think of an absolute eternity. Thus (Joel 3:20), "But Judah shall dwell forever, and Jerusalem from generation to generation"—where the last clause, being parallel, is explanatory, and assumes a succession of generations not to be thought of in the heavenly state.——So the parallel clause in Isa. 60:15—"I will make thee an eternal excellency, a joy of many generations."——Note also the indications of time in the "new heavens and new earth" of Isa. 65:22, where you might expect an absolutely eternal state—"For

as the days of a tree are the days of my people, and mine elect shall long enjoy the work of their hands."——The passage (Ezek. 37 : 21–28) expresses the duration of its events by "forever" (v. 25), and by "for evermore" (vs. 26, 28), but it also locates the Lord's people "in the land upon the mountains of Israel;" affirms that "the heathen shall know that I the Lord do sanctify Israel," assuming that some heathen still live on the earth and are cognizant of her condition; and also declares—"I will set my sanctuary in the midst of them for evermore"—"yea, I will be their God and they shall be my people"—a passage which Paul (2 Cor. 6 : 16) manifestly assumes to have its fulfilment in the Christian age of the world.——Thus it might be shown that many of these prophecies which affirm eternal duration most strongly embrace points which locate their fulfilment on earth, in time, and not in heaven during the eternal state.——(3.) None of these prophecies give us any marks by which we can distinguish between what belongs to this world and what to the next, the heavenly. The New Testament descriptions of heaven never fail to furnish these marks of discrimination, as is apparent in Matt. 25 : 34; Luke 16 : 22, 25, 26; and even in Rev. 21 and 22, which chapters follow the final judgment: the first heaven and the first earth have passed away; the holy city is the *New* Jerusalem, built in heaven, and has no temple in it; the wicked are all in the lake that burneth with fire; the righteous enjoy the beatific presence of God and the Lamb.——Criteria of this sort are wholly wanting in the millennial prophecies of the Old Testament.——(4.) Unlike the New Testament descriptions of heaven, these prophecies give us no intimation that their scenes transpire *after* death, the resurrection, and the general judgment.——(5.) The prophetic state which is said to continue "forever," is in many cases described with Jewish costume; in other words, the Jews dwell in their own land, with their temple and ritual institutions complete; the Gentiles come up to Jerusalem to build and beautify that temple, and to worship therein—all legitimate as descriptions of the millennial state on earth, but scarcely admissible as descriptions of the real heaven beyond death and the judgment.——(6.) The New Testament does not locate heaven upon this earth, but elsewhere. Always it is a place to which residents of earth are said to "*go*" and to "*depart;*" of which Christ said, "I go to prepare a place for you." But of this more fully hereafter.——(7.) The only uniform and reliable principle by which the terms "everlasting, "forever," &c., can be explained, is that which makes them *relative*, *i. e.*, as long as the nature of the subject which they qualify will admit. Thus "eternal punishment," under the government of God must be as long as God's government exists; "everlasting mountains" will stand while the world stands; "an ordinance forever" will remain only so long as the system to which it pertains. It is only on this principle that the Jewish festivals (Lev. 23 : 14, 21, 31, 41) are everlasting, or the Aaronic priesthood (Ex. 40 : 15 and Num. 25 : 13), for they ceased with the passing away of the system of which they formed a part.——On this principle the millennial "forever" would be indefinitely long, yet would, or at least *might* close, in that special form, with the end of this world.

3. To the argument that the Old Testament reveals nothing of the heavenly state except in these prophecies; that the results of Messiah's reign are altogether incomplete without a somewhat full revelation of its heavenly state; and that therefore we have a right to expect something definite of heaven in these Old Testament prophecies—I answer;——(1.) The first statement is not strictly correct. The real heaven stands forth revealed in such passages as the following: "Thou wilt show me the path of life: in thy presence is fulness of joy; at thy right hand there are pleasures for evermore" (Ps. 16:11).——"As for me, I shall behold thy face in righteousness; I shall be satisfied when I awake with thy likeness" (Ps. 17:15).—"Thou shalt guide me with thy counsel, and afterward receive me to glory. Whom have I in heaven but thee, and there is none upon earth that I desire besides thee. My flesh and my heart faileth; but God is the strength of my heart, and my portion forever" (Ps. 73:24–26).——"Many of them that sleep in the dust of the earth shall awake, some to everlasting life, and some to shame and everlasting contempt. And they that be wise shall shine as the brightness of the firmament; and they that turn many to righteousness as the stars for ever and ever."——(2.) Of the other points, I remark, (*a.*) that the revelations of the Old Testament must be admitted to be incomplete compared with those of the New, especially in respect to the future world; the resurrection, the final judgment, and the ultimate destiny of the righteous and of the wicked.——(*b.*) It is rather the genius of the Old Testament to reveal the great fact of a *present moral government* over nations, and also largely over individuals as well—administered *in this world* by present rewards and penalties; and then to leave the future destiny of men *to be inferred from this great fact of present retribution.*——(*c.*) Remarkably, the future existence of the soul, the future blessedness of the righteous, and misery of the wicked, are rather *assumed* than *affirmed*, *e. g.*, the existence of the soul after death, in Exodus 3:6: "I am the God of thy fathers, the God of Abraham, the God of Isaac, and the God of Jacob." Our divine Lord teaches us how to bring out from this passage the underlying assumption of the soul's continued existence (Matt. 22:32): "God is not the God of the dead but of the living"—where "*dead*" must be taken in the Sadducean sense—*non-existent.* Jehovah could not be the God of nonentities; hence Abraham, Isaac, and Jacob are shown to be still living.——So the resurrection is assumed to be known in those striking passages where it is used as a figure to represent analogous changes in the state of the nations, viz., Isa. 26:14, 19: "They" (God's enemies) are dead, they shall not live; they are deceased, they shall not rise." "Thy dead men shall live, together with my dead body shall they arise. Awake and sing, ye

that dwell in dust, for thy dew is as the dew of herbs, and the earth shall cast out the dead."——Or the well-known passage, Ezek. 37:1-14, the vision of the valley of dry bones, raised from the dead, and figuratively representing how God revives the hope and the national spirit of his captive people.——Dan. 12:2, recently cited, comes nearer to a formal affirmation of the resurrection than any thing else in the Old Testament, and yet it was not the design of that passage to affirm the *universal* resurrection. The Old Testament nowhere teaches this doctrine in a didactic, elementary way, as our Saviour does (John 5:28, 29). It is quietly assumed. ——So the future blessedness of the righteous is assumed—inferrible from his blessedness here in time—and on the same principle, the final woe of the wicked.——(*d.*) It should not be forgotten that according to the New Testament, Jesus Christ "brought life and immortality to light through the gospel." This cannot mean less than that life and immortality were not really *brought to light* until Christ came. Those great truths had lain in comparative obscurity, with only dim and flickering rays falling around.——(*e.*) It is not altogether safe or wise for us to assume that certain things *ought* to appear in the Old Testament. The Lord has his own views and plans as to the order and method of his revelations to man.

Second Theory.—This theory denies all reference of these prophecies to the New Testament age, and locates their fulfilment *as to time*, after the resurrection and judgment day;—*as to space*, upon this earth purified by the fires of the last day, and made the eternal abode of the righteous. It excludes all promise of the conversion of the world to Christ.

Of this I have to say—1. If it be true, it is doubtless susceptible of very clear and strong proof. The points it assumes to be true are entirely tangible. If taught in the Scriptures at all, they would be likely to appear in tangible forms.——2. A theory which robs the Church of God of so many of her glorious hopes for the future prosperity of Zion, and for the Saviour's joy in the travail of his soul;—which smites down so many of her best impulses and motives to missionary zeal and self-sacrifice, *ought* to be well grounded, or else not be believed at all. A theory which so eclipses the glories of heaven as well as the best hopes for our present earth, can have but small hold, it would seem, on our Christian sympathies. Yet, if it be true, let us bear it in submission, though in sorrow; but if it be not true, let us hurl it from us as the robber of our best heritage.——3. This theory cannot be true and must be false, because the conversion of the world to Christ is taught and implied in the word of God most abundantly.——(1.) It is the plain significance of those prophecies which are clothed most fully in Jewish costume and figures, representing Israel and Judah in the gospel age as dwelling in their own land with their temple standing and ritual service entire; and Gentiles coming up from all the ends of the earth to worship the one Lord there.——See notes on Hos.

1:10, 11, and on Zech. 12:1–9.——(2.) In another class of prophecies which have far less of Jewish costume, the same great truth is undeniably taught;—*e. g.*, Ps. 2:8—"I will give thee (the Messiah) the heathen for thine inheritance, and the uttermost parts of the earth for thy possession." Ps. 22:27, 28: "All the ends of the earth shall remember and turn unto the Lord, and all the kindreds of the nations shall worship before thee. For the kingdom is the Lord's, and he is Governor among the nations." Ps. 72:8, 17: "He shall have dominion also from sea to sea, and from the river to the ends of the earth." .... "And men shall be blessed in him; all nations shall call him blessed."——Mal. 1:11: "For from the rising of the sun even to the going down of the same my name shall be great among the Gentiles, and in every place, incense shall be offered to my name, and a pure offering; for my name shall be great among the heathen, saith the Lord of hosts." See also Gen. 22: 18, and 49:10.——(3.) Such passages as Isa. 52:13–15, and 53:10–12, show that the Messiah shall be gloriously successful *relatively to Satan and sin* in the very work of saving men—shall be exalted high in triumph because of his great humiliation and sufferings, and in view of the fruits thereof; "shall sprinkle many nations;" "shall see of the travail of his soul till he is satisfied;" shall have the great for his portion, and a large share of the spoil after the battle with sin and Satan is fought through.——Gen. 3: 15 runs in the same strain, confirming the glorious truth that the masses of the human family are to be ultimately for Christ and not for Satan. Of course, no such result can be without an indefinitely long millennial state upon this earth.——(4.) The New Testament confirms this view by teaching the same thing. See Rom. 11:15, 25, 26: "For if the casting away of them *be* the reconciling of the world, what *shall* the receiving *of them be*, but life from the dead? For I would not, brethren, that ye should be ignorant of this mystery, lest ye should be wise in your own conceits; that blindness in part is happened to Israel, until the fulness of the Gentiles be come in. And so all Israel shall be saved: as it is written, There shall come out of Sion the Deliverer, and shall turn away ungodliness from Jacob." And Rev. 11:15: "And the seventh angel sounded; and there were great voices in heaven, saying, The kingdoms of this world are become *the kingdoms* of our Lord, and of his Christ; and he shall reign for ever and ever." These predictions are exceedingly definite and explicit. It need not surprise us that their number is no greater. The New Testament writers believed in Old Testament prophecy, and held its testimony to this point to be abundantly adequate.——(5.) Yet further, the New Testament most fully endorses the application of these prophecies to the gospel age, and especially to the conversion of the Gentiles, and to the ultimate union of Jews and Gentiles in the same earthly Church and kingdom of God. It is not easy to conceive how they could more strongly endorse both this interpretation of these prophecies and its reliability, than by quoting them as proof of these very points.

Here let us note how Paul (Acts 13 : 47) quotes Isa. 49 : 6 : "We turn to the Gentiles; for so hath the Lord commanded us: I have set thee (the Messiah) to be a light of the Gentiles, that thou shouldest be for salvation unto the ends of the earth."

The chapter here quoted from is one of the most decisive and rich prophecies of the world's conversion. Note also how James (Acts 15: 15–18) cites Amos 9: 11, 12: "Simon (Peter) hath declared how God at first did visit the Gentiles, &c., and to this agree the words of the prophet, as it is written: After this I will return, and will build again the tabernacle of David, which is fallen down; and I will build again the ruins thereof, and I will set it up, that the residue of men might seek after the Lord, and all the Gentiles, upon whom my name is called, saith the Lord, who doeth all these things. Known unto God are all his works from the beginning of the world;" as if he would intimate that God had planned the conversion of the Gentiles from the very creation of man.——In the same way Paul (Rom. 11 : 26, 27) quotes Isa. 59: 20, and in Rom. 15 : 18–12 quotes several prophecies, and among them Isa. 11—one of the first-class prophecies of the conversion of the world.——Thus do the apostles, after being fully taught by the Spirit, see in these prophecies that God had purposed and foretold the conversion of the Gentiles to Christ, and the ultimate union of both Jews and Gentiles in the Christian Church. They make the same use of these prophecies that we ought to make now, as the ground of faith and the fountain of impulse to self-denying labor for the gathering of all nations into the Messiah's kingdom. It never entered their mind that these prophecies teach nothing about the conversion of men, but only promise a sort of heavenly paradise on this earth after probation shall have closed. *They never cite these prophecies as teaching and proving this modern doctrine.* They do continually cite them to prove that, through the effusions of the Spirit and the preaching of the gospel, Gentiles and Jews shall be converted to Christ. That they expected the fulfilment of these prophecies in the present world by means of these gospel agencies, the divine and the human, is beyond all doubt. Hence, if their testimony be admitted, it decides the question.

4. If it be fully admitted that these prophecies pledge the conversion of the world to Christ, the further question respecting the locality of the future heavenly state loses most of its importance. Not all of it, however, for the natural tendency of the notion that the future heaven is to be on this earth, is material as opposed to spiritual—not to say even sensual and carnal—exceedingly unlike the tendency and influence of those New Testament descriptions which make heaven consist essentially in being "forever with the Lord," and in so "beholding his glory" that we become thereby forever "like him." See 1 John 3 : 2, and Thess. 4 : 17.——It may not be superfluous, therefore, to say, that the evidence in the Scriptures to prove that

this earth is to be the future heaven of the saints is exceedingly meagre.——The heaven of the Scriptures is already in existence, long before this earth is purified. Myriads have already gone before to that other better world. Everywhere in the Scriptures it is a place to which one *goes from* this world. As said by our Lord: "In my father's house are many mansions; I go to prepare a place for you." (Did he mean by these words that he was then going to burn *this world* up, and purify it for a heaven?) He adds: "I will come again, and (*not* dwell with you on this earth, but) receive you to myself, that where I am, there ye may be also" (John 14: 2, 3.)

Paul "desired to *depart*, and to be with Christ." At the very time when the theory in question would plant the saints in this glorified earth, Paul assigns them a very different location: "Them also that sleep in Jesus *will God bring with him*, *i. e.*, up to heaven; and those who are then alive (not having tasted death) shall be *caught up* together with"—the previously dead now raised—"in the clouds, to meet the Lord in the air," and "they inherit the kingdom prepared for them (not *at the end* of the world, but) from the foundation of the world."——But it is claimed that Isaiah, Peter, and John teach this doctrine under the phrase, "The new heavens and the new earth" (Isa. 65: 17, 18; 2 Pet. 3: 13, and Rev. 21 and 22.)——In few words as possible, I reply: (*a*.) The important declarations in Isaiah are: "Behold, I create new heavens and a new earth; the former shall not be remembered nor come into mind. . . . But be ye glad and rejoice forever in that which I create, for, behold, I create Jerusalem a rejoicing, and her people a joy," &c.——This is obviously a great moral change, and not a physical one, as when Paul says, "If any man be in Christ, there is a new creation." (This is the original.) Isaiah himself explains it to mean "I create Jerusalem a rejoicing, and her people a joy," *i. e.*, a cause or ground of joy to all who love God and holiness. The context still further proves that the prophet speaks of the millennial state in this world of probation as produced under the gospel, and not of the state of retribution subsequent to the resurrection and final judgment.——(*b*.) Peter, having described the burning of the earth and the works that are therein, adds, "Nevertheless we, according to his promise, look for a new heaven and a new earth, wherein dwelleth righteousness." But this falls far short of affirming that the saints shall dwell forever in this new earth. It just as much affirms that they shall dwell forever in these new heavens. It does not specially affirm either. Hence this text will scarcely suffice for a cornerstone of any entire system of doctrine respecting the future location of the saints. There are too many doubtful points in its interpretation. It is doubtful what Peter refers to by "*his promise*." He may refer to some unwritten promise from the Saviour's own lips; or to Isa. 65: 17; or possibly to Rev. 21.——(*c*.) John, in Rev. 21 and 22, most distinctly locates the saints before and around the throne of God and of the Lamb; represents them as dwelling in a great and glorious city—the new Jerusalem (which manifestly must be taken as Jewish costume)—but is very far indeed from affirming that the location of this heavenly state is on this earth. Indeed, he does not tell us where this holy city is located. It was no part of his design to give its celestial geography.

If these brief suggestions shall conduce to save the millennial prophecies from the perverting influence of unfounded theories, and leave them to stand forth before the Church in their full strength and glory, my main purpose will be accomplished.

CHRONOLOGICAL TABLES.

I. KINGS OF JUDAH.

	Began to reign B. C.	Reigned years.
Rehoboam	975	17
Abijam	958	3
Asa	955	41
Jehoshaphat,	914	25
Jehoram	891	7
Ahaziah	884	½
Athaliah	884	7
Joash	877	39
Amaziah	838	27
Uzziah	811	52
Jotham	759	16
Ahaz	743	15
Hezekiah	728	29
Manasseh	699	55
Amon	644	2
Josiah	642	31
Jehoahaz	611	¼
Jehoiakim	611	11
Jehoiachin	600	—
Zedekiah	600	12
End of the kingdom	588	

II. KINGS OF ISRAEL.

	Began to reign B. C.	Reigned years.
Jeroboam I.	975	22
Nadab	954	2
Baasha	952	22
Elah	930	1
Omri	929	11
Ahab	918	21
Ahaziah	897	1
Jehoram	896	12
Jehu	884	28
Jehoahaz	856	16
Joash	840	15
Jeroboam II	825	41
Interregnum	784	11
Zachariah	773	½
Shallum	773	1/12
Menahem	773	12
Pekahiah	761	2
Pekah	759	19
Interregnum	740	9
Hoshea	731	9
End of the kingdom	722	

III. HEBREW PROPHETS.

	B. C.
Joel (supposed)	830–825
Jonah	823
Amos	825–759
Hosea between 825 and 699	
Isaiah	759–699
Micah	758–699
Nahum	700
Jeremiah	629–580
Zephaniah	624
Habakkuk	610–588
Daniel	603–533
Ezekiel	595–573
Obadiah	588–580
Haggai	520
Zechariah	520
Ezra	457–432
Nehemiah in Judah	444–432 & 408–400
Malachi (supposed)	408–400

N. B.—In a few of these cases no certain data exist. The figures should be regarded as only the nearest approximation to truth possible under the circumstances.

IV. GREAT EVENTS,

	B. C.
Revolt of the ten tribes	975
Shishak, king of Egypt, at Jerusalem	970
Omri builds Samaria	929
Famine under Ahab 3½ y'rs.	913–910
Homer	907
Carthage built	885
First Olympiad	776
Rome founded	753
End of kingdom of ten tribes	722
Nineveh destroyed	625
First captives to Babylon	606
Jerusalem destroyed	588
Confucius	551
Restoration from Babylon	536
Rome a republic	525
Temple finished	515
Pythagoras	497
Esther	478
Themistocles	514–449
Herodotus	484–444
Socrates	469–399

The Harvest of the Sea. A Contribution to the Natural and Economic History of the British Food Fishes.

By James G. Bertram. With 50 illustrations. One large vol. 8vo, 520 pages. Cloth. Price $7.50.

"This is the first work in which an attempt has been made to bring before the public in one view the present position and future prospects of the Food Fishes. Great pains have been taken to obtain reliable information and correct statistics."—*Editor's Note.*

"Contains a large amount of highly interesting information and curious matter."—*The Athenæum.*

"For beauty of illustration, excellence of workmanship, and instructiveness of contents, has not been surpassed by any similar work lately issued."—*New York Times.*

The Works of Lord Macaulay

Complete. Edited by his sister, Lady Trevelyan. With Portrait, engraved on steel, by W. Hull. 8 vols. large 8vo, cloth. Price $40; half calf extra, $56.

In preparing for publication a complete and uniform edition of Lord Macaulay's works, it has been thought right to include some portion of what he placed on record as a jurist in the East. The papers selected are the Introductory Report upon the Indian Penal Code, and the notes appended to that Code, in which most of its leading provisions were explained and defended. These papers were entirely written by Lord Macaulay.

The contents are arranged in this edition as follows: Vols. I. to IV., History of England since the Accession of James the Second; Vols. V., VI, and VII., Critical and Historical Essays, Biographies, Report and Notes on the Indian Penal Code, and contributions to Knight's Quarterly Magazine; Vol. VIII., Speeches, Lays of Ancient Rome, and Miscellaneous Poems.

A Treatise on the Steam-Engine

in its Various Applications to Mines, Mills, Steam Navigation, Railways, and Agriculture, with Theoretical Investigations respecting the Motive Power of Heat and the proper proportions of Steam-Engines, Elaborate Tables of the Right Dimensions of every part, and Practical Instructions for the Manufacture and Management of every species of Engine in Actual Use. By John Bourne. Being the Seventh Edition of "A Treatise on the Steam-Engine," by the "Artisan Club." Illustrated by 37 plates and 546 woodcuts. 1 vol. 4to, cloth. Price $18.00.

"The author is well known as an accomplished engineer; what he says will be accepted as truth."—*New York Commercial Advertiser.*

"The eminence of the author in his profession makes this work authority on the subjects of which it treats."—*Eastern Argus.*

Homes Without Hands, being a

description of the habitations of animals, classed according to their principles of construction. By the Rev. J. G. Wood, M. A. F. L. S., author of the "Illustrated Natural History," etc., with new designs by W. E. Keyl and E. Smith. Engraved by G. Pearson. 1 vol. large 8vo, 21 full-page drawings and 85 illustrations; 632 pages. Cloth. Price $7.50.

"One of the most charming Natural History books we have ever read."—*Glasgow Herald.*

"A clever original work on Natural History, which is certain to take its place among permanent literature."—*Globe.*

"A really more instructive and entertaining work on Natural History has not been published."—*Leeds Intelligencer.*

"'Homes Without Hands' is one of the most interesting and instructive works on Natural History."—*Observer.*

"No volume lately published contains so much curious and interesting information, presented in so attractive a form, as Mr. Wood's work, which he has aptly and happily named 'Homes Without Hands.'"—*New York Times.*

Mythology of Ancient Greece

and Italy. By Thomas Keightley, author of "The History of Greece," "The History of Rome," "Fairy Mythology," "Tales and Popular Fictions," etc. Third edition. Revised and augmented. With 12 plates from the antique. 1 vol., large 8vo, 512 pages, cloth. Price $6.00.

This work has reached its third edition, and has been carefully revised, and has received numerous additions. Mr. Pococke, in his late work, terms it "the best compendium of Hellenic mythology that has appeared, and will always deservedly maintain its high position as the exponent of what the Greeks thought and wrote about and believed."

The Horse. By Wm. Youatt.

With a Treatise on Draught. Revised and enlarged. By Walker Watson, M. R. C. V. S. With numerous illustrations. 1 vol. 8vo, 589 pages. Price, cloth, $4.00.

" * * * The present edition will be found to have undergone a thorough revision and arrangement, many fresh diseases have been introduced, and the nature and treatment of others considered in accordance with the principles of veterinary science at the present day."

"This is an excellent and comprehensive work on the subject of which it treats."—*Philadelphia Inquirer.*

"We hope every lover and owner of a horse will secure a copy, and learn how to treat the faithful beast."—*Troy Times.*

The Treasury of Bible Knowledge.

Being a Dictionary of the Books, Persons, Places, Events, and other Matters of which Mention is made in Holy Scripture. Intended to establish its Authority and Illustrate its Contents. By Rev. John Ayre, M. A., of Gonville and Caius College, Cambridge. With 15 full-page engravings, 5 colored maps, and many hundred woodcuts. 1 vol., thick 18mo, 944 pages, cloth. Price $5.

"The best of the new books. * * * We know of none more valuable than 'The Treasury of Bible Knowledge.' It is in all respects the best, as it is the most convenient manual for the Biblical student yet published. Especial attention has been given to the clear and full presentation of the evidence of Christianity, and the latest and most complete arguments in regard to the authenticity and inspiration of the various books of the Bible."—*American Baptist.*

" * * * One of the most valuable publications ever issued by that house. In fact, the book may be pronounced an Encyclopædia or Library of Scriptural Information."—*New Yorker.*

A Smaller Classical Dictionary

of Biography, Mythology, and Geography. By William Smith, LL.D., Editor of the Dictionaries of "Greek and Roman Antiquities," "Biography and Mythology, etc. Abridged from the larger Dictionary. Illustrated by 200 engravings on wood. 1 vol. 12mo, 464 pages, cloth. Price $3.00.

"It will fill admirably a want heretofore much felt in school and classical literature."—*New Yorker.*

"It will be found a very desirable work for students."—*New York Commercial Advertiser.*

The Old Testament History.

From the Creation to the return of the Jews from Captivity. Edited by William Smith, LL.D., with 10 maps and numerous woodcuts. 619 pages. 1 vol. 12mo, cloth. Price $3.00.

" * * * Besides giving the history recorded in the Old Testament, with the necessary explanations, notes, references, and citations, this work contains information on a large number of other subjects. Among these may be mentioned an account of each of the Books of the Bible, the geography of the Holy Land and of other countries, together with the political and ecclesiastical antiquities of the Jews, Historical and Genealogical Tables, etc."—*Extract from Preface.*

www.ingramcontent.com/pod-product-compliance
Lightning Source LLC
LaVergne TN
LVHW021139110826
845150LV00005B/1073

* 9 7 8 1 4 2 5 5 4 9 4 6 6 *